THE BUDDHIST PHILOSOPHY OF THE MIDDLE

Studies in Indian and Tibetan Buddhism

THIS SERIES WAS CONCEIVED to provide a forum for publishing outstanding new contributions to scholarship on Indian and Tibetan Buddhism and also to make accessible seminal research not widely known outside a narrow specialist audience, including translations of appropriate monographs and collections of articles from other languages. The series strives to shed light on the Indic Buddhist traditions by exposing them to historical-critical inquiry, illuminating through contextualization and analysis these traditions' unique heritage and the significance of their contribution to the world's religious and philosophical achievements.

STUDIES IN INDIAN AND TIBETAN BUDDHISM

THE BUDDHIST PHILOSOPHY OF THE MIDDLE

Essays on Indian and Tibetan Madhyamaka

David Seyfort Ruegg

WISDOM PUBLICATIONS • BOSTON

Wisdom Publications
199 Elm Street
Somerville MA 02144 USA
www.wisdompubs.org

Library of Congress Cataloging-in-Publication Data

Ruegg, David Seyfort.
The Buddhist philosphy of the middle : essays on Indian and Tibetan Madhyamaka / David Seyfort Ruegg.
p. cm.
Includes bibliographical references and index.
ISBN 0-86171-590-X (pbk. : alk. paper)
1. Madhyamika (Buddhism) I. Title.
BQ7457.R835 2010
294.3'92—dc22
2010007996

15 14 13 12 11 10
6 5 4 3 2 1
eBook ISBN 978-0-86171-936-5

Cover and interior design by Gopa & Ted2, Inc.

Wisdom Publications' books are printed on acid-free paper and meet the guidelines for permanence and durability of the Production Guidelines for Book Longevity of the Council on Library Resources.

Printed in the United States of America.

This book was produced with environmental mindfulness. We have elected to print this title on 30 percent PCW recycled paper. As a result, we have saved the following resources: 15 trees, 5 million BTUs of energy, 1,417 pounds of greenhouse gases, 6,822 gallons of water, and 414 pounds of solid waste. For more information, please visit our website, www.wisdompubs.org. This paper is also FSC certified. For more information, please visit www.fscus.org.

Publisher's Acknowledgment

THE PUBLISHER gratefully acknowledges the generous help of the Hershey Family Foundation in sponsoring the publication of this book.

Contents

Foreword

WITH THE PRESENT VOLUME, Wisdom Publications and the Studies in Indian and Tibetan Buddhism series have the honor of making available some of the finest scholarship in Buddhist Studies, fifteen key essays by David Seyfort Ruegg. The subject of the book is Madhyamaka, the "philosophy of the middle," a school of thought founded by Nāgārjuna and Āryadeva in about the second century C.E. and going on to Candrakīrti and Bhā(va)viveka in the sixth century, Kamalaśīla and Śāntarakṣita in the eighth, and a host of illustrious Tibetan exponents. Numerous are the Western writers who have been fascinated by its promise, notably the critique of realism, the wide-ranging dialectical method, and the philosophical quietism it produces. David Seyfort Ruegg is one of the most outstanding of these scholars, and he has consecrated much of his life to the study of Madhyamaka thought.

Seyfort Ruegg was born in 1931 in New York. His university education was primarily in Paris, where he studied Indology under Jean Filliozat and Louis Renou and Tibetology under Marcelle Lalou and Rolf Stein. He has a strong connection with the French tradition of scholarship on Madhyamaka, a tradition that includes figures such as Louis de la Vallée Poussin, Étienne Lamotte, J. W. de Jong, and Jacques May. Another strong connection he has maintained throughout his career is with Tibetans. He has collaborated with high-level Tibetan scholars, in Europe, the United States, and also in India. Among others these include the Buryat/Mongolian Dge bshes Ngag dbang nyi ma, an abbot of Sgo mang college who taught in Leiden in the 1960s when Seyfort Ruegg was there, as well as Dge bshes Dge 'dun blo gros, whom Seyfort Ruegg knew in Kalimpong and who later became a professor at the University of Hamburg. Indeed, early on in his career Seyfort Ruegg adopted the perspective that the great scholars of Tibet were themselves scholars of Indian Buddhism. They were, as he once put it, Indologists *avant la lettre*.

Seyfort Ruegg's work—as the list of publications appended to the present book amply shows—has ranged over most aspects of Indian and Tibetan Studies. However two interests come back repeatedly: the philosophy of the buddha-nature (*tathāgatagarbha*) and the philosophy of the middle. The first was the subject of his 1969 doctoral thesis, *La théorie du tathāgatagarbha et du gotra*. In 1973 he published a translation of Bu ston Rin chen grub's treatise on the *tathāgatagarbha*, and in 1989 *Buddha-Nature, Mind and the Problem of Gradualism in a Comparative Perspective*. As for the Madhyamaka, besides the articles in the present book and recent publications in Vienna, we should especially mention Seyfort Ruegg's *Literature of the Madhyamaka School in India* (Wiesbaden, 1981). As the present book attests, buddha-nature and the Madhyamaka are in one way or another closely linked in later Indian Buddhism, and very much so in Tibetan philosophies.

David Seyfort Ruegg has held professorial positions in several major universities—Leiden, Seattle, Hamburg, and now the School of Oriental and African Studies of the University of London. He is a Sanskritist and a Tibetologist and at one time or another has held chairs in Indian Philosophy, Buddhist Studies, and Tibetan. Indeed virtually all his publications are proof that Buddhist Studies profits greatly from the double perspective that knowing both Tibetan and Sanskrit brings.

I first met David Seyfort Ruegg in the early 1980s and have been his admirer ever since. What has always impressed me is how he combines philological precision, extraordinary erudition in Western philosophy, hermeneutics, linguistics, and other subjects, and an ability to distill and illuminate broad trends within the field. The fifteen articles presented here show the richness of Indian and Tibetan Buddhist philosophy and the impressive scope of a remarkable career. We are reprinting them here that they may be readily accessible and continue to serve as a model for Buddhist Studies.

This book would not have seen the light of day without the invaluable help of several people. Above all, special thanks are due to David Seyfort Ruegg for his willingness to undertake this project and his patience throughout. We are greatly indebted to Burkhard Quessel of the British Library, who contributed to the book at every stage—he computerized the articles, corrected the scans, checked proofs, and so on. David Kittelstrom was the indefatigable editor at Wisdom Publications. Other Wisdom resources from whose help we benefitted are Laura Cunningham, Lea Groth-Wilson, Megan Anderson, and Tony Lulek. Finally, thanks are due to Professor David Jackson, who provided much useful biographical information.

The articles were reprinted with the kind permission of the original publishers. Full references are given in the initial note to each chapter. The Elisabet de Boer Fund of the University of Lausanne, Switzerland, helped in defraying the costs of this publication. All that remains is to offer the traditional dedication: *dge legs 'phel.*

Tom J. F. Tillemans

Preface

THE PRESENT VOLUME comprises reprints of a selection of studies concerned with the Madhyamaka school of Buddhist thought in India and Tibet. For this volume misprints in the original articles have been corrected. The transliteration of Tibetan has been altered by the publishers, who have also made a number of editorial changes. To the paper on linguistic and mathematical models (no. 1) a postscript has been appended listing some newer publications dealing with the relative places of linguistic and mathematical models in Indian thought and providing references to some recent treatments of Indian mathematics and astronomy.

These papers were written in parallel with, and thus complement, their author's *Literature of the Madhyamaka school of philosophy in India* (1981) and *Three studies in the history of Indian and Tibetan Madhyamaka philosophy* (Part 1 of *Studies in Indian and Tibetan Madhyamaka thought*, 2000). The latter volume contains an outline history of earlier Madhyamaka in Tibet, a study on the place of propositional assertions or theses *(pratijñā)*, philosophical positions (*mata, pakṣa*, etc.), and non-contentiousness or eirenicism in Madhyamaka thought (an earlier article on the subject published in 1983 is therefore not reproduced here) and a study on epistemological-logical *(pramāṇa)* theory and the ontic in Tsong kha pa's (1357–1419) Madhyamaka philosophy (an earlier version published in 1991 is therefore not reprinted here). Part 2 of *Studies in Indian and Tibetan Madhyamaka thought* (2002) is comprised of a translation of Candrakīrti's (seventh-century) comment in his *Prasannapadā* on the first stanza of Nāgārjuna's great *Mūlamadhyamakakārikā*s and a translation of a treatise going back to Tsong kha pa, but recorded by his immediate disciple Rgyal tshab Dar ma rin chen (1364–1432), on the eight Crucial Points *(dka' gnad or dka' gnas brgyad)* in Madhyamaka philosophy.

Since the original publication of the article on the Tibetan Jo nang pas (no. 12)—the first of its kind on the subject—original texts composed by many of this remarkable school's principal authorities have very fortunately come to light and been made more readily available in printed form; at the time of writing of this article in the early 1960s, the oldest such works known to be accessible in a public collection in the West were probably some manuscripts held by the Reiss Museum in Mannheim. The article reprinted here will serve the purpose of providing the reader with two examples of the Tibetan historiography and doxography of this school, including a critique, by an eighteenth-century master of the Dga' ldan pa school, of the Jo nang pa doctrine of Emptiness of the other (Tib. *gzhan stong,* i.e., Emptiness of the heterogeneous, as opposed to Emptiness of self[-existence], *rang stong* or *svabhāvaśūnyatā*).

Concerning the negation of the so-called tetralemma (*catuṣkoṭi*), a characteristic and very fundamental procedure in Buddhist thought studied in the third article in this volume, further observations on it—and also on non-presuppositional and non-implicative negation *(prasajyapratiṣedha)* sometimes also referred to as propositional or extemal negation—are included in both parts of the present writer's *Studies in Indian and Tibetan Madhyamaka thought* (especially Part 1, pp. 109–12, 142–44, on the tetralemma itself, with Part 2, pp. 19–24, on the two types of negation: *paryudāsa* and *prasajyapratiṣedha*).

These papers were written over a time-span of several decades, and the reader will doubtless notice in them a gradual evolution in the translations of Indian and Tibetan technical terminology as well as in the description of systems of Buddhist philosophical thought. In the original of the earliest article reprinted here (no. 12), technical terms were often rendered by European equivalents with initial capitalized (following a style once introduced by the great Indologist Sylvain Lévi). In later papers, this style has been used more sparingly, exceptions still being, e.g., "Emptiness (of self-existence)" for *(svabhāva)śūnyatā,* "Gnosis" for *jñāna,* "Truth/Reality" for *satya,* and "Middle" for *madhyamaka.* It seems appropriate to retain this typographical convention at least in the case of European equivalents of terms having technical meanings in Buddhist thought where no single translation-equivalent seems to be entirely satisfactory and any rendering is an approximation. (Especially problematical is the matter of the translation of *satya* [Tib. *bden pa*] by "truth" in the Tibetan expression *bden par grub pa* [or *bden grub*] meaning "hypostatically established" or "reified.") Capitalization of a term serves to underscore the fact that it is not in the first place a definition in an English dictionary of the equivalent selected for an original Sanskrit or Tibetan term that will be determinative of its technical meaning in a given passage but, rather, definitions and uses of the term in our Sanskrit and Tibetan sources.

It is evident that studies in Indian, and in particular Buddhist, thought have long been complicated, sometimes obfuscated, and occasionally severely hampered by the fact that no system of technical equivalents—however conventional these must in many cases be—has been agreed upon by modern scholars. The development of a system of equivalents was, however, something achieved by Tibetan scholars and translators at a very early stage of their endeavours at the turn of the ninth century.

A case in point is the not infrequently found description of Nāgārjuna's Madhyamaka philosophy as "nihilism." Now, it is anything but clear how in modern English his philosophy of the Middle could be fittingly described as nihilism, a word that has as its closest equivalent Skt. *nāstikya* (even if Apte's English-Sanskrit dictionary has very curiously translated "nihilism" by Skt. *śūnyavāda*—while rendering "atheism" by *nāstikya* although this English word corresponds most closely to *anīśvara/nirīśvaravāda*—thus creating an inextricably confused skein of concepts and terms!). The very purpose of Nāgārjuna and his followers, the Mādhyamikas, was precisely to steer clear of the twin positions of nihilism and substantialism (metaphysical essentialism), each of which they regarded as an extreme (Sanskrit *anta* = Tibetan *mtha'*) to be carefully eschewed by the philosopher-practiser. (Many have indeed considered nihilism to be at least as dangerous as substantialism, if not more so; see *Kāśyapaparivarta* §§ 64–65 on *śūnyatādṛṣṭi* in relation to *pudgaladṛṣṭi,* as well as Nāgārjuna's *Mūlamadhyamakakārikā*s xiii.8 and xxiv.11 on *śūnyatādṛṣṭi.*) At the very same time Mādhyamikas have refused to adopt and entrench themselves in some putative middle position (*pakṣa,* etc.) or speculative view *(dṛṣṭi)* between two extremes (see *Samādhirājasūtra* ix.27). If, then, the Mādhyamikas are "centrists," they are so in a special sense. And Madhyamaka is strictly speaking no "third way." Buddhists in general have indeed ever sought to avoid the twin extremes of destructionism *(ucchedānta)* and eternalism *(śāśvatānta),* nihilism and substantialism. Those who explain *śūnya* and *śūnyatā* in terms of nihilism and nihility—or the *néant*—overlook the fact that the two Sanskrit expressions are as it were shorthand for *svabhāvaśūnya(tā),* so that what the Mādhyamika is speaking about is not nihilism but, rather, the fact of emptiness of self-existence. Thus a *śūnyatāvādin* is a *niḥsvabhāvavādin,* one who considers all factors of existence *(dharma),* all entities *(bhāva),* to be without self-existence *(svabhāva).* But he does not consider everything to be a mere nothing *(abhāva),* which would of course be an extreme position in terms of Madhyamaka.

The two extremes thus rejected are equivalent to the first two positions of a tetralemma *(catuṣkoṭi),* namely the positively expressed one and the negatively expressed one. And the notion of a "third way"—i.e., a putative intermediate position or view between two extremes, which is also rejected—is reducible to the fourth ("neither...nor") position, or perhaps to the third ("both...and") position, of a tetralemma. Now, in Madhyamaka thought, all four positions of the tetralemma are in fact negated (through non-presuppositional and non-implicative negation, *prasajyapratiṣedha*).

Most of the branches of Madhyamaka philosophy are, moreover, not philosophically idealist in so far as the pure Madhyamaka admits pragmatically the relative existence of an object of cognition (the *bāhyārtha*) external to mind *(citta, vijñāna)* (the Yogācāra-Madhyamaka tradition being something of an exception in this regard). And in this sense Mādhyamikas might be described as realists. But they are realists of a very particular kind, ones who posit the ultimate reality neither of an external, objective, world, nor of an internal, mental, world; hence, in some respects, they have been described as anti-realists as well as anti-foundationalists. In what sense the Yogacara-Vijñānavādins—the advocates of the Cittamātra (Tib. *sems tsam*) who make up the second main school of Mahāyāna philosophy alongside the Madhyamaka—are "idealists" (cf. *vijñānamātra*), "mentalists" (cf. *cittamātra*), or "representationists" (cf. *vijñaptimātra*) has equally been the subject of discussion among historians of Indian and Buddhist thought. Very interestingly, early in the history of the Madhyamaka, authors belonging to the Vijñānavāda movement apparently wrote commentaries on Nāgārjuna (now extant only in Chinese versions), examples being Asaṅga and Sthiramati.

Because of the very considerable problems we encounter in employing terms borrowed from Westem philosophy, or from the ordinary linguistic usage of some idiom of "Standard Average European," some writers have preferred to retain the original (Sanskrit or Tibetan) technical terms, which they then explain in a glossary, note, or monograph. But this solution is not really available when translating from Sanskrit and Tibetan.

It is clear, then, that an adequate philosophical description of the traditions and systems of Buddhist thought, and in particular of the Madhyamaka, is a matter of the utmost importance because it raises a number of critical and complex issues, as does the translation of the technical vocabulary of these traditions and systems. There are required both a sort of modern (meta)language capable of describing specific (and perhaps fairly unfamiliar) systems of thought and a coherent set of established and agreed technical European-language equivalents for translating the relevant philosophical vocabularies. In this regard—and concerning the unavoidable conventionality of such renderings—reference may be made to the present writer's "Some

Reflections on Translating Buddhist Philosophical Texts from Sanskrit and Tibetan" (1992: pp. 367–91) and "La traduction de la terminologie technique de la pensée indienne et bouddhique depuis Sylvain Lévi" (2007: pp. 145–71).

The glossary appended to the present book seeks to clarify some of the above-mentioned issues with particular reference to a selection of important technical terms in Madhyamaka thought.

Concerning the proper names Bhāviveka, Bhāvaviveka, Bhāvin, and Bhavya,—Legs ldan (')byed, Snang 'bral, and Skal ldan in Tibetan—, they have often been seen as alternative appellations of a single person, the sixth-century Mādhyamika known to Candrakīrti. And in some articles in this collection the appellations Bhā(va)viveka and Bhavya have been used as appellations for the same person. The name found in Candrakīrti's metrical *Madhyamakaśāstrastuti* is Bhāvin (rendered Legs ldan byed in the Tibetan translation published by de Jong); but in the prose of the *Prasannapadā* by the same authority we find Bhāvaviveka in the edition published by La Vallée Poussin. The form Bhāviveka is now widely accepted. It seems appropriate to refer to the author of the *Prajñāpradīpa*, a commentary on Nāgārjuna's *Mūlamadhyamakakārikā*s, and of the *Madhyamakahṛdaya*(*kārikā*s), an independent text, as Bhāviveka. Whether this Bhāviveka was also the author of the *Madhyamakārthasaṃgraha* is perhaps not altogether settled yet. The *Madhyamakaratnapradīpa* is evidently to be assigned to a later Bhavya. The authorship of the *(Madhyamakahṛdayavṛtti-)Tarkajvālā* ascribed in the Tibetan Bstan 'gyur to Bhavya—and very often assigned to Bhāviveka, which, if correct, would make this very extensive work an autocommentary—raises problems discussed in section 5 of the present publication. The main source of the "Svātantrika" branch of the Madhyamaka was, of course, the author of the *Prajñāpradīpa*. On these matters see also sections 2, 6, 11, and 15 in this publication. When reading the relevant articles in this book, these points are to be kept in mind. As for Bhavyakīrti and Bhavyarāja, they are different, and later, figures.

My sincere thanks go to those connected with the publication of this volume, and in particular to Tom Tillemans and Burkhard Quessel, both of whom have spared no pains in arranging for the reprinting of these articles.

D.S.R.

Abbreviations

A	Aṅguttaranikāya
AA	*Abhisamayālaṃkāra* ascribed to Maitreya(nātha). Edited by Th. Stcherbatsky and E. Obermiller, Bibliotheca Buddhica xxiii, Leningrad, 1929.
AAĀ	*Abhisamayālaṃkārālokā Prajñāpāramitāvyākhyā* of Haribhadra. Edited, together with the text of the *Aṣṭasāhasrikā Prajñāpāramitā,* by U. Wogihara, Tokyo, 1932.
AAWG	Abhandlungen der Akademie der Wissenschaften zu Göttingen
ABORI	*Annals of the Bhandarkar Oriental Research Institute*
AK	*Abhidharmakośa* of Vasubandhu. Edited by P. Pradhan, Tibetan Sanskrit Works Series, volume VIII, Patna, 1967.
AKBh	*Abhidharmakośabhāṣya* of Vasubandhu. Edited by P. Pradhan, Tibetan Sanskrit Works Series, volume VIII, Patna, 1967.
AKV	*Abhidharmakośavyākhyā* of Yaśomitra. Edited together with *AK* and *AKBh* by Svāmī Dvārikādāsa Śāstrī in four parts, Bauddha Bhāratī Series 5–7, 8/9, Vārāṇasī, 1970–73.
ALB	*Adyar Library Bulletin*
AM	*Asia Major*
AO	*Acta Orientalia*
AOH	*Acta Orientalia Academiae Scientiarum Hungaricae*
BEFEO	*Bulletin de l'École française d'Extrême-Orient*
BHSD	Franklin Edgerton, *Buddhist Hybrid Sanskrit Dictionary*
BNTh	*Bu ston rnam thar* by Sgra tshad pa Rin chen rnam rgyal (1318–88). Contained in volume sha of the Gsung 'bum of Bu ston Rin chen grub (1290–1364).

BrCh	*'Brug pa chos 'byung* of 'Brug chen Padma dkar po (1527–92)
BSOAS	*Bulletin of the School of Oriental and African Studies, University of London*
BSOS	*Bulletin of the School of Oriental Studies, London*
C	Co ne edition of the Bstan 'gyur. Microfiche from the Institute for Advanced Study of World Religions, New York, 1974.
CŚ	*Catuḥśataka* of Ārya-Deva. Chapters 8–16 edited with Candrakīrti's commentary by Vidhushekhara Bhattacharya, Visva-Bharati Series No. 2, Calcutta, 1931. Edited by K. Lang, Copenhagen, 1986.
D	Sde dge edition of the Bka' 'gyur and Bstan 'gyur
DNg	*Deb ther sngon po* of 'Gos lo tsā ba Gzhon nu dpal (1392–1481). Kun bde gling xylograph; published in facsimile by Lokesh Chandra, New Delhi, 1974.
EB	*Eastern Buddhist*
EW	*East and West*
GK	Gauḍapāda, *Gauḍapadīyakārikā*s
HJAS	*Harvard Journal of Asiatic Studies*
IBK	*Indogaku-Bukkyōgaku Kenkyū*
IHQ	*Indian Historical Quarterly*
IIJ	*Indo-Iranian Journal*
IT	*Indologica Taurinensa*
JA	*Journal Asiatique*
JAOS	*Journal of the American Oriental Society*
JASB	*Journal of the Asiatic Society of Bengal*
JBBRAS	*Journal of the Bombay Branch of the Royal Asiatic Society*
JIABS	*Journal of the International Association of Buddhist Studies*
JIBS	*Journal of Indian and Buddhist Studies (Indogaku Bukkyōgaku Kenkyū)*
JIP	*Journal of Indian Philosophy*
JPASB	*Journal and Proceedings of the Asiatic Society of Bengal*
JPTS	*Journal of the Pali Text Society*
JRAS	*Journal of the Royal Asiatic Society*
JRASB	*Journal of the Royal Asiatic Society of Bengal*

KD	Gsung 'bum of Klong rdol bla ma Ngag dbang blo bzang (1719–94). lHa sa xylograph.
KhG	*Chos 'byung mkhas pa'i dga' ston* of Dpa' bo Gtsug lag phreng ba (1504–66). Published by Lokesh Chandra, New Delhi, 1959–65.
KNZB	*Dka' gnad/gnad brgyad kyi zin bris* of Tsong kha pa / Rgyal tshab Dar ma rin chen
KSS	Kāśī Sanskrit Series
KZ	*Zeitschrift für vergleichende Sprachforschung*
M	Manuscrit Pelliot tibétain 814, Bibliothèque Nationale, Paris
MA	*Madhyamakāvatāra* of Candrakīrti. Edited with the author's own *Bhāṣya (MABh)* by L. de La Vallée Poussin, Bibliotheca Buddhica IX, St. Petersburg, 1907–12.
MAV	*Madhyāntavibhāga* ascribed to Maitreya(nātha). Edited by G. M. Nagao, Tokyo, 1964.
MAVBh	*Madhyāntavibhāgabhāṣya* of Vasubandhu. Edited together with *MAV* by G. M. Nagao, Tokyo, 1964.
MAVṬ	*Madhyāntavibhāgaṭīkā* of Sthiramati. Edited by Ramachandra Pandeya, *Madhyānta-Vibhāga-Śāstra,* Delhi, 1971.
MCB	*Mélanges chinois et bouddhiques*
MMK	*Mūlamadhyamakakārikā*s of Nāgārjuna. Edited by L. de La Vallée Poussin, Bibliotheca Buddhica IV, St. Petersburg, 1903–13; edited by J. W. de Jong, Adyar Library Series, vol. 109, Adyar, 1977.
MSA	*Mahāyānasūtrālaṃkāra* ascribed to Maitreya(nātha). Edited by S. Lévi, Paris, 1907.
MSABh	*Mahāyānasūtrālaṃkārabhāṣya* ascribed to Vasubandhu. Edited together with the *MSA* by S. Lévi, Paris, 1907.
N	Narthang edition of the Bka' 'gyur and Bstan 'gyur
NS	*Nyāyasūtra*s
OLZ	*Orientalistische Literaturzeitung*
P	Peking edition of the Bka' 'gyur and Bstan 'gyur
PEW	*Philosophy East and West*
PPMV	*Prasannapadā Madhyamakavṛttiḥ* of Candrakīrti. Edited together with the *MMK* by L. de La Vallée Poussin, Bibliotheca Buddhica IV, St. Petersburg, 1903–1913.

PSJZ	*Dpag bsam ljon bzang* of Sum pa mkhan po Ye shes dpal 'byor (1704–88). Published by Sarat Chandra Das, Calcutta, 1908.
RGV	*Ratnagotravibhāga Mahāyānottaratantraśāstra* ascribed to Maitreya(nātha). Sanskrit text edited by E. H. Johnston and T. Chowdhury, Patna, 1950, together with the *RGVV*, the commentary (Vṛtti, or Vyākhyā = Tib. *Rnam par bshad pa*) ascribed to Asaṅga. Tibetan translation edited by Z. Nakamura, Tokyo, 1967. (In the Chinese tradition the Śāstra is attributed to a certain *Sāramati.)
RGVV	*Ratnagotravibhāga-Vyākhyā.* Edited by E. H. Johnston, Patna, 1950.
RM	*Re'u mig* of Sum pa mkhan po. Appended to this author's *PSJZ,* and published as *dPag-bsam-ljon-bzaṅ,* Part III, by Lokesh Chandra, New Delhi, 1959.
RO	*Rocznik Orientalistyczny*
S-P	Svātantrika-Prāsaṅgika
StII	*Studien zur Indologie und Iranistik*
T	Taishō canon
ThG	*Thu'u bkvan Grub mtha' = Grub mtha' shel gyi me long* of Thu'u bkwan Blo bzang Chos kyi nyi ma (1732–1802)
TP	*T'oung Pao*
TPS	*Tibetan Painted Scrolls* by Giuseppe Tucci, Roma, 1949.
TS	*Tattvasaṃgraha* of Śāntarakṣita. Edited by Svāmī Dvārikādāsa Śāstrī, Bauddha Bhāratī Series volumes 1–2, Vārāṇasī, 1968.
TSP	*Tattvasaṃgrahapañjikā* of Kamalaśīla. Edited together with *TS.*
VP	*Vākyapadīya*
VV	*Vigrahavyāvartanī* of Nāgārjuna. Edited with the author's commentary by E. H. Johnston and A. Kunst in *Mélanges chinois et bouddhiques* 9 (1951); reprinted together with an English translation by K. Bhattacharya, *The dialectical method of Nāgārjuna,* Delhi, 1978.
WZKS	*Wiener Zeitschrift für die Kunde Südasiens*
WZKSO	*Wiener Zeitschrift für die Kunde Süd- und Ostasiens*
ZDMG	*Zeitschrift der Deutschen Morgenländischen Gesellschaft*

1. Mathematical and Linguistic Models in Indian Thought: The Case of Zero and *Śūnyatā**

I

BEGINNING WITH the ancient Greek thinkers, the exact sciences have played what may be called a paradigmatic role in the formation and development of Western thought. And as the exact science par excellence, mathematics has indubitably exercised there a fundamental influence not only in the natural sciences but also by extension in the sciences of man inclusive of the "humanities." Especially in linguistics and philosophical logic mathematical models, formalizations, and calculi occupy a prominent place. And despite the fact that Saussurean structuralism was not derived from mathematics, the mathematical mode of thought has clearly not been without impact in the development of some forms of structuralism. At the same time linguistics and the linguistically based form of structuralism have also exercised very considerable influence, so that a linguistically inspired paradigm has taken an important place in the main stream of modern Western thought.[1]

In this respect a certain convergence has arisen, consciously or unconsciously,[2] between modern Western thought and classical Indian thought. For when the Indologist looks for ideas and methods that have played a modelling and paradigmatic role in the history of Indian thought, it is probably

* First published in *Wiener Zeitschrift für die Kunde Südasiens* 22 (1978), pp. 171–81.

1. Cf. C. Lévi-Strauss, *Anthropologie structurale* (Paris, 1958), chap. iii; *L'homme nu* (Paris, 1971), "Finale"; J. Piaget, *Le structuralisme* (Paris, 1968), p. 17; R. Jakobson, *Main Trends in the Science of Language* (London and New York, 1973). Cf. J. Lyons, *Semantics* (Cambridge, 1977), pp. 230–31.

2. Cf. J. F. Staal, *Euclides en Pāṇini* (Amsterdam, 1963); *Philosophy East and West* 15 (1965), pp. 99–116; S. Al-George, in *Actes du Xᵉ Congrès international des linguistes* (1970), 2, pp. 235–40; T. de Mauro, ed., F. de Saussure, *Cours de linguistique générale* (Paris, 1972), p. 380.

above all to the grammatical śāstra that he would turn. The Indian thinkers have indeed themselves pointed to the paradigmatic significance of grammar in their civilization, and one of them has referred to it as a universal science *(sarvapārṣada-śāstra)*.[3] Mathematics appears on the contrary to have generally occupied a relatively less prominent place in the history of Indian thought taken as a whole.

II

At least one interesting exception to this general tendency may, however, be recalled here. As is well known, the Abhidharma schools of Buddhism developed a theory of elements or factors *(dharma)*, each of which is considered to bear its own specific characteristic that determines it.[4] But the precise nature of the *dharmas* was the subject of much discussion in the Buddhist schools, which differed appreciably as to their ontological status; and one of the major problems that arose concerned the nature of a *dharma* with respect to its efficiency *(kāritra)* in the three times, namely present, past, and future. The Sarvāstivāda or Vaibhāṣika school maintained that the *dharmas* exist in all three times, which are in fact determined by just this efficiency. Thus, when a *dharma* exercises its *kāritra*, it is said to be present; when it does not yet exercise it, it is said to be future; and when having exercised its efficiency it has ceased, it is said to be past.[5] But there was disagreement among the Ābhidharmikas as to how such a *dharma* goes from one point in the time-scale to another.

Four distinct solutions to the problem have been recorded by Vasubandhu in his *Abhidharmakośabhāṣya* (v.26). One solution is ascribed to Dharmatrāta, who maintained that there takes place in time a change of condition *(bhāvānyathātva)* rather than of substance *(dravya)*, like in the Sāṃkhya system; this change is then compared to the change *(pariṇāma)* of

3. Helārāja on Bhartṛhari, *Vākyapadīya* iii.3.1. (Cf. the term *sarvavedapāriṣada* in Patañjali's *Mahābhāṣya* ii.1.58, vt. 1, and vi.3.14, vt. 2?)

4. *Abhidharmakośabhāṣya* I.1 (ed. Pradhan, p. 2.9): *nirvacanaṃ tu svalakṣaṇadhāraṇād dharmaḥ*. See Th. Stcherbatsky, *Central Conception of Buddhism* (London, 1923), p. 26, with O. Rosenberg, *Probleme der buddhistischen Philosophie* (Heidelberg, 1924), pp. 72, 81. Cf. M. und W. Geiger, *Pāli: dhamma* (Ab. Bayer. Ak. d. Wiss., Phil. Kl. xxxi/1, Munich, 1921); H. von Glasenapp, *ZDMG* 92 (1938), pp. 383ff.

5. See *Abhidharmakośa* v.26d: *adhvānaḥ kāritreṇa vyavasthitāḥ; Abhidharmakośabhāṣya* ii.46 (p. 76.12ff.); ii.56 (p. 95.3: *ko 'yaṃ puruṣakāro nāma / yasya dharmasya yat kāritram*); v.26d (*yadā sa dharmaḥ kāritraṃ na karoti tadânāgataḥ / yadā karoti tadā pratyutpannaḥ / yadā kṛtvā niruddhas tadâtīta iti /*).

milk to curd, which involves a change of one property—e.g., taste—but not of another—e.g., colour. The solution connected with the name of Ghoṣaka maintained that the change in question is one of characteristic *(lakṣaṇa),* which does not involve a change of condition; the process is then compared to the case where a man becomes enamoured of one woman without being free of passion for others. Another solution is ascribed to Buddhadeva, who spoke of relational otherness, explaining that a *dharma* that evolves in time may be said to be other *(anya)* with respect to the preceding and the subsequent without this involving a change of substance, just as one and the same woman is said to be a mother in relation to her child and a daughter in relation to her own mother.[6] In each of the three solutions thus offered, the example adduced to illustrate the process of change in time remains of an everyday, non-scientific kind.

The case is somewhat different in the fourth solution connected with a certain Bhadanta Vasumitra, who is probably to be identified as one of the leading figures at the time of Kaniṣka's Great Council.[7] Vasumitra explained the process in question by saying: "A *dharma* evolving in the [three] times is stated to be other according to the different states it enters, [the change in question being then] due to otherness of state *(avasthāntarataḥ)* but not of substance." The example adduced to illustrate this is that of a marker or counter *(vartikā)* in reckoning which in the unit position has the value of a unit, in the hundred's position that of a hundred, and in the thousand's position that of a thousand.[8] It is this explanation by Vasumitra that the *Kośakāra* has described (v.26c)—provisionally—as correct, although as a Sautrāntika Vasubandhu would criticize all these solutions (v.27).

Vasumitra's explanation is of interest to us both because it adduces a more "scientific" example, and because it provides us with one of the earliest available references to arithmetical place-value and hence to one of the functions of zero.[9]

6. In his *Vyākhyā* on the *Abhidharmakośabhāṣya* v.26, Yaśomitra remarks that Buddhadeva's view would entail the existence of all three times in a given time. This is a view rejected by the Sautrāntika.

7. Kaniṣka's year 1 is placed either in 78 C.E. or in the first part of the second century (other dates have also been proposed). Cf. G. Fussmann, *BEFEO* 1974, pp. 48ff.

8. P. Pradhan reads *vartikā* in his edition of *Abhidharmakośabhāṣya* v.26 (p. 296): *dharmo 'dhvasu pravartamāno 'vasthām avasthāṃ prāpyānyo nirdiśyate, avasthāntarato na dravyāntarataḥ/ yathâikā vartikā ekāṅke nikṣiptā ekam ity ucyate, śatāṅke śataṃ, sahasrāṅke sahasram iti/* But Dvarikadas Shastri in his edition (p. 806) reads *gulikā,* following Yaśomitra's *Vyākhyā.*

9. For a discussion see W. E. Clark, "Hindu-Arabic Numerals," in *Indian Studies in Honor*

This example is indeed quite well known in Indian thought and it turns up in a number of later texts. An equivalent term—*nikṣepavartikā*—is to be found in the *Vibhāṣāprabhāvṛtti*.[10] Yaśomitra in his *Vyākhyā* uses the term *gulikā* "ball, bead"; and in his *Pañjikā* on the *Tattvasaṃgraha* (1786), Kamalaśīla specifies that the counter was of clay *(mṛdguḍikā)*. On the other hand the *Vyāsabhāṣya* on the *Yogasūtra* has the term *rekhā* "line, stroke";[11] and Vijñānabhikṣu glosses *rekhā* as the *aṅkaviśeṣa*, which denotes 100 when joined with two zeros *(bindu)*, but 10 when joined with only one zero. The *Vyāsabhāṣya* differs from Vasubandhu by connecting the example of the *rekhā* in the different places and the example of a woman who may be either a mother or daughter according to the particular relationship in question (which in the *Abhidharmakośabhāṣya* was connected with Buddhadeva's solution). The term *rekhā* in the same context is also found in Śaṃkara's commentary on the *Brahmasūtras* (ii.2.17).

The terms *vartikā* and *gulikā/guḍikā* seem to presuppose the abacus system of reckoning, whereas the term *rekhā* evidently refers to a written zero (cf. Vijñānabhikṣu's explanation).

III

In view of the fact that in the Sanskrit mathematical and astronomical literature the word *śūnya* has the meaning of zero, there exists another point in the history of Indian thought where, at least in principle, it might be supposed that mathematics has had some influence on philosophy: the Buddhist theory of the emptiness *(śūnyatā)* of *dharmas*. And some scholars have in fact suggested a connexion between the Madhyamaka theory of *śūnyatā* developed by Nāgārjuna and the mathematical zero.[12]

---

of C. R. Lanman (Cambridge MA, 1929), pp. 223ff. See also the studies cited below in note 14.

10. Ed. P. Jaini, p. 260: *yathā nikṣepavartikâikāṅkavinyastâikêty ucyate, sâiva śatāṅke śataṃ sahasrāṅke sahasram iti.*

11. Vyāsabhāṣya on *Yogasūtra* iii.13: *na dharmī tryadhvā/ dharmās tu tryadhvānaḥ/ te lakṣitā alakṣitāś ca tāṃ tām avasthām prāpnuvanto 'nyatvena pratinirdiśyante 'vasthāntarato na dravyāntarataḥ/ yathâikā rekhā śatasthāne śataṃ daśasthāne daśâikā câikasthāne/ yathā câikatve 'pi strī mātā cocyate duhitā ca svasā cêti/* (variant reading: ... *lakṣitā alakṣitāḥ/ tatra lakṣitāḥ tāṃ tām avasthām* ...).

12. See P. T. Raju, "The Principle of Four-Cornered Negation," in *Review of Metaphysics* 7 (1953–54), p. 701 (on zero as an indeterminate number); B. K. Matilal, *Epistemology, Grammar, and Logic in Indian Philosophical Analysis* (The Hague, 1971), pp. 151–52 ("it

It has however to be noted in the first place that *śūnya* as a term for zero appears much later in our sources than the canonical Buddhist concept, and also after Nāgārjuna (no later than ca. 200 C.E.). The earliest datable attestations of *śūnya* in the meaning of zero seem to be in the Paitāmahasiddhānta of the *Viṣṇudharmottarapurāṇa*, which apparently goes back to the early fifth century, in the *Bṛhatsaṃhitā* (viii.20) of Varāhamihira (sixth century),[13] and in another work by the same author based on five astronomical siddhāntas—the Pauliśa, Romaka, Vāsiṣṭha, Saura (Sūrya), and Paitāmaha—entitled *Pañcasiddhāntikā*.[14] In Sphujidhvaja's *Yavanajātaka*—a versified version, made in 269/270 C.E., of another Sanskrit work (the source of which was an Alexandrine manuscript in Greek) going back to 149/150 C.E.—the words used for zero are *kha* and *bindu*, terms that were to remain in regular use later.[15] In the new *Sūryasiddhānta* (i.29) *kha* is used for zero.[16] Amongst literary works, the *Vāsavadattā* of Subandhu (ca. sixth century) employs the expression *śūnyabindu* for the symbol for zero.[17]

As already observed above, however, place-value (and hence a function of zero) was known to Vasumitra. And if this Vasumitra is the well-known contemporary of Kaniṣka, as may be the case, he could also be the contemporary of Nāgārjuna (if not older), and also of Sphujidhvaja's Sanskrit source of 149/150.[18]

---

was left to Nāgārjuna to make a very significant use of this mathematical concept [viz. zero] in philosophy").

13. Cf. W. E. Clark, loc. cit., pp. 227–28.

14. For a discussion of early uses of zero and its symbols see also B. Datta and A. N. Singh, *History of Hindu Mathematics* (Lahore, 1935), i, pp. 75ff.; D. M. Bose, S. N. Sen, and B. V. Subbarayyappa, *Concise History of Science in India* (New Delhi, 1971), pp. 175, 586; P. V. Kane, *History of Dharmaśāstra,* V/I[2] (Poona, 1974), pp. 699–702; O. Neugebauer and D. Pingree, eds., *Pañcasiddhāntika* (Copenhagen, 1970–71), p. 11n12. On the *Paitāmahasiddhānta* of the *Viṣṇudharmottarapurāṇa,* see D. Pingree, *Journal for the History of Astronomy* 7 (1976), pp. 109–23. On *śūnya* in the *Chandaḥsūtra* see below.

15. See D. Pingree, *Yavanajātaka* (Cambridge MA, 1978), § 79, 6d and § 79, 7d. I wish to thank Professor Pingree for kindly giving me this reference to his forthcoming volume. He also points out to me that, in some instances, a place-value system was used by Sphujidhvaja (whose practice in this matter was, however, mixed).

16. Cf. W. E. Clark, loc. cit., pp. 226–27.

17. *Vāsavadattā,* ed. L. H. Gray, p. 174 ("cipher"). Cf. W. E. Clark, loc. cit., pp. 225, 229.

18. The evidence concerning Vasumitra has not been considered by Clark and some other more recent writers on the subject of zero in ancient India. Clark (loc. cit., p. 236), for example, refers only to the *Yogabhāṣya* passage. The date of the Bakhshālī manuscript, which uses zero, is not established; cf. Clark, loc. cit., pp. 224–25.

A few words need now to be said about *śūnya* and some cognate or semantically equivalent words.

Already in the *Ṛgveda* the cognate word *śū́na* appears, as a neuter noun, with the meaning of "lack, absence, emptiness" (in sentences introduced by the negative particle *mā́*). Later it is found as an adjective meaning "swollen, increased."[19] As for the word *śūnyá,* it appears as an adjective in the Brāhmaṇa literature with the meaning "hollow, deserted," and then in the Epic with the meaning "empty, vacant (of a look); devoid," etc. In the Epic *śūnya* is in addition attested as a noun meaning "desert; empty place."

In the meaning of "nought, cipher, zero," *śūnya* has as a synonym the word *kha* as well as such words as *ākāśa, ambara,* and *viyat,* all denoting empty space. The word *kha* is attested from the *Ṛgveda* in the sense of "hollow, cavity," and from the Brāhmaṇa literature in the meaning of "empty space, sky, air."[20]

It is to be remarked that, as a word denoting the unlimited *(apeiron), ākāśa* served in ancient Indian thought so to speak as a model for the concept of *bráhman.* And *ākāśa* and *kha* are in fact attested as names for *bráhman.*[21]

The word *śūnya* has been usually derived from the root *śvi- (śū-)* "to swell, increase, grow." Hence, both etymologically and in its actual usage, *śūnya* is linked with the ideas of swelling and blowing up and hence of hollowing out.[22]

Finally, just as according to the *Bṛhadāraṇyakopaniṣad* (v.1.1) the full or "plenum" *(pūrṇa,* i.e., *bráhman)* is subject to neither increase nor decrease, in Buddhist thought the absolute element *(dhātu)*—which is empty *(śūnya)* only of all adventitious factors but *aśūnya* of certain constitutive informing factors—is subject to neither diminishing nor increase (*Ratnagotravibhāga* i.154–55). In this connexion it is interesting that the word *pūrṇa* has been used for zero by Bhāskara (twelfth century) in the Gaṇitādhyāya of his *Siddhāntaśiromaṇi.*[23]

But concerning the question whether the theory of *śūnyatā* was inspired by or modelled on a mathematical concept, in the present state of our knowledge we can only say that neither the history of the Buddhist doctrine

19. Cf. the commentaries on Pāṇini's *Aṣṭādhyāyī* vii.2.14.

20. Cf. A. K. Coomaraswamy, *BSOS* 7 (1934), pp. 487–97; P. V. Kane, op. cit., p. 702.

21. Cf. *Bṛhadāraṇyakopaniṣad* v.1.1 *(kha); Chāndogyopaniṣad* iii.18.1 *(ākāśa)* and iv.10.5 *(kha).*

22. Cf. M. Mayrhofer, *Kurzgefaßtes etymologisches Wörterbuch des Altindischen,* s.v. *śū́nam.*

23. Cf. P. V. Kane, op. cit., p. 702n.

starting with the canonical scriptures, nor the semantic history in Sanskrit of the words *śūnya* and *śūnyatā,* nor the history of mathematics and astronomy in India appears to establish that the philosophical concept of *śūnyatā* in the Madhyamaka or elsewhere in Buddhism has anything to do directly with the mathematical zero. This is consistent with our initial observation that in ancient India mathematical concepts did not often serve as models or paradigms in philosophy. At the most one could perhaps speak only of a subjacent and remote resemblance or cognitive homology between independently developed concepts.

IV

It may now be asked whether the theory of *śūnyatā* has connexions with the other model and paradigmatic type of thinking mentioned above: ancient Indian linguistic theory.

It is to be observed in the first place that the *Chandaḥsūtra,* a treatise on metrics attributed to Piṅgala, employs the word *śūnya* (viii.28–31). There the expression is used when a unit is not to be halved (since this would produce a fraction), so that it is there the sign of absence of a metrical operation.[24] But although the *Chandaḥsūtra* has sometimes been dated as early as 200 B.C.,[25] its date is uncertain, and the relevance of its testimony for the early history of the philosophical notion of *śūnyatā* is accordingly doubtful. Moreover, while *śūnya* in this text does clearly enough relate to the voidness of a particular operation so that its use might be compared with the philosophical *śūnya* which concerns a certain kind of inoperativeness—namely that of all entities since they are empty of own-being (i.e., aseitic existence, *svabhāvaśūnya*)—this usage has no bearing on the meaning of the term in the older Buddhist literature, where the allusion is in the first place to emptiness.

In grammatical theory going back to Pāṇini too we meet with certain concepts which are of interest in the present context, even though their historical links with the *śūnyatā* theory are anything but perspicuous.

In the *Aṣṭādhyāyī* we find the term *lopa* "elision, syncope" defined as non-appearance of a linguistic element (*adarśana,* i.1.60). The term refers to the non-realization in the actual speech *(bhāṣā)* of ordinary usage *(laukikaprayoga)* of an element posited in grammar as existing on the level

24. See A. Weber, *Indische Studien,* VIII (Berlin, 1863), p. 446. Cf. W. E. Clark, loc. cit., p. 227; P. V. Kane, op. cit., p. 700.

25. Cf. W. E. Clark, loc. cit., p. 227; P. V. Kane, op. cit., p. 701.

of the *sthānin,* i.e., the theoretically postulated form. In other words, what is postulated on the level of the *sthānin* may, according to grammatical theory, not in fact be represented on the level of the *ādeśa* "substitute," i.e., the linguistic element which is in actual speech substituted for the *sthānin.*[26] And *lopa* as a zero substitute is then opposed to *śravaṇa* "hearing," that is, realization of the *sthānin* by means of a full substitute-morph in actual speech.

Lopa = *adarśana* affects the postulated grammatical element that is termed *prasakta* "applicable"—or *prasaṅgavat* "having application"—on the level of the *sthānin.*[27] And the *sthānaśabda* is then termed *prasaṅgavācin,*[28] *sthānin* and *prasakta* being thus largely equivalent expressions.[29]

The concept of *lopa* thus corresponds, at least in part, to that of zero in modern linguistics.[30] Furthermore, through *lopa* the *sthānin* might be regarded as in some sense void or empty on the level of real speech-usage. And perhaps to this extent a parallel (though a very limited one) presents itself with the *dharmas* which serve as theoretical factors of philosophical analysis, although in fact they are empty of own-being *(svabhāvaśūnya)* according to the Mahāyāna.

Despite the fact that the word *śūnya* does not form a part of the grammarian's technical vocabulary, it is remarkable that the notion of a linguistic zero appears in close association with the idea of the *prasakta/prasaṅgavat.* Now in the Madhyamaka the theory of *śūnyatā* is quite closely linked with concepts expressed by terms derived from *pra-saj-*. Thus the Mādhyamika speaks of the *prasakta* (that which arises or applies within the frame of discursive development and dichotomizing conceptualization);[31] of a *prasaṅga* (the unde-

26. See Patañjali, *Mahābhāṣya* i.1.62, vt. 14: *lopo 'py ādeśaḥ/ katham/ ādiśyate yaḥ sa ādeśaḥ/ lopo 'py ādiśyate . . .* Cf. P. Thieme, *Mélanges d'indianisme à la mémoire de L. Renou* (Paris, 1968), pp. 715–23; A. Wezler, *KZ* 86 (1972), pp. 7–20. For the application of i.1.60 see vi.1.66ff.

27. *Mahābhāṣya* i.1.60, vt. 4: *prasaktādarśanaṃ lopasaṃjñaṃ bhavati.*

28. *Mahābhāṣya* i.1.51, vt. 3. *Prasaṅga* glosses *sthāna.*

29. Cf. A. Wezler, loc. cit., pp. 12–13.

30. For a discussion of this subject cf. W. S. Allen, "Zero and Pāṇini," in *Indian Linguistics* 16 (1955), pp. 107–13; S. Al-George, "The Semiosis of Zero according to Pāṇini," *EW* 17 (1967), pp. 115–24. Cf. T. de Mauro, ed., F. de Saussure, *Cours de linguistique générale* (Paris, 1972), p. 380.

31. In Candrakīrti's *Prasannapadā* vii.2 (ed. La Vallée Poussin, p. 147.8) *prasakta* = *prāpta* (cf. *prasajyate* ~ *prāpnoti* and *prasaṅga* ~ *prāpti*). See also *Prasannapadā* ii.8 and ii.11; ii.23.

sired consequence resulting within this frame);[32] of *prasaṅgāpādana* (a form of reasoning based on a reduction to absurdity or logical impossibility of a conceptual position postulating some entity);[33] and of the *prasajyapratiṣedha* (absolute non-presuppositional negation which, contrary to relative or choice negation, does not commit one to asserting the contrary of what one has denied within the frame of discursive development and dichotomizing conceptualization, since it is shown by philosophical analysis that the subject of the negated proposition is null and empty and that no predicate or property whatsoever can therefore be ascribed to it).[34]

This terminological convergence is at least worthy of note even if it is difficult to pursue it further by showing that the two systems of thought in question—the Vaiyākaraṇa's and the Mādhyamika's—are directly related historically or systematically comparable.

At the same time there are undeniably very considerable differences between the grammarian's zeroing of a postulated form and the philosopher's "zeroing" of conceptual entities and factors of analysis *(niḥsvabhāvatā, dharmanairātmya).*

As has been noted above, the *prasakta/prasaṅgavat* form belongs in grammatical theory to the postulated level of the *sthānin,* which in the event of *lopa* is not actually realized by means of a full *ādeśa* in speech-usage. In the Śūnyavāda of the Madhyamaka school it is the *saṃvṛti* or *vyavahāra* level of transactional usage that is comprised of the conceptual entities and the analytical factors which are postulated and applicable (*"prasakta"* so to say) in the frame either of conceptual thinking *(prapañca* and *vikalpa)* with its associated speculative views *(dṛṣṭi),* or of philosophical analysis. But in reality these entities and factors are empty of own-being; and on the *paramārtha* level they are simply not "realized."[35]

32. With the grammarians, *prasaṅga* "(provisional) occurrence" refers to the domain of application of a rule, operation, or word, which may be annulled by the actual conditions or a subsequent rule; cf. L. Renou, *Terminologie grammaticale du sanskrit* (Paris, 1957), p. 230. More generally, *prasaṅga* may also mean "occasion, application."

33. Concerning the question of reasoning by the absurd in the grammatical tradition, see P. Boudon, *JA* 1938, pp. 358–91.

34. The term *prasajyapratiṣedha* was used also by the grammarians and ritualists. In grammar the term is used to denote a prohibition that operates after provisional (or virtual) application, and where negation pure and simple rather than the affirmation of the contrary (as in *paryudāsa* negation) predominates; it is then defined as verbally bound negation. Cf. J. F. Staal, *BSOAS* 25 (1962), pp. 58ff.; G. Cardona, *Language* 43 (1967), pp. 34ff.

35. Cf. Nāgārjuna, *Mūlamadhyamakakārikās*, chap. xxiv.

Hence the relation between the two levels in question—the subjacent one of the postulated ideal *sthānin* and the actual speech-usage one of the *ādeśa* (with the *prasakta* on the *sthānin* level in grammar), and the absolute *paramārtha* level and the relative transactional one (with the so-to-say applicable *prasakta* factors on the *saṃvṛti* level in the Madhyamaka)—is not congruent in the two systems.

Most importantly, according to the Mādhyamika, *śūnyatā* does not refer to any kind of entity, ultimate or conventional. Nor is it another factor in philosophical analysis on the same level as the *dharma*s, and it transcends the duality of conditioned *(saṃskṛta)* and unconditioned *(asaṃskṛta).* It is then comparable with a higher-level principle that directs the correct analysis of the (lower-level) entities and factors, and that describes the ultimately real state of affairs, viz. the non-substantiality and emptiness of all *dharma*s. In the grammatical theory of *lopa,* there does not seem to be a place for anything corresponding to *śūnyatā,* which refers metalinguistically to the fact, or truth, that all conceptual entities and analytic factors are empty "ciphers" in philosophical and psychological description.

Furthermore, the conceptual process of construction or *(abhi)saṃskāra* in Buddhist philosophy and the linguistic process of word formation or *śabdasaṃskāra* in Indian grammar are hardly isomorphic or directly comparable.

V

While it has been possible to adduce an interesting link between mathematical and philosophical thought in the case of Vasumitra's theory of the phases of a *dharma,* it has not so far been possible to establish any clear and direct influence of the arithmetical zero on the theory of *śūnyatā.* It has been noted, however, that in the *Chandaḥsūtra* the term *śūnya* is evidently used in connexion with the absence of an operation. And it has also been possible to point to a certain parallel, albeit a very limited one, between the *lopa* of a *prasakta* linguistic form in grammar and some important features of the Madhyamaka; but this parallel rests largely on a terminological convergence that scarcely suffices to demonstrate the dependence of the philosophical notion on a grammatical concept.

The main point of contact between the Śūnyavāda and the departments of Indian thought examined above appears, then, to lie with the grammarians' (and the ritualists') *prasajyapratiṣedha* and the theory of absolute negation as developed by the Mādhyamikas, especially from the time of Bhā(va)viveka (sixth century) and Candrakīrti (seventh century), who both elaborate on it. The (onto-)logical use to which the Mādhyamika puts the *prasajyapratiṣedha* is of course distinct from the more limited application it had elsewhere.

If our search for either a mathematical or a linguistic background or epistemic homology for the philosophical theory of *śūnyatā* has thus resulted largely in a *non liquet,* the outcome of the investigation has at least the usefulness of underscoring the specificity—indeed the uniqueness—of the philosophical concept. The theory of *śūnyatā* evidently represents a new threshold in the history of Indian thought. And this uniqueness may help to account for the fact that, in the course of the development of Indian philosophy, the theory has raised many a problem—and perhaps also for the fact that, so often, it has been the object of misunderstanding on the part of philosophers, Buddhist as well as non-Buddhist, belonging to other tendencies who were unfamiliar with its background, significance, and implications.

Postscript (2008)

In the decades intervening since the first publication of the preceding article, the theme of Indian grammar in relation to geometry and mathematics has been taken up by J. Bronkhorst, "Pāṇini and Euclid: Reflections on Indian Geometry" in *Journal of Indian Philosophy* 29 (2001), 43–80 (containing an extensive bibliography of secondary literature). J. F. Staal, who had raised the question in his *Euclides en Pāṇini* (Amsterdam, 1963, cited in note 2 above), again addressed these topics in the frame of the idea of mathematics and Pāṇinian grammar as what he terms artificial languages; see his "Artificial Languages across Sciences and Civilisations" in *Journal of Indian Philosophy* 34 (2006), 89–141 (including a critique of Bronkhorst, and in note 10 a rejection of Joseph Needham's curious suggestion that zero originated in Southeast Asia), and "Artificial Languages between Innate Faculties," *Journal of Indian Philosophy* 35 (2007), 577–96. None of these articles considers the matter of *śūnyatā* in Buddhist thought, however. Beginning in 1980 Kamaleswar Bhattacharya published a series of articles relating to the place of grammar in Nāgārjuna's and Candrakīrti's thought: "Nāgārjuna's Arguments against Motion: Their Grammatical Basis," *A Corpus of Indian Studies* (Essays in honour of Professor Gaurinath Sastri, Calcutta, 1980), pp. 85–95, and "The Grammatical Basis of Nāgārjuna's Arguments: Some Further Considerations," *Indologica Taurinensia* 8–9 (1980–81, Dr. Ludwig Sternbach Commemoration Volume), 35–43; the relevant articles are listed in his "A Note on Nāgārjuna's Sanskrit," *Śemuṣī* (Baldev Upādhyāya

Janmaśatī Volume, Varanasi, 2004), p. 659, including his "Nāgārjuna's Arguments against Motion," *Journal of the International Association of Sanskrit Studies* 8 (1985), 7–15, and (the last of the series) "Back to Nāgārjuna and Grammar," *Adyar Library Bulletin* 59 (1995, C. Kunhan Raja Birth Centenary Volume), 178–89.

Concerning zero—which marks place value (known already to the Babylonians)—and numerals in general, see K. Menninger, *Zahlwort und Ziffer, eine Kulturgeschichte der Zahl* (Göttingen, 1958), G. Ifrah, *The Universal History of Numbers* (London, 1998), and R. Kaplan, *The Nothing That Is: A Natural History of Zero* (London 1999). For the transmission of the Indo-Arabic numerals, see recently C. Burnett, "Indian Numerals in Arabic, Greek and Latin," in *Journal of Indian Philosophy* 34 (2006), pp. 25–26. According to M. Yano, *Journal of Indian Philosophy* 34 (2006), p. 154, Brahmagupta (sixth century) was the first Indian mathematician to have defined zero as one of the numbers.

Regarding grammar as a universal science and model for other Indian knowledge systems, to the references in note 3 above may be added Ānandavardhana's observation in his *Dhvanyāloka* i.13 (KSS, pp. 132–33): *prathame hi vidvāṃso vaiyākaraṇāḥ, vyākaraṇamūlatvāt sarvavidyānām.*

2. Towards a Chronology of the Madhyamaka School*

IN INVESTIGATING the literary, religious, and philosophical history of a school of thought it is necessary to attempt to establish its chronology. Three chronological frames basically come into question for this purpose: (1) the internal chronology of the masters and texts of the school relative to each other, (2) the external chronology of these masters and texts relative to those of other schools, allied and opposed, and (3) their absolute chronology. The determination of an absolute chronology will normally involve both the fixing of the relative chronology, in either or both of the above-mentioned forms, of authors and texts and the establishment of correlations with events known otherwise that can serve as independent historical landmarks with which these authors and texts can be brought into either a synchronic or a diachronic relation *(terminus ante quem* or *post quem).* In the case of the Madhyamaka literature, as with so much of Indian literature, it is, however, only occasionally that we are in the fortunate position of being able to bring external, historically verifiable data actually to bear on an author or text with a view to establishing a date with any high degree of precision and certainty. Frequently the historian has to satisfy himself with approximations, and datings to within the nearest century or two are often the best that can be achieved with the available documentation.

I

For Nāgārjuna, the source of the Madhyamaka school, we have certain traditionally accepted synchronisms. Thus his contemporaneousness, and even the

* First published in *Indological and Buddhist Studies, Volume in Honour of Professor J. W. de Jong.* Ed. L. Hercus et al., pp. 505–30. Canberra: Faculty of Asian Studies (Australian National University), 1982.

existence of a personal relationship, with a Sātavāhana monarch are reported by authorities belonging to the seventh century. These are the *Harṣacarita* of Bāṇa (chapter VIII), the *Hsi-yü-chi* of Hsüan-tsang, and the *Nan-hai chi-kuei nei-fa ch'uan* of I-ching. The possibility of such a royal link is indeed suggested by two works ascribed to Nāgārjuna: the *Suhṛllekha,* a paraenetic epistle addressed to a king, and the *Ratnāvalī,* an ethico-philosophical treatise also addressed to a king *(rājaparikathā).*[1]

A later commentary on the *Suhṛllekha* by Mahāmati and one on the *Ratnāvalī* by Ajitamitra, both of which are extant in Tibetan versions, mention Bde spyod as the name of the king with whom Nāgārjuna was in contact.[2]

On the basis of this information modern scholars have variously identified the Sātavāhana monarch in question as Hāla, Gautamīputra Śātakarṇi, Vāsiṣṭhīputra Pulumāyi II, and Yajñaśrī Śātakarṇi. The fact that several different kings whose reigns cover a period of about a century have thus been

1. See S. Beal, *Si-yu-ki: Buddhist Records of the Western World,* II (London, 1884), pp. 210–16 (cf. T. Watters, *On Yuan Chwang's Travels,* II [London, 1905], pp. 200f); and J. Takakusu, *A Record of the Buddhist Religion As Practised in India and the Malay Archipelago by I-tsing* (Oxford, 1896), pp. 159 f. See also the title of the Chinese translation by Paramārtha (500–69) of the *Ratnāvalī* (*Pao-hsing wang,* T 1656); cf. J. W. de Jong, *IIJ* 20 (1978), p. 137.

The reference in Hsüan-tsang and I-ching as well as Bāṇa is to a Nāgārjuna who was also a physician. In Hsüan-tsang he is in addition an alchemist (Beal, op. cit., II, p. 216; cf. S. Lévi, *JA* 1936, pp. 105–6; J. Filliozat, *Yogaśataka* [Pondichéry, 1979], pp. xiii f). On other evidence from I-ching see below, note 20.

For the Jaina tradition see Kutūhala, *Līlāvaī,* verse 1008; cf. A. K. Warder, *Indian Kāvya Literature,* II (Delhi, 1974), pp. 183, 213–14.

2. These two commentaries are contained in the Tibetan Bstan 'gyur. In verse 14 of the Tibetan translation of the *Suhṛllekha* itself we find the name Bde byed.

The Sanskrit original of Bde spyod (bzang po) poses a problem. In his translation of Tāranātha's *Rgya gar chos 'byung,* A. Schiefner has given Udayana (*Târanâtha's Geschichte des Buddhismus in Indien* [St. Petersburg, 1869], p. 2n2); and in the index to the Peking Bstan 'gyur we find Udayi(bhadra) (see P. Cordier, *Catalogue du fonds tibétain de la Bibliothèque Nationale,* III [Paris, 1915], Mdo 'grel, gi, no. 32 [*Suhṛllekha*] and nge, no. 27 [id.] and no. 35 [*Suhṛllekhaṭīkā*]). Cf. S. Lévi, *JA* 1936, pp. 103–10, and É. Lamotte, *Le traité de la Grande Vertu de Sagesse,* III (Louvain, 1970), pp. liii–liv (referring to both Udayana and *Jantaka). But it appears that Bde spyod corresponds properly to Sātavāhana (Sāta). Another Tibetan equivalent seems to be Mthar 'gro zhon, to which correspond Śālivāhana (*Mahāvyutpatti* 3654) and *Antīvāhana (? which is found in Bu ston's *Chos 'byung,* fol. 100b [Obermiller, II, p. 127]); here *mtha'* "end" may be intended to render *sāta* understood as meaning "ended" (root *sā-/so-* "to end, finish, destroy"?). Recently J. Filliozat has suggested that *Jantaka represents *Sā(ṃ)taka(ṇi) ~ Śātakarṇi (*Yogaśataka,* p. xviii, referring to I-ching).

suggested shows, however, how unhelpful such a synchronism is by itself for the purpose of obtaining a precise dating.

A further synchronism between Nāgārjuna and (a) Kaniṣka has been mentioned by Kalhaṇa, the twelfth-century historian of Kaśmīr, in his *Rājataraṅgiṇī*. There (i. 170) the Kaniṣka in question is described as a Turuṣka king, alongside Huṣka and Juṣka;[3] and the context refers to the Ṣaḍarhadvana (Harvan). The difficulties here are not easier to solve than in the case of the synchronism with the Sātavāhana; for not only do we not know precisely which Kaniṣka should be considered, but modern scholars remain divided concerning the date of Kaniṣka I and the beginning of the Kuṣāṇa dynasty, which they have placed between the year 78 and the third century of the Christian era.

In one passage of his *Hsi-yü-chi,* Hsüan-tsang seems furthermore to have made Nāgārjuna a contemporary of Aśvaghoṣa and Kumāralāta.[4] But in other Chinese records of the Indian masters of Buddhism, Aśvaghoṣa, the so-called twelfth patriarch who is frequently linked with Kaniṣka I, is placed before Nāgārjuna, who is counted as the fourteenth patriarch.[5]

The dates of Kumārajīva (344–413 or 350–409?), the founder of the Chinese Madhyamaka (San-lun) school who was of Serindian origin but studied as a boy in Kaśmīr (Chi-pin), also hardly allow any precise chronological determination; they can provide us only with a *terminus ante quem* for Nāgārjuna and his followers Āryadeva and Rāhulabhadra.[6] It has furthermore to be noted that the commentary on the *Daśabhūmikasūtra* attributed to Nāgārjuna, and now extant only in Kumārajīva's Chinese translation (T. 1521), is reported to have been translated earlier, in the second half of the third century, by Dharmarakṣa, who also translated the sūtra itself;[7] this translator arrived in Ch'ang-an in 265 and worked there until about 313. But the ascription of this commentary to Nāgārjuna has been the subject of debate;

3. On Kaniṣka and the Turuṣkas see, e.g., Buddha Prakash, *Studies in Indo-Asian Art and Culture,* 1 (ed. Perala Ratnam, Śatapiṭaka Series 95, New Delhi, 1972), pp. 32–33.

4. See S. Beal, *Si-yu-ki,* II, p. 302 (cf. pp. 97–101); T. Watters, *On Yuan Chwang's Travels,* I (London, 1904), p. 245. See also J. Takakusu, *Record of the Buddhist Religion,* p. 181. —This synchronism has been dismissed by É. Lamotte, *Le traité,* III, p. 1n1.

5. Cf. É. Lamotte, *L'enseignement de Vimalakīrti* (Louvain, 1962), pp. 73–74; *Le traité,* III, pp. xlvi, li f.

6. On the basis of information originating in Kumārajīva's school, É. Lamotte and J. May have, however, proposed 243 C.E. as the precise date of Nāgārjuna's birth (see below).

7. See R. Hikata, *Suvikrāntavikrāmi-Paripṛcchā Prajñāpāramitā-Sūtra* (Fukuoka, 1958), p. lii; É. Lamotte, *L'enseignement de Vimalakīrti,* p. 76, and *Le traité,* III, pp. xl, li f.

and the relevance of this report, even if accurate, to the date of Nāgārjuna is therefore uncertain.[8]

The name Bhadanta Nāgārjunācārya is found mentioned in an inscription discovered a century ago near the Jaggayyapeṭa Stūpa in South India.[9] But because of the relative lateness of its script this reference unfortunately cannot help much in establishing the date of Nāgārjuna, the author of the *Mūlamadhyamakakārikās* etc.[10]

In sum, it is likely that Nāgārjuna flourished at some time when the Sātavāhana and Kuṣāṇa dynasties were holding sway in India. But of just which king(s) of either of these dynasties he was the contemporary, and whether he had personal links with any of them, it is hardly possible to determine either by means of criteria internal to the works ascribed to him or on the basis of the Indian and Chinese reports mentioned above. On balance it seems appropriate to place Nāgārjuna ca. 150–200 C.E. (with E. Frauwallner and a number of other scholars). The dating proposed by É. Lamotte and J. May, who place his birth precisely in 243 C.E.,[11] even if not intrinsically impossible, is based on an inference drawn from the complex, and rather hypothetical, chronological calculations originating in Kumārajīva's school.

Recently it has also been suggested by É. Lamotte that a later Indian author—perhaps a second Nāgārjuna originally trained in the Sarvāstivādin Abhidharma and living in northwestern India somewhat later than the author of the *Mūlamadhyamakakārikās*—was the author of the *Ta-chih-tu-lun* (T 1509). This encyclopaedic commentary on the large *Prajñāpāramitāsūtra* traditionally ascribed to Nāgārjuna was translated into Chinese by Kumārajīva at the beginning of the fifth century. Lamotte's suggestion is based in part on the fact that both Āryadeva's *Catuḥśataka* and Rāhulabhadra's *Prajñāpāramitāstotra* are cited in the *Ta-chih-tu-lun*. Lamotte observes, moreover, that such an extensive and encyclopaedic work referring to some thirty

8. See A. Hirakawa, *IBK* 5.2 (1957), pp. 504 f. But cf. R. Hikata, op. cit., pp. lxxii f; S. Yamaguchi, *EB* 1 (1966), pp. 45–47.

9. See J. Burgess, *Notes on the Amarāvatī Stūpa* (Madras, 1882), p. 57, and *The Buddhist Stupas of Amaravati and Jaggayyapeta* (Archaeological Survey of Southern India, London, 1887), pp. 111–12.

10. Burgess dated the writing of this inscription to ca. 600; but G. Tucci has suggested the earlier dating of 450–500 (*Minor Buddhist Texts,* II [Rome, 1958], p. 284). T. N. Ramachandran thinks the inscription refers to the tantric Siddha Nāgārjuna (see *Nagarjunakonda 1938,* Memoirs of the Archaeological Survey of India 71 [Delhi, 1953], pp. 28–29), on whom see below.

11. É. Lamotte, *L'enseignement de Vimalakīrti,* pp. 74–76; J. May, *Hōbōgirin* V, pp. 473a, 478b.

Mahāyāna sūtras cannot be ascribed to Nāgārjuna I and hence placed at the very beginning of "Madhyamaka Buddhism."[12] Now this enormous treatise appears to be quite unknown to the Indo-Tibetan traditions; and it seems in any case to be generally agreed among specialists on the subject that the extant text of the *Ta-chih-tu-lun* is in large part a composite work which is not even of exclusively Indian origin.[13] Could it then be that its text as we now have it was the product of Serindian scholarship,[14] and that it was subjected to a final process of Sinification at the time of its translation by Kumārajīva and his Chinese colleagues?[15] The work could then have been ascribed to Nāgārjuna because its basic ideas—and perhaps even its core—go back to this Indian source of the Madhyamaka school without his having been the author, in the strict sense, of this work. Thus, although Lamotte's hypothesis concerning the authorship of the *Ta-chih-tu-lun* is certainly not in itself impossible, it seems at least as simple—and certainly more economical than postulating an early Deutero-Nāgārjuna living quite soon after Nāgārjuna I—to account for references to Mādhyamikas later than Nāgārjuna I, as well as for other apparently later elements in this work, by attributing them to the activity of Serindian scholars and Chinese redactors.

The date of Āryadeva is to be determined in relation to that of Nāgārjuna I, whose direct disciple he is universally considered to have been. The relationship between Rāhulabhadra and Nāgārjuna will be discussed below (§ II).

12. É. Lamotte, *Le traité,* III, pp. xiv f; IV, pp. xiii, xv.

13. See R. Hikata, op. cit., pp. lii f; R. H. Robinson, *Early Mādhyamika in India and China* (Madison, 1967), pp. 34–39. Cf. also P. Demiéville, *JA* 1950, pp. 383n, 386, and *L'Inde classique,* ed. L. Renou and J. Filliozat, II (Paris, 1954), § 2130. In *Le traité,* III, p. lv, n. 2, Lamotte has, however, declined to express an opinion on this subject (but see *Le traité,* III, pp. xlix–l).

14. This could have been the "Indian" version referred to by Kumārajīva's disciple Seng-jui (352–436), since some Serindian scholars at least might well have been capable of writing in Sanskrit.

On this original of the *Ta-chih-tu-lun,* see *Le traité,* III, pp. xlvii–xlviii; cf. P. Demiéville, *JA* 1950, pp. 387 f.

15. While Lamotte accepts that parts of the *Ta-chih-tu-lun* are by Kumārajīva (*Le traité,* III, pp. xlix–l), he considers that neither a Chinese nor even a Serindian author could have been as well informed about things Indian as certain sections of this treatise show its author to have been (p. xxvi). (On this see also R. Hikata, op. cit., p. lxvi.) But given the importance of Indian culture in Central Asia and, in addition, the fact that Kumārajīva had family links with Kaśmīr and studied there as a boy, it does not seem impossible to ascribe even such sections to a Serindian like him.

Bhā(va)viveka (Bhavya), the founder of what later came to be known as the Svātantrika-Madhyamaka school, wrote a major commentary on Nāgārjuna's *Mūlamadhyamakakārikās*, the *Prajñāpradīpa,* which was translated into Chinese in the fourth decade of the seventh century by Prabhākaramitra (T 1566). Later in the same century his "Jewel in hand treatise" was translated into Chinese by Hsüan-tsang (*Ta-ch'eng chang-chen lun,* T 1578). Bhā(va)-viveka has been shown to be the elder contemporary of both Sthiramati (ca. 510–70) and Dharmapāla (ca. 530–61).[16]

Buddhapālita, the master of what later came to be known as the Prāsaṅgika branch of the Madhyamaka and the target of Bhā(va)viveka's criticism, as well as Candrakīrti, the main authority of this Prāsaṅgika branch and Bhāvaviveka's great opponent, are both unknown to the classical tradition of the Chinese San-lun school. And external historical evidence of the above-mentioned kind making it possible to determine precisely their absolute chronology seems to be lacking.

The historical records of Tibet, on the contrary, permit reasonably accurate datings of several Indian Mādhyamikas living during the early propagation *(snga dar)* of Buddhism in that country. Thus they indicate that Śāntarakṣita, the great apostle of Tibet during the reign of Khri Srong lde btsan, arrived there for the first time ca. 763, and that he resided there a second time from about 775 to his death in about 788. He was closely associated with the foundation of Bsam yas (ca. 775 or 779?) and was in fact the first abbot *(upādhyāya)* of this great Tibetan monastic centre. On the death of Śāntarakṣita his disciple and commentator Kamalaśīla was invited to Tibet to continue and consolidate his master's work there. He was in Tibet during at least part of the "Council of Tibet" (or "Council of Bsam yas") in about 792–94, and he died there in about 795.[17]

The Tibetan records also make it possible to date with a fair degree of accuracy several important later Indian Mādhyamikas living during the earliest period of the later propagation *(phyi dar)* of the Dharma in Tibet. Dīpaṃkaraśrījñāna (ca. 982–1054) was the contemporary of Rin chen bzang po (958–1055), the senior monk-scholar of the kingdom of Western Tibet and the teacher of 'Brom ston pa (1005–64), the master from Central Tibet who founded the Bka' gdams pa school. Jayānanda, a Kāśmīrī Mādhyamika and the commentator on Candrakīrti's *Madhyamakāvatāra,* was closely

16. On Bhā(va)viveka's relation to Dharmapāla, see S. Beal, op. cit., II, p. 223; cf. T. Watters, op. cit., II, p. 215, and Y. Kajiyama, *WZKSO* 12–13 (1968/69), pp. 194 f, 199 f.

17. Cf. E. Frauwallner, *WZKSO* 5 (1961), pp. 141–43; G. Tucci, *Minor Buddhist Texts,* II, pp. 28–31.

associated with the Tibetan translator Pa tshab Nyi ma grags (born in 1055) in the establishment on a solid basis in Tibet of the Prāsaṅgika branch of the Madhyamaka. And Abhayākaragupta, a later authority who developed a synthesis of the Madhyamaka with the Yogācāra, Prajñāpāramitā, and Vajrayāna, composed his *Munimatālaṃkāra* in the thirtieth year of the reign of the Pāla king Rāmapāla (r. ca. 1077–1130 or 1072–1126) according to the colophon of its Tibetan translation contained in the Bstan 'gyur.

II

Having surveyed some external historical evidence for the absolute chronology of the Mādhyamikas, let us now turn to evidence to be derived from internal analysis of their works for the relative chronology of their school.

A serious difficulty in the chronology of the texts and authors of the Madhyamaka arises, to begin with, from the fact that a large number of works of varied, and quite distinct, contents are traditionally ascribed to Nāgārjuna. Some of them are independent scholastic treatises *(śāstra)* such as the *Mūlamadhyamakakārikās*, the *Vigrahavyāvartanī* and the *Yuktiṣaṣṭikā.* Others are commentaries on sūtras, for example the *Vibhāṣā* on the *Daśabhūmikasūtra* (T 1521) and the above-mentioned commentary on the large *Prajñāpāramitāsūtra* (the *Ta-chih-tu-lun,* T 1509). Still others are epistles and homilies, such as the *Suhṛllekha* and *Ratnāvalī,* and hymns *(stava).* A classification of Nāgārjuna's works traditionally adopted in Tibet has divided them into a scholastic corpus *(rigs tshogs),* a hymnic corpus *(bstod tshogs),* and a homiletic corpus *(gtam tshogs).* But despite the differences it recognized between them not only as to literary genre but also, to a considerable degree, in contents, this tradition has nevertheless ascribed all the works included in these three categories to one and the same author.[18]

In such circumstances, one means of establishing authorship in the case of works of uncertain provenance, and hence also a relative chronology of texts and their authors, would be to attempt to apply to them terminological and philosophic criteria of the kind employed by Paul Hacker and his successors for determining the authenticity of works ascribed to Śaṃkara. In the case of Nāgārjuna, however, there are special difficulties. In the first place, most of the works in question are now available to us only in Chinese and/or Tibetan translations, so that the use of the usual literary, stylistic,

18. On this subject, see our article in *Études tibétaines dédiées à la mémoire de Marcelle Lalou* (Paris, 1971), pp. 448–71, reprinted as chapter 4 of the present volume.

and terminological criteria for establishing authorship becomes either problematic or simply impossible. No less important is the consideration that even when we do possess indubitable evidence of differences in style, terminology, and ideas, it is by no means certain that works that so differ have necessarily to be by different authors. It can in fact be just as legitimately supposed that they belong to different periods in the development of the thinking of a single author, or even that they represent one author's complementary (rather than opposed) approaches to certain difficult philosophical problems. An example could be the treatment of reality in an apophatic manner (e.g., in the major portion of the *Mūlamadhyamakakārikā*s and the related treatises ascribed to Nāgārjuna), in a cataphatic manner (e.g., in several of the hymns ascribed to him), and by the philosopher's silence (*āryatūṣṇībhāva,* e.g., in a few passages of the *Mūlamadhyamakakārikā*s and of the hymns). When seeking to establish authorship in such cases, then, it would clearly be begging the question were one to argue that, because of differences of style or terminology, such texts must necessarily be by different authors. Indeed, the question is precisely to define the full range of an author's religious and philosophical thought; and this can surely be done only by taking into account all his works, without any text ascribed to him being excluded *a priori* on purely stylistic or terminological grounds. We have, in other words, to determine what styles an author has employed and what religious and philosophical ideas he has accepted on the basis of the entire corpus of his works; and to proceed the other way round can all too easily involve prejudgements and circular reasoning. In sum, we must be prepared to recognize the full range of historical, philological, and philosophical problems that arise in discussing the authenticity of the works ascribed to Nāgārjuna.

Even when our sources clearly refer to authors as famous in the history of the Madhyamaka as Nāgārjuna, Bhā(va)viveka (Bhavya), and Candrakīrti, further difficulties can arise owing to the fact that these names have been borne by two (or sometimes even more) different masters of the school who lived at quite different times. As a consequence, otherwise valuable sources have on occasion attributed improbably long lifespans to a single master, placing the same name/person at what are evidently quite different points in the history of the school. The resulting uncertainty as to whether such names are to be understood as designating one or more persons constitutes an additional major difficulty standing in the way of establishing a secure chronology of the Madhyamaka.

This problem is encountered in an acute form in the case of the relation between Nāgārjuna and Rāhulabhadra, whose names appear linked together at what clearly appear to be widely separated periods in the history of their school. And the difficulty is compounded by the fact that Rāhulabhadra is sometimes described in our sources as the successor and disciple of Nāgārjuna, whereas at other times he is stated to be his predecessor and master. Modern scholars have arrived at diametrically opposed solutions to this difficulty, which thus presents the historian with an intriguing and instructive problem.[19]

Scrutiny of the evidence seems to indicate that Nāgārjuna I was the source and originator of the Madhyamaka as a distinct school of thought and that (a) Rāhulabhadra was his successor. This Rāhulabhadra may have been the direct disciple of both Nāgārjuna and Āryadeva or of Āryadeva alone: the evidence is not clear on this point. (As already mentioned, both these masters are cited in the *Ta-chih-tu-lun* ascribed to Nāgārjuna and translated by Kumārajīva at the beginning of the fifth century.)

The statements that make Rāhulabhadra the master rather than the follower of Nāgārjuna can, however, be satisfactorily explained as referring to the Siddha Rāhulabhadra (= Sarahapāda), the master of the Deutero-Nāgārjuna who we have very good reason to believe lived no later than the seventh century.[20] This Nāgārjunapāda, also one of the Siddhas, played a leading role in the development of the synthesis of the Madhyamaka and Vajrayāna which came into prominence at that time; and he is presumably to be identified with the source of the Ārya tradition of the *Guhyasamājatantra*. Supposing this Siddha Nāgārjuna to have been the disciple of Rāhulabhadra = Sarahapāda while Nāgārjuna I, the author of the *Mūlamadhyamakakārikā*s etc., was on the contrary the predecessor of the Rāhulabhadra known to the *Ta-chih-tu-lun*—as well as to Asaṅga's commentary on the *Madhyamakaśāstra* (T 1565) and *Sāramati's **Mahāyānāvatāraśāstra* (T 1634)[21]—we are in a position to resolve an apparent conflict in the evidence concerning the relationship between these two names and the persons they designate.

This solution does not of course dispose of all our chronological or other historical problems. And the question of the precise identity of Nāgārjuna

19. See G. Tucci, *JPASB* 26 (1930), p. 141 (= *Opera minora*, II, p. 211 f); R. Hikata, op. cit., pp. lxxi–lxxii; H. Nakamura, *Acta asiatica* 1 (1960), p. 63; É. Lamotte, *L'enseignement de Vimalakīrti*, pp. 76–77, and *Le traité*, III, pp. xl, 1373–74; J. W. de Jong, *AM* 17 (1971), pp. 107–8.

20. I-ching (635–713), who left Tāmralipti about 685, already mentions Nāgārjuna's having studied the Vidyādharapiṭaka. See E. Chavannes, *Mémoire composé à l'époque de la grande dynastie T'ang sur les religieux éminents qui allèrent chercher la loi dans les pays d'Occident* (Paris, 1894), p. 102. In I-ching's *Record* (translated by Takakusu, p. 35), Nāgārjuna appears only as a physician and, perhaps, alchemist.

21. See É. Lamotte, *Le traité*, III, p. 1374.

in relation to "Nāga" *(Nāgāhvaya)* and perhaps also Nāgabodhi continues to raise questions. Sometimes we find mention of a "Nāga" who appears to be identical with Nāgārjuna; but at other times "Nāga" figures as a distinct person. His precise identity thus remains uncertain, but since no works are known to be by him he ceases to be a subject of major concern to the historian of Madhyamaka literature.[22] As for Nāgabodhi, being reported to be the teacher of Vajrabodhi (ca. 671–741?) and Amoghavajra (ca. 705–74), the Indian masters who helped introduce the Vajrayāna into China and whose dates can be determined from Chinese sources,[23] he has to be placed much later. (Whether Nāgabodhi and the Vajrayānist Nāgārjunapāda mentioned above were identical it is difficult to say; the dates could support such an identification, but their identity is not established.)[24]

So that the long period of time separating Nāgārjuna, the author of basic treatises of the Madhyamaka school, and the Siddha Nāgārjuna(pāda), who lived approximately half a millennium later, might be bridged, those sources which do not distinguish between these two persons have ascribed to their single Nāgārjuna an unusually long lifespan (of six hundred years).

In the main line of Madhyamaka masters, Nāgārjuna I and his disciple Āryadeva were followed by Buddhapālita. As already noted, in the present state of our knowledge it is not possible to establish precisely the date of this master of what was later known as the Prāsaṅgika branch of the Madhyamaka; but the evidence points reasonably clearly to the period about 500 as the time when Buddhapālita flourished.[25]

The next major figure in the history of the Madhyamaka, Bhā(va)viveka or Bhavya, has already been mentioned above in connexion with the Chinese translations of two of his works. He found fault with Buddhapālita's philosophical procedure founded on the exclusive use of *prasaṅga*-type reasoning to reveal the inapplicability of any thesis presupposing the existence

22. The authorship of the **Trikāyastotra/stava* or **Kāyatrayastotra/stava* ascribed to Nāga by Tāranātha (*Rgya gar chos 'byung*, p. 68) is uncertain. A *Kāyatrayastotra* is ascribed to (a) Nāgārjuna in the Bstan 'gyur; but it is doubtful that a hymn concerning the three *kāya*s can be attributed to Nāgārjuna I. In addition, the *Kāyatrayāvatāramukha* is ascribed to Nāgamitra in the Bstan 'gyur.

23. See G. Tucci, *JPASB* 26 (1930), p. 142 (= *Opera minora*, I, p. 212); P. Demiéville, in *L'Inde classique*, II §§ 2092–93; Chou Yi-liang, *HJAS* 8 (1944/45), pp. 281 f, 313–14.

24. It is probably preferable to regard Nāgabodhi as a follower of Ārya Nāgārjunapāda, the tantric Siddha.

25. Ārya Vimuktisena may have been a younger contemporary of Buddhapālita; cf. D. Seyfort Ruegg, *WZKSO* 12–13 (1968/69), p. 306.

of some kind of entity, and he sought to formulate independent inferences *(svatantrānumāna)* and syllogisms *(prayoga)* for this same purpose. Bhā(va)viveka was in his turn severely criticized by Candrakīrti, who came to Buddhapālita's defence. As already noted also, Bhā(va)viveka was the elder contemporary of Sthiramati, the master of the Valabhī school of the Vijñānavāda who criticised him and wrote a commentary on Nāgārjuna's *Mūlamadhyamakakārikās* (T 1567), and of Dharmapāla, the master of the Nālandā school of the Vijñānavāda who also criticised him in his commentary on Āryadeva's *Catuḥśataka* (T 1571). On the basis of these interrelationships Bhā(va)viveka can be placed ca. 500–570, a dating compatible with what has been noted above concerning the external historical evidence provided by the Chinese translations of two of his works, the first of which is dated to 630–32.[26]

For lack of external historical evidence, Candrakīrti's date has to be fixed relatively to that of his predecessor Bhā(va)viveka, whom he criticised by name in his *Prasannapadā Madhyamakavṛttiḥ* and whose own dates thus provide a *terminus a quo,* and to later developments in the Madhyamaka school. Since Candrakīrti's works were not translated into Chinese, the external evidence from that source, which has so often proved invaluable in other cases, is unavailable to us; an argument from silence is provided by the fact that Bhā(va)viveka, but not Candrakīrti, has been mentioned by I-ching, who left India about 685. Candrakīrti has then presumably to be placed some time in the seventh century.[27] This is about the same time as Dharmakīrti (ca. 600–660), to whom Candrakīrti does not, however, seem to refer when criticizing some doctrines of the Buddhist logico-epistemological school founded by Dignāga (cf. *Prasannapadā* i, pp. 59f).

Here a problem arises owing to the fact that the *Madhyamakaratnapradīpa,* a treatise ascribed to Bhavya, refers to Candrakīrti. Because of this reference Candrakīrti's date has even been put back by a recent writer to ca. 500–560, the time of Bhā(va)viveka/Bhavya.[28] But this earlier dating appears in fact to be quite unnecessary on the grounds adduced by its proponent, and intrinsically it is quite improbable. In the first place, the

26. See Y. Kajiyama, *WZKSO* 12–13 (1968/69), pp. 193–203, for the dates of Bhā(va)viveka and Sthiramati.

27. Candrakīrti was, however, placed in the sixth century by M. Winternitz, *History of Indian Literature,* II (Calcutta, 1933), p. 363, because he held him to be the pupil of Dharmapāla: but he gives no source for this statement (this may be Tāranātha's *Rgya gar chos 'byung,* p. 133.18, which is, however, altogether obscure).

28. See C. Lindtner, *AO* 40 (1979), p. 91.

Madhyamakaratnapradīpa refers also to Dharmakīrti, whose date would for the same reason have to be pushed back to the same time when he would have been an only slightly younger contemporary of Dignāga (ca. 480–540); but such a dating for Dharmakīrti is most improbable. It is true that the *Madhyamakaratnapradīpa* has itself stated that its author also wrote the *Tarkajvālā,* the commentary on the *Madhyamakahṛdayakārikās* ascribed, like the basic text, to Bhā(va)viveka. We thus seem to have to choose between regarding this statement as incorrect and ascribing the *Tarkajvālā* to a second, later Bhā(va)viveka/Bhavya. However this may be, in view of the reference to Dharmakīrti in the *Madhyamakaratnapradīpa,* it seems impossible to ascribe this text as a whole to Bhā(va)viveka I, the author of the *Prajñāpradīpa,* who has to be placed in the sixth century since he was a contemporary of Sthiramati and Dharmapāla. And there is every reason to suppose that the *Madhyamakaratnapradīpa* was composed by a second Bhavya who lived later than the middle of the seventh century.[29] There is therefore no need to make the author of the *Madhyamakāvatāra* and *Prasannapadā* a contemporary of Bhā(va)viveka I.

In the case of Candrakīrti, just as in that of Nāgārjuna and Bhavya, it appears that we have, moreover, to reckon with more than one important master bearing this illustrious name. Thus the author of the *Pradīpoddyotana,* a commentary on the *Guhyasamājatantra,* has presumably to be distinguished from the author of the *Madhyamakāvatāra* and *Prasannapadā.* And still another Candrakīrti lived in the eleventh century, when he translated his **Madhyamakaprajñāvatāra* (or **Madhyamakāvatāra-prajñā?*) into Tibetan together with the *lo tsā ba* 'Gos khug pa Lha(s) btsas.

The relative position of Śāntideva in the history of the Madhyamaka can be determined from the fact that he is quoted by Śāntarakṣita; but he is not mentioned by I-ching. His contribution to the Madhyamaka can be regarded as a continuation of Candrakīrti's, and he is usually counted as an exponent of the latter's Prāsaṅgika school. It is thus likely that Śāntideva flourished about 700.[30] His *Bodhicaryāvatāra* was already translated into Tibetan by Dpal brtsegs and his *Śikṣāsamuccaya* by Ye shes sde (ca. 800).

Śāntarakṣita has been credited in some sources with almost as long a lifespan as Nāgārjuna. But in the case of Śāntarakṣita the reason lies in the fact that he has been held by some doxographers to be not only the main representative but also the founder (*shing rta'i srol 'byed* "way-opener" or "pathfinder")

29. It has to be noted that the *Madhyamakaratnapradīpa* refers to Vajrayānist ideas and to the Vidyādharapiṭaka.

30. Cf. J. W. de Jong, *IIJ* 16 (1975), pp. 179–80.

of the Yogācāra-(Svātantrika-)Madhyamaka school, while Ārya Vimuktisena was reckoned to be a member of this same school. Now Ārya Vimuktisena, a commentator on the *Pañcaviṃśatisāhasrikā Prajñāpāramitā* following the system of the *Abhisamayālaṃkāra,* is stated to have been a younger contemporary of Buddhapālita (fl. ca. 500) and a disciple of Vasubandhu (ca. 400–480) or of Dignāga (480–540) and Bhavya (ca. 500–70). But, as the putative founder of the school to which Ārya Vimuktisena belonged, Śāntarakṣita had for historical-doxographical reasons to be regarded as the latter's predecessor, and his birth had therefore to be put some time before that of his supposed disciple; he thus came to be credited with a very long life beginning in the fifth/sixth century and extending almost to the end of the eighth century.[31] Accordingly, whereas Nāgārjuna was assigned an extraordinarily long lifespan because (at least) two distinct persons of special importance in the Madhyamaka school bore his name, the reason for crediting Śāntarakṣita with almost as long a life was essentially doxographical in origin. It should however be noted that this relative chronology (mentioned, e.g., by Mkhas grub Dge legs dpal bzang in his *Rgyud sde spyi rnam,* fol. 26a) has not been accepted by the majority of the Tibetan historians and doxographers.

The dates of Śāntarakṣita's grand-teacher Śrīgupta, who is counted sometimes as a Svātantrika-Mādhyamika and sometimes as a Yogācāra-Mādhyamika, and of Jñānagarbha can also be determined relatively to his own. Śāntarakṣita's teacher Jñānagarbha, a disciple of Śrīgupta, apparently has to be distinguished from the Jñānagarbha who lived a little later, about 800, and translated into Tibetan several Madhyamaka texts (including the commentary on Jñānagarbha's *Satyadvayavibhaṅga* ascribed to Śāntarakṣita) with the Tibetan translators Dpal brtsegs, Klu'i rgyal mtshan, and Ye shes sde.

In several other cases of importance for the history of the Madhyamaka also the same name has been borne by more than one master. Thus the name Jitāri/Jetāri designates a master living ca. 800 and another living at the end of the tenth century. Dharmamitra, the Mādhyamika author of a commentary on Haribhadra's *Abhisamayālaṃkārakārikā-śāstravṛtti* (the "*Sphuṭārthā*") who lived ca. 800, has to be distinguished from an earlier Dharmamitra who commented on Guṇaprabha's *Vinayasūtra.* Buddhajñāna(pāda), a representative of the Yogācāra-Madhyamaka school and a disciple of Haribhadra, has to be distinguished from Buddhaśrījñāna, the author of the *Jinamārgāvatāra* who lived ca. 1200. Dānaśīla was the name of at least three different masters, the first of whom lived at the end of the eighth century, the second at

31. For references see D. Seyfort Ruegg, *WZKSO* 12–13 (1968/69), p. 307n18.

the end of the tenth century, and the third in the twelfth century. Still other examples could be given of a single name designating two or more masters; in some cases only a minute study of the works attributed to the masters bearing such names will allow us to assign them correctly, whereas in others the date of a translation and the identification of the co-translator(s) of an author-translator, if accurately known, make possible the correct attribution (examples are the cases of Jñānagarbha and Candrakīrti mentioned above).

The chronological results summed up above prompt an observation concerning the question of the reliability of Tāranātha's History of the Dharma in India *(Rgya gar chos 'byung).* Since this work was first published and translated in Europe in the 1860s, attempts have been made to exploit for chronological purposes the information that this work contains, and which Tāranātha collected from both his own extensive reading and from the Indian paṇḍits with whom he was in contact.[32] These attempts have, however, been often frustrated by a failure to understand how Tāranātha proceeded in recording his information and by our consequent inability to interpret this information; and chronological results based on Tāranātha's works have consequently been impugned by scholars who have called into question all of Tāranātha's statements. Tāranātha's alleged unreliability has then been contrasted with the reliability of the Chinese pilgrims to India, especially Hsüan-tsang and I-ching. It has, however, to be recalled that the Chinese sources too are sometimes in serious error. Thus I-ching's dating of Bhartṛhari's death to ca. 651[33] brought considerable confusion into the history of Indian philosophy until it was finally corrected as late as the 1950s.[34] Moreover, once the chronology of the Mādhyamikas has been examined on the basis of both internal and external evidence, some of the information that Tāranātha has provided falls into place, and it turns out to be quite compatible with results reached on the basis of other evidence. Thus, with regard to Tāranātha's statements that Rāhulabhadra was a disci-

32. Cf. Paṇ chen Blo bzang dpal ldan ye shes, *Shambha la'i lam yig,* fol. 18a–b; G. Tucci, *IHQ* 7 (1931), pp. 683–702 (= *Opera, minora,* II, pp. 305–19); *Tibetan Painted Scrolls* (Rome, 1949), pp. 137 and 164.

33. See J. Takakusu, *A Record of the Buddhist Religion,* pp. 179–80. (I-ching has also made Bhartṛhari a contemporary of Dharmapāla!)

34. See H. R. Rangaswami Iyengar, *JBBRAS* 26 (1951), pp. 147–49; H. Nakamura, *Studies in Indology and Buddhology* (Festschrift S. Yamaguchi, Kyoto, 1955), pp. 122–36; D. Seyfort Ruegg, *Contributions à l'histoire de la philosophie linguistique indienne* (Paris, 1959), p. 59; E. Frauwallner, *WZKSO* 3 (1959), pp. 107 f, and 5 (1961), pp. 134–35. Cf. also J. Brough, *BSOAS* 36 (1973), pp. 248–60.

ple[35] of Nāgārjuna and his master,[36] we now have reason to think that both statements are true provided that they are understood to refer to two different sets of masters bearing the names Nāgārjuna and Rāhulabhadra. The difficulty arose because Tāranātha has not clearly distinguished between the two sets of names and persons, so that the true historical situation could hardly be reconstructed from his statements on the subject alone. But even though his two statements require interpretation in the light of data from other sources, it nevertheless turns out that, once put in context, they are not contradictory as they at first appeared to be.[37]

III

Beside the absolute chronology discussed in § I and the internal relative chronology of the Madhyamaka discussed in § II above, it will be of interest also to consider briefly the external relative chronology of the Madhyamaka school vis-à-vis the great treatises and masters of other schools of Indian thought, non-Buddhist as well as Buddhist.

Nāgārjuna's *Mūlamadhyamakakārikā*s are in large part a critique of philosophical ideas current among the Buddhist Ābhidhārmikas. And the *Ta-chih-tu-lun* seems to represent an attempt to construct what might be called a Mahāyānist Abhidharma in place of the Sarvāstivādin Abhidharma. Nāgārjuna's *Ratnāvalī* (I.61) alludes to the Sāṃkhya, Aulūkya (i.e., Vaiśeṣika?),[38] and Nirgrantha (i.e., Jaina) schools of thought; but unfortunately it is not possible to determine precisely to what period of these schools such a passing reference pertains. In addition to Kapila, the sage of

35. *Rgya gar chos 'byung* (ed. A. Schiefner), pp. 68, 73. See also Bu ston, *Chos 'byung,* fol. 94a1 (Obermiller, II, p. 109, reads Bāhula, which is presumably a misprint for Rāhula).

36. *Rgya gar chos 'byung,* pp. 53, 83; Tāranātha, *Bka' babs bdun ldan gyi brgyud pa'i rnam thar,* fols. 181 f. See also Bu ston, *Chos 'byung,* fol. 99a (Obermiller, II, p. 123).

37. Sometimes, of course, Tāranātha does explicitly distinguish between two masters having the same name. In addition to Ārya Vimuktisena and Bhadanta Vimuktisena, a case in point is that of Dharmamitra, the Mādhyamika interpreter of the Prajñāpāramitā (ca. 800), whom Tāranātha distinguishes from the Vaibhāṣika and Vinaya master of the same name who lived earlier (see above). Tāranātha distinguishes also between two Mātṛceṭas (p. 75; cf. p. 152).

38. Ulūka is also mentioned in lists of Sāṃkhya teachers, however; cf. P. Chakravarti, *Origin and Development of the Sāṃkhya System of Thought* (Calcutta, 1951), p. 131. In the *Vaidalyaprakaraṇa* (§ 8) his name appears beside those of Kapila, Maṭhara, Vyāsa, et al.

the Sāṃkhya, and Ulūka, the *Vaidalyaprakaraṇa* (§ 8) mentions Maṭhara.[39] This treatise enumerates and refutes point by point the sixteen categories *(padārtha)* of *Nyāyasūtra* I.i.1; and it also mentions (§ 19) the twelve factors of I.i.9. Of special importance for a comparison with the *Nyāyasūtras* is Nāgārjuna's *Vigrahavyāvartanī,* which, unlike the *Vaidalyaprakaraṇa,* is extant in Sanskrit. The editors and translators of this work have noted connections between *VV* 31f. and *NS* II.i.16–19, between *VV* 64 and *NS* II.i.13, and between *VV* 20 and 69 and *NS* II.i.8–12. In his study of ancient Indian eristic *(vāda),* G. Oberhammer has argued that the view expressed in *NS* V.i.10 is rejected in *VV* 31 f., which is then answered in *NS* II.i.19, and that the view expressed in *NS* V.i.18–20 is mentioned in *VV* 20 and 69.[40] Recently, however, K. Bhattacharya has maintained that *VV* 31 f. indeed refer to *NS* II.i.19, and that *VV* 20 and 69 refer to NS II.i.12 f.[41] A close historical proximity between Nāgārjuna's discussion of the *pramāṇas* and several *Nyāyasūtras* seems in any case to be established, and G. Tucci has convincingly spoken of interdependence.[42] More precise chronological results are difficult to obtain because of the paucity and ambiguity of the documents.

Similar problems arise concerning the question of the precise relationship

39. The *Māṭharavṛtti* itself is of course dated to a much later time. On the Māṭharas in a treatise ascribed to Āryadeva (and extant only in a Chinese translation by Bodhiruci [T. 1640], see H. Nakamura, *HJAS* 18 (1955), p. 99, who also notes an identification with Vyāsa. See also P. Chakravarti, op. cit., p. 159. As already noted, in the *Vaidalyaprakaraṇa* (§ 8), Maṭhara and Vyāsa are listed separately, beside Ulūka et al.

40. *WZKSO* 7 (1963), pp. 64–70. See also G. Tucci, *Pre-Diṅnāga Buddhist Texts on Logic from Chinese Sources* (Baroda, 1929), Notes on the *Vigrahavyāvartanī,* pp. 36 f, who considers that *NS* II.i contains replies to Nāgārjuna. According to Vācaspatimiśra's *Tātparyaṭīkā,* the opponent in II.i.8 is a Mādhyamika.

41. *Journal of Indo-European Studies* 5 (1977), pp. 265–73. B. K. Matilal, *Nyāya-Vaiśeṣika* (*A History of Indian Literature,* Otto Harrassowitz, VI,2, Wiesbaden, 1977), p. 79, has suggested that *NS* IV.i.38 may be a reply to Nāgārjuna's critique of *svabhāva.* But, contrary to W. Ruben's opinion (*Die Nyāyasūtra's,* Leipzig, 1928, p. 106), *itaretarābhāva* in the preceding sūtra can hardly apply to Nāgārjuna's theory; and the *Laṅkāvatārasūtra* (p. 75) indeed condemns *itaretaraśūnyatā* as the most inferior emptiness.

42. *Pre-Diṅnāga Buddhist Texts,* p. xxvii. The above-mentioned discussions of the *Vigrahavyāvartanī* have mostly been conducted without reference to the *Vaidalya-"Sūtra"* and *Prakaraṇa,* both of which are ascribed to Nāgārjuna and are therefore of the highest relevance.

of Āryadeva to the Nyāya and Vaiśeṣika, discussed by G. Tucci,[43] and to the Sāṃkhya, discussed by E. Frauwallner[44] and M. Honda.[45]

Even the relatively abundant materials to be found in the *Ta-chih-tu-lun* do not easily yield clear results for chronology and the question of the historical relationship between the early Mādhyamikas and other schools. A great deal of this material has now been made available and annotated in E. Lamotte's monumental translation of this encyclopaedic treatise (see in particular *Le traité,* III, pp. xiv–xxvi), and some of it has also been discussed in K. Venkata Ramanan's *Nāgārjuna's Philosophy as Presented in the Mahā-Prajñāpāramitā-Śāstra* (Tokyo, 1966). On the Buddhist side, the author(s) of this treatise have made much use of the Sarvāstivādin Abhidharma as well as of a large number of Mahāyānist sūtras.[46] As for non-Buddhist schools, although this work argues against the Sāṃkhya and Vaiśeṣika as well as against the theists, it is hardly possible to identify precisely the targets of its criticism.[47]

Buddhapālita's commentary on the *Mūlamadhyamakakārikās* has still to be studied in detail from the present point of view.

The historical position of Bhā(va)viveka is somewhat clearer. Notably in his *Madhyamakahṛdayakārikās*, and in the accompanying *Tarkajvālā,* the doctrines of the Sāṃkhya, Vaiśeṣika, and Mīmāṃsā, as well as those of the Śrāvakas and Yogācāras, have been discussed in some detail. Even a reference to the Persian Magi is to be found in chapter IX of the *Tarkajvālā.* Bhā(va)viveka seems, moreover, to have been the first Mādhyamika to discuss the Vedānta, which he criticises in chapter VIII of his *Madhyamakahṛdayakārikās*.[48] But at the same time, in chapter III of the same work, Bhā(va)viveka has virtually assimilated the supreme *brahman* and the *dharmakāya* (verses 278–83), which he describes as cessation of discursive development *(prapañca)* and as inaccessible to those who engage in hypothetical reasoning (*tārkika,* 280); and he goes on to say that this *brahman* corresponds to the supreme reality

43. *Pre-Diṅnāga Buddhist Texts,* p. xxvii.

44. *WZKSO* 2 (1958), p. 131.

45. *IBK* 23.1 (1974), pp. 7–12. On the later *Sāṃkhyasūtra* and the Madhyamaka see R. Garbe, *Die Sâṃkhya-Philosophie* (Leipzig, 1917), p. 146n265.

46. Cf. *Le traité,* III, pp. xiv–xxv, xxxii–xxxvii; *Le traité,* IV, pp. x–xii.

47. Cf. *Le traité,* III, pp. xxv–xxvi; R. H. Robinson, *Early Mādhyamika,* pp. 68 f, 90, 94. R. Hikata, *Suvikrāntavikrāmiparipṛcchā,* pp. lxiv f, places the *Nyāyasūtra* later than the *Ta-chih-tu-lun.*

48. This older form of Vedānta has been discussed by H. Nakamura, *Shoki no Vedānta tetsugaku* I (Tokyo, 1950), pp. 238–332 (cf. *HJAS* 18 [1955], pp. 103–4) and V. V. Gokhale, *IIJ* 2 (1958), pp. 165 f.

of which the Muni (i.e., the Buddha) spoke (283), and that Sages *(ārya)* such as Avalokiteśa, Maitreya, and the rest "approach" *(upās-)* it precisely through the mode of non-worship (*anupāsanayogena,* 284).[49]

In formulating his independent inferences and syllogisms to establish the Mādhyamika's doctrines, Bhā(va)viveka was influenced by the Buddhist logico-epistemological school going back to Dignāga.[50] He strongly opposed the Vijñānavāda of Guṇamati, the master of the Valabhī school; and he was in his turn criticized by Guṇamati's disciple Sthiramati, as well as by Dharmapāla, a master of the Nālandā school of the Vijñānavāda. Bhā(va)viveka approved the doctrine of Devaśarman, a commentator on the *Mūlamadhyamakakārikās* whose work is no longer extant.[51] The commentary on the *Prajñāpradīpa* by Avalokitavrata also provides much interesting information on the history of Indian philosophy which awaits analysis.

Candrakīrti criticizes the Sāṃkhya[52] and Vaiśeṣika and mentions the Vedānta in his *Madhyamakāvatāra.* He followed and developed Buddhapālita's Prāsaṅgika interpretation of Nāgārjuna's philosophy; and he criticized both Bhā(va)viveka's logical innovations in the Madhyamaka and Dignāga's school. He does not seem to refer to Dharmakīrti, but it is not certain what chronological significance this silence has.[53] In the course of his critique of his opponents' epistemology, Candrakīrti has also quoted (*Prasannapadā* i, p.65) the *Madhyāntavibhāga* (i.9), one of the fundamental treatises of the Vijñānavāda school traditionally ascribed to Maitreyanātha and commented on by Vasubandhu.

In the following centuries explicit or implicit allusions to and discussions of opposed schools, Buddhist and non-Buddhist, become abundant in the literature of the Madhyamaka. In particular, Śāntarakṣita's *Tattvasaṃgraha* and Kamalaśīla's *Pañjikā* on it provide much information about Indian philosophy and its masters in the seventh and eighth centuries. Kamalaśīla's

49. See V. V. Gokhale, *IIJ* 5 (1961/62), pp. 271 f. On Bhā(va)viveka and Maitreya and Avalokiteśvara, compare Hsüan-tsang's remarks in his *Hsi-yü-chi* (trans. S. Beal, *Si-yu-ki,* II, pp. 223–26). And on his closeness to the "Sāṃkhya" see ibid., p. 223, and T. Watters, *On Yuan Chwang's Travels,* II, pp. 215, 223.

50. Cf. Y. Kajiyama, *WZKSO* 7–8 (1963–64); 12–13 (1968/69), p. 198.

51. The information that Tāranātha has given on Devaśarman in his *Rgya gar chos 'byung* (p. 133.18) is hardly intelligible.

52. See R. Garbe, *Die Sâṃkhya-Philosophie,* pp. 391–92 (where most of Candrakīrti's information has been described as untraceable in the Sāṃkhya sources).

53. According to I-ching (see J. Takakusu, *A Record of the Buddhist Religion,* p. 186), Dignāga's treatises were still in use in his time as basic works on logic.

Pañjikā (328), for example, contains what appears to be the earliest mention in a Buddhist treatise of the Advaitadarśana; this mention in a work composed in the second half of the eighth century is consistent with the dating of Śaṃkarācārya in the early eighth century. The *Nibandhana* by Bodhibhadra (tenth century) on Āryadeva's *Jñānasārasamuccaya* also supplies information of value on Indian philosophy of the late classical period. As for the mention of the Upaniṣadvādins in the *Pañjikā* by Prajñākaramati (ca. 1000?) on Śāntideva's *Bodhicaryāvatāra* (ix.60), it refers back to Śāntarakṣita's *Tattvasaṃgraha* (328–29). From the eleventh century we have a mention of the Vedāntin Bhāskara in Advayavajra's *Tattvaratnāvalī* (p. 19).[54]

Turning now to some of the great classics of Brāhmanical thought, we find in Kumārila's *Ślokavārttika* a chapter entitled Śūnyavāda that follows immediately on another entitled Nirālambanavāda. Kumārila was evidently a contemporary of Dharmakīrti, whose doctrine he criticises, and he is dated to ca. 600–660; thus he is in all likelihood also a contemporary of Candrakīrti, but he does not seem to refer to this Madhyamaka master anywhere. Contrary to what one might expect of a text called Śūnyavāda, it is not devoted primarily to a discussion of the Madhyamaka school. In the Śūnyavāda chapter (verse 259), just as in the Nirālambanavāda chapter (e.g., verse 3), the term *śūnya* refers not to the Madhyamaka theory but to the absence of any separately real objective correlate *(artha)* in a cognition; and these two chapters of the *Ślokavārttika* are in fact concerned mostly with a criticism of Dharmakīrti's logico-epistemological doctrine. It is true that Kumārila's criticism in the Nirālambanavāda (5–10) of the Buddhist theory of the two *satya*s—the *saṃvṛtisatya* and the *paramārthasatya*—and of the idea that the *saṃvṛti* is really false *(mṛṣā, mithyā)* can be applied to Madhyamaka doctrine also; and when commenting on verse 5 of this chapter, Uṃveka (eighth century) and Pārthasārathimiśra in fact quote *Mūlamadhyamakakārikā* xxiv.8 *(dve satye samupāśritya buddhānāṃ dharmadeśanā/ loke* [sic] *saṃvṛtisatyaṃ ca satyaṃ ca paramārthataḥ//)*.[55] But it is at the same time clear that Kumārila had in mind the doctrine of the unreality of the external object, which—contrary to what has sometimes been maintained—is not a tenet of the pure Madhyamaka schools (in contradistinction to the synthesising Yogācāra-Madhyamaka). In verse 14 Kumārila distinguishes between the Yogācāras and the Mādhyamikavādins, explaining that the first accept a

54. See H. Nakamura, *ABORI* 48–49 (1968), pp. 119–22.

55. Cf. also Bhāsarvajña, *Nyāyabhūṣaṇa* (Ṣaḍdarśanaprakāśanagranthamālā, Banaras, 1968), pp. 518 f on *saṃvṛti*.

cognition empty of an object *(arthaśūnya vijñāna),* whereas the latter maintain the non-existence of even such a *vijñāna.*[56] Kumārila's doctrines were subsequently discussed and criticized in Śāntarakṣita's *Tattvasaṃgraha* and Kamalaśīla's *Pañjikā* on it.

The relationship between the Vedānta and the Madhyamaka poses a number of interesting questions which can be only briefly touched on here.[57] Reference has already been made above to Bhā(va)viveka's critique of the Vedānta and to his very remarkable comparison of the supreme *brahman* with the Buddhist idea of ultimate reality.

On the Brāhmaṇical side, Gauḍapāda—who is dated to ca. 500 but is sometimes considered to have been Śaṃkarācārya's teacher's teacher—shows clear and unmistakable links with Buddhist thought in chapter IV of his *Māṇḍūkyakārikā*s, in particular with the Vijñānavāda and also with the Madhyamaka. However, in the other chapters of this work, starting with the third and culminating in the first, there is to be found a progressive movement away from Buddhist ideas and towards the Vedāntic sources.[58]

In his attitude towards what he terms Śūnyavāda (which in this case is unquestionably the Madhyamaka), Śaṃkarācārya has taken up a negative stance in his *Bhāṣya* on the *Gauḍapādīyakārikā*s (see ii.32; cf. i.7 and iv.28).[59] His position on the subject is especially clear in his *Bhāṣya*s on the *Brahmasūtra* and the *Bṛhadāraṇyakopaniṣad,* where he has simply rejected the Śūnyavāda, without discussion or analysis, as contrary to all means of correct knowledge *(sarvapramāṇavipratiṣiddha)* and as therefore unworthy of

56. For references to the Mādhyamikas see Uṃveka, *Ślokavārttika-Tātparyaṭīkā* on Śūnyavāda 1 and 245, as well as on Nirālambanavāda 14–18. Kumārila mentions Śūnyavādins in his Nirālambanavāda 129.

57. On the early Madhyamaka of Nāgārjuna and Āryadeva and the Vedānta see H. Nakamura, *HJAS* 18 (1955), pp. 89–102; K. Venkataramanan, *Nāgārjuna's Philosophy as Presented in the Mahā-Prajñāpāramitā-Śāstra* (Tokyo, 1966), pp. 319–21.

58. For a recent discussion and analysis of the *Gauḍapadīya-* or *Māṇḍūkya-Kārikā*s see T. Vetter, *WZKS* 22 (1978), 95–131. Vetter, who places this work ca. 500, thinks (p. 95n1) that Bhā(va)viveka's *Madhyamakahṛdayakārikā* viii.12 may presuppose *GK* iii.5. At the same time he recognizes the Buddhist background to chapter IV of *GK,* considering it to be the earliest of the four chapters; and he suggests that the other chapters of the *GK* reflect Gauḍapāda's progressive development away from the Mahāyāna, the first chapter of the *GK* being then the one least indebted to Buddhist thought and closest to the Upaniṣadic source (the *Māṇḍūkyopaniṣad*).

59. See T. Vetter, *Studien zur Lehre und Entwicklung Śaṅkaras* (Vienna, 1979), pp. 50, 53 f, 73–74.

serious attention and refutation;[60] according to the great Advaitin, it is simply the teaching of nihilists *(vaināśika)* and thus like a sandy, dried-up well.[61] It is indeed strange to find the Madhyamaka being dismissed out of hand for teaching something it has rejected. In fact, according to the Mādhyamika, nihilism *(ucchedānta)* is just as unacceptable a philosophical extreme as eternalism *(śāśvatānta)*; and from the soteriological point of view it is perhaps an even more pernicious extreme than its opposite. Beginning with Nāgārjuna, the Mādhyamikas have furthermore accepted *saṃvṛtisatya* and *lokavyavahāra* as necessary to philosophical thought and as duly recognized in the Buddha's teaching.[62] For Śaṃkarācārya to characterise the Madhyamaka as being in opposition to all means of philosophical knowledge is then at least an oversimplification demonstrating his lack of familiarity with the Madhyamaka as set out in the very large body of literature that it had produced by his time. How this is to be accounted for it is now difficult to say. It may have been the result of inveterate hostility—perhaps more theological and sociological than philosophical—to Buddhist thought. Moreover, Śaṃkarācārya may have felt himself obliged to distance himself from Buddhist thought as much as possible, not least because of the links that seem to have connected certain earlier Vedāntic ideas and Buddhist thought.[63] A contributing factor may, finally, have been real unfamiliarity with Madhyamaka literature and philosophy due to a scarcity of this school's books, at least in the places Śaṃkarācārya was living.

Quite different in his attitude to the Madhyamaka was Śrīharṣa, the twelfth-century Vedāntin author of the *Khaṇḍanakhaṇḍakhādya,* who employed a method he termed deconstructive reasoning *(khaṇḍanayukti)*. This form of

60. *Brahmasūtrabhāṣya* II.ii.31 and *Bṛhadāraṇyakopaniṣad-bhāṣya* IV.iii.7.

61. *Brahmasūtrabhāṣya* II.ii.32. Cf. *Bṛhadāraṇyakopaniṣad-bhāṣya* I.ii.1 where, in a discussion of causality and the reality of *kāraṇa* in relation to *kārya,* a Śūnyavādin holding the tenet *sarvasyaivâbhāvo 'stu* is supposed to be the opponent. But this passage in fact tells us nothing pertinent to the Madhyamaka as we know it from its own sources.

62. See, e.g., *Mūlamadhyamakakārikā,* chapter XXIV, especially verses 8–10. It is true that Candrakīrti has not invested *vyavahāra* and *saṃvṛtisatya* with ultimate reality and "truth," for he considers that it cannot resist ontological analysis and that any attempt to investigate it in such a way is fraught with paradoxes and insoluble logical antinomies. But in itself this theory need not imply either indulgence in paralogisms and nihilism, or the taking up of an anti-philosophical position.

63. D. Ingalls has suggested that even if, metaphysically, the distance between "idealistic" Buddhism and Śaṃkara was but little, the psychological and historical chasm separating them was nevertheless deep (*PEW* 3 [1953], pp. 291 f). See also T. Vetter, *WZKSO* 12–13 (1968/69), p. 409, and *Studien,* pp. 53 f, on Śaṃkara's differences with Buddhism.

reasoning has been recognized to be closely related to the Mādhyamika's dialectic and to his *prasaṅga*-type reasoning. Śrīharṣa has moreover accepted the *vitaṇḍā*,[64] which is certainly to be understood in this case not as referring to the form of argument employed by an unprincipled opponent merely to win an argument at any cost, but as philosophical criticism and reduction to the impossible.[65] Rather than a cavil, then, *vitaṇḍā* is here an acceptable form of discussion which may be required by a true philosopher when he confronts the onto-logically indeterminate relative.[66]

In philosophical works of the Jainas, including doxographical texts like Haribhadrasūri's *Ṣaḍdarśanasamuccaya*, as well as in later Hindu doxographical works such as Mādhava's *Sarvadarśanasaṃgraha*, we find more or less condensed accounts of some form of Madhyamaka, and in particular of its epistemology and gnoseology. No comprehensive analysis of the Madhyamaka by a classical Indian authority of an opposed school seems to exist, however.

Many of the above-mentioned sources have not hitherto been systematically studied in detail from a comparative viewpoint for the purpose of

64. Kāśī Sanskrit Series no. 197 (Banaras, 1970), pp. 126–27 (= Chowkhamba Sanskrit Series ed. § 168). Cf. pp. 7, 12.

65. In the *Nyāyasūtras*, *vitaṇḍā* is mentioned together with *jalpa* (IV.ii.49) and also *hetvābhāsa* and other faults in debate (I.i.1). In I.ii.3 it has been defined as a *jalpa* that lacks the assertion of a counter-thesis *(pratipakṣasthāpanāhīna)*. K. Bhattacharya, *JA* 1975, pp. 99–102, has denied that Śrīharṣa ever described himself as a *vaitaṇḍika* (which seems to be true); but he does not mention the above-mentioned passages of the *Khaṇḍanakhaṇḍakhādya*, where Śrīharṣa speaks favourably of the employment of *vitaṇḍā*. It seems necessary, then, to distinguish between *vitaṇḍā* as a cavil used to gain a debating point by demolishing the opponent's thesis and *vitaṇḍā* as a form of reasoning and argument where a serious philosopher refrains from asserting a counter-thesis. (See also *NS* IV.ii.48: *pratipakṣahīnam api vā prayojanārtham arthitve.*) While he would no doubt reject a *vitaṇḍā* used in the first way, Śrīharṣa appears to be ready to accept the second use since, with the sole exception of *brahman* as *vijñāna*, everything is different from both existence and non-existence *(vijñānavyatiriktaṃ punar idaṃ viśvaṃ sadasadbhyāṃ vilakṣaṇaṃ brahmavādinaḥ saṃgirante)*, much as is stated in the *Laṅkāvatārasūtra*.

In their comments on *NS* I.ii.3, Uddyotakara and Vācaspatimiśra discuss in addition the question whether the *vitaṇḍā*, defined as a *jalpa* that is *pratipakṣasthāpanāhīna*, can constitute proof by residue *(pāriśeṣyāt pakṣasiddhiḥ)* arrived at by excluding all opposed theses. In this case the Vaitaṇḍika would indeed have a thesis, even if it is established exclusively by refuting other theses.

66. It should be recalled here that the *Vaidalyaprakaraṇa* (§ 56) has rejected *vitaṇḍā* together with the other fifteen topics enumerated in *Nyāyasūtra* I.i.1. Though he uses *prasaṅga*-arguments, its author does not, therefore, identify himself with the Vaitaṇḍika who uses the *vitaṇḍā* in the first way mentioned in the previous note.

tracing historical influences operating between the Mādhyamikas and the other philosophers of India.[67] Once it has been carried out, such study can be expected to yield a rich harvest for our understanding of the history of Indian thought in its diverse forms; and it will at the same time no doubt resolve many a thorny chronological problem.

In conclusion, it is possible to state that the internal relative chronology of the Indian Madhyamaka school is clear in its broad outlines. But the exact place in this overall scheme of a few masters still remains doubtful; and it has not been possible to attribute a number of texts to specific authors in certain cases where the same name has been borne by more than one master. The absolute chronology of several masters also has not been settled beyond doubt, especially in the earlier period. Finally, the external relative chronology continues to pose problems, and in some cases it has not yet been possible to connect allusions made anonymously and without particulars with specific masters and texts known to us. Further detailed and patient research may be able to clear up many of the outstanding obscurities.

Postscript to pages 23–24

In a further article in *Acta Orientalia* 41 (1980), 27–37, in support of his dating of Bhavya's *Madhyamakaratnapradīpa* to 570 (p. 33) and of Candrakīrti to the sixth century (see above, note 28), Christian Lindtner has now put back the date of Dharmakīrti also to ca. 530–600. He describes (pp. 31–32) Hsüan-tsang's silence as "the apparently only objection to an earlier date of Dharmakīrti than ca. 600–660"; and in support of his earlier dating he refers to E. Frauwallner's article on Kumārila's lost *Bṛhaṭṭīkā,* where it is argued that this treatise must have been written about 630 as a reply to Dharmakīrti's theory of inference and the necessary connection between cause and effect. But in his article (*WZKSO* 6 [1962], p. 89) Frauwallner sought in particular to show that Dharmakīrti's work on this point is to be placed between Kumārila's *Ślokavārttika,* which does not know of it and still treats the relation in question in terms of *vyāpti,* and the *Bṛhaṭṭīkā,* the *niyama* theory of

67. T. R. V. Murti, *Central Philosophy of Buddhism* (London, 1955), provides an interesting philosophical comparison between what he calls the two traditions of Indian philosophy embodied respectively in Buddhism and Vedānta. But Murti was not concerned with chronological sequences and interrelationships. Nor did he make use of the Chinese and Tibetan sources that are now, owing to the loss of the Sanskrit originals of so many works of Indian philosophy, our principal documents not only for the history of the Madhyamaka but also for so much of classical Indian thought.

which must have been a response to Dharmakīrti's theory of inference and the necessary connection between cause and effect. According to Frauwallner, then, Dharmakīrti and Kumārila must have been contemporaries; and Lindtner's new dating of Dharmakīrti would as a consequence entail putting Kumārila's date back to the sixth century too. (It might of course be supposed that Dharmakīrti's contribution came to Kumārila's attention only after he had finished his *Ślokavārttika* although Dharmakīrti preceded him by a long period of time; but this line of argument has not been followed by Lindtner.) Whether the (relatively minor) difficulty of the authorship and date of the *Madhyamakaratnapradīpa* in fact necessitates and justifies the chronological revisions involved by Christian Lindtner's new datings will require further investigation and discussion which cannot be undertaken until he has presented in full the evidence announced in his last article.

3. The Uses of the Four Positions of the *Catuṣkoṭi* and the Problem of the Description of Reality in Mahāyāna Buddhism*

I. *The Four Positions in Early Buddhist Thought*

IN THE EARLY philosophical literature of Buddhism the notion of four alternative positions *(koṭi)* making up what is often termed a *catuṣkoṭi* or "tetralemma" appears in discussions on the questions whether a *tathāgata* exists after death, whether the world has an end, and whether the world is eternal. In each of these cases the nature of a postulated entity and its relation to a predicate is investigated in such a way that all conceptually imaginable positions are exhausted; for an entity and its predicate can be conceptually related only in terms of these four limiting positions. Thus it is asked whether a *tathāgata* exists, does not exist, both exists and does not exist, or neither exists nor does not exist after death;[1] whether the world (of living beings, *loka*) is finite, infinite, both finite and infinite, or neither finite nor infinite; and whether the world (of living beings) is eternal, not eternal, both eternal and not eternal, or neither eternal nor not eternal.[2] In addition

* First published in *Journal of Indian Philosophy* 5 (1977), pp. 1–71.

1. The word *tathāgata* here may refer to the *buddha* (see for example *MMK* xxv.17 and xxii.214); see below, notes 54 and 62. But it is also taken in the sense of "person"; and it is then sometimes interpreted as equivalent to *pudgala* (see for example Vasubandhu, *AKBh ix*, p. 471). E. W. Hopkins pointed out that in the usage of the Epic *tathāgata* means "in so (grievous) a condition," i.e., practically dead or dead (*American J. of Philology* [1911], pp. 205–9).

2. Sometimes *śāśvata* "eternal" is taken as referring to the past *(pūrvānta)* and *ananta* "infinite" as referring to the future *(aparānta);* cf. Candrakīrti, *PPMV* xxvii.15, 21; xxv.21. In *PPMV* xxvii.1 *aparānta* refers to *vartamāna-ātmabhāva* (below n. 64>. But Vasubandhu speaks of the thesis of the *śāśvata* nature of the *loka* being incompatible with attainment

to these questions, the canonical literature mentions that of the relationship between a vital principle (*jīva* "soul") and the body, which is envisaged under only two headings, viz. whether they are different or not different.

Thus in the Buddhist canonical texts up to fourteen points have been mentioned, twelve concerning three topics each investigated with respect to four positions and two relating to a single topic investigated in terms of only two positions. In the canon the Buddha is represented as having declined to answer any of these moot points when questioned about them by Māluṅkyāputta, Vacchagotta (Vatsagotra), and other questioners; and he has thus come to be suspected of either ignorance or agnosticism. However, these questions are treated in Buddhist thought rather as ones to be set aside *(sthāpanīya, ṭhapanīya)* because they cannot be explicated either usefully or meaningfully, and for this reason they are frequently referred to as the unexplicated points *(avyākṛtavastu)*.

Such questions cannot be *usefully* answered and are to be set aside since, from the soteriological point of view, their solution can contribute nothing to progress on the path to Awakening.[3] And they cannot be *meaningfully* decided because of a certain logical and semantic vagueness in their terms. These questions are met in one form or another throughout Buddhist literature beginning with the canonical texts, and they have accordingly been extensively discussed also in the modern literature on Buddhism and Indian philosophy.[4]

---

of *parinirvāṇa,* which would appear to make the term refer to the future; see *AKBh* ix (pp. 470–71).

As for *loka,* it seems here to mean the world of living beings (cf. *jagat*) (below, n. 54); cf. L. de La Vallée Poussin, *Nirvāṇa* (Paris, 1925), p. 92. In Candrakīrti's *Madhyamakāvatāra* (vi.129) *loka* is explained as *skandha;* cf. *MMK* xxvii.22. A few canonical sources add *ātman (attā)* before *loka,* e.g., Dīghanikāya I, p. 16 and Majjhimanikāya II, p. 233. On *loka = ātman* see *AKBh* ix, pp. 470–71; *ātman* is also to be found in the *Ta chih tu lun (*Mahāprajñāpāramitopadeśa),* transl. É. Lamotte, *Le traité de la Grande Vertu de Sagesse de Nāgārjuna,* i (Louvain, 1944), p. 155.

3. Cf. Dīghanikāya I, pp. 188–89, and III, p. 136; Majjhimanikāya I, p. 431; Saṃyuttanikāya II, pp. 222–23.

4. On the *catuṣkoṭi (cātuṣkoṭika),* often translated in the modern Western literature as "tetralemma," see S. Schayer, *Ausgewählte Kapitel aus der Prasannapadā* (Kraków, 1931), pp. xxv–xxvi, L. de La Vallée Poussin, *L'Abhidharmakośa* (Louvain, 1923ff.) v, pp. 43–46; ix, pp. 262–69 (on the *avyākṛtas*); É. Lamotte, *Le traité de la Grande Vertu de Sagesse* (Louvain, 1944), i, pp. 154, 422–23; T. R. V. Murti, *Central Philosophy of Buddhism* (London, 1960), pp. 129ff.; K. N. Jayatilleke, *Early Buddhist Theory of Knowledge* (London, 1963), p. 344 and passim. On the *koṭis* see also L. Schmithausen, *Der Nirvāṇa-Abschnitt der Viniścayasaṃgrahaṇī* (Vienna, 1969), pp. 183ff.

In the following pages certain uses and interpretations of the last two positions *(koṭi)* of the "tetralemma," and of "neither . . . nor" sentences in particular, will be examined with respect to their applications in the philosophical analysis of linguistic and conceptual fictions, the conditioned *(saṃskṛta)* factors of existence on the relative level of dependent origination, and the unconditioned *(asaṃskṛta)* factors on the level of ultimate reality *(paramārtha)*. And the question whether the Mahāyāna śāstras developed a special language and logic of mysticism[5] apart and quite distinct from the language and logic of philosophical analysis as well as ordinary usage will be touched on in connexion with certain uses of the "neither . . . nor" formula. This study will be based on some older treatises of the Madhyamaka and

---

Instead of fourteen unexplicated *(avyākṛta)* points, some canonical sources enumerate only ten points. In such enumerations only the question about the *tathāgata's* survival after death is put in the form of the *catuṣkoṭi,* all the other questions having only two alternatives each. See Dighanikāya I, pp. 187ff., and III, pp. 134–36; Majjhimanikāya I, pp. 426ff. (Māluṅkyāputta) and 484ff. (Vacchagotta); Saṃyuttanikāya III, p. 258.

The Buddhist exegetical tradition recognizes in the Buddha's teaching four kinds of explanation *(vyākaraṇa):* the explicit and definitive *(ekāṃśa),* that which introduces a distinction *(vibhajya),* that which consists in a counter-question *(paripṛcchā),* and that which involves setting aside a question *(sthāpanīya).* See for example *Abhidharmakośa* v.22. The last form is known in Pāli as *ṭhapanīya* and is mentioned, e.g., in Dīghanikāya III, p. 229, and Aṅguttaranikāya I, p. 197. Such a question is then unexplicated *(avyākṛta;* Pāli *avyākata).*

The fact that certain questions have been set aside and left unexplicated can be motivated both pedagogically and psychologically—with regard to the propensities *(āśaya)* etc. of the questioner—and logically and semantically—owing to the empty (null, *nirvastuka*) nature of the subject term and its relation to a predicate. Cf. *AKBh 9* (pp. 470–71; *praṣṭur āśayāpekṣayā*) and *PPMV* xxii.12 (which compares the subjects in question to the empty notion of the son of a barren woman, *vandhyāputra,* to which no qualification can be applied meaningfully).

On the *avyākṛtavastus* see *AKBh* v.22 and 9 (pp. 469–11); *MMK* xxii.12ff. and xxv.17ff.; *Madhyamakāvatāra* vi.129; L. de La Vallée Poussin, *L'Abhidharmakośa* v, p. 43; ix, pp. 262–69; E. Lamotte, *Le traité de la Grande Vertu de Sagesse,* i, pp. 154, 423; G. Nagao, "The Silence of the Buddha," *Studies in Indology and Buddhology* (S. Yamaguchi Volume; Kyoto, 1955), pp. 137ff.; N. Tatia, "The Avyākṛtas," *Nava-Nālandā Mahāvihāra Research Publication,* II, pp. 47–73; T. R. V. Murti, *Central Philosophy of Buddhism* (London, 1960), chap. ii; K. N. Jayatilleke, *Early Buddhist Theory of Knowledge,* passim; R. H. Robinson, *Philosophy East and West* 22 (1972), pp. 309–23.

The *avyākṛtavastus* partly correspond to some of the sixteen speculative opinions *(dṛṣṭi)* of the *Brahmajālasuttanta;* cf. *MMK* xxvii, especially verses 18ff.

5. On this question see for example J. F. Staal, *Exploring Mysticism* (Berkeley, 1975). See also below, pp. 90, 99, and n. 182.

Vijñānavāda schools and on the *Ratnagotravibhāga,* an old Mahāyānist text that deals especially with the positive characterization of ultimate reality.

II. The Uses of the Catuṣkoṭi *in the Madhyamaka*

In the literature of the Madhyamaka school the term *catuṣkoṭi(kā)* has not actually been employed by Nāgārjuna in the *Mūlamadhyamakakārikā*s, by Āryadeva in the *Catuḥśataka,* and by Candrakīrti in the *Prasannapadā.*[6] But the four positions of the "tetralemma" frequently appear from the earliest times in the literature of this school, where they are usually negated either explicitly or implicitly.[7] That is, each position (or *koṭi*)—the positive one (I), the negative one (II), the one consisting in a combination or conjunction of the positive and negative (III), and the one consisting in the binegation of the positive and negative (IV)—is negated, the usual term used for such negation being *pratiṣedha.*

The negation may be expressed either in a single grammatical word—namely a descriptive *(karmadhāraya)* or possessive *(bahuvrīhi)* compound made up of a term preceded by the negative member *a(n)*—or in a sentence predicate containing a verbally bound negative particle—i.e., *na* + verb[8] in Sanskrit. The negation is therefore formally either term-negation or predicate-negation. While the first syntactic form corresponds to relational negation *(paryudāsa)* as defined by the Indian grammarians, the second syntactic form answers to the definition of absolute negation *(prasajyapratiṣedha)* as given by them.[9]

The positions of a "tetralemma" have been variously used in the *Mūlamadhyamakakārikā*s for analysing the concept of causation, the totality of factors on the level of the relative and conventional *(saṃvṛti),* conditionship in the context of reality *(tattva)* or the ultimate *(paramārtha),* the existence of a *tathāgata,* and *nirvāṇa.* With the sole exception of the case of

6. The word *catuṣkoṭi* appears in Prajñākaramati's *Bodhicaryāvatārapañjikā* ix.2 in a quotation.

7. For an exception see below on *MMK* xviii.8, which is phrased in the form of a *catuṣkoṭi* but differs from the other examples we have to consider since it concerns the Buddha's graded teaching, which is progressively accommodated to the various levels of his disciples' understanding.

8. The copula may be unexpressed but implied.

9. See Patañjali, *Mahābhāṣya* i.4.57 and iii.3.19.

the totality of factors on the level of the relative (§ 2 below), the analyses in question are carried out by negating all the positions or *koṭis*.

1. *Causation*

The four positions appear in the analysis of causation in *Mūlamadhyamakakārikā* i.1:

> *na svato nâpi parato na dvābhyāṃ nâpy ahetutaḥ /*
> *utpannā jātu vidyante bhāvāḥ kvacana ke cana //*
>
> Entities of any kind are not ever found anywhere produced from themselves, from another, from both [themselves and another], and also from no cause.

The leading commentators of the two main branches of the Madhyamaka school—Bhā(va)viveka for the Svātantrika branch and Candrakīrti for the Prāsaṅgika branch—agree that the statements in question here are to be interpreted as negations that do not commit the person accepting them to an affirmation of their contradictory. In other words they are regarded as cases of absolute negation *(prasajyapratiṣedha)* as defined by the logicians, so that the negation of a sentence stating production from self, for example, does not commit one to the affirmation of a sentence stating production from another, etc.[10]

10. In philosophical usage *prasajyapratiṣedha* is pure negation in which no opposed (contradictory) thing is posited even by implication.

MMK i.1 is explained by Candrakīrti in the following manner in *PPMV* (pp. 13, 36, and 38–39): *naiva svata utpannā ity avadhāryamāṇe parata utpannā ity aniṣṭaṃ prāpnoti / na prāpnoti, prasajyapratiṣedhasya vivakṣitatvāt, parato 'py utpādasya pratiṣetsyamānatvāt / ... parato 'pi nôtpadyante bhāvāḥ ... dvābhyāṃ api nôpajanyante bhāvāḥ ... ahetuto 'pi nôtpadyante.* (Compare Buddhapālita, *Mūlamadhyamakakārikāvṛtti,* fol. 182a [ed. Walleser, pp. 11–12].) And for Bhā(va)viveka's explanation see his *Prajñāpradīpa,* fol. 48a (ed. Walleser, p. 10). (The Tibetan translation of *MMK* i.1 is syntactically noteworthy: *bdag las ma yin gzhan las min // gnyis las ma yin rgyu med min // dngos po gang dag gang na yang // skye ba nam yang yod ma yin//*, the use of *ma yin* corresponding formally to the *paryudāsa* type of negation whereas *med* corresponds to the *prasajyapratiṣedha.* The Tibetan exegetical tradition takes the negation to be of the *prasajya* type, following the Indian commentators.)

On the subject of the *prasajyapratiṣedha* in Indian thought, see F. Kielhorn, trans., Nāgojībhaṭṭa, *Paribhāṣenduśekara*[2] (Poona, 1960), p. 10; F. Edgerton, *Mīmāṃsānyāyaprakāśa* (New Haven, 1929), §§ 330ff.; L. Renou, *Terminologie grammaticale du sanskrit* (Paris, 1957), p. 230, and *JA* 1957, p. 131; Y. Ojihara and L. Renou, *La Kāśikā-Vṛtti*

In the same body of texts we also meet with statements where the negative is not verbally bound but forms part of a compound, so that such a sentence would correspond formally to the Indian grammarians' definition of relational negation *(paryudāsa)*. This is the case for example in the eight negations which relate to dependent origination *(pratītyasamutpāda)* in the introductory verses to the *Mūlamadhyamakakārikās*. The question then arises whether this syntactical difference reflects a semantic one and in particular whether, from the logical point of view, we have to do in this second type of sentence with a proposition committing the person accepting it to the affirmation of the contradictory of what he has negated, as is to be expected normally in the case of *paryudāsa* negation. In other words, do the eight (negated) epithets referring to *pratītyasamutpāda* in the introductory verse of the *Madhyamakaśāstra*

anirodham anutpādam anucchedam aśāśvatam /
anekārtham anānārtham anāgamam anirgamam //

commit the Mādhyamika to a positive statement equivalent to the contradictory of what is here negated because these epithets appear in the syntactical form usually associated with *paryudāsa* negation?

For the Mādhyamika the reply is evidently "no." Candrakīrti indeed observes that, by using the epithets *anutpāda* etc., the Buddha, who has indicated that entities arise in dependence on causes and conditions, has denied *(ni-ṣidh-)* that an entity arises from no cause, one cause, or disparate causes, or that it is produced from itself, another, or both together. The surface nature *(sāṃvṛta-svarūpa)* of conventional things is thus revealed *(udbhāvita)* by this negation *(niṣedha)* in a way that is applicable to the conventional *pratītyasamutpāda*—although in point of fact, for the pure Gnosis of the saints *(āryajñāna)*, there is no cessation *(nirodha)* because no entity has ever been produced through own-being (*svabhāva* "aseitas").[11]

Moreover, the explanations offered by the exegetical tradition of the

(Paris, 1960), pp. 119ff.; J. F. Staal, *BSOAS* 25 (1962), pp. 58ff.; G. Cardona, *Language* 43 (1967), pp. 34ff.; B. K. Matilal, *The Navyanyāya Doctrine of Negation* (Cambridge, Mass., 1968), pp. 156–57, and *Epistemology, Logic, and Grammar in Indian Philosophical Analysis* (The Hague, 1971), pp. 163–64; D. Seyfort Ruegg, *La théorie du tathāgatagarbha et du gotra* (Paris, 1969), Index s.v. *prasajyapratiṣedha;* Y. Kajiyama, *WZKS* 17 (1973), pp. 162ff.

11. *PPMV,* pp. 10–11: . . . sa *evedānīṃ sāṃvṛtaḥ pratītyasamutpādaḥ, svabhāvenânutpannatvād āryajñānāpekṣayā nâsmin nirodho vidyate. . .*

Madhyamaka do not appear to suggest the existence of any correlation of the syntactically variant forms of negation mentioned above—viz. nominally bound term-negation and verbally bound predicate-negation—with the logical differentiation between implicitly affirming (presuppositional or choice) negation and denying (non-presuppositional or exclusion) negation, or between the negation of a proposition and the negation of a predicate. In other words, in the usage of the Mādhyamika authors, it does not seem to be the case that negation which is of the *paryudāsa* type on the syntactic level—i.e., nominally bound negation—has the logical value of relational negation, in contradistinction to absolute negation as expressed by the verbally bound *prasajya* type of negation; and both syntactic schemata appear to have been interpreted by these exegetes as involving, from the logical point of view, what they term absolute *(prasajya)* negation.[12] The linguistic formulae expressing the opposed positions (and *koṭis*) in question are furthermore sometimes regarded as involving conflict and contradiction *(virodha)*.[13]

Although it has been alleged that Buddhist philosophers—and, indeed, other Indian thinkers as well—ignore or reject the principles of non-contradiction and excluded middle, this contention certainly cannot be sustained as concerns Nāgārjuna and his school, whose entire reasoning is in fact founded on them. It is true that paradoxical and antiphrastic formulations are not infrequent in some Mahāyāna sūtras, and in particular in the Prajñāparamitā texts of which the Madhyamaka school has made abundant use; and Nāgārjuna was evidently convinced of the paradoxicality of many so-called common-sense views of the world and the real based on the assumption of entities or essences possessing own-being *(svabhāva)* as maintained by many of his predecessors and contemporaries.[14] But at least in his theoretical scholastic treatises *(rigs tshogs)*, of which the *MMK* is most

12. In *PPMV*, p. 12.4, Candrakīrti speaks of the *pratiṣedha* of *nirodha* being mentioned in the verse before that of *utpāda*, but he does not go into the logical nature of this negation.

13. See *PPMV* xviii.6 (p. 355.7) on the contradictory opposition *(virodha) ātman/anātman* (below, p. 47. According to *PPMV* vii.30 and xxv.14, *bhāva* and *abhāva* are mutually exclusive *(parasparaviruddha)* contraries, like light and darkness (which are also *parasparāsaṃgata* in *PPMV* xx.11, p. 400.5). Similarly *sad* and *asad* are *parasparaviruddha* according to *PPMV* i.7. See further *PPMV* vi.4 and xx.11 concerning the opposition *saṃsāra/nirvāṇa*, and *PPMV* xvi.8 concerning *bandha/mokṣa*.

That *sad* and *asad* are *parasparaviruddha* has been stated by Nāgārjuna himself in *MMK* viii.7.

14. Compare Nāgārjuna's use of dilemmas to destroy the substantialist views of his opponents based on the assumption of a *svabhāva*, etc.

representative, he does not seem to have himself employed paradoxes as such in an attempt to speak of reality.[15]

2. *The totality of factors in relative truth*

In the *MMK* the following has been said with regard to transactional and relative truth (xviii.8):

> *sarvaṃ tathyaṃ (na vā tathyaṃ) tathyaṃ câtathyam eva ca /*
> *naivâtathyaṃ naiva tathyam etad buddhānuśāsanam //*

> All[16] is just so,[17] or[18] not just so, both just so and not just so, neither just so nor not just so: this is the graded teaching of the Buddhas.

This statement might at first sight seem to be a paradox, or perhaps even an example of the outright rejection of the rule of non-contradiction. However, to understand the purport of the statement it is in the first place necessary to note that the use of the word *anuśāsana*—with the preverb *anu-* meaning "progressive" or "fitted"—for the teachings in question may be crucial. Candrakīrti at least clearly thought so, for he explains *anuśāsana* with due regard to its etymology either as a teaching that proceeds progressively *(anupūrvyā śāsanam)* in introducing its recipients to reality *(tattvāmṛtāvatāradeśanānupūrvī),* or as a teaching fitted to those who are to be instructed *(vineyajanānurūpyeṇa vā*

15. On the somewhat different language of the stotras and stavas *(bstod tshogs)* attributed to Nāgārjuna, however, see D. Seyfort Ruegg, "Le *Dharmadhātustava,*" in *Études tibétaines dédiées à la mémoire de M. Lalou* (Paris, 1971), pp. 448–71, reprinted as chapter 4 of the present volume. On the use of paradox and antiphrasis in certain sūtras, see D. Seyfort Ruegg, *Le traité du tathāgatagarbha de Bu ston Rin chen grub* (Paris, 1973), pp. 87–88, 114n3, 118n2, 134n3. The aim seems on occasion to be to produce perplexity *(the tshom = saṃśaya)*—a kind of intellectual "torsional" tension—which would permit one somehow to comprehend reality (see also *Théorie du tathāgatagarbha,* p. 387). (For a similar process in Zen cf. C. Y. Cheng, *Journ. of Chinese Philosophy* 1 [1973], pp. 77ff.)

16. *Sarva* can refer to all *saṃskṛtadharmas:* Saṃyuttanikāya IV, p. 15; *Mahāniddesa* i; p. 132, and *AKBh* v.27 (p. 301.7–8) and ix, p. 465. Candrakīrti glosses *sarva* by *skandha, dhātu, āyatana,* etc.

17. The antonym of *tathya* is *mṛṣā* (see below). Candrakīrti explains *tathya* here as that for which there is not otherness (change), and *atathya* as that for which there is otherness (change). For the present use of *tathya,* cf. the *Kālakārāma-suttanta* (Aṅguttaranikāya II, p. 24).

18. *Vā = ca* according to *PPMV,* p. 371.6.

śāsanam).[19] In his discourses the Buddha is in fact represented as not seeking to dispute with people however much they may quarrel with him, and as disposed to adhere to usually accepted conventions from which he would depart only when replying to well-defined and semantically well-formed questions put to him by informed questioners.[20] Candrakīrti emphasizes the progressive and also complementary nature of these teachings by stating that the particle *vā* used in the verse is equivalent to *ca* in the sense that the teachings in question are cumulative *(deśanāsamuccaya).*[21]

It is furthermore important to observe that the context clearly shows that such a method of teaching that takes "all" to be just so, etc., according to the situation, does not represent an attempt to define ultimate and ineffable reality. On the contrary, it is accommodated to conventional ways of speaking used by the majority of people with respect to ordinary topics of discourse, ways which the Buddha himself adopted in order to guide people away from doctrinal bypaths and ethical abysses and set them on the main road towards their particular, albeit interim, destinations. Candrakīrti accordingly observes that, when teaching in this manner that "all" is just so, etc., the Buddha has ordinary unintelligent folk in mind in the first statement, and the *ārya*s in the statement to the effect that all is false *(mṛṣā: atathya).* As for the teaching that "all" is neither *tathya* nor *atathya,* it is intended for persons who have for a long time cultivated insight into reality but have not yet totally eradicated the obstacles *(āvaraṇa);*[22] such a use of the "neither . . . nor" type of

19. These are the two most usual meanings of *anu.* This is certainly not to deny that the word *anuśāsana* is regularly used in Sanskrit, including in Buddhist literature, to mean teaching, instruction, without any specific reference to progressivity or fitness, as is also *anusāsana* in Pāli. It is not possible to determine with absolute certainty what value Nāgārjuna assigns to this word in *MMK* xviii.8; we can only observe that in xviii.11 he uses *śāsana,* and that if xviii.8 were to be understood as referring to the standardized classical *catuṣkoṭi,* this would be the only passage where it is not negated.

20. See Majjhimanikāya I, p. 499. This particular situation differs from that of the *avyākṛtavastus* in which a reply is to be set aside; for in this case the Buddha *is* able to answer either by an explicit and definitive *(ekāṃśa)* explanation, or by introducing a distinction *(vibhajya),* or perhaps by asking a counter-question *(paripṛcchā),* in other words by employing one of the accepted modes of *vyākaraṇa* (see above, n. 4).

21. For the idea, compare Aṅguttaranikāya II, pp. 25–26, where it is explained that because the *tathāgata* does not construe as either true or false the perceptions and concepts people have but knows them just as they are, he is *tādī.*

22. Similarly, we might say of something that it is roughly so, i.e. neither just so nor quite the opposite, although if analysed it would require further qualification. It is to be noted that the "neither . . . nor" form of statement is here intended for a category of

statement is held to be appropriate because it is applied when speaking of a subject that is empty (null) like the son of a barren woman *(vandhyāsuta),* so long as the particular disciples addressed have only partially understood the non-substantiality of all *dharmas*.[23] (We would say that a sentence containing such an empty subject is not well formed semantically, and that any qualification is therefore inapplicable.) Such a method of progressive and accommodated teaching is, then, considered to be simply a useful device *(upāya)* employed by the compassionate Buddha to introduce people in a preliminary manner to the quintessence of reality *(tattvāmṛtāvatāra).*[24]

Āryadeva has us observe in the chapter of his *Catuḥśataka* dealing with the practice of the disciple that any references in the Buddha's teaching to existence, non-existence, both existence and non-existence, and neither existence nor non-existence are to be regarded as "remedies" employed according to the nature of the "disease" to be treated in each specific case (viii.20):

> *sad asat sadasac cêti nôbhayaṃ cêti kathyate /*
> *nanu vyādhivaśāt sarvam auṣadhaṃ nāma jāyate //*

> Reference is made to existence, non-existence, [both] existence and non-existence, and neither. Is it not that everything, according to the disease, comes to be what is called a medicine?[25]

The progressive nature of the teachings has also been emphasized by Āryadeva (*CŚ* viii.15):

---

persons inferior to those in question under *MMK* xviii.6; for here this formulation does not refer to the highest level of the understanding of reality.

23. *PPMV,* p. 371: *vandhyāsutasyâvadātaśyāmatāpratiṣedhavad ubhayam etat pratiṣiddham* "as in the case of the negation of the paleness and darkness of the son of a barren woman, both *[tathya* and *atathya]* are negated." On the *vandhyāsuta* (or *vandhyāputra*) see *PPMV* xiii.3, xxii.12, xxiv.1, and xxvii.28. Bhā(va)viveka's explanation differs in some respects, but these differences do not concern the question being treated here. See Appendix I below.

24. *PPMV,* p. 369.13 and 370.1. *MMK* xviii.8 could also be interpreted according to the *māyā* comparison; that is, the world is neither "so" ("true") because it is not as it appears, nor is it "not so" ("false") because of origination in dependence *(pratītyasamutpāda).* According to the *marīci* comparison, we should be wrong to look for water in a mirage; and this cannot even be the object of strict negation since the very possibility of water simply does not arise in the case of the mirage.

25. Quoted in *PPMV* xviii.6. Cf. *CŚ* xvi.10, according to which each of the four positions involves a fault; and *CŚ* xiv.21 and xvi.24–25 quoted below.

vāraṇaṃ prāg apuṇyasya madhye vāraṇam ātmanaḥ /
sarvasya vāraṇaṃ paścād yo jānīte sa buddhimān //

First demerit is excluded, in the middle self is excluded, and finally all is excluded; he who knows [this] is a wise person.[26]

3. *Ātman*

Analysis by means of the positions including binegation in the "neither . . . nor" form is moreover applied to the variant teachings concerning a self *(ātman)* alluded to in the Buddhist canon. The *MMK* states (xviii.6):

ātmêty api prajñapitam anātmêty api deśitam /
buddhair nâtmā na cânātmā kaścid ity api deśitam //

On the one hand the designation "self" has been made, and on the other "non-self" has been taught, and the Awakened ones have taught also "[there is] no self and no non-self."[27]

In his comment Candrakīrti has pointed out that the two opposed doctrines of *ātman* and *anātman* are to be found not only outside the Buddhist teaching (for example in the Sāṃkhya and Lokāyata respectively),[28] but even within the Buddhist canon. In some places the Buddha in fact refers positively to an *ātman* as a protection,[29] and also to acts belonging to an *ātman;*[30] whereas elsewhere he explicitly states that there is here no *ātman* having any conceivable connexion with the psycho-somatic groups *(skandha)* through a relation of identity, possession, or inclusion.[31] Since a conflict *(virodha)* can

26. Quoted in *PPMV* xviii.6. In his commentary on this verse of the *CŚ*, Candrakīrti explains that "all" refers to all things *(dngos po thams cad)* as excluded.

27. *PPMV*, p. 358.9: *evam nâsty ātmā kaścin na câpy anātmā kaścid astîti deśitam.* Compare *MMK* xxvii.13:

evaṃ dṛṣṭir atīte yā nâbhūm aham abhūm aham /
ubhayaṃ nôbhayaṃ cêti naiṣā samupapadyate //

and *Ratnāvalī ii.*3:

naivam ātmā na cânātmā yāthābhūtyena labhyate /
ātmānatmakṛtadṛṣṭī varvārâsmān mahāmuniḥ //

28. *PPMV* xviii.6 (p. 360).

29. Here the word *ātman* seems to be used practically as a reflexive pronoun.

30. *Samādhirājasūtra* xxxvii.35, quoted in *PPMV* xviii.5 (pp. 354–55).

31. See *MMK* xvi.2; xviii.1; xxii.1, 8 (and cf. x.14–15); *PPMV* xviii.5 (p. 355). Cf.

arise only when both opposed teachings are ascribed to the same source (here the Buddha),[32] it is of course only with this case that one is concerned here. However, this is not in itself a sufficient condition for a conflict because, in addition, the teachings in question would have to relate to exactly the same thing in the same respect. But this is not considered to be so, and the intentions of the teachings *(deśanābhiprāya)* in question have therefore to be elicited to begin with.[33] According to Candrakīrti these are as follows. In accordance with the first, positive, position, the buddhas have sometimes employed the designation *ātman* in order to turn disciples of a lower type *(hīna-vineya)* away from unwholesome actions. But they have also spoken, in accordance with the second position, of *anātman,* in their desire to assist disciples of the middling type *(madhya-vineya),* whose conceptual attachment *(abhiniveśa)* to the speculative view positing a real substantial self *(satkāyadṛṣṭi)* must be weakened so that they may achieve *nirvāṇa.*[34] Nevertheless, the buddhas have in fact also taught that there is neither self nor non-self to superior disciples *(utkṛṣṭa-vineya)* after having established their superior convinced adhesion *(adhimukti)* with respect to *nirvāṇa;* for such disciples are not attached to a self, and they are able to penetrate the very kernel of the most profound teachings as a consequence of having through previous superior exercises ripened the seeds of convinced adhesion to the profound *dharma.*[35] This explanation is then connected by Candrakīrti with the *Kāśyapaparivarta* (§ 57), where it is stated that the affirmation of *ātman* and *nairātmya* both represent extremes, the Middle Way being formless, invisible, incommensurable, etc.; and with Nāgārjuna's *Ratnāvalī* (ii.3–4), which says that the Buddha has qualified the visual and auditory as neither true nor false because a conceptual position *(pakṣa)* necessarily involves its counter-position *(pratipakṣa)* and both are thus untrue. And just as the view

Samyuttanikāya III, p. 44, and IV, p. 287, on the *caturdhā vicāraḥ (rūpaṃ [vedanām,* etc.] *attato samanupassati, rūpavantaṃ samanupassati, attani rūpam, rūpasmiṃ attānaṃ samanupassati).*

32. See *PPMV* xviii.5 (p. 355).

33. *PPMV* xviii.5–6.

34. As has been observed by Vasubandhu *(Abhidharmakośabhāṣya* ix, p. 470), the buddhas teach the *dharma* with the same care as a feline carries its young, neither holding them too tightly between its teeth nor letting them drop. So the Buddha sometimes teaches an *ātman* to exclude nihilism, and sometimes he teaches the *anātman* to exclude eternalism, the two philosophical extreme positions.

35. To be noted is the difference between the persons for whom the "neither... nor" statement is intended here and in *PPMV* xviii.8 quoted above.

of the existence of an *ātman* does not correspond to reality, so also its opposite, the view of the existence of non-self, would not do so. Hence the teaching that there exists neither self nor non-self is appropriate because it alone allows one to avoid positing a speculative entity—be it a positive *ātman* or a negative *anātman*—as the propositional subject of the substantive verb *asti* "exists."[36] Candrakīrti's explanation emphasizes the point that the binegation contained in the last position does not apply two opposed predicates simultaneously to some entity or essence regarded as indeterminate.

We have to do here with three distinct approaches fitting the predispositions and needs of three different types of disciples. Whereas the first two types are provided with remedies *(pratipakṣa)* against the "ills" of nihilism and eternalism, the highest type receives the teaching to the effect that in fact neither of the opposed views is valid because both are devoid of reality (*atattva,* p. 358.8). Either term of the conceptual dichotomy *(vikalpa) ātman/ anātman* is an extreme deriving from discursive development *(prapañca)* and related to either eternalism or nihilism, the twin extreme positions that the Middle Way eschews by its very definition.[37] To say that these two doctrinal extremes are nothing but polarizations of discursive and dichotomizing conceptualization no doubt amounts to saying that they relate in the final analysis to empty (null) subjects.[38]

With regard to analysis by means of the four positions, a verse by Āryadeva may be quoted in which it is said that, in considering oneness (i.e., identity), otherness (i.e., difference), both oneness and otherness, and neither oneness nor otherness, it is necessary in addition to consider the fourfold question as to whether we have, in each case, existence, non-existence, both existence and non-existence, and neither existence nor non-existence (*CŚ* xiv.21):

> *sad asat sadasac cêti sadasan nêti ca kramaḥ /*
> *eṣa prayojyo vidvadbhir ekatvādiṣu nityaśaḥ //*

In his comment on this verse Candrakīrti first gives as examples of oneness, otherness, their conjunction, and their binegation respectively the *satkāryavāda,* the *asatkāryavāda,* the *sadasatkāryavāda,* and the doctrine

36. Cf. *MMK* xxvii.8 and ix.12 on the *ātman (upādātṛ)* as neither existing nor not existing.

37. Here then, contrary to the case under *MMK* xviii.8, the "neither . . . nor" statement is intended for the superior disciples.

38. This point has been made elsewhere; see *PPMV* xiii.3, xviii.8, xxii.12, 24.1, and xxvii.29 for the *vandhyāputra* (etc.) comparison. Cf. also *PPMV* xxvii.8.

of the indeterminate *(brjod du med pa)* nature of the relation of oneness/ otherness between products and their causes. And he next gives as examples of the four-term set *ātman* (: *sat*), *anātman* (: *asat*), both *ātman* and the absence of *ātman* (i.e., *anātman: sat* and *asat*), and *nâtmâpi na cânatmâpi* (: *na san nâsat*).[39]

This type of analysis of a problem thus constitutes one of the basic methods used by the Mādhyamikas to establish the inapplicability of any imaginable conceptual position—positive, negative, or some combination of these—that might be taken as the subject of an existential proposition and become one of a set of binary doctrinal extremes *(antadvaya).*[40]

4. *Dependent origination and reality*

An important use of the "neither . . . nor" form of statement is to be found in *MMK* xviii.10:

> *pratītya yad yad bhavati na hi tāvad tad eva tat /*
> *na cânyad api tat tasmān nôcchinnaṃ nâpi śāśvatam //*

> Whatever exists in dependence [on a cause] is not that [cause] nor is it different [from that cause]. Therefore [the cause on which there is dependence] is neither destroyed nor eternal.

This point indeed constitutes the very kernel of the teaching of the buddhas (xviii.11).

39. Cf. *CŚ* xvi.10 according to which each of the four positions involves a fault.

40. Cf. *CŚ* xvi.24–25:
gcig yod gcig med ces bya ba // de nyid min 'jig rten pa'ang min //
des na 'di yod 'di ces med // brjod pa nyid du nus ma yin //
yod dang med dang yod me zhes // gang la phyogs ni yod min pa //
de la yun ni ring po na'ang // klan ka brjod pa nus ma yin //
To say something is and something is not is neither really true nor [a] worldly [conventional statement]; therefore it cannot be said that this is [but] that this is not. He who has no thesis stating existence, non-existence, and [both] existence and non-existence cannot ever be criticized.
CŚ xvi.25 is quoted in *PPMV*, p. 16:
sad asat sadasac cêti yasya pakṣo na vidyate /
upālambhaś cireṇâpi tasya vaktuṃ na śakyate //
Cf. Nāgārjuna's *MMK* xxiv.3 and *Vigrahavyāvartanī* 29 and 59, where there is however no explicit reference to the *catuṣkoṭi,* and the subject is a proposition *(pratijñā)* demonstrating some particular thesis that involves onto-logical faults (as opposed to Emptiness against which no objection can be properly urged).

The problem here is what Candrakīrti has termed the conventional "worldly" characteristic of reality *(laukikaṃ tattvalakṣaṇam),* i.e., the relation between cause and effect once the Mādhyamika has been able to establish that neither the non-causal and eternalistic *śāśvatavāda* nor the causal and non-eternalistic *satkāryavāda* withstands philosophical analysis. This verse then refers to what might be called the antinomic and even irrational nature of any concept of production so long as the factors in question are supposed to be existent entities *(bhāva).*[41]

But when seen in the light of the true nature of reality *(tattvalakṣaṇa)* as it is accessible to the *ārya*s, the real itself is not antinomic and becomes intelligible (xviii.9):

> *aparapratyayaṃ śāntaṃ prapañcair aprapañcitam /*
> *nirvikalpam anānārtham etat tattvasya lakṣaṇam //*
>
> Independent of another,[42] still, not discursively developed through discursive developments, without dichotomizing conceptualization, and free from multiplicity:[43] this is the characteristic of reality.

With this should be compared what is said about conditionship, the real nature of dependent origination (*MMK* vii.16):

> *pratītya yad yad bhavati tat tac chāntaṃ svabhāvataḥ /*
> *tasmād utpadyamānaṃ ca śāntam utpattir eva ca //*
>
> Whatever exists in dependence [on a cause] is still in its own nature; therefore what is produced is still, as is the very process of production.

Here then a "neither . . . nor" form of statement is used to reveal the irrationality of something, that is, the antinomic and logically inconsistent character

41. Cf. *PPMV* i, p. 26.

42. This word is interpreted as meaning "not learnt from another" *(nâsmin parapratyayo 'stîty aparapratyayaṃ paropadeśāgamyaṃ svayam evâdhigantavyam, PPMV,* p. 373.1; cf. *PPMV,* p. 493.10–11: *sa hi paramārtho 'parapratyayaḥ śāntaḥ pratyātmavedya āryāṇāṃ sarvaprapañcātītaḥ).*

43. *Anānārtha* = Tib. *don tha med min.* Cf. the introductory verses to the *MMK* (pp. 3–4) where the *pratītyasamutpāda* is also so qualified.

of a theory of causality operating with the concept of *bhāva*s endowed with real natures *(svabhāva)*. (That this is not the Mādhyamika's own theory of causation does not require reiteration.[44])

In sum, to say that something is neither *A* nor non-*A* *(Ā)* does not represent an attempt on the part of the Mādhyamika to define some entity *(bhāva,* i.e., a thing possessing *svabhāva)* that is neither *A* nor *Ā* (i.e., indeterminate) but rather a way of stating the Buddhist theory of conditionship in terms of the Madhyamaka doctrine of emptiness of own-being *(svabhāvaśūnyatā)* and non-substantiality of all factors *(dharmanairātmya)*. And both eternalism (non-destruction) and nihilism (non-production) are thus excluded as at the same time extreme and complementary positions based solely on dichotomizing conceptualization.

To the extent that it applies to the conventional worldly domain of the surface level, the Mādhyamika's Middle Way does not, when seen in this light, involve either the ignoring or the rejection of the principle of noncontradiction. And the fact, or truth, of the interdependent origination of things is then referred to by the term *śūnyatā,* "Emptiness," a designation not belonging to the object-language applied conditionally to this state of affairs.[45] Such is accordingly the Middle Way (*MMK* xxiv.18):

> *yaḥ pratītyasamutpādaḥ śūnyatāṃ tāṃ pracakṣmahe /*
> *sā prajñaptir upādāya pratipat sâiva madhyamā //*[46]

In addition to their uses reviewed above both for analysing fictional constructs, such as dichotomous conceptions based on the idea of *ātman* (in, e.g., *MMK* xviii.6), and also for discussing the conventional surface-level

44. For the Mādhyamika, *pratītyasamutpāda* does not operate on *dharmas* or *bhāvas* having real and immutable natures, and the causal process is therefore in a certain sense indeterminate and irrational. See the introductory verses to the *MMK* and *PPMV,* pp. 9ff.; and the *pratītyasamutpāda* is described as *sāmvṛta* (*PPMV,* pp. 10–11).

Bhā(va)viveka for his part considers that the *pratītyasamutpāda* has two aspects, the absolute one and the relative one. See his *Madhyamakahṛdayakārikā* ii.10 (ed. Gokhale, *IIJ* 15 [1973], p. 44).

45. The term *śūnyatā* could then be described as metalinguistic since it does not refer to any given (first-order) object or thing. Indeed, because it allows the Mādhyamika philosopher to analyse the terms of the Ābhidharmika's philosophical parlance, which are second-order terms inasmuch as they do not refer directly to objects in the world but rather to analytical concepts such as the *dharma* lists, *śūnyatā* might even be called a third-order term.

46. Cf. Nāgārjuna's commentary on his *Vigrahavyāvartanī* 70, at the end.

origination of *dharmas* in dependence on causes and conditions on the plane of the *laukikatattvalakṣaṇa* (in, e.g., *MMK* xviii.10), the *koṭis*—and especially the binegation of opposed but complementary positive and negative terms in the "neither . . . nor" form of statement—appear also in the Mādhyamika's discussion of terms used to indicate ultimate reality. This is the domain of what Candrakīrti terms *tattvalakṣaṇa* proper, as accessible to the Gnosis *(jñāna)* of the perfected saints *(ārya)*.[47]

An essential characteristic of reality is, Nāgārjuna has stated, to be uncommunicated by one to another,[48] to be still, to be not the object of discursive development, to be free from dichotomizing conceptualization, and to be without differentiation (*MMK* xviii.9 quoted above, p. 51). Candrakīrti observes that whereas *vikalpa* comprises a "running forth" of thinking *(cittapracāra)*, it can be said that reality *(tattva)* is not only verbally inexpressible but that it resides in absence of the "running forth" even of pure knowledge *(jñānasyâpy apracāraḥ)*.[49] The *paramārtha* is neither taught nor is it even cognized *(sa nôpadiśyate, na câpi jñāyate)*.[50] And the fact that the *tattva* is free from multiplicity is to be recognized because of the fact that it has the value of Emptiness *(anānārthatā tattvasya lakṣaṇaṃ veditavyaṃ śūnyatayâikarasatvāt)*. In sum, the *paramārtha* finds its only appropriate "expression" in the silence of the saint *(āryatūṣṇībhāva)*,[51] propositions being applicable only to entities within the sphere of discursive development *(prapañca)* and dichotomizing conceptualization *(vikalpa)*. Such then is *tattvalakṣaṇa* for the perfected *āryas*, with respect to whose Gnosis there can be no cessation of things because things are in fact not produced in respect of own-being *(svabhāva)*.[52]

The negation of the opposed predicates "originated" and "destroyed" for a grammatical "subject" that refers to the level of absolute reality—*dharmatā, nirvāṇa,* etc.—is then a way of saying that outside the domain of discursive and conceptual thinking there is no propositional naming (*MMK* xviii.7):

> *nivṛttam abhidhātavyaṃ nivṛtte cittagocare /*
> *anutpannāniruddhā hi nirvāṇam iva dharmatā //*

47. *PPMV* xviii.9, p. 375.9; cf. p. 11.1.

48. See above, note 42 .

49. *PPMV,* p. 374.

50. *PPMV* xxiv.8 (p. 493.11); cf. xxv.24.

51. *PPMV* i.1 (p. 57.8).

52. *PPMV,* p. 11.1 (quoted above, note 11).

> The denotatum has ceased once what is in the domain of thinking has ceased; for *dharma*-nature is non-produced and non-destroyed, like *nirvāṇa.*[53]

Candrakīrti comments:

> If there existed here any denotatum whatsoever, it would be set forth; but once the denotatum is stopped and there is no object of words, then no thing at all is taught by the buddhas .... Were any thing within the domain of thinking, there would be verbal activity consequent on the imputation to it of some phenomenal mark *(nimitta).* But when the very object of thinking is not possible, where then is a phenomenal mark imputed in virtue of which there might be verbal activity? . . . And because, like *nirvāṇa, dharmatā*—the own-being *(svabhāva)* of the *dharmas*, the nature *(prakṛti)* of the *dharmas*—is established as non-produced and non-destroyed, thinking consequently does not operate there. And when there is no thinking activity, how can there be imputation of phenomenal marks? Hence it is fully established that no thing at all has been taught by the buddhas.

It is for this reason then that only the silence of the saint is in conformity with absolute reality.

Nāgārjuna makes the point again in his chapter on *nirvāṇa* (*MMK* xxv.24):

> *sarvopalambhopaśamaḥ prapañcopaśamaḥ śivaḥ /*
> *na kva cit kasya cit kaś cid dharmo buddhena deśitaḥ //*

> The quieting of all cognitive grasping, the quieting of all discursive development, still: no *dharma* has been taught anywhere by the Buddha to anybody.

5. *The tathāgata and nirvāṇa*

An idea related to the preceding is expressed by Nāgārjuna in his chapter on the *tathāgata* (*MMK* xxii.15):

53. Cf. L. de La Vallée Poussin, "Réflexions sur le Madhyamaka," *MCB* 2 (1933), p. 39.

prapañcayanti ye buddhaṃ prapañcātītam avyayam /
te prapañcahatāḥ sarve na paśyanti tathāgatam //

Those who make the *buddha*—beyond discursive development and unchanging—the object of discursive development are all ruined by discursive development, and they do not see the *tathāgata.*

Candrakīrti notes that all discursive development is dependent on a substantial thing *(vastu);* but the *tathāgata* is no substantial thing *(avastuka).* In the next verse Nāgārjuna adds that the world (of living beings) has the same nature as the *tathāgata* and that it is consequently without own-being, just like the *tathāgata* (xxii.16):

tathāgato yatsvabhāvas tatsvabhāvam idaṃ jagat /
tathāgato niḥsvabhāvo niḥsvabhāvam idaṃ jagat //

These two verses follow a section where Nāgārjuna discusses the application of the negation of the four positions of the *catuṣkoṭi* to the question of the existence after cessation of a *tathāgata* and to the questions whether the world *(loka)* has an end *(anta)* and is eternal *(śāśvata).* These are of course the questions dealt with in twelve of the fourteen unexplicated points *(avyākṛtavastu).*[54]

In this connexion Nāgārjuna has explained that the application of the four positions based on the idea of the empty *(śūnya)* is not valid from the point of view of absolute reality (*MMK* xxii.11):

<śūnyam iti na vaktavyam> aśūnyam iti vā bhavet /
ubhayaṃ nôbhayaṃ cêti prajñaptyarthaṃ tu kathyate //

One must not say "empty," or else there would be "not empty," both ["empty" and "not empty"], and neither. Yet for the sake of designation [such] is stated.[55]

54. It is to be noted that Nāgārjuna here takes *tathāgata* as a synonym of *buddha,* and *loka* as a synonym of *jagat* "world (of living beings)." Cf. above, notes 1 and 2.

55. This and the following predicates refer to the masculine noun *tathāgata* according to the context; La Vallée Poussin however reads *aśūnyaṃ* and restores *śūnyam* (cf. *PPMV* xv.2, p. 264). The Tibetan translation reads:

The scholiast[56] has observed:

> All this [viz. the four positions] is not to be said by us. However, if unspoken, knowers are unable to understand own-being as it is *(yathāvadavasthitam).* So, relying on transactional truth *(vyavahārasatya),* by imputation *(āropataḥ)* we say "empty" with a view to transactional usage by accommodation to people who are to be trained. And we also say "not empty," "empty and not empty," and "neither empty nor not empty."[57] Hence [Nāgārjuna] has said: "Yet for the sake of designation [such] is stated." As the Lord [Buddha] declared, "All factors of existence are without own-being . . . ." Elsewhere the not empty is spoken of, [as when it was said:] "O monks, were a past visible form *(rūpa)* non-existent, a learned Auditor-Saint *(ārya-śrāvaka)* would not have desired [that] past visible form. O monks, because there is a past visible form, a learned Auditor-Saint therefore desires that past visible form." "Were a future visible form non-existent . . . ." "O monks, were past consciousness non-existent . . . ."[58] Thus, in the Sautrāntika doctrine, the past and future are empty, the remainder [i.e., the present] being not empty; dissociated[59] communicative behaviour *(vijñapti)* is empty.[60] In the Vijñānavāda also the imaginary nature has the property of being empty because it is not produced in dependence, as in the case of a person suffering from eye disease who sees a double moon.

---

stong ngo zhes kyang mi brjod de // mi stong zhes kyang mi bya zhing //
gnyis dang gnyis min mi bya ste // gdags pa 'i don de brjod par bya //

J. W. de Jong translates (*Cinq chapitres de la Prasannapadā* [Paris, 1949], p. 80): "Ne peut dire ni qu'il est vide, ni qu'il est non-vide . . . ." The meaning given in our translation above, following the Sanskrit, seems to be appropriate, since saying "empty" involves the logically complementary (and opposite) idea of "not empty" etc., within the frame of dichotomizing conceptualization *(vikalpa),* which involves pairs of binary concepts *(pratidvandvin, pratibandhin,* etc.). See *MMK* xiii.7 (quoted below, p. 109).

56. This development is not to be found in the Tibetan translation of *PPMV.*

57. Cf. *PPMV* xv.2 (p. 264).

58. Cf. L. de La Vallée Poussin, "Documents d'Abhidharma," *MCB* 5 (1937), p. 54.

59. *Viprayuktā.* Cf. *Abhidharmakośa* ii.35–36.

60. Cf. *Abhidharmakośa* iv.2–3; É. Lamotte, "Traité de l'acte," *MCB* 4 (1936), p. 165.

Here the scholiast quotes *Madhyāntavibhāga* i.3[61] and then concludes by saying: "All these constructions (*kalpanā*, viz. the four positions) are impossible *(na sambhavanti)* in the case of the *tathāgata* free from discursive development *(prapañca)*."

Just as the four positions based on the property of being empty and its opposite are said to be impossible in the case of the *tathāgata*, so also the four positions based on the concept of the eternal *(śāśvata)* and its opposite, and on that of an end *(anta)* and its opposite, are inapplicable to what is tranquil (*MMK* xxii.12):

> *śāśvatāśāśvatādy atra kutaḥ śānte catuṣṭayam /*
> *antānantādi câpy atra kutaḥ śānte catuṣṭayam //*

In his comment Candrakīrti first enumerates the fourteen *avyākṛtavastus* in which the eternality of the world, the end of the world, and the existence of the *tathāgata* after death[62] are each considered in terms of the four limiting positions, while the relation between a life principle *(jīva)* and the body is considered in terms of only two limiting positions (identity and difference). Candrakīrti then explains that just as the tetrad of *śūnyatva* etc. is not possible *(na sambhavati)* in the case of the *tathāgata* tranquil by nature and without own-being *(niḥsvabhāva)*, so the tetrad of the eternal is not possible in this case. Indeed, it is just because of this impossibility *(asambhava)* that this set of four questions was not explicated by the Buddha in the case of the world of living beings *(loka)*, the case being just like attributing darkness or paleness to the son of a barren woman *(vandhyāputra)*.[63] And just as this tetrad is impossible in the case of the *tathāgata*, so is that which is based on the idea of an end and its opposite impossible for the tranquil *tathāgata*.

In sum, suppositions *(cintā)* or constructions *(kalpanā)* based on the four positions of the *catuṣkoṭi* do not fit what is empty of own-being (*MMK* xxii.14ab):

> *svabhāvataś ca śūnye 'smiṃś cintā naivopapadyate /*

61. See below, pp. 68, 71–72.

62. Here *tathāgata* = *bhagavant* (cf. *MMK* xxv.17) or *buddha* (xxii.15). *MMK* xxv.17 and 21, but not *PPMV* xxii.12–3, have *paraṃ nirodhāt* (instead of *maraṇāt*). Cf. above, notes 1 and 54.

63. Cf. *PPMV* xiii.3, xviii.8, xxii.12, xxiv.1, and xxvii.29.

Nāgārjuna and Candrakīrti consider that the four *koṭis* relating to the *tathāgata*'s existence after cessation *(nirodha)* were developed with reference to speculation on *nirvāṇa,* and that the other two questions also analysed in terms of four *koṭis*—the world's end and eternality—were developed respectively with reference to whether the world and the self come to a final end *(aparānta)* and whether they have a beginning *(pūrvānta)* (*MMK* xxv.21):

> *paraṃ nirodhād antādyāḥ śāśvatādyāś ca dr̥ṣṭayaḥ /*
> *nirvāṇam aparāntaṃ ca pūrvāntaṃ ca samāśritāḥ //*[64]

The negation of the four positions based on the concept of entity (essence or *aseitas*) and absence of entity is furthermore applied to the term which has been used above all others in Buddhist thought to refer to reality: *nirvāṇa.*

After having demonstrated the inapplicability of the first three positions—entity (or essence, *bhāva* = *dngos po*), absence of entity (or essence, *abhāva* = *dngos med*), and both entity and absence of entity—in verses 4 to 14 of his chapter on *nirvāṇa* in the *Mūlamadhyamakakārikās*, Nāgārjuna takes up the question of the last position, consisting in binegation of entity and absence of entity, in the following pair of verses (*MMK* xxv.15–16):

> *naivâbhāvo naiva bhāvo nirvāṇam iti yâñjanā /*
> *abhāve caiva bhāve ca sā siddhe sati sidhyati //*
> *naivâbhāvo naiva bhāvo nirvāṇaṃ yadi vidyate /*
> *naivâbhāvo naiva bhāva iti kena tad ajyate //*

> The showing that *nirvāṇa* is neither entity nor absence of entity is established on condition that absence of entity and also entity be established. [But] if *nirvāṇa* exists neither as absence of entity nor as entity, what shows it to be neither absence of entity nor entity?[65]

Candrakīrti has provided the following comment:

> Were there some thing such as an entity, then, as its negation

64. Cf. *MMK* xxvii. In *PPMV* the *aparānta* is connected with the *vartamāna-ātmabhāva* (p. 572.14–15). For *MMK* xxv.17 on the *bhagavant,* see below, p. 60.

65. *Añjanā* = Tib. *ston pa,* "show, reveal"; and *ajyate* = Tib. *mngon byed.* The Tibetan version does not translate *vidyate: gal te mya ngan 'das pa ni // dngos min dngos po med min na//*

(pratiṣedha), there is the construction that *nirvāṇa* is no entity *(naiva bhāva nirvāṇam ity eṣā kalpanā).* And were there absence of entity, then, as the negation of this, *nirvāṇa* might be no absence of entity *(naivâbhāvo nirvāṇaṃ syāt).* But when entity and absence of entity do not exist, their negation also does not exist. Therefore even the construction that *nirvāṇa* is neither entity nor absence of entity is altogether not applicable, so that is not logically correct.[66] Moreover, if it be supposed that this *nirvāṇa* exists having the nature of neither absence of entity nor entity, what shows, makes cognitively perceived, and reveals that this *nirvāṇa* of such a kind having neither [absence of entity and entity] as its nature *(nobhayarūpa)* exists? Is there in this case some knower *(pratipattṛ)* of such a kind in *nirvāṇa,* or is there not? (a) If there were, a self would exist in *nirvāṇa* even; but [this] is not admitted because of the absence of existence *(astitvābhāva)* of a self without an appropriated substratum *(nirupādāna)* [in *nirvāṇa*]. (b) If there were not, who determines that there exists this *nirvāṇa* of such a kind?—Perhaps [somebody] situated in *saṃsāra* does so?—If [somebody] situated in *saṃsāra* determines this, does he do so through Gnosis *(jñāna)* or by analytical knowledge *(vijñāna)*? If you suppose that it is by *vijñāna,* that is not logically correct because *vijñāna* has as its object a phenomenal mark *(nimitta)* and there is no phenomenal mark in *nirvāṇa;* therefore, to begin with, this is not objectivized by *vijñāna.* Nor is it known through *jñāna;* this is so because *jñāna* will necessarily have emptiness as its object *(śūnyatālambana);* and since this [*jñāna* will then have] the nature of non-production *(anutpādarūpa)* exclusively, how does such *[jñāna]* whose own nature is non-existent *(avidyamānasvarūpa)* cognitively grasp that *nirvāṇa* is neither absence of entity nor entity, *jñāna* having [precisely] the nature of being beyond all discursive development *(prapañca)?*

Therefore nothing shows *nirvāṇa* to be neither absence of entity nor entity. And it is not logically correct to say that what is unshown, unrevealed, and unperceived cognitively exists in this way [i.e., in terms of the "neither . . . nor" position]. And just as

66. *Tasmān naiva bhāvo naivâbhāvo nirvāṇam iti yā kalpanā sâpi nôpapadyate evêti na yuktam etat.* This supposition also is not possible because it still presupposes that *bhāva* and *abhāva* are real *(siddha),* and that *nirvāṇa* is some sort of entity that consists in the binegation of these two reals.

these four constructions (*kalpanā,* viz. the *koṭis*) are altogether not possible *(na sambhavanti)* in the case of *nirvāṇa,* so are these constructions not possible either in the case of the *tathāgata,* who is the comprehender *(adhigantṛ)* of *nirvāṇa.* To demonstrate this it has been said [*MMK* xxv.17]:

paraṃ nirodhād bhagavān bhavatîty eva nôhyate /
na bhavaty ubhayaṃ cêti nôbhayaṃ ceti nôhyate //

That the Lord exists after cessation is not understood, and it is not understood that he does not exist, both [exists and does not exist], and neither.[67]

6. The dual function of "neither . . . nor" sentences

Only a few verses earlier Nāgārjuna has himself stated that once the Teacher has set out the elimination of becoming and passing away, it is logically correct to say that *nirvāṇa* is neither entity nor absence of entity (*MMK* xxv.10):

prahāṇaṃ câbravīc chāstā bhavasya vibhavasya ca /
tasmān na bhāvo nâbhāvo nirvāṇam iti yujyate //

Does this statement not therefore conflict with his rejection of the applicability to *nirvāṇa* of the fourth position consisting in the binegation of both existence and non-existence (*MMK* xxv.15–16)?

Linguistically, the difference between what Nāgārjuna has stated in xxv.10cd and xxv.15–16 is perhaps not as clear as might be wished; indeed the negation of the fourth *koṭi* is only formally distinguished from the negation mentioned in xxv.10cd by use of the correlative particles *eva . . . eva* (in *naiva . . . naiva* as against *na . . . na*).[68] Nevertheless, that there is a difference between the two statements despite the circumstance that both can be rendered by the "neither . . . nor" formula is shown by the context and the course of Nāgārjuna's discussion. For xxv.15–16 clearly represent the fourth *koṭi,* the applicability of which to *nirvāṇa* Nāgārjuna rejects; whereas xxv.10 equally clearly represents

67. *Ūhyate* (?) = Tib. *mngon pa,* "be clearly seen." Read *ajyate* as in xxv.16?

68. Cf. *PPMV* xxii.12 (p. 446): *naiva śāśvato nâśāśvataś ca lokaḥ; naivântavān nânantavāṃś ca lokaḥ; naiva bhavati na na bhavati tathāgataḥ paraṃ maraṇāt;* xxv.21 (p. 536): *naivântavān nânantavān lokaḥ; naiva śāśvato naivâśāśvato lokaḥ.* For the positive formula see *PPMV* xxvii.15: *sa eva deva sa eva manuṣyaḥ.*

the negation of the first and second *koṭis*, which Nāgārjuna had just been discussing (xxv.4–9). And only in the following verses (xxv.11ff.) does Nāgārjuna actually take up the discussion of the last two *koṭis*.

The semantic and logical difference between the two statements is no less evident: whereas the negation of the first and second *koṭis* (stated in xxv.10cd) does not, as a *prasajyapratiṣedha,* commit the Mādhyamika to the contrary statement about the existence of *nirvāṇa* (as either a positive or a negative entity), the fourth *koṭi* was evidently regarded as an attempt to present a description of some kind of entity, albeit one that is indeterminate, in terms of the opposition positive ("existence")/negative ("non-existence"). And it is for this reason that the Mādhyamika rejects its applicability by negating the fourth *koṭi* in addition to the other three *koṭis*.

This interpretation appears to agree with what Candrakīrti said concerning the statement that has the form "neither so nor not so" in *MMK* xviii.8.[69] There the "neither . . . nor" statement has been syntactically formulated in just the way that the fourth position of the *catuṣkoṭi* has been formulated elsewhere (for example in xxv.15–16), namely by means of the correlative particles *naiva . . . naiva.* This statement is considered to be an accommodation to the needs of the category of persons who have not yet completely eliminated the obstacles *(āvaraṇa);*[70] and one can no doubt conclude that, like the fourth *koṭi,* this "neither . . . nor" statement has also in the last analysis to be negated, for it refers simply to a fictional construct.[71]

The function of "neither . . . nor" sentences is then twofold inasmuch as they can be used either to formulate the fourth position of the *catuṣkoṭi* or to

69. Above, pp. 44ff.

70. See Candrakīrti's commentary quoted above, pp. 44–45.

71. Still, Candrakīrti's explanation of *MMK* xviii.8, which compares the case to the negation of the qualifications "pale" and "dark" with respect to the son of a barren woman (*vandhyāsuta,* i.e. an empty subject), does not seem to have made this point absolutely clear. For the binegation of these qualifications in the case of the *vandhyāsuta* would apparently correspond to the fourth *koṭi before* its negation, whereas (as seen above) it too has to be, and in fact is, negated by the Mādhyamikas. The discrepancy is puzzling, and may be due to an oversight or to inaccurate composition on Candrakīrti's part; or the point may have seemed to him so obvious in view of what is said elsewhere that he did not feel it necessary to dwell on it. Again, it might be that Candrakīrti switched just here from thinking of the "neither . . . nor" form of statement represented by the fourth position of the *catuṣkoṭi* to the "neither . . . nor" type of statement to be found for example in *MMK* 25.10cd.

It is interesting to note that the *Laṅkāvatārasūtra* (3, p. 188) equates the *cātuṣkoṭika* with the *lokavyavahāra,* outside which anything is a mere *flatus vocis (vāgmātra),* just like the "son of a barren woman".

state that neither of the positions of a conceptual schema based on a binary opposition of the type *A/Ā* (i.e., *koṭi*s I and II) is applicable according to the Madhyamaka, and that the Middle Way does not therefore postulate the existence of any entity of which something might then be predicated in positive or negative terms.[72]

On the logical and semantic levels it accordingly appears necessary to distinguish clearly between (a) a "neither . . . nor" sentence expressing the last position of the *catuṣkoṭi,* by which some entity would be postulated as indeterminate,[73] and (b) a "neither . . . nor" sentence where not even an indeterminate entity is posited, and which serves simply to exclude, by the *prasajya* type of negation, all positions resulting from dichotomizing conceptualization that polarizes itself as *A/Ā* (and sometimes also in the imaginable combinations "both *A* and *Ā*" and "neither *A* nor *Ā*").

7. *The third koṭi and the question of the coincidence of opposites*

Just as the Mādhyamikas did not accept the fourth *koṭi* as applicable to the description of a real, it is equally clear that they did not posit a real combining opposite (contrary if not contradictory) properties to which opposed predicates are applicable in terms of the third *koṭi.* Ultimate reality *(paramārtha)* may indeed be sometimes described in the literature of the Mahāyāna as undeterminable and inexpressible *(anabhilāpya);* but this does not imply according to the Madhyamaka that reality may be represented as a *coincidentia oppositorum,* where opposite properties converge together in some entity or essence that is to be described as both *A* and *Ā.*

For the Mādhyamika reality is as free from the third position of the *catuṣkoṭi* as it is from the others. This point has been discussed in *MMK* xxv.11–14 with regard to *nirvāṇa* as both *bhāva* and *abhāva,* a position that is rejected by Nāgārjuna. And in *MMK* xxvii.17, 22, and 25 Nāgārjuna has rejected the conjunction (even distributed) of the qualifications *śāśvata/aśāśvata* and *antavat/anantavat.*

72. The use of binegation to refer to a high level of realization may have been suggested by the highest of the four *ārūpyas,* the *naivasaṃjñānāsaṃjñāsamāpatti,* "attainment of neither notion nor non-notion." However, this *samāpatti* does *not* represent in Buddhism the highest level of *samāpatti* (the *saṃjñāveditanirodha* or *nirodhasamāpatti*), and it certainly does not therefore correspond to *nirvāṇa.*

73. Compare the Vātsīputrīya theory of the *pudgala* that is neither identical with nor different from the *skandhas,* the relation between the two being then undeterminable *(avaktavya)?*

8. *Inexpressibility and non-duality*

From the point of view of the Madhyamaka doctrine of emptiness of own-being *(svabhāvaśūnyatā)* and the non-substantiality of all factors *(dharmanairātmya),* exclusively *cataphatic* language taking the form of the third as well as the first *koṭi* and exclusively *apophatic* language taking the form of the fourth as well as the second *koṭi* are equally inapplicable to reality. However, a "neither . . . nor" sentence may on occasion be pressed into service in an attempt to indicate or reveal the *paramārtha;* but it cannot then be supposed to correspond to the (unnegated) fourth *koṭi.* And such a formulation is used because it constitutes the closest linguistic approximation available to the semioticized silence of the *ārya,* the only kind of "sign" that conforms to ultimate reality as it truly is.

It is accordingly necessary not to confound ultimate reality *(paramārtha),* which may be described as inexpressible *(anabhilāpya),* and even as undeterminable (cf. Tib. *ma nges pa*), with an entity conceived of and defined as indescribable, undecidable, or indeterminate which, instead of being free of all four positions of the *catuṣkoṭi,* would simply correspond to the (unnegated) fourth *koṭi.*

Furthermore, because *śūnyatā* applies to all *dharma*s without exception, no differentiation whatsoever exists between *saṃsāra* and *nirvāṇa* (*MMK* xxv.19):

> *na saṃsārasya nirvāṇāt kiṃcid asti viśeṣaṇam /*
> *na nirvāṇasya saṃsārāt kiṃcid asti viśeṣaṇam //*

Hence also their "limit" *(koṭi* = Tib. *mtha')* is the same (*MMK* xxv.20):

> *nirvāṇasya ca yā koṭiḥ koṭiḥ saṃsaraṇasya ca /*
> *na tayor antaraṃ kiṃcit susūkṣmam api vidyate //*

Here a clear distinction has to be drawn between the Buddhist theory of non-duality *(advaya),* based on the emptiness of all *dharma*s, and the monism for example of the Vedāntic *advaita,* which posits one unique spiritual entity from which there is no real differentiation.[74]

The fact that the Mādhyamika does not find the four positions to be applicable and that he negates the statements in which these positions are accepted

74. It is to be recalled that in the Vedānta school the term *anirvacanīya* "indeterminable" is applied not to the absolute *brahman*—which is unique and without a second—but to *avidyā* and *nāmarūpa.* Cf. P. Hacker, *ZDMG* 100 (1950), p. 255.

does not of course imply that he considers the method of analysis based on the *catuṣkoṭi* useless. On the contrary, when properly employed for the purpose of the investigation of concepts and (pseudo-)entities, they prove to be an eminently valuable instrument for philosophical analysis, of which the Mādhyamika has made abundant use. Such analyses on occasion bring the Mādhyamika to a consideration of transactional linguistic usage (e.g., in *MMK* xxiv.18 on *prajñapti* and xviii.10 on the *abhidhātavya*) and of discursive development that is linguistic as well as conceptual (e.g., *MMK* xviii.9 and xxiv.24), although the purely linguistic aspect of philosophical analysis has not been pursued in special detail by the earlier Mādhyamikas.

9. *Canonical sources*

In the foregoing the discussion has been concerned with the uses and interpretations of the *koṭis* by the older masters of the Madhyamaka school, but as observed at the beginning, the basic principles we have been considering were known earlier since they appear in some parts of the Āgamas/Nikāyas.

In this connexion Nāgārjuna has referred in *MMK* xv.7 to the only Āgama text which he explicitly mentions by name in this treatise, the *Kātyāyanāvavāda* of the Saṃyuktāgama. In that canonical text it has been said that conventional transactional usage in the world is based on the set of dichotomous concepts comprised by the pair existence/non-existence, which the Buddha is shown in that sūtra to have analysed and rejected.[75] This pair of concepts makes up two of the most frequently discussed *koṭis* or positions. Candrakīrti has remarked that this canonical text has been recognized by all the Buddhist schools *(sarvanikāya),* an observation that is supported by the fact that a parallel passage is found in the Saṃyuttanikāya transmitted by the Theravāda school.[76] And he aptly concludes that, since speculation based on the dichotomies of own-being *(svabhāva)*/other-being *(parabhāva)* and existence/non-existence are equally in conflict with the Buddha's teaching, intelligent people will attach themselves to neither of these speculative opinions.[77]

The rejection of the positions that postulate the existence of *ātman* and

75. Cf. *Kāśyapaparivarta* § 60 and *Samādhirājasūtra* ix.27.

76. Saṃyuttanikāya II, p. 17 *(Kacchānagotta-suttanta).*

77. Cf. *MMK* xv.6. According to Candrakīrti's *Madhyamakāvatāra* i.8 (p. 22), moreover, the *Kātyāyanāvavāda* helps also to establish one of the most important tenets of the Madhyamaka school from both the soteriological and gnoseological standpoints, namely that knowledge *(jñāna)* of *nairātmya* and *śūnyatā* is common to both the ārya-śrāvaka and the bodhisattva. Cf. *PPMV* xviii.5.

anātman mentioned in *MMK* xviii.6 (cf. xxvii.12–3 and *Ratnāvalī* ii.3) is supported by *Kāśyapaparivarta* § 57, which Candrakīrti has quoted in his comment.

10. *The logical structure of the* catuṣkoṭi *and its negation*

As already mentioned, the Mādhyamika commentators of both the Svātantrika and Prāsaṅgika schools, Bhā(va)viveka and Candrakīrti, have taken the negation of the four positions to be of the *prasajya* or absolute kind. This means that the negation of the first position does not commit the person who maintains it to the affirmation of the opposite statement, corresponding to the second position. And the same principle holds for the negation of the other positions. This point has been emphasized by the Mādhyamikas at least since the sixth century, the time of Bhā(va)viveka.[78]

It is noteworthy also that Bhā(va)viveka regards the Madhyamaka propositions *(pratijñā)* consisting in the negation of the four positions as belonging, despite their verbalized form and consequent discursivity *(prapañca),* not to the level of surface convention *(saṃvṛti)* to which the *prapañca* is normally assigned, but rather to a special form of *paramārtha* that entails construction *(abhisaṃskāra).* This level is termed pure worldly knowledge *(śuddhalaukikajñāna)* in order to distinguish it from the supramundane *(lokottara)* nature of the supreme *paramārtha,* which is quite free from *prapañca* and cannot therefore be verbalized.[79]

With respect to the syntactical and logical structure of the *catuṣkoṭi,* on the other hand, the Madhyamaka school has had very little to say. This attitude of the school, which so markedly sets it apart from many modern writers on the subject, indicates that the questions raised by these modern writers as to whether the four *koṭi*s stand in a relation of conjunction or disjunction and whether the terms are contraries or contradictories were not of primary importance to the school. Now this attitude of the school appears intelligible and valid when we consider that the Mādhyamikas have negated all four positions because they maintained that, severally or in combination, they do not ultimately apply to any *dharma;* and the universe of discourse along with all dichotomizing conceptualization is thus annulled.[80]

The formulation given to the statement of the *catuṣkoṭi* by the Mādhyamika

78. For references see note 10 above. This interpretation of the commentators would suggest that they regarded the sentences and *koṭi*s in question as contradictory rather than as contraries.

79. Bhā(va)viveka, *Tarkajvālā* iii.26 (fol. 63b–64a; cf. fol. 63a) referring to *MMK* i.1.

80. See *MMK* xviii.7 quoted above, pp. 53–54.

masters is moreover variable. Nāgārjuna has connected some of the positions in *MMK* xxv.17–18 and xxvii.13 by the particle *ca* "and"; but in xxii.11 *vā* "or" appears side by side with *ca.*[81] In *Catuḥśataka* viii.20, xiv.21, and xvi.25 we find only *ca.* In *MMK* i.1 some of the positions have been linked by the correlative particles *api* . . . *api.* Similarly, in xviii.6 Nāgārjuna has linked the two positions *ātmêti* and *anātmêti,* taught in differing circumstances by the Buddha, by the particles *api* . . . *api;* and in introducing this verse Candrakīrti has mentioned the possibility of a conflict *(virodha)* between these two teachings emanating from the same source.[82]

With regard to the "both . . . and" formulation, in *MMK* xxv.14 the relation between existence *(bhāva)* and non-existence *(abhāva)* is compared to the mutually exclusive relation between light and darkness in one time and place, i.e., to contrariety *(virodha);* this explanation is given with respect to the supposition that *nirvāṇa* might be definable in terms of the third *koṭi* as both *bhāva* and *abhāva.*[83] In *MMK* xxvii.17 and 25, which deal with the inapplicability of the opposites *divya/mānuṣa, śāśvata/aśāśvata,* and *antavat/anantavat,* Nāgārjuna alludes to and rejects an interpretation of the third position that distributes the terms of the conjunction by using the words *ekadeśaḥ* . . . *ekadeśaḥ* (= *aṃśena* . . . *aṃśena*) "part(ly) . . . part(ly)."

As for the fourth position referred to in *MMK* xxvii.18, it is suggested that only on the assumption that both the eternal and non-eternal were established *(siddha)* would something be said to be neither eternal nor non-eternal. But Candrakīrti observes that such a supposition does not in fact apply since things are never actually so established.

The Madhyamaka materials cited above do not then support the contention that the connexion between the *koṭi*s is regularly one of exclusive disjunction rather than of conjunction.[84] As for the idea that the pairs of terms in

81. *MMK* xxii.14 also links by means of the particle *vā* the first two *koṭi*s relating to a *buddha's* existence after *nirodha.* See xviii.8, where the reading *na vā tathyam* is, however, La Vallée Poussin's reconstruction. In *Ratnāvalī* ii.6 the positions are linked by *athavā* and *vā.*

82. On *naiva* . . . *na(iva)* sentences see above, p. 61.

83. Bhā(va)viveka (*Madhyamakahṛdayakārikā* iii.124ff.) discusses the negation of the so-called *ubhayavāda* (*gnyi gar smra ba,* "doctrine of both [positions maintained simultaneously]"), the conjunction of two opposed—and contradictory (: *virodha*)—positions which he ascribes to the Nirgranthakas. And he applies this case to the idea of the existence-cum-non-existence of the self, substantiality, and permanence (*Tarkajvālā* iii.26; P, vol. ja, fol. 94b).

84. Compare Jayatilleke and R. Robinson discussed (below, pp. 93–98).

the third and fourth *koṭis* are contraries rather than contradictories,[85] there is indeed some support for it here and there in the sources; but these sources do not make the point explicitly, and in any case in certain contexts the terms are evidently contradictories. (Nor, as already observed, does it appear that the point was of major concern to the school because of the fact that all the *koṭis* are to be negated with a view to breaking down the dichotomizing universe of conceptualization and discourse.) Whereas Nāgārjuna and his school have alluded to an interpretation according to which in the third *koṭi* the terms may be distributed, this interpretation has in fact been considered inapplicable by them; and there seems to be no clear evidence for regular logical distribution and quantification in our sources.[86] Finally, there does not appear to be any support at all in the Madhyamaka sources for the contention that the fourth *koṭi* supposes a neutral third position between opposites.[87]

III. Conjunction and Negation of Opposed Terms in Vijñānavāda Definitions of Reality

A basic concept in the Yogācāra/Vijñānavāda school is the *abhūtaparikalpa* which is identified as the dependent nature *(paratantrasvabhāva),* the second of the three natures postulated by this school.[88] It is represented as both existent in virtue of the third aspect or nature—the *pariniṣpannasvabhāva*—and without existence with respect to the first aspect or nature—the *parikalpitasvabhāva,* i.e., the duality of cognized and cognizer *(grahyagrāhaka).*[89] In other words, on the negative side of the empty *(śūnya),* although *abhūtaparikalpa* becomes associated with the imaginarily constructed duality of subject and object, it is in fact really free of it and empty. And on the positive side, *abhūtaparikalpa* represents real *(paramārthatas)* existence in virtue of own-nature *(svabhāvatas)* and even *substantialiter*

85. Compare Raju, Robinson, *et al.* (below, pp. 89–99).

86. Cf. R. H. Robinson's criticism of Jayatilleke in *PEW* 19 (1969), p. 75 (below, pp. 97–98).

87. Compare Jayatilleke (below, p. 97). (For the "neither . . . nor" formulation in *MMK* xxv.10, see above, p. 60).

88. *MAVBh* i.6.

89. *MAV* i.3cd.

(dravyatas).[90] The concept is therefore bound up with a "both . . . and" position.

Abhūtaparikalpa is moreover described as being neither empty nor not empty, and the concept thus involves also a "neither . . . nor" position.[91]

The question therefore arises as to what the attitude of the Yogācāras/ Vijñānavādins is towards these two positions in respect to their theory of reality.

1. *The "both . . . and" formula in relation to* abhūtaparikalpa *and* upalabdhi

On the ontological level the Vijñānavādin speaks both of *sattva* "existence" with respect to *abhūtaparikalpa* and *śūnyatā,* and of *asattva* "non-existence" with respect to duality. In fact, for the Vijñānavāda, this is what constitutes the Middle Way. Thus we read in the *Madhyāntavibhāga* (i.3cd):

> *sattvād asattvāt sattvāc ca madhyamā pratipac ca* sā //
>
> Because of existence [of *abhūtaparikalpa*], non-existence [of duality in *abhūtaparikalpa*], and existence [of *śūnyatā* in *abhūtaparikalpa* and of *abhūtaparikalpa* in *śūnyatā*], this is the Middle Way.[92]

Accordingly, the Middle Way is so called because it avoids both denial *(apavāda)* of the real—i.e., the dependent and absolute natures *(paratantra°* and *pariniṣpanna-svabhāva)*—and imputation *(samāropa)* of the unreal—i.e., the imaginarily constructed nature *(parikalpitasvabhāva).*

On the gnoseological level also the Vijñānavādin speaks both of non-apprehension based on apprehension and of non-apprehension based on non-apprehension (*MAV* i.7):

> *upalabdhiṃ samāśritya nopalabdhiḥ prajāyate /*
> *nopalabdhiṃ samāśritya nopalabdhiḥ prajāyate //*

90. *MAVṬ* i.2 (pp. 9–10).

91. *MAV* i.3a.

92. Cf. *MAVBh* i.3cd: *sattvād abhūtaparikalpasya, asattvād dvayasya, sattvāc ca śūnyatāyā abhūtaparikalpe tasyāṃ câbhūtaparikalpasya/ sā ca madhyamā pratipat/ yat sarvaṃ naikāntena śūnyaṃ naikāntenâśūnyam/ evam ayaṃ pāṭhaḥ prajñāpāramitādiṣv anulomito bhavati: sarvam idaṃ na śūnyaṃ nâpi câśūnyam iti//*

On the relation between duality—the imaginarily constructed—and *abhūtaparikalpa,* see *MAVṬ* i.4 quoted below. For Candrakīrti's critique of this passage of the *MAV,* see *PPMV* xxii.11 (p. 445).

That is, non-apprehension of an object apart from cognition is established in a first phase, on the basis of apprehension of pure representation *(vijñaptimātra).*[93] But in a second phase, on the basis of this non-apprehension of an object, non-apprehension of *vijñaptimātra* itself is established; for the latter would only have reality, in terms of the subject/object dichotomy, if its object were real, which has been seen not to be the case in the first phase (*MAVBh* i.7).[94] The fact that apprehension has the own-being of non-apprehension is thus established, and this in turn leads to what is termed equality of apprehension and non-apprehension (*MAV* i.8):

> *upalabdheḥ tataḥ siddhā nopalabdhisvabhāvatā /*
> *tasmāc ca samatā jñeyā nopalambhopalambhayoḥ //*

This concept of the equality of the two as constituting the real nature of knowledge accordingly introduces once again a "both . . . and" formulation, the real being thought of here as determinable in terms of both presence and absence of apprehension *(upalabdhi, upalambha).*

Since the Vijñānavādin thus appears to be quite prepared to qualify what he considers real by two sets of dichotomously opposed terms, it is necessary to enquire what this signifies in the frame of his philosophical system.

In his commentary on this passage Vasubandhu has simply stated that apprehension is not established as being apprehension *(upalabdhir upalabdhitvenâsiddhā).* Yet, he adds, apprehension is still mentioned here because an unreal object does appear *(abhūtārthapratibhāsatayā),* even though it has the nature of non-apprehension *(anupalabdhisvabhāvā)* (*MAVBh* i.8).

Sthiramati for his part is clearly aware of our present problem, for he explains that there is here no contradiction *(virodha)* between the two propositions. He writes:

> "Hence," i.e. because of absence of apprehension in the absence of an *artha* to be apprehended. When speaking of apprehension, one

93. "Representation" here has to be taken in the active sense. This "representation" is pure *(mātra),* i.e., consciousness altogether free from the subjective as well as from the objective side of cognition. Although grammatically a causative form, *vijñapti* does not seem here actually to have a causative meaning (cf. Tib. *rnam par rig pa* instead of *rnam par rig byed*).

94. That is, if there is in fact no real object of cognition established separately from cognition, there can be no corresponding subject or cognizer either. Consciousness is therefore pure and simple, without the duality of subject and object, cognizer and cognized thing.

> supposes one of [three factors]: action, agent, and instrument.[95] But because of the absence of an object[96] this triad is not possible here . . . [97] Apprehension having non-apprehension for its nature, *samatā*—i.e., equivalence *(tulyatā)*—is therefore to be recognized; for there is no difference given the fact that there is neither non-apprehension of an object nor apprehension which is pure representation *(vijñaptimātropalambha)*.[98] In order to exclude mutual contradiction between the terms "apprehension" and "non-apprehension" [Vasubandhu] has said: "Yet apprehension is mentioned because an unreal *artha* appears." However, nothing at all is apprehended by this [apprehension] because of the absence of an object. Hence, from the point of view of the absolute *(paramārtha)* [it is said in the *MAVBh*]: "Though having the nature of non-apprehension"; and there is therefore no contradiction *(virodha)* (*MAVṬ* i.8).

According to some authorities cited by Sthiramati, apprehension and non-apprehension function as counteragents against imputation *(samāropa)* and denial *(apavāda)*; and the pair of them is equal in virtue of the absence of dichotomizing conceptualization (*samam etad ubhayaṃ nirvikalpatayā,* p. 23). Now, because of the fact that apprehension and non-apprehension are exempt from imputation and denial, introspective equality

95. Apprehension *(upalabdhi)* involves (1) the "processive being" *(bhāva)* or action of apprehension, (2) the apprehender or cognizing agent *(kartṛ)*, and (3) the means or instrument of apprehension *(karaṇa)*. On these three expressions in the terminology of Indian grammar, see L. Renou, *Terminologie grammaticale du sanskrit* (Paris, 1957), s.vv. The *bhāvasādhana* (Renou: "qui a pour mode de réalisation l'entrée dans un état" [p. 244], "qui a pour mode de réalisation la production [d'un phénomène nouveau]" [p. 125]) is opposed to the *karmasādhana* (Renou: "qui a l'objet-transitif [i.e., une action passive] pour mode de réalisation" [p. 125]). Thus, taking as examples the words *śeṣa* and *vidhi,* as *bhāvasādhana* they mean "the leaving [of something: *śeṣaṇa*]" and "enjoining [of something new: *(asato) vidhānam*]," and as *karmasādhana* they mean "remainder" (: *śiṣyate*) and "the enjoined" (: *vidhīyate*); cf. Patañjali, *Mahābhāṣya* i.1.57 (i, p. 144) and Kaiyaṭa, *Pradīpa* i.2.64. Here *sādhana* may be taken in the active sense of "realizer." The term *bhāva* has been studied by A. Wezler, *Bestimmung und Angabe der Funktion von Sekundär-Suffixen durch Pāṇini* (Wiesbaden, 1975), pp. 103ff.

96. Tib. *las* = *karman* "object," i.e., the object to be apprehended *(upalabhyārtha)*. As seen above, the Vijñānavāda maintains that such an object does not exist independently.

97. Tib.: *las med pas de gsum char yang mi rung ste.*

98. Tib. (D, fol. 202b): *de'i phyir mnyam mo // don mi dmigs pa dang rnam par rig pa tsam du dmigs pa yang med par bye brag med pa'i phyir mtshungs pa nyid du shes par bya'o//*

(pratyātmasamatā) is to be recognized, this being according to the authorities cited what is expressed by the well-known verse

> *nâpaneyam ataḥ kiṃcit prakṣepta<vyam na kiṃcana /*
> *draṣṭavyaṃ bhūtato bhūtaṃ bhūtadarśī vimucyate> //*
>
> Nothing is to be removed from it and nothing is to be added:
> the real is to be seen as real, and the seer of the real is released.[99]

2. *The "neither . . . nor" formula in relation to* abhūtaparikalpa

To turn now to the "neither . . . nor" type of statement in the Vijñānavāda, we find that Vasubandhu has the following to say on the subject of *abhūtaparikalpa.* Since, following *MAV* i.4, there is no object separate from cognition, and since cognition as the correlate of an object in a subject/object relation is therefore itself unreal, Vasubandhu affirms that the nature of *abhūtaparikalpa* is not as it appears. Still, it is not altogether non-existent because there exists the arising of error as such *(bhrāntimātra),* and because the existence of *abhūtaparikalpa* is required for release to be achieved.[100] In other words, were *abhūtaparikalpa* non-existent, neither bondage nor release would be known (*MAVBh* i.5). Moreover, if *abhūtaparikalpa* is then *neither* as it appears—i.e., as affected by duality—*nor* altogether non-existent—because it is the condition for error and for release—this is to be understood in terms of the theory of the three natures *(svabhāva)* of the Yogācāra. That is, *abhūtaparikalpa* as *paratantrasvabhāva* exists as such: whereas it is *not* as it appears when affected by the subject/object duality of the *parikalpitasvabhāva,* once freed from the latter it is the perfect nature of the *pariniṣpannasvabhāva* (*MAVBh* i.6).

This is then the meaning of the following key passage of the *MAV* (i.2–3ab):

> *abhūtaparikalpo 'sti dvayaṃ tatra na vidyate /*
> *śūnyatā vidyate tv atra, tasyām api sa vidyate //*
> *na śūnyaṃ nâpi câśūnyaṃ tasmāt sarvaṃ vidhīyate /*

99. See *Abhisamayālaṃkāra* v.21. Cf. *RGV* i.154 (which reads in *pāda b: upaneyaṃ na kiṃcana*). On this verse and its significance for the Mahāyānist theory of ultimate reality, cf. D. Seyfort Ruegg, *Théorie du tathāgatagarbha et du gotra,* pp. 313, 333ff.

100. Sthiramati alludes here to an inference: *kim tarhi kleśavyavadānapakṣasāmarthyāt tadastitvam anumīyate/ "anyathā" iti yadi tasya sarvathābhāva evêṣyate "na bandho na mokṣa" iti/* (*MAVṬ* i.5, pp. 17–18).

> The *abhūtaparikalpa* exists. Duality is not found therein.
> But here *śūnyatā* is found, and this [*abhūtaparikalpa*] is found in this [*śūnyatā*] also.
> Therefore all is set forth as neither empty nor non-empty.[101]

The Vijñānavāda system thus differs from the Madhyamaka inasmuch as for it the "both . . . and" and "neither . . . nor" formulae refer to a *vastu:* the *paratantrasvabhāva* or *abhūtaparikalpa* that is real *qua* substantive thing *(dravyatas).*[102] It is nevertheless far from certain that in this case the Vijñānavāda school was attempting to establish some entity as *per se* either *both* existent *and* non-existent or *neither* existent *nor* non-existent. On the contrary, the school insists that this *vastu* is real and existent. And it is said to be non-existent only to the limited—and indeed quite illusory—degree to which its appearances are unreal because they belong to the realm of duality and imaginary construction; but this unreality clearly does not apply to the real *per se.* Given what is intended by the school, then, it would seem that in the matter of the definition of reality, the Vijñānavādins have rejected neither the principle of non-contradiction nor the principle of the excluded middle. For in one respect the *abhūtaparikalpa* is existent and non-empty—namely with regard to the *paratantra* and *pariniṣpanna* natures—and in another respect it is non-existent and empty—namely with regard to the *parikalpita* nature and its duality;[103] and there seems therefore to be no question here of attributing to one and the same entity opposed properties on the same level of reference and from the same point of view.

101. Vasubandhu explains (*MAVBh* i.3): *na śūnyaṃ śūnyatayā câbhūtaparikalpena ca/ na câśūnyaṃ dvayena grāhyena grāhakena ca/ "sarvaṃ" saṃskṛtaṃ câbhūtaparikalpākhyam, asaṃskṛtaṃ ca śūnyatākhyam/* "Not empty with respect to Emptiness [: *pariniṣpanna*] and *abhūtaparikalpa* [: *paratantra*], and not non-empty with respect to duality—viz. the cognized and cognizer [: *parikalpita*]. 'All': the conditioned known as *abhūtaparikalpa* and also the unconditioned known as Emptiness."

102. The *parikalpita* on the contrary is non-existent *substantialiter (dravyatas);* but it nevertheless exists conventionally *(vyavahāratas)* so that it is counted as one of the three *svabhāvas* (*MAVṬ* i.6, p. 19.1; cf. i.14, p. 37.1). On the *abhūtaparikalpa* or *paratantra* as a *vastu* existing substantially *(dravyatas)* and by own-nature *(svabhāvatas),* see *MAVṬ* i.2 (pp. 9–10; on p. 10.14 *vastumātra* is probably to be read instead of *bhāvamātra,* as in Pandeya's edition).

The *Tattvaprakāśa* attributed to Advayavajra (ed. H. P. Shastri, p. 46) seems to suggest that the Yogācāra position does not altogether go beyond the *catuṣkoṭi,* as does the Mādhyamika's.

103. Contrast the relation between the *paratantra* and the *pariniṣpanna* in *MSABh* vi.1 (below, p. 80).

3. *The "neither . . . nor" formula and* śūnyatā

The "neither . . . nor" formula reappears, together with simple affirmation and negation, in connexion with the discussion of the defining characteristic *(lakṣaṇa)* of Emptiness (*MAV* i.14):

> *dvayābhāvo hy abhāvasya bhāvaḥ śūnyasya lakṣaṇam /*
> *na bhāvo nâpi câbhāvaḥ na pṛthaktvaikalakṣaṇam //*

> Indeed [there is] non-ens *(abhāva: dngos po med pa)* of duality (*dvaya* "couple") [consisting in] ens *(bhāva: dngos po)* of [this] non-ens, the characteristic of Empti[ness].[104] There is neither existence *(bhāva: yod pa)* nor non-existence *(abhāva: med pa)*.[105] There is no characteristic of [either] difference [or] identity.

Vasubandhu explains: i. There is non-ens of object and subject as a duality. ii. And since the ens of this non-ens is the characteristic of Emptiness, it is indicated that emptiness has the own-being *(svabhāva)* of non-ens *(abhāva)*. iii. This own-being comprised of the non-ens of a duality is "neither existence nor non-existence," (a) In what way is there not existence? Because there is non-ens of a duality, (b) And in what way is there not non-existence? Because there is ens of the non-ens of a duality. Such is the characteristic of Emptiness. iv. It is for this reason that [it is said in the *MAV*] "There is no characteristic of [either] difference [or] identity" in relation to *abhūtaparikalpa.* Were there difference, there would arise the impossibility consisting in real nature *(dharmatā)* being other than the thing (*dharma,* to which it relates)—like impermanence and painfulness *(anityatāduḥkhatāvat)* [of what is impermanent and painful].[106] And [conversely,] were there identity, there would be

104. Tib.: *gnyis dngos med pa'i dngos med pa'i // dngos po stong pa'i mtshan nyid do//* But *MAVBh* and *MAVṬ* take *dvayābhāva* and *abhāvasya bhāvaḥ* as two coordinate things; and in the verse, instead of *gnyis dngos med pa'i,* there is found the variant reading *gnyis dngos med dang* adopted by S. Yamaguchi in his edition. (The Sde dge edition of *MAVṬ* curiously reads in the first *pāda: gnyis dngos med pa'i dngos po yi.)*

Although *śūnya* and *śūnyatā* are not normally synonyms, Vasubandhu and Sthiramati take *śūnya* here as equivalent to *śūnyatā,* with metrical elision of the *bhāvapratyaya -tā-* (*kārikānuguṇyena* as Sthiramati remarks). Further on (p. 38.6–7) Sthiramati observes that *śūnyatā* is not different from what is *śūnya.*

105. It is to be noted that *bhāva* and *abhāva* are here translated in Tibetan according to the sense either as *dngos po* and *dngos (po) med pa,* or as *yod pa* and *med pa.*

106. See Sthiramati's explanation quoted below.

no objective base for purification *(viśuddhyālambana)*—Gnosis *(jñāna)*[107]—and no general characteristic *(sāmānyalakṣaṇa)*.[108] In this way the characteristic free from identity and difference *(tattvānyatvavinirmukta)* has been indicated.

Sthiramati analyses this verse and Vasubandhu's explanation in his sub-commentary. He first takes up single negation and affirmation (points i and ii above), making the following observations:

1. There is non-existence *(abhāva)* with respect to *vastu*-nature because duality—i.e., the cognized and cognizer—is imaginarily constructed *(parikalpita)* (a) in *abhūtaparikalpa* or (b) by *abhūtaparikalpa*.[109]
2. Concerning *bhāva (dngos po)* of *abhāva (dngos po med pa)*, the essential nature of the non-ens of duality is existence. Otherwise the empty ens of non-ens would not exist, and the ens of duality would then exist. For this reason Vasubandhu has referred to *śūnyatā*'s having the characteristic of the own-being of *abhāva (abhāvasvabhāvalakṣaṇatva)*, rather than a characteristic consisting of *bhāva (bhāvarūpalakṣaṇa)*.[110]
3. Some hold the opinion that the word *bhāva* is redundant when the term *abhāva* serves, as it does here, to negate *bhāva*, so that even if the word *bhāva* were lacking here, its sense would be understood implicitly. But Sthiramati observes that it is in fact not redundant; for if nothing more were indicated than *dvayābhāva* being the characteristic of emptiness, it would be principally the non-ens of duality that would be understood—like the non-ens of a hare's horn—but not what has to be understood, namely the fact of being real nature *(dharmatā)*—like the painfulness *(duḥkhatā)*, etc., of what is painful *(duḥkha)*, etc. Therefore non-ens of duality is *śūnyatā*; it is present in *abhūtaparikalpa* and is known as *śūnyatā*. Here reference has been made to *dharmatā*-nature because of the inclusion of the characteristic of the *bhāva* of

107. *Jñāna* is omitted by both Sthiramati and the Tibetan translation of *MAVBh*.

108. E.g., *dharmatā* of the *dharma*s and *śūnyatā* of empty things; see *MAVṬ* quoted below.

109. Sthiramati thus interprets the grammatical construction of *abhūtaparikalpa* in two ways, taking it either as locative or as instrumental. See *MAVṬ* i.2 (p. 11.30–31) on the *abhūta°* as the locus for the construction of duality or as the instrument for the construction of unreal duality.

110. Tib. (D, fol. 212a): *dngos po med pa'i dngos po zhes bya ba de dag gang yin/ dngos po med pa'i bdag nyid ni yod pa nyid do // gzhan du na de'i dngos po med pa'i dngos po stong pa med pa'i phyir ro // gnyis kyi dngos po yod pa nyid du 'gyur ro // de'i phyir de ltar dngos po med pa'i ngo bo nyid stong pa nyid kyi mtshan nyid du yongs su bstan pa yin no zhes bya ba smos te / dngos po'i ngo bo'i mtshan nyid du ni ma yin no//* The Sanskrit of Pandeya's edition differs.

abhāva. Alternatively, it can be held that when *dvayābhāva* is spoken of as *śūnyatā,* the word non-existence *(abhāva = med pa)* designates the general *(sāmānyavācin),* so that it is not known what *abhāva* is meant. Therefore, in order to indicate absolute absence *(atyantābhāva = gtan med pa),* it has been stated that in *abhūtaparikalpa* there is *bhāva (dngos po)* of *abhāva (dngos po med pa)* of duality.[111] Because in this case the characteristic of the *abhāva* of *bhāva* is assumed, *atyantābhāva (gtan dngos po med pa)* of the cognized and cognizer is indicated as *śūnyatā.*

Next binegation is taken up by Sthiramati in the following observations which relate to points iii and iv above:

1. In reply to the question as to how an absolute *(paramārtha)* is spoken of if *śūnyatā* in fact consists in non-existence *(abhāva: med pa),* Sthiramati explains: It is spoken of because this *paramārtha* is the object of supreme Gnosis *(paramajñāna)*[112]—like in the case of the impermanence [of what is impermanent]—but not because it is a substantive thing *(vastu).*[113]
2. If *śūnyatā* had the quality of being an existent *(bhāvatva: yod pa),* there would be no absolute absence *(atyantābhāva)* of duality *(dvayabhāva),* no being the real nature *(dharmatā)* of *abhūtaparikalpa;* and so it has been stated that it is not existent.
3. As for its not being non-existent either, non-ens of duality does not consist of *abhāva* having the form of *abhāva* of duality *(dvayabhāva).* Were it such *abhāva* pure and simple, there would be existence of duality; and there would be no *dharmatā* of *abhūtaparikalpa*—like the impermanence and painfulness [of what is impermanent and painful].
4. Reference has then been made to neither existence nor non-existence because this represents the nature of the non-ens of a permanent *(nitya)* and blissful substance imputed in error by a living being *(sems can phyin ci log tu gyur pas sgro btags pa'i rtag pa dang/ bde ba'i dngos po'i dngos po med pa'i ngo bo nyid yin pas).*

111. Here *prāgabhāva* and *pradhvaṃsābhāva* would be possible only if there were self-appropriation *(svopādāna).* And *anyonyābhāva* is not possible because it implies mutual support.

112. Cf. *MAVBh* i.16: *āryajñānagocaratvāt paramārthaḥ, paramajñānaviṣayatvāt.* Cf. *MAV* iii.11.

113. Thus, for the Vijñānavādin, the *paratantrasvabhāva* (: *abhūtaparikalpa*) and the *pariniṣpannasvabhāva* (or *śūnyatā*) are both real; but while the former is a *vastu* existing substantially as seen above, the latter is not.

5. Now, if *śūnyatā* of *abhūtaparikalpa* is *dharmatā*, is this stateable *(vaktavya)* as other *(anya)* than *abhūtaparikalpa* or as not other *(ananya)*?[114]

(a) Vasubandhu has stated: "Were there difference, there would arise the impossibility consisting in the real nature *(dharmatā)* being other than the thing (*dharma*, to which it relates)."—What would be the incongruence *(ayoga)* here?—The real nature (of a thing, *dharmatā*) becomes another thing by having a characteristic different from the thing to which it relates, just like any thing other than it. Now one thing cannot be the real nature of another thing; for there would then be infinite regress *(anavasthā)* since still another thing would then have to be sought for [as the real nature of the second thing]. "Just as in the case of impermanence and painfulness": i.e., just as *anityatā* is not other than what is impermanent *(anitya)* and *duḥkhatā* is not other than what is painful *(duḥkha)*, so *śūnyatā* is not other than what is empty *(śūnya)*.

(b) Vasubandhu has furthermore stated: "Were there identity, there would be no objective base for purification *(viśuddhyālambana)* and no general characteristic *(sāmānyalakṣaṇa)*." That is, the path being purification inasmuch as it is the means for purification, there would be no objectification of the path, like the specific characteristic of a *dharma*, because there is no difference from the specific characteristic *(svalakṣaṇa)* of that *dharma*. Nor is any general characteristic *(sāmānyalakṣaṇa)* therefore possible because it is not other than the specific characteristic. Also commonness *(sāmānyatā: mnyam pa nyid)* is lost, there being mutual difference just as in the case of the nature of a *dharma*.—Alternatively, because the specific characteristic is not other than this [general one] there is absence of difference, just as in the case of the nature of an entity. Nor would there be any general characteristic either, because the general characteristic is by definition dependent on difference [between it and the particular things having a specific characteristic].—Alternatively, the expression *viśuddhyālambana* means an objective base for realizing purification *(rnam par dag par*

114. D, fol. 212b: *gal te yang dag pa ma yin pa kun rtog pa'i stong pa nyid chos nyid yin na/ ci ste de las gzhan zhes bya ba'am/ 'on te gzhan ma yin zhe na/ de'i phyir de ni stong pa nyid kyi mtshan nyid do zhes bya ba smos te/ dngos po med pa'i no bo nyid kho na'o//* The Sanskrit of Pandeya's text is hardly intelligible since, if the subject is *śūnyatā/dharmatā*, the forms *anya, ananya,* and *vaktavya* would be expected to be feminine to accord with their subject (as on p. 38.15).

byed pa'i phyir). And purification is not attained through objectification of a specific characteristic; for all sentient beings would then be already purified.[115]

6. As for *śūnyatā* being indefinable *(avaktavyā)* with respect to difference and identity[116] in relation to *abhūtaparikalpa,* Sthiramati observes that the Vijñānavāda notion of indefinability is not reducible here to the Nirgrantha's concept of non-determinateness because the Nirgrantha doctrine posits an existent *bhāva (dngos po)* which is in fact determinable as being neither different nor identical *(bhāvasya satas tattvānyatvam).* But *śūnyatā* is no such *bhāva (dngos po),* and there is therefore no difficulty in the Vijñānavāda theory.[117]

It is, Sthiramati concludes, for these reasons that *śūnyatā* has been indicated in *MAV* i.14 as (i) having the characteristic of *abhāva (med pa'i mtshan nyid)* [of duality] (ii) having the characteristic of the own-being of *abhāva* [of duality] *(dngos po med pa'i ngo bo nyid kyi mtshan nyid),* (iii) having the characteristic of no duality (i.e., *na bhāvo nâpy abhāvaḥ*) *(mi gnyis pa'i mtshan nyid),* and (iv) having the characteristic of being free from identity and difference *(tattvānyatva) (de nyid dang gzhan las rnam par grol ba'i mtshan nyid).*

Thus, in contradistinction to his procedure in the case of the *abhūtaparikalpa* or *paratantrasvabhāva* to which he has not applied the "both . . . and" or the "neither . . . nor" formula on the same level of reference and from the same point of view (see above), here in the case of *śūnyatā* or the *pariniṣpannasvabhāva* the Vijñānavādin has made use of a statement negating simultaneously two opposed qualities. It should nevertheless be observed that, unlike *abhūtaparikalpa,* which is regarded as a real *vastu, śūnyatā* or *paramārtha* is stated by Sthiramati not to be a *vastu* or *bhāva.*[118] This difference in the metaphysical status of the two factors may be crucial in deciding

115. See below, p. 79. Cf. *MAV* i.22–23; *MAVṬ* i.2 (p. 10.21: *śūnyatā hi viśuddhyālambanā*[?]: *stong pa nyid ni rnam par dag pa'i dmigs pa ste*).

116. *Anyānanyatva* = *gzhan dang gzhan ma yin pa.* Cf. Candrakīrti, *PPMV,* p. 64.

117. But cf. *MAVṬ* i.21 (p. 46.14–15): *yady abhāvasvabhāvaśūnyatā nôcyeta śūnyatāyā abhāva eva prasajyeta/ tadabhāvāc ca pudgaladharmayoḥ pūrvavad bhāvaḥ syāt/* "Were Emptiness having *abhāva* as its own nature not stated, there would result the nonexistence of Emptiness; and because of its non-existence, *pudgala* and *dharma* would exist as before," i.e., before their Emptiness was realized.

118. *MAVṬ* i.14 (p. 37.18): *yady abhāvātmika śūnyatā katham paramārtha ucyate/ paramajñānaviṣayatvād anityatāvat, na tu vastutvāt/*; i.14 (p. 38.16): *śūnyatā tu na bhāvaḥ.*

whether opposed qualities are predicable of it even in the form of their binegation in the "neither . . . nor" type of formula. If so, this could well account for the difference in treatment of the two levels of reality.

But the Vijñānavāda concept of *śūnyatā* continues to pose problems since not infrequently *śūnyatā* is presented as virtually some kind of entity. This view of *śūnyatā* comes to the fore for example in the commentaries on *MAV* i.21:

> *pudgalasyâtha dharmāṇām abhāvaḥ śūnyatâtra hi /*
> *tadabhāvasya sadbhāvas tasmin sā śūnyatâparā //*
>
> The non-ens *(abhāva: dngos po med pa)* of the individual as well as of the factors of existence is indeed here *śūnyatā*. The real existence in this[119] of their *abhāva* is another *śūnyatā*.

Vasubandhu explains: The non-ens of *pudgala* and *dharma*s is *śūnyatā*. And the existence *(sadbhāva: dngos po yod pa)* of their non-ens in this aforementioned enjoyer, etc., is another *śūnyatā*. For the purpose of making known this characteristic of *śūnyatā*, a twofold *śūnyatā* has been set out—viz. *abhāvaśūnyatā* and *abhāvasvabhāvaśūnyatā*[120]—which serve to exclude respectively the imputation *(samāropa)* of *pudgala* and *dharma*s and the negation *(apavāda)* of their emptiness (*MAVBh* i.21).

Now, in commenting on this passage, Sthiramati stresses the notion of *śūnyatā* as some kind of existent. Had the *abhāvaśūnyatā* not been stated, he writes, the undesired consequence would have been that *pudgala*s and *dharma*s having an imaginarily constructed *(parikalpita)* nature would exist. And had the *abhāvasvabhāvaśūnyatā* not been stated, the undesired consequence would have arisen of the non-existence of *śūnyatā*, as a result of which *pudgala* and *dharma*s would in fact exist (*MAVṬ* i.21). In other words, while the fifteenth aspect of *śūnyatā* serves to cancel the existence of *pudgala* and *dharma*s, the sixteenth aspect imparts to emptiness a kind of own-being without which the existence of *pudgala* and *dharma*s would not be cancelled.

119. Viz. the enjoyer *(bhoktṛ)*, etc., according to *MAV* i.18, i.e., the inner bases *(ādhyātmikāny āyatanāni, MAVBh)*.

120. These are respectively numbers 15 and 16 in the lists of the sixteen aspects of *śūnyatā* (see *MAV* i.18–21). Cf. E. Obermiller, *IHQ* 9 (1933), pp. 170ff.; É. Lamotte, *Le traité de la Grande Vertu de Sagesse,* iv, pp. 2031, 2035, 2039, 2149ff. (who takes *abhāvasvabhāva* as a *dvandva* compound!).

This notion of *śūnyatā* as some kind of existent is clearly quite different from that of the Madhyamaka theory, which stresses the fact that it is not the function of *śūnyatā* to make *dharma*s empty but that *śūnyatā* simply reveals that *dharma*s are empty.[121] But, as already observed, in another place Sthiramati has himself taken care to state that *śūnyatā* is not to be regarded as a *vastu* or *bhāva*.[122]

4. *The "neither . . . nor" formula in the description of ultimate reality*
The concept of the absolute as neither some thing nor not that thing appears elsewhere in the literature of the Vijñānavāda.

In Vasubandhu's *Triṃśikā*—which has been supposed to be by another Vasubandhu than the author of the *MAVBh*[123]—the *pariniṣpanna* or absolute nature is described as neither different nor not different from the *paratantra* or dependent nature (22):

> *ata eva sa naivânyo nânanyaḥ paratantrataḥ /*
> *anityatādivad vācyo nâdr̥ṣṭe 'smin sa dr̥śyate //*

> This [absolutely perfect nature] is consequently neither different nor not different from the dependent [nature]. It is to be described as like impermanence, etc. [in relation to what is impermanent, etc.]; and the [dependent nature] is not known when this [absolutely perfect nature] is unknown.

In his comment Sthiramati explains that *dharmatā*—namely the *paratantra*'s exemption (*rahitatā,* corresponding to the *pariniṣpanna* level) from the imaginarily constructed *(parikalpita)* nature—is properly neither different nor not different from the [corresponding] *dharma;* and consequently, since the *pariniṣpanna* is *paratantradharmatā,* it is neither different nor not different from the *paratantra.* Indeed, he adds, if the *pariniṣpanna* were different

121. Cf. Candrakīrti, *PPMV* xiii.8 (which quotes *Kāśyapaparivarta* § 63–65); *Madhyamakāvatāra vi.*34.

122. Above, pp. 75, 77.

123. Cf. E. Frauwallner, *Die Philosophie des Buddhismus*[3] (Berlin, 1969), p. 351. The objections against Frauwallner's view on this point made by P. Jaini (*BSOAS* 21 [1956], pp. 48–53) and A. Hirakawa (*Index to the Abhidharmakośabhāṣya* [Tokyo, 1973], p. ii) are indecisive (and the latter author has not correctly interpreted Frauwallner's position on the authorship of the *Triṃśikā,* which he suggests ascribing not to his Vasubandhu I but to his Vasubandhu II, the author of the *Abhidharmakośa*).

from the *paratantra,* the latter would not be empty *(śūnya)* of the *parikalpita.* But on the other hand, were it not different, the *pariniṣpanna* could not be the support of purification *(viśuddhyālambana)* because it would comprise defilements *(kleśa),* just like the *paratantra;* while at the same time, because the *paratantra* would not be different from the *pariniṣpanna,* it would not comprise defilement. Here, just as in his commentary on the *MAV,* Sthiramati, following the lead of Vasubandhu,[124] draws a comparison with impermanence, painfulness, and absence of self *(anātmyatā)* as the generic characteristics respectively of what is impermanent, painful, and non-self.

In this connexion attention needs to be drawn also to the treatment of the defining characteristic of ultimate reality in the *Mahāyānasūtrālaṃkāra* (vi.1):

> *na san na câsan na tathā na cânyathā na jāyate vyeti na câvahīyate /*
> *na vardhate nâpi viśudhyate punar viśudhyate tat paramārtha-lakṣaṇam //*

> Neither existent nor non-existent, neither so nor otherwise, it neither comes into existence nor passes away, it neither decreases nor increases, and it is not purified yet is purified: this is the characteristic of the absolute.[125]

The Bhāṣya specifies that since the *paramārtha* has non-duality *(advaya)* as its sense, it has been set out in these five aspects: (i) neither existent, i.e. by the *parikalpita°* and *paratantra-lakṣaṇa,* nor non-existent, i.e. by the *pariniṣpanna-lakṣaṇa;* (ii) neither so, owing to absence of identity of the *pariniṣpanna* with the *parikalpita* and *paratantra,* nor otherwise, owing to absence of difference from them; (iii) neither coming into existence nor passing away, because the *dharmadhātu* is causally unconstructed *(anabhisaṃskṛta);* (iv) neither decrease nor increase, because the *paramārtha* remains as it is when Affects *(saṃkleśa)* come to a stop and purification *(vyavadāna)* manifests; and (v) neither is it purified, owing to natural non-defilement, nor is it not purified, owing to the dispersal of the adventitious defilements *(āgantukopakleśa).* It

124. See *MAVBh* i.14.

125. Such descriptions of reality are also to be found, e.g., in the Prajñāpāramitā-Sūtras. See for example the *Saptaśatikā* (ed. Masuda, p. 195) with regard to both *tathatā* and *tathāgata.*

is in this way, the Bhāṣya concludes, that the fivefold characteristic of non-duality *(advayalakṣaṇa)* is the *paramārtha-lakṣaṇa.*[126]

In this way the Bhāṣya has made it clear that the negation of opposite predicates with respect to the *paramārtha* has the purpose of showing that it is characterized by non-duality. In other words, both terms of the conceptually opposed pairs are negated because either fails to apply to the *paramārtha,* which the Mahāyāna always holds to be beyond the binary tension of *vikalpa* and *prapañca.*

IV. Negation of Opposed Terms in the Description of the Absolute in the Ratnagotravibhāga

The *dharma(ratna)*—the second of the seven adamantine planes *(vajrapada)* treated in the *Ratnagotravibhāga*—is described in one of the *kārikā*s or basic verses of this text in terms of the negation of all four positions making up a *catuṣkoṭi* (i.9ab):

126. Here, accordingly, we again find that the binegation of opposed predicates of the *paramārtha* is stated with respect to different natures, namely the *parikalpita* and *paratantra svabhāva*s on the one side and the *pariniṣpanna svabhāva* on the other side. Cf. above, pp. 68, 71–72, 79.

Particularly noteworthy is the fact that here the *paratantra* is taken together with the *parikalpita* and that it is therefore on the side of the unreal, whereas in the passages quoted above from the *MAV* and its commentaries it is taken together with the *pariniṣpanna* and is therefore on the side of the real. (As a consequence, in the *MSABh* it is the *pariniṣpanna* that evidently serves as what the later exegetical traditions refers to as the "ground of emptiness" [*stong gzhi*]; for it is empty of the *paratantra* as well as of the *parikalpita.* But in the *MAV* and the standard Vijñānavāda doctrine as codified by the doxographers, it is the *paratantra* that serves as the "ground of emptiness"; for once it is realized as empty of the imaginarily constructed, it is the *pariniṣpanna.*) This appears to be a major difference between the standard Vijñānavāda and the *MSABh* and seems to set the latter text apart from the main tradition of the school. (On these two theories see also D. Seyfort Ruegg, *Théorie du tathāgatagarbha et du gotra,* pp. 326ff.)

This fact is of importance in determining the authorship of the *MSABh,* which has been ascribed by a later Indo-Tibetan tradition to Vasubandhu, who is considered by it as the author of both the *MAVBh* and the *Triṃśikā.* In view of the doctrinal difference noted here, however, the uncertainty concerning the ascription is strengthened. It may be recalled that Ārya Vimuktisena appears to ascribe a passage found in the *MSABh* (xii.9) to Asaṅga; see his *Abhisamayālaṃkāravṛtti* i.72–73 (ed. C. Pensa, pp. 113–15). (On the other hand, agreement between the *Triṃśikā* and the *MAVBh* on the point under discussion is not absolutely conclusive as to the identity of the author of these two texts, since it is only natural that a standard treatise of the Vijñānavāda like the *Triṃśikā* should agree on such a point with basic śāstras of the school like the *MAV* and the *MAVBh.*)

> *yo nâsan na ca san na câpi sadasan nânyaḥ sato nâsataḥ śakyas*
> *tarkayitum niruktyapagataḥ pratyātmavedyaḥ śivaḥ* /

If we adopt in the second part of this verse the manuscript reading *śakyas*, which is confirmed by the Tibetan translation, the sense corresponds largely with that of the passage of the *Mahāyānasūtrālaṃkāra* (vi.1) discussed above.[127] And this interpretation is supported by *RGV* i.12, where it is stated that the truth of cessation *(nirodhasatya)*—which is what the *dharma* is in its ultimate aspect[128]—is inconceivable *(acintya)* because it is not within the purview of speculative (hypothetical) thinking *(tarka)*, which would necessarily take it as being non-existent, existent, both existent and non-existent, or neither the one nor the other *(asatsatsadasannobhayaprakārais caturbhiḥ api tarkāgocaratvāt, RGVV* i.12).[129] According to this reading and interpretation, the meaning of verse i.9ab then is:

> [That sun-like Dharma *(dharmadivākara)*] cannot be thought of speculatively as non-existent, existent, [both] existent and non-existent, and also as other than the existent and non-existent; it is free from verbalization, to be known directly and still . . . .

That is, the four limiting positions, singly or in combination, are the only modes under which an entity can be discursively and speculatively conceived. But either singly or in combination they are not applicable to the absolute.[130]

127. E. H. Johnston in his edition of the text read *sato nâsato 'śakyas tarkayitum*. The Tibetan translation has: *gang zhig med min yod min yod med ma yin yod med las gzhan du'ang // brtag par mi nus* . . . L. Schmithausen has proposed accordingly the correction *sataś câsataḥ* (*WZKS* 15 [1971], p. 136). Johnston noted that the reading *śakyas* instead of *aśakyas* is found in his manuscript B.

128. *RGV* i.10–12.

129. Here *tarka* is not synonymous with reasoning in general (*yukti = rigs pa*, etc.) but signifies hypothetical thinking within the domain of dichotomizing speculation. Absolute reality is always considered by the Mahāyāna to be beyond this type of thinking; but this would not necessarily imply that it is irrational.

130. If Johnston's reading *aśakyas tarkayitum* were to be accepted, we would seemingly have a double negation of the four positions, in which case the *RGV* would be going a step further than the *MSA* and other comparable Mahāyānist texts. What precisely such a double negation could be intended to mean is by no means clear, however; and this interpretation is supported neither by the manuscript B and the Sanskrit commentary nor by the Tibetan translation.

Elsewhere also the *RGV* has stressed the inexpressibility in words and the conceptual unthinkability of the *paramārtha.*[131]

The terminology employed in the *RGV* as well as the idea expressed is quite in line with the bulk of the Mahāyānist literature, both sūtras and śāstras. To mention only a few parallels with passages of the *Mūlamadhyamakakārikās* already discussed above, the use of the epithet *śiva* to refer to absolute reality as "tranquil" or "still," and thus beyond the binary tension of discursive development *(prapañca)* and dichotomizing conceptualization *(vikalpa),* recalls *MMK* xxv.24 and xviii.9 (where we find *śānta* instead of *śiva*).[132] And the expression *niruktyapagata* "free from verbalization"—which the commentator glosses by *anabhilāpya* "inexpressible" (*RGVV* i.12)—may be compared with *prapañcātīta* in *MMK* xxii.15 and *aprapañcita* in xviii.9.[133] Also, the notion of *tarka* as speculative (hypothetical) thinking is not without connexion with *vikalpa.*[134] As such, the *paramārtha* is only to be known directly and immediately *(pratyātmavedya);* as the *MMK* (xviii.7) puts it, on the level of *dharmatā* or *nirvāṇa* the nameable *(abhidhātavya)* ceases when what is in the scope of discursive thinking has ceased.

Still, there seems to be no suggestion here that reality—*dharma* as *nirodhasatya*—is some kind of illogical and irrational entity, only that it cannot be categorized in terms of the binary tension of discursive thinking and that it may therefore be appropriately treated in an apophatic manner.[135]

At the same time other passages of our *RGV* as well as of the sūtras on which it is based, with the sūtras treating of the *tathāgatagarbha* in the forefront, certainly do not eschew cataphaticism. Thus, especially in treatments of the *paramārtha* (which are by their very nature so to speak "raids on the unspeakable"), apophaticism and cataphaticism come to be used in "torsional" complementarity in the (no doubt paradoxical) attempt to lend conceptual form and verbal expression to the *paramārtha.* This "torsional" complementarity is also perhaps to be found in another form in the Vijñānavāda theory of

131. See *RGV* ii.69ff., v.1. Cf. D. Seyfort Ruegg, "On the Knowability and Expressibility of Absolute Reality in Buddhism," *IBK* 20.1 (1971), pp. 1–7.

A "neither . . . nor" form of statement appears in the *RGV* also in the chapter on the qualities characteristic and constitutive of the *buddha* (iv.30).

132. Cf. also *MMK* v.8 and vii.16.

133. Cf. also *MMK* xviii.5.

134. In *MMK* xviii.5 and 9, for example.

135. Cf. D. Seyfort Ruegg, *Théorie du ta thāgatagarbha et du gotra,* pp. 319ff.; "Le Dharmadhātustava" in *Etudes tibétaines dédiées à la mémoire de M. Lalou* (Paris, 1971), pp. 448–71, reprinted in chapter 4 of the present collection.

śūnyatā discussed above. But in the scholastic treatises of the Madhyamaka with which we started our discussion and in which all four "positions" of the *catuṣkoṭi* are negated, the approach of Nāgārjuna and his followers has been thoroughly apophatic.

V. The Vātsīputrīya Conception of the Indeterminate

The Vātsīputrīyas defined the *pudgala* or "individual" they posited as neither different nor not different from the five groups *(skandha)* and hence as indeterminate *(avaktavya, avācya)*.

The doctrine of this school is known to us mainly from accounts and refutations of it by other Buddhists, one of the earlier sources being the ninth chapter of Vasubandhu's *Abhidharmakośabhāṣya* (ca. sixth century). There it is stated that the Vātsīputrīya theory entails postulating a fifth category called the indeterminate (*avaktavya,* literally "unstateable") in addition to the three within the conditioned *(saṃskṛta)*—viz. past, present, and future—and the unconditioned *(asaṃskṛta)*. But as an indeterminate factor it is not stateable as either a fifth category or not a fifth category in relation to the four abovementioned categories.[136]

In the same chapter Vasubandhu has also alluded to the question of the *jīva,* one of the factors contained in the list of *avyākṛtavastu*s discussed at the beginning of this paper. Vasubandhu explains that the Blessed One has not spoken of a *jīva* in terms of either identity or difference *(tattvānyatva)* since it does not exist. Nor has he ascribed non-existence to it lest a nominal *(prājñaptika)* or fictitious entity possess the property of even non-existence.[137]

A comparable approach to the question of an indeterminate factor that cannot be defined in terms of identity and difference has been adopted by Candrakīrti. In his *Prasannapadā* he observes that when establishing a characterized thing along with its defining characteristic *(lakṣaṇa),* one would

136. *AKBh* ix, pp. 462–63: *yadi câyaṃ [pudgalaḥ] anyaḥ skandhebhyo na vaktavyaḥ 'pañcavidhaṃ jñeyam atītānāgataṃ pratyutpannam asaṃskṛtam avaktavyam iti' na vaktavyaṃ prāpnoti/ naiva hi tad atītādibhyaḥ pañcamaṃ nâpañcamaṃ vaktavyam/*

137. *AKBh* ix, p. 470. Yaśomitra remarks that the *pudgala* is not even existent on the surface level *(saṃvṛtisat);* and as an empty term it cannot therefore even be said to have the property of non-existence.

For a discussion of the relation between *jīva* and *śarīra,* see also *AKBh* v.22 (p. 294.3); pp. 465.12 and 469.9ff.

have to resort to the category of identity and difference because there is no other course *(gati);* and when this proves impossible, the conclusion is that the thing does not exist.[138] Indeed, whatever cannot be determined in terms of identity and difference in relation to some entity cannot be said to exist even on the surface level *(saṃvṛti).*[139] The five speculative theses concerning the relation between an *ātman* and the *skandha*s, which are discussed also in Candrakīrti's *Madhyamakāvatāra* (vi.142–44), are said to be subsumed under the thesis of identity and difference *(tattvānyatvapakṣa).*[140]

In the eighth century, in a discussion of the Vātsīputrīya doctrine in his *Tattvasaṃgraha,*[141] Śāntarakṣita has noted that the *pudgala* was held by this school to be free of both identity and difference *(tattvānyatva)* in relation to the *skandha*s (336) and that it was therefore supposed to have the property of indeterminateness *(avācyatā)* (337). But Śāntarakṣita immediately reminds his reader that a real entity *(vastu)* does not transcend the category of identity and difference (339–42); for there is in fact no other course *(gatyantara)* for a real thing, as Kamalaśīla observes in agreement with other masters.[142] The conclusion is accordingly that no ultimately real *(pāramārthika) pudgala* exists; being indeterminate, its ontological status is that of a water-lily growing in empty space (338).

Śāntarakṣita has moreover observed (344) that union with two opposed properties *(viruddhadharma)* must entail a difference between entities (rather than something like a coincidence of opposites). Consequently, since the *skandha*s are recognized to be not only impermanent but also determinable *(vācya)* with respect to their mutual identity/difference whereas the *pudgala* is supposed not to be so determinable, such a *pudgala* would have to be different from the *skandha*s, contrary to what the Vatsīputrīyas have supposed (346).

In his discussion of certain canonical passages containing specified negation *(viśeṣapratiṣedha)* of a relation between a self and the *skandha*s to which Śāntarakṣita has referred at the end of his section on the Vātsīputrīya doctrine, finally, Kamalaśīla notes that in contradistinction to general negation *(sāmānyapratiṣedha),* specified negation entails the affirmation of the

138. *PPMV* i.1 (p. 64). On the absence of a third alternative, see also Śāntideva's *Bodhicaryāvatāra* ix.35 discussed below, pp. 101 and 104–5.

139. *PPMV* xxi.4 (p. 413.8–9).

140. *PPMV* xxii.1 (p. 435.3). On the supposed relations between an *ātman* and the *skandhas*, see above, note 31.

141. Cf. S. Schayer, *RO* 8 (1931–32), pp. 68–93.

142. *TSP* 339. See above, note 138.

opposite *(anyavidhināntarīyaka)*. For example, when I say "I do not see with my left eye," it is implicitly understood that I see with my right eye; for were I totally blind I should simply say "I do not see," without the above-mentioned specification. Now, since in the sūtras it has been stated that *ātman* is not the *skandha*s, is it not implicitly indicated *(sūcita)* by the use of specified negation that there in fact exists a self which has some other characteristic *(vilakṣaṇa)* and which is indeterminate *(avācya)* in relation to the *skandha*s? The answer suggested is that such specified negation simply serves to reject the twenty specific kinds of speculative views postulating a self, namely the views that *ātman* is *rūpa* (or *vedanā, saṃjñā, saṃskāras, vijñāna*), is in *rūpa* (etc.), possesses *rūpa* (etc.), or is the locus of *rūpa* (etc.).

This explanation has been given by Kamalaśīla in reply to a claim made by Uddyotakara to the effect that the Tathāgata's negation of *ātman* in relation to the *skandha*s cannot be established as meaningful if the negation of the self is considered to be an overall one according to *sāmānyapratiṣedha,* and that it is therefore a *viśeṣapratiṣedha* which implies the affirmation of the self in another respect. And Kamalaśīla concludes by characterizing the negative statements in question in the canon as "illustrative" *(anūdya)* rather than as "operative" affirmations *(vidhi)* of something else.[143]

It is interesting to find here that the old Mīmāṃsā and grammatical concept of *anuvāda* as distinct from *vidhi* has thus been linked with the distinction between *sāmānyapratiṣedha* and *viśeṣapratiṣedha.* This last distinction is in its turn parallel to that between the absolute *prasajyapratiṣedha* and the relative *paryudāsa* negation referred to elsewhere in this paper. Perhaps the distinction between *anuvāda* and *vidhi* can best be explained in terms of a comprehensive theory of speech acts; whereas the distinction between *prasajya* and *paryudāsa* negation, and that between *sāmānyapratiṣedha* and *viśeṣapratiṣedha,* is essentially a logical and semantic difference.

In concluding, it is to be noted that the concept of the indeterminate is not identical with that of inexpressibility discussed elsewhere in this paper: the use of the term *avaktavya* or *avācya* evidently presupposed the existence of some entity, however hard to define, whereas the term *anabhilāpya* relates to absence of own-being *(niḥsvabhāvatā),* non-substantiality *(nairātmya),* and Emptiness *(śūnyatā)*.[144]

143. *TSP* 349.

144. *anabhilāpya* can also be used differently (see, e.g., *AKBh* ii.47, p. 82.4). For Sthiramati's observations on the indeterminate, see above, pp. 77, 79.

Appendix I. Commentarial Interpretations of Mūlamadhyamakakārikā *xviii.8*

The **Akutobhayā* describes the four positions in the Buddha's teaching mentioned in *MMK* xviii.8 as successive graded stages *(rim pa = krama)* that have been utilized by the Teacher so that sentient beings may attain their aim progressively. These stages have been taught by the Buddha in accordance with his disciples' mental faculties, propensities *(bsam pa = āśaya)*, inclinations *(bag la nyal = anuśaya)*, temporal circumstances, etc.[145]

For his part Buddhapālita has not, in his interpretation of this passage, laid emphasis on any special force to be assigned to the prefix *anu-* in *anuśāsana;* but he states that what Nāgārjuna refers to in this verse has its source in worldly distinctions.[146] Thus, the Buddha has allowed that what is held in the world to be *tathya* is true (I), and what is held in the world to be not *tathya* is not true (II). The same principle of accommodation to worldly consensual usage holds also in the case of the conjunction of both, which is represented in the third position (III): what is held in the world to be both *tathya* and not *tathya* the Buddha has allowed to be true and not true. That is, although the Buddha has realized that all things *(bhāva)* are empty of own-being, by virtue of worldly transactional convention *(lokavyavahāra)* they have nevertheless been treated as "true" in some respect. As for the binegation of both positions (IV), it holds good for all *bhāva*s in the absolute sense *(paramārtha);* for while empty of own-being (i.e., not "true"), they are still as real as an illusory projection *(māyā),* a dream, a mirage, a reflection, an echo, etc. (i.e., not altogether "untrue" hallucinations).[147]

Buddhapālita mentions next the following alternative interpretation of these four positions. Some persons hold that "all" *(sarva)* are produced from an existent (*yod pa = sat,* i.e., according to the *satkāryavāda,* e.g., of the Sāṃkhya) (I), others hold that "all" are produced from causes in which the result is not yet existent (*rgyu la 'bras bu snga na med pa dag las,* i.e., according to the *ārambhavāda* of the Nyāya) (II), and still others hold that "all" are produced from the existent-cum-non-existent (III). But the Buddha-Bhagavats themselves have taught that all *bhāva*s, which are nothing but designations founded on causes and conditions in interdependence, neither exist nor do they not exist *(dngos po rgyu dang rkyen las gdags par zad kyi*

145. **Akutobhayā,* tsa, fol. 83b (Peking edition in the Japanese photographic reprint).

146. Cf. Candrakīrti, *PPMV* xviii.8 (p. 372.1).

147. Buddhapālita, *Mūlamadhyamakakārikāvṛtti,* tsa, fol. 276a–277a.

yod pa dang med pa ni ma yin te) (IV). Consequently the Buddha-Bhagavats have said this and that by accommodation to worldly transactional convention; but persons wishing to see reality as it is must not attach themselves conceptually *(abhiniviś-)* to what has been said in accordance with any worldly convention, and they must rather apprehend the real *(de kho na = tattva)*.[148]

While this second interpretation does not perhaps presuppose a series of progressively more "correct" positions, in the first explanation position IV is clearly the most "correct" inasmuch as it is the closest approximation to reality, so that one can even in this interpretation speak of successive graded positions, the last of which approximates best, within the limits of discursive linguistic usage, to reality.

Bhā(va)viveka in his interpretation of the verse also does not lay emphasis on any special force of the prefix *anu-*. But when he comes to the conjunction of *tathya* and not *tathya* (III), he states (like the author of the **Akutobhayā*)[149] that it is dependent on the two truth-levels *(satyadvaya)*. As for binegation (IV), according to Bhā(va)viveka it refers to the fact that during meditative intuition *(mngon par rtogs pa = abhisamaya)* the yogin does not engage in dichotomizing conceptualization concerning the reality *(tattva)* of all *dharmas*.[150]

In an alternative explanation he gives next (also in agreement with the **Akutobhayā*), Bhā(va)viveka points out that, from one point of view, one may speak of *tathya* (I) but from another of not *tathya* (II). The conjunction of the two (III) is dependent on the difference between worldly transactional convention and the convention established in the philosophical treatises *(śāstravyavahāra)*. And since, in Mahāyāna thought, all *dharmas* are unborn, any analytic view *(mam par brtag pa: vicāra)* that takes them as *tathya* and so forth in virtue of some supposed *bhāva* within the domain of either *savikalpaka* or *nirvikalpaka* cognition does not really exist as such. For this reason, then, their binegation has been stated (IV).[151]

In other words, we have here not some indeterminate, irrational, or mysterious entity that is (or appears as) simultaneously *tathya* and not *tathya* (III), or neither (IV), but rather reality to which an approximation has been made by the various schools of thought by means of certain discursively

148. Buddhapālita, vol. tsa, fol. 277a. See, e.g., *MMK* xviii.9 for the *tattvalakṣaṇa*.

149. Fol. 83a6.

150. Bhā(va)viveka, *Prajñāpradīpa*, tsha, fol. 236a–b.

151. Ibid., fol. 236b. Cf. **Akutobhayā*, fol. 83b.

expressible positions, such as holding it to be *tathya,* not *tathya,* both, and finally neither. This approximation to reality is sometimes (but evidently not always) regarded as progressive and graded; and when it is so regarded, position IV may be considered closer to reality than position III. The commentaries quoted above do not, therefore, present reality as being in itself some *coincidentia oppositorum* (though they do indeed support a kind of *docta ignorantia* in the *āryatūṣṇībhāva*): conjunction (III) derives from the juxtaposition of either *lokavyavahāra* and *śāstravyavahāra* or *saṃvṛti* and *paramārthasatya.*

It is to be noted that Bhā(va)viveka's explanation generally agrees with the **Akutobhayā,* although he does not explicitly refer to successive stages as does this commentary.

For Candrakīrti's interpretation, see above (pp. 44–46).

While the preceding explanations tend to regard the four positions as approximations, the fourth being sometimes considered as the best, a section of the *Ta chih tu lun (*Mahāprajñāpāramitā-Upadeśa)* has quoted *MMK* xviii.8 in reply to the question: "If all views are false, what is the absolute point of view?"[152]

Appendix II. Some Modern Interpretations of the Catuṣkoṭi

1. *Logical aspects*

Over the last two decades in particular, the logical structure of the *catuṣkoṭi* has been the subject of a considerable amount of discussion and controversy, and also of some speculation in the context of what is sometimes called "East-West" philosophical comparison. In the following pages some points in the principal attempts at an explication of its structure are briefly reviewed.

Since the early 1930s (Schayer 1933, 93) the *catuṣkoṭi* has come to be referred to as the tetralemma, each *koṭi* being regarded as a proposition. And the *catuṣkoṭi* as a whole has been termed a "quadruple proposition" (Robinson 1969, 76).

An impetus for much of the discussion that has taken place during the last two decades in the English-speaking world at least seems to have been

152. See É. Lamotte, *Le traité de la Grande Vertu de Sagesse de Nāgārjuna* (Louvain, 1944), i, pp. 45–46. (Cf. Sêng-chao's view below, p. 95).

As seen above, in certain cases a sentence having the "neither . . . nor" form (in common with the fourth *koṭi*) has been used in the texts of the Indian Madhyamaka to describe absolute reality.

supplied by P. T. Raju's essay entitled "The Principle of Four-Cornered Negation in Indian Philosophy" (1953–54). Raju there reviewed briefly the fourfold schema as used in Indian thought at a time just previous to the rise of Buddhism (Sañjaya, and the "sophists" or *amarāvikkhepikas*) and during the earlier period of the development of Buddhism (*vitaṇḍāvādins* in the Nyāya literature), as well as its use by Nāgārjuna and Śaṃkara. He singled out the concept of the modal relativity of truth and knowledge *(nayavāda, syādvāda)* in Jaina thought and showed how, in the seven-fold conditional predication *(saptabhaṅgī)* employed by this school, a subject in addition to being (1) existent and (2) non-existent may also be (3) both existent and non-existent, (4) simply indescribable *(avaktavya),* and (5–7) both indescribable and either P, not P, or both P and not P. Raju pointed out further that for the Jaina these seven *nayas* or "tropes" are non-exclusive alternatives rather than exclusive disjunctives.[153] With respect to the Śūnyavāda of the Mādhyamika, Raju noted that the word *śūnya* "empty" also denotes the zero in Indian mathematics, and that zero is mathematically an indeterminate number since it is neither positive nor negative.[154] Concerning the logical problem posed by the fourth *koṭi,* Raju suggested that "it can be explained with the help of the difference between contrary and contradictory opposition of western logic. Two contraries can both be negated, but not the contradictories" (710). And after pointing out that Sanskrit did not have separate terms to express the difference between a contrary and a contradictory (710)[155] he added:

> We may say that if the principle of double negation is applicable to an opposition, it is contradictory; otherwise, contrary. In the case of propositions with quantified subjects, it is easy for us to deter-

153. A connexion between the Buddhist *catuṣkoṭi* and the Jaina *saptabhaṅgī* has been disputed by K. N. Jayatilleke, *Early Buddhist Theory of Knowledge,* pp. 347ff. This is due to his interpreting the fourth *koṭi* as consisting of a real subject, such that it does not have the characteristic P or its contrary not-P but a neutral value. On the *saptabhaṅgī,* see op. cit., pp. 138ff., 156, 338. The Jaina position of course differs from the Buddhist since, for the Jaina, all seven positions are true for a given subject in respect to different modes.

154. It should be noted, however, that there is no evidence in the basic texts of the Madhyamaka school that a mathematical model (and place value) had any immediate bearing on their theory of *śūnyatā.* In the Madhyamaka the term *śūnya* refers to the fact that any *dharma* is empty of own-being *(svabhāvaśūnya),* in which notion there is no mathematical connotation.

155. Cf. Staal 1962, 53.

> mine which is a contrary and which a contradictory negation. But in the others it is extremely difficult (711).

Raju concluded that

> double negation is not necessarily the original affirmation .... The followers of Sankara, like Nāgārjuna, did not accept the principle of double negation (712).[156]

At about the same time C. T. K. Chari brought into the discussion of the *catuṣkoṭi* the question of a logic of mysticism (cf. R. Otto) along with that of the applicability in this context of multi-valued logics, Brouwerian logic as distinct from "classical Boolean logic," and (following H. Reichenbach) the principles of uncertainty and complementarity as evolved in quantum physics. He observed:

> The function of Brouwer's logic and Reichenbach's logic is to introduce into mathematics and mathematical physics, respectively, a domain of "restricted assertability" .... This is just what mystical dialectic proposes to do in the much larger field of human thinking (1954, 323).[157]

Later A. Bahm took up the discussion again, but since he confined himself to the Jaina *syādvāda* we need only note that he also held that "non-*a*" is the contrary rather than the contradictory of "*a*" (1957, 128). This view was accepted by K. N. Jayatilleke (1963, 337) and others and has come to be a cornerstone of their interpretations of the problem of the *catuṣkoṭi.*

In 1958 H. Nakamura published an English version of a study that first appeared in 1954 in Japanese dealing with the formalization of Buddhist logic by means of symbolic logic, in this case Boolean algebra. Nakamura

156. As concerns Nāgārjuna, Raju's conclusion is to say the least questionable in view of what is known of his system from his many surviving works.

157. D. Ingalls has pointed out that the germ of a multi-valued logic may be found in Śaṃkara's idea of *avidyā,* which is *anirvacanīya* (*PEW* 3 [1953], pp. 69ff.). But with respect to the idea of a separate logic of mysticism, however valid the idea of a "mystical dialectic" may be in some domains its applicability here is highly questionable. Indeed it seems to be formally ruled out by the statements of the Madhyamaka masters themselves whose reasoning is based on the *prasaṅga* method which would fail when there are more than two truth-values, as Chari in fact himself remarked (1955, 67). Cf. below, pp. 102, 107.

acknowledged that Nāgārjuna used in his arguments the laws of contradiction and excluded middle but contended that his "arguments clearly show errors from the standpoint of olden time Western traditional logic" (1958, 9). Nakamura suggested that "when viewed from the standpoint of the two-valued logical algebra of Schröder, there are occasions when they are not fallacies and become true arguments" (9). For example, in *MMK* xiii.7

> *yady aśūnyaṃ bhavet kiṃcit syāc chūnyam iti kiṃcana /*
> *na kiṃcid asty aśūnyaṃ ca kutaḥ śūnyaṃ bhaviṣyati //*[158]

which he regards as a hypothetical judgement, Nakamura finds the fallacy of the denial of the consequent based on the negation of the antecedent, which would constitute an infringement of the law of conversion by contraposition (8–9).[159] Nakamura nevertheless suggests a reformulation in terms of Schröder's logical algebra and holds that

> although the first sentence by Nāgārjuna may be wrong, when expressed with the figures of symbolic logic which designate classes, there is no fallacy with regard to conversion by contraposition; i.e., the conclusion entails no fallacy of contradicting to the first sentence set forth by Nāgārjuna. The fact that the abovementioned logistical formation as such is fallacious proves that the doctrine of voidness as such held by ancient Buddhists has something that can not be explained away by the method of symbolic logic alone (10).[160]

As for the *catuṣkoṭi,* it should be noted that Nakamura treats the four *koṭi*s as conjunctive in his formalization $a+(-a)+[a(-a)] + [-a(-a)]$ and speaks of a logic of four alternative propositions (12). Finally, noting that *śūnya* has the same meaning as 0 in logical algebra, he concludes: "It must be permitted after all to indicate Voidness by '0,'" for in two-valued logic "all that does

158. "If something not empty existed, something called 'empty' would exist; something not empty does not exist, and how will there [then] exist something empty?"

159. For a discussion of this point see Appendix III below.

160. Nakamura also claims that if, following Ingalls (*PEW* 3 [1953], pp. 69ff.), the germ of a multi-valued logic is to be found in Śaṃkara's idea of *avidyā,* "then the same significance can be held for the *avidyā* of Buddhism" (p. 2n2).

not exist is expressed by 'o' and is called the 'null class,' indicating something that cannot exist and expressing falsehood" (14–15).[161]

In 1957 R. H. Robinson took up the subject in a paper entitled "Some Logical Aspects of Nāgārjuna's System," in which he gave a brief survey of earlier opinions. He there discussed Nakamura's suggestions as set out in his original article of 1954, from which he acknowledged having drawn some of his material despite certain differences (1957, 295). Very significantly, Robinson stressed that his article was to consider only the formal structure of Nāgārjuna's argumentation, excluding epistemology, psychology, and ontology (295). First Robinson showed that Nāgārjuna recognized and used the principles of non-contradiction and excluded middle, as well as the law of identity (295–96). Then he went on to claim that Nāgārjuna's principal form of inference is the hypothetical syllogism. And from the fact that in, for example, *MMK* xix.6

bhāvaṃ pratītya kālaś cet kālo bhāvād ṛte kutaḥ /
na ca kaścana bhāvo 'sti kutaḥ kālo bhaviṣyati //[162]

Nāgārjuna virtually states the rule of denying the consequent, Robinson deduces that he "was aware to some degree of the principle of conversion" (296). But, citing as examples *MMK* xiii.7 (quoted above) and also vii.17 and x.7, Robinson goes on to argue that by negating the antecedent Nāgārjuna violated the law of conversion (297).[163] Next Robinson takes up Nakamura's suggestion that these examples would be valid in terms of the logical algebra of Schröder but finds that transcribing them in this manner does not remove the logical difficulties (298).

With regard to the *catuṣkoṭi,* Robinson considers that its four members are in a relation of exclusive disjunction (301), and that taken together they are supposed to be exhaustive (302). Robinson then maintains that while the first two alternative propositions are to be quantified universally ("All *x* is *A*";

161. Here Nakamura does not clearly distinguish in his translation between *śūnya* (and *śūnyatva*) on the one hand and *śūnyatā* on the other. (This failure to distinguish between the two concepts is especially characteristic of scholars influenced by the Sino-Japanese tradition of Buddhism, the Chinese word *kung* rendering both concepts. On the problem in Indian texts see above, note 104.)

162. "If time is dependent on an entity, how without an entity could there be time? Now no entity exists. How [then] will time exist?"

163. But as will be seen in Appendix III, there is no reason to suppose that Nāgārjuna has in fact committed this error here.

"All *x* is not *A*"), the third is to be quantified as "Some *x* is *A* and some *x* is not *A*"; in the fourth alternative *x* is null ("No *x* is *A* and no *x* is not *A*") (302). Robinson points out that, given Schayer's transcription (~*p*.~(~*p*): 1933, 93) for the fourth alternative, "not-*p* and not-not-*p*" implies that the four alternatives are propositional functions.

> However, it is apparent that negations and conjunctions of the basic proposition do not transcribe [*MMK* xxv.15–18], and, if the terms of the other examples are quantified in the same way, do not transcribe them. "Not-*p*" is the contradictory of "*p*," but "some *x* is *A*" is not the contradictory of "some *x* is not *A*" (302).

Concerning Nakamura's (1954) interpretation of the *catuṣkoṭi* in algebraic notation, Robinson observes that the third ("*a* –*a*") and fourth ("–(*a*–*a*)") alternatives would be redundant and senseless; "however, if the subject is not totally distributed in either conjunct in the third alternative, then this form need no longer be considered redundant" (302–3); and it is noted that Stcherbatsky's translation in *Conception of Buddhist Nirvāṇa* (p. 90) in fact implicitly quantified the third alternative (303 note). The third and fourth *koṭis* then "are not simple propositions, but conjunctions" of the Aristotelian I and O and E and A forms (in Boole–Schröder notation respectively $ab \neq 0 . a\bar{b} \neq 0$ and $ab = 0 . a\bar{b} = 0$) (303).[164] Robinson concludes that "Nāgārjuna's reason for negating each of the alternatives is that its terms are null, as defined by his opponents" (303). The way of escape from the consequences of the dilemmas pointed out by Nāgārjuna is to

> "take them by the horns," to repudiate the definitions which they presuppose. In so doing, one rejects the whole set of propositions which Nāgārjuna calls "views" *(dṛṣṭi),* and arrives at the meaning of emptiness (304).

Finally, concerning Nakamura's definition of "voidness" as being itself the null class, Robinson proposes a correction when he observes that in a fundamental verse (*MMK* xxiv.14) "'everything' means 'all mundane and transmundane dharmas'" (305); accordingly,

> the entire point of Nāgārjuna's argument is that the class of entities

164. In 1957 (p. 301) Robinson recalls Nāgārjuna's denial of other cases of existential quantification, e.g., in *MMK* xxvii.17 and 26–27.

> that possess own-being is null. Thus the class of empty phenomena, *pratītya-samutpāda,* is the complement of the own-being, or null, class. The "emptiness" class has "designations" as members, and some designations are cogent. Thus the emptiness class is not null, but is co-extensive with the universal class (306).
>
> The Śūnyavāda is in fact a kind of theory of fictions. The concept of designation *(prajñapti)* provides a way of handling abstracts without concretizing them, or assigning ontological value to them (307–8).

In a supplement dealing with Sêng-chao, the Chinese San-lun master who lived from 374 to 414, Robinson suggests that several passages in the *Chao lun* support the supposition that its author "understood the tetralemma as involving quantification" (1958, 114) and that he thus had some knowledge of the logic of classes (119). Sêng-chao employed the lemmas as "heuristic designations," but unlike Nāgārjuna he may not have been aware of the rules of non-contradiction and of the excluded middle (119). Indeed, Sêng-chao seems to have held that the fourth lemma is "speech about Absolute Truth" (115).[165] In this article Robinson interprets the fourth *koṭi* as "All *x* is *A* and all *x* is non-*A*" (113); though this formulation differs from his formulation of 1957 ("No *x* is *A* and no *x* is not *A*"), he remarked in a later publication that "No *x* is not *A*" equals "All *x* is *A*" (1967, 57).[166]

The early history of the *catuṣkoṭi* was studied, mainly on the basis of materials drawn from the Pāli Nikāyas and their commentaries and from Jaina sources, in the course of a large work entitled *Early Buddhist Theory of Knowledge* by K. N. Jayatilleke (1963). In this book the author developed ideas he had already outlined in an article of 1950 entitled "Some Problems of Translation and Interpretation II."[167]

Jayatilleke objected to calling the *catuṣkoṭi* a tetralemma; and regarding the *koṭis* as propositional functions he usually referred to them as four alternatives; indeed, since he considered them as basic to an entire system of logic, he proposed the appelation of fourfold logic of the four alternatives (1963, 350). He also objected to Robinson's statement that the *catuṣkoṭi* resembles the four Aristotelian forms, adding that Robinson's proposal to interpret the

165. See above, p. 89.

166. On this see Jayatilleke 1967, 75.

167. *University of Ceylon Review* 7 (1950), pp. 45–55.

fourth alternative as "No x is A and no x is not A," which is true "when x is null," is contradicted by usage in the Pāli Nikāyas (351). Jayatilleke maintained in addition that in the case of

> a ṭhapanīya pañha or meaningless question all four alternatives were *rejected* rather than *negated* because the question in each of the alternatives was not considered to be a proper question *(kallo pañho)* . . . . The replies to each of these questions is of the form "mā h'evaṃ," i.e. do not say so (A. 11.161).

Rather than "four-cornered negation" (Raju) this should, therefore, properly be called "four-cornered rejection" (346).

Jayatilleke returned to the "Logic of the Four Alternatives" a last time in 1967 when he discussed once again the significance of these alternatives in the Nikāyas and ventured the observation that the problem has baffled not only modern scholars but also Nāgārjuna himself (1967, 69). Given his opinion that "Nāgārjuna and some of his commentators, ancient and modern, refer to this logic with little understanding of its real nature and significance" and that "there is little evidence that Nāgārjuna understood the logic of the four alternatives as formulated and utilized in early Buddhism" (82), his article cannot be expected to contribute much to an understanding of the Madhyamaka school.[168] Suffice it then to note that, according to Jayatilleke, the four alternatives are mutually exclusive and together exhaustive (70). While in some examples all four alternatives are rejected, sometimes in the Nikāyas if one of the four alternatives is true then the others are false; but it is historically incorrect to say (with Robinson) that Gautama has negated each of the alternatives (70–71). In particular, Jayatilleke criticized Robinson's interpretation of the third lemma as a conjunction of the Aristotelian I and O forms and of the fourth as a conjunction of the contraries of the conjuncts of the third lemma, and he concluded: "It can be shown that if Robinson's analysis is correct, the alternatives are not mutually exclusive or together exhaustive, contradicting his claim . . . " (74). "But the difficulty is with the fourth lemma, since E and A, being contraries, cannot both be true" (75). In Jayatilleke's view

> the second alternative is to be taken as the contrary of the first. We designate this by non-P instead of not-P[169] . . . . It is evident that the

168. Jayatilleke's treatment of Nāgārjuna is unfortunately superficial, and rather presumptuous.

169. In 1963 (pp. 136, 350) Jayatilleke wrote this as "notp" (rather than as -p) since "notp"

> third alternative is not a conjunction of the first two alternatives or of the contradictories of the first two alternatives (on the analogy of the quantified propositions) . . . . When the statement "the universe is both finite and infinite" is made, it is explained as "the universe is finite in one dimension and infinite in another." In general, the third alternative is, therefore, of the form: "*S* is *partly P* and *partly* non-*P*." (78–79)

As for the fourth *koṭi,*

> since the second alternative is the contrary and not the contradictory of *P* and the third asserts that the subject has a combination of some of the contrary characteristics, there is left a part of the determinable constituting the universe of discourse which is referred to by the fourth alternative (80).

For example,

> happiness *(sukha)* . . . is a determinate quality characterizing a person's *hedonic tone (vedanā).* When we remove the qualities of "happiness," "unhappiness" *(dukkha),* or a mixture of the two, we are left with "neutral hedonic tone" *(adukkha-m-asukha vedanā).* So a person who is "neither happy nor unhappy" comprises the class of people experiencing a neutral hedonic tone. Such a class need not necessarily be a null class, although it could be so sometimes (80).[170]

Jayatilleke observes finally that it would

> be self-contradictory to negate all the alternatives. The apparent instances in which this is done in early Buddhism are those in which, for some reason or other, each of the alternatives is misleading, being based on false assumptions, and therefore is to be rejected. This rejection is not the same as negation (81).[171]

---

is not the contradictory of "*p*." On the first and second alternatives as contrary and opposite (rather than contradictory), see also his 1963, pp. 341ff.

170. "This is another reason why Robinson's proposal to translate non-quantified propositions into quantified ones . . . is unsatisfactory," Jayatilleke adds (p. 80).

171. Although the distinction made by Jayatilleke between rejection and negation is of logical importance, it does not in fact seem to serve a purpose in the explication of the

In 1969 Robinson published a review of Jayatilleke's *Early Buddhist Theory of Knowledge* in which he also refers to his article of 1967 just summarized. Amongst other points he takes up Jayatilleke's interpretation of the fourth alternative as referring to a neutral position in a series of non-contradictory predicates and points out some flaws in it. Moreover, the examples of the *catuṣkoṭi* in the Nikāyas are not homogeneous (75), and in the third *koṭi* the subject is undistributed (76). Already earlier Robinson had maintained that the four lemmas are not modes of a single proposition ("either *p*, or not-*p*, or *p*-and-not-*p*, or not-*p*-and-not-not-*p*"), and that since they differ in the quantity of their constituent terms they are four propositions with different internal structures ("All *x* is *A*"; "No *x* is *A*"; "Some *x* is *A*, and some *x* is not *A*"; "No *x* is *A*, and no *x* is not *A*") (1967, 57).

In 1969 (76–78) Robinson, searching for the widest ground of agreement with Jayatilleke, concluded in eirenic vein by enumerating a number of points on the *catuṣkoṭi* as used in the Nikāyas. The third *koṭi* is a conjunction of contraries, so that there is no violation of the rule of contradiction. The fourth *koṭi* is

> meaningful when *X* exists and when *Y* and non-*Y* are contraries rather than contradictories. The non-existence of *X* may have been sufficient reason for rejecting the fourth lemma, though this one, like the first three, was evidently rejected wherever the Buddhist took exception to the questioner's or listener's *concept* of *X*. This . . . is Nāgārjuna's position. As he considers own-being *(svabhāva)* to be a self-contradictory concept, any proposition containing a term to which own-being is ascribed is to be denied.
>
> Each of the four alternatives is intended to exclude the other three

and

> the four lemmas were intended to be jointly exhaustive.
>
> The predicates of the first two *koṭis* are sometimes contradictories ("finite or infinite in all respects"), sometimes contraries ("east or west"), and sometimes just phrases containing opposites ("torments himself, or torments another").
>
> The *catuṣkoṭi*, like other Buddhist dialectic, assumes a two-value logic. No truth-values other than true and false are countenanced either in Early Buddhism or in Nāgārjuna. As the silence

Madhyamaka and Vijñānavāda texts considered above. And its usefulness in analysing the doctrines of the Nikāyas has not been sufficiently well established by Jayatilleke.

> of the *ārya*s is non-propositional, it is out of order to consider inexpressibility as a true-value.

Finally, in a posthumously published paper dealing with the *avyākṛtavastu*s, Robinson has noted that, for the early Buddhists, the fourth lemma seems to have meant equivocation:

> the rejection of this lemma, together with the explicit statements attributed to Gotama and his disciples to the effect that he knew what was to be known, should dispel the view that Gotama refused to assert the unexplained points because he was agnostic about them (1972, 318–19).

As already seen above, the distinction between *prasajya* and *paryudāsa* negation is of importance for the problem of the *catuṣkoṭi.*[172] B. K. Matilal has claimed that when interpreted in terms of exclusion negation—i.e., the *prasajya* kind—"the apparent contradiction of the joint negation of the fourfold alternatives will disappear" (1971, 164).[173] In this form of negation as used by the Mādhyamika, "denial of a position does not necessarily involve commitment to any other position" (164). While the last point is of fundamental importance, the suggestion that in *prasajya* negation contradiction will disappear overlooks the fact that the Madhyamaka method works precisely because positions I and II and the terms of positions III and IV are contradictorily opposed. The Mādhyamika is certainly not working towards some ontological or logical third value between contradictories any more than he is seeking a dialectical synthesis. Indeed, if there really existed such a dialectical synthesis or third value, there would be something on which conceptual thinking could base itself and cling, and the entire purpose of the Madhyamaka method could then no longer be achieved. In other words, contradiction must not disappear; and all the four *koṭi*s are to be negated or rejected (see below, pp. 101, 104, 107–8).

In an article on the relationship between religion and logic, S. Ichimura has discussed the logical interpretations of the *catuṣkoṭi* proposed by several scholars, and he has accepted for early Buddhism Jayatilleke's analysis of the *koṭi*s as propositional and disjunctive, the third and fourth assertions being respectively not a conjunction of the first and second and not their binegation (1973, 44). But Jayatilleke's demonstration is not final, and it is not exhaustive

172. Cf. above, note 10.

173. But see F. Staal, *Exploring Mysticism* 1975, 38.

since it did not touch on the Mahāyāna (45). As for Nāgārjuna, his method is intended to reveal the limitations of logic and language, and the principle of the negative application of the *catuṣkoṭi* "derives from the conceptual scheme which consists of the four dyadic propositions such that their totality leads to contradiction and hence to total annihilation, i.e., the breakdown of symbolism" (47–48). The negative use of the *catuṣkoṭi* was then developed for a religious reason, to transcend the limits of our logical and linguistic conventions (50),demonstrating the self-contradictory nature of the referential object of a proposition (51).[174]

Taking up a theme he had broached already in 1962 in an article entitled "Negation and the Law of Contradiction in Indian Thought," F. Staal has on two subsequent occasions considered the question of the *catuṣkoṭi.* While in the earlier discussion, an appendix to a study on analyticity, he has merely offered a formalization of *MMK* i.1 together with a brief account of three varieties of negation (1966, 90–92), in his most recent work Staal has devoted a chapter to the *catuṣkoṭi* in the context of a discussion on whether "Oriental mysticism" and the Madhyamaka are to be regarded as rational or irrational (1975, 32–46).

Staal notes that the type of negation used by the Mādhyamika is the *prasajya* kind. But contrary to Matilal he considers that this by no means disposes of the fact that contradictions arise between *prasajya* negations, for "the principle of noncontradiction applies only to such negations" (Staal 1975, 38). And he concludes that Raju's, Robinson's and Matilal's "logical attempts to save the *catuṣkoṭi* from inconsistency are . . . unsatisfactory" (38). Nevertheless, "a sensible interpretation offered by Robinson, following Candrakīrti . . . , would be to regard the *catuṣkoṭi* not as a statement, but as a pedagogical or therapeutic device" (40). Staal also describes Nāgārjuna's statement that all is *tathya,* not *tathya,* both, and neither (*MMK* xviii.8) as "the central teaching of the Buddha" (36), although this is anything but certain in the context of what Nāgārjuna has written.[175]

Staal however acknowledges that the Mādhyamikas have not in fact thrown overboard the principle of non-contradiction, and in so doing he has gone a long way towards dispelling the nonsense so often talked about a

174. In his *Buddhist Formal Logic* (London, 1969), R. S. Y. Chi devoted a section to the *catuṣkoṭi* (pp. 156–63); but in his foreword to the book, he has himself repudiated this treatment, describing it as "far from correct" (p. viii) and even as "erroneous" (p. ix). See now R. Chi, "Topics on Being and Logical Reasoning," *PEW* 24 (1974), pp. 295–98.

175. See above, pp. 44ff., 86–89.

so-called "Buddhist irrationalism." Yet he still thinks that the Mādhyamikas "do in fact reject the principle of the excluded middle" (39). He explains:

> If we reject the fourth clause [of the *catuṣkoṭi*], as the Mādhyamika philosophers did, we are free to accept the principle of excluded middle. But we don't have to, since denying the denial of the excluded middle only implies the excluded middle if we accept the principle of double negation, which is itself equivalent to the excluded middle (39).

Staal then concludes:

> When the Mādhyamika philosopher negates a proposition, it does not follow that he himself accepts the negation of that proposition. Accordingly, there are other alternatives than *A* and not-*A*, and the principle of the excluded middle does not hold (44).

In this connexion Staal has introduced the question of intuitionistic logic, and he writes:

> According to Brouwer, when we are dealing with sets of infinitely many objects, we may not be in a position to determine whether *A* or not-*A* is valid. Hence in this logic there are more than two values (39).

Staal's interpretation is then tantamount to affirming that, for the Mādhyamikas, there exists some third position or value between the affirmation and the negation of a predicate (or proposition).

Now, that this was not the opinion of the Madhyamaka school *as a whole* is eloquently shown by Śāntideva's statement (*Bodhicaryāvatāra* ix.35):

> *yadā na bhāvo nâbhāvo mateḥ saṃtiṣṭhate puraḥ /*
> *tadânyagatyabhāvena nirālambā praśāmyati //*

> When neither existence nor non-existence presents itself before the mind, then, being without a support because of the absence of any other recourse, [the mind] is still.

Staal does not refer to this very important statement at all in his chapter on the *catuṣkoṭi* and "Buddhist irrationalism"; and when he quotes it much later in quite another context (160) he does not draw the conclusion that, for this important Madhyamaka master at least, the principle of the excluded third is not only valid but altogether fundamental in the philosophical thought of his school.[176]

Nāgārjuna has not, it is true, expressed himself quite so clearly on the matter in his *Mūlamadhyamakakārikās* or *Vigrahavyāvartanī;* and his statements in *MMK* vii.30 and viii.7, quoted by Staal (34), have to do rather with non-contradiction. But in *MMK* ii.8 and 15 as well as in xxi.14, Nāgārjuna seems to have recognized the principle clearly enough; Candrakīrti has also stated the principle of the exclusion of the third in his *Prasannapadā* (e.g., xxiii.14; cf. Seyfort Ruegg 1969, 384–85). That the principle involved in the *tertium non datur* is indeed fundamental in Madhyamaka thought follows from the consideration that, if a third position or value really existed, the mind could cling to it as some kind of thing, albeit one beyond the two values of "classical" logic. But if this were to happen, there could be no "stillness" or "tranquillity" on the level of the *paramārtha,* i.e., no absence of *vikalpa* and *prapañca.* And this would be radically opposed to Madhyamaka theory.

Staal next considers the problem of the use of paradox, which is especially frequent when the Mahāyāna literature treats absolute reality. About Nāgārjuna's statement in the *Vigrahavyāvartanī* (29) "But I have no proposition" *(nâsti ca mama pratijñā),* Staal writes: "Unless this statement itself is not a proposition, we have a paradox here" (45). However, this interpretation assimilates two distinct uses of the term "proposition"; and it would hold good only if *pratijñā* meant here any sentence or statement ("*nâsti ca mama pratijñā*" being of course indubitably a sentence). But this sentence is not a *pratijñā* in Nāgārjuna's sense; for in his usage *pratijñā* denotes an assertion and more specifically a thesis (e.g., of an inference or syllogism) which seeks to establish something.[177] What Nāgārjuna is saying here, then, is surely not that he is not uttering a meaningful sentence (something that would be not

176. This idea is supported also by *Samādhirājasūtra* ix.27:
[astîti] nâstîti ubhe 'pi antā
[śuddhī] aśuddhîti ime 'pi antā /
tasmād ubhe anta vivarjayitvā
madhye 'pi sthānaṃ na karoti paṇḍitaḥ //

177. In his autocommentary on *Vigrahavyāvartanī* 29 Nāgārjuna explains: *sarvabhāveṣu śūnyeṣv atyantopaśānteṣu prakṛtivivikteṣu kutaḥ pratijñā* "when all entities are empty, altogether still and devoid of a nature, how could there be a proposition [presenting them as being some thing or other]?" Cf. Candrakīrti, *PPMV,* p. 16.

merely paradoxical[178] but quite absurd), but rather that he is not propounding a proposition claiming probative force concerning the (positive or even negative) own-being *(svabhāva)* of any thing. Whatever other logical problems may arise in connexion with Nāgārjuna's procedure in this respect, there would appear to be no paradox here at all.

To return to the exclusion of the middle, as an onto-logical principle it is therefore one of the very foundations of Madhyamaka thought. And if the logical principle of the excluded middle (understood as meaning that one of a set of two contradictory sentences must be true according to the principle of bivalence) is not accepted in the Mādhyamika's procedure based on the use of the *prasaṅga,* this is because he considers that the subject of such sentences is in fact null; hence, to use modern terminology, such a proposition is not semantically well-formed. But from this it is not possible to argue that the Mādhyamika does not recognize the principle as valid: he simply does not find that the thing in question can be the subject of a qualification in any appropriate and meaningful way (as Staal himself has indeed correctly noted [45] following Schayer 1931, xxvi).[179]

In the light of the foregoing, it turns out that the cases Staal has considered problematic (though not as signs of irrationalism) and as possibly indicating non-acceptance of the principle of the excluded middle do not require such an interpretation. This of course only strengthens his general thesis that an irrationalist interpretation of Nāgārjuna and the Madhyamaka is quite unfounded. At the same time, it should make us extremely wary of injecting into the thought of the Madhyamaka school the modern concepts of multivalued logic. There is no evidence that the main stream of this school admitted a third position as valid either logically or ontologically; and an analysis of the use of the negation of position IV of the *catuṣkoṭi* certainly does not support such an idea. Nāgārjuna's use referred to above of what amounts to a two-valued logic is consonant with the Mahāyānist theory of alternatives in a (binary or quaternary) conceptual system *(vikalpa),* where the affirmation of one member of a dichotomously structured pair involves the negation of the other member. And there appears to be no doubt that Nāgārjuna and his successors in the Madhyamaka school founded many of their analyses of concepts and entities and their arguments based on reasoning by undesired consequences *(prasaṅga)* on the twin principles of non-contradiction and the excluded middle, before going on to show that in fact none of the members of a conceptual pair or tetralemma can in fact apply in reality.

178. As in the paradox of the liar for example (the paradox of Epimenides).

179. Cf. the remarks above on the empty (null) class.

Now a three-valued logic may be based on the non-fulfilment of referential presuppositions;[180] and in this case an aspect of three-valued logic could indeed have a certain bearing on Nāgārjuna's philosophy. For him, any and all presuppositions according to which propositions are constructed concerning the (positive or even negative) own-being *(svabhāva)* of a thing are necessarily unfulfilled because all *dharma*s are really empty of own-being *(svabhāvaśūnya)* and non-substantial *(niḥsvabhāva)*. Production or existence through own-being of any thing of which some property could properly be predicated thus clearly constitutes an unfulfilled condition in the Madhyamaka. Consequently, a thing may be said, following Mahāyānist theory, to be *like* a magical projection *(māyā)* (not in a nihilistic sense but in the sense that it is imagined to be otherwise than it is in its true nature of dependent origination and emptiness); and it is just in this way that things may be regarded as indeterminate or indefinite in the Mahāyāna. But it has to be observed at the same time that in no circumstances are *dharma*s ever anything but ontologically and logically undetermined in the sense just described; for never are they real entities *(bhāva)* of which some property could (eventually) be predicated. No *bhāva* can therefore ultimately have the truth-value "true"/"false."

When the Mādhyamika describes a *dharma* as being like a flower in the sky *(khapuṣpa)*, the son of a barren woman *(vandhyāputra)*, etc., he is thus evidently operating with a notion comparable with that of non-referentiality according to which the relevant presuppositions are unfulfilled. But it appears that his system is not otherwise strictly based on a three-valued logic in which the concept of falseness may be divided into (a) "false" and (b) "indeterminate," and in which a predicate may possess a third and neutral area in addition to "true" and "false."

If, as has been suggested by U. Blau in his work on three-valued linguistic analysis and logic, informal thinking is best reconstructed within the frame of three-valued logic, it is possible that such a logic might have left traces in Nāgārjuna's writings since his language could no doubt be described as

180. See for example U. Blau, *Dreiwertige Sprachanalyse und Logik* (Munich, 1974), according to whom two-valued logic is a special case of three-valued logic, the latter being characteristic of informal thinking and ordinary language and not incompatible with two-valued logic. Cf. also W. Stegmüller, *Hauptströmungen der Gegenwartsphilosophie,* II (Stuttgart, 1975), pp. 186–91, 216–18. Sentences with unfulfilled presuppositions arise when non-referential terms or ill-defined and vague concepts are contained in them. And elementary sentences have the truth-value of "indeterminate" (rather than "true" or "false") when the subject lies in the region of vagueness of the predicate, or when the referential presuppositions are not fulfilled.

"ordinary" language. But at the same time it has to be recalled that the logical method used by Nāgārjuna is firmly based on a "classical" two-valued logic founded on the dichotomously structured binary nature of discursive thinking in terms of alternatives *(vikalpa);* for only in this way can the concepts of discursive thinking, and along with them the categories of language, be shown to be self-cancelling and "zeroed." This point, which has been made by Śāntideva in his *Bodhicaryāvatāra* (ix.35, quoted above), emerges also from Nāgārjuna's analytic procedure.

To sum up, the logical investigations to which the *catuṣkoṭi* and related concepts have been submitted have no doubt succeeded in demonstrating that the principles of non-contradiction and of the excluded middle have been recognized by the Mādhyamika thinkers, and that their reasoning *(yukti)* in particular is in fact based on them. (There also seems now to be reason to think that the principle of double negation was also understood by them.[181]) Concerning the structure and functions of the *catuṣkoṭi,* however, while a great deal of ingenuity has been expended in these discussions with a view to clarifying its logical background, the applications of this set of four positions in Buddhist thought have perhaps received short shrift or been sometimes obscured in the dust of argument between the proponents of variant interpretations. In fact, much of the discussion was admittedly conducted mainly with a view to establishing the logical structure of the *catuṣkoṭi* and its parts to the exclusion of its other philosophical aspects (cf. Robinson 1957, 295). It has also been made a stock topic for a certain style of "East-West philosophy" and for what Jayatilleke referred to as a typical "East-West problem" (1967, 69 and 82). A problematic has thus tended to be imposed on Buddhist thought in a form that does not in fact seem to be essential to the questions with which the Buddhist thinkers were actually concerned. It would seem obvious that such prejudgement in terms of another problematic imported from elsewhere is a rather ethnocentric procedure inasmuch as it is determined not by the system of thought being studied but by the modern analyst's culture and presuppositions. Hermeneutically it may be that such a tendency is difficult to avoid, but the difficulties require to be noted and taken careful account of. With regard to Nāgārjuna in particular, one basic source of misunderstanding has probably been the inclination of many writers to regard him first and foremost as a dialectician.[182]

181. Staal (1975, 39), however, still has doubts about this.

182. The attempt to improve this description by referring to a mystical dialectic is hardly calculated to clarify the matter. Against this view Robinson (1957, 291) already entered a

Another example of the importing of a logical problem from outside will be briefly considered in Appendix III.

2. *The semiotic aspect*

Beside the essentially logical approaches reviewed above, the second half of the 1960s saw the beginnings of an application of semiotics to the study of the Śūnyavāda and the *catuṣkoṭi.*

In the course of an interpretation of the Śūnyavāda as a "zero way" or "zerology," L. Mäll (1965, 190) proposed analysing the *catuṣkoṭi* as a conjunction $A_1 = A+(-A)+[A+(-A)]+\{-[A+(-A)]\}$. In a subsequent article (Kull and Mäll 1967, 63) the tetralemma was presented, with a slightly different interpretation, both as disjunction and as conjunction.

Mäll has defined zerology as involving a lifting of the opposition between an affirmative and a negative judgement (between + and −), which means that relations are considered as indefinite (1968, 58–59). Thus, on the highest level of *prajñā,* as opposed to that of *vijñāna,* no logically determined relations would exist between concepts. While the *vijñāna* level corresponds to logical thought, the *prajñā* level would represent a variety of thought that is "post-logical"—or a different logic which can be marked by the formula A ⟲ B[183] (1968, 61–62; cf. 1965, 191). Mäll adduces statements drawn from the Prajñāpāramitā literature which he interprets as: A is A because it is $\bar{A}$ (1968, 62).

Mäll does not regard what he terms Oriental pragmatics as directly reducible to Occidental schemata, and he questions the substitution of modern philosophical and psychological terminology for Buddhist terminology. This is, however, not to deny the existence of parallels between the two; but in many domains of culture the Orient has attained altogether exceptional results (1968, 55).

Following the approach to the Śūnyavāda outlined by Mäll, J. Kristeva has considered the "zero way" or "zerology" in the frame of her semiotic theory of paragrammatism. In one place she has in fact formalized paragrammatic practice by means of a conjunctive tetralemma: $\pi = D+(-D)+[D+(-D)]+\{-[D+(-D)]\} = 0$ (where π is the paragrammatic sequence and D a denotatum) or, in mathematical notation, as $A \quad B$ (i.e., a non-synthetic union of sometimes

caveat (cf. J. May, "Kant et le Mādhyamika," *IIJ* 3 [1959], pp. 108ff.). See also J. W. de Jong, "Emptiness," *JIP* 2 (1972), pp. 10ff. On mystical intuition in the Madhyamaka, see J. W. de Jong, "The Problem of the Absolute," *JIP* 2 (1972), p. 5; J. May, *Prasannapadā,* p. 20.

183. This sign symbolizes a non-synthetic union of different factors that may be contradictory (cf. Kristeva 1969, 197 and 253). See further below.

contradictory formulae) (1969, 197 and 253). Elsewhere she has used the formula $A = B+(-B)+[B+(-B)]+\{-[B+(-B)]\} = 0$ to resume the two sides of the twofold truth which then neutralize each other (1969, 85). In her general theory of semiotics Kristeva has assimilated the kind of negation found in the language of poetry with an annihilative type of negation that has nothing to do with the negation found in a proposition of ordinary language governed by the linguistic sign, the negativity constituting a judgement (as in the case of Aufhebung), or the negation internal to a judgement (as in Boolean 0–1 logic). She concludes that a "zerological subject"—i.e., ultimately a non-subject—comes to assume thought which annuls itself. Such a "zerological subject" is exterior to the space governed by the linguistic sign; the subject vanishes when the thought of the sign disappears, i.e., when the relation of the sign to the denotatum is reduced to zero (1969, 273–74). Kristeva has also employed the concept of orthocomplementary structure to describe the relations of elements in the paragrammatic space of poetic language to the extent that the latter goes beyond the 0–1 opposition of ordinary language and logic (1969, 265 and 273). Kristeva's theory of paragrammatism, in the light of her comparison of it with the "zerology" of the Śūnyavāda, would tend to bridge the gulf of incommensurability between at least certain Occidental and Oriental schemata and notations.[184]

The semiotic interpretation of Mahāyānist, and in particular Madhyamaka, thought has still to be elaborated and made more precise. Certain points also are in need of clarification, for example what exactly is meant when it is said that the four members of the tetralemma "equal" 0. But it seems that semiotics can accommodate within its theory the idea of the tetralemma and its negation, and it appears to be worth exploring further for its potential contribution to an approach to Mahāyānist thought.

In a discussion of the Mahāyānist treatment of absolute reality, Seyfort Ruegg (1969, 383ff.) emphasized the point that, contrary to the opinion of some scholars,[185] Madhyamaka reasoning *(yukti)* is based on the twin pillars of the

184. A link between poetry and trans-linguistic and trans-logical philosophy has also been pointed to for example by Chari (1954, 325) following I. H. Parsons' *Poesiens logik.* And the notion of a "metapoetics" is undergoing further development at the present time with reference to logic, philosophy, etc. J. Kristeva herself has not pursued this matter further in her more recent *La révolution du langage poétique* (Paris, 1974). On the question of a mathematical connotation in the theory of *śūnyatā,* see note 154 above.

185. Cf. A. Kunst, "The Principle of Excluded Middle in Buddhism," *RO* 21 (1957), pp. 141–47; H. Nakamura, *IBK* 7.1 (1958), pp. 1ff.; J. F. Staal, *BSOAS* 25 (1962), p. 68n6; Y. Kajiyama, *Nava-Nālandā-Mahāvihāra Research Publication,* I (1957), pp. 293ff.; T. R. V.

principles of non-contradiction and excluded middle; and the negation of the four *koṭis* then serves to bring to a stop all discursive thinking consisting of conceptual development *(prapañca)* and dichotomizing conceptualization *(vikalpa)* involving the solidarity of complementary opposites expressed as affirmation *(vidhi)* and negation *(pratiṣedha)*. When the four *koṭis*—taken as being exhaustive of all imaginable positive and negative positions within discursive thought—have been used up, there remains no "third" (indeterminate or putatively dialectical) position between the positive and negative which discursive thought could then seize on and cling to; and the mind therefore becomes still.[186] This exhaustion—and "zeroing"[187]—of all the discursively conceivable extreme positions by means of the negation[188] of all four *koṭis* corresponds to the Middle Way, and to reality understood by the Mādhyamika as emptiness of own-being and non-substantiality of all factors of existence.

Now, as already noted, it is found that reality has on occasion been indicated by a sentence that corresponds in its verbal formulation with the (unnegated) fourth *koṭi*. Nevertheless, since the *paramārtha* is regarded by the Mahāyāna as free from all the positions of the *catuṣkoṭi*, it is clearly necessary to distinguish between the use of the "neither . . . nor" formula (which is not then negated) to indicate the *paramārtha* and binegation as found in the "neither . . . nor" formula of the fourth *koṭi* (which is to be negated). And there does not seem to be any reason to suppose that the philosophers of the classical Madhyamaka school ever used the fourth position of the *catuṣkoṭi* to characterize or indicate the *paramārtha;* by definition, absolute reality is free from all positions comprising worldly transactional usage *(lokavyavahāra)* (Seyfort Ruegg 1969, 384 and 57).[189]

Murti, *Central Philosophy of Buddhism* (London, 1955), pp. 146ff. But see L. de La Vallée Poussin, *Way to Nirvāṇa* (Cambridge, 1917), p. 111.

186. See Candrakīrti, *PPMV* xv.7 (p. 270) quoting the *Kāśyapaparivarta* (§ 57); and *Samādhirājasūtra* ix.27 and Śāntideva, *Bodhicaryāvatāra* ix.35 quoted above.

187. Here the expression "to zero" is being used not with a mathematical reference but in a more general sense of an*null*ing. (Cf. above, n. 154.)

188. Jayatilleke's distinction between negation and rejection does not appear to serve any useful purpose here.

189. The *Laṅkāvatārasūtra* has stated that since *lokavyavahāra* "worldly transactional usage" belongs to the domain of the "tetralemma" *(cātuṣkoṭika)*, everything outside the *cātuṣkoṭika* is a mere *flatus vocis (vāgmātra)*, such as "the son of a barren woman" *(vandhyāputra)* (iii, p. 188). This evidently applies to entities and concepts on the worldly level. The same sūtra adds that the *tathāgata* is beyond *prapañca* and that the *tathāgata* is neither permanent *(nitya)* nor impermanent *(anitya)* (iii, p. 190; v, p. 217). The *tathāgata*

Appendix III. The Logical Error of Negation of the Antecedent and the Mūlamadhyamakakārikās

An extraneous logical problem has been injected by some writers into the discussion of Nāgārjuna's thought when they raise the question of the hypothetical judgement (Nakamura 1958, 9) or hypothetical syllogism (Robinson 1957, 296) when analysing such statements as *MMK* vii.17

> *yadi kaścid anutpanno bhāvaḥ saṃvidyate kvacit /*
> *utpadyeta sa kiṃ tasmin bhāva utpadyate 'sati //*
>
> If any unproduced entity were *found* anywhere it *would* be produced, but when this entity does not exist, what is produced?

MMK x.7

> *anya evêndhanād agnir indhanaṃ kāmam āpnuyāt /*
> *agnīndhane yadi syātām anyonyena tiraskṛte //*
>
> If fire and fuel were mutually independent,[190] fire being other than fuel might well touch the fuel.

or *MMK* xiii.7

> *yady aśūnyaṃ bhavet kiṃcit syāc chūnyam iti kiṃcana /*
> *na kiṃcid asty aśūnyaṃ ca kutaḥ śūnyaṃ bhaviṣyati //*
>
> If something not empty existed, something called "empty" would exist; something not empty does not exist, and how will there [then] exist something empty?

If such statements are regarded as proper hypothetical syllogisms (the form of which is in *modus ponens* $p \supset q. \supset .{\sim}q \supset {\sim}p; \therefore {\sim}p$, and in *modus tollens* $p \supset q; {\sim}q; \therefore {\sim}p$), it indeed turns out that the proposition would have the

is in fact undetermined (*ma nges pa; Mahāparinirvāṇasūtra,* Lha sa ed., kha, fol. 10a–b, quoted in Bu ston's *Mdzes rgyan,* fol. 33a–b; see our *Le traité du tathāgatagarbha de Bu ston Rin chen grub* [Paris, 1973], p. 136).

190. *Anyonyena tiraskṛte* = Tib. *gcig gis gcig ni bsal 'gyur na.* Candrakīrti explains by the concept of dependence.

form $p \supset q; \sim p; \therefore \sim q$. And on this assumption the statement would involve the fallacy of negation of the antecedent, violating the principle of conversion by contraposition (Nakamura 1958, 10; Robinson 1957, 297).

However, there seems to exist no justification for injecting the question of the hypothetical syllogism and the fallacy of negation of the antecedent into the discussion of Nāgārjuna's statements in question. In fact such an interpretation substitutes an altogether extraneous problem, and apparently it has thereby missed Nāgārjuna's point by failing to appreciate what he is saying in terms of his system and methods.

If we apply here the well-known Madhyamaka principle of the complementarity of binary concepts and terms, what Nāgārjuna is saying becomes clear and, in terms of his system, valid: if two opposite concepts or terms stand in a relation of complementary correlation in the framework of dichotomous conceptualization—that is, if they are *pratidvandvins* (Tib. *'gran zla* or *'gal zla*)[191]—the negation of one necessarily involves the negation of the other, without the problem of the antecedent and consequent in a hypothetical syllogism ever arising. Thus *MMK* xiii.7 is parallel to xxii.11 quoted above.[192] It may or may not be the case that Nāgārjuna did not here observe the principle of conversion, as claimed by Nakamura and Robinson; but given Nāgārjuna's evident purpose, his statements in question simply do not allow us to draw a conclusion (and the question is in any case hardly relevant to the analysis and understanding of what Nāgārjuna has said in the passages impugned). We are dealing here not with a schema intended to make possible the deduction or inference of *B* from *A,* but with a nexus of complementary terms which are conceptually, linguistically, and logically, but not causally, interrelated.[193]

191. See Candrakīrti, *PPMV* ii.15 (p. 101.13ff.). Cf. the concept of the *pratipakṣa (gnyen po).* See S. Schayer, *Ausgewählte Kapitel aus der Prasannapadā,* Index s.v. *pratidvandvin;* J. May, *Prasannapadā,* p. 16 and n. 68.

192. Above, p. 55. Cf. for example *MMK* vii.33cd: *saṃskṛtasyâprasiddhau ca kathaṃ setsyaty asaṃskṛtam* "when the conditioned is unestablished, how will one establish the unconditioned?"

193. Robinson (1967, 53) has himself referred to the theory of the *pratidvandvin.* Cf. Robinson's remark in *PEW* 17 (1967), p. 149. (Compare the question of the dilemma discussed by Robinson 1957, 303–4.) It is probably significant that in his work of 1967 Robinson does not advert to this supposed fallacy in the *MMK.*

Bibliography
(Appendices II and III)

Bahm, A. J. (1957) "Does Seven-Fold Predication Equal Four-Cornered Negation Reversed?," in *Philosophy East and West* 7, 127–30.

Chari, C. T. K. (1954) "On the Dialectical Affinities Between East and West II," in *Philosophy East and West* 3/4, 321–36.

Chari, C. T. K. (1955) "Quantum Physics and East-West Rapprochement," in *Philosophy East and West* 5, 61–67.

Chang Chung-yuan (1967) "Ch'an Buddhism: Logical and Illogical," in *Philosophy East and West* 17, 37–49.

Chi, R. S. Y. (1974) "Topics on Being and Logical Reasoning," in *Philosophy East and West* 24, 295–98.

Ichimura Shohei (1973) "Buddhist Thoughts on the Relationship Between Religion and Logical Thinking Especially in Theravāda and Zen," *The Mahā Bodhi* 1973, 42–54.

Jayatilleke, K. N. (1950) "Some Problems of Translation and Interpretation II," in *University of Ceylon Review* 7, 45–55.

Jayatilleke, K. N. (1963) *Early Buddhist Theory of Knowledge* (London: George Allen and Unwin).

Jayatilleke, K. N. (1967) "The Logic of Four Alternatives," in *Philosophy East and West* 17, 69–83.

Kristeva, J. (1969) Σημειωτική *Recherches pour une sémanalyse* (Paris: Editions du Seuil).

Kull, I. and Mjall, L. (1967) "K probleme tetralemmy," in Σημειωτική *Trudy po znakovym sistemam* (Tartu) 3, 60–63.

Kunst, A. (1957) "The Principle of Excluded Middle in Buddhism," in *Rocznik Orientalistyczny* 21, 141–47.

Mäll (Mjall), L. (1965) "Nulevoï put," in Σημειωτική *Trudy po znakovym sistemam* (Tartu) 2, 189–91. English version in: L. Mäll, *Studies in the Aṣṭasāhasrikā Prajñāpāramitā and other essays*, Studia Orientalia Tartuensia, Series Nova, vol. 1 (Tartu, 2003), pp. 13–15.

Mäll (Mjall), L. (1968) "Une approche possible du Śūnyavāda," in *Tel Quel* 32 (Hiver 1968), 54–62 (French version of "Ob odnom vozmožnom podxode k ponimaniju Śūnyavāda," in *Terminologia indica* 1 [Tartu, 1967] 13–24).

Matilal, B. K. (1971) *Epistemology, Logic, and Grammar in Indian Philosophical Analysis* (Janua linguarum, Series minor, 111) (The Hague: Mouton).

Nakamura Hajime (1954) "Kūkan no kigo-ronrigaku-teki ketsumei," in *Indogaku-Bukkyōgaku Kenkyū* 5, 219–31.

Nakamura Hajime (1958) "Buddhist Logic Expounded by Means of Symbolic Logic," in *Indogaku-Bukkyōgaku Kenkyū* 7/1, 1–21.

Raju, P. T. (1954) "The Principle of Four-Cornered Negation in Indian Philosophy," in *Review of Metaphysics* 7, 694–713.

Robinson, R. H. (1957) "Some Logical Aspects of Nāgārjuna's System," in *Philosophy East and West* 6, 291–308.

Robinson, R. H. (1958) "Mysticism and Logic in Sêng-chao's Thought," in *Philosophy East and West* 8, 99–120.

Robinson, R. H. (1967) *Early Mādhyamika in India and China* (Madison: University of Wisconsin Press).

Robinson, R. H. (1969) Review of: K. N. Jayatilleke, *Early Buddhist Theory of Knowledge,* in *Philosophy East and West* 19, 69–81.

Robinson, R. H. (1972) "Some Methodological Approaches to the Unexplained Points," in *Philosophy East and West* 22, 309–23.

Schayer, St. (1931) *Ausgewähle Kapitel aus der Prasannapadā* (Kraków: Polska Akademja Umiejętności, Prace Komisji Orjentalistyznej, No. 14).

Schayer, St. (1933) "Altindische Antizipationen der Aussagenlogik," in *Bulletin de l'Académie Polonaise,* Classe de Philologie, 1933, 90–96.

Seyfort Ruegg, D. (1969) *La théorie du tathāgatagarbha et du gotra* (Publications de l'École française d'Extrême-Orient, volume LXX, Paris: Adrien-Maisonneuve).

Seyfort Ruegg, D. (1971) "On the Knowability and Expressibility of Absolute Reality in Buddhism," in *Indogaku-Bukkyōgaku Kenkyū* 20/1, 1–7.

Staal, J. F. (1962) "Negation and the Law of Contradiction in Indian Thought," in *Bulletin of the School of Oriental and African Studies* 25, 52–71.

Staal, J. F. (1966) "Analyticity," in *Foundations of Language* 2, 89–92.

Staal, J. F. (1975) *Exploring Mysticism* (Berkeley: Univ. of California Press).

4. Le *Dharmadhātustava* de Nāgārjuna*

PARMI LES NOMBREUX écrits attribués par la tradition bouddhique à Nāgārjuna, le grand maître du Mahāyāna que suit l'école des Mādhyamika, plusieurs catégories d'ouvrages se laissent distinguer au point de vue de la forme aussi bien que du fond. En premier lieu il y a l'ouvrage fondamental de Nāgārjuna, les *Mūlamadhyamakakārikā* dont les 27 chapitres traitent des problèmes les plus importants pour la doctrine des Mādhyamika. Et à son côté on range plusieurs traités plus courts consacrés à des exposés portant sur un ou plusieurs aspects de cette doctrine; cinq ouvrages mineurs sont ainsi énumérés par les historiens bouddhistes: la *Yuktiṣaṣṭikā,* la *Śūnyatāsaptati,* la *Vigrahavyāvartanī,* le *Vaidalyaprakaraṇa,* et la *Vyavahārasiddhi* (texte qui n'a pas été inclus dans les recueils des śāstra et auquel on substitue parfois la *Ratnāvalī*).[1] Ces six textes, qui sont censés constituer le corpus des traités scolastiques fondamentaux de l'école des Mādhyamika, sont connus des doxographes bouddhistes comme le groupe des traités fondés sur le raisonnement *(yukti)* ou *rigs tshogs.*[2] Puis il y a une autre catégorie d'ouvrages connue de ces mêmes autorités comme le groupe des discours *(kathā?)* ou *gtam tshogs;* il semble s'agir de textes traitant de la morale et de la bonne conduite, et destinés peut-être surtout aux laïques. On inclut dans cette catégorie l'«Épître amicale» *(Suhṛllekha)* adressée à

* First published in *Études tibétaines dédiées à la mémoire de Marcelle Lalou,* pp. 448–71. Paris: Librairie d'Amérique et d'Orient Adrien Maisonneuve, 1971.

1. Pour une brève description du contenu de ces ouvrages cf. Bu ston, *Chos 'byung,* fol. 19b (Obermiller, I, p. 50–51), et Mkhas grub rje, *Stong thun chen mo,* fol. 35a–36a.—Sur la question de savoir s'il faut mettre la *Ratnāvalī* à la place de la *Vyavahārasiddhi* v. Mkhas grub rje, *Rgyud sde spyi rnam,* fol. 24a–b (Lessing-Wayman, p. 86). Voir aussi Tsong kha pa, *Legs bshad gser phreng,* I, fol. 4a, et ci-dessous.

2. Voir les différentes histoires de la philosophie bouddhique *(Grub mtha'),* qui s'appuient notamment sur ce que Candrakīrti écrit dans l'autocommentaire de son *Madhyamakāvatāra* vi.3.

un certain roi Udayana(bhadra);[3] Nāgārjuna figure d'ailleurs comme l'un des ascètes chargés des affaires du royaume *(yatayo rājyavṛttinaḥ).*[4] Et il est possible d'y ajouter d'autres écrits traitant de morale et de *nīti* comme le *Prajñāśataka,* le *Jantupoṣaṇabindu* et le *Prajñādaṇḍa.* Dans cette même catégorie on peut classer aussi la *Ratnāvalī* puisque, comme le montre son titre complet de *Rājaparikathā-Ratnāvalī,* il s'agit d'une instruction composée pour un roi et que son quatrième chapitre s'intitule le Rājavṛttopadeśa «instruction sur la fonction royale»;[5] cependant, comme on vient de le voir, dans certaines listes la *Ratnāvalī* figure au nombre des six traités scolastiques de Nāgārjuna, classification que justifie le contenu essentiellement philosophique de l'ouvrage dans son ensemble.[6] Enfin, la troisième catégorie d'ouvrages attribués à Nāgārjuna se compose d'hymnes *(stava* et *stotra),* et elle est donc connue comme le groupe des hymnes *(bstod tshogs).*

Cette classification tripartite, qui est à la fois formelle et synchronique, ne tient compte qu'assez imparfaitement de l'histoire de la philosophie et de la relation entre les traités scolastiques *(rigs tshogs)* et les hymnes *(bstod tshogs).* La question se pose donc de savoir si tous ces ouvrages—ou à tout le moins

3. V. H. Wenzel, Bçes pai phrin yig, *JPTS* 1886, p. 1–32; S. Beal, *The Suhṛillekha* (Londres, 1892).

Sur Bde spyod (bzang po)/Udayana(bhadra) = Sātavāhana (Śāta°) ~ *Antivāhana/ Mthar 'gro zhon cf. les colophons du Bstan 'gyur (P), Mdo 'grel, tome gi, n° 32 *(Suhṛllekha),* et tome nge, n° 35 *(Suhṛllekhaṭīkā);* Bu ston, *Chos 'byung,* fol. 100b (II, p. 127); la note de Wassiljew in A. Schiefner, *Tāranātha's Geschichte des Buddhismus,* p. 303. Cf. aussi Bāṇa, *Harṣacarita* (chap. VIII).

Selon Yi-tsing, le destinataire du *Suhṛllekha* fut un certain roi Jetaka; v. J. Takakusu, *Record of the Buddhist Religion* (Oxford, 1896), p. 158, et S. Lévi, Kaniṣka et Sātavāhana, *JA* 1936, p. 107, sur Jetaka et Śātavāhana.

4. V. *Mañjuśrīmūlakalpa* 53.867.

5. Selon Ajitamitra, le commentateur de la *Ratnāvalī,* le destinataire de cet ouvrage fut le même Bde spyod à qui Nāgārjuna envoya le *Suhṛllekha.* Selon Bu ston la *Ratnavalī* fut adressée à Jetaka ~ Jitaka (v. *Chos 'byung,* fol, 99a [II, p. 125]).

6. Mentionnons en outre l'existence d'un autre type de *kathā (gtam)* qui aurait des liens avec Nāgārjuna, les contes du Vetāla. Bien qu'aucune version indienne ne soit connue où Nāgārjuna et son ami le roi Bde spyod bzang po jouent un rôle, dans des versions tibétaines et mongoles—le *Ro sgrung* et le *Siditü kegür (Siddhi kür)*—ils sont les principaux personnages dans le récit cadre et ailleurs. En tibétain ces contes s'appellent *gtam rgyud.* Bien que ces contes aient un caractère édifiant qui leur a fait jouer un rôle important dans l'instruction religieuse au Tibet, ils n'ont pas trouvé une place dans le Bstan 'gyur. Peut-être la connexion de ces contes avec Nāgārjuna s'explique-t-elle, au moins en partie, par le fait qu'ils se rapportent à la production de l'or par un procédé «alchimique», au moyen du *vetāla,* Nāgārjuna étant souvent considéré comme un alchimiste (voir ci-dessous, n. 22).

les ouvrages les plus importants dans chaque catégorie—peuvent être mis au compte d'un seul et même auteur, car les textes en question diffèrent non seulement par leur forme littéraire mais aussi au point de vue doctrinal.

Si la tradition historiographique et doxographique du bouddhisme ne semble pas avoir conservé un souvenir précis de l'existence de plusieurs maîtres ayant porté le nom de Nāgārjuna parmi lesquels il faudrait répartir les écrits en question, elle n'en fait pas moins état de trois périodes distinctes dans l'activité du Bodhisattva Nāgārjuna, qu'elle considère comme une seule et même personne dont la vie n'aurait pas duré moins de plusieurs siècles.[7]

Selon une tradition qui s'appuie sur certaines écritures canoniques mahāyānistes renfermant des prophéties *(vyākaraṇa)* touchant l'avenir de la Loi, dans les 400 ans après le *nirvāṇa* du Buddha Nāgārjuna prit naissance dans le Sud de l'Inde[8] et pendant 100 ans il œuvra pour le bien des gens; c'est alors qu'eut lieu ce qu'on a appelé sa première grande proclamation de la Loi *(chos kyi sgra chen po)*.[9] Les sources ne donnent pas de précisions concernant les

7. Il est vrai que quelques sources parlent d'un certain Nāgāhvaya différent de Nāgārjuna. Ainsi, selon Tāranātha (*Rgya gar chos 'byung,* p. 66 et 68), il fut un contemporain d'Āryadeva et serait identique à Tathāgatabhadra; selon cet historien et Sum pa mkhan po (*Dpag bsam ljon bzang,* p. 89–90), il fut un disciple de Nāgārjuna. Les mêmes autorités précisent qu'il soutint le Vijñapti-Madhyamaka *(rnam rig gi dbu ma* ou *rnam rig pa'i dbu ma)*; et Tāranātha nous dit même qu'il composa un hymne au *garbha (snying po'i bstod pa)*. Il est donc possible que cette différenciation constitue, dans la tradition tibétaine, la trace d'une distinction entre plusieurs Nāgārjuna. Cependant, le *Kāyatrayastotra* que Tāranātha lui attribue (p. 68) est de Nāgārjuna lui-même selon le Bstan 'gyur. Un Nāgāhvaya est mentionné dans le *Laṅkāvatārasūtra,* Sagāthaka 165; dans son autocommentaire du *Madhyamakāvatāra* (vi.3, p. 76) Candrakīrti cite ce vers en le mettant en rapport avec Nāgārjuna, comme le fait Bu ston (*Chos 'byung,* 94b [II, p. 110]). Voir aussi *Mañjuśrīmūlakalpa* 53.449 et 869 (avec Bu ston, *Chos 'byung,* fol. 94b–95a et 95b [II, p. 111 et 113]); *Mahāmeghasūtra* cité par Candrakīrti, *op. cit.,* vi.3, (p. 76–77: Klu zhes bya ba); Nāropā, *Sekoddeśaṭīkā,* p. 57 (v. *infra,* n. 46).

8. Plusieurs sources précisent qu'il naquit au Vidarbha (Berār); v. Bu ston, *Chos 'byung,* fol. 98b; Tāranātha, *Bka' babs bdun lda,* p. 2; Sum pa mkhan po, *Dpag bsam ljon bzang,* p. 85.

9. V. le *Mahāmeghasūtra* cité dans *Madhyamakāvatāra* vi.3 (p. 76–77) (le chiffre de 400 ans manque dans la version de ce sūtra dans le Bka' 'gyur [H], fol. 294a–295a); *Mañjuśrīmūlakalpa* 53.449. —Cf. P. Demiéville, *BEFEO (*1924), p. 227; G. Tucci, Animadversiones indicae, *JASB* 26 (1931), p. 146 (et S. Lévi, *BSOS* 6 [1930–32], p. 417–29). Sur la relation du *Mahāmeghasūtra* avec Nāgārjuna v. R. Hikata, *Suvikrāntavikrāmiparipṛcchā* (Fukuoka, 1958), p. LVI–LVII, qui discute le problème posé par le fait qu'un *Mahāmeghasūtra* est mentionné dans le *Ta tche tou louen* attribué à Nāgārjuna.

Notons cependant que Bu ston écrit (*Chos 'byung,* fol. 101a [II, p. 129–30]) qu'il n'est pas clairement établi que le *Mahāmeghasūtra* se réfère à Nāgārjuna, et qu'il faut

traités composés par Nāgārjuna à cette occasion; et elles se bornent à dire qu'il purifia alors la communauté des moines *(saṃgha)* en frappant de suspension *(bskrad pa = pravāsanīya)* des bhikṣu coupables d'infractions à leur règle, et qu'il conféra à un certain moine nommé Bde byed (Śaṃkara?) les douze *dhūtaguṇa.*[10] Puisqu'il s'agit donc d'une activité portant sur la discipline monastique et sur la morale, il serait peut-être possible de mettre cette première période de l'activité de Nāgārjuna en rapport avec au moins certains ouvrages du *gtam tshogs,* dont on dit qu'ils traitaient de la morale et de la bonne conduite laïque. A la fin de cette période qui dura 100 ans, Nāgārjuna se rendit, selon la même tradition, au royaume des Nāga, où il séjourna pendant 100 ans; il y obtint les Prajñāpāramitāsūtra, qui avaient été inaccessibles dans le Jambudvīpa depuis peu de temps après le *nirvāṇa* du Buddha, et les apporta au Jambudvīpa méridional où il avait vécu auparavant.[11] Son deuxième séjour au Jambudvīpa, qui comme le premier dura 100 ans, vit la prédication des Écritures que Nāgārjuna eut rapportées du royaume des Nāga ainsi que la composition de ses traités scolastiques *(rigs tshogs)* où il expliqua l'enseignement de ces sūtra; c'était donc sa deuxième grande proclamation de la Loi, laquelle fut ainsi consacrée à la doctrine de la *śūnyatā.*[12] Ensuite, après avoir prédit en l'an 700 p.N. au jeune garçon Jetaka (ou Jitaka) qu'il serait un jour un grand roi, Nāgārjuna disparut de nouveau, cette fois dans l'Uttarakuru; et dans ce continent septentrional il passa 200 ans[13] avant de revenir une dernière fois au Jambudvīpa méridional,

---

examiner la question de savoir si le *Mahābherīsūtra* se réfère à lui. (M. Tucci estime que le *Mahāmegha* ne se réfère effectivement pas, dans sa version tibétaine, au fondateur de l'école des Mādhyamika; v. *ibid.,* p. 146–47.)

10. Cf. *Mahābherīsūtra* (H, fol. 201a7): *rung ba ma yin pa'i gzhi chen po yongs su spangs te chos chen po sgrog pa.* Cf. 'Jam dbyangs bzhad pa, *Dbu ma chen mo,* fol. 195b–196a, et *Grub mtha' chen mo,* ca, fol. 5a–b.

Sur la purification du Saṃgha par Nāgārjuna v. *Grub mtha' chen mo,* ca, fol. 5a4–b1; Sum pa mkhan po, *Dpag bsam ljon bzang,* p. 86.17–18. Selon Bu ston, Tāranātha, *Bka' babs bdun ldan,* p. 4.23, et Sum pa mkhan po, le moine Bde byed fut un ennemi du Mahāyāna et l'auteur du *Rig rgyan* (cf. *Rgya gar chos 'byung,* p. 57).

11. Cf. *Grub mtha' chen mo,* ca, fol. 3b4–5 (qui renvoie au *Mahāmeghasūtra).* Selon Bu ston, *Chos 'byung,* fol. 99b4 et 71a (II, p. 124 et 50), et Tāranātha, *Bka' babs bdun ldan,* p. 4.21, quelques sections manquaient à cette *Prajñāpāramitā* rapportée par Nāgārjuna.

12. C'est le *stong pa nyid kyi gtam* (*Mahābherīsūtra,* H, fol. 202a1) ou le *theg chen gyi stong nyid kyi chos sgra* (*Dbu ma chen mo,* fol. 196a) = *theg chen gyi stong nyid kyi gtam gyi chos sgra chen po* (*ibid.,* fol. 195b).

13. Tāranātha (*Bka' babs bdun ldan,* p. 5.5) et Sum pa mkhan po (*Dpag bsam ljon bzang,* p. 86.15) parlent de 12 ans.

où Jetaka régnait comme le grand roi Udayana-Sātavāhana. De ce voyage au Nord Nāgārjuna rapporta de nouveau des Écritures canoniques, cette fois-ci le *Mahābherīsūtra* et le *Mahāmeghasūtra* qui sont les deux principales sources scripturaires qui nous renseignent sur ces trois périodes dans l'activité de Nāgārjuna sous la forme de *vyākaraṇa* touchant l'avenir de la Loi; puis il diffusa ces sūtra, et pour les expliquer il composa un groupe d'hymnes *(bstod tshogs)* dont le *Dharmadhātustava* est considéré comme l'un des plus importants. C'était la troisième grande proclamation de la Loi remplissant les 100 dernières années de sa vie.[14] Selon cette tradition biographique quelque peu schématique la vie de Nāgārjuna dura donc 600 ans au total.[15]

Selon 'Jam dbyangs bzhad pa, l'auteur du *Grub mtha' chen mo* et l'un des meilleurs historiens de la philosophie bouddhique, cette dernière proclamation a pour thème principal l'existence chez tous les êtres animés de l'Élément spirituel *(khams = dhātu)* du *buddha.* Or, comme cette autorité considère que le *dhātu* est identique à la *śūnyatā,* la troisième proclamation serait essentiellement en harmonie avec la deuxième proclamation relative à la *śūnyatā,* et avec le deuxième cycle de la prédication du Buddha consistant en les Prajñāpāramitāsūtra;[16] mais à la différence de la deuxième proclamation, et du deuxième cycle de la prédication, la troisième proclamation de Nāgārjuna enseigne, comme le font certains sūtra du troisième cycle, que le *buddha* est permanent par continuité,[17] et qu'au sens certain *(nītārtha)*

14. C'est le *sems can gyi khams rtag pa'i gtam (Mahābherīsūtra,* fol. 202a1, cité dans *Grub mtha' chen mo,* ca, fol. 6b, qui porte *btags pa* [lire *brtags pa*] au lieu de *rtag pa)* ou le *khams brtags pa'i gtam* (*Dbu ma chen mo,* fol. 196b5). Cf. *Mañjuśrīmūlakalpa* 53.450: *nānāśāstrārthadhātvartham niḥsvabhāvatattvavit.*

Sur les trois *chos kyi sgra* cf. aussi *Mahāmeghasūtra,* H, fol. 284b4, 297a3, 299al; Sum pa mkhan po, *Dpag bsam ljon bzang,* p. 86.

15. Cf. *Mañjuśrīmūlakalpa* 53.449; Bu ston, *Chos 'byung,* fol. 100b1 (II, p. 127); *Grub mtha' chen mo,* ca, fol. 4a3, 6a–b.

Tāranātha se réfère à un comput différent; v. *Bka' babs bdun ldan,* p. 5.10, et *Rgya gar chos 'byung,* p. 58; Sum pa mkan po, *Dpag bsam ljon bzang,* p. 86.16. Cf. E. Lamotte, Sur la formation du Mahāyāna, *Asiatica* (Festschrift F. Weller, Leipzig, 1954), p. 388.

16. 'Jam dbyangs bzhad pa, *Grub mtha' chen mo,* ca, fol. 6a–b. Cf. *Dbu ma chen mo,* fol. 196a.

17. **prabandhanitya (rgyun gyi rtag pa),* à l'opposé de *kūṭasthanitya* «permanent de façon absolue et immuable» (comme le *puruṣa* du Sāṃkhya ou le *brahman* du Vedānta etc.) et aussi de *pariṇāminitya* «permanent dans ses transformations matérielles» (comme la *prakṛti* du Sāṃkhya).—Sur la *prabandhanityatā v. Mahāyānasūtrālaṃkāra* ix.66 au sujet du *nirmāṇakāya.*

il n'entre pas dans l'extinction.[18] 'Jam dbyangs bzhad pa considère donc que la doctrine du *Dharmadhātustava* est conforme à l'enseignement du *Dhāraṇīśvararājasūtra* et du *Ratnagotravibhāga* relatif au *(tathāgata)dhātu* et au *tathāgatagarbha.*[19]

De ce résumé de la légende de Nāgārjuna il ressort que la tradition bouddhique n'était pas insensible aux problèmes posés par la vie de Nāgārjuna et par la variété des ouvrages qui lui sont attribués. Il va sans dire que seuls les aspects doctrinaux et systématiques de la question ainsi que l'hagiographie revêtaient une importance capitale pour cette tradition, qui prenait peu d'intérêt à l'histoire et à la biographie au sens moderne. Mais il demeure que la tradition historiographique et doxographique faisant état de trois périodes distinctes dans l'activité de Nāgārjuna qui sont échelonnées dans le temps et qui diffèrent par leurs doctrines rejoint, au moins partiellement, les conclusions auxquelles ont abouti des historiens modernes du bouddhisme; car ceux-ci ont aussi distingué entre l'auteur des traités scolastiques, qui vécut entre le Ie et le IIIe siècle[20] et fonda l'école des Mādhyamika, et un ou plusieurs maîtres plus récents ayant porté le même nom et auxquels on incline généralement à attribuer les

18. Voir plus loin, n. 60.

19. *Grub mtha' chen mo,* ca, fol. 6b: *'dir chos dbyings bstod pa rgyud bla ma gzungs rgyal gyi mdo rnams kyi don ston lugs 'dra bar kho bo smra la de yang 'di rnams kyis sems can thams cad la 'tshang rgya ba'i khams yod cing/ de yang stong nyid la 'jog pa dang/ mthar thug theg pa gcig tu bsgrub pas 'khor lo bar pa dang mthun kyang sangs rgyas la rgyun gyi rtag pa dang/ mya ngan las nges don mi 'da' tshul byas par chos kyi sgra gnyis pa las zur du gsum par byas so//*

Bu ston observe que si le raisonnement *(yukti)* prédomine dans les traités scolastiques de Nāgārjuna, ses stotra et stava reposent directement sur l'Écriture *(āgama)* *(Chos 'byung,* fol. 100a: *lta ba gtso bor ston pa la mtha' bral gyi dbu ma lung gis ston pa dbu ma bstod pa'i skor/ rigs pas ston pa rigs pa'i skor* «pour ce qui est de l'enseignement consacré principalement à la théorie, le cycle des hymnes du Madhyamaka enseigne par l'*āgama* du Madhyamaka et le cycle du raisonnement enseigne par la *yukti»).*

20. Les opinions des historiens diffèrent sur la date de Nāgārjuna. On le place tantôt au Ier s. (v. S. Lévi, *JA* 1936, p. 61–121; S. Bailey, *Śatapañcāśatka of Mātṛceṭa* [Cambridge, 1951], p. 9); tantôt au IIe siècle (v. M. Winternitz, *History of Indian Literature,* II [Calcutta, 1933], p. 342; E. Lamotte, *Le traité de la Grande Vertu de Sagesse* [Louvain, 1944], p. x; T. R. V. Murti, *Central Philosophy of Buddhism* [Londres, 1955], p. 87); et tantôt au IIIe siècle (v. M. Walleser, Life of Nāgārjuna, *Asia Major, Hirt Anniversary Vol.* [1923], p. 423; E. Frauwallner, *Philosophie des Buddhismus* [Berlin, 1936], p. 170 [um 200 n.u.Z.]). Mgr. E. Lamotte a récemment opté pour la chronologie de l'école de Kumārajīva, qui place Nāgārjuna et son disciple Āryadeva dans les 800 ans p. N., c'est-à-dire au IIIe siècle de l'ère chrétienne; v. *L'enseignement de Vimalakīrti* (Louvain, 1962), p. 74–77. Cf. R. H. Robinson, *Early Mādhyamika in India and China* (Madison, 1967), p. 22 et suiv.

ouvrages tântriques, médicaux[21] et alchimiques[22] rattachés par la tradition au nom de Nāgārjuna.[23] Ainsi donc il n'est pas impossible que la tradition relative aux trois périodes dans l'activité de Nāgārjuna traduise à sa façon une réalité historique et doctrinale; et la classification des ouvrages attribués à Nāgārjuna en trois catégories semble bien recouvrir grosso modo les différences non seulement littéraires mais aussi doctrinales qu'on constate en lisant ces textes.[24] Au demeurant, il ne faut pas perdre de vue le fait que les maîtres qui ont transmis ces traditions étaient au moins aussi sensibles que nous aux différences doctrinales entre certains des ouvrages en question et, partant, aux problèmes d'exégèse historico-systématique posés par ceux-ci. Certes, nos sources sont loin de parler le même langage que l'historien moderne; mais si l'on est trop prompt à en écarter le témoignage, qui somme toute n'est pas sans intérêt, on risque de se priver d'indices qui peuvent être utiles lorsqu'on cherche à apprécier la pensée de Nāgārjuna ou à extraire l'essentiel de l'affabulation légendaire qui entoure sa Vie.

Pourtant, le simple fait d'admettre l'existence de plusieurs Nāgārjuna et de distinguer le grand fondateur de l'école des Mādhyamika des maîtres plus tardifs qui ont pu porter le même nom et subir l'influence plus ou moins forte d'un Mahāyāna plus avancé ainsi que du Vajrayāna ne résout nullement le problème posé par la multiplicité et la variété des ouvrages qui lui sont attribués; et dans plusieurs cas il reste malaisé de dire auquel de ces Nāgārjuna il faudrait attribuer tel texte.

21. Cf. Bu ston, *Chos 'byung,* fol. 100a5 (II, p. 126); J. Filliozat, *L'inde classique* § 1628, 1635, 1662; P. Ch. Rây, *History of Chemistry in Ancient and Medieval India,* ed. P. Rây (Calcutta, 1956), p. 61.

22. Cf. Bu ston, *Chos 'byung,* fol. 100a6–7 (II, p. 126); J. Filliozat, *L'inde classique,* § 1690; Rây, *History of Chemistry,* p. 116 et suiv. (qui situe l'alchimiste au VIIe–VIIIe s.). Voir aussi S. Lévi, *JA* 1936, p. 104–6; M. Eliade, *Le Yoga* (Paris, 1960), p. 277, 398.

23. Voir en dernier É. Lamotte, *Le traité,* p. xi, et Sur la formation du Mahāyāna, p. 388; Mgr. Lamotte envisage la possibilité de distinguer entre quatre Nāgārjuna différents. Sur le tāntrika (qu'on incline à placer au VIIe s.) v. S. Lévi, *BSOS* 6 (1930–32), p. 417–29; G. Tucci, *JRASB* 26 (1930), p. 138–55, et *Tibetan Painted Scrolls* (Rome, 1949), p. 214, 231; H. Hoffmann, *Beiträge zur indischen Philologie und Altertumskunde* (Festschrift Schubring, Hamburg, 1951), p. 142.

24. Dans le cas parallèle de Candrakīrti les autorités tibétaines distinguent entre les ouvrages relevant d'une phase des sūtra *(mdo skabs)* et ceux qui appartiennent à une phase des tantra *(rgyud skabs).* Cette distinction semble bien traduire dans des termes synchroniques et systématiques la différence historique et biographique entre le maître de l'école des Prāsaṅgika-Mādhyamika qui composa la *Prasannapadā* et le *Madhyamakāvatāra,* et le tāntrika qui composa le *Pradīpoddyotana* sur le *Guhyasamājatantra.*

Les *Mūlamadhyamakakārikā* sont en grande partie une critique des philosophèmes courants au début de l'ère chrétienne dans les écoles bouddhiques et non bouddhiques de l'Inde. Et même lorsque Nāgārjuna y expose les principes fondamentaux des Mādhyamika il adopte normalement la voie de la négation ou du «silence méthodique», si bien que ses adversaires indiens aussi bien que plusieurs historiens modernes l'ont souvent considéré, sans doute à tort, comme un simple nihiliste. Mais quelques savants récents n'ont pas manqué de signaler le contenu positif de sa théorie et d'insister sur son caractère «absolutiste»; et St. Schayer a notamment cru pouvoir attribuer le *Dharmadhātustava* à l'auteur des *Mūlamadhyamakakārikā,* car il considérait la doctrine de celui-ci comme une combinaison de mystique absolutiste avec une dialectique tenant à la fois de la négation et de l'*epoché.*[25] Pourtant, si le *Dharmadhātustava* est à considérer comme un ouvrage authentique de l'auteur des *Kārikā,* sa forme hymnique aussi bien que son contenu doctrinal ne laissent pas de surprendre à première vue; et encore que cet hymne soit adressé à un principe aussi impersonnel et abstrait que le *dharmadhātu,*[26] on serait peut-être plutôt enclin, au premier abord du moins, à placer à une époque sensiblement plus tardive de l'histoire de l'école des Mādhyamika la composition d'un hymne où le *dharmadhātu* figure comme la réalité absolue positive susceptible d'être qualifiée d'une façon non apophatique et quasi substantialiste.[27]

* * * *

Considérons d'abord brièvement le rôle du genre hymnique dans la littérature ancienne du Mahāyāna ainsi que quelques motifs qui ont pu présider au choix de ce genre. Au début de plusieurs manuscrits des Prajñāpāramitāsūtra on trouve un hymne adressé à la *prajñāpāramitā* et attribué à Rāhulabhadra, qui passe pour être le maître de Nāgārjuna.[28] Parce que la *prajñāpāramitā*

25. St. Schayer, Das mahāyānistische Absolutum, *OLZ (*1935), col. 402 et 406; cf. C. Regamey, *Three Chapters from the Samādhirājasūtra* (Varsovie, 1938), p. 25; K. Venkata Ramanan, *Nāgārjuna's Philosophy as Presented in the Mahā-Prajñāpāramitā-Śāstra* (Rutland et Tokyo, 1966), p. 37, 368a; R. H. Robinson, *Early Mādhyamika,* p. 27.

26. V. v.1, 89–90.

27. Sur le point de vue plus «positif» du *Ta tche tou louen* attribué à Nāgārjuna (mais dont des portions au moins sont probablement d'autres auteurs), v. K. Venkata Ramanan, *Nāgārjuna's Philosophy,* p. 16, 44–45, 251 et suiv.

28. V. *Aṣṭasāhasrikā* (éd. Mitra), p. 3; *Pañcaviṃśatisāhasrikā* (version de Dutt), p. 3; *Suvikrāntavikrāmiparipṛcchā* (éd. Hikata, p. 2; cf. l'introduction de l'éditeur, p. LXXI). La version chinoise incorporée dans le *Ta tche tou louen* a été traduite par Lamotte (*Le traité,* p. 1060 et suiv.), qui attribue l'hymne au maître du fondateur de l'école des Mādhyamika

est—tout comme le *dharmadhātu*—transcendante, inconcevable, ineffable, etc. *(nirvikalpā, sudurbodhā, niṣprapañcā, nirakṣarā),* l'auteur de cet hymne dit que c'est seulement par le truchement d'un langage conventionnel qu'il pourrait louer Celle qui est vraiment sans marque distinctive et qui surpasse donc toute louange (19–20):

śaktas kas tvām iha stotuṃ nirnimittāṃ nirañjanām /
sarvavāgviṣayātītāṃ yā tvaṃ kvacid aniśritā //
saty evam api saṃvṛtyā vākpathair vayam īdṛśaiḥ //
tvām astutyām api stutvā tustūṣantaḥ sunirvṛtāḥ //[29]

Du reste, c'est en recourant au langage conventionnel, et en vue des désignations nécessaires pour l'instruction des êtres incarnés, que les Maîtres du monde, par compassion, ont eux aussi parlé de la *prajñāpāramitā,* mais sans en parler en fait (18):

vyavahāraṃ puraskṛtya prajñaptyarthaṃ śarīriṇām /
kṛpayā lokanāthais tvam ucyase ca na côcyase //

Et dans une autre stance il est dit que sans la voir de telle ou telle manière[30] on recourt *(prapad-)* selon sa nature (? *bhāva*)[31] à la *prajñāpāramitā* et qu'on trouve alors la libération, ce qui est une très grande merveille (14):

ye tvām evaṃ na paśyanti prapadyante ca bhāvataḥ /
prapadya ca vimucyante tad idaṃ mahad adbhutam //[32]

(v. *L'enseignement de Vimalakīrti,* p. 76–77). Dans la traduction tibétaine incluse dans le Bstan 'gyur, Bstod tshogs, l'hymne est cependant attribué à Nāgārjuna.—Cf. G. Tucci, *JRASB* 26 (1930), p. 141; W. Baruch, *AM* 3 (1953), p. 112.

29. Cf. *Aṣṭasāhasrikā,* chapitres III–IV, et *Abhisamayālaṃkāra* ii.18–19 avec le commentaire de Haribhadra.

30. Hikata lit *eva* au lieu de *evam.*

31. Dans le *Dharmasaṃgraha* (75) le *bhāva* est énuméré comme un des *bala* du bodhisattva, à côté de la *pratipatti (sgrub pa;* voir la note suivante). Le mot *bhāva* a plusieurs sens, ceux qui entrent en ligne de compte ici étant surtout: nature, disposition et inclination mentale *(bsam pa : āśaya).* Dans la littérature sanskrite le mot s'emploie au sens d'«état» mental ou physique (sentiment, émotion; affection, amour; geste, comportement) ainsi qu'au sens de cœur ou esprit (le siège de ces «états»).

32. La version tibétaine de ce vers dans le Bstod tshogs du Bstan 'gyur est (P, fol. 88a): *gang khyod de ltar ma 'khums nas // bsam pa yis ni bsgrubs pa dang // bsgrubs pa las ni rnam grol ba // de 'dir rmad byung chen po lags //* Ainsi le verbe *prapad-* a été traduit par

Le même problème de la louange et, partant, de la description de la Réalité absolue indescriptible est mentionné par Nāgārjuna lui-même dans son «Hymne au Sans-pareil».[33] Dans ce *Niraupamyastava* il observe que le Buddha est vu dans les mondes innombrables par ses fidèles *(bhaktāḥ = gus rnams)* qui sont attachés *(lālasāḥ = mos rnams)* à l'idée des actes que le Buddha y a accomplis, à savoir son départ du ciel Tuṣita pour entrer dans la matrice de sa mère, sa naissance, son Éveil, sa prédication de la Loi, et son *nirvāṇa* (23):

> *lokadhātuṣv ameyeṣu tvadbhaktaiḥ punar īkṣyase /*
> *cyutijanmābhisambodhicakranirvr̥tilālasaiḥ //*

Et c'est ainsi que, dans son hymne, l'auteur se fait fort de répandre sur le Buddha vraiment inconcevable et incommensurable les «fleurs des qualités» (25ab):

> *iti sugatam acintyam aprameyaṃ guṇakusumair avakīrya . . .* [34]

Pareillement, dans son «Hymne au Véritable», Nāgārjuna précise que l'Absolu tel qu'il est n'est accessible que dans le seul domaine du sens de l'Ainsité, mais qu'il va pourtant le louer, en tant que *guru,* avec *bhakti (gus pa)* en recourant aux désignations conventionnelles de l'usage ordinaire (*Paramārthastava* 1–2):

> *kathaṃ stoṣyāmi te nātham anutpannam anālayam /*
> *lokopamām atikrāntaṃ vākpathātītagocaram //*
> *tathâpi yādr̥śo vâsi tathatārtheṣu gocaraḥ /*
> *lokaprajñaptim āgamya stoṣye 'ham bhaktito gurum //*[35]

---

sgrub pa «réaliser»; et *bhāva* a été rendu par *bsam pa* (qui peut aussi traduire *āśaya* «disposition d'esprit», etc.).—Cette stance manque dans le *Ta tche tou louen* (Lamotte, *Le traité,* p. 1064.)

33. Le *Niraupamyastava* (ou *Nirupamastava*) a été édité par G. Tucci, *JRAS* (1932), p. 312–20. (Le vers 13 de l'hymne est cité dans la *Prasannapadā* de Candrakīrti.)

34. Cf. Mātr̥ceṭa, *Varṇārhavarṇastotra,* Aśakyastava 22: *pracīya guṇapuṣpāni tvanmatād eva paṭalāt/ phullaṃ tvâvakariṣyāmi taruṃ svakusumair iva//* (v. S. Bailey, *BSOAS* 13 [1949–50], p. 676; B. Pauly, *JA* 1964, p. 246), «Ayant cueilli les fleurs des qualités de la collection (?) qu'est ta doctrine, je te couvrirai de fleurs, comme un arbre de ses propres fleurs». Voir aussi v. 23–24 (ci-dessous).

35. Selon le commentaire d'Amr̥tākara (*Samāsārtha,* éd. G. Tucci, *Minor Buddhist Texts*

Encore qu'il ne puisse pas être vraiment loué, l'absolu est néanmoins à louer par une telle louange. Mais tous les *dharma* étant vides *(śūnya),* qui est loué, et par qui? En fait, on ne saurait louer ce qui est sans naissance, sans destruction, sans limites spatiales, etc. (9–10):

evaṃ stute stuto bhūyās athavā kiṃ bata stutaḥ /[36]
śūnyeṣu sarvadharmeṣu kaḥ stutaḥ kena vā stutaḥ //
kas tvāṃ śaknoti saṃstotum utpādavyayavarjitam /
yasya nânto na madhyaṃ vā grāho grāhyaṃ na vidyate //[37]

Presque à la même époque où vécut le fondateur de l'école des Mādhyamika un des plus grands poètes bouddhistes, Mātṛceṭa, qui a incorporé un Nirupamastava dans son *Śatapañcāśatka,* met en œuvre le paradoxe et d'autres procédés de la poétique pour être en mesure de louer le Buddha, qui est en réalité au-delà de toute louange. Et dans sa «Louange de Celui qui ne saurait être loué» (Aśakyastava), le premier hymne d'une collection dédiée à «Celui qui est digne de louange tout en étant vraiment inaccessible à la louange», Mātṛceṭa écrit (*Varṇārhavarṇastotra* i.9 et 12):

sa kenôpanayāmi tvânupameyo 'si nāyaka /
hṛtopamāvakāśāya namo 'stv anupamāya te //
kaḥ saṃkhyāsyaty asaṃkhyeyān ko 'prameyān pramāsyati /
na hi saṃkhyāprabhāvābhyāṃ vyavasthâsti guṇeṣu te //

I, p. 245), le vers 2 introduit la réponse à une objection consistant à dire que l'Absolu est ineffable, cette réponse étant donnée au point de vue de la relativité *(saṃvṛti).*

36. Amṛtākara (ibid., p. 245) lit *evaṃ stute stuto bhūyās,* et explique: *saṃvṛtyeti śeṣaḥ, 'athavā kiṃ bata stutaḥ' paramārthena.*

37. Selon Amṛtākara (ibid., p. 245–46), à partir du vers 10 du *Paramārthastava* Nāgārjuna montre que la louange est impossible même au point de vue de la relativité: *idānīṃ saṃvṛtyâpi stuter asambhavaṃ pratipādayann āha 'kas tvaṃ śaknoti saṃstotum' ityādi/ utpādavyayavarjito bhagavān/ stotā côtpādavyayayuktaḥ/ anādyantamadhyo bhagavān/ sa ca trikāṇḍapratītyasamutpādasaṃgṛhītaḥ/ grāhakagrāhyanirmukto bhagavān/ sa ca grāhake grāhye ca caratîti/ saṃvṛtyâpi bhūtaguṇākhyānarūpāyāḥ stuter asambhavaḥ/ acintyapratītyasamutpādadharmatayā saty advaye 'pi prakṛter abhāvād iti// svabhāvapariśuddhyadhimuktyâpi vastuno 'nupalambhena pravṛttas tu mahāphala iti/ mahān asambhavo bhavatîti pratyetavyam//*

Cf. le *Stutyatītastava* 1 (P, fol. 91a): *bla med lam las gshegs pa yi // de bzhin gshegs pa bstod 'das kyang // gus shong spro ba'i sems kyi ni // bdag gis bstod 'das bstod par bgyid //; Pañcakrama* iii.1 (éd. La Vallée Poussin): *evaṃ stute namas te 'stu kaḥ stotā kaś ca saṃstutaḥ//*

> Comment te présenterai-je? O Seigneur, tu es incomparable; hommage à toi qui ne donnes pas de prise à la louange et qui es sans comparaison.—Qui dénombrera [tes qualités] innombrables, qui mesurera [tes qualités] incommensurables? Car en vertu de leur nombre et de leur pouvoir tes qualités ne font pas l'objet d'une délimitation.[38]

Et Mātṛceṭa d'ajouter plus loin (23–24):

> *svaratnair ākaram iva svadhātubhir ivâcalam /*
> *candanaṃ svarasenêva saraḥ svajalajair iva //*
> *guṇais tvâbhyarcayiṣyāmi tvanmatād eva nirhṛtaiḥ /*
> *svanirvāntena hemnêva kāñcanaṣṭhīvinaṃ maṇim //*

> Telle une mine [qu'on compare uniquement] avec ses propres pierres précieuses, telle une montagne [métallifère] avec ses propres minerais, tel le santal avec sa propre essence, tel un lac avec ses propres lotus, je te célébrerai avec les qualités prises à ta doctrine elle-même—à l'instar de la pierre précieuse qui émet l'or [et qui est seulement comparable] avec l'or qu'elle a elle-même émis.[39]

En effet, seul le *dharma* du Buddha fournit, dans le monde, un analogue avec lequel on peut comparer Celui qui est vraiment supramondain et partant incomparable (6).[40] Mātṛceṭa prend donc soin de distinguer toute qualité mondaine, si excellente soit-elle, d'un vrai *buddhadharma* (*Śatapañcāśatka* 39):

38. Cf. *Śatapañcāśatka* 8.

39. Cf. *Śatapañcāśatka* 151: *aprameyam asaṃkhyeyam acintyam anidarśanam// svayam evâtmanâtmānaṃ tvam eva jñātum arhasi//* «Seul tu peux te connaître toi-même par toi-même comme incommensurable, innombrable, inconcevable et invisible *(bstan min)* (ou: sans exemple)».

40. V. v. 6 et 22 (cité plus haut, n. 34), et *Śatapañcāśatka* 40.—Le *dharma* est d'ailleurs un écoulement *(niṣyanda)* du *dharmakāya;* cf. *Ratnagotravibhāga* i.145 et i.20.

Pour l'idée selon laquelle le *buddha* est à voir par le truchment de son *dharma* voir *Vajracchedikā* (p. 57): *dharmato buddhā draṣṭavyā dharmakāyā hi nāyakāḥ/ dharmatā na vijñeyā na sā śakyā vijānitum//* (cf. Candrakīrti, *Prasannapadā* ad *Mūlamadhyamakakārikā* xxii.15 [p. 448] et *Madhyamakāvatāra* p. 361; Prajñākaramati, *Bodhicaryāvatārapañjikā* ix.38 [p. 421.10]); *Aṣṭasāhasrikā* 4 (p. 94), 17 (p. 338–39), 28 (p. 462), et 31 (p. 513); *Samādhirājasūtra* xxii.21 et suiv.; *Udānavarga* xxii.12; *Theragāthā* 469.

anena sarvaṃ vyākhyātaṃ yat kiṃcit sādhu laukikam /
dūre hi buddhadharmāṇāṃ lokadharmās tapasvinaḥ //

Le poète termine son Aśakyastava en faisant lui aussi allusion à la *bhakti,* qui fait incliner vers le Buddha les facultés des chanteurs de louange (*bhaktiprahvendriya,* 28). Au lieu de la *bhakti* Mātr̥ceṭa parle ailleurs, dans un contexte identique, de la tranquillité pellucide *(prasāda)* de l'esprit plein de foi qui est tourné vers le Muni; c'est ce *prasāda* qui confère au poète l'inspiration *(pratibhā)* qui lui permet de créer sa bonne œuvre (*Śatapañcāśatka* 153):

phalodayenâsya śubhasya karmaṇo muniprasādapratibhodbhavasya me /

Dignāga, qui a incorporé les vers du *Śatapañcāśatka* de Mātr̥ceṭa à son *Prasādapratibhodbhavastotra* (dit par conséquent *Miśrakastotra*), reprend cette notion de la *pratibhā* issue du *prasāda* et termine avec elle son hymne au Buddha.[41]

Le rôle assigné ainsi aux désignations *(prajñapti),* à la relativité *(saṃvr̥ti),* au développement discursif *(prapañca),* etc., n'appelle guère de commentaire puisque ces notions se rencontrent si fréquemment dans la pensée bouddhique. Plus remarquable est l'allusion que font Nāgārjuna et Mātr̥ceṭa à la *bhakti,* car l'emploi de ce mot ne manque pas d'évoquer la notion de la dévotion à Dieu si bien connue de l'hindouïsme. Et l'allusion, dans l'hymne de Rāhulabhadra, à l'action de «recourir» *(prapad-)* selon sa nature (? *bhāvataḥ*) à la *prajñāpāramitā* mérite également l'attention parce que les termes de *prapatti* et *bhāva* devaient désigner, dans la théorie du *rasa* et dans la dévotion viṣṇouïte et kr̥ṣṇaïte, respectivement la prise de refuge ou l'abandon dévoué et l'affection ou l'amour de Dieu; encore serait-il anachronique et abusif d'identifier la *bhakti,* le *bhāva* et la **prapatti* de ces auteurs bouddhistes aux notions que ces termes désignent dans l'hindouïsme. Enfin le terme de *pratibhā* est intéressant à un autre point de vue, car les grammairiens, les poéticiens et les philosophes l'ont employé pour exprimer l'idée de l'intuition ou de l'inspiration, notion qui est d'ailleurs liée au *pratibhāna* (pāli: *paṭibhāna*) bouddhique.

41. Le *prasāda* peut procéder de la vue immédiate du Muni (cf. *Śatapañcāśatka* 92: *te prasādayati darśanam*). (Le *prasāda* joue aussi un rôle important dans la théorie du *rasa.*)

Sur le *preman* et le *gaurava* ayant pour objet le Buddha, voir aussi *Aṣṭasāhasrikā* 17 (p. 338–39) et 28 (p. 462). (Sur la *bhakti* dans le Madhyamaka cf. É. Lamotte, *La concentration de la Marche Héroïque* [Bruxelles, 1965], p. 56–58.)

En résumé, dans le *Niraupamyastava* (23), le *Stutyatītastava* (fol. 91a5) et le *Paramārthastava* (2) de Nāgārjuna ainsi que dans le *Varṇārhavarṇastotra* de Mātṛceṭa la louange du Buddha jointe à la description positive et quasi ontologique de la réalité absolue à laquelle correspond le niveau du Buddha parfait procède de la *bhakti,* s'appuie sur la *prajñapti* et ressortit donc à la *saṃvṛti.* Par ailleurs, on peut «recourir» à la *prajñāpāramitā* qui est en soi absolument transcendante; et le *prasāda* confère au poète la *pratibhā* qui lui est nécessaire pour créer sa bonne oeuvre consistant, quelque peu paradoxalement, à attribuer des qualités à Celui qui est sans comparaison et qui surpasse donc toute qualité mondaine.[42]

Si la description et la qualification de la réalité inexprimable relèvent dans ces cas de la simple convention linguistique, ou si elles procèdent d'un besoin religieux où l'on impute à cette réalité des attributs qui ne lui reviennent pas en vérité, la description positive que le *Dharmadhātustava* donne de l'Absolu semble devoir s'expliquer, au moins en partie, d'une autre façon. En effet, selon un certain courant dans la pensée bouddhique qui est représenté aussi bien par des sūtra que par des śāstra, la réalité absolue est inséparable *(avinirbhāga)* de ses qualités *(guṇa)* ou propriétés *(dharma)* supramondaines *(lokottara)* et de Sens absolu qui lui sont intrinsèques, et par lesquelles elle est «constituée» *(prabhāvita).* En d'autres termes, dans cette ligne de pensée, l'attribution de qualités à la réalité ineffable et inconcevable ne s'impose pas faute de mieux à un poète ou à un philosophe qui se voit obligé d'utiliser les moyens disponibles dans l'usage ordinaire du monde du discours, et elle ne s'explique pas non plus par la seule ferveur religieuse. Bien au contraire, elle correspond à ce qu'on pourrait peut-être nommer la constitution métaphysique et gnoséologique de l'Absolu.[43] Du reste, selon le *Dharmadhātustava,*

42. Selon le *Mahāyānasūtrālaṃkāra* (ix.36), vouloir décrire et définir la profondeur de l'Absolu au niveau de l'*amaladhātu* se ramène à vouloir peindre l'espace vide avec des couleurs *(raṅgair ākāśacitraṇā),* car l'Absolu exempt de développement discursif *(niṣprapañca)* est pareil à l'*ākāśa.*

En revanche, la révérence (? *citrīkāra*) pour la Conductrice des Tathāgata *(tathāgatanetrī)*—la *Prajñāpāramitā*—consiste en une forme élevée de la dévotion *(bhaktiviśeṣa)* ou en la tranquillité pellucide de l'esprit *(prasāda);* v. Haribhadra, *Abhisamayālaṃkārālokā* ii.18–19, p. 267, et p. 939. (Le sens précis de *citrīkāra* n'est pas certain. En sanskrit classique ce mot peut désigner l'émerveillement, et en bouddhique il désigne la révérence [v. F. Edgerton, *BHSD,* s.u.]; cf. en sanskrit classique *citrya* «qui est à honorer, adorer» [Apte-Gode-Karve]. Remarquons que selon la traduction tibétaine de *citrīkāra, ri mor byed pa,* il s'agit précisément d'une représentation ou d'une «délinéation».)

43. Cf. notre *Théorie du tathāgatagarbha et du gotra* (Paris, 1969), p. 319 et suiv.

bien qu'étant en soi ineffable et inconcevable (89), le *dharmadhātu* est accessible d'une certaine manière à la connaissance mentale (*manojñāna,* 90), et il est donc un connaissable *(jñeya).*[44] La relation de (ou des) Nāgārjuna avec ce courant de pensée reste à préciser.

* * * *

Lorsque nous cherchons à situer le *Dharmadhātustava* dans l'histoire de la pensée bouddhique en général, et de l'école des Mādhyamika en particulier, et à trancher la question de savoir si un pareil texte a pu être composé par le fondateur de cette école, la mise à contribution des critères philologiques usuels est malaisée sinon exclue parce que—abstraction faite des quelque six vers (19–24) cités dans la *Sekoddeśaṭīkā* de Nāropā—la version originale sanskrite de l'hymne n'est pas accessible et qu'il est par conséquent impossible d'entreprendre une analyse stylistique ou métrique de l'ensemble de l'ouvrage; et il est donc impossible de déceler ainsi l'existence éventuelle d'interpolations. Cependant, la fidélité des traductions tibétaines permet sans doute l'application à ce texte de critères terminologiques et philosophiques.

Or nous constatons que le vocabulaire philosophique du *Dharmadhātustava* diffère sensiblement de celui des *Mūlamadhyamakakārikā* (un texte beaucoup plus étendu), des termes aussi caractéristiques de l'hymne que *dharmadhātu* et *dharmakāya* étant inconnus de ces *Kārikā* comme le sont d'autres termes importants comme *pāramitā, bhūmi, bodhicitta,* etc.[45] Cette constatation n'est guère décisive, cependant, et à elle seule elle n'autoriserait sans doute pas la conclusion que le *Dharmadhātustava* ne pourrait en aucun cas être l'ouvrage de l'auteur des *Mūlamadhyamakakārikā.* Du reste, le *Niraupamyastava* (vi.21), l'*Acintyastava* (fol. 90a7) et le *Paramārthastava* (8)—c'est-à-dire des textes qu'on attribue généralement à Nāgārjuna I—ont effectivement employé le mot *dharmadhātu;* et tandis que le *dharmakāya* est implicitement mentionné dans le premier de ces *stava* au moyen de l'expression *kāyo dharmamayaḥ* (22), le mot *dharmaśarīra* y est attesté à côté du mot *janmaśarīra* (12) et le terme de *dharmatā* y figure également (3).[46]

44. Sur l'Absolu connaissable encore qu'inaccessible à la connaissance *discursive,* v. *Théorie,* p. 297 et suiv.

45. Cf. E. Frauwallner, *Philosophie des Buddhismus,* p. 174; R. H. Robinson, *Early Mādhyamika,* p. 63.

46. Le *Kāyatrayastotra,* qui est attribué à Nāgāhvaya par Nāropā (*Sekoddeśaṭīkā,* p. 57) et par Tāranātha (v. *supra,* n. 7), mais à Nāgārjuna dans le Bstan 'gyur, fait naturellement état du *dharmakāya,* du *sambhogakāya* et du *nirmāṇakāya,* le *dharmakāya* étant qualifié

Par ailleurs, dans l'autocommentaire de son *Madhyamakāvatāra* Candrakīrti cite, en les attribuant à l'école des Pūrvaśaila, sept stances dont deux méritent d'être relevées ici puisqu'elles ont trait au *dharmadhātu* et à sa relation avec le *sattvadhātu:*[47]

> *zhig pa med cing skye med la/ /chos dbyings dang mnyam par gyur kyang//*
> *sreg pa'i bskal pa brjod mdzad pa/ /'di ni 'jig rten mthun 'jug yin//*
> *dus gsum dag tu sems can gyi/ /rang bzhin dmigs pa ma yin la//*
> *sems can khams kyang ston mdzad pa/ /'di ni 'jig rten mthun 'jug yin//*

> Exempt de destruction et de naissance, [le monde est][48] égal au *dharmadhātu,* et [tout de même le Maître] parle de l'embrasement à la fin d'une période cosmique:[49] c'est se conformer à [l'usage ordinaire du] monde.[50] Une nature des êtres animés n'est pas perçue dans les trois temps, et [tout de même le Maître] enseigne l'Élément des êtres animés:[51] c'est se conformer à [l'usage ordinaire du] monde.

---

d'immuable *(nirvikāra),* de tranquille *(śiva),* d'omniprésent *(vyāpin),* et de connaissable par la seule intuition directe *(pratyātmavedya).*

47. *Madhyamakāvatāra* vi.44 (p. 134–35).

48. Le mot *jagat* «monde» manque dans la version tibétaine du *Madhyamakāvatāra,* mais il figure dans la version sanskrite du vers citée dans la *Prasannapadā* (voir ci-dessous). Ce mot désigne par excellence le monde des êtres animés *(sattva)* et il est ainsi presque équivalent à *sattvadhātu* «plan des êtres animés». En tant qu'Élément *(dhātu)* des *sattva* le *sattvadhātu* peut être qualifié d'exempt de destruction et de naissance (v. *infra,* notes 49 et 54).

49. Dans la mesure où le *jagat,* qui correspond au *sattvadhātu,* participe du *(dharma) dhātu,* il est incomposé *(asaṃskṛta)* et ne saurait être détruit. —L'allusion au *kalpoddāha* sert à contrecarrer la notion de la permanence *(nityasaṃjñā)* selon le *Vimalakīrtinirdeśa* (trad. de Lamotte, p. 296); cf. *Śikṣāsamuccaya,* p. 324. La version sanskrite parle ici du *sattvadhātu* et non pas du *sreg pa'i bskal pa.* (Sur ce dernier cf. *Mahābherīsūtra* [H], fol. 206a: *'jig rten gyi khams 'di nyid sreg pa'i bskal pa byung na mi tshig pa* «ce *lokadhātu* [du Buddha] n'est pas embrasé même lorsque vient l'âge où le monde est détruit par le feu».)

50. Sur la *lokānuvṛtti* cf. *Niraupamyastava* 19.

51. Le mot *sattvadhātu* peut être pris ici dans ses deux valeurs, l'une cosmologique—«plan des êtres animés» (parallèle à *lokadhātu, kāmadhātu,* etc.)—et l'autre ontologique—Élément des êtres animés» (voir ci-dessous).

Deux stances analogues se trouvent dans la *Prasannapadā* de Candrakīrti (ad *Mūlamadhyamakakārikā* xxvi.2, p. 548):[52]

> *avināśam anutpannaṃ dharmadhātusamaṃ jagat /*
> *sattvadhātuṃ ca deśeti eṣā lokānuvartanā //*
> *triṣu adhvasu sattvānāṃ prakṛtiṃ nôpalambhati /*
> *sattvadhātuṃ ca deśeti eṣā lokānuvartanā //*

> Exempt de destruction et de naissance, le monde est égal au *dharmadhātu,* et tout de même [le Maître] enseigne l'Élément de l'être animé: c'est se conformer au monde.[53] Il ne perçoit pas une nature des êtres animés dans les trois temps, et tout de même [le Maître] enseigne l'Élément des êtres animés: c'est se conformer au monde.[54]

Nāgārjuna, le fondateur de l'école des Mādhyamika, vécut, selon la tradition, dans l'Andhra, le fief des sectes et sous-sectes de l'école des Mahāsāṃghika dont les Pūrvaśaila étaient parmi les plus importants.[55]

52. La version originale de cette stance en sanskrit hybride, ou plutôt sans doute en prākrit, la langue des Mahāsāṃghika/Pūrvaśaila, transmise sous une forme méconnaissable, a été rétablie par La Vallée Poussin; voir la note de son édition de la *Prasannapadā,* p. 548.

53. Dans son édition de la *Prasannapadā* (p. 548) La Vallée Poussin estimait que les «scribes ont peut-être pris induement le troisième pāda de la strophe suivante; on peut lire *tejaḥkalpam ca . . .* » (Mais la leçon attestée dans la *Prasannapadā* n'est pas incompréhensible; car si le *jagat* sans naissance et sans destruction est le *dharmadhātu,* il n'y aurait pas lieu de parler du *sattvadhātu* sauf dans la mesure où l'on veut se conformer à l'usage ordinaire qui admet l'existence d'un *sattvadhātu.*)

54. La Vallée Poussin a traduit *sattvadhātu* par «l'existence des êtres» (*Vijñaptimātratāsiddhi: La Siddhi de Hiuan-tsang* [Paris, 1928–29], p. 752), mais cette traduction n'est guère probante; M. J. May, qui traduit «plan des êtres» (*Candrakīrti, Prasannapadā Madhyamakavṛtti* [Paris, 1959], p. 257), ne rend qu'une seule des deux valeurs du mot *sattvadhātu* relevées plus haut, et qui doivent probablement être retenues simultanément ici. A vrai dire, puisque le *sattvadhātu* est ici la contrepartie du *dharmadhātu,* il est possible que dans ce contexte l'acception «ontologique» («Élément des êtres animés») prime l'acception «cosmologique».

55. V. L. de La Vallée Poussin, Réflexions sur le Madhyamaka, *MCB* 2 (1933), p. 38; É. Lamotte, *Asiatica* (Festschrift Weller), p. 386–87.

Pour un bref historique de la notion du *dharmadhātu* voir L. de La Vallée Poussin, *Vijñaptimātratāsiddhi*, p. 751–53. Cf. É. Lamotte, *Le traité,* p. 711n1, et p. 939n1; M. et W. Geiger, *Pāli Dhamma* (München, 1921), p. 69; K. Kawada, *IBK* 11.2 (1963), p. 9–24; J. Takasaki, *IBK* 14.2 (1966), p. 78–94.

De plus, comme le *dharmadhātu* ainsi que d'autres notions étroitement apparentées sont mentionnés dans l'*Aṣṭasāhasrikā* et d'autres Prajñāpāramitāsūtra, dans le *Samādhirājasūtra,* etc.,[56] Nāgārjuna, qui a dû connaître des versions de ces sūtra, aurait très bien pu les mentionner—si tant est qu'il ait voulu parler de la réalité absolue.[57]

Que le *Dharmadhātustava* ne soit pas entièrement isolé parmi les hymnes attribués à Nāgārjuna[58] non seulement au point de vue de la terminologie mais aussi à celui de la doctrine, c'est ce que montrent deux vers du *Niraupamyastava* (21–22):

> *dharmadhātor asambhedād yānabhedo 'sti na prabho /*
> *yānatritayam ākhyātaṃ tvayā sattvāvatārataḥ //*
> *nityo dhruvaḥ śivaḥ kāyas tava dharmamayo jina /*
> *vineyajanahetoś ca darśitā nirvṛtis tvayā //*

> Seigneur, comme le *dharmadhātu* est sans différenciation il n'y a pas de différence [réelle] entre les Véhicules, et tu as proclamé la triade des Véhicules [seulement] en vue d'introduire [dans la doctrine] les êtres animés.[59] Ton Corps est permanent, stable et tran-

56. Cf. les passages de l'*Aṣṭasāhasrikā* relevés ci-dessus, note 40, et *Samādhirājasūtra,* chapitres III (Bhūtaguṇavarṇaprakāśana), XXII (Tathāgatakāyanirdeśa) et XXIII (Tathāgatācintyanirdeśa).

57. Plusieurs de ces termes se rencontrent dans le *Ta tche tou louen;* cf. K. Venkata Ramanan, *Nāgārjuna's Philosophy,* p. 251 et suiv.

58. Il est bien entendu impossible de tenir compte ici de tous les ouvrages attribués à Nāgārjuna.

59. Cf. la notion de l'arrière-pensée d'introduction *(avatāraṇābhisaṃdhi).* V. *Ratnāvalī* iv.88: *tathāgatābhisaṃdhyoktāny asukhaṃ jñātum.*

Sur le *dharmadhātu* cf. *Paramārthastava* 8, et *Niraupamyastava* 6:

> *tvaṃ vivedaikarasatāṃ saṃkleśavyavadānayoḥ /*
> *dharmadhātvavinirbhedād viśuddhaś câsi sarvataḥ //*
> Tu as connu la Valeur unique de la souillure et de la pureté;
> et tu es entièrement pur en vertu de l'indifférenciation du *dharmadhātu.*

Cf. *Abhisamayālaṃkāra* i.39ab:

> *dharmadhātor asambhedād gotrabhedo na yujyate /*
> En raison de l'indifférenciation du *dharmadhātu* une différence [réelle] du *gotra* n'est pas possible.

V. *Théorie du tathāgatagarbha et du gotra,* p. 129 et suiv., 179 et suiv.; et Ārya and Bhadanta Vimuktisena on the Gotra-Theory of the Prajñāpāramitā, *WZKSO* 12–13 (1968, Festschrift Frauwallner), p. 303–17.

quille et consiste en *dharma:* c'est à l'intention des gens à instruire que tu as manifesté la cessation [le *nirvāṇa*].[60]

De son côté l'*Acintyastava* va jusqu'à parler de la réalité, du Sens absolu et de l'Ainsité comme une «chose» véritable et non trompeuse, et il ajoute qu'on est Éveillé *(buddha)* quand on l'a connu (39):[61]

tat tattvaṃ paramārtho 'pi tathatā dravyaṃ iṣyate /
bhūtaṃ tad avisaṃvādi tadbodhād buddha ucyate //

Mais comme les sūtra qui enseignent la doctrine du *(tathāgata)dhātu* et du *tathāgatagarbha,* le *Niraupamyastava* insiste (10) sur le fait que l'esprit du sage ne s'attache pas à la conceptualisation différenciatrice *(vikalpa)* qui oppose le permanent *(nitya)* et l'impermanent *(anitya),* la béatitude *(sukha)* et la douleur *(duḥkha),* le soi *(ātman)* et le non-soi *(anātman, nairātmya),* etc. De même, selon le *Dharmadhātustava* (35), la réalité absolue dépasse toute dichotomie opposant le soi et le non-soi (cf. 24, 65), car la dichotomie procède du *vikalpa* (28, 48).

Ainsi donc, dans l'état actuel de nos connaissances, il n'est guère possible d'affirmer catégoriquement que le *Dharmadhātustava* (ou tout au moins son noyau) ainsi que les passages parallèles dans d'autres hymnes attribués à Nāgārjuna ne pourraient pas être des compositions du fondateur de l'école des Mādhyamika, encore qu'il ne soit pas absolument exclu que ce stava ait été composé plus tard par un Deutéro-Nāgārjuna ayant subi l'influence des tendances ontologiques qui se sont accentuées dans le Mahāyāna développé et notamment dans le Vajrayāna, où la dévotion au maître joue par ailleurs un rôle capital. En tout état de cause le courant de pensée représenté par le *Dharmadhātustava* remonte assez loin dans l'histoire du Mahāyāna et embrasse notamment les nombreux sūtra enseignant le *(tathāgata)dhātu* et le *tathāgatagarbha* ainsi que le *Ratnagotravibhāga.*

Quoi qu'il en soit de cette question, il demeure que, à la différence des *Mūlamadhyamakakārikā* et des autres ouvrages analogues de Nāgārjuna constituant le groupe des traités scolastiques *(rigs tshogs)* qui ne posent pas une réalité positive et quasi substantielle et qui procèdent surtout par la voie de la négation, le *Dharmadhātustava* fait état d'une réalité absolue qualifiée

60. La notion de l'immutabilité et de la permanence du *buddha* est caractéristique du *Mahāparinirvāṇasūtra* mahāyāniste, etc.; cf. aussi la théorie docétiste du *Ratnagotravibhāga* i.80 et suiv. Cf. ci-dessus, p.117–18.

61. Fol. 90a6–7, cité par Prajñākaramati, *Bodhicaryāvatārapañjikā* ix.106 (p. 528).

d'une façon positive, si bien qu'on l'a parfois considérée comme une entité substantielle.[62] Pareillement, alors que les Prajñāpāramitāsūtra qui constituent, selon la classification tripartite des écritures canoniques du bouddhisme, le cycle intermédiaire de la prédication du Buddha enseignent surtout la *śūnyatā*, encore d'autres sūtra ainsi que le *Ratnagotravibhāga* relevant du dernier cycle traitent de la théorie du *(tathāgata)dhātu* et du *tathāgatagarbha* et enseignent par là l'existence chez tous les êtres de l'Élément spirituel, ou de l'Embryon essentiel, du *tathāgata* qui rend certaine l'obtention future de l'Éveil et de l'état de *buddha* par tous les êtres animés sans exception. Ainsi le parallélisme entre la deuxième grande proclamation de la Loi de Nāgārjuna consacrée à la *prajñāpāramitā* et à la *śūnyatā* et le deuxième cycle de la prédication bouddhique d'une part, et de l'autre entre la troisième grande proclamation de la Loi de Nāgārjuna traitant notamment du *dharmadhātu (chos kyi dbyings)* et du *dhātu* spirituel *(khams)* de l'être animé et le troisième cycle de la prédication bouddhique ressort très clairement, mais sans qu'il soit possible, dans l'état actuel de nos connaissances, d'affirmer que le schéma des trois proclamations démarque simplement la classification mieux connue en trois cycles.[63] En tout état de cause, le schéma des trois proclamations est mentionné dans le *Mahābherīsūtra* et le *Mahāmeghasūtra*.

Ces deux points de vue, lesquels sont parfois considérés comme deux doctrines différentes et exclusives, rappellent la différence entre la *via eminentiae* et la *via negationis* ou entre la *κατάφασις* et l'*απόφασις*. Et l'école tibétaine des Jo nang pa est effectivement allée jusqu'à opposer la *svabhāvaśūnyatā (rang stong)*, qui est enseignée par les traités scolastiques *(rigs tshogs)* de Nāgārjuna et qu'ils considèrent comme une Vacuité de destruction *(chad stong)*, à la *śūnyatā* «véritable»—c'est-à-dire la Vacuité des seuls facteurs relatifs et hétérogènes à l'absolu *(gzhan stong)*—enseignée dans les hymnes *(bstod tshogs)* de Nāgārjuna. Ainsi, selon les Jo nang pa, l'enseignement des Prajñāpāramitāsūtra et du *rigs tshogs* relatif au *rang stong* «nihiliste» est intentionnel *(ābhiprāyika)* et de sens indirect *(neyārtha)*, et c'est la théorie du *gzhan stong* des sūtra du troisième cycle enseignant le *garbha (snying po'i mdo)* et du *bstod tshogs* qui est de sens direct et certain *(nītārtha)*.[64]

62. Cf. la doctrine des Jo nang pa (voir ci-dessous).

63. Cf. la remarque de Bu ston citée plus haut (n. 19) selon laquelle les hymnes de Nāgārjuna reposent directement sur l'Écriture alors que ses traités scolastiques s'appuient plutôt sur le raisonnement.

64. Sur l'interprétation ontologiste et substantialiste de la réalité absolue du *Dharmadhātustava* qui a été préconisée par les Jo nang pa et par d'autres écoles apparentées voir les critiques de Bu ston, *Bde snying mdzes rgyan*, de Thu'u bkwan Blo bzang chos kyi nyi

Aucun commentaire indien du *Dharmadhātustava* n'étant connu, il est impossible de dire comment les Mādhyamika indiens auraient abordé les nombreux problèmes qu'il pose.[65]

* * * *

Une version chinoise du *Dharmadhātustava* fut exécutée par Che-hou (*Dānapāla ou *Dānarakṣita?), un traducteur originaire de l'Uḍḍiyāna qui travailla à K'ai-fong après 980.[66] Un peu plus tard, au milieu du XIe s., il fut traduit en tibétain par Kṛṣṇa Paṇḍita et Nag tsho lo tsā ba Tshul khrims rgyal ba (né en 1011);[67] ces mêmes traducteurs ont aussi traduit en tibétain le *Niraupamyastava,* le *Paramārthastava,* etc.

Voici un résumé de la théorie de la réalité absolue à la fois transcendante et immanente selon le *Dharmadhātustava.*[68]

Après une invocation adressée à Mañjuśrī Kumārabhūta qui sert, d'après l'interprétation tibétaine usuelle, à marquer l'appartenance de l'ouvrage à la catégorie des śāstra relevant de l'*abhidharma* au sens large—c'est-à-dire des traités relatifs à la *prajñā* dont Mañjuśrī est la maître[69]—le stava commence par un hommage à l'Élément de(s) *dharma (chos kyi dbyings = dharmadhātu)* qui, si l'on ne le connaît pas complètement, tourne dans les trois plans de

ma, *Grub mtha' shel gyi me long* (chapitre des Jo nang pa, traduit dans *JAOS* 83 [1963], p. 73–91), de Mkhas grub rje, *Rgyud sde spyi rnam,* fol. 10b–12b, et de Klong rdol bla ma, *Theg chen gyi mngon pa'i sde snod las byung ba'i dbu ma'i skor gyi ming gi rnam grangs,* fol. 14a–15a (passages traduits dans "On the dGe-lugs-pa Theory of the tathāgatagarbha" in: J. Heesterman et al.(éd.) *Pratidānam* [La Haye, 1968], p. 500–509).—Selon d'autres écoles, les doctrines du *tathāgatagarbha/tathāgatadhātu* et de la *śūnyatā* sont en dernière analyse équivalentes; v. *supra,* p. 117, et *Théorie,* p. 313 et suiv., 400 et suiv.

65. *L'Āryadharmadhātugarbhavivaraṇa* attribué à Nāgārjuna dans le Bstan 'gyur est un commentaire de la formule *ye dharmā hetuprabhavah . . .* et n'a aucun rapport direct avec le *Dharmadhātustava.*

66. Taishō n° 1675. La date tardive de cette traduction chinoise pourrait certes être considérée comme un indice en faveur de l'hypothèse selon laquelle le *Dharmadhātustava* est d'un Deutéro-Nāgārjuna postérieur à l'auteur des *Madhyamakakārikā* déjà traduites par Kumārajīva au Ve siècle. Che-hou a aussi traduit des ouvrages tântriques. Mais il est le traducteur d'autres ouvrages attribués à Nāgārjuna, y compris la *Bhavasaṃkrānti* et la *Yuktiṣaṣṭikā;* or ce dernier texte est généralement considéré comme un ouvrage authentique du fondateur de l'école des Mādhyamika.

67. V. 'Gos lo tsā ba Gzhon nu dpal, *Deb ther sngon po,* ca, fol. 3b (I, p. 247).

68. Dans la suite les chiffres entre parenthèses renvoient aux vers du *Dharmadhātustava.*

69. Cf. les remarques de Tsong kha pa, *Legs bshad gser phreng,* I, fol. 9b, et de Gung thang Dkon mchog bstan pa'i sgron me, *Legs bshad snying po'i mchan,* fol. 1b. L'invocation initiale peut aussi être du traducteur, qui salue ainsi sa divinité tutélaire *(iṣṭadevatā).*

l'existence relative *(tribhava),* et qui se trouve chez tous les êtres animés *(sattva)* (1).[70] Tantôt il est la cause *(hetu)* du cycle des existences *(saṃsāra);* et tantôt, lorsqu'il est pur *(śuddha)* en vertu de l'action purificatrice, il est le *nirvāṇa* ainsi que le *dharmakāya* (2).[71] De même que le beurre clarifié encore mêlé au lait n'est pas visible, ainsi le *dharmadhātu* encore mêlé aux souillures *(kleśa)* n'est pas visible; mais de même que le beurre clarifié devient pur grâce à la purification du lait, ainsi le *dharmadhātu* devient pur grâce à la purification des *kleśa* (3–4). De même qu'une lampe dans un vase ne rayonne pas, ainsi le *dharmadhātu* n'est pas visible dans le vase des *kleśa;* mais la nature de la lumière apparaîtra là où l'on pratique une ouverture dans ce vase, et lorsque le vase des *kleśa* a été cassé par la pierre de la composition d'esprit *(samādhi)* le *dharmadhātu* rayonne jusqu'aux confins de l'espace (5–7).[72] Le *dharmadhātu* ne naît pas, et il n'est pas arrêté: toujours sans *kleśa* au début, au milieu et à la fin, il est exempt d'impureté (8). Bien que la pierre précieuse de béryl *(vaiḍūrya)* soit toujours brillante, tant qu'elle se trouve dans le roc sa lumière n'éclate pas; pareillement, encore que le *dharmadhātu* recouvert des *kleśa* soit absolument immaculé en soi, sa lumière n'éclate pas dans le *saṃsāra;*

70. Sur le sens de *dharma* dans le terme de *dharmadhātu* cf. *infra,* v. 43–45 et 90. Le mot sanskrit *dhātu* est traduit en tibétain par *dbyings* quand il désigne l'Élément absolu en tant que tel, au niveau de la réalité suprême, comme dans l'expression *nirvāṇadhātu.* Le mot *dbyings* est glosé par *ngang* «nature essentielle» et *klong* (= *dkyil*) «milieu; noyau quintessentiel» (dans le vocabulaire philosophique; cf. *byings,* qui traduit *dhātu* «racine grammaticale»). L'équivalent *khams* (voir ci-dessous) se rapporte en revanche à l'Élément spirituel au niveau de la relativité, chez le *sattva* dans le *saṃsāra;* et ainsi *tathāgatadhātu (~ tathāgatagarbha)* est normalement traduit par *de bzhin gshegs pa'i khams* puisqu'il s'agit de l'Élément existant chez les *sattva;* cf. *sems can gyi khams = sattvadhātu.* On peut cependant constater des flottements dans l'usage.

Le *dharmadhātu* figure ici comme l'équivalent du *tathāgatadhātu* et du *tathāgatagarbha* existant chez tous les *sattva* selon le *Tathāgatagarbhasūtra,* le *Ratnagotravibhāga,* etc., et du *prakṛtisthagotra* de l' *Abhisamayālaṃkāra.*

71. Il s'agit de la *vaimalyapariśuddhi* (ou *vaimalyaviśuddhi*) de la Vyākhyā du *Ratnagotravibhāga,* c'est-à-dire de la pureté résultant de la pratique du chemin et consistant en l'absence totale des impuretés adventices, à la différence de la pureté naturelle *(prakṛtipariśuddhi, prakṛtiviśuddhi)* qui est originelle mais obscurcie par les *kleśa* adventices *(āgantuka).*

Cf. aussi l'*Abhidharmasūtra* mahāyāniste cité dans la Vyākhyā du *Ratnagotravibhāga* (i.149–52), etc.:

anādikāliko dhātuḥ sarvadharmasamāśrayaḥ /
tasmin sati gatiḥ sarvā nirvāṇādhigamo 'pi ca //

72. La comparaison de la lampe cachée dans un vase est appliquée au *dhātu* dans le *Mahābherīsūtra* (H, fol. 181a–182b).

c'est dans le *nirvāṇa* que sa lumière éclate (9–10).[73] Étant donné l'existence de l'élément (minéral, *khams = dhātu*), on verra l'or pur grâce au nettoyage; mais s'il n'y avait pas d'Élément (spirituel, *khams = dhātu*), même si l'on procédait au nettoyage on ne produirait que des *kleśa* (11).[74] De même que l'on ne tient pas le riz non décortiqué pour la graine, ainsi on ne considère pas ce *dhātu* recouvert de *kleśa* comme le *buddha;* mais de même que la graine elle-même apparaîtra une fois qu'on l'a décortiquée, ainsi le *dharmakāya* brille lorsqu'il est séparé des *kleśa* (12–13).[75] Encore que la comparaison de la tige du bananier *(kadalīstamba)* illustre, dans l'usage ordinaire, ce qui n'est pas solide *(asāra),*[76] on mange son fruit—le noyau solide—qui est doux; pareillement, quand il est séparé de la cage des *kleśa,* c'est-à-dire du *saṃsāra* qui n'est

73. La comparaison du *(tathāgata-)dhātu* avec le *vaiḍūryamaṇi* se trouve dans le *Dhāraṇīśvararājasūtra* (cité dans la Vyākhyā du *Ratnagotravibhāga* i.2; la version tibétaine se trouve dans le *Tathāgatamahākaruṇānirdeśasūtra* [P], fol. 176b).

Au sujet de l'Élément précieux caché dans sa «gangue» on peut citer deux vers. L'un se trouve dans la Vyākhyā du *Ratnagotravibhāga* i.2 (p. 6), où il est question du *viśuddhagotra* et du *tathāgatadhātu:*

> *yathā pattharacuṇṇamhi jātarūpaṃ na dissati /*
> *parikammeṇa tad diṭṭhaṃ evaṃ loke tathāgatā //*
> De même que l'or n'est pas visible dans la poussière des pierres alors
> qu'on le voit après qu'on l'a nettoyé, ainsi les Tathāgata [lire *tathāgato* «le
> Tathāgata»?] [sont (est) vu(s)] dans le monde.

L'autre vers est cité par Yaśomitra dans son *Abhidharmakośavyākhyā* i.1 (p. 5) et vii.36 (p. 644, où l'édition de Wogihara porte *svasūkṣma* au lieu de *susūkṣma*):

> *mokṣabījam ahaṃ hy asya susūkṣmam upalakṣaye /*
> *dhātupāṣāṇavivare nilīnam iva kāñcanam //*
> J'aperçois son très subtil germe de délivrance, tel l'or caché dans les pierres
> contenant une substance précieuse.

74. Le terme de *dhātu* désignant l'Élément spirituel du *sattva* dans le *saṃsāra,* qui est comparé au minéral précieux *(dhātu = khams)* dans sa gangue, est ainsi traduit en tibétain par *khams* et non pas par *dbyings.* Cette comparaison est sans doute sous-jacente à la notion selon laquelle la transmutation de l'esprit est une transmutation alchimique, notion qui figure dans la littérature tântrique.

La comparaison du *dharmadhātu (fa sing),* ou du *nirvāṇa,* avec la «nature» *(sing)* de l'or ou de l'argent dans sa gangue ainsi que l'allusion au processus quasi alchimique de sa transmutation se retrouve dans le *Ta tche tou louen* (cf. 298b, cité par K. Venkata Ramanan, *Nāgārjuna's Philosophy,* p. 261–62). La présence de ces notions dans le *Dharmadhātustava* ne saurait donc pas être considérée comme un indice prouvant l'origine tardive du stava.

75. Voir la troisième comparaison du *Tathāgatagarbhasūtra* (H, fol. 9a–10a) et du *Ratnagotravibhāga* (i.105–7).

76. Voir par exemple *Ratnāvalī* ii.1, et la *Yuktiṣaṣṭikā;* cf. *Samādhirājasūtra* xxix.14.

pas solide *(asāra)*, le Fruit qui est le solide même[77] devient l'élixir de tous les êtres incarnés *(dehin)* (14–15). De tout germe *(bīja)* naît un fruit pareil à sa cause; or, s'il n'y avait pas de germe quelle personne, si experte soit-elle, saurait établir que le fruit existera? On estime que ce *dhātu*, qui est un «germe», est le point d'appui *(āśraya)* de toutes les choses *(dharma)*; après avoir été progressivement purifié il atteindra le plan de l'éveillé *(buddhapada)* (16–17).[78] Le soleil et la lune immaculés sont obscurcis par cinq obscurcissements: le nuage, la nuée, la fumée, l'éclipse, et la poussière; pareillement, la pensée *(citta)* qui est lumineuse *(prabhāsvara)* est obscurcie par les cinq obscurcissements que sont la concupiscence, la malignité, la langueur, la dissipation et l'incertitude.[79] Le feu étant pureté, quand un vêtement souillé par des impuretés diverses est placé dans le feu, ce sont les impuretés qui sont brûlées et non point le vêtement en soi *(vastratā)*;[80] pareillement, le *citta* lumineux est souillé par les impuretés de la concupiscence etc., et c'est l'impureté qui est alors brûlée par le feu de la Gnose *(jñāna)* et non point ce *[citta]* qui est lumineux. C'est par les sūtra enseignant la Vacuité et énoncés par les *jina* que les *kleśa* sont éliminés; et le *dhātu* n'est pas détruit. De même que l'eau souterraine reste sans impureté, ainsi la Gnose cachée dans les *kleśa* reste elle aussi sans impureté (18–23).[81]

Comme le *dharmadhātu*, qui n'est ni soi *(ātman)*, ni femme, ni homme,

77. Alors que P, N et C portent *snying po nyid*, D donne *sangs rgyas nyid* (= *buddhatva* ou *buddhatā*) «bouddhaté».

78. Cf. la Vyākhyā du *Ratnagotravibhāga* (i.26) sur le *dhātu* comme *bīja*. Et sur le *dhātu* comme le point d'appui des choses cf. le vers de l'*Abhidharmasūtra* mahāyāniste cité plus haut, n. 71.

79. V. Aṅguttaranikāya I, p. 10, sur le *citta* lumineux et les cinq *nīvaraṇa* qui le recouvrent.

80. S'agit-il d'un vêtement fait de fibres d'amiante pouvant être nettoyé par le feu?

81. Le texte sanskrit de ces six vers est cité dans la *Sekoddeśaṭīkā* de Nāropā (p. 66):
nirmalau candrasūryau hy āvṛtau pañcabhir malaiḥ /
abhranīhāradhūmena rāhuvaktrarajomalaiḥ //
evaṃ prabhāsvaraṃ cittam āvṛtam pañcabhir malaiḥ /
kāmavyāpādamiddhena auddhatyavicikitsayā //
agniśaucaṃ yathā vastraṃ malinaṃ vividhair malaiḥ /
agnimadhye yathâkṣiptaṃ malaṃ dagdhaṃ na vastratā //
evaṃ prabhāsvaraṃ cittaṃ malinaṃ rāgajair malaiḥ /
jñānāgninā malaṃ dagdhaṃ na dagdhaṃ tat prabhāsvaraṃ //
śūnyatāhārakāḥ sūtrā ye kecid bhāṣitā jinaiḥ /
sarvais taiḥ kleśavyāvṛttir naiva dhātuvināśanam //
pṛthivyantarhitaṃ toyaṃ yathā tiṣṭhati nirmalam /
kleśair antarhitaṃ jñānaṃ tathā tiṣṭhati nirmalam //

est exempt de tout objet saisi,[82] comment imaginerait-on *(brtag pa)* qu'il est soi ? Dans toutes les choses *(dharma)* exemptes d'attachement *(asaṅga)* on ne perçoit ni femme ni homme; c'est en vue des disciples à instruire *(vineya)* tourmentés[83] par la concupiscence qu'on a fait état de femme, d'homme et de *prajñā*. On nettoie le *citta* par les trois facteurs nommés l'impermanent *(anitya)*, la douleur *(duḥkha)* et le Vide *(śūnya)*;[84] le *dharma* qui nettoie le *citta* par-dessus tout, c'est l'absence d'être propre (: *niḥsvabhāvatā*) (24–26).

De même que l'enfant dans la matrice de la femme enceinte est invisible bien qu'il s'y trouve, ainsi le *dharmadhātu* recouvert des *kleśa* n'est pas visible (27).[85]

Les vers suivants traitent entre autres de la conceptualisation différenciatrice *(vikalpa)*, de la «notion» aperceptive *(saṃjñā)*, et de la désignation *(prajñapti)*[86] (28–32).

Par l'exemple des cornes du lièvre et du bœuf on établit que les qualités du *tathāgata (sugatadharma)* ne sont autres que le Milieu *(madhyama)*,[87]

82. *Gzung ba* = *grāhya* «objet» *(gzung bar bya ba)* ou *grāha* «saisie, position» (: *'dzin pa*).

83. *Gdungs* (P, N, C); D porte *ldongs* «aveuglés».

84. Cf. trois des quatre sommaires de la loi *(dharmoddāna)* et des quatre aspects du *duḥkhasatya*. Selon le *Dhāraṇīśvararājasūtra* (cité dans la Vyākhyā du *Ratnagotravibhāga* i.2), la prédication relative à l'*anitya*, au *duḥkha*, à l'*anātman*, et à l'*aśubha* sert à «ébranler» les gens qui se plaisent au *saṃsāra* et à les introduire dans l'enseignement; cette prédication n'est cependant pas finale, et elle est suivie d'abord de la prédication relative aux trois *vimokṣamukha (śūnyatā, ānimitta* et *apraṇihita)* et ensuite de la prédication portant sur le *dharmacakra* irréversible.

85. Dans la *Dharmadhātudarśanagīti* d'Atisha ce vers se trouve immédiatement après le vers 13 (cf. *infra*, p. 142). Cf. *Laṅkāvatārasūtra*, Sagāthaka 760:
yathā hi garbho garbhiṇyā vidyate na ca dṛśyate /
ātmā hi tadvat skandheṣu ayuktijño na paśyati //
dont la version tibétaine est (H, fol. 299b):
ji ltar sbrum par gyur pa'i bu/ yod bzhin du yang mi snang ba//
de bzhin bdag nyid phung po la/ /rig<s> pa mi shes pas mi mthong//
Cf. Sagāthaka 833.

86. D et la *Gīti* d'Atisha portent *brtags pa* < *rtog pa* «imaginer» au lieu de *btags pa* < *'dogs pa* «attacher (un nom), désigner». L'alternance *btags pa / brtags pa* est assez fréquente dans les textes tibétains et se rencontre plusieurs fois dans les éditions du *Dharmadhātustava*.

87. Les *buddhadharma*, qui sont *asaṃskṛta* «incomposés», ne sont ni inexistants et purement nominaux comme la corne du lièvre, ni des entités existantes et, partant, *saṃskṛta* comme la corne du bœuf. Cf. *Mahāparinirvāṇasūtra*, kha (H), fol. 340a (cité par Bu ston, *Mdzes rgyan*, fol. 25b).

Ce vers n'a que trois *pāda* dans les versions du Bstan 'gyur.

et la forme du soleil, de la lune et des étoiles est vue comme une réflexion dans l'eau d'un réceptacle propre; le caractère *(lakṣaṇa)* parfaitement achevé *(rdzogs pa)*[88] est pareil (33–34). Ce qui est bon au début, au milieu et à la fin, et qui est non trompeur, stable *(dhruva)* et aussi non-soi *(anātman)*, comment l'imaginerait-on *(brtag pa)* comme soi *(ātman)* ou comme appartenant au soi *(ātmīya)* (35)?[89] De même qu'on dit que l'eau est chaude en été et qu'elle est froide en hiver, ainsi on parle d'un être animé *(sattva)* lorsque les *kleśa* le recouvre, mais d'un *buddha* lorsqu'il est délivré des *kleśa* (36–37).[90]

Suit une discussion du processus de la perception des objets des cinq sens et de la connexion entre la connaissance de ces objets et la réalité absolue, le *dharmadhātu* sans naissance, sans arrêt, sans caractère *(lakṣaṇa)*. Par exemple, l'être propre de la langue est la *śūnyatā*, et l'élément de la saveur *(rasadhātu)* est Absolutisé;[91] par la nature du *dharmadhātu*[92] la connaissance *(vijñāna)* ne se fixe pas. Et c'est en éliminant la conceptualisation et la construction imaginaire qu'on devra réaliser en méditation que les *dharma* sont le *dharmadhātu*. Ainsi, une fois que le yogin a connu le visible, l'audible, l'odeur, la saveur, le tangible, et les choses (*dharma*, qui sont les objets de la pensée), leur caractère est parfaitement achevé. Et quand elles sont purifiées les six bases internes *(ādhyātmikāyatana)*—l'œil, l'oreille, le nez, la langue, le corps, et l'esprit *(manas)*—ont ce même caractère[93] (38–45).

Le *citta* en tant que tel *(sems nyid)* est élevé[94] de deux manières: le *saṃsāra* procède du fait qu'on saisit comme soi (: *ātmagrāha*) le mondain *(laukika)* et le supramondain *(lokottara)*, mais pour la connaissance intuitive c'est la réalité même[95] (46). Par suite de l'épuisement *(kṣaya)* de la concupiscence, de la

88. Voir plus loin, v. 44.

89. Ce vers et le vers parallèle 24 insistent ainsi sur le fait qu'il ne convient pas de ramener la réalité absolue au Soi des hétérodoxes, car il ne saurait faire l'objet de la «saisie» *(grāha)* et de la conceptualisation différenciatrice *(vikalpa)*. Cf. *Niraupamyastava* 10 et 22 (*supra*, p. 130–31).

90. Cf. les trois conditions *(avasthā)* du *dhātu*—celles du *sattva(dhātu)*, du *bodhisattva* et du *tathāgata*—qui sont énumérées dans le *Ratnagotravibhāga* (i.45 et suiv.) et dans le sūtra cité dans sa Vyākhyā (i.48).

91. *Dben pa = vivikta*, un terme qui se rapporte à la réalité en tant qu'«absolu».

92. *Chos kyi dbyings kyi ngo bo yis*. D porte *ngo bo yin* «c'est la nature du *dharmadhātu*».

93. Le caractère de l'absence d'être propre *(niḥsvabhāvatā: dharmadhātu)*.

94. *Mtho*. Selon D, qui porte *mthong*, il faut traduire: «on voit que le *citta* est double».

95. *De nyid = tattva?* V. *Mūlamadhyamakakārikā* xviii.9 pour une définition du *tattva* selon le Madhyamaka. Sur le *citta* cf. *Ta tche tou louen* 276b (cité par Venkata Ramanan,

haine et de la confusion il y a *nirvāṇa;* en vertu de leur arrêt *(nirodha)* il y a l'état de l'Éveillé *(buddhatva),* qui est le refuge même de tous les êtres incarnés (47). Tout procède en dernière analyse de la dichotomie de savoir et non-savoir, et on est lié par la conceptualisation différenciatrice *(vikalpa)* portant sur soi-même;[96] quand on a connu le soi *(ātman)* on est délivré (48).[97] L'Éveil *(bodhi)* n'est ni proche ni lointain;[98] mais dans la cage des *kleśa* il y a la dichotomie de vue et non-vue (49). Dans les sūtra il est dit que celui qui a atteint la tranquillité suprême en s'établissant dans la *prajñā* flambante doit s'établir toujours dans le soi[99] (50).

Suivent des vers sur l'action salvifique du *buddha,* qui est invisible aux êtres inférieurs obnubilés par les *kleśa* de l'ignorance *(avidyā);* au contraire, pour les êtres qui ont acquis des mérites, ses trente-deux marques *(lakṣaṇa)* sont rayonnantes (51–54). En effet, le Corps Formel *(rūpakāya)* du Seigneur *(nātha)* a duré pendant de nombreuses périodes cosmiques *(kalpa),* et c'est en vue de l'entraînement des disciples que le *dhātu (dbyings)* est diversifié (55).[100] Parmi les enfantins *(bāla)* il y a l'omniscient *(sarvajña),* et parmi les saints *(ārya)* il y a l'universel:[101] Maheśvara-Amitāyus est la cause de la vie *(āyus)* qui dure toute une période cosmique.[102] Celui qui a protégé tout au

---

Nāgārjuna's Philosophy, p. 71–72), qui va encore plus loin que le *Daśabhūmikasūtra,* chap. VI, où il est dit: *cittamātram idaṃ yad idaṃ traidhātukam.*

96. Cf. *Mūlamadhyamakakārikā* xviii.5, et ci-dessous, n. 107.

97. Rappelons que le mot *ātman* s'emploie aussi bien comme un pronom réfléchi que comme un substantif («soi»).

98. L'état de *buddha* n'est ni une entité immanente ni une entité transcendante. Voir aussi plus loin, v. 61. Cf. *Mahāparinirvāṇasūtra,* kha (H), fol. 172a–b (cité par Bu ston dans son *Mdzes rgyan,* fol. 16b–17a) sur la Nature de *buddha.*

99. *Bdag la rtag par gnas bya* (P, C et N [qui porte *rtag pa]).* D porte *bdag la brtags pas gnas bya.*

100. V. *Niraupamyastava* 21 (*supra,* p. 130) et *Abhisamayālaṃkāra* i.39 (*supra,* n. 59).

101. *Sna tshogs nyid;* traduction incertaine. Le texte fait peut-être allusion à la possibilité qu'ont tous les ārya des trois Véhicules *(yāna)* de comprendre la réalité absolue; cf. *Théorie,* p. 171n, 177 et suiv.

102. Amitābha est mentionné par Nāgārjuna dans le *Suhṛllekha* (§ 121); et le *Laṅkāvatārasūtra* (Sagāthaka 166) et le *Mañjuśrīmūlakalpa* (53.451) disent que Nāgārjuna naîtra dans la Sukhāvatī après avoir quitté son corps.—Il semble exister un lien particulier entre Amitābha et la doctrine du *dhātu;* v. *Ratnagotravibhāga* v.25 et le *Ta tch'eng k'i sin louen* (dans ces conditions, les remarques de W. Liebenthal, *TP* 46 [1958], p. 189 et 197, sont probablement à reconsidérer).—Sur les liens entre la *bhakti* et le culte d'Amitābha, cf. É. Lamotte, *La concentration de la Marche Héroïque,* p. 56–58.

Le monde de Maheśvara *(maheśvarabhuvana)* est la résidence des bodhisattva de

long d'une période incommensurable *(asaṃkhyeyakalpa)* la vie des êtres animés est le principe vital *(srog = jīva)* de tous les êtres vivants. Cette cause est inépuisable: ce en vertu de quoi le Fruit *(phala)* ne s'épuise pas agit en vue de la *prajñā* moyennant une particularité sans apparence *(nirābhāsa)* (58–60).[103] Sans penser que la *bodhi* soit lointaine, on ne doit pas penser qu'elle soit proche; on connaîtra exactement et conformément à la réalité *(yathāvat)* que les six objets *(viṣaya)* sont sans apparence (61).[104]

D'un mélange de lait et d'eau contenu dans un seul vase le *haṃsa* ne boit que le lait et laisse l'eau;[105] pareillement, dans ce corps la Gnose *(jñāna)* recouverte de *kleśa* existe ensemble [avec ce qui lui est étranger], mais le yogin prend la Gnose et laisse l'ignorance *(avidyā)* (62–63).

Dans la mesure où l'on saisit *(grah-)* le soi *(ātman)* et ce qui appartient au soi *(ātmīya)* on construit par désignation;[106] mais quand on a vu l'Insubstantialité de la personne *(pudgalanairātmya)* et des choses *(dharmanairātmya)* le germe de l'existence *(bhava)* est arrêté (64). A cause de la base pure qui est propre *(śuci)*, permanente *(nitya)* et bonne et en vertu de laquelle le *buddha* est nirvâné l'enfantin construit par désignation la dualité; sa non-dualité est le séjour du *yoga* (65).[107]

---

la dixième *bhūmi;* v. *Daśabhūmikasūtra* 10J et *Yogācārabhūmi,* p. 76 (cf. L. de La Vallée Poussin, *Vijñaptimātratāsiddhi,* p. 440–42, 493–94).

103. Cf. par exemple *Mahāyānasūtrālaṃkārabhāṣya* xi.32–33 *([a]dvayābhāsa = gnyis su snang ba [med pa]).*

104. Voir plus haut, v. 49 et 45.

105. Cf. Asaṅga, *Mahāyānasaṃgraha* i.49.

106. Comme plus haut D porte *brtags pa* «imaginer».

107. P, N et C portent: *gang phyir sangs rgyas mya ngan 'das // gtsang ba rtag pa dge ba'i gzhi // dag phyir gnyis ni byis pas btags // de yi gnyis med rnal 'byor gnas//* Mais D donne la variante *gang phyir gnyis ni byis pas brtags.* En suivant cette variante on pourrait traduire: La non-dualité de ce en vertu de quoi le *nirvāṇa* du *buddha* est une chose propre *(śuci)*, permanente *(nitya)* et bonne et de ce en raison de quoi l'enfantin imagine la dualité est le séjour du *yoga.* En d'autres termes, le *yoga* serait la coïncidence et, partant, l'abolition des oppositions dichotomiques et discursives portant sur l'impermanent/permanent, etc., et l'*advaya* est donc le séjour du *yoga.* Cf. Candrakīrti, *Madhyamakāvatāra* vi.117:

so so'i skye bo rnams ni rtog pas bcing//
mi rtog rnal 'byor pa ni grol 'gyur bas//
rtog rnams log par 'gyur ba gang yin te//
rnam par dpyod pa'i 'bras bur mkhas rnams gsungs//
Les profanes *(pṛthagjana)* sont liés par l'imagination constructive *(kalpanā)*,
et le yogin qui ne s'adonne pas à l'imagination constructive est délivré; les sages
ont donc déclaré que l'inversion (: *bkag pa*) de l'imagination est le fruit
de l'examen.

Suivent des vers sur les perfections *(pāramitā)* dont les trois premières—la libéralité *(dāna),* la discipline *(śīla)* et la patience *(kṣānti)*—servent à développer l'Élément spirituel *(khams),* tandis que les trois dernières—l'énergie *(vīrya),* la méditation *(dhyāna)* et la *prajñā*—développent la *bodhi* (66–67). Le *dhātu* est également développé par quatre facteurs: la *prajñā* jointe au moyen *(upāya),* la très parfaite résolution, et la Gnose bien établie dans la force (68).[108] Dire que le *bodhicitta* n'est pas à honorer, c'est dire ce qui est mauvais; car aussi longtemps que le bodhisattva ne naît pas il n'y aura pas de *dharmakāya* (69).[109]

Ensuite vient une série de vers sur la production du *bodhicitta* et sur les terres spirituelles *(bhūmi)* du bodhisattva qui mènent à la *buddhabhūmi* (70–87). Comme il contient le séjour des *buddha*—le Fruit de la conduite *(caryā)* des bodhisattva—on appelle le séjour métamorphosé *(yongs su gyur pa: parivṛtta* ou *parāvṛtta)* le Corps de Dharma *(dharmakāya)* (88).[110]

Ce qui est délivré des prédispositions *(vāsanā)* est inconcevable *(acintya),* alors que la *vāsanā* du *saṃsāra* est concevable. Tu es entièrement inconcevable, et qui pourrait te connaître (89)! Hommage avec louange à ce qui dépasse tout le domaine verbal, qui est inaccessible à toutes les facultés sensorielles *(indriya)*[111] et qui est à connaître par la connaissance mentale (90)![112]

Par cette méthode de progression les fils renommés du Buddha arrivent à voir la *dharmatā* Vide *(śūnya)* au moyen de la Gnose *(jñāna)* du Nuage du Dharma *(dharmamegha)* (91).[113] Suivent des vers sur la délivrance des bodhisattva suprêmes, qui possèdent sans dépérissement les qualités de *buddha (buddhadharma)* inconcevables *(acintya)* et sans développement discursif *(niṣprapañca)* (92–98). Tandis que ceux qui n'ont obtenu que le *nirvāṇa* avec reste *(sopadhiśeṣa)* pensent avoir le *nirvāṇa* sans reste *(nirupadhiśeṣa),* le *nirvāṇa* dont il est question ici comporte la métamorphose de la pensée

108. Sur le développement de l'Élément *(dhātupuṣṭi)* voir notamment *Mahāyānasūtrālaṃkāra* xi.61–73.

109. Cf. *Madhyamakāvatāra* i.1 avec l'autocommentaire de Candrakīrti, qui cite le *Kāśyapaparivarta* § 88.

110. Cf. plus loin, v. 99.

111. Cf. la fin du *Prajñāpāramitāstotra* de Rāhulabhadra.

112. Rappelons que dans le système des dix-huit *dhātu* de l'Abhidharma les *dharmāḥ* (= *dharmadhātu*) sont le *viṣaya* du *manas,* le point d'appui du *manovijñāna.* Cf. *Abhidharmakośa* i.16 et suiv.

Selon le *Kāyatrayastotra* le *dharmakāya* est à connaître intuitivement *(pratyātmavedanīya);* v. *supra,* n. 44, et n. 46.

113. *Dharmameghā,* la dixième *bhūmi.*

(citta) dans la pureté (99).[114] Le bodhisattva voit la nature insubstantielle de tous les êtres animés, laquelle lui est accessible, ainsi que le *dharmakāya* très pur (100). Et l'océan de la Gnose étant métamorphosé en le *dharmakāya* très pur, c'est à l'instar de la pierre précieuse universelle[115] qu'il fait le bien de l'être animé (101).

* * * *

Le texte de la version tibétaine du *Dharmadhātustava* n'est pas sans poser des problèmes. Ainsi, à côté du vers 33 qui n'a que trois *pāda,* le vers 99 a un *pāda* de trop, sans doute par dittographie.[116] En ce qui concerne la structure de l'hymne, des vers traitant du même thème sont parfois séparés par un ou plusieurs vers parlant de tout autre chose. C'est ainsi que le vers 91 semble bien développer l'idée exprimée dans 88, les deux vers 89–90—qui contiennent un hommage au *dharmadhātu* inaccessible à la connaissance sensorielle et à la pensée discursive—paraissant alors comme une intercalation qui interrompt la continuité; et le vers 61, dont le premier hémistiche répète ce qui est dit dans le premier hémistische de 49, amplifie l'idée développée dans 38–45. En outre, à en juger d'après le contexte, le vers 27—qui ajoute encore une autre comparaison pour illustrer la notion de l'Élément caché exposée dans 3–23—pourrait ne pas être à sa place, conjecture qu'appuie peut-être le fait que dans la *Dharmadhātudarśanagīti* d'Atisha ce vers suit le vers 13 du *Dharmadhātustava.*[117]

114. Voir plus haut, v. 88. —Sur le *nirvāṇa* des *śrāvaka* qui ne cherchent que la tranquillité du *samādhi* et s'installent donc dans une sorte d'extinction provisoire, voir *Ratnagotravibhāga* ii.58, et l'*Abhisamayālaṃkārālokā* de Haribhadra qui cite (ii.1) un vers où il est dit que les personnes qui craignent l'existence et s'établissent dans une condition qu'ils tiennent pour le *nirvāṇa* seront un jour réveillées par les *buddha* et obtiendront ainsi enfin l'Éveil suprême; selon Haribhadra, c'est Amitābha qui les réveille. Une version du vers en question se trouve dans le *Bodhicittavivaraṇa* de Nāgārjuna. Cf. *Théorie,* p. 194 et 211.

Selon le *Pañcakrama* (vi.9), quand on a atteint le stade de l'Intégration *(yuganaddha)* on ne construit pas de différence entre le *sopadhiśesa*° *et* le *nirupadhiśeṣanirvāṇa.* Cf. aussi L. de La Vallée Poussin, *Vijñaptimātratāsiddhi,* p. 508 et 671–73 (et l'*Abhidharmakośa* 6, p. 211).

115. *Sna tshogs nor bu = *citramaṇi (= cintāmaṇi?).*

116. Ce *pāda* additionnel, qui dans P, N et C constitue le premier *pāda* du vers et est identique au *pāda d* de ces éditions, a été supprimé dans D. D'ailleurs, ainsi qu'on a pu le constater plus haut, D présente plusieurs remaniements et corrections du texte transmis (avec quelques variantes) dans P, N et C.

117. La traduction chinoise ne semble cependant pas confirmer cette conjecture.

Cette *Dharmadhātudarśanagīti* fut traduite en tibétain par l'auteur lui-même avec Nag tsho lo tsā ba, qui traduisit le *Dharmadhātustava;* elle reprend, avec quelques variantes sans grande importance, la majorité des stances de la première partie du *Dharmadhātustava.*[118]

Cependant, même si l'on suppose que le texte du *Dharmadhātustava* renferme des interpolations, il n'est sans doute pas possible d'expliquer par l'hypothèse de remaniements ultérieurs la présence, dans cet ouvrage attribué au fondateur de l'école du Madhyamaka, d'une théorie positive de la réalité, car cette théorie caractérise l'hymne dans son ensemble. D'ailleurs, des traces d'une notion positive de la réalité se trouvent dans d'autres hymnes attribués à Nāgārjuna, et notamment dans le *Niraupamyastava,* ainsi que dans le **Mahāprajñāpāramitopadeśa (Ta tche tou louen)* qui, même s'il n'est pas à attribuer dans sa totalité à Nāgārjuna, n'en remonte pas moins à une période assez ancienne dans l'histoire de l'école du Madhyamaka. Il est donc clair que le *Dharmadhātustava* revêt une importance considérable pour l'étude de la doctrine des Mādhyamikas.

118. Les stances du *Dharmadhātustava* reprises par Atisha se trouvent au début de la *Dharmadhātudarśanagīti* dans l'ordre suivant (numérotation du *Dharmadhātustava*): 1, x, x (9 pāda au total, sans équivalent dans le *Dharmadhātustava*), 2, 3, 4, 5, 6, 7, 8, 9, 10ac (!), 12, 13, 27 *(ji ltar sbrum ma'i lto na bu . . .),* 24 (avec une variante), 26ab (avec une variante), 22, 22cd (avec une variante), 30, 31, 32. Le reste de la *Dharmadhātudarśanagīti,* approximativement 6/7 de l'ouvrage entier, n'a aucun rapport direct avec le *Dharmadhātustava.*

5. On the Authorship of Some Works Ascribed to Bhā(va)viveka/Bhavya*

INDOLOGISTS HAVE REPEATEDLY been confronted by the difficult problem of the correct assignment of literary works to their authors. In the history of the Vedānta the attribution of works to Śaṃkara has been frequently debated, whilst in the Alaṃkāraśāstra there is the thorny question whether Ānandavardhana was the author of the *Dhvanikārikā*s as well as of the commentary on them, the *Dhvanyāloka.* Another well-known discussion has centred on the question whether one and the same Vasubandhu was the author of the *Abhidharmakośa,* the *Viṃśatikā,* and the *Triṃśikā* on the one side and of texts such as the *Madhyāntavibhāgabhāṣya* and of other commentaries on Mahāyānist sūtras and śāstras on the other side. Similarly, in the early history of the Madhyamaka, we are faced with the question whether one and the same Nāgārjuna was the author not only of the *Mūlamadhyamakakārikā*s, and of other closely related works considered to form part of a "Scholastic Corpus," but also of the *Ratnāvalī* and, above all, of a "Hymnic Corpus."

A more recent arrival on the scene as a subject of discussion is the authorship of the *Tarkajvālā,* the commentary on Bhā(va)viveka's *Madhyamakahṛdayakārikā*s, of the *Madhyamakārthasaṃgraha,* and of the *Madhyamakaratnapradīpa,* all texts ascribed by some writers to the same Bhā(va)viveka/Bhavya who lived in the sixth century C.E.[1]

* First published in *Earliest Buddhism and Madhyamaka,* pp. 59–71. Ed. D. Seyfort Ruegg and L. Schmithausen. Leiden: E. J. Brill, 1990.

1. See Y. Kajiyama, *WZKSO* 12–13 (1968/69), pp. 193ff.; D. Seyfort Ruegg, *The Literature of the Madhyamaka School of Philosophy in India* (Wiesbaden, 1981), pp. 61–62.

Whether the fact that the names Bhāvaviveka, Bhāviveka, and Bhavya are all either retrievable or reconstructable from the Indian, Chinese, and Tibetan sources, and that they are sometimes used in alternation, has anything to do with the existence of more

In the case of authors like Śaṃkara and Ānandavardhana, and even to a large extent Nāgārjuna and Vasubandhu, the fact that their relevant works have survived in the original Sanskrit makes it possible to apply to them both stylometric and terminological criteria with a view to establishing authorship. But the case of Bhā(va)viveka is different because of the fact that with the sole exception of the *Madhyamakahṛdayakārikās*—a photograph of which text was taken at Zha lu in Tibet by Giuseppe Tucci after a hand copy had earlier been made there by Rāhula Sāṅkṛtyāyana—none of the works ascribed to him is now accessible in the original. This circumstance of course makes impossible the use of stylometric analysis. As for the application of terminological criteria, it is fraught with difficulty. For even though Paul Hacker and his followers have for example developed fine terminological and related doctrinal criteria for the study of Śaṃkara, it is well known how difficult it can be to extract conclusive arguments from such distinctions. For one thing, our frequently imperfect knowledge of the history of Indian philosophical ideas, arguments, and terms may not place us in a position safely and confidently to affirm that a given doctrine, reasoning, or expression could not, in any circumstance, have been accepted by the author to whom a text is traditionally ascribed. With regard to Nāgārjuna, for example, the predominantly positive ideas and the cataphatic language found in the hymns ascribed to him stand in marked contrast to the largely negative theory and apophatic approach of Nāgārjuna's scholastic works such as the *Mūlamadhyamakakārikās*; and we can say that there indeed exists a clear and significant difference in philosophical ideas and methods between the "Scholastic Corpus" and the "Hymnic Corpus" and that the works in question can be divided into two distinct categories (as has in fact been done by the Indo-Tibetan doxographical traditions as well as by modern scholars). But from this it by no means follows necessarily that the same Nāgārjuna could in no circumstances have been the author of both these sets of works. For the difference could be one of genre or it could be the reflection of parallel traditions drawn on by the same author; or again it could be the result of a development in his thinking.

than a single Mādhyamika master bearing one (or more) of these names is quite uncertain because of the loss of most of the relevant Indian-language documents in the original. The distribution in the Tibetan sources of the Tibetan equivalents of these names—Legs ldan 'byed (pa), Legs ldan, Snang bral, Skal ldan, Bha bya—does not appear definitely to establish such a supposition. In Candrakīrti's *Prasannapadā* as edited by L. de la Vallée Poussin, the Mādhyamika master who commented on Nāgārjuna's *Mūlamadhyamakakārikās* is referred to as Bhāvaviveka; and in Candrakīrti's *Madhyamakaśāstrastuti* (11) we find the name Bhāvin. (Bhāvivikta—a formation comparable to Bhāviveka—was the name of a Naiyāyika who lived probably in the sixth or seventh century.)

This kind of difficulty is compounded when the texts in question are available only in translation, as is the case for almost all the works ascribed to Bhā(va)viveka. Even in the case of Vasubandhu, although it might have been hoped that the problem of authorship would be less difficult to resolve because so many of the works ascribed to him that have been under scrutiny are extant in Sanskrit and thus lend themselves to stylometric and terminological analysis, this expectation has not actually been fulfilled. And the availability of such means of analysis has not hitherto been of decisive help in arriving at clear conclusions as to authorship, or indeed even in reaching a working consensus among all scholars. This is due in part to the very nature of the materials scrutinized: they reveal few conclusive and unassailable arguments for or against identity of authorship that are accepted by all scholars in the present state of knowledge.

For deciding identity of authorship between a basic text *(mūla)* and its commentary, the often-cited exegetical principle of avoiding *utsūtravyākhyāna*, according to which a commentator should not go beyond the master's intent as found in the *mūla* being commented on, would if strictly observed make difficult, or even precarious, any conclusion as to authorship based on doctrinal content. But it is of course necessary to determine whether this principle has been observed, and indeed the extent to which a good commentator is in a position to observe it. Conversely, if an author were to feel free to go beyond his own *mūla* in his explanation of it in a *svopajñavṛtti* etc., the frontier between an auto-commentary and a commentary by another author who did not observe the principle of avoiding *utsūtravyākhyāna* would be an uncertain one with respect to doctrinal content. P. V. Kane once observed: "[An author of an autocommentary] can very well say 'my sūtra is brief and I am expanding its meaning for the sake of clear grasp of the subject.' Or he may say in the vṛtti that what he has stated in the sūtra is due only to his following old writers and that his own real opinion is different."[2] This last alternative in fact represents what Vasubandhu has done in his *Abhidharmakośabhāṣya*, where he has given the Sautrāntika doctrine as his own, whereas in the *kārikā*s he has stated the Kāśmīra-Vaibhāṣika view (see *Kośa* viii.40). In such a case the principle of avoiding *utsūtravyākhyāna* is clearly not operative.

In this connection there moreover arises the often awkward question as to when *adhyāhāra*—that is, the frequently necessary, and quite legitimate, supplying by a commentator of words missing in the *mūla* for reasons of brevity etc.—may turn into *utsūtravyākhyāna*.

2. P. V. Kane, *History of Sanskrit Poetics*[3] (Delhi, 1961), p. 174.

References in a text to Mantrayāna/Vajrayāna ideas, or to tantric works, have sometimes been cited as a further criterion for differentiating between compositions ascribed to an author. Here an important distinction requires, however, to be made explicit. Given the fact that Mantrayāna is after all fairly old in India, and that tantric texts were no doubt in existence well before what might be called the main Vajrayāna efflorescence beginning in, approximately, the seventh century C.E., an allusion to such ideas or texts cannot by itself be a sufficient ground for establishing that a text is not by a given author if he is posterior to, say, the fourth century at the latest. Only a traceable quotation from a homogeneous work of a known later date could serve this purpose. It is, then, the *kind* of Mantrayāna material mentioned, and the *way* it has been used in a text, that can be revealing; for it may contribute at least to a balance of probability one way or the other in respect to the authorship and date of a work.

In the specific case of Bhā(va)viveka/Bhavya, therefore, the mere mention of *dhāraṇī*s *(gzungs sngags), mantra*s *(gsang sngags),* and *vidyā*s *(rig sngags)* in the *Tarkajvālā*[3] is very clearly not conclusive in assigning authorship to a Deutero-Bhā(va)viveka/Bhavya. On the contrary, the quotation of a "prophecy" *(vyākaraṇa)* concerning Nāgārjuna from the *Mañjuśrīmūlatantra* in the *Madhyamakaratnapradīpa*[4] is quite another matter. This is because our text of the *Mañjuśrīmūlakalpa* in its Rājavyākaraṇaparivarta—which in fact contains a "prophecy" concerning Nāgārjuna, though not in the precise words quoted in the *Madhyamakaratnapradīpa*—mentions King Gopāla, the founder of the Pāla dynasty and the predecessor of Dharmapāla (r. ca. 770–810 or 775–812) in whose time Śāntarakṣita, Kamalaśīla, and Haribhadra also flourished.[5] The citation of the *Mañjuśrīmūlatantra* in the *Madhyamakaratnapradīpa* thus possesses greater weight than the simple allusion to *dhāraṇī*s etc. in the *Tarkajvālā* (especially in view of the uncer-

3. *Tarkajvālā* iii.12–13, P, fol. 60a6; iv, P, fol. 199b2. On *dhāraṇī* according to the Madhyamaka and other traditions, see É. Lamotte, *Le traité de la Grande Vertu de Sagesse,* I (Louvain, 1944), pp. 316–21, 328; IV (Louvain, 1976), pp. 1854–69. And on Bhā(va) viveka and *dhāraṇī*s according to Hsüan-tsang, see T. Watters, *On Yuan Chwang's Travels in India,* II (London, 1905), pp. 215, 223–24.

4. *Madhyamakaratnapradīpa,* P, fol. 361b4–5.

5. See *Mañjuśrīmūlakalpa,* chap. liii.449–51 (ed. T. Gaṇapati Śāstrī, Trivandrum, 1925) = 491–93 (ed. Rāhula Sāṅkṛtyāyana, in: K. P. Jayaswal, *An Imperial History of India,* Lahore, 1934) for Nāgārjuna; chap. liii.628 and 816 = 683 and 883 for Gopāla.

tainty as to whether this tantra was extant, as the constituted work we now know, as early as the sixth century).[6]

In regard to the authorship and date of the *Madhyamakaratnapradīpa,* it is moreover to be noted that when quoting (P f. 354a3–4) a verse to be found in Saraha's Apabhraṃśa *Dohākośa,*[7] Bhavya has referred to the author of this verse as "teacher's teacher" *(bla ma'i bla ma: guru-guru).*[8] This description can be interpreted as indicating that Bhavya, the author of the *Madhyamakaratnapradīpa,* was the grandpupil of Saraha. Now this Saraha may be identical with Rāhulabhadra, the master of Ārya Nāgārjuna, i.e., of the Deutero-Nāgārjuna who would seem to have lived in the seventh century. This would be consonant with the references in the *Madhyamakaratnapradīpa* to Dharmakīrti and Candrakīrti, who are also usually placed in the seventh century (see below).

Now, if we may suppose that the *Madhyamakaratnapradīpa* was actually referring to this Apabhraṃśa verse by Saraha, and that the latter was its author's teacher's teacher—a supposition which appears not to be historically implausible and is in accord with the Vinaya lineage Rāhula → Nāgārjuna → Bhā(va)viveka → Śrīgupta → Jñānagarbha → Śāntarakṣita found in some sources[9]—the question arises as to the date of the Apabhraṃśa composition by Saraha known as the *Dohākośa.* By its first editor, M. Shahidullah,

6. The *Mañjuśrīmūlakalpa* was translated into Chinese by T'ien-hsi-tsai at the end of the tenth century (T 1192), and into Tibetan by Kumārakalaśa and Shākya Blo gros at the command of Byang chub 'od in the eleventh century. On earlier versions in Chinese, see recently Y. Matsunaga, in M. Strickmann, ed., *Tantrik and Taoist Studies in Honour of R. A. Stein,* III (= *Mélanges chinois et bouddhiques* 22 [1985]), pp. 882–94. (It is however conceivable that the version of this tantra cited in the *Madhyamakaratnapradīpa* did not contain the *vyākaraṇa* concerning King Gopāla; but it is of course impossible to prove this.)

7. Ed. P. Ch. Bagchi, *Journal of the Department of Letters, Calcutta University* 28 (Calcutta, 1935), p. 82; ed. Rāhula Sāṃkṛtyāyana, *Dohākoś* (Patna, 1957), p. 6; Tibetan translation, P, fol. 77a2. This quotation has already been noted by C. Lindtner, *WZKS* 26 (1982), p. 175.

8. *Madhyamakaratnapradīpa,* P, fol. 354a3–4: *bla ma'i bla mas kyang don dam par rigs pa'i glu las/ rang gi sems nyid kun gyi sa bon te // gang la srid dang myang 'das 'phro ba // 'dod pa'i 'bras bu ster bar byed pa yi // yid bzhin 'dra ba'i sems la phyag 'tshal lo // zhes gsungs pas* .... The version in the Tibetan translation of Saraha's *Dohākośa* reads: *sems nyid gcig pu kun gyi sa bon te // ... yid bzhin nor 'dra'i sems la phyag 'tshal lo//*

9. See Bu ston, *Chos 'byung,* fol. 127a6. Cf. D. Seyfort Ruegg, *Literature of the Madhyamaka School,* p. 89; "Über die Nikāyas der Śrāvakas," in H. Bechert, ed., *Zur Schulzugehörigkeit von Werken der Hīnayāna-Literatur* (AAWG, Göttingen, 1985), pp. 123–24.

this collection was dated to ca. 1000 C.E.;[10] and the tenth century has been maintained by several subsequent writers on Apabhraṃśa and the history of Middle Indo-Aryan.[11] A *terminus ante quem* is provided by the *Dohākośa* commentary by Advayavajra (Maitrīpāda), probably the author of that name who lived in the early eleventh century. But the tenth century, although perhaps within the bounds of possibility, would seem to be a rather late date for Saraha; for as already mentioned he may well be identical with Saraha/Rāhulabhadra, the master of Ārya Nāgārjuna who may have lived in the seventh century.[12]

As for Apabhraṃśa, it is known as a literary language from the seventh century by references to it in Bhāmaha's *Kāvyālaṃkāra* (i.16, 28) and Daṇḍin's *Kāvyādarśa* (i.32, 36), as well as in an inscription of Dharasena II of Valabhī (ca. 600). But texts composed in Apabhraṃśa have mostly been dated by historians of Middle Indo-Aryan no earlier than the tenth century, although the language is attested earlier, for example in the *Bhaṭṭikāvya* (a seventh-century text from Valabhī) and in Uddyotana's *Kuvalayamālā* (eighth century). Moreover, according to Śākyaprabha's autocommentary on his *Ārya[mūla]sarvāstivādiśrāmaṇerakārikās*, Apabhraṃśa was the language

10. M. Shahidullah, *Les chants mystiques de Kāṇha et de Saraha* (Paris, 1928), p. 31.

11. See G. V. Tagare, *Historical Grammar of Apabhraṃśa* (Poona, 1948), p. 20; R. A. Singh, *Syntax of Apabhraṃśa* (Calcutta, 1980), p. 3. Cf. J. Bloch, *Indo-aryan* (Paris, 1965), p. 21; L. Renou, J. Filliozat, and P. Meile, *L'Inde classique,* I (Paris, 1947), §§ 116, 940; II (Paris, 1953) § 2030; S. K. Chatterji, *Origin and Development of the Bengali Language*[2] (London, 1970), I, pp. 110 f., 123; III, pp. 26–27; P. Kværne, *An Anthology of Buddhist Tantric Songs* (Oslo, 1977), pp. 5–7.

On the question of "Eastern Apabhraṃśa" as the designation of the language in which Saraha's *Dohākośa* is written, see S. N. Ghosal, *JASB*, 22 (1956). S. R. Banerjee, *Eastern School of Prakrit Grammarians* (Calcutta, 1977), p. 86, would date Saraha's *Dohākośa* in the tenth or at the latest the twelfth century but adds that it is better to take 700–1200 as the period of the Apabhraṃśa texts he is considering.

12. Saraha has been placed in the eighth century by A. Wayman, *The Buddhist Tantras* (New York, 1973), pp. 13–14. J. Naudou, *Les bouddhistes kaśmīriens au Moyen Age* (Paris, 1968), p. 82, and P. Kvaerne, *Anthology,* p. 7, speak of a ninth-century date. Such datings are however perhaps too late in view of the mention by I-ching (635–713) of a Nāgārjuna who had studied the Vidyādharapiṭaka (see E. Chavannes, *Mémoire composé à l'époque de la grande dynastie T'ang sur les religieux éminents qui allèrent chercher la Loi dans les pays d'Occident* [Paris, 1894], p. 102), and of the time of Vajrabodhi (ca. 671–741)—a disciple of Nāgabodhi—and of Amoghavajra (ca. 705–74). On this complicated question, which has still to be wholly clarified, see D. Seyfort Ruegg, *Literature of the Madhyamaka School,* pp. 104–5, and "Towards a Chronology of the Madhyamaka School," p. 511 (chapter 2 of the present volume, p. 21), where the seventh century has been suggested for Ārya Nāgārjunapāda, the disciple of Rāhulabhadra = Saraha.

of the canon of an (unspecified) Buddhist school *(nikāya)*; this Śākyaprabha lived at the latest in the eighth century.[13] (Later sources have connected the Apabhraṃśa canon in question with specific Nikāyas.)[14] Although the evidence bearing on the use of Apabhraṃśa as a literary language is accordingly hardly sufficient in the present state of knowledge to date Saraha's *Dohā*s on the basis of linguistic criteria, a date later than that of Bhā(va)viveka I—the sixth century—seems very likely. As already noted above, Saraha could have lived in the seventh (or at the very earliest perhaps in the late sixth) century if the above-mentiond Ārya Nāgārjuna lived in the seventh century.

Hence, although again not conclusive by itself, the evidence provided by the quotation in the *Madhyamakaratnapradīpa* of a verse identical with one found in Saraha's Apabhraṃśa *Dohākośa* points to a time later (and perhaps even much later) than that of Bhā(va)viveka I, the author of the *Prajñāpradīpa* and the *Madhyamakahṛdayakārikā*s.[15]

It is to be noted further that a quotation from Bhā(va)viveka's *Madhyamakahṛdayakārikā*s (iii.259) has been introduced by the author of the *Madhyamakaratnapradīpa* by saying: "In order to set out the Middle Way by eliminating the two extremes, I therefore negate also this *abhāva* [with the verse iii.259]."[16] In other words, to judge by the only available version of this text in Tibetan, it appears that the author of the *Madhyamakaratnapradīpa* claimed that he was also the author of *Madhyamakahṛdayakārikā* iii.259. The *Madhyamakaratnapradīpa* contains other quotations from the *Madhyamakahṛdayakārikā*s too.

13. See D. Seyfort Ruegg, "Über die Nikāyas," in: H. Bechert (ed.), *Zur Schulzugehörigkeit von Werken der Hīnayāna-literatur*, p. 114.

14. See D. Seyfort Ruegg, "Über die Nikāyas," pp. 116–17. This tradition, found in Tibetan sources, is not to be found in either Śākyaprabha or Padmākaraghoṣa. (And the indication on the subject in O. von Hinüber, *Das ältere Mittelindisch im Überblick* [Vienna, 1986], § 102, citing A. Yuyama in H. Bechert (ed.), *Die Sprache der älteren buddhistischen Überlieferung* [AAWG, Göttingen, 1980], pp. 175–81, evidently needs to be modified accordingly.)

15. In the appendix on Yogācāra to chap. xxv of his *Prajñāpradīpa*, Bhā(va)viveka in fact refers to his *Madhyamakahṛdaya-tattvāvatāra* (D, fol. 248a6).

16. *Madhyamakaratnapradīpa*, P, fol. 345a3–4: *gang gi phyir kho bo mtha' gnyis spangs pas/ dbu ma'i lam ston pa'i phyir med pa nyid kyang 'gog par byed de: "dngos rnams med ces bya ba'i blo // don bzhin yin par mi 'dod de // rtog pa'i sgo nas grub pa'i phyir // mtho yor la ni mi blo bzhin//"* The Sanskrit text of *Madhyamakahṛdayakārikā* iii.259 in the edition of Y. Ejima (*Chūgan shisō no tenkai - Bhāvaviveka kenkyū*, Tokyo, 1981) reads: *na santi bhāvā iti vā yathārthā na matir matā/ kalpanādvāranirvṛtteḥ sthāṇoḥ puruṣabuddhivat//.*

In another passage of the Tibetan translation of the *Madhyamakaratnapradīpa,* the author has stated that he composed the *Tarkajvālā.*[17]

Before pursuing this matter further, it will be of interest to enquire whether, apart from literary-historical criteria, data of a formal kind are available that will assist us in deciding the question of the authorship of works ascribed to Bhā(va)viveka.

In the *Tarkajvālā* there is found a curious feature that is of importance in this respect. On several occasions this work has referred to the author of the *Madhyamakahṛdayakārikā* being commented on not only in the third person but also as "Ācārya" *(slob dpon).*[18] That the author of a *mūla* should in his autocommentary refer to himself in the third person is of course very usual.[19] But that an author of an autocommentary should refer to himself as "Ācārya" is, if not unprecedented, at least rare.

It is true that in his *Abhidharmakośabhāṣya* (*avatāraṇikā* on i.3) Vasubandhu has put in the mouth of a questioner a sentence in which the author of the *Abhidharmakośakārikā*s is referred to as "Ācārya." But the decisive point in this case is the fact that another person is here supposed to be speaking and using the appellation "Ācārya" for Vasubandhu, so that this example can scarcely be regarded as a precedent for the usage found in the *Tarkajvālā.* An example where a Sanskrit writer has in an autocommentary referred to the author of the *mūla*—in other words to himself—as "Ācārya" is nevertheless to be found in the Jaina Haribhadrasūri's (eighth century?) *Anekāntajayapatākā.*[20] How frequent this convention is has not to my knowledge been established, but it would appear to be quite rare.[21] The question for us is then whether Bhā(va)viveka has actually employed this convention.

17. *Madhyamakaratnapradīpa,* P, fol. 335b3: *bdag gis bkod pa rtog ge 'bar ba.*

18. E.g., *Madhyamakahṛdayavṛtti-Tarkajvālā,* i.21 (P, fol. 50a5); iii.58 (fol. 75a1), 97 (fol. 86a2), 176 (fol. 107a2), 196 (fol. 112b6), etc.

19. As has been observed by P. V. Kane, *History of Dharmaśāstra, I²* (Poona, 1968), p. 195, "in order to avoid looking egoistic, ancient authors generally put their own views in the third person as said by early writers like Medhātithi [ad Manu i.4] and Viśvarūpa [ad Yājñavalkya i.2]." In his *History of Sanskrit Poetics³,* p. 270, Kane has remarked that "ancient writers regarded it as too dogmatic to express their opinions in the first person," observing on page 171 that "it is clear that there is no prohibition against an author saying that he himself composed the sūtra and the vṛtti, even when he speaks of himself in the third person in the vṛtti."

20. Ed. H. R. Kāpadīā, Gaekwad's Oriental Series (Baroda, 1940), vol. 1, p. 2.12.

21. The author of the *Pratītyasamutpādahṛdayavyākhyāna* has also referred to the author of the *mūla*—the *Pratītyasamutpādahṛdayakārikā*s—as *slob dpon = ācārya.* Both these

Because of his recognition of its rarity, V. V. Gokhale has suggested that Nag tsho Tshul khrims rgyal ba, Atisha's Tibetan collaborator in the translation of the *Tarkajvālā,* may have inserted explanations given by Atisha, introducing them by the appellation *ācārya.*[22] This is of course not in itself impossible, but it must be considered an unusual procedure. It would moreover seem that the word *ācārya* in the *Tarkajvālā* refers in such cases not to Atisha but to the author of the *mūla.*

Here, then, it is a formal feature rather than either a literary-historical or a doctrinal one that could lead to the conclusion that the author of the *Tarkajvālā* was not identical with the author of the *Madhyamakahṛdayakārikās* in question.[23]

If this is the case, nothing stands in the way of supposing that the name of the author of the *Tarkajvālā*—and of the *Madhyamakaratnapradīpa* too—was Bhā(va)viveka/Bhavya also. And the problem would be one not of authenticity as against forgery, but of identifying to which of two or more Bhā(va)vivekas/Bhavyas these works are to be ascribed.

What is then to be made of the disparate, and sometimes apparently conflicting, evidence gathered above?

In several Indo-Tibetan sources the three works in question—the *Madhyamakahṛdayakārikās*, the *Tarkajvālā,* and the *Madhyamakaratnapradīpa*—have evidently been ascribed, implicitly if not explicitly, to one and the same author.

Y. Ejima has however distinguished between an *"Ur-Tarkajvālā"* and a revised *Tarkajvālā,* which is the text included in the Tibetan Bstan 'gyur. In Ejima's opinion, while the *"Ur-Tarkajvālā"* was by the author of the *Madhyamakahṛdayakārikās*, the revised version is by the author of the *Madhyamakaratnapradīpa,* who has referred favourably to Candrakīrti and Dharmakīrti, both of whom are usually placed in the seventh century, as well as to a number of tantric texts generally dated to after the sixth century.

works have been ascribed to Nāgārjuna in the Bstan 'gyur. C. Lindtner has expressed doubt as to Nāgārjuna's authorship of the *Vyākhyāna;* see *WZKS* 26 (1982), p. 172. On these two works see recently C. Dragonetti, *WZKS* 30 (1986), pp. 110 f.

22. V. V. Gokhale in: C. Lindtner (ed.), *Miscellanea buddhica* (Copenhagen, 1985), pp. 77 and 99n44.

23. See Y. Ejima, *Chūgan shisō no tenkai—Bhāvaviveka kenkyū.* See also Ejima's views reported in C. Lindtner, *WZKS* 26 (1982), pp. 182–83.

The opposite situation is to be found for example in the *Yogasūtrabhāṣya,* whose author as it were incorporates certain sūtras into his *bhāṣya* by introducing them as if he had composed them himself (saying, e.g., *vakṣyāma* in ii.40 and 46).

Ejima has supposed that this Bhavya lived no earlier than Śāntarakṣita and Kamalaśīla (eighth century).[24]

C. Lindtner has taken the opposite course of ascribing all three works in question, as well as the *Madhyamakārthasaṃgraha* to be considered below, to one and the same sixth-century author, placing both Candrakīrti and Dharmakīrti accordingly in the sixth rather than in the seventh century and also giving the sixth century as the lower limit for all the tantric sources cited in the *Madhyamakaratnapradīpa.*[25]

Now, on the basis of any of the above-mentioned data taken separately, it may indeed not be possible conclusively to demonstrate either that, negatively, the *Tarkajvālā* and the *Madhyamakaratnapradīpa* can *not* be by the author of the *Madhyamakahṛdayakārikā*s or that, positively, these two works *are* by an author different from the Bhā(va)viveka who composed the *Madhyamakahṛdayakārikā*s. Nevertheless, it still has to be said, I think, that the cumulative weight of the various data constituting our body of evidence must lead one very carefully to consider the possibility that these texts are in fact not by the author of the *Madhyamakahṛdayakārikā*s and the *Prajñāpradīpa.* The balance of evidence seems to incline in favour of this conclusion, even if it cannot be held to prove it conclusively: what is possible in logical deduction will indeed seldom be possible in such difficult cases of historical and philological induction.

At the same time, following an old philosopher's maxim which the historian has also to bear in mind, *entia non sunt multiplicanda praeter necessitatem* "entities are not to be multiplied beyond need." The question here is then what is need and what corresponds to parsimony—to *lāghava* as opposed to *gaurava.*

The problems posed by assuming identity of authorship for these three works seem to outweigh any that result from assuming different authorship. That is, to suppose that all three are by one and the same sixth-century author appears to involve making more difficult assumptions—e.g., putting back

24. See Y. Ejima, op. cit., and *Indogaku bukkyōgaku kenkyū* 28.2 (1980), pp. (37)–(43). See also Ejima's views reported in C. Lindtner, *WZKS* 26 (1982), pp. 182–83.

25. See C. Lindtner *AO* 40 (1979), p. 90, and 41 (1980), pp. 27–37; *WZKS* 26 (1982), pp. 167–84; *Indologica Taurinensia* 12 (1984), pp. 163–84; and most recently in E. Kahrs (ed.), *Kalyāṇamitrārāgaṇam, Essays in Honour of Nils Simonsson* (Oslo, 1986), pp. 179–202, and in B. K. Matilal (ed.), *Buddhist Logic and Epistemology* (Dordrecht, 1986), pp. 239–63.

the dates not only of Candrakīrti and Dharmakīrti but also of Kumārila,[26] making Dharmakīrti virtually a younger contemporary (or an immediate successor) of Dignāga, and placing the *Mañjuśrīmūlatantra/kalpa* as a constituted text bearing this title no later than ca. 500 C.E. together with all the tantric and other sources cited in the *Madhyamakaratnapradīpa* including the Apabhraṃśa *dohā* discussed above—than to suppose, on the balance of the evidence, a difference of authorship. A point of no little importance is also the fact that the author of the *Madhyamakaratnapradīpa* regarded (a) Candrakīrti favourably and quoted him as an authority; whereas the author of the *Prasannapadā* was perhaps the chief opponent of Bhā(va)viveka, the author of the *Prajñāpradīpa.*

Beside the two opposed views advocated by Ejima and Lindtner, there exists a third, theoretical, possibility of resolving at least the literary-historical problems raised by the authorship of the three texts. This would consist in supposing that Bhā(va)viveka/Bhavya had an extremely—and unusually—long life-span beginning in the sixth century, before Sthiramati, when he composed the *Prajñāpradīpa,* and extending to a very advanced age in the seventh century, the time of Candrakīrti and Dharmakīrti and of masters such as Saraha/Rāhulabhadra and Ārya-Nāgārjunapāda, when he might have composed the *Madhyamakaratnapradīpa.*

Such a solution does not, however, account for the author of the *Madhyamakahṛdayakārikās* being evidently referred to in the *Tarkajvālā* with the title *ācārya.* Nor does it explain how the author of the *Madhyamakaratnapradīpa* came to refer to Candrakīrti as an authority to be followed, especially when there is evidence that Candrakīrti lived in the seventh century.[27]

Could it be, then, that the author of the *Madhyamakahṛdayakārikās* and the *Prajñāpradīpa* was indeed different from the Bhā(va)viveka/Bhavya who composed the *Tarkajvālā* and the *Madhyamakaratnapradīpa,* but that the author of the latter work considered himself to belong to the same mental and spiritual continuum *(cittasaṃtāna)* as his earlier namesake(s) so that he

26. See D. Seyfort Ruegg, "Towards a Chronology of the Madhyamaka School" (chapter 2 of the present volume) in: L. A. Hercus et al. (eds.), *Indological and Buddhist Studies,* p. 530 (where in the words "It must of course be supposed . . . " *must* is a misprint for *might*).

27. If, however, the reference in the *Madhyamakaratnapradīpa* were not to Candrakīrti, the author of the *Prasannapadā* and the chief critic of Bhā(va)viveka I, but to the Deutero-Candrakīrti, a disciple presumably of the tāntrika Ārya-Nāgārjunapāda, the *Madhyamakaratnapradīpa* could not be ascribed to the sixth-century Bhā(va)viveka I; and it could hardly be placed before the seventh or eighth century.

could evidently claim the authorship of the *Madhyamakahṛdayakārikās* and explicitly state that he composed the *Tarkajvālā*?

If so, our problem would be as much one of religious ideas as of literary history and the development of philosophical doctrine. This relationship could apply even if it turns out that the *Tarkajvālā* has a different author from both the *Madhyamakahṛdayakārikās* and the *Madhyamakaratnapradīpa,* that is, if we have to do with three rather than with two authors sharing the name Bhā(va)viveka/Bhavya and all belonging to the same spiritual lineage.

How does the hypothesis that the author of the *Madhyamakaratnapradīpa* was not Bhā(va)viveka I square with the historical and doxographical traditions of Buddhism? For, as already mentioned, certain Indo-Tibetan traditions have proceeded, at least tacitly, as if all three texts in question were composed by the same author. And the *Tarkajvālā* has in any case been regularly regarded as Bhā(va)viveka's *rang 'grel* or autocommentary on the *Madhyamakahṛdayakārikās.*

The traditions are not, however, all agreed that the *Madhyamakaratnapradīpa* was composed by Bhā(va)viveka I, as has sometimes been supposed on the basis of the Bstan 'gyur catalogues etc.

Thus, while Lcang skya Rol pa'i rdo rje (1717–86) regards the *Tarkajvālā* as an autocommentary on the *Madhyamakahṛdayakārikās*, he explicitly states that the *Madhyamakaratnapradīpa* was not composed by the same author but by a master known as the Junior Bhavya (Legs ldan chung ba).[28] And in an important historical and doxographical work completed in 1801/1802 by Thu'u bkwan Blo bzang Chos kyi nyi ma (1737–1802) mention is also made of a later, or younger, Bhā(va)viveka who lived after Candrakīrti and belonged very significantly to the lineage of the *zab mo lta ba'i brgyud pa* or *klu sgrub nye brgyud.*[29] A related tradition is attested earlier in the *Rgya nag chos 'byung* by Mgon po skyabs (eighteenth century).[30]

Turning now to the *Madhyamakārthasaṃgraha* ascribed also to Bhā(va)-viveka/Bhavya, it can be observed that starting with its introductory verse of salutation, this text is quite closely related to the *Satyadvayavibhaṅga* by

28. Lcang skya Rol pa'i rdo rje, *Grub pa'i mtha' rnam par bzhag pa gsal bar bshad pa,* kha, fol. 6a (= p. 283): *legs ldan chung bar grags pas mdzad pa yin gyi slob dpon 'dis mdzad pa min no.*

29. Thu'u bkwan Blo bzang chos kyi nyi ma, *Grub mtha' shel gyi me long,* Rgya nag chapter, fol. 9b3: *legs ldan 'byed phyi ma'am legs ldan 'byed chung ma.*

30. Mgon po skyabs, *Rgya nag chos 'byung* (Sichuan ed., 1983), p. 123.

Jñānagarbha (eighth century), the master mentioned above who belonged to a lineage in which he linked Bhā(va)viveka and Śrīgupta with Śāntarakṣita.

The theory of the two levels—*paramārtha* and *saṃvṛti*—and of the two *satya*s in the *Madhyamakārthasaṃgraha* appears at least as advanced as Jñānagarbha's, and as rather more elaborate than that of chapter iii of the *Madhyamakahṛdayakārikās* and the *Tarkajvālā*. On the level of the *paramārthasatya,* it operates with a division between the "non-modal" (i.e., non-conceptualizable and non-verbalizable) Absolute *(rnam grangs ma yin don dam: *aparyāya/niṣparyāya-paramārtha)* and a "modal" Absolute *(rnam grangs kyi don dam: *saparyāya-paramārtha),* the latter being in its turn subdivided into the **saparyāya-paramārtha* of reasoning (*rigs pa: nyāya* or *yukti*?) and that of the negation of real origination *(skye ba bkag pa'i don dam).* This developed terminology is not to be found in the *Tarkajvālā,* chapter iii (which does however, like the *Madhyamakārthasaṃgraha,* distinguish between a *paramārtha* without *prapañca* and one with);[31] nor indeed is it found even in Jñānagarbha's text (see however *Satyadvayavibhaṅga* 4ab on *rigs pa* as *don dam*). As for the *saṃvṛti* level, the *Madhyamakārthasaṃgraha* mentions the division between true *saṃvṛti (yang dag pa'i kun rdzob: tathyasaṃvṛti)* and false *saṃvṛti (log pa'i kun rdzob: mithyāsaṃvṛti),* a distinction seemingly implied in the *Tarkajvālā* (iii.7, which however mentions only the *tathyasaṃvṛti*) and explicitly mentioned by Jñānagarbha (8d, where the latter is referred to as the *yang dag pa ma yin pa'i kun rdzob* etc.). The *Madhyamakārthasaṃgraha*'s very important, indeed criterial, definition of true *saṃvṛti* in terms of a thing *(dngos po = vastu)* that is causally efficient *(don byed nus pa = arthakriyāsamartha)*—an idea presumably taken from Dharmakīrti[32]—is to be found also in the *Satyadvayavibhaṅga* (8 and 12). According to the *Madhyamakārthasaṃgraha,* false *saṃvṛti* may be either conceptually constructed (*rtog bcas: savikalpa,* as in the case of a rope misapprehended as a snake) or not so constructed (*rtog med,* e.g., when somebody suffering from eye-disease sees the moon as double without any conceptual construction entering into this apprehension).

The *Madhyamakārthasaṃgraha* would accordingly seem to fit very well into the philosophical thought of the eighth century (if not later).[33] And it can

31. The present writer's observation in *Literature of the Madhyamaka School of Philosophy in India,* p. 64n202, therefore requires reconsideration.

32. Cf. M. Nagatomi, *ALB* 31–32 (1967/68), pp. 52–72. On this definition in Jñānagarbha's *Satyadvayavibhaṅga,* see now M. D. Eckel *Jñānagarbha's Commentary on the Distinction between the Two Truths* (Albany, 1987).

33. See also Y. Ejima, *Chūgan shisō no tenkai—Bhāvaviveka kenkyū.*

perhaps be dated to about the same period as the *Madhyamakaratnapradīpa.* This very short text does not cite any sources or authorities, and it does not therefore allow any literary-historical inferences to be drawn.

Further research is required to determine how far back the Tibetan tradition on two Bhā(va)vivekas goes and what its ultimate sources were. In any case, the existence of this tradition demonstrates very clearly that the *Madhyamakaratnapradīpa* has not been unanimously attributed in Buddhist sources to the Bhā(va)viveka who lived in the sixth century. Further investigation of the relation between the *Tarkajvālā,* the *Madhyamakārthasaṃgraha,* and the *Madhyamakaratnapradīpa* will also be necessary.

For many purposes it would in the final analysis seem to be more interesting to seek to understand and explain texts and religious and philosophical ideas, and to study the traditions to which they belong, rather than to concentrate one-sidedly on trying to determine authorship, especially when the very nature of the evidence makes the latter enterprise so uncertain. Although clarifying authorship is of very considerable help in understanding and interpreting a text, this latter goal can still be effectively pursued even when authorship is uncertain or unknown, as is often the case in the history of Indian literature.

6. The *Svātantrika-Prāsaṅgika* Distinction in the History of Madhyamaka Thought*

I

IN PHILOSOPHICAL TRADITIONS later thinkers—the authors of "mere" commentaries as well as of original treatises—have regularly expended much effort on unpacking and explicating the ideas of the textual sources and the institutor(s) of their traditions. In both Indian and Tibetan civilization it is very often to commentary that noteworthy developments in philosophical thought are owed.

For almost a millennium now, the doxographical and philosophical distinction drawn by later commentators and doxographers between *Svātantrika and *Prāsaṅgika has been in use among Mādhyamikas in Tibet in order to mark a bifurcation of Madhyamaka thought into two branches each tracing its origins back to Ārya Nāgārjuna and his disciple Āryadeva, who had flourished about a millennium earlier. At the head of these two branches of the pure Madhyamaka tradition in its middle period were Bhā(va)viveka/ Bhāvin/Bhavya (sixth century C.E.) for the *Svātantrikas and Buddhapālita (ca. 500) and Candrakīrti (seventh century) for the *Prāsaṅgikas.[1] By

* First published in *Indo-Iranian Journal* 49 (2006), pp. 319–46.

1. For reasons given below, the terms Svāntantrika and Prāsaṅgika should strictly speaking be marked with an asterisk (*). But the two words have become so frequent in discussions of Madhyamaka thought that the asterisk is often dispensed with, as it will be in the following.

As for the source of the Svātantrika-Madhyamaka school, the names Bhāviveka, Bhāvin, Bhāvaviveka, and Bhavya have all been transmitted in the sources. Regarding the form Bhāviveka, comparison can be made with the name Bhāvivikta (compare also the name Bhāsarvajña). Bhāviveka (along perhaps with Bhavya) is probably the form to be preferred. See D. Seyfort Ruegg, *The Literature of the Madhyamaka School of Philosophy in India* (Wiesbaden, 1981), p. 61n183; id. "On the Authorship of Some Works ascribed to Bhāvaviveka/Bhavya," p. 69n1, reprinted in the present volume, p. 145n1; id., *Three Studies in the History of Indian and Tibetan Madhyamaka Philoshophy* (Studies

contrast, in the period of Madhyamaka thought preceding the appearance of these two branches—namely at the time of Nāgārjuna and Āryadeva—the textual sources of the Madhyamaka have been considered to be "matrix sources" *(mātṛkā,* Tib. *phyi mo),* that is, works not assignable to either of these two "wings" *(pakṣa,* Tib. *phyogs)* and therefore not limited to them. The integration into Madhyamaka thought of "autonomous" *(svatantra)* inference *(anumāna)* and formal reasoning *(prayoga),* attributable to Bhāviveka, is thought to have been due to the impact on Buddhist thought of the work of the epistemologists and logicians, in particular Dignāga (ca. 480–540) whom Candrakīrti has mentioned (at the end of his *Madhyamakāvatārabhāṣya*) and criticized (in his *Prasannapadā Madhyamakavṛttiḥ [PPMV]* but without actually naming him).

Two questions at least legitimately arise at this point. (1) Historically speaking, was the nomenclature in question—viz. "Svātantrika" and "Prāsaṅgika"—actually in use among Indian masters of the Madhyamaka? And (2) philosophically speaking, is this terminology—found as it is in later Tibetan commentaries and in the doxographical (Grub mtha' = Siddhānta) literature—a well-founded and hence fruitful one for the purposes of describing and analysing the classical Indian Madhyamaka? This second problem proves to be not only a historical and philosophical one but also a methodological one (that is in some respects reminiscent of the modern distinction between the "emic" and the "etic" in the study of cultures[2]).

(1) The answer to the first question seems fairly clear. The terms Svātantrika and Prāsaṅgika have not been employed by Buddhapālita, Bhāviveka, and Candrakīrti either as self-designations, or as the names of their branches of the Madhyamaka, or as nouns designating an opposed branch of the Madhyamaka. The term *svātantrika*—a lexeme seemingly unattested in Sanskrit as a derivative of *svatantra*—is in fact a retrotranslation of the Tibetan expression *rang rgyud pa;* and in its use as a designation for a master or branch of the Madhyamaka the word *prāsaṅgika*—a derivative attested in Sanskrit of *prasaṅga*—is a retrotranslation of Tib. *thal 'gyur ba.* This doxographic terminology seems to be prefigured in a work by Jayānanda, a Kaśmīrī scholar active in Tibet and Central Asia in the eleventh century; and it was then apparently in use by his Tibetan disciple (S)Pa tshab Nyi ma grags (b. 1055), whose writings are however now accessible only in fragments.

---

in Indian and Tibetan Madhyamaka thought, Part 1; Vienna, 2000), pp. 12–13; and Y. Ejima, "Bhāvaviveka/Bhavya/Bhāviveka," *IBK* 38.2 (1990), pp. 846–38.

2. For some remarks on the "emic" and "etic," and on metatheoretical description, see section III and p. 188 below.

In Jayānanda's large commentary *('grel bshad* or *ṭīkā)* on Candrakīrti's *Madhyamakāvatāra(bhāṣya)*—now unavailable in the original Sanskrit but happily extant in a Tibetan translation in which its author collaborated (D 3870)—the expression *rang rgyud pa* has been used to designate a characteristic feature of Madhyamaka philosophical procedure in Bhāviveka's school, and *dbu ma rang rgyud pa* and *rang rgyud du smra ba (*svatantra-vādin)* refer to one employing it.[3] The name Thal 'gyur ba = Prāsaṅgika is, however, not found in Jayānanda's commentary, or in any other classical Madhyamaka source of Indian origin, as a designation for Buddhapālita's and Candrakīrti's branch of the Madhyamaka.[4]

In view, then, of the fact that the terms Svātantrika and Prāsaṅgika are unattested in writings of Indian origin as specific designations for the two wings of the pure Madhyamaka, some scholars have fastidiously felt obliged to question, and even to reject in a mood of radical and sceptical historicism, both their historical justification and their philosophical suitability as names for the Madhyamaka traditions of Bhāviveka and Buddhapālita/Candrakīrti respectively.[5]

In Indian works dating from the seventh to the eleventh century—i.e., previously to the time of Dīpaṃkaraśrījñāna (Atisha, 982–1054)—the Madhyamaka master Candrakīrti seems to be mentioned already in Avalokitavrata's commentary on Bhāviveka's *Prajñāpradīpa* (D, wa, fol. 73a, 102a, but without any detailed discussion of his doctrines) and several times in Bhavya's

3. For the terms *(dbu ma) rang rgyud pa* and *rang rgyud du smra ba*, see Seyfort Ruegg, *Three Studies*, p. 20n38.

4. Cf. *Three Studies*, pp. 13–14, 20n38. Whilst Buddhapālita is considered to have already been in effect a Prāsaṅgika, Candrakīrti is regarded by some Tibetan doxographers as the main source of this branch of the Madhyamaka.

5. See section IV below. In *The Literature of the Madhyamaka School of Philosophy in India*, while often noting the Tibetan classification of an Indian Mādhyamika thinker as a Svātantrika, Prāsaṅgika, etc., the present writer did not make the Svātantrika-Prāsaṅgika distinction the organizing principle for the history of the Madhyamaka in India. But in section I of his *Three Studies in the History of Indian and Tibetan Madhyamaka Philosophy* devoted to the history of Madhyamaka in Tibet, this taxonomy has been adopted as a convenient device given its wide currency in Tibetan doxography from the eleventh century onwards. The adoption of such a traditional (and "emic") distinction is not, however, to be understood as implying that Tibetan authorities counted as Prāsaṅgikas did not (following Dharmakīrti) make use of *anumāna*s and formal reasoning, and also that some of them did not hold a thesis *(pratijñā)* or philosophical position *(mata)* provided that this did not involve the reification of *bhāva*s. These two issues, which are mentioned below, have been explored in *Three Studies*, sections II and III.

Madhyamakaratnapradīpa (D, fol. 260b–261a, 271a, 272a, 279a).[6] Then, in Dīpaṃkaraśrījñāna's *Satyadvayāvatāra* (verse 15; D, a, fol. 72b), Candrakīrti is named as a master whose theory of *dharmatā* is to be adopted by the Mādhyamika; and his *Madhyamakāvatāra* vi.80 is cited in verse 19. As for the Svātantrika-Prāsaṅgika distinction, it has not been mentioned in the *Lta ba'i khyad par* by Ye shes sde (ca. 800), the *Jñānasārasamuccayanibandhana* by Bodhibhadra (a teacher of Dīpaṃkaraśrījñāna), and the *Tattvaratnāvalī* by Advayavajra (Maitrīpāda, early eleventh century). Nor has Candrakīrti's name been mentioned in these last sources. Indeed, in the transmission lineages of Indo-Tibetan teachers of the Madhyamaka, the line of Indian Prāsaṅgika masters following Candrakīrti is anything but perfectly clear and includes names which are hard to identify precisely.[7] With the exception of Jayānanda's commentary on the *Madhyamakāvatāra,* no Indian commentaries on Candrakīrti's Madhyamaka works are known to us.[8]

By contrast, Indian masters connected by later doxography with the Svātantrika-Madhyamaka were more numerous, Śrīgupta (seventh century?) and his disciple Jñānagarbha being in the forefront. Śāntarakṣita (eighth century) belonged to their lineage. There also exists, in Tibetan translation, the enormous subcommentary by Avalokitavrata (seventh or eighth century?) on the *Prajñāpradīpa,* Bhāviveka's comment on Nāgārjuna's

6. On this text and its author—who is evidently different from, and considerably later than, Bhāviveka, the author of the *Prajñāpradīpa* and the *Madhyamakahṛdayakārikās*—see D. Seyfort Ruegg, "On the authorship" (as in n. 1), reprinted as chapter 5 of the present volume; and *Buddha-Nature, Mind and the Problem of Gradualism in a Comparative Perspective: On the Transmission and Reception of Buddhism in India and Tibet* (London, 1989), pp. 206 f. This Bhavya's date is uncertain.

7. For such lineages, see *Three Studies,* p. 9n10 and p. 17n29.

The *Lta ba'i khyad par* of Ye shes sde (ca. 800) does know Bhavya/Bhāviveka and the Svātantrika-Madhyamaka (which it terms the *mdo sde [spyod] pa'i dbu ma*) as well as Śāntarakṣita and the Yogācāra-Madhyamaka (which it terms the *rnal 'byor spyod pa'i dbu ma*) but not Candrakīrti and the Prāsaṅgika. In its section on the Madhyamaka, Bodhibhadra's *Nibandhana* (on *k.* 28) also mentions Bhavya. Advayavajra distinguishes between the *māyopamādvayavādin (sgyu ma rigs grub pa)* and the *sarvadharmāpratiṣṭhānavādin (rab tu mi gnas par smra ba)* in his *Tattvaratnāvalī* (ed. Ui, p. 5). Tibetan doxographers have discussed the question of the identification of these two schools in terms of the standard doxographical categories; see *Three Studies . . .,* esp. pp. 32 f, 60, 96 f.

With the exception of his *Yuktiṣaṣṭikāvṛtti,* translated into Tibetan in the ninth century—i.e., in the Earlier Propagation of the Dharma *(snga dar)*—Candrakīrti's works were translated into Tibetan only during the Later Propagation *(phyi dar).*

8. For the so-called **Lakṣaṇaṭīkā* on the first part of the *Prasannapadā,* however, see note 9 below.

*Mūlamadhyamakakārikā*s. The extent to which Śāntideva/Śāntadeva (ca. 700?), the author of the *Bodhi(sattva)caryāvatāra,* is to be counted as a Prāsaṅgika is perhaps not quite certain; his commentator Prajñākaramati (ca. 1000) has, however, quoted Candrakīrti on several occasions.

How the historical situation of Candrakīrti and his writings in the development of Madhyamaka is best to be explained is not clear. We know little about the sociology of knowledge and the particulars of knowledge-transmission in India in the centuries following this master of the Madhyamaka. We do know, however, that manuscripts were fragile and fairly rare things in India, and that even an important text could be lost and its author become half forgotten. (For example, the comment on Patañjali's *Mahābhāṣya* by the great scholar Bhartṛhari [fourth–fifth centuries] was almost lost; and at the end of the second chapter of his *Vākyapadīya,* Bhartṛhari tells of the vicissitudes undergone by the text and study of the *Mahābhāṣya* itself.) In other words, the rarity of manuscripts of a work by a given author is not necessarily a reliable indicator of its inherent worth, nor of the importance that was subsequently to be attributed to a text and its author in a given tradition. For the later Indo-Tibetan Madhyamaka, Candrakīrti indeed occupied a central position. But in the conditions prevailing at certain times in India, a major work could run the risk of being almost forgotten along with detailed and accurate information about its author, however important.

(2) The second question concerns the more difficult problem of the philosophical appropriateness of adopting the distinction in question from the Tibetan tradition going back to Jayānanda's disciple Pa tshab. Do the two terms Svātantrika and Prāsaṅgika truly describe and define characteristic features of the philosophical procedures of the two branches of pure Madhyamaka?

On this vexed point there has existed some difference of opinion if not confusion. That Bhāviveka employed "autonomous" *(svatantra)* forms of reasoning, in the shape of inferences *(anumāna)* and of formal reasoning *(svatantraprayoga[vākya]),* is of course clear from his commentary on Nāgārjuna's *Mūlamadhyamakakārikā*s (the *Prajñāpradīpa*), now extant only in a Tibetan translation, as well as from his independent treatise entitled *Madhyamakahṛdayakārikā*s, which is available in Sanskrit. But there still remains the fact that the word *svatantrānumāna* is not actually attested as an independent compound in Bhāviveka's extant Sanskrit works, even though it is found embedded in the compound *svatantrānumānābhidhāyitva* in a quotation in Candrakīrti's *Prasannapadā* (*PPMV,* ed. La Vallée Poussin, pp. 16.11 and 18.5). The compound *svatantraprayogavākya* is, moreover, attested in the *PPMV* (p. 25). (Compare the expression *svatantrasā<dha>navādin[?]* in a

Sanskrit note on the last text in a work provisionally entitled **Lakṣaṇaṭīkā,* dated to a time several centuries after Bhāviveka.)[9] And the syntagmas *svatantram anumānam* and *svatantrā pratijñā* (*PPMV,* p. 16.12) are well attested.

Concerning the appropriateness and significance of the terms *rang rgyud pa* = **svātantrika* and *thal 'gyur ba* = *prāsaṅgika,* the Tibetan scholar Tsong kha pa (1357–1419)—who has fully acknowledged the fact that the terms are not found in the earlier sources as names for the two branches of the Madhyamaka or their masters—remarks specifically and pointedly that they refer to the two procedures by which an understanding of ultimate reality—*śūnyatā*—is generated in the conscious stream *(saṃtāna)* of the philosopher-practiser. And he adds that the two terms are in conformity and consistent *(mthun pa)* with Candrakīrti's procedure in the *Prasannapadā,* and that they are accordingly no mere arbitrary creations *(rang bzo)* of later scholars in the period of the second propagatation *(phyi dar)* of Buddhism in Tibet.[10] Tsong kha pa has devoted many pages of his writings to demonstrate this. In sum, the pair of terms may indeed not describe and define the philosophies of Bhāviveka and Candrakīrti in their entirety; and, in particular, they circumscribe neither their respective theories of the surface-level *(saṃvṛti)* nor their views on ultimate reality *(paramārtha)* as such. It is also maintained that, as Mādhyamika followers of Nāgārjuna, Bhāviveka and Candrakīrti were in broad agreement as to the ontic and epistemological (gnoseological) status of the *paramārtha,* and that the disagreement to be found in their respective treatments of *saṃvṛti* was of somewhat subordinate importance compared with their basic agreement concerning the kernel of Madhyamaka thought. Despite his important points of difference with Bhāviveka, Candrakīrti has not in fact systematically rejected the latter's views on all matters. And Tsong ka pa, although he regarded himself as a Prāsaṅgika, has explicitly referred to Bhāviveka as a leading Mādhyamika; yet—and perhaps somewhat paradoxically—he has also described him as a substantialist *(dngos por smra ba: *vastu-vādin,* i.e., *vastusatpadārthavādin),* meaning that Bhāviveka ascribed to *saṃvṛti* an ontic-epistemological status, one which, according to Tsong

9. See Y. Yonezawa, "*Lakṣaṇatīkā: Sanskrit Notes on the *Prasannapadā* [1]," *J. Naritasan Institute for Buddhist Studies* 27 (2004), pp. 121, 131.

10. *Lam rim chen mo* (Mtsho sngon ed. of 1985), p. 573 (= Gtsang ed., fol. 343a): *gangs ri'i khrod kyi phyi dar gyi mkhas pa rnams dbu ma la thal 'gyur ba dang rang rgyud pa gnyis kyi tha snyad byed pa ni tshig gsal dang mthun pas rang bzor mi bsam mo // des na tha snyad du phyi rol 'dod mi 'dod gnyis su nges la don dam pa stong pa nyid nges pa'i lta ba rgyud la skyed tshul gyi sgo nas ming 'dogs na'ang thal rang gnyis su nges pa yin no//* Cf. *Three Studies,* p. 95.

kha pa, a Prāsaṅgika-Mādhyamika could not—and a follower of Nāgārjuna should not—attribute to it.[11]

Moreover, the characteristic philosophical procedure because of which Bhāviveka has been described by Candrakīrti as being fond of inference (*priyānumānatā, PPMV,* p. 16) and as a syllogist or ratiocinative speculator (*tārkika, PPMV,* pp. 25 and 31), whilst for their part both Buddhapālita and Candrakīrti relied basically on apagogic reasoning (i.e., negative *prasaṅga*-type arguments), does not *of necessity* mean that no Prāsaṅgika could ever hold a thesis *(pratijñā)* of his own. Nor does it imply that the Mādhyamika may never employ *anumāna* or formal reasoning without ceasing to be a Prāsaṅgika.[12] Some later followers of Candrakīrti—and in particular a large body of Tibetan Mādhyamikas regarded as Prāsaṅgikas—do in fact make use of such reasonings (see below). And in this way they in effect combined Madhyamaka thought *(dbu ma)* with the epistemology and logic *(pramāṇa-vāda, tshad ma)* of Dignāga's great successor Dharmakīrti (seventh century) into what came to be known under the name of *dbu tshad* "Madhyamaka and Pramāṇa." Tsong kha pa among many others was a leading exponent of this convergence of the two traditions in Buddhist thought which in fact had antecedents in India (for instance with Jitāri, who flourished in the tenth century).[13]

II

For the Svātantrika-Prāsaṅgika (S-P) distinction there evidently existed more than a single criterion. Listed below are several features that have served to define currents in Madhyamaka thought and which either have been considered characteristic of Svātantrikas or are found in writings by Indian authors classified by later doxographers as Svātantrikas.[14]

11. See below, pp. 167, 169, 173, 186–87 on Tsong kha pa's attribution to Bhāviveka of the doctrine of a *rang (gi) mtshan (nyid)* = *svalakṣaṇa*$_3$.

12. The Mādhyamika's disowning of theses concerns both any *pratijñā* presumed to possess probative self-nature *(svabhāva)*—as distinct from purely communicative *(jñāpaka)* force (see Nāgārjuna's *Vigrahavyāvartanī*)—and any *pratijñā* where the self-existence *(svabhāva)* of entities *(bhāva)* is posited in terms of the positions of the *catuṣkoṭi* (see ibid., and *Mūlamadhyamakakārikā* i.1). See the discussion in *Three Studies,* section II.

13. See *Three Studies,* index s.v. Jitāri.

14. Further details can be found in the second section of the present writer's *Two Prolegomena to Madhyamaka Philosophy: Candrakīrti's Prasannapadā Madhyamakavṛttiḥ on*

1) Whether or not, on the transactional-pragmatic level of *vyavahāra* or *saṃvṛti,* the philosopher-practiser employs autonomous *(svatantra)* inference *(anumāna)* and formal reasoning *(prayoga[vākya])* when achieving understanding of reality *(paramārtha).* The term *svatantra* has been so used by Bhāviveka in his *Prajñāpradīpa* commentary on the *MMK;* and the philosophical and methodological issue is discussed at length by Candrakīrti, *Prasannapadā* i.1 (see above, pp. 163–64).

On the face of it, this feature would appear to constitute the fundamental criterion for the S-P distinction. Additional more or less distinctive issues are listed below.

2) Whether or not the restrictive modifier "in ultimate reality" *(paramārthatas)* is to be affixed to the four negated propositions into which *MMK* i.1 is divided, namely that no entity *(bhāva = dngos po)* originates either from itself (i), or from another entity (ii), or from both i and ii (iii), or from neither (iv). The addition of the restriction *paramārthatas* by Bhāviveka in his *Prajñāpradīpa* (see also his *Madhyamakahṛdayakārikā* iii.26) has been discussed by Candrakīrti in *PPMV* i.1; according to him, this addition is unnecessary and unfounded because, in fact, origination *(utpāda, utpatti)* of a hypostatized entity *(bhāva)* does not take place in terms of any of the aforementioned alternatives of the tetralemma *(catuṣkoṭi, catuṣkoṭikā, cātuṣkoṭika),* and the restriction of the negation of origination to the level of *paramārtha* is not consistent with this fact. But for Bhāviveka such origination can evidently take place in an intelligible fashion on the level of *saṃvṛti.* The use of the modifier *paramārthatas* has been linked, e.g., in Haribhadra's *Abhisamayālaṃkārālokā prajñāpāramitāvyākhyā* iv.29–31 (ed. Wogihara, p. 636), with the so-called "concordant ultimate" *(paramārthānukūla);* and this connexion appears to go back to the *Tarkajvālā*'s interpretation of *paramārtha* as a *bahuvrīhi* compound (see below under point 5a).

3) Whether or not there exist external objects *(bāhyārtha, bahirartha)* on the surface level.[15] The Svātantrikas and Prāsaṅgikas agree that there exist external objects on the level of *saṃvṛti.*[16] But, given their links with

Madhyamakakārikā i.1 and Tsong kha pa Blo bzang grags pa / rGyal tshab Dar ma rin chen's dKa' gnad/gnas brgyad kyi zin bris (Studies in Indian and Tibetan Madhyamaka thought, Part 2, Vienna, 2002), under the index entries Svātantrika and Prāsaṅgika.

15. See Tsong kha pa / Rgyal tshab Dar ma rin chen, *Dka' gnad/gnad brgyad kyi zin bris (KNZB),* § 3. Bhadanta Śubhagupta (eighth century), described as a Vaibhāṣika, devoted a short treatise to this subject, the *Bāhyārthasiddhi.*

16. Concerning, then, the significance for the Mādhyamika of the canonical *cittamātra* doctrine, see *Two Prolegomena,* pp. 202f.

Vijñānavāda, those philosophers classified by doxographers as Yogācāra-(Svātantrika-)Mādhyamikas disagree on this point even on the *saṃvṛti* level (see Śāntarakṣita, *Tattvasaṃgraha k.* 1971 ff.).[17]

4) Whether or not the transactional-pragmatic level of *saṃvṛti* represents ontically and epistemologically a foundational (i.e., objectively existent) ground or given. (This is what Bhāviveka's just-mentioned restriction of the negated propositions of *MMK* i.1 could lead his reader to think.) In the parlance of later Mādhyamikas, the question then becomes whether such an ontic-epistemological existent is established, on the level of *saṃvṛti/vyavahāra,* by self-characteristic *(rang gi mtshan nyid: *svalakṣaṇa).* (Concerning the *paramārtha,* according to both Svātantrika and Prāsaṅgika Mādhyamikas, as such and on its own level, it is empty of hypostatized existence *[svabhāvaśūnya, niḥsvabhāva]* and free from all conceptualization and verbalization.) This matter has been treated as one of the eight crucial points *(dka' gnad/gnas brgyad)* of the Madhyamaka in Tsong kha pa / Rgyal tshab Dar ma rin chen's *Dka' gnad/gnas brgyad kyi zin bris (KNZB),* § 2.[18] And there then arises the question as to how this postulated *rang gi mtshan nyid* (abbreviated as *rang mtshan*) may relate to the *svalakṣaṇa* "specific feature [of a *dharma*]" in Abhidharma thought and the *svalakṣaṇa* "particular" in the philosophy of Dignāga and Dharmakīrti (see below, p. 187).

At the same time, nevertheless, the level of *saṃvṛti* cannot, according to Mādhyamika thinkers, really withstand close philosophical analysis *(dpyad bzod):* it is in fact describable as *dpyod du mi bzod pa* "not susceptible of analysis *(vicāra = dpyad/dpyod pa).*" And, according to Svātantrika authorities, it is so to say ontically undeterminable and epistemologically undecidable (that is, it is uncertain) in terms of the analysis *(vicāra = rnam par dpyad/dpyod pa, brtag pa)* of reality, contrary to the presupposition of the naïve realist and the expectation of the substantialist *(*vastu-vādin: dngos por smra ba).*[19] As such, it could therefore be regarded as analytically and philosophically satisfying only so long as no such analysis is undertaken *(avicāra-[eka]ramaṇīya/ramya = ma brtags gcig pu na dga' ba; avicāra-[eka]manohara = ma brtags gcig pu na yid du 'ong ba).* (See Haribhadra, *Abhisamayālaṃkārālokā* iv.24–26, p. 594: ... *tathyātathyabhedena saṃvṛtisatyadvayam avicāraikaramyam* ...

17. See also M. Ichigō, "Śāntarakṣita and Bhāviveka as Opponents of the Mādhyamika in the *Madhyamakāloka,*" in J. Silk, ed., *Wisdom, Compassion, and the Search for Understanding* (G. M. Nagao Felicitation Volume; Honolulu, 2000), pp. 163ff.

18. Cf. *Two Prolegomena,* pp. 139ff., 168ff.

19. Regarding the significance of the expressions "indeterminate" and "uncertain" see section III below.

nirdiśya, tathyasaṃvṛtau sthitvā yathādarśanaṃ māyāpuruṣeṇêva dānādy ācaritavyam . . . ; and *Two Prolegomena,* p. 180. Compare the worldling *pṛthagjana*'s cognition described as *rangga ba* "ordinary" *[phal pa],* i.e., untutored, or as *rang dga' ba* "self-contented," i.e., self-sufficient, arbitrary, and wilful, even autarkic.) At the most, then, and philosophically speaking, *(tathya) saṃvṛti* is acceptable "just as cognitively presented" (*yathādarśanam = ji ltar snang ba;* for *tathya* as opposed to *mithyā,* see below under point 6.) Earlier Bhāviveka had compared the *tathyasaṃvṛti* with steps enabling one to ascend to the top of the lofty mansion of reality *(Madhyamakahṛdayakārikā* iii.12: *tattvaprāsādaśikharārohaṇaṃ na hi yujyate/ tathyasaṃvṛtisopānam antareṇa yatas tataḥ//).*[20]

In a somewhat different philosophical frame, the aforementioned point would be acceptable to some Prāsaṅgika thinkers also: as seen under point 2 above, the Prāsaṅgika does not posit the *real* origination of entities *(bhāva)* in terms of any of the four positions of the tetralemma *(catuṣkoṭi).* And, according to Prajñākaramati's *Bodhicaryāvatārapañjikā* ix.2 (p. 357), causality understood as *idampratyayatāmātra* "simple conditionality on this" can be treated as *avicāramanohara.* Concerning *vicāra,* compare *PPMV* p. 27: . . . *loko hi svataḥ parata ity evamādikaṃ vicāram anavatārya kāraṇāt kāryam utpadyata ity etāvanmātraṃ pratipannaḥ/ evam ācāryo [nāgārjuno] 'pi vyavasthāpayām āsa, iti sarvathā [paramārtha-]viśeṣaṇavaiphalyam eva niścīyate;* and ibid., p. 67.7.

Now, *prima facie,* there would seem to exist a certain at least latent tension between the Mādhyamikas' view that *(tathya) saṃvṛti* cannot be meaningfully subjected to philosophical analysis *(vicāra)* and the view, attributed to the Svātantrika, that *saṃvṛti* has an ontic-espistemological structure that allows it to be made the object of rational discourse and examination in terms

20. For *yatas tataḥ* the citation in Haribhadra's *Abhisamayālaṃkārālokā,* p. 169, reads *vipaścitaḥ,* and it inverts *pāda*s ab and cd of the verse. The simile of the *sopāna* recurs in Kambalapāda's *Ālokamālā* 176, where *upāya*s enabling us to attain the *paramārtha* are the *upameya.*

Bhāviveka has not here specified whether, once they have served their pupose, the steps are dispensed with, as in the parable of the raft *(kulla)* in the *Alagaddūpamasutta* (Majjhimanikāya i.134–35)—or indeed in the metaphor of the steps in L. Wittgenstein's *Tractatus logico-philosophicus* (§ 6.54). An interesting comparison (not of course an equivalence) might perhaps be drawn between the relation of *(tathya)saṃvṛti* with *paramārtha* and Wittgenstein's logical propositions, which are expressible and said, with the unsaid, but shown, inexpressible (unaussprechlich) alluded to at the end of the *Tractatus,* at least following one understanding of this aphoristic work. See, e.g., P. Hadot, *Wittgenstein et les limites du langage* (Paris, 2005).

of a valid means of correct knowledge/cognition in the form of autonomous *(svatantra)* inference and formal reasoning based on the three-fold logical mark *(trirūpa-liṅga, trairūpya).* This tension seems resolvable, however, once consideration is given to the fact that being truly susceptible of such *vicāra* would, in principle, confer on *saṃvṛti* the status of being ultimately real (i.e., of being, quite paradoxically, *pāramārthika*); but, of course, the Svātantrika has done no such thing, for he has in fact ascribed no self-existence *(svabhāva)* to entities *(bhāva),* which (as seen above) do not originate "ultimately" *(paramārthatas)* in terms of any of the positions of the tetralemma. (Tsong kha pa's ascription to the Svātantrika of an ontic-epistemological *rang mtshan* on the transactional-pragmatic level of *saṃvṛti* does not need to derogate from this fundamental point.) In the case of the Prāsaṅgika too, it might at first sight seem that there exists a tension between denying that *saṃvṛti* is susceptible of analysis and the view—adopted in Prāsaṅgika tradition by Tsong kha pa for instance—that this level can still be thought of and examined in terms of valid means of correct knowledge/cognition *(pramāṇa = tshad ma).* But this tension too seems resolvable once consideration is given to the fact that the correct knowledge/cognition in question here is, precisely, a transactional-pragmatic one *(tha snyad pa'i tshad ma, *vyāvahārika-pramāṇa);* and this form of *pramāṇa* does not engage close philosophical analysis *(vicāra)* in the strict sense, which is thought of as relating rather to ultimate reality. (In *PPMV* i.1, pp. 27f., Candrakīrti did not develop this particular line of thinking, the origination of all *bhāvas* being simply negated by him without the restrictive modifier *"paramārthatas"* being invoked. And unlike Tsong kha pa, Candrakīrti did not elaborate in detail the concept of **vyāvahārika-pramāṇa,*[21] however much he of course recognized the level of *vyavahāra/saṃvṛti.*)[22]

5a) Whether or not the philosopher-practiser posits what is termed the "concordant ultimate" *(paramārthānukūla = don dam pa dang mthun/'thun pa).* This very noteworthy concept—denoted by means of a special term—appears with later Mādhyamikas, for example Śāntarakṣita (*Madhyamakālaṃkāra k.* 70) and Kamalaśīla (*Bhāvanākrama I* [ed. Tucci], p. 199); see also Haribhadra's *Abhisamayālaṃkārālokā* iv.29–31 (p. 636.22: *sakalaprapañcaparivarjitaparamārthasyânukulatvād yathoktabuddheḥ paramārthatvam*).

21. On Tsong kha pa's concept of *tha snyad pa 'i tshad ma,* see *Three Studies,* section III; also K. Yotsuya, *The Critique of Svatantra Reasoning by Candrakīrti and Tsong-kha-pa* (Stuttgart, 1999).

22. See, e.g., *PPMV* i.1, p. 70. And see p. 35 for *nyāya,* and p. 75 for *pramāṇa* at the level of *lokavyavahāra/saṃvṛti.*

It evidently corresponds to the third definition of *paramārtha* as a possessive *(bahuvrīhi)* compound in the *Tarkajvālā* (D, fol. 59b: *don dam pa dang mthun pa ste don dam pa rtogs pa dang rjes su mthun pa'i shes rab la don dam pa de yod pas don dam pa dang mthun pa'o*), the reference here being to a superior form of cognition.[23] (For the link between *paramārthānukūla* and Bhāviveka's use of the restrictive modifier *"paramārthataḥ,"* see above under point 2.)

5b) Whether or not, in the same vein, there is to be postulated a discursive—that is, a notional and notational—ultimate *([sa]paryāya-paramārtha = rnam grangs pa'i don dam pa),* i.e., a *paramārtha* consisting in conceptual and verbalized representation of ultimate reality, as distinct from *paramārtha* as such which, by definition, is entirely non-discursive *(rnam grangs ma yin pa; aparyāya, niṣparyāya),* i.e., trans-conceptual and unverbalizable *(anabhilāpya* [etc.] = *brjod du med pa).* These forms have been referred to in the *Madhyamakārthasaṃgraha* (verse 4).[24] The theme is connected with the very important distinction between two forms of a Buddha's Gnosis *(jñāna),* namely the *yāvadbhāvikatā* = *ji snyed pa yod pa* (i.e., the *ji snyed pa mkhyen pa'i ye shes*) and *yathāvadbhāvikatā* = *ji lta ba yod pa* (i.e., the *ji lta ba mkhyen pa'i ye shes*), and also between the *pṛṣṭhalabdha* "post-concentrative" and the *samāhita* "concentrative" (which two factors belong to the *vyavahāra/saṃvṛti* level). (This topic is treated among the eight crucial points of the Madhyamaka in *KNZB* § 8; cf. *Three Studies,* p. 32n; and *Two Prolegomena,* pp. 191, 251ff.) In its turn this theme engages the topic of reasoned analytical knowledge (*rigs shes* = *rigs pa'i shes pa* in Jñānagarbha's *Satyadvayavibhaṅga* 26), which is

23. At D, fol. 329b, this major commentary on the *Madhyamakahṛdayakārikās* is ascribed to the *slob dpon chen po* Bhavya (i.e., Bhāviveka I?). On authorship problems connected with the *Tarkajvālā,* see "On the authorship . . . " (as in note 1 above), pp. 59ff., reprinted as chapter 5 of this volume.

For the *paramārthānukūla* see H. Tauscher, *Die Lehre von den zwei Wirklichkeiten in Tsoṅ kha pas Madhyamaka-Werken* (Vienna, 1995), index, p. 418, s.v. *don dam (pa): mthun pa'i don dam pa / don dam (pa) rjes mthun pa;* D. Seyfort Ruegg, *Three Studies,* pp. 97n207; and *Two Prolegomena,* pp. 190–91, 252. Cf. D. Lopez, *A Study of Svātantrika* (Ithaca, 1987), pp. 326f.

24. On this work traditionally ascribed to the *slob dpon chen po* Bhavya see "On the authorship . . . ," pp. 67–68, reprinted as chapter 5, pp. 156–58.

For the *(sa)paryāyaparamārtha* and the *aparyāyaparamārtha,* see "On the authorship . . . ," p. 67, reprinted in this volume as chapter 5, p. 157; *Three Studies,* index s.v. *saparyāya; Two Prolegomena,* index s.v. *paryāya;* and H. Tauscher, *"Paryāyaparamārtha* as an Object of Cognition," in H. Uebach et al., ed., *Tibetan Studies: Proceedings of the 4th Seminar of the International Association of Tibetan Studies* (Hohenkammer-München, 1985) (Munich, 1988), pp. 483–90; id., *Die Lehre von den zwei Wirklichkeiten in Tsoṅ kha pas Madhyamaka-Werken,* index s.v. *paryāyaparamārtha.*

directed towards the analytical understanding of non-substantiality *(niḥsvabhāvatā = ngo bo nyid med pa / rang bzhin med pa,* and *nairātmya = bdag med pa)* and Emptiness of self-being *([svabhāva]śūnyatā = stong pa nyid)* by reason of origination in dependence *(pratītyasamutpāda).*[25]

In parallel, a highly significant differentiation has been made between *saṃvṛtisatya (kun rdzob pa'i bden pa)* and *saṃvṛtimātra (kun rdzob tsam)* "simple (or pure) *saṃvṛti,*" the latter being the object of the *ārya*'s and the *buddha*'s Gnosis in so far as it relates to the relative level of the transactional-pragmatic. (This topic, which derives from *Madhyamakāvatārabhāṣya* vi.28, has been addressed in *KNZB* § 2.3.3; cf. *Two Prolegomena,* pp. 194ff.)

6) The surface-level of *saṃvṛti* has been divided by Svātantrikas into the correct *(tathya = yang dag pa)* and the mistaken *(mithyā = log pa).*[26] This two-fold division of *saṃvṛti* has been taken up also in Prajñākaramati's *Bodhicaryāvatārapañjikā* ix.2. (The topic is discussed in *KNZB* § 2; cf. *Two Prolegomena,* pp. 174ff.; and p. 253n184. In addition, the above points have a bearing on the fundamental epistemological and gnoseological topic of the *rigs shes,* or reasoned analytical knowledge, and on the *tha snyad pa'i tshad ma, *vyāvahārika-pramāṇa,* as distinct from the *pāramārthika.*) This feature relating to epistemology, gnoseology, and buddhology is one of the most complex in Buddhist thought. In India its elaboration owed much to thinkers classified by doxographers as Svātantrikas; in Tibet it was further developed by Prāsaṅgika-Mādhyamikas, who drew both on Dharmakīrti's logic and epistemology and on the work of these Svātantrika-Mādhyamikas.

The points just listed are interrelated in so far as they all in some way pose the question of the status of the transactional-pragmatic level of *saṃvṛti/vyavahāra,* which could be said to be ontically undeterminable (indeterminate) and epistemologically undecidable (uncertain). Even point 1 concerns the relevance of inference *(anumāna)* and formal reasoning (*prayoga[vākya],* the so-called "syllogism") to the understanding of reality; it moreover implicitly raises the question as to whether a true Mādhyamika can ever be in a position, within the frame of his philosophy, to maintain an assertion or thesis *(pratijñā)* or a philosophical position (*mata, abhyupagama,* etc.) (see above, p. 166 with note 12). In the final analysis, as already observed, *saṃvṛti/vyavahāra* cannot resist searching analysis (it is *dpyod du mi bzod pa*); and it thus falls within the domain of the undeterminable and undecidable and

25. Cf. *Three Studies,* pp. 97–98, 212–13, 301; *Two Prolegomena,* pp. 189f.

26. See above under point 4; "On the authorship," pp. 67–68 (p. 157 in this volume); *Two Prolegomena,* pp. 179f.

within the scope of ordinary—untutored and self-contented—thought *(avicāra-ramaṇīya; avicāra-manohara).*

Points 1, 2, and 4 have evidently been criterial in some way for the S-P distinction, although no. 4 was to be fully elaborated only at a later period in the history of the Madhyamaka. The two-fold division of *saṃvṛti* (see under point 6) has usually been regarded as distinctively Svātantrika; and it appears to be meaningful above all when a **svalakṣaṇa (rang mtshan)* is ascribed to the level of *saṃvṛti.* But sometimes this division came also to be considered in works usually regarded by doxographers as composed by Prāsaṅgika authors. As for points 5a and 5b, among Mādhyamikas they came into prominence in works by authors regarded by doxographers as Svātantrikas, but they too have been addressed by later thinkers classified as Prāsaṅgikas.

In points 5a–b, the problem addressed from several angles is how a higher form of knowledge—the Gnosis *(jñāna = ye shes)* of a *buddha,* or of an advanced *ārya*—can possibly relate to the level of *saṃvṛti/vyavahāra,* it being understood that neither a *buddha* nor an *ārya*-bodhisattva is totally dissociated from the relative level of transactional-pragmatic usage, and that at some stage their cognition (the *pṛṣṭhalabdha* or post-concentrative one) must have this level as a discrete cognitive object. And points 4–6 all concern in some fashion the ways in which ultimate reality *(paramārtha = don dam pa)* can be said to comport with the conventional level of the relative *(saṃvṛti = kun rdzob),* i.e., with the transactional-pragmatic level *(vyāvahārika = tha snyad pa),* or *vice versa;* and, equally, how the discursive and conceptual knowledge *(jñāna = shes pa)* of the philosopher-practiser along with its verbal expression are able to engage with *paramārtha* which as such transcends, by definition, all concepts and words and is therefore non-discursive. Relevant here too are the two sorts of *saṃvṛti,* mentioned under point 6, one of which is described as correct *(tathya = yang dag pa)* on its own (relative) level; whereas, in terms even of the ontic-epistemological situation of the relative, the second is erroneous *(log pa = mithyā),* and indeed false, *saṃvṛti.* (Furthermore, although the ultimate and the conventional levels receive respectively the designations *paramārthasatya* and *saṃvṛtisatya,* it is only *paramārthasatya* that is in the proper sense *satya,* whilst *saṃvṛtisatya* reveals itself under philosophical investigation to be false *[rdzun pa = alīka].*)

As noted above, these points were elaborated by Mādhyamikas classified by later doxographers as Svātantrikas. But in the present state of our knowledge, it is not entirely clear just how defining in an exclusive sense all these issues were for Bhāviveka and his Svātantrika tradition, that is, the extent to which, in Madhyamaka thought, they were specific to, even criterial for, the Svātantrika alone. At all events, they were not explored by

Buddhapālita and Candrakīrti, the standard-bearers of the branch of the Madhyamaka described as Prāsaṅgika by later doxographers. Yet they relate to crucial issues in gnoseology/epistemology, soteriology, and buddhology; and they thus came to be of considerable interest also to later thinkers counted as Prāsaṅgika-Mādhyamikas. Thus, points 5a and 5b, and even occasionally point 6, were investigated also by later writers regarded as Prāsaṅgikas, either before or after the S-P distinction had been explicitly formulated in the eleventh century. Inference *(anumāna)* and formal argument *(prayoga[vākya])*, comparable to what is included under point 1, were equally to occupy a conspicuous place in the writings of later thinkers classified as Prāsaṅgikas. (These particular kinds of *anumāna* and *prayoga* do not, however, seem to have been specifically described as *rang rgyud pa* = **svātantrika* by the Prāsaṅgika-Mādhyamikas who were to make use of them, and who employed the S-P distinction.) Concerning point 2, in order to steer clear of the twin extremes *(anta = mtha')* of substantialism and nihilism and, therefore, to remain true to the Middle Way *(madhyamā pratipat = dbu ma'i lam)*, Tsong kha pa for one was to make ample use of the modifiers *don dam du / don dam par* and *kun rdzob tu / tha snyad du* for the purpose of clearly distinguishing between (ultimate) non-existence (*med pa,* etc.) on the level of *don dam = paramārtha,* and (cognitively presented) existence *(yod pa)* on the conventional and transactional-pragmatic level of *kun rdzob = saṃvṛti* and *tha snyad = vyavahāra;* but, as a follower of Candrakīrti, he did not make use of the restriction "ultimately" to limit the negation of origination found in *Mūlamadhyamakakārikā* i.1. As for point 4, it is perhaps the most difficult of the points listed above. And the ascription to Bhāviveka and the Svātantrikas of the postulation of some thing described as "established by self-characteristic" *(rang gi mtshan nyid kyis grub pa = *svalakṣaṇasiddha)* has been the outcome of philosophic reconstruction of this master's philosophy; in the case of Tsong kha pa, it was dependent on his internal reconstruction, and systematic reading, of Bhāviveka's philosophy, and of course on his systematic Madhyamaka hermeneutics as a whole.[27]

27. Examples of such discussion are to be found in *KNZB,* § 2; see the annotation to the present writer's translation of this work in *Two Prolegomena.* Concerning internal philosophic reconstruction, see id., "The Indian and the Indic in Tibetan cultural history, and Tsong kha pa's achievement as a scholar and thinker: An essay on the concepts of Buddhism in Tibet and Tibetan Buddhism," *JIP* 32 (2004), pp. 338–39, reprinted as chapter 15 of the present volume, pp. 393–94.

III

The indulgence of some readers will no doubt be required when there is introduced into the discussion (pp. 167–68, 171–72 above) a pair of concepts—indeterminacy and uncertainty—that may be reminiscent of the language which has been used for describing the theoretical foundations of quantum physics. Now, of course, neither Nāgārjuna nor his Mādhyamika followers were microphysicists.[28] Nor in their deconstruction of then current constructs *(vikalpa, kalpanā),* popular or even philosophical, concerning causality conceived of as operating between hypostatized entites *(bhāva;* Tib. *dngos po)* were they mathematical probabilists. And it is not being suggested here that Madhyamaka thought was somehow an anticipation or precursor of quantum theory. Yet, in regard to the conditioned origination *(pratītyasamutpāda)* of things on the relative, transactional-pragmatic *(vyāvahārika),* level of *saṃvṛti,* Mādhyamikas do in their own way have a sense of what might be called the probabilistic, as well as of the impossibility of setting up any unified theory of things in the frame of an ontology predicated on the substantial existence of reified entities *(bhāva).* Their philosophy does not, however, amount to some hyper-sceptical view based on randomness and the radically aleatoric; for the Madhyamaka thinker has regularly worked within the philosophical frame, not of entities conceived of as produced fortuitously *(adhītyasamutpanna)* but, rather, of things—i.e., phenomenal events—thought of as originating in dependence on causes and conditions *(pratītyasamutpanna).* These are accordingly described as Empty of self-existence *(niḥsvabhāva, svabhāvaśūnya).* The Mādhyamika's theory of causality does not, then, amount to "playing dice" with the world (to recall Albert Einstein's famous objection to one interpretation of quantum mechanics). Nonetheless, the descriptive language once employed by Werner Heisenberg—invoking in quantum physics the principle of *indeterminacy (Unbestimmtheitsrelation)* or *uncertainty (Unsicherheitsrelation),* and also the dependence of scientific observations and their measurement on the experimental procedures being adopted by the observer (the physicist) himself—would seem to lend itself, *mutatis mutandis,* to describing (if only by analogy and approximation) certain ideas met with in Madhyamaka

28. By Indian tradition Nāgārjuna is credited with an interest in chemistry and *rasāyana.* A text on medicine is also traditionally attributed to him, the *Yogaśataka* (edited and translated by J. Filliozat, Pondichéry, 1979).

thinking, notwithstanding the clear differences in their respective problematics and contents.[29]

Regarding the Mādhyamika's S-P distinction, the approach adopted will be defined (at least in part) in dependence on the respective analytical and meditative procedures adopted by philosopher-practisers. (To say this is not, of course, to minimize the significance of theoretical distinctions between the two branches of Madhyamaka thought described as Svātantrika and Prāsaṅgika.)

Nor is it being suggested here that Mādhyamikas presupposed or relied on a three-valued (a so-called "quantum") logic. In fact, contrary to what has sometimes been supposed, the reasonings advanced by Nāgārjuna and his Mādhyamika followers appear to be founded on a two-valued logic. (Whether some sort of multi-valued logic is latent in the thinking of this school is a separate issue that cannot be addressed here.[30])

The *uncertainty* principle in quantum physics just mentioned appears as a special case of the *complementarity* principle, which was invoked for instance in Niels Bohr's "Copenhagen interpretation" of quantum theory and the duality of wave and particle, of momentum and position. Now, in Madhyamaka thought, the idea of complementarity lends itself to describing—either synchronically or diachronically—the complex, indeed vexed, relationship between the way of apophaticism and the negative (apagogic) procedure followed in *prasaṅga*-type reasoning and adopted in Nāgārjuna's scholastic treatises (the so-called *Rigs tshogs*) on one side, and on the other side the way of cataphaticism and the positive (thetic) procedure adopted for pointing to highest reality (*paramārtha, dharmadhātu,* etc.) in certain hymnic works ascribed to Nāgārjuna (the so-called *Bstod tshogs*).[31] In the history of Madhyamaka thought, these two approaches to apprehending

29. For some observations on indeterminateness and on inexpressibility in Madhyamaka thought in connexion with the negation of the tetralemma *(catuṣkoṭi),* and with non-presuppositional and non-implicative negation *(prasajyapratiṣedha)* as opposed to presuppositional and implicative negation *(paryudāsa),* see D. Seyfort Ruegg, "The Uses of the Four positions of the *catuṣkoṭi* and the problem of the description of reality in Mahāyāna Buddhism," *JIP* 5 (1977), pp. 1–71, reprinted as chapter 3 of the present volume; and "Theses, Philosophical Positions and Contention in Madhyamaka Thought," in *Three Studies.*

30. Cf. D. Seyfort Ruegg, "The uses of the four positions of the *catuṣkoṭi* and the problem of the description of reality in Mahāyāna Buddhism," pp. 50ff., reprinted as chapter 3 of the present volume, pp. 102ff.

31. See the remarks in D. Seyfort Ruegg, "Le *Dharmadhātustava* de Nagārjuna," in *Études tibétaines dédiées à la mémoire de Marcelle Lalou* (Paris, 1971), pp. 448ff., reprinted in

reality—namely the apophatic-apagogic and the cataphatic-thetic, which might be described as "incommensurable"—appear sometimes as opposed and sometimes as complementary, if only in two distinct universes or levels of discourse. (This is especially so if the same Nāgārjuna is taken to be the author of both the aforementioned scholastic and hymnic compositions traditionally ascribed to him.) The same may also hold for the *rang stong (svabhāvaśūnyatā) / gzhan stong (parabhāva-śūnyatā)* duality (see below). In these two cases, the complementarity relation between distinct theories has no doubt to do with the fact that, as such, the *paramārtha* is considered to be unconceptualizable and unverbalizable (*anabhilāpya* "inexpressible," etc., as noted under point 5b in section II above). Concerning the polar opposition between apophaticism and cataphaticism, and between the *rang stong* and the *gzhan stong,* under a possible interpretation each pole has its proper part to play in distinct stages of philosophical apprehension and meditation gone through by the philosopher-meditator. In a certain sense, then, the rôle of the Mādhyamika philosopher-meditator might, *mutatis mutandis,* be compared (though of course not equated) with the part played by the observer in experiments in physics: each apprehends the object of investigation in different ways depending on the procedure being adopted at a given time and for a given purpose. Needless to repeat, this statement is not intended to minimize, or relativize, the opposed polar terms in the distinctions under discussion. And the situation is probably rather different from the thought experiment known as "Schrödinger's cat" (wherein a quantum mechanical system exists in a "superposition" of two states until an observation is made whereby the system is found to exist in one or the other of these states).[32]

---

chapter 4 of the present volume, and in *The Literature of the Madhyamaka School of Philosophy in India* (Wiesbaden, 1981), pp. 33f.

32. A further case where there has arisen the question of incompatibility and contradiction *vs.* complementarity (if only in distinct universes of discourse and on different levels) is the hermeneutical relation between the doctrine of the Prajñāpāramitā sūtras (viz. *svabhāvaśūnyatā* "Emptiness of self-nature," or *rang stong,* assigned to the Second Cycle of the Dharma-Wheel) and the doctrine of the *Tathāgatagarbha* sūtras (viz. the *dhātu, prakṛtisthagotra,* and *tathāgatagarbha*—and also the "Emptiness of the heterogeneous," *gzhan stong*—assigned to the Third Cycle). Here the question is whether the two are opposed and contradictory—and hence whether one doctrine, that said to be of definitive meaning *(nītārtha),* cancels the other, which will then be considered to be only "intentional" *(ābhiprāyika)* and provisional in meaning *(neyārtha)*—or whether, on the contrary, the two doctrines, distinct though they indeed are, somehow complement each other. The views of the Buddhist hermeneuts and doxographers in Tibet have differed significantly on this subject which has considerably exercised their hermeneutical skills. Cf. below.

Concerning the level of *paramārtha,* of inexpressible ultimate reality, might the "singularity" that is *śūnyatā*—"Emptiness" for which empty space *(ākāśa)* appears as an analogue or metaphor *(upamāna, dṛṣṭānta)*—be understood as a sort of unifying principle, being as it were the ground for the processes of *saṃvṛti*—the relative surface-level—in a kind of field (as it were in a field theory)? Might it possibly even be the base for some "theory of everything" (so to say as in unifying string theory, now emerging)? As already stated, any parallel or virtual homology between Madhyamaka thought and physics need not be seen as a Madhyamaka anticipation of, much less equivalence with, the contents of modern physics. Rather, this would be a matter of possible parallels in respect to discursive descriptions of two quite different areas: the Mādhyamika and the modern physicist would indeed part company given their very different starting points and concerns. (All this has very little to do with a universal language of "unified science" such as, in the twentieth

---

Concerning the concept of incommensurability, there is no reason why *per se* it should automatically presuppose or be linked with irrationality and philosophical relativism (or ethical antinomianism). In the context discussed above, two theories that are conceptually contrary (being descriptively incompatible) but also philosophically complementary can meaningfully be referred to as incommensurable. That is because the two theories which are complementary and incommensurable in the sense under discussion here relate to two distinct universes or levels of discourse. Hence the concept of contradiction will not be pertinent here; for by definition contradiction arises when, to the same thing, something is both attributed and not attributed in the same respect. A case of complementarity and descriptive incommensurability—such as discursive descriptions of the really unconceptualizable and unverbalizable *paramārtha,* which the Madhyamaka does not of course posit as a substantive entity—need not, then, preclude philosophical analysis and rational discussion. Intellectual relativism would intervene only if all relevant descriptive propositions were to relate in the same respect to one and the same thing in the same universe of discourse. (Incidentally, just as "black" is the contrary of "white"—the contradictory of which is: "not white"—the pair of theoretical descriptions in question are conceptually complementary; and the two might then perhaps be regarded as what have been termed *contrapletes* [for which term see D. Runes, *Dictionary of Philosophy* s.v. (1962)].)

Hence, when distinct universes or levels of discourse are in play—e.g., in the above-mentioned cases of the *Rigs tshogs* and *Bstod tshogs* both traditionally ascribed to Nāgārjuna—complementary (and incommensurable) descriptions are not equivalent to the third position of the Mādhyamika's tetralemma (*catuṣkoṭi,* i.e., the "both ... and" position, which is negated by Nāgārjuna). Further, in Madhyamaka thought, a description in terms of binegation ("neither ... nor") need not be related to the fourth position of the *catuṣkoṭi* (i.e., the "neither ... nor" position, also negated by Nāgārjuna). See D. Seyfort Ruegg, "The uses of the four positions of the *catuṣkoṭi* and the problem of the description of reality in Mahāyāna Buddhism" especially pp. 16ff., reprinted as chapter 3 of the present volume (some further uses of the "neither ... nor" formula have been discussed in section II of *Three Studies*).

century, the *Einheitswissenschaft* with its *Einheitssprache* of the Neopositivists in the Wiener Kreis. What in the final analysis it might have to do with L. Wittgenstein's thought—for instance with his distinction between saying and showing, with his idea of the inexpressible [*das Unaussprechliche*] and the mystical [*das Mystische*], with his concept of philosophy as clarificatory activity and therapeutic and of the disposal of the ladder-steps of philosophical propositions once they have served their purpose, or finally with his notion of language games—is of course a quite different matter.)

This recognition of a difference and discontinuity nevertheless leaves intact the question as to whether a theoretical vocabulary originating in one area of enquiry may meaningfully be revalued and deployed, *mutatis mutandis,* in another area. That is, can one field of thought yield a metalanguage or metatheory (and possibly an "etic" perspective) that can prove useful, when thus transposed, for exploring another field of thought quite distinct in its content and methodologies? Of some relevance when considering such issues is no doubt the matter of models.

Such issues of discursive description, (meta)theoretical or (meta)linguistic, as well as of theoretical modelling, are separate from the kind of problem arising in intercultural and interlinguistic translation of technical terminologies (for example those of philosophy). This will be the case even if it is conceded that the elaboration in a target-language (e.g., English) of a system of regular translation-equivalents for the technical terminology of the source language (e.g., Sanskrit) may possibly be influenced by semantic structures embedded in the thought patterns and terminology of the language and culture from which the new (English) translation-equivalents are being taken. Still, any regular system of target-language (e.g., English) translation-equivalents for the philosophical terminology of the source language (e.g., Sanskrit) will probably necessitate the establishment of new, consistent and systematic, semantic conventions. And being therefore system-determined, these *conventional* equivalents should be basically "emic" (and not be determined solely by definitions of the chosen equivalent already found in a preexisting English dictionary). Whereas, on the contrary, a description might very well involve the identification in one area of thought of a homology or parallel with an other, exogenous, area of thought, and the employment on this basis of a new, non-endogenous, discursive description (which will of course then be "etic" rather than "emic"). The conventionalism invoked here for translation can be thought of in terms of language games, where everything will depend on how words are actually used in their contexts.[33]

33. Concerning systematic, and conventional, translation suitable for Indian philosophical

Finally, to avoid misunderstanding, a word is in order concerning the expression "deconstruct(ion)" employed above (p. 174) in connexion with a characteristic type of thinking frequently adopted in Madhyamaka. No more than the use of the word "incommensurable" should the use of this expression be mistaken for a borrowing from modern (e.g., Derridan) usage. For it is motivated and explicable entirely in terms of Madhyamaka thought itself. What in his analyses the Mādhyamika deconstructs and "zeroes"—rather than simply refuting or denying—are unfounded, distorted, perceptions or views supervening on discursive construction inherent to conceptualizion *(kalpanā, vikalpa)* and language, and in the final analysis on mis-knowledge *(avidyā)* and its accompanying substantialist reifications *(svabhāvavāda).*

IV

An effort has been made above (section II) to bring together, if only schematically, a number of points that are of interest for the division between Svātantrika and Prāsaṅgika. Schematization of course risks flattening out a complex history of philosophical discovery and elaboration. Widely distributed in the original Indian (and Tibetan) sources, these points are now found scattered piecemeal in the secondary literature. Further research and analysis may show how these concepts originated and developed historically in the vast literature of Buddhism, and of the Madhyamaka in particular.

Several of the issues listed above have now been examined, or at least

terminology, see D. Seyfort Ruegg, "La traduction de la terminologie technique de la pensée indienne et bouddhique depuis Sylvain Lévi," in the forthcoming Proceedings of the Colloque Sylvain Lévi held in Paris in October 2003.

It may be recalled that T. Stcherbatsky once understood the Mahāyānist and Madhyamaka concept of *śūnyatā* in terms of *relativity;* but in his *Conception of Buddhist Nirvāṇa* (Leningrad, 1927) he was evidently not thinking of, e.g., Einstein's theory of relativity (on p. 53 he has emphasized a link with Hegel). For the view of S. Schayer on translation, see "La traduction de la terminologie technique . . . ." In the 1960s and 1970s, efforts were made to understand *śūnyatā* and the tetralemma in terms of a "zerology," and of modern semiotics; see L. Mäll, *Studies in the Aṣṭasāhasrikā Prajñāpāramitā and Other Essays* (Tartu, 2003). Cf. "The uses of the four positions of the *catuṣkoṭi*" (as in n. 29), pp. 52–54, reprinted in chapter 3 of the present volume, pp. 105–7. Stcherbatsky's approach does not appear to have brought us very far (in spite of the well-established link between *śūnyatā* and *pratītyasamutpāda*), and it has been largely set aside in more recent studies. As for the semiotic appoach, it does not seem to have been fully followed up in recent years.

touched on, in *The Svātantrika-Prāsaṅgika Distinction.*[34] This collection of articles by different authors represents a major contribution to the study of these issues, which are examined historically, on the basis of a goodly number of Sanskrit and Tibetan sources, and philosophically, where a laudable degree of sophistication is demonstrated.

The book is divided into two parts: "Examining the Distinction in the Indian Tradition" and "Examining the Distinction in the Tibetan Tradition."

In part 1, W. Ames, "Bhāvaviveka's Own View of His Differences with Buddhapālita" (pp. 41–66), carefully considers his subject's self-understanding as a Mādhyamika together with his relation to his predecessor Buddhapālita, whom Bhāviveka criticized for not having adequately propounded and defended Nāgārjuna's Madhyamaka view because of his failure to employ "autonomous" inferential arguments of the kind already being relied on at the time by other Buddhist and non-Buddhist philosophers in India. "[I]n Bhāvaviveka's own view, his differences with Buddhapālita were almost entirely methodological rather than substantive. [. . .] [H]e seems to interpret *prasaṅga* arguments differently depending on whether they are found in Nāgārjuna's verses or Buddhapālita' s commentary. This shift in interpretation enables him to criticize Buddhapālita without subjecting Nāgārjuna to the same criticism" (p. 56).

C. W. Huntington, "Was Candrakīrti a Prāsaṅgika?" (pp. 67–91), takes a highly sceptical view of the historical justification and philosophical appropriateness of the S-P distinction. "First, the labels *Thal 'gyur ba* and *Rang rgyud pa* [. . .] must be judged not only anachronistic but philosophically problematic as applied to a period in the intellectual history of Indian Buddhism when [. . .] not one of Nāgārjuna's commentators was prepared to acknowledge, even provisionally, the existence of two distinct and viable interpretations of the MMK" (p. 83). Furthermore, "[i]f [. . .] we are interested in understanding Candrakīrti, [. . .] then I believe we must begin by seeing and accepting the fact that he excluded uncategorically [*sic*] Bhāvaviveka from membership in this [Madhyamaka] school" (p. 83). The view adopted in this article seems to make the distinction between Svātantrika and Prāsaṅgika a dichotomy that would require its user to operate a final and definitive choice between two immutably fixed and mutually exclusive doctrinal positions rather than to opt provisionally, and at a certain point,

34. G. Dreyfus and S. McClintock, eds., *The Svātantrika-Prāsaṅgika Distinction* (Boston, 2003).

between two alternative (though of couse not simply equivalent) approaches to philosopical and meditative procedure.

T. Tillemans, "Metaphysics for Mādhyamikas" (pp. 93–123) provides a philosophically well-informed and sophisticated analysis. He writes (pp. 113–14): "I see two ways to take Candrakīrti's philosophy. First of all, the Svātantrika might be depicted as claiming that judgments about customary truth *[saṃvṛtisatya]* should be like what the first Kantian *Critique* had termed *convictions (Überzeugung),* valid for all rational beings [. . .] The corresponding depiction of the Prāsaṅgika would be to say that he recognizes only *persuasions (Überredung)* that work for particular groups of people in particular contexts, but not for all objectively in an idealized audience. This advocacy of persuasions to the exclusion of convictions could then be taken pejoratively, in keeping with the Kantian spirit, as resulting in a kind of skepticism, i.e., a view that understandings are always nothing but a 'mere semblance' *(ein blosser Schein)* with only 'private validity' *(Privatgültigkeit),* never justified by the objective facts and the metaphysical underpinnings they would need to have in order to be serious and genuine. [. . .] A second, more sympathetic picture [. . .] would be to say that Candrakīrti accepts that the world has its own agreed-upon standards of true and false, real and unreal, and that these common criteria do lead to shared understandings, and perhaps even new and more sophisticated knowledge. Still this consensus or shared 'persuasions' about customary truth would not be underpinned by objective facts, appearances-cum-particulars, or any such metaphysical constructs. [. . .] If that's right, Candrakīrti could well be a genuinely extraordinary figure in Indian philosophy: a type of quietist, or perhaps minimalist, whose philosophy promotes only *le libre retour à l'empirique sublimé,* and recognizes neither possibility nor need for metaphysics at all." In his note 47, Tillemans has observed that a "more interesting way to take the 'no-theory' stance is 'no theory accepting metaphysical entities.'"[35] This article has much to say also about the Tibetan Tsong kha pa's contribution to the subject.

S. McClintock, "The Role of the 'Given' in the Classification of Śāntarakṣita and Kamalaśīla as Svātantrika-Mādhyamikas" (pp. 125–71), examines the question "does postulating the given on the model of the Buddhist epistemologists necessarily imply an ontological commitment on the part of a Mādhyamika that, from a Madhyamaka perspective, should be deemed in Tsong kha pa's terms 'unsuitable'?" (p. 130). "Thus, anyone who accepts what could be described as the given cannot be a [. . .] Mādhyamika in the

35. See note 12 above.

truest and best sense of the term, but must instead be some type of 'realist' *(dngos por smra ba),* i.e., a philosopher who accepts unassailable reality in any form, whether objective or subjective" (p. 131). She concludes: "All this lends support to an interpretation of these authors [namely Śāntarakṣita and Kamalaśīla] as making some kind of implicit, albeit provisional, commitment on the conventional level. But is this really an ontological commitment [. . .]? It seems more like an epistemological or perhaps even a rhetorical commitment, which would lead the authors to an ontological commitment only if they accepted that perception is nonerroneous on all levels of analysis (which they seem *not* to do). [. . .] [T]he given is less a foundation for knowledge than a testing ground for reason, an experience one investigates to discover ultimate or metaphysical realities, the most important of these being [. . .] the utter absence of all forms of unassailable reality, conventionally and ultimately" (pp. 151–52).

M. Eckel, "The Satisfaction of No Analysis: On Tsong kha pa's Approach to Svātantrika-Madhyamaka" (pp. 173–203) offers a thoughtful and sensitive analysis of this important Tibetan master's reading of Bhāviveka and his followers. For the term *grags pa* Eckel has chosen without explanation the interpretation "common sense" (p. 181); in the relevant contexts, the term is usually understood to mean what is commonly acknowledged or accepted (Skt. *[pra]siddha*) in the transactional-pragmatic usage of people in the world *(loka)* (compare the closely related, but not entirely synonymous, *mthun snang du grub pa* "established [in agreement by people] in concordant presentation [in cognition]"). On p. 180 read *Saṃgrahaṇī* (instead of *Saṃgraha*). Eckel writes that his article is "an essay [. . .] about the creative appropriation of tradition" (p. 175) and that he is concerned with "cross-cultural transmission" (p. 195).[36] For Tsong kha pa's key concept in his analysis of Bhāviveka's philosophy, *rang (gi) mtshan (nyid) (*svalakṣaṇa)*, Eckel has adopted the translation-interpretation "identity" (p. 179), rather than, e.g., "self-characteristic."[37] He concludes: "Tsong kha pa has forced Bhāvaviveka in a direction that is foreign to his own way of thinking. Bhāvaviveka does not refer to conventional reality as 'established with its own identity,' and there are good reasons to think that he would have resisted this approach.

36. To describe this very important matter, the present writer has employed the concepts of dynamic transmission, integration, and enculturation; see "The Indian and the Indic in Tibetan Cultural History, and Tsong kha pa's achievement as a scholar and thinker: An essay on the concepts of Buddhism in Tibet and Tibetan Buddhism," *JIP* 32 (2004), pp. 321–43, reprinted as chapter 15 in the present volume.

37. Cf. loc. cit., pp. 338–39 (pp. 393–94 in the present volume).

On the other hand, there is no question that Bhāvaviveka thinks it useful and even logically necessary to specify the reference of conventional terms. You can argue that Tsong kha pa distorts Bhāvaviveka's position for his own intellectual purposes, but you can argue just as plausibly that Tsong kha pa draws implications from Bhāvaviveka's work that would have eluded even Bhāvaviveka, but were present implicitly in his work. Either way, whether Tsong kha pa's argument is read as a distortion of the Indian sources or as a careful elaboration of their implications, it is clear that Tsong kha pa's text is more than a slavish reproduction of the Indian tradition. It is a strong act of philosophical interpretation [. . .]" (p. 187). Concerning the principle of "satisfaction of no analysis," Eckel writes that his concept of analysis "lets Tsong kha pa draw a sharp distinction between the Svātantrikas and the Prāsaṅgikas: one group *analyzes* things conventionally and the other does not. [. . .] If we look closely at Tsong kha pa's Indian sources, we find that the distinction is not as sharp as it appears in Tsong kha pa's text. By the eighth century, the concept of no analysis seems to have become a standard feature of Madhyamaka, regardless of a thinker's traditional affiliation" (p. 190).

In part 2, H. Tauscher, "Phya pa chos kyi seng ge as a Svātantrika" (pp. 208–55), points out that, in his only work now accessible entitled *Dbu ma shar gsum gyi stong thun*—the Tibetan text of which Tauscher published in Vienna in 1999—Phya pa does not deal with this distinction directly, but only with the validity of the *prasaṅga* and *svatantra* reasonings in Madhyamaka. "Therefore this paper has to be restricted primarily to the question of how, to what extent, and according to which criteria Phya pa is to be classified as a Svātantrika" (p. 207). Tauscher concludes (pp. 237–38): "In regard to the Prāsaṅgika-Svātantrika distinction [. . .] one has to distinguish two methods. [. . .] The 'old' method centers on the question of whether an own thesis *(pratijñā)* is denied or maintained, and it takes any proof by means of the triply characterized *(trairūpya)* logical reason established by valid cognition to be *svatantra* reasoning. The second method, i.e., the 'dGe lugs pa distinction,' on the other hand, concentrates on the question of whether an own character *(svalakṣaṇa)* established in itself is denied or accepted—with all its ontological and epistemological implications—and it takes only a reasoning where the triple characterization of the logical reason is established by valid cognition autonomously, without depending on what is acknowledged by others to be *svatantra.* Phya pa chos kyi seng ge appears to be somewhere in between these. On the one hand he is [. . .] clearly indebted to the 'old' distinction, and according to it he is a Svātantrika. On the other hand his views show a number of correspondences in particular with the ontological and epistemological position of Tsong kha pa, and at the present stage I cannot see any convincing reason to classify him as a Svātantrika according to the 'dGe lugs pa distinction' [. . .]."

C. Yoshimizu, "Tsong kha pa's Reevaluation of Candrakīrti's Criticism of Autonomous Inference" (pp. 257–88) sets out "to reveal Tsong kha pa's systematic shifting of the values of autonomous inference, as well as his interpretation of Candrakīrti's arguments against it" (p. 257). Her investigation results in the enumeration of five main points she has detected in Tsong kha pa's reinterpretation or re-evaluation of Candrakīrti's criticism of autonomous inference (p. 274).

J. Cabezón, "Two Views on the Svātantrika-Prāsaṅgika Distinction in Fourteenth-Century Tibet" (pp. 289–315) examines the positions of Rong ston (1367–1449) and his disciple Go rams pa Bsod nams sen ge (1429–89) in relation to some of their predecessors, including Rngog Blo ldan shes rab (1059–1109) and his immediate disciples, and to Klong chen Dri med 'od zer (1308–63) and Tsong kha pa. "Our discussion [. . .] will focus on the debates between Sa skya pas and dGe lugs pas in the fourteenth and fifteenth centuries" (p. 292). Cabezón distinguishes between a Sa skya pa "soft" doxography, which de-emphasizes the radical difference between Svātantrikas and Prāsaṅgikas (pp. 296ff.), and the "hard" doxography of Tsong kha pa and the Dge lugs pa school, which holds this distinction to be of major and substantial importance. Hence (p. 307): "[O]ne cannot help but see in the soft doxographical position of Rong ston pa and Go rams pa not only a disagreement with Tsong kha pa over how substantial the Svātantrika-Prāsaṅgika distinction really is, but, given Tsong kha pa's position, a challenge to the very foundation of his interpretation of the Madhyamaka, and therefore to the viability of the dGe lugs pa tradition as a whole. [. . .] Of course, it is one thing to say that the debate [. . .] had potential social and political consequences [. . .], and quite another to claim that the debate can be reduced to socio-political factors."

G. Dreyfus, "Would the True Prāsaṅgika Please Stand? The Case of 'Ju Mi pham" (pp. 317–47) examines the views on the subject of 'Ju Mi pham rgya mtsho (1846–1912), a modern scholar of great repute from Khams province in eastern Tibet who had links with the eighteenth- and nineteenth-century universalist or oecumenical *(ris med)*—perhaps even "inclusivist" (in P. Hacker's sense)—movement in philosophy and religion, and who composed an extensive commentary on Śāntarakṣita's *Madhyamakālaṃkāra.* This work brought Mi pham into the ambit of the synthesizing Yogācāra-Madhyamaka; and it justifies raising the question as to the extent to which it is appropriate to classify Mi pham as a Prāsaṅgika (pp. 338f.), even if he himself considered himself to be one (p. 339) (perhaps in the frame of some "soft" doxography?). Dreyfus points out (pp. 330f.) that Mi pham minimized differences between Śāntarakṣita and Candrakīrti. His article throws light on a number of theoretical issues in their historical and philosophical contexts: the eight crucial—i.e., difficult *(dka' ba)* and uncommon *(thun mong ma yin pa)*—points *(dka' gnad/gnas brgyad)* of Madhyamaka and Go rams pa's parallel list of sixteen points (p. 325), the *rang mtshan* "self-characteristic" in the history of Madhyamaka thought and in relation to the anti-foundationalism of Madhyamaka, Mi pham's critique of Tsong kha pa's concept of the negandum *(dgag bya),* the status in Madhyamaka thought of *svasaṃvedana/svasaṃvitti* (*rang rig* "self-cognition") and the link it might possibly have with the concept of *pratyātmavedanīya* "direct, intuitive, knowledge" or "self-awareness" (p. 333),[38] the discursive (i.e., conceptualized and verbalized *rnam grangs pa: [sa]paryāya*) and the non-discursive *(rnam grangs ma yin pa) paramārtha* (pp. 334f., 338f.), the convergence or syzygy of the Luminous and Empty (*gsal stong,* p. 329) and of presented Appearance and the Empty (*snang stong,* p. 336), gradualism and simultaneism (p. 337), and much else. Concerning Mi pham's own philosophical view, Dreyfus observes (p. 339): "Mi pham is not deluded when he claims to be a Prāsaṅgika, but his Prāsaṅgika view is of a particular kind. It is in certain respects a *tantric Madhyamaka view,* based on the combination of an extensive investigation of the figurative ultimate [i.e., the *saparyāya-paramārtha*] with a vision of the luminosity [i.e., the *prabhāsvaratā,* etc.] of the mind. [. . .] This use of Madhyamaka as a preparation for tantric practice and the role of tantra in the completion of the view further explain why Mi pham is inclusive of and comfortable with approaches such as Śāntarakṣita's, despite their being classified as Svātantrika by Tibetan doxographers." Regarding the interpreters of the main theme of this volume, the S-P distinction, Dreyfus concludes (p. 341): "[N]o side [i.e., Tsong kha pa, Go rams pa, Shākya mchog ldan, Mi pham, et al.] is completely right but each brings important insights"; and regarding certain issues involved he does not hesitate to speak of "slipperiness" and "shiftiness" (p. 343). In discussing Mi pham's Madhyamaka view, Dreyfus has interestingly touched on the complex hermeneutical question of the relationship between the theories of *rang stong (svabhāvaśūnyatā)* in classical Madhyamaka and of *gzhan stong* (*parabhāva-śūnyatā,* etc.) as accepted by certain Mādhyamikas. Instead of envisaging in their interrelationship the

38. Notwithstanding Dreyfus's note 33, the question arises as to whether the bringing together of self-cognition and interiorized awareness—which correspond to two quite distinct terms and concepts in both Sanskrit and Tibetan—is due to inadvertence or deliberate conflation. Cf. *Two Prolegomena,* pp. 221–22n, 243n.

possibility of complementarity and of a duality of universes of discourse (on which see the remarks in section III above), Dreyfus here invokes the ideas of a broad-minded, inclusive, and non-sectarian—and also eclectic—synthesis; and he postulates the presence in Mi pham's thought of a distinctive "tantric Madhyamaka view" (pp. 320–21, 339–40).

The introductory chapter (pp. 1–37) identifies significant points made in the individual articles. Here Dreyfus adds noteworthy theoretical, contextual, and historical comments.

In this volume, the name of the sixth-century source of the Svātantrika-Madhyamaka has been standardized to "Bhāvaviveka," although the preferred form appears to have been Bhāviveka (or perhaps Bhavya; see note 1 above). Occasionally a rendering of a term or concept raises a difficulty not resolved in the discussion. Thus *bden pa* is usually rendered in this volume by "real, true (existent)" or the like. But, although Tibetan *bden pa* (= Skt. *satya*) can indeed mean "real, true, veridical," in the terms *bden (par) grub (pa)* and *bden (pas) stong (pa)*, and taken by itself as a technical expression in Madhyamaka, the reference is to what is (putatively) existent hypostatically, or reified, and which is accordingly treated by the Mādhyamika as the negandum for reasoning *(rigs pa'i dgag bya)*. This *dgag bya* is, then, not so much an "object of refutation" (as it has sometimes been rendered in this volume) as the "object of negation" (Skt. **niṣedhya, *pratiṣedhya*). The point is that the *dgag bya*—self-existence and substantialism—may be negated and "zeroed" by rational means—i.e., through reasoned analytical knowledge *(rigs shes)*—but that this is not necessarily achieved by means of a refutation *(sun 'byin pa = dūṣay-) sensu stricto* which would identify and refute logical flaws *(dūṣaṇa = skyon)*. As for the technical term *bden stong*, it means not exactly "lacking true existence" but "Empty of hypostatized (reified) existence." The expression *bden pa rnam bcad tsam gyi bden med* then means "absence of hypostatization consisting in simple exclusion/negation *(rnam par bcad pa = vyavaccheda)* of [imputed] hypostatic existence" (the translation "being true is simply negated" on page 122 does not seem to catch the full force of the intended meaning). Similarly, a *dngos por smra ba (*bhāva-vādin, *vastu-vādin)* is not so much a "realist" as a substantialist, that is, one who postulates the reified existence of a substantialistically—i.e., hypostatically—established entity *(dngos po = bhāva, vastu)*, on the level at least of *saṃvṛti*, as in the case of Bhāviveka according to Tsong kha pa's systematic reading. Very many Mādhyamikas are indeed describable as "realists" in so far as they admit the existence of an external object (and are therefore not "idealists").[39] As observed above, the term *rang gi mtshan nyid* denotes

39. See point 2 in section II above; and *KNZB* § 3.

the concept of "self-characteristic" which Tsong kha pa has attributed to Bhāviveka. For Ābhidhārmikas, however, the term designated a specific characteristic or feature of a *dharma;* and in the logico-epistemological usage of the school of Dignāga and Dharmakīrti, the *svalakṣaṇa* is the particular, as opposed to the *sāmānyalakṣaṇa* or generic. These three distinct uses of the word might be marked respectively as *svalakṣaṇa*$_3$, *svalakṣaṇa*$_1$, and *svalakṣaṇa*$_2$. The semantic history of these three uses of the lexeme still remains to be reconstructed in detail.[40]—A *cig car ba* is no doubt better described as a "simultaneist" (rather than a "suddenist," p. 337) inasmuch as he holds that two mental events may arise together rather than only serially (*rim gyis* = *krameṇa* "gradually"), or alternatingly *(res 'jog),* as was often supposed in traditional Buddhist psychological and philosophical analysis.[41] — It is not entirely accurate to write that Dge lugs pa scholars have argued that the Buddha's "Third Cycle of the Dharma-Wheel" was limited to Yogācāra (p. 345); actually, like other Tibetan scholars, Dge lugs pa scholars have assigned the sūtras teaching the *tathāgatagarbha* to the Third Cycle, but they have nonetheless held this teaching to be of definitive meaning (*nges don* = *nītārtha,* like the Prajñāpāramita sūtras of the Second Cycle), while at the same time considering the Yogācāra/Cittamātra doctrine belonging to the Third Cycle to be of provisional meaning *(drang don = neyārtha).*[42]—Concerning Dreyfus's identification in Mi pham's thought

40. Chizuko Yoshimizu has, however, devoted several valuable publications to the *rang mtshan* = *svalakṣaṇa* in Madhyamaka thought and elsewhere, most recently in her article "Defining and Redefining *Svalakṣaṇa:* Dharmakīrti's Concept and Its Tibetan Modification," in S. Hino and T. Wada, eds., *Three Mountains and Seven Rivers* (Musashi Tachikawa Felicitation Volume; Delhi, 2004), pp. 117–33.

41. On sequentiality and alternation as opposed to simultaneity in connexion with the *pṛṣṭhalabdha-jñāna* relative to the *samāhita-jñāna,* and on *yāvadbhāvikatā*-Gnosis in relation to the *yathāvadbhāvikatā* of a *buddha,* see *Two Prolegomena,* p. 252 (cf. pp. 243, 254, 274). And on "simultaneism" in Indo-Tibetan thought, see D. Seyfort Ruegg, *Buddha-nature, Mind and the Problem of Gradualism,* index s.v. *yugapad* and *(g)cig c(h) ar (ba), cig char 'jug pa.*

Whether it is possible for two mental events to arise together in the same moment in the same conscious continuum was discussed in the old Nikāyas; see the table on p. 277 in A. Bareau, *Les sectes bouddhiques du Petit Véhicule* (Paris, 1955), with pp. 72, 73. The particular terminology in question here has its origin (in part at least) in discussions on the question of the simultaneous *(yugapad = cig car)* existence or activity of more than one *vijñāna.* See L. de La Vallée Poussin, *Vijñaptimātratāsiddhi: La Siddhi de Hiuan-tsang,* I (Paris, 1928), pp. 184n, 186; and L. Schmithausen, *Ālayavijñāna* (Tōkyō, 1987), pp. 45f.

42. See *Théorie du tathāgatagarbha et du gotra* (Paris, 1969) (esp. chapters vii and ix). Cf. *Le traité du tathāgatagarbha de Bu ston Rin chen grub* (Paris, 1973), pp. 49ff.

of a broad-minded and non-sectarian eclectic synthesis, and his postulation there of a "tantric Madhyamaka view" (noted above, p. 185), it is of course clear that the cataphatic approach to ultimate reality, expressed notably in the *gzhan stong* theory, was frequently connected with the Vajrayāna, and with the Kālacakra in particular (in the case of the Jo nang pas); but it has to be made clear that a cataphatic approach to reality as well as the *tathāgatagarbha* doctrine are not necessarily attributable to the Vajrayāna alone (see also the remark in section III above).

In discussing its historical and philosophical legitimacy, some articles in this volume seem to reflect various degrees of discomfort or dissatisfaction with the S-P distinction (and thus, if only indirectly, with the difference mentioned above on p. 160 between an analysis that is "emic"—i.e., systemic, synchronic, and rooted in an indigenous tradition—and one that is "etic"—i.e., historical, trans-cultural, and comparative). The question is whether the S-P distinction defines two frozen, and diametrically opposed, doctrinal positions, or two distinct approaches on the levels of philosophy and meditation. If the first alternative were correct, there would exist a fixed and uncrossable frontier between the two rather than the much more complex situation actually encountered in the history of the Madhyamaka (sketched above in section II). Surprisingly, in the discussions concerning the use made in Tibet of the S-P distinction, attention has not been directed to Tsong kha pa's crucial view that this distinction is consistent with Candrakīrti's own treatment of the generation in the philosopher-practiser's conscious stream *(saṃtāna)* of the apprehension of ultimate reality, even though the relevant terminology is not attested in the foundational treatises of the great Indian masters of the Madhyamaka including Candrakīrti's *Prasannapadā*.[43] Tsong kha pa certainly adopted the approach of Candrakīrti, and he regarded himself as a Prāsaṅgika; yet he paid considerable attention to the doctrine of the Svātantrika Bhāviveka, whom he recognized as a Mādhyamika despite his having accepted (according to Tsong kha pa) a *rang mtshan* and being therefore described by him as a *dngos [por] smra ba* "substantialist" (see above, pp. 164 and 186).

The volume is accompanied by an excellent analytical index. Only occasionally has an important term or concept evaded its compiler. Examples are: *avicāramanohara/avicāraramaṇīya* (see pp. 189, 191, 201); corresponding ultimate = *paramārthānukūla* (see p. 210); *paramārthatas* (see pp. 342f.). Concerning the entries "emptiness" and "*śūnyatā*" in this index, it is useful to distinguish between the noun Emptiness *(śūnyatā = stong pa*

43. See above, p. 164 with n. 10.

nyid)—equivalent to ultimate reality (*paramārtha, dharmatā, nairātmya,* etc.)—and the attribute Empty *(śūnya = stong pa)*—a feature of all entities *(bhāva)* and *dharma*s, and which is then an attribute of things belonging to the level of *saṃvṛti;* this distinction is normally (if not invariably) made in the Sanskrit and Tibetan languages (except perhaps in some metrical passages), but it is often either overlooked or ignored in Western publications. Only very rarely are misprints to be found in the transliteration of the Tibetan, and they will seldom cause misunderstanding (but on p. 133 line 3 correct *gtags* to *rtags* "evidence, logical reason").

In this volume there are assembled materials of great significance for the history of Buddhist, and Indian, thought. Because of the complexity of these materials, and also of the quantity of insights proposed in the various articles, it has not been possible to summarize here all that is of interest in the volume. It has indubitably carried the study of these materials a significant step forward, even if some contributions were evidently prepared in the 1990s and are therefore not entirely up to date. In view of publishing delays, it would be well worth considering dating contributions in such collective publications so that the reader is better able to judge what literature was available at the time of writing.

As indicated above, there still exist a considerable number of problems that do not easily lend themselves to examination within the constraints of the kind of discourse that has been customary in Indian and Buddhist studies. And, as is indeed to be expected, there remain unresolved some well-known problems which are inherent to technical philosophical translation from Sanskrit and Tibetan into a modern European language.

V

In an article[44] published just a year after the volume discussed in section IV, J. Nagashima has considered several historical questions posed by the absence of explicit references to the terms Svātantrika and Prāsaṅgika designating the two branches of the Madhyamaka in the literature of this school from the sixth/seventh century (the time of Bhāviveka and Candrakīrti) to the time of Dīpaṃkaraśrījñāna (Atisha, 982–1054). He has also sought to account for

44. Jundo Nagashima, "The Distinction between Svātantrika and Prāsaṅgika in Late Madhyamaka: Atiśa and Bhavya as Prāsaṅgikas," *Nagoya Studies in Indian Culture and Buddhism—Saṃbhāṣa 24* (Department of Indian Studies, Nagoya University, 2004), pp. 65–98.

the remarkable fact that Candrakīrti and the Prāsaṅgika appear to have been largely ignored in our sources during this long span of several centuries (see pp. 160–61 above). Nagashima's conclusion is that Candrakīrti must have played a quite inconspicuous rôle in this period of the history of the Indian and Tibetan Madhyamaka, indeed that he remained practically unknown to other important Mādhyamikas whose writings are now accessible to us. Furthermore, pointing out the fact that the compound *svatantrānumana* is unattested in Bhāviveka's writings now accessible in the original Sanskrit, and that we there find only the syntagma *svatantram anumānam,* Nagashima arrives at the conclusion that *svatantram* is used here not as an adjective but rather as an adverb meaning "autonomously." And somewhat surprisingly he adds (p. 69n): "it is possible that there is no such type of inference as *svatantrānumāna* mentioned in the *Prasannapadā*." But he has not explained just what he considers is to be gained by this unusual view of the matter. Nor indeed has he stated how he would interpret the compound *svatantraprayogavākya* attested at *PPMV,* p. 25.8 (see p. 163 above).

Nagashima considers that a definition and determination of the Svātantrika solely in terms of the use of "autonomous" *(svatantra)* inference and formal reasoning (considered at length by Candrakīrti in *PPMV* i.1) would be one-sided, and that for defining the Svātantrika the postulation of the *paramārthānukūla* "concordant ultimate" (see above under points 2 and 5a in section II) can be of crucial, and criterial, importance (pp. 68–78; cf. pp. 92–94). And on page 93 he goes so far as to hold that the non-postulation of this "concordant ultimate" by the author of the *Madhyamakaratnapradīpa* is an indication that he was a Prāsaṅgika.[45] Nagashima also points out (pp. 72–73) the link existing between the postulation of the *paramārthānukūla* and Bhāviveka's affixing of the restrictive modifier "*paramārthatas*" to an autonomous inference or argument.

Herein lie some problems. Did Dīpaṃkaraśrījñāna, the Indian master considered to have contributed so much to the establishment of Buddhism in Tibet, know the S-P nomenclature, and did he recognize the existence of a specific Prāsaṅgika branch of the Madhyamaka? As seen in section I above, there exists no textual evidence for the use of the S-P nomenclature before

45. If accepted, this criterion would in addition establish that this Bhavya was not the same person as the author of the *Tarkajvālā,* a work which evidently does operate with the concept (if not the term) in question. However, as seen under point 5a in section II above, it is perhaps not perfectly clear whether, in later Madhyamaka, the non-postulation (or alternatively the postulation) of the *paramārthānukūla* by an author will necessarily decide his having to be classified as a Prāsaṅgika (or alternatively as a Svātantrika).

the end of the eleventh century, at the time of Jayānanda and his disciple Pa tshab. Moreover, Nagashima correctly observes (p. 83): "It is clear that he [Atisha] does not regard Bhāviveka and Candrakīrti as rivals who have opposing views on the two truths." (This is true of other sources also, and Tsong kha pa for one does not systematically oppose the views of the two masters.) Furthermore, Dīpaṃkaraśrījñāna does not seem clearly to separate the author of the *Madhyamakaratnapradīpa* (namely Bhavya, who has cited Candrakīrti favourably) and the author of the *Prajñāpradīpa* and the *Madhyamakahṛdayakārikās* (Bhāviveka, who is cited and criticized by Candrakīrti). Yet in his *Ratnakaraṇḍodghāṭa-Madhyamakopadeśa* Dīpaṃkaraśrījñāna has seemingly placed Candrakīrti before Bhavya. Now the implication of this could be either that he did in fact distinguish between them (on page 90 Nagashima mentions but does not countenance this possibility) or that at the time of writing he had not seen Candrakīrti's *Prasannapadā* where Bhāviveka is named and criticized (Nagashima does not examine this second alternative which, if it were to prove to be the case, would tell us much about the fate in India of this major work of Candrakīrti's).

Nagashima observes (p. 82): "Atiśa does not hold the concordant ultimate [i.e., the *paramārthānukūla*] and does not adopt the valid means of knowledge *(pramāṇa)* including inference *(anumāna)* in order to reach emptiness. These pieces of evidence indicate that Atiśa should be classified as a Prāsaṅgika." (On page 85 he has somewhat qualified this statement.) Nagashima shows that Bhavya's views expressed in his *Madhyamakaratnapradīpa* occupied a central place in Atisha Dīpaṃkaraśrījñāna's own view of Madhyamaka. And he concludes (p. 94): "Atiśa considers that Bhavya (Bhāviveka) and Candrakīrti belong to the lineage that descends from Nāgārjuna to Atiśa himself. However, this does not mean that there was no distinction between the Svātantrika and the Prāsaṅgika in his period. His attitude towards inferential reasoning is surely regarded as that of the Prāsaṅgika, and is based on the *Madhyamakaratnapradīpa* of Bhavya. [...] It is clear that there was a shift in Madhyamaka history around the ninth–tenth century C.E."

Nagashima has reviewed some recent scholarly work on the S-P division, concentrating almost exclusively, however, on Japanese publications. It is certainly useful to have a survey of Japanese secondary literature on the subject, since this body of scholarly work is available in the West only in a very limited number of major libraries. By largely excluding modern Western publications on the subject this article, although written by Nagashima when resident at a British university, has in several respects left philosophical studies in Madhyamaka as they were some fifteen or more years ago.[46] It nonetheless very usefully complements *The Svātantrika-Prāsaṅgika Distinction* (before the publication of which it was written) by providing a valuable overview of some important historical issues regarding the division between Bhāviveka's and Candrakīrti's branches of the Indian Madhyamaka.

VI

From the observations made above it can be perceived that the S-P distinction developed by Tibetan doxographers beginning in the late eleventh century does not supply us with a simple hard-and-fast line of doctrinal demarcation, and a ready-made and fool-proof tool for distinguishing between doxographically discrete, and radically opposed, branches of the pure Indian Madhyamaka. Very many of the issues mentioned above have been addressed mainly in later Indian sources assigned by doxographers to the Svātantrika branch of the Madhyamaka, as well as to the synthesizing Yogācāra-(Svātantrika-)Madhyamaka of Śāntarakṣita and Kamalaśīla and their successors.[47] But these issues were to acquire very considerable importance also for Tibetan Mādhyamikas counted as Prāsaṅgikas. It is, then, texts or sets of texts, together with their contexts, that require study and analysis in the first place; and on the basis of such historical and philosophical analysis, it will be possible to consider the intricate, and sometimes vexed, problems of authorship along with the precise doctrinal affiliation of each author and his contribution to Madhyamaka thought. The problem of authorship arises in a particularly acute form in relation to the many works that have been ascribed to Bhā[va]viveka/Bhavya; it arises too in connexion with works ascribed to (a) Candrakīrti such as the *Triśaraṇasaptati* (not to speak of Vajrayānist works ascribed to a Candrakīrti).

Historically, in terms of preceptorial lineage and textual tradition, a Prāsaṅgika may be described as a follower of Candrakīrti, and as a Mādhyamika who makes this scholar's *Prasannapadā* and *Madhyamakāvatāra(bhāṣya)* the centre-pieces of his Madhyamaka exegesis. And from the same standpoint a Svātantrika may be described as a follower of Bhāviveka and as a Mādhyamika

46. Nagashima has made no reference to the publications on *paryāyaparamārtha* and *paramārthānukūla* cited in notes 23 and 24 above.

47. Concerning the Yogācāra-Madhyamaka of Śāntarakṣita and Kamalaśīla, and the latter's relation to Bhāviveka, see recently M. Ichigō, "Śāntarakṣita and Bhāviveka as Opponents of the Mādhyamika in the *Madhyamakāloka*" (as in note 17 above), pp. 147ff.

who makes this scholar's *Prajñāpradīpa* and *Madhyamakahṛdaya* the centrepieces of his Madhyamaka exegesis. *Methodologically* and *doctrinally,* the former may be described as a Mādhyamika who makes apagogic *prasaṅga*-type thinking the linchpin of his philosophical procedure, and the latter as a Mādhyamika who makes probative *svatantra*-type thinking the linchpin of his philosophical procedure. Further, whilst both kinds of Mādhyamika accept ultimately the Emptiness of self-existence *(svabhāvaśūnyatā)* and non-substantiality *(niḥsvabhāvatā, nairātmya)* of all things, in Tsong kha pa's reading, for instance, the Svātantrika is characterized by his postulation of the so-called "self-characteristic" (*rang gi mtshan nyid, svalakṣaṇa*$_3$) on the level of *saṃvṛti,* while the Prāsaṅgika does not postulate this. This view also dispenses with non-acceptance of theses *(pratijñā),* etc., as the criterion for being a Prāsaṅgika.

Recognition of the constraints and limitations of the Svātantrika-Prāsaṅgika distinction as applied in the sources need not lead inexorably to the conclusion that it is arbitrary historically and worthless philosophically, that it has neither descriptive (taxonomic and doxographic) nor analytical and heuristic usefulness. Provided it is handled with due care, and with an appreciation of its historical limits, it can prove interesting even for the study of the Indian sources, in spite of the fact that the distinction as such has not been mentioned there. And it remains serviceable for tracing the history of the Madhyamaka in Tibet, although there too it may sometimes be necessary to proceed with caution. This is demonstrated in the earlier history of the Tibetan Madhyamaka by the case of the Jo nang pas and their doctrine of an authentic *gzhan stong* opposed to Candrakīrti's, and the Prāsaṅgika's, *rang stong* (or *nyi tshe ba'i stong pa = prādeśikaśūnya*), and much later, in the nineteenth century, by the case of Mi pham rgya mtsho (as shown by G. Dreyfus in his article referred to above in section IV). Furthermore, in Tibetan doxography, Svātantrika is not an immutable monolithic block of doctrine (as shown by H. Tauscher in his article). *Formally* and *systemically,* hermeneutics in Tibet has *inter alia* attached the commentarial tradition of the *Abhisamayālaṃkāra* to the Svātantrika, and the ultimate intent *(dgongs pa)* of the *Ratnagotravibhāga* to the Prāsaṅgika-Madhyamaka.[48] For elucidating

48. That the ultimate theory of the *Abhisamayālaṃkāra* should also be attached to Prāsaṅgika-Madhyamaka is, however, the argument of the title *Shes rab kyi pha rol tu phyin pa'i man ngag gi bstan bcos mngon par rtogs pa'i rgyan gyi mthar thug pa'i lta ba thal 'gyur du 'grel tshul, Gnad don gsal ba'i zla zer* included in vol. ka of the Gsung 'bum of Mkhas grub Dge legs dpal bzang, as well as of the latter's *Stong thun chen mo,* fol. 119b ff. This is, then, an example of the adaptability of the S-P distinction, which here is systemically doxographical rather than historical.

these matters, questions of theoretical description and technical translation (such as those sketched above in section III) are also relevant.

Concerning Tsong kha pa, who very clearly regarded himself as a follower of Candrakīrti and as a Prāsaṅgika, he has integrated into his Madhyamaka thought the logico-epistemological findings of Dharmakīrti, thus drawing extensively on Pramāṇavidyā. He accordingly did something that is comparable with what Bhāviveka had done almost a millennium earlier when he adopted methods of Pramāṇavidyā and became the source of the Svātantrika branch of the Madhyamaka. In his writings Tsong kha pa has in addition made much use of the findings of later Indian thinkers classified doxographically as Svātantrika-Mādhyamikas (e.g., Jñānagarbha) and Yogācāra-(Svātantrika-)Mādhyamikas (Śāntarakṣita and Kamalaśīla, Haribhadra, et al.). Thus, in their own discussions as well as in their critique of Svātantrika, Tibetan Prāsaṅgikas have addressed issues surveyed above in section II, even though in Madhyamaka these issues were originally investigated mainly by authors classified by them as Svātantrikas. Tsong kha pa has done this in the frame of his philosophically elaborated systematic reading of Buddhapālita's and (above all) Candrakīrti's exegeses of Nāgārjuna, as well as of his interpretation of the canonical sources of the Madhyamaka, and within the philosophical-hermeneutical frame of his use of the Thal 'gyur ba = Prāsaṅgika and Rang rgyud pa = Svātantrika distinction.[49]

July 2005

49. For one of Tsong kha pa's important statements concerning the S-P distinction, see the citation in note 10 above. Cf. D. Seyfort Ruegg, "The Indian and the Indic . . . " (as in n. 27 above), reprinted as chapter 15 of the present volume.

7. Purport, Implicature, and Presupposition: Sanskrit *abhiprāya* and Tibetan *dgongs pa* / *dgongs gzhi* as Hermeneutical Concepts*

I

THE TIBETAN HERMENEUTICAL term *dgongs gzhi* has no known Sanskrit original, nor does it seem to be attested in the literature translated into Tibetan from Sanskrit. It is in fact likely to be a terminological development of the Tibetan hermeneuticians, who have employed it alongside the terms—both well attested in extant Sanskrit works as well as in Tibetan translations from the Sanskrit—*dgongs pa* = *abhiprāya* "intention, intended meaning, purport"[1] and *dgongs pa can* = *ābhiprāyika* "pertaining to intention, intentional," said of a sūtra text the surface meaning of which does not reflect the ultimate and definitive intention *(abhiprāya)* of the Buddha.[2]

Beside the rendering "intentional (i.e., purportive) foundation, ground," the expression deep meaning (in contrast to surface meaning) may serve to paraphrase *dgongs gzhi.*[3] It is, according to the hermeneuticians, what the Buddha ultimately and definitively had in mind even when communicating

* First published in *Journal of Indian Philosophy* 13 (1985), pp. 309–25.

1. The Tibetan word *dgongs pa* is an honorific and is used to translate Skt. *abhiprāya* when the "intention" of an honoured, recognized, and authoritative speaker or author such as the Buddha is being referred to. *Abhiprāya* may be translated into Tibetan also by the (non-honorific) word *bsam pa,* which also renders *bhāva* "meaning," as well as *āśaya* "proclivity, disposition." For Skt. *abhiprāya,* cf. Pāli *adhippāya.*

2. See F. Edgerton, *Buddhist Hybrid Sanskrit Dictionary,* s.v. *ābhiprāyika* "(specially, esoterically) intentional, intended." Edgerton renders *abhiprāya* by "intention" (and also, in some contexts, "difference," for which meaning compare Pāli *adhippāya*).

3. In *Le traité du tathāgatagarbha de Bu ston Rin chen grub* (Paris, 1973), the present writer has translated *dgongs gzhi* by "fondation intentionnelle." For references see below, note 11.

quite other (sometimes opposed) teachings in sūtras that these hermeneuticians have accordingly described as *ābhiprāyika* and as having for their motivation *(dgos pa = prayojana)* certain purposes envisioned by the Buddha—in conformity with the salvific principle governed by his skill in means *(upāyakauśalya)*—intended to aid these addressees, who are thus defined as the special and specific trainees *(gdul bya = vineya)* of a particular *ābhiprāyika* (and *neyārtha*) sūtra.

In Buddhist exegesis and hermeneutical theory the concept of intended purport thus underlies the categories of the *ābhiprāyika (dgongs pa can)* in sūtra interpretation, and of the intentionally communicated *(dgongs bshad: saṃdhyā bhāṣita-, saṃdh(y)āya bhāṣita-)* in tantra interpretation. On the contrary, a sūtra or tantra that is not *ābhiprāyika* in this way is described as "non-intentional" *(dgongs min)*. Coupled with two further sets of contrasting categories—the literal (*sgra ji bzhin pa = yathāruta,* i.e., standard linguistic usage) as against the non-literal (*sgra ji bzhin pa ma yin pa = na yathāruta,* i.e., non-standard linguistic convention or special code),[4] and the provisional meaning requiring to be further (i.e., otherwise) interpreted *(drang [ba'i] don = neyārtha)* as against the meaning that is definitive and certain *(nges [pa'i] don = nītārtha)*—the *dgongs bshad* and the *dgongs min* make up a set of six points *(mtha' drug = ṣaṭkoṭi)*. This *ṣaṭkoṭi* is well known in tantric hermeneutics, and is treated in the commentarial literature on the *Guhyasamāja* in particular.[5]

It is interesting to note that Sa skya paṇḍi ta Kun dga' rgyal mtshan (1182–1251) has however not restricted the term *ṣaṭkoṭi* and the six points making it up to tantric hermeneutics alone. For when discussing, in his *Mkhas pa rnams 'jug pa 'i sgo,* the matter of rebutting objections *(brgal lan)* in the interpretation of the Buddha's teachings, he has used the term *mtha' drug* with reference to textual exegesis *(gzhung bshad pa)* in general, even while quoting Candrakīrti's tantrik *Pradīpoddyotana* as his source.[6] Indeed, Sa skya paṇḍi ta observes, if one's understanding does not follow the *ṣaṭkoṭi,* mistakes will be

4. Here *ruta = sgra* is opposed to *artha = don* as the letter is to sense or purport.

5. In the tradition of the *Guhyasamāja* for example, the *ṣaṭkoṭi* is included as one of the seven *alaṃkāras (rgyan bdun),* a further set of hermeneutical categories. See Y. Matsunaga, *Journal of Indian and Buddhist Studies* 11.2 (1963), pp. 470–76; and 12.2 (1964) pp. 19 f.; E. Steinkellner, in L. Ligeti, ed., *Proceedings of the Csoma de Kőrös Memorial Symposium* (Budapest, 1978), pp. 445ff.; M. Broido, *Journal of the Tibet Society* 2 (1982), pp. 18 f., and in E. Steinkellner et al., eds., *Contributions on Tibetan and Buddhist Religion and Philosophy,* Proceedings of the Csoma de Kőrös Symposium (Vienna, 1983), pp. 19 f., as well as the article cited below, note 10.

6. Sa paṇ, *Mkhas pa (rnams) jug pa'i sgo,* chap. ii, fol. 41b–42a = pp. 106–8.

made whether one is explaining sūtra or tantra. According to the *Mkhas 'jug*, the *ṣaṭkoṭi* consists of *dgongs pa* / *dgongs pa bshad pa* and *dgongs pa ma yin pa, nges pa 'i don* and *drang ba 'i don, sgra ji bzhin pa* and *sgra ji bzhin ma yin pa.* In this connexion Sa skya paṇḍi ta expounds *dgongs pa bshad pa* by means of the four *abhiprāya*s *(dgongs pa)* and four *abhisaṃdhi*s *(ldem por dgongs pa)* set forth in the *Mahāyānasūtrālaṃkāra* (xii.16–18) for example.[7] As for exegesis of the non-intentional *(dgongs pa ma yin pa),* he specifies that this variety of interpretation is employed when the Buddha's intention *(dgongs pa)* is directly recognized through the words-and-sense (*tshig don,* of a given sūtra passage) themselves, without there being any need to search out a further *abhiprāya.*[8] Sa skya paṇḍi ta's *Mkhas 'jug*—a work that may have been composed in the third decade of the thirteenth century[9]—is accordingly one of the oldest available original Tibetan sources concerned with the subject of *abhiprāya* in the context of scriptural exegesis and hermeneutics. And the fact that it extends to general exegesis the points of the *ṣaṭkoṭi* attested in the Indian sources as devices in tantric hermeneutics is noteworthy.[10]

The *dgongs gzhi* is however not included amongst the points of the *ṣaṭkoṭi,* and it has accordingly not been treated in the relevant section of the *Mkhas 'jug.* But this term appears elsewhere in Sa skya paṇḍi ta's works, with Bu ston (1290–1364), in the commentary on the *Mahāyānasūtrālaṃkāra* by Rgyal sras Thogs med (1295–1369), and already somewhat earlier with Bsod nams rtse mo (1142–82).

Among the instances of *dgongs gzhi* cited by Bu ston Rin chen grub in his treatise on the *tathāgatagarbha,* we find non-substantiality *(nairātmya* or *niḥsvabhāvatā)* and Emptiness *(śūnyatā). Śūnyatā* is regarded as the *dgongs gzhi* "intentional foundation or ground" for an *ābhiprāyika* teaching of the Buddha (rather than as the expressed content of his teaching) in cases where

7. Cf. É. Lamotte, "La critique d'interprétation dans le bouddhisme," *Annuaire de l'Institut de Philologie et d'Histoire Orientales et Slaves* 9 (Mélanges Grégoire, Brussels, 1949), pp. 341–61; D. Seyfort Ruegg, *La théorie du tathāgatagarbha et du gotra* (Paris, 1969), pp. 165–66, and *Le traité du tathāgatagarbha de Bu ston Rin chen grub,* pp. 83ff.

8. *Dgongs pa gzhan btsal mi dgos par tshig don de nyid kyis sangs rgyas kyi dgongs pa dngos su 'phrod pa'o.*

9. A thesis on chapter iii of the *Mkhas 'jug* has just been completed under my supervision by Dr. David Jackson. See also L. van der Kuijp, *JIABS* 7 (1984), pp. 47–48.

10. Padma dkar po (1527–92) also regards the *ṣaṭkoṭi* as applicable to general exegesis in his *Dbu ma gzhung lugs gsum gsal bar byed pa, nges don grub pa'i shing rta,* fol. 9b–10b. Instead of the ("tantric") term *dgongs bshad,* Padma dkar po uses *dgongs pa can (gyi mdo)* for his third category, and for his fourth he uses *dgongs pa can ma yin pa('i mdo).* Cf. M. Broido, *JIP* 12 (1984), pp. 25–26.

he is thought by the hermeneuticians to have considered it inappropriate to express and communicate Emptiness and non-substantiality to his addressee, either directly and explicitly *(dngos su: mukhya)* or by implication *(shugs kyis = sāmarthyāt,* or *don gyis = arthāt),* because this specific auditor was (at that particular time) unprepared for such a teaching owing, e.g., to the fact that he was disturbed and frightened by the idea of Emptiness.[11]

The existence of a *dgongs gzhi* is one of three criteria required so that a sūtra can be properly and legitimately identified by the hermeneutician as intentional *(ābhiprāyika)* and needing further interpretation in another sense *(neyārtha).* The other two criteria are the Buddha's motive *(prayojana)* in communicating it, already mentioned above, and incompatibility between the primary, surface meaning *(dngos la gnod byed;* cf. Sanskrit *mukhyārthabādha)* of a given sūtra or sūtra passage and the real purport of the Buddha's teaching established by interpretation of the whole of the Buddha's Word *(buddhavacana),* i.e., the entire canonical corpus.[12]

11. Emptiness *(śūnyatā)* is of course not the only *dgongs gzhi* possible for an *ābhiprāyika* sūtra. For other examples of *dgongs gzhi* see for example Bu ston's *Bde gshegs snying po gsal ba'i rgyan (Mdzes rgyan),* fol. 8b–9a, 10b–11a, 12a1, 15a5, 18b6, 24b3, 27a5, 32a4, and 37b3, translated in our *Traité du tathāgatagarbha de Bu ston Rin chen grub.*

When discussing the *ābhiprāyika* character of (at least one form of) the *tathāgatagarbha* doctrine in his *Sdom gsum rab dbye* (fol. 9a), Sa skya paṇḍi ta considers the *dgongs gzhi* to be *śūnyatā;* see our *Traité du tathāgatagarbha,* p. 32. For examples of *dgongs gzhi* according to the Vijñānavāda tradition as found in Rgyal sras Thogs med's commentary on the *Mahāyānasūtrālaṃkāra* (fol. 132b f.), see M. Broido, *JIP* 12 (1984), pp. 24–25. And for further examples of *dgongs gzhi* from other sources, see below, note 12.

12. See Bu ston, *Mdzes rgyan,* fol. 12a ff. (and *Le traité du tathāgatagarbha,* pp. 90ff.).

The triad of *dgongs gzhi, dgos pa,* and *dngos la gnod byed* is to be found earlier in Sa skya paṇḍi ta's *Sdom gsum rab dbye,* fol. 9a (see *Le traité du tathāgatagarbha* . . . , p. 32) and in his *Thub pa'i dgongs pa rab tu gsal ba,* fol. 54a. For a still earlier use of the term *dgongs gzhi* see Bsod nams rtse mo (1142–82), *Byang chub sems dpa'i spyod pa la 'jug pa'i 'grel pa,* fol. 74a (the last reference I owe to Dr. David Jackson). In these texts the *dgongs gzhi* is, respectively, *stong pa nyid (śūnyatā), chos kyi sku'i sangs rgyas (dharmakāya-buddha),* and *kun rdzob par yod pa* (existence of things on the relative, surface level of *saṃvṛti*).

As for the third criterion, that of incompatibility with the primary meaning, in addition to the expression *dngos la gnod byed* we find in Bsod nams rtse mo (loc. cit.) *dngos kyi don la gnod pa,* which corresponds to Skt. *mukhyārthabādha.* Other equivalent expressions to be found are *sgra ji bzhin pa la gnod byed* and *sgras zin la gnod byed.* On this criterion see *Théorie du tathāgatagarbha et du gotra,* pp. 158, 220–21, and *Traité du tathāgatagarbha,* pp. 104–5.

II

In a closely reasoned article recently published in the *Journal of Indian Philosophy* (12 [1984], 1ff.), Michael Broido has argued in favour of rendering *dgongs gzhi* by "implication$_C$"—that is, the content of an implication (pp. 4–5 and 28 of his article). And the noun *dgongs pa* Broido renders by "implication$_A$"—that is, the act of implication (p. 4). Implication$_C$ he then describes as referring to the "fact or state of affairs or proposition implied by an implicative utterance, as against the topic or subject-matter or what the utterance is about" (p. 5) and as against the "'implied object' (e.g., a topic or a thing implicitly referred to)" (p. 28). The question whether *śūnyatā* is a fact or a thing he leaves open (p. 5); but he observes that the *dgongs gzhi* "seems to be the content . . . and not, say, the topic implied" (p. 5).[13]

Now the problem—and indeed the potential difficulty—that arises if we are to use the term and concept of implication in analysing the theory of *ābhiprāyika* utterances, which are often understood as having a meaning that has to be *further* (i.e., otherwise) interpreted *(gzhan du drang ba'i don,* also *bkri ba'i don,* i.e., *neyārtha)*—and which are provisional in so far as the obvious (surface or "literal") meaning is not the one that is in the Buddha's mind in the final analysis—rather than a meaning that is certain and definitive *(nges pa'i don,* i.e., *nītārtha),* is that this Buddhist hermeneutical theory has nothing to do with either of the kinds of implication usually recognized in logic and semantics, namely logical implication and semantic implication.[14]

13. The significance in the present context of the distinction being made by Dr. Broido on page 5 and also on page 28 of his article is not wholly clear to me. He illustrates his distinction, however, when he adds (p. 5): "Borderline cases are possible, such as *śūnyatā:* is this—in its technical, madhyamaka use—a fact or a thing?"

One could answer this question by observing that, if by "thing" a *bhāva* is meant, then *śūnyatā* is not a thing, this having been made amply clear, e.g., in Nāgārjuna's *Mūlamadhyamakakārikā*s as well as in many a Mahāyāna sūtra. The status of *śūnyatā* as a *dharma* is on the other hand complicated. *Ākāśa, (apratisaṃkhyā)nirodha,* and *nirvāṇa* = *pratisaṃkhyānirodha* are indeed all included in the Sarvāstivādins' list of 75 *dharma*s and in the Vijñānavādins' list of 100.

14. In his article cited above (note 5), p. 447, E. Steinkellner has described *neyārtha* as implicit meaning and *nītārtha* as explicit meaning in the context of the *Akṣayamatinirdeśa-sūtra* and the Madhyamaka. However, that for this sūtra—and for the Mādhyamika who bases his definitions of *neyārtha* and *nītārtha* on it—the relation between these two terms has nothing at all to do with the opposition implicit/explicit should be clear from the very fact that this sūtra states that a canonical text teaching *śūnyatā* and non-substantiality is *nītārtha* whereas one that does not do so is *neyārtha.* In other words, the criterion here is the *content* of the teaching, and not the (explicit or implicit) *mode of expression* of a

(1) The *dgongs gzhi* which, in a given hermeneutical system, is regarded as corresponding to what is intended in the ultimate sense *(pāramārthika)* by the Buddha—and hence to the *nītārtha*—is not according to this theory something to be logically inferred (*rjes su dpag par bya ba* = *anumeya* "inferendum") through the means of right knowledge known in Buddhist philosophy as inference *(rjes su dpag pa* = *anumāna)*. That is, it is not a logical consequent known by inference from an antecedent within the sūtra passage in question. (2) Nor does the *dgongs gzhi* represent the content of semantic implication in the standard sense of this term. This kind of implication is in fact regularly designated in Indian and Tibetan philosophical language by the specific terms *shugs kyis* = *sāmarthyāt* or, sometimes, *don gyis* = *arthāt*. And what is thus implicitly communicated—the implication$_C$—is designated in Tibetan not by the term *dgongs gzhi* but by the term *shugs bstan*, the antonym to *dngos bstan* which designates what is explicitly conveyed by the primary meanings of words. What is implicitly communicated in this way is sometimes described in Sanskrit as *utsūtra*, in contradistinction to what is explicitly conveyed *expressis verbis*, that is, *granthatas* "textually" and *sūtratas* "in the sūtra's own words."[15] Semantic implication may, moreover, be considered

---

teaching. For the Vijñānavādins, and to a degree for the Yogācāra-Mādhyamikas, on the other hand, the difference between *neyārtha* and *nītārtha* is indeed connected with the distinction between non-literal and literal *(yathāruta)*, and accordingly with the opposition implicit/explicit.

For a consequence of this important difference between the pure Mādhyamikas and Bu ston, who apparently follows here the Yogācāra-Madhyamaka view, see *Traité du tathāgatagarbha de Bu ston Rin chen grub*, pp. 57–58.

15. See Vasubandhu, *Abhidharmakośabhāṣya* iii.28ab and vi.3 (p. 333). In his *Abhidharmakośavyākhyā* (i.20) Yaśomitra has glossed *utsūtra* by *utkrāntaṃ sūtrāt* "exceeding the sūtra."

In *Abhidharmakośabhāṣya* iii.28ab, the concept of *utsūtra*—as opposed to *sūtrārtha*—appears in parallel with that of *neyārtha*—in contradistinction to the *nītārtha* (= *vibhaktārtha* according to Yaśomitra) that conforms with the *sūtrārtha*, which excludes *utsūtra* interpretation. In the context of *utsūtra* Vasubandhu has furthermore mentioned the *iṣṭi* (iii.28ab)—a term which, in grammatical exegesis, denotes a desideratum to be extracted from a sūtra formulation by means of interpretation, as opposed to what is immediately realized through a sūtra in grammar (cf. *prāptijña* in contradistinction to *iṣṭijña*).

Now, in Indian exegetical theory, explanations and meanings that are *utsūtra* are normally considered to be unjustified and unacceptable; see for example Patañjali, *Mahābhāṣya*, Paspaśāhnika, p. 12.27, and Māgha, *Śiśupālavadha* ii.112 (with F. Kielhorn, *JRAS* 1908, pp. 501–2). The term *utsūtra* has been explained as *sūtrād udgatam*, i.e., *sūtrānārūḍha* "not found in/based on the sūtra"; see Śivarāmendra Sarasvatī, *Mahābhāṣyasiddhāntaratnaprakāśa* (ed. M. S. Narasimhacharya; Pondicherry, 1973), p.

to be linguistically secondary in relation to what is explicitly expressed. In the Buddhist hermeneutical theory under consideration here, however, the *dgongs gzhi* is clearly primary from the hermeneutician's systematical point of view; for it corresponds to the *pāramārthika* and to the *nītārtha*—i.e., to what the Buddha has in mind in the final analysis (within a given hermeneutical system)—whereas the meaning of an *ābhiprāyika* sūtra passage is secondary in this frame and corresponds to the *neyārtha* which the Buddha puts provisionally to use, in a perlocutionary fashion, as it were, for a given purpose and in a particular pragmatic situation relative to specific addressees (the *vineya*s or "trainees" of the particular sūtra passage in question).

Finally, it is not the case that in *ābhiprāyika* or *neyārtha* sūtra passages the *dgongs gzhi* is communicated to the *vineya* by implication in addition to the obvious surface content that is explicitly expressed. The trainees for whom the *ābhiprāyika* or *neyārtha* sūtra utterance is specifically destined by the Buddha are indeed not expected to be yet able to grasp the *dgongs gzhi,* i.e., the certain and definitive meaning the Buddha has in mind. For if they were, there could be little purpose in teaching them the *ābhiprāyika* and *neyārtha* sūtra passage.

For the reasons stated, then, the *dgongs gzhi* cannot be an implication in the standard logical or semantic senses of the term.[16]

However, even though the *dgongs gzhi* is not conveyed to the specific *vineya* of an *ābhiprāyika* or *neyārtha* sūtra by means of either of these kinds

106. According to a maxim cited by Nāgeśa in his *Uddyota* on the above passage from the *Mahābhāṣya* concerning *utsūtra* explanation, what is found in a *vṛtti* or *vārttika* is [i.e., must be considered] present in the basic sūtras themselves *(sūtreṣv eva hi tat sarvaṃ yad vṛttau yac ca vārttike).* For some observations on *utsūtravyākhyāna,* see P. V. Kane, *History of Sanskrit Poetics* (Delhi, 1961), pp. 170ff. (Compare further P. Hacker, "Notes on the Māṇḍūkyopaniṣad and Śaṁkara's Āgamaśāstravivaraṇa," in *India Maior* [Festschrift J. Gonda; Leiden, 1972], p. 115, who observes that *utsūtra* material has been used in a non-condemnatory fashion.)

The problem posed by the legitimacy or otherwise of *utsūtra* explanation appears to be reflected in the Tibetan terminology as attested in the Tibetan translation of Vasubandhu's *Abhidharmakośabhāṣya,* where we find both the evaluative and condemnatory *mdo dang 'gal ba* "contrary to the sūtra" and the more neutral renderings *mdo las 'das pa* and *mdo las thal ba* "exceeding the sūtra."

16. It is important to note that in tantric texts on the other hand, the *ābhiprāyika* and non-*ābhiprāyika*—and the *neyārtha* and *nītārtha*—may *both* be fully intended and be in full force together. That is, whereas in systematical sūtra hermeneutics, a given sūtra passage can (within a single hermeneutical system) *finally and definitively* bear only one value (the non-*ābhiprāyika* and *nītārtha* one), in tantric hermeneutics a single passage can be meant to convey both the intentional and non-intentional—*neyārtha* and *nītārtha*—values.

of implication, it may be said that, from the point of view of the competent systematical hermeneutician as well as from that of the Buddha, the *dgongs gzhi* is, in a very special sense, an implicate in the Buddha's teaching insofar as it is considered as a system. And just as the Buddha has it in mind when he gives other quite different and non-concordant—or even incompatible—teachings to specific *vineya*s unable yet to comprehend what he actually has in mind, so that competent exegete, who has at his disposal the corpus of the Buddha's teachings (together, eventually, with the oral and/or written commentarial tradition), is able to discover—to "calculate" as it were—the *dgongs gzhi* by means of the systematical interpretation of this corpus.

Thus, while for the Buddha the *dgongs gzhi* is a kind of *presupposition* underlying his utterances as an experienced teacher, for the hermeneutician it can perhaps also be described as an *implicature* (see section VI below) discoverable through the systematical interpretation of the corpus of the Buddha's teachings having regard to his motive *(prayojana)* in a particular pragmatic and communicative situation of teaching.

III

If we now look for a parallel (if not the immediate source) for the notion of *dgongs gzhi* in the literature of Indian semantics, it could no doubt be best compared with suggestive force *(vyañjanā)* and poetic resonance *(dhvani)*. Thus, where the surface meaning of an *ābhiprāyika* or *neyārtha* sūtra, or sūtra passage, is clearly and totally discordant with the sense and purport of the Buddha's teaching taken as a whole and as established by systematical interpretation of the canonical corpus—e.g., in the case of *pariṇāmanābhisaṃdhi* where the meaning is to be transmuted or cancelled[17]—the form of *dhvani* which is most closely comparable is the one in which the obvious surface

17. As an example of *pariṇāmanābhisaṃdhi* the *Mahāyānasutrālaṃkārabhāṣya* and the authorities following it quote the verse

asāre sāramatayo viparyāse ca susthitāḥ /
kleśena ca susaṃkliṣṭā labhante bodhim uttamām //

See *La theorie du tathāgatagarbha et du gotra,* pp. 375–76. According to certain authorities, moreover, we have a further example of this type of *abhisaṃdhi* in the verse

mātaraṃ pitaraṃ hatvā rājānaṃ dvau ca śrotriyau /
rāṣṭraṃ sānucaraṃ hatvā śuddha ity ucyate naraḥ //

See *Le traité du tathāgatagarbha de Bu ston Rin chen grub,* pp. 83–84. Both of these verses, together with a third one, are cited in Asaṅga's *Abhidharmasamuccaya* (ed. P. Pradhan; Santiniketan, 1950), p. 107.

content is altogether unintended *(avivakṣitavācya),* this surface meaning being then either totally annulled *(atyantatiraskṛtavācya)* or transmuted into another meaning *(arthāntarasaṃkramitavācya).* On the other hand, in those cases where the *ābhiprāyika* or *neyārtha* meaning is compatible with the total corpus of the Buddha's teaching within the frame of a given hermeneutical and doctrinal system and where it is therefore at least provisionally acceptable, comparison can be made with that form of suggestion where the expressed content is still meant even though another, unexpressed, meaning is actually the one intended *(vivakṣitānyaparavācya).*[18]

Moreover, the philosopher-hermeneutician able by means of systematical exegesis to grasp the *dgongs gzhi* in an *ābhiprāyika* or *neyārtha* sūtra is, in certain respects, not unlike the cultivated and expert *sahṛdaya,* that is, the aesthetically sensitive and cultivated connoisseur of Indian poetics.

But there nonetheless appears to exist an important difference in this matter between *kāvya* and *alaṃkāraśāstra* on the one side and Buddhist philosophical hermeneutics on the other. For poetics does not have a place for a listener or reader corresponding to the specific trainees *(vineya)* for whom the Buddha's *ābhiprāyika* and *neyārtha* utterances are specially destined as useful and thoroughly motivated—even though provisional—propaedeutic devices.

IV

It is interesting to note that the terms *dgongs gzhi* and *dgongs pa* = *abhiprāya* as well as *dgos pa* = *prayojana* can all be glossed by the English words "intent" or "intention" in one or the other of their historically attested uses. Thus, for "intent" the *Shorter Oxford English Dictionary* records the meanings (1) act of intending; (4) understanding; frame of mind, spirit; thought of any kind; (5) meaning; purport; (7) intended subject, theme; and (6) end purposed; aim, purpose. And for "intention" it records (3) meaning, import; (4) the act of intending; (5) that which is intended; a purpose, design.

The Sanskrit word *ābhiprāyika*—an adjective derived from the noun *abhiprāya* by means of the suffix *-ika-* denoting belonging to (see L. Renou,

18. The intended meaning in question is closely related to another concept in Indian semantics, that of *tātparya* "purport." According to some writers on the subject, *tātparya* is quite simply identical with suggestive force *(vyañjanā, dhvani),* whereas according to other authorities it represents an additional force *(vṛtti)* of words. This point need not detain us here.

Grammaire sanscrite, p. 247: appartenance; J. Wackernagel and A. Debrunner, *Altindische Grammatik* II/2, p. 311: Zugehörigkeit) with *vṛddhi* of the base—means "intentional" in the sense of "pertaining to intention."[19] An *ābhiprāyika* sūtra passage is intentional too in the sense that it is governed by a purpose, that is, the Buddha's motive(s) *(prayojana)* in communicating a provisional, surface teaching intended specially for the specific addressee of such a sūtra. (Additionally, an *ābhiprāyika* sūtra may be intentional in the sense that intentionality attaches to it, that is, that pointing beyond its provisional, surface meaning it is directed towards the definitive, deep meaning, in other words towards the *dgongs gzhi.*)

As the "intentional ground," the *dgongs gzhi* is intentional in the first sense of pertaining to the Buddha's definitive, deep meaning or intention: it is that towards which the Buddha's communicative act in teaching is ultimately and finally directed, even though it is not expressed directly in an *ābhiprāyika* and *neyārtha* sūtra and is accordingly not conveyed to the specific and special addressee—the trainee *(vineya)*—of such a sūtra. But the *dgongs gzhi* is of course not itself motivated in the special sense noticed above of being governed by a salvific and propaedeutic *prayojana (dgos pa)* as defined by the hermeneutical theory under consideration here.

The definition of the word "intentional" given in the *Shorter Oxford English Dictionary*—i.e., "of or pertaining to intention or purpose"—appears to take into account at least the first two of the above-mentioned uses of the word. While the meaning "governed by an intention, or purpose" is doubtless a usual one in everyday English (as it also is of the French word "intentionnel"), the term "intentional" is being used here simply as an adjective to the noun "intention."

The use of this word to describe one particular category of sūtra—namely that category which has an underlying but unexpressed ultimate *abhiprāya*—need not be nullified or rendered inappropriate by the fact that *any* utterance may be described as intentional insofar as it conveys a speaker's or author's intended meaning, and that it is motivated by the purpose he has in making his utterance. In this wider sense, every sūtra serves to convey, directly or indirectly, the Buddha's intention *(abhiprāya,* understood either as *dgongs pa* or as *dgongs gzhi).*

If sūtras in general have sometimes been described in the Abhidharma literature as being *ābhiprāyika,* this is in contradistinction to the Abhidharma which is said in this literature to be *lākṣaṇika* = *mtshan nyid pa* "comprising

19. See Yaśomitra, *Abhidharmakośavyākhyā* vi.3, who glosses *ābhiprāyika* by *abhiprāye bhavaḥ.*

technical definitions, technical." In other words, the adjective *lākṣaṇika* is to be understood in this case as derived not from *lakṣaṇā* "figurative meaning" but from *lakṣaṇa* "characteristic, definition."[20] As for the *neyārtha,* it is contrasted by Yaśomitra with that the meaning of which is analysed and clarified *(vibhaktārtha,* i.e., *nītārtha).*[21]

V

In his commentary on the *Mahāyānasūtrālaṃkāra* (fol. 133b) Rgyal sras Thogs med points out that the category of the *neyārtha* is not coextensive with the twin categories of *abhiprāya* and *abhisaṃdhi,* for Asaṅga has stated in his *Mahāyānasaṃgraha* (ii.31) that it is the whole of the corpus of the Buddha's word (and not just that portion of it which may be regarded as *neyārtha*) that is to be understood in terms of the four *abhiprāya*s and the four *abhisaṃdhi*s. Moreover, Rgyal sras Thogs med explains, this corpus in all its sections serves as a counteragent *(gnyen po = pratipakṣa)* against the wrong practices of disciples, so that it may be subsumed in its entirety under the *pratipakṣābhisaṃdhi.* Rgyal sras Thogs med then explains that this view is not contradicted by the passage of the *Abhidharmasamuccaya* (p. 106) where Asaṅga has defined *abhisaṃdhi* as a semantic transmutation of linguistic forms *(nāmapadavyañjana);* for this definition relates to *pariṇāmanābhisaṃdhi* only. This view expressed by Rgyal sras Thogs med is supported by the three examples given in the *Abhidharmasamuccaya* (p. 107).

However, as seen above, the main hermeneutical schools do in fact recognize the existence of utterances of the Buddha which are neither *dgongs bshad* nor *dgongs pa can* inasmuch as no further intention additional to the one expressed and conveyed by the words of the utterance itself has to be sought for. Such utterances—which do then contain a *dgongs pa (abhiprāya)* in the wide sense but no *dgongs gzhi* or unexpressed intentional ground—are accordingly described as non-intentional *(dgongs min = dgongs pa ma yin pa* or *dgongs pa can ma yin pa).*

20. See Vasubandhu, *Abhidharmakośa* vi.3 with Yaśomitra's *Vyākhyā.* Yaśomitra glosses *lākṣaṇika* by *lakṣaṇe bhavaḥ.*

21. See Yaśomitra, *Abhidharmakośavyākhyā* iii.28ab.

VI

Given the requirement, from the point of view of systematical hermeneutics, to postulate an unexpressed *dgongs gzhi* in certain of the Buddha's utterances which are in some specific way non-concordant or incompatible with the final and definitive doctrine within the frame of a given philosophical system—namely in those sūtras or sūtra passages which the hermeneuticians describe as *ābhiprāyika* and *neyārtha* and as being motivated by particular salvific purposes *(prayojana)* entertained by the Buddha in order provisionally to help the specific and special addressees *(vineya)* of these sūtras—it may be useful to consider here what H. P. Grice has termed conversational implicature. Grice's notion cannot, however, be simply borrowed without modification and adaptation to the hermeneutical concerns being studied in this paper.[22] The sūtras in question are in the first place scarcely conversational in Grice's sense. Nor, more importantly, do Grice's four categories associated with what he has called the Co-operative Principle—namely the categories of Quality, Quantity, Relevance, and Manner—all apply in every *ābhiprāyika* (and *neyārtha*) sūtra because of the existence in them of a deliberately unexpressed intentional ground, the *dgongs gzhi.* In fact Grice's Co-operative Principle yields in such sūtras to what we might call a *Salvific Principle* put to use in a perlocutionary manner.

Still, in conformity even with this Salvific Principle of the Buddha, "flouting"—or more specifically *upāya*-governed salvific exploitation—of the Conversational Maxims are to be found in *ābhiprāyika* and *neyārtha* sūtras, just as they have been recognized in Grice's second type of conversational implicature involving exploitation of the maxims.[23] Thus, in the case of *pariṇāmanābhisaṃdhi,* there is obvious exploitation of the maxims of Quality and Manner; while in other forms of *ābhiprāyika* utterance exploitation is detected through systematical hermeneutics. And both in the pragmatic situation of the Buddha's communicating an *ābhiprāyika* teaching to specific trainees according to their particular intellectual and spiritual dispositions *(bsam pa = āśaya)* and within the frame of the systematical interpretation

22. That Grice's Maxims are not wholly applicable in the analysis of utterances whose function is something other than that of augmenting the addressee's store of propositional knowledge has indeed been noted by J. Lyons, *Semantics,* vol. 2 (Cambridge, 1977), p. 593. For recent discussions of implicature, apart from Lyon's book just cited see S. C. Levinson, *Pragmatics* (Cambridge, 1983), and G. N. Leech, *Principles of Pragmatics* (London, 1983).

23. See Levinson, *Pragmatics,* pp. 109ff.

of the Word of the Buddha *(buddhavacana)* as a whole, the *dgongs gzhi* does involve something that might be compared with *implicature,* thus distinguishing it on the one side from logical implication, entailment, and consequence and on the other side from semantic implication. The implicature being considered here will not be *inferred* in terms of either logical or semantic inference and implication; yet it will be *elicited* both with regard to a given pragmatic situation—i.e., the speaker, addressee(s), and other contextual factors affecting the communication of the sūtra—and in terms of a systematical hermeneutics. This elicitation of meaning will satisfy the hermeneutic maxim that meaning is not to be inferred but elicited *(sensus non est inferendus sed efferendus).*[24]

In an interesting way, then, and within the frame of a given system of philosophical hermeneutics, the *dgongs gzhi* is a kind of *presupposition* for the speaker—the Buddha as teacher—when uttering an *ābhiprāyika* (and *neyārtha*) sūtra, and even for the hermeneutician—who is of course not the specific and special *vineya* of the intentional sūtra. Each of them will, in his own way, be committed to the *truth* of the proposition corresponding to the *dgongs gzhi* and to the *reality* of the corresponding fact or state of affairs. But from the point of view of the addressee of the *ābhiprāyika* sūtra—i.e., the specific *vineya* to whom it is in particular being communicated—the *dgongs gzhi* would not normally be recognized as existent; and *a fortiori* it would not be regarded by him as satisfying a truth-condition.

At the same time the *dgongs gzhi* figures as the condition for the Buddha's employment of the *ābhiprāyika* sūtra in an effective manner as a useful salvific propaedeutic. And it will function also as a kind of felicity-condition for both the speaker and hermeneutician, but again not normally for the addressee. In both these ways, then, the *dgongs gzhi* is for the hermeneutician a *systemic implicature*—or a *systemic presupposition*—in the particular communicative situation where the Buddha teaches a special (type of) addressee by means of an utterance having above all a perlocutionary effect, and where the hermeneutician then submits it to systematical interpretation.[25]

Finally, as a *dgongs gzhi,* Emptiness *(śūnyatā)*—whether described as a fact, a state of affairs, or otherwise—appears as a kind of reality-condition

24. See E. Betti, *Die Hermeneutik als allgemeine Methodik der Geisteswissenschaften*[2] (Tübingen, 1972), p. 14. Cf. J. Bleicher, *Contemporary Hermeneutics* (London, 1980), p. 58.

25. On the relation between implicature and presupposition and connected problems, see, e.g., J. Lyons, *Semantics,* pp. 592–606; S. C. Levinson, *Pragmatics,* pp. 9–10, 25–27, 100ff.

rather than as a truth-condition involving a propositional content (which *śūnyatā* can hardly be).

For the teacher when uttering an *ābhiprāyika* and *neyārtha* sūtra, and also for the hermeneutician when interpreting such an utterance in the context of the total corpus of sūtras, such intentional sūtra passages requiring further interpretation are, within the given hermeneutical frame, finally *neutralized* by the non-*ābhiprāyika* and *nītārtha* sūtras.

VII

Turning now to the question of the relation between *dgongs pa = abhiprāya* and *dgongs gzhi,* it appears from our sources that the concept of *dgongs gzhi* is appreciably narrower than that of *dgongs pa* but that the two terms nevertheless refer to the intention of the Buddha in a canonical utterance. That is, whereas *any* sūtra at all can properly be said to contain an intention (see section IV above), *only* such sūtras in which the Buddha's ultimate intention is not directly expressed and communicated *(dngos bstan)* and the surface teaching of which is destined by the Buddha to serve as a provisional (and perlocutionary) propaedeutic device for the corresponding specific *vineya*s may be said to have the *dgongs gzhi* being discussed here. And it is only this latter kind of sūtra that is termed *dgongs pa can = ābhiprāyika* by most hermeneuticians, even though it is true that all sūtras, including also those that are non-*ābhiprāyika* and *nītārtha,* convey the Buddha's intention and have as their motivation his purpose of helping living beings by his teaching. In other words, while the terms *dgongs pa* and *dgongs gzhi* have basically the same meaning, the latter has a much more restricted scope since it is reserved for a particular category of utterance within *buddhavacana.*

It appears moreover that the non-literal *(sgra ji bzhin ma yin pa = na yathāruta-) ābhiprāyika* sūtra differs significantly from the *neyārtha* one above all in one case. This is that of the Mādhyamika who accepts the definitions of the *Akṣayamatinirdeśasūtra* and *Samādhirājasūtra* according to which the difference between *neyārtha* and *nītārtha* is stated to result from a difference in content—that is, whether a sūtra teaches *śūnyatā* or the equivalent (in which case it is *nītārtha*) or teaches something else (in which case it is *neyārtha*)—and does not depend on whether the expression-level is explicit and literal or not.[26] In other respects, and for philosopher-hermeneuticians following other definitions of this difference, the categories of *ābhiprāyika*

26. See above, note 14.

and *neyārtha* seem to have largely converged in sūtra hermeneutics at least; and the difference in terminology appears mainly to reflect originally distinct historical antecedents and exegetical traditions. Further research is required on this point.

In the case of the four kinds of *abhiprāya (dgongs pa)* mentioned in the *Mahāyānasūtrālaṃkāra* and related texts alongside the four *abhisaṃdhi*s *(ldem por dgongs pa)* (see section I above), however, the word *abhiprāya* has been used in a significantly narrower and more specific way that sets it off from the wider and more general use where *abhiprāya* is an equivalent of *bhāva, āśaya,* and *artha* "meaning, purport." For these four kinds of *abhiprāya* are located by the hermeneuticians only in certain sūtra passages which are intentional *(ābhiprāyika)* in the technical sense identified above, whereas in its wide sense the word *abhiprāya* denotes the intended meaning of any and every sūtra text (see section IV above). Whilst no *dgongs gzhi* is specified by the Tibetan hermeneuticians in the case of the wide use of *dgongs pa = abhiprāya,* a *dgongs gzhi* is identified by them in the case of the set of four *abhiprāya*s listed in the *Mahayānasūtrālaṃkāra* etc. (It has at the same time to be recalled that Asaṅga has stated in his *Mahāyānasaṃgraha* that all the Buddha's teaching *[buddhavacana]*—and not just that portion of it which is regarded as *neyārtha* and *ābhiprāyika* in the technical sense—has to be understood in terms of the four *abhiprāya*s and four *abhisaṃdhi*s. See section V above.)

With regard to the relation between the concept of *ābhiprāyika* and that of *neyārtha,* a possibly useful differentiation from the analytic point of view might be to say that the latter is, in some cases at least, a more purely semantic and content-oriented notion whilst the former is perhaps more readily understood in terms of pragmatics and speech-act theory.

VIII

It might seem attractive to approach the analysis of the Buddha's intention in its form of *dgongs gzhi* in *ābhiprāyika* and *neyārtha* sūtras by identifying it—as well as its direct expression (as *abhiprāya = dgongs pa* in the wide sense noted above) in non-*ābhiprāyika* and *nītārtha* sūtras—with the actual *kerygma* of the Buddha's word *(buddhavacana),* as opposed (rather in the manner of Bultmannian demythologization) to the *ābhiprāyika* utterances and *neyārtha* formulations to be found in *buddhavacana.*

This would however seem to involve us in an oversimplification. That part of the Buddhist canon that is *ābhiprāyika* and *neyārtha* is very clearly not to be rationalized or interpreted away in the view of the Buddhist hermeneuticians: interpretation in terms of a further, unexpressed meaning which is resorted to by them in order to calculate a *dgongs gzhi* and to elicit the Buddha's final and definitive intention, or deep meaning, is indeed quite different from just interpreting away the provisional surface meaning. The *dgongs gzhi* is, then, a text-transcendent teleological goal or focus of the Buddha's teaching, rather than the text-immanent meaning of an *ābhiprāyika* or *neyārtha* sūtra. Its addressee—the specific and special *vineya* of the sūtra passage in question—will be ultimately brought to an understanding of the *dgongs gzhi* or "intentional ground"—as well as of the direct expression of the Buddha's *abhiprāya* found in the non-*ābhiprāyika* and *nītārtha* sūtras—precisely through the mediation of the *ābhiprāyika* utterance and *neyārtha* formulation, which work with and through the specific trainee's conceptual fore-structure of understanding (Vorverständnis), i.e., his pre-suppositions (Voraussetzungen) and pre-judgements (Vorurteile). (These pre-suppositions need of course have nothing to do with the semantic notion of presupposition dealt with above, any more than these pre-judgements need have anything to do with prejudice in the current sense.)

IX

In sum, the *dgongs gzhi* of our sources functions neither as a standard inferential implicate nor as a semantic-linguistic implicate of an *ābhiprāyika* or *neyārtha* sūtra passage, of which it is rather the intentional (i.e., purportive and teleological) foundation or ground. It thus occupies the place of a systemic implicature and presupposition in a canonical whole—linguistic and also pragmatic, and inclusive of non-*ābhiprāyika* and *nītārtha* sūtras too—of which the *ābhiprāyika* and *neyārtha* sūtras are but a part. (In the technical language of Indian exegetical theory, moreover, the unexpressed intention is semantically *utsūtra* "text-transcendent" as opposed to *sūtrārtha* or text-immanent.) And insofar as it is not directly expressed or conveyed within an utterance or text by means of inferential or semantic implication, it is the function of systematical hermeneutics to calculate and elicit it.

The term *dgongs gzhi* is not used in our sources in such a way that we may simply translate it by the words unexpressed presupposition or implicature or by suggested meaning (on the model of *dhvani* and *vyañjanā*). And it thus appears necessary to render it by the expression "intentional foundation" or "intentional ground" (the term *intentional* being understood here as explained in section IV above).

It should be noted finally that in Modern Tibetan the word *dgongs gzhi* is used in the sense of "(undeclared) intention, idea, plan."[27] It is thus both related to and different from the nouns *'char gzhi* "idea" and *rtsis gzhi* "plan" (as well as the verbal auxiliary *rtsis* "intend, plan, expect," French "compter"), where the connotation of undeclared is not present.

27. The meaning "intention" is duly registered in M. Goldstein, *Tibetan-English Dictionary of Modern Tibetan* (Kathmandu, 1975). The term is not listed under "intent"/"intention" in M. Goldstein and N. Narkyid, *English-Tibetan Dictionary of Modern Tibetan* (Berkeley, 1984).

8. An Indian Source for the Tibetan Hermeneutical Term *dgongs gzhi,* "Intentional Ground"*

THE FOREGOING ARTICLE in this volume discussed the Tibetan term *dgongs gzhi,* a word used by the Tibetan hermeneuticians to designate the ultimately intended, but not immediately conveyed, purport or import of an utterance described as *ābhiprāyika* "intentional"—or "allusive"—and as involving the cancellation or neutralization of the utterance's directly expressed surface meaning *(dngos la gnod byed: mukhyārthabādha),* the one that is prima facie conveyed to the addressee. As such, the *dgongs gzhi* can be described as the "deep meaning" of an *ābhiprāyika* utterance (and of one that is described as *neyārtha* = *drang [ba'i] don* or *bkri ba'i don*), inasmuch as the latter requires to be interpreted in a sense other than the obvious surface meaning in order to elicit its intended sense. In that article it was suggested that, as a term designating one of the three criterial factors required for establishing that an utterance is *ābhiprāyika* and *neyārtha* in the frame of a given system of philosophical hermeneutics,[1] the compound word *dgongs gzhi* may have been a terminological development of the Tibetan hermeneuticians. Attention has nevertheless to be drawn to the source of this compound, the analytical expression *dgongs pa'i gzhi.*

In a passage of the *Prasphuṭapadā,* a commentary by Dharmamitra (ca. 800) on Haribhadra's Vṛtti on the *Abhisamayālaṃkāra,*[2] we read in chapter

* First published in *Journal of Indian Philosophy* 16 (1988), pp. 1–4.

1. With the Tibetan hermeneuticians these criterial factors are, in addition to the *dgongs gzhi,* the motive *(dgos pa = prayojana)* governing the giving of an *ābhiprāyika* teaching and systematic incompatibility with the primary and directly expressed meaning of a text-passage *(dngos la gnod byed: mukhyārthabādha).*

2. On Dharmamitra and his *Abhisamayālaṃkārakārikāprajñāpāramitopadeśaśāstraṭīkā Prasphuṭapadā,* see D. Seyfort Ruegg, "The *gotra, ekayāna* and *tathāgatagarbha* Theories of the Prajñāpāramitā According to Dharmamitra and Abhayākaragupta," in L. Lancaster

vii (Peking edition of the Bstan 'gyur, Mdo 'grel, nya, fol. 105b–106a; Sde dge edition, Shes phyin, nya, fol. 91a5–6):

> *rtag pa dang chad pa la sogs pa'i lta ba las (b)zlog pa'i phyir bdag dang kun gzhi sogs pa ni/ chos kyi dbyings dgongs pa'i gzhir bzhag las...*
>
> in order to remove views *(dṛṣṭi)* such as the eternalist *(śāśvata)* and nihilist *(uccheda)* ones, [teachings given in the canon pertaining to an] *ātman, ālaya[vijñāna],* etc., took as [their] intentional ground the *dharmadhātu...*

This passage from the *Prasphuṭapadā* provides a valuable parallel to explanations later given by the Tibetan hermeneuticians of the Madhyamaka school according to which canonical allusions both to an *ātman* and to the *ālayavijñāna* (and also sometimes even to the *tathāgatagarbha*) are *ābhiprāyika* and *neyārtha* utterances that are governed by specific—and legitimate—salvific motives *(prayojana = dgos pa)* of the Buddha and have as their *dgongs gzhi* "intentional ground" non-substantiality *(nairātmya),* Emptiness *(śūnyatā),* and ultimate reality *(bhūtakoṭi),* that is, equivalents of *dharmadhātu* in Dharmamitra's text.[3]

It is true that no reference has been explicitly made here by Dharmamitra to the cancellation of the directly expressed surface meaning in favour of a deep meaning conveyed by indirection, or to the *ābhiprāyika* and *neyārtha* character (within the frame of the Mādhyamika's systematic interpretation of the total canonical corpus of the Buddha's teaching) of those teachings that bear on an *ātman* (for example in the Mahāyānist *Mahāparinirvāṇasūtra* and in other doctrinally related sūtras) or on the *ālayavijñāna* (in sūtras linked with the Vijñānavāda). However, the notion of motive *(prayojana)*—which is, together with the *dgongs gzhi,* the second fundamental criterial condition that must be satisfied to establish that an utterance is *ābhiprāyika* and *neyārtha*—is very clearly represented in the *Prasphuṭapadā* by the words "in order to remove views such as the eternalist and nihilist ones."

(ed.), *The Prajñāpāramitā and Related Systems* (Studies in honor of E. Conze, Berkeley, 1977), pp. 283ff.

3. This idea can be found already in the *Laṅkāvatārasūtra,* chap. ii (ed. B. Nanjio, pp. 78–79), as well as in Candrakīrti's observations in his *Madhyamakāvatārabhāṣya* (vi.42, 85, and 95f). But the hermeneutical theory based on the three criteria mentioned above was only fully elaborated later.

Since the compound *dgongs gzhi* regularly employed by the Tibetan hermeneuticians is simply a convenient abbreviation of the analytical expression *dgongs pa'i gzhi,* this passage of the *Prasphuṭapadā* provides us with a ninth-century source both for the "intentional ground" in the hermeneutical theory discussed earlier and for the term *dgongs gzhi* that designates it.

Because the Sanskrit original of the *Prasphuṭapadā* is not available, the exact Sanskrit equivalent of the expression *dgongs pa'i gzhi* unfortunately remains uncertain, and all that can be said at present on the basis of the materials available to this writer is that it presumably contained the word *abhiprāya* or a derivative of this word. It is to be hoped that the precise Sanskrit form can, sooner or later, be located in some text the Sanskrit original of which is extant. As the Sanskrit equivalent of *dgongs pa'i gzhi, abhipretavastu* might be tentatively suggested.

In closing, attention can be drawn to interesting parallels between Buddhist hermeneutical terminology in Sanskrit and Tibetan and some Greek terms. Thus, to *abhiprāya* = *dgongs pa* "intention, purport" there correspond *νοῦς, διάνοια,* and *βούλημα.* And *ὑπόνοια* corresponds not only to this term but also to *dgongs pa'i gzhi.*[4] These are parallels and it is being suggested neither that the Buddhist and Greek theories converge nor that one is derived from the other. (If ultimately the English word "intentional" is felt to be inappropriate to render Sanskrit *ābhiprāyika* and Tibetan *dgongs pa can* because of its semantic overlap with the word "deliberate," "dianoetic" could be introduced to express what is denoted by these terms in their wider use. And when the reference is specifically to a covert "intentional ground," i.e., to one not immediately conveyed to the addressee of an utterance, "hyponoetic" could be introduced to express this meaning. It should however be noted that the Greek words *διανοητικός* and *ὑπονοητικός* do not appear to be attested as adjectives to the above-mentioned Greek hermeneutical terms. If we wish to avoid employing such neologisms, the word "allusive" can be used to paraphrase *ābhiprāyika* = *dgongs pa can.*)

4. See for example H. de Lubac, *Exégèse médiévale,* I (Paris, 1959), especially pp. 373ff., 382–83, 392n3, and also II/2 (Paris, 1964), pp. 182ff. (on the problem of the *integumentum* and *involucrum,* and *exegesis per integumentum*). See also recently M. Harl, *Origène: Philocalie 1–20* (Paris, 1983), pp. 47 (on the "spirit" of a text as opposed to its literal meaning, the *lexis* [λέξις] or *historia* [ἱστορία]), and 122 (on *huponoia* [ὑπόνοια] as the hidden sense of a text).

9. Some Reflections on the Place of Philosophy in the Study of Buddhism*

I

IT IS SURELY no exaggeration to say that philosophical thinking constitutes a major component in Buddhism. To say this is of course not to claim that Buddhism is reducible to any single philosophy in some more or less restrictive sense but, rather, to say that what can be meaningfully described as philosophical thinking comprises a major part of its procedures and intentionality, and also that due attention to this dimension is heuristically necessary in the study of Buddhism. If this proposition were to be regarded as problematic, the difficulty would seem to be due to certain assumptions and prejudgements which it may be worthwhile to consider here.

In the first place, even though the philosophical component in Buddhism has been recognized by many investigators since the inception of Buddhist studies as a modern scholarly discipline more than a century and a half ago, it has to be acknowledged that the main stream of these studies has, nevertheless, quite often paid little attention to the philosophical. The idea somehow appears to have gained currency in some quarters that it is possible to deal with Buddhism in a serious and scholarly manner without being obliged to concern oneself with philosophical content. One has only to look at several dictionaries to see that the European terminology so often employed to render Pāli, Sanskrit, and Tibetan technical terms is on occasion hardly coherent and did not reflect the state of philosophical knowledge even at the time these dictionaries were first published. This impression is reinforced by many a translation from these three languages as well as by some work on texts written in them.

* This article is an expanded version of the presidential address delivered at the 11th International Conference of the International Association of Buddhist Studies at Mexico City in October 1994. It was first published in the *Journal of the International Association of Buddhist Studies* 18 (1995), pp. 145–81.

An example of such lexical incoherence is the rendering of Sanskrit *saṃjñā* and Pāli *saññā* "idea, notion" by the English word "perception" if, at the same time, the epistemological term *pratyakṣa (pramāṇa)* is to be rendered as "(direct) perception"; for if in a well thought-out and coherent terminology *saṃjñā* is to be translated by "perception," *pratyakṣa* could not be, and conversely. A somewhat more difficult case is the rendering "form" for *rūpa,* rather than the more precise "(elementary [*mahābhūta* = *dhātu*] and derived [*bhautika*], resistant) matter (for *rūpaskandha*) / visible matter (having colour and shape) (for *rūpāyatana*)." In the Abhidharma, *rūpa* is the first of the five *skandha*s "Groups"; and in the *āyatana* classification of the Sarvāstivādins, the *rūpin* Bases are numbers 1–5 and 7–11, the *rūpāyatana* or visible matter Base being number 7, which is the sense object of the *cakṣurindriyāyatana* (Base 1); and in the *dhātu* classification, the *rūpin* Elements are numbers 1–5 and 7–11, the *rūpadhātu* Element being number 7 in relation to the *cakṣurdhātu* (Element 1) and the *cakṣurvijñānadhātu* (Element 13). Hence, when adopting the rendering "form" for *rūpa* one is obliged to consider whether, in philosophical usage, this equivalent can actually bear the required meanings; a glance at a good dictionary of philosophical terminology will reveal that the term "form" in fact very seldom does.[1] These are, then, fundamental terms

1. In the list of *khandhas/skandhas*, even while rendering *saññā* by "idea" the philosopher K. N. Jayatilleke retained "form" for *rūpa* in his *Early Buddhist Theory of Knowledge* (London, 1963), e.g., p. 283. Conversely, Y. Karunadasa rendered *rūpa* by "matter" while continuing to use "perception" for *saññā* in his *Buddhist Analysis of Matter* (Colombo, 1967). Bhikkhu Ñāṇānanda, *Concept and Reality in Early Buddhist Thought* (Kandy, 1971), also kept "perception" for *saññā*. These translations were given in *The Pali Text Society's Pali-English Dictionary* (London, 1921–25), and earlier in R. C. Childers, *A Dictionary of the Pali Language* (London, 1875). Already in 1939 the *Critical Pāli Dictionary* (Copenhagen, 1924ff.) s.v. *arūpa* had rendered *rūpa* by "corporeal, material" (beside "form"!); it however curiously conflated *saññā* and *viññāṇa,* translating both terms by "conscious(ness)" s.vv. *asañña* and *aviññāṇa.* The rendering "corporeality" for *rūpa(skandha)* was adopted by Nyanatiloka/Nyanaponika, *Buddhist Dictionary*[4] (Kandy, 1980), which used "perception" for *saññā.* Much earlier, T. Stcherbatsky had employed "matter," "ideas," and "consciousness" to render these three *skandha*-terms in his *Central Conception of Buddhism* (London, 1923), elaborating on results obtained previously by O. Rosenberg (see *Die Probleme der buddhistischen Philosophie* [Heidelberg, 1924], where the renderings "das Sinnliche," "Unterscheidung," and "Bewußtsein" have been used). L. de La Vallée Poussin has frequently used "matière" and "notion" in his translations. In his note "Saṃjñā," in C. Vogel, ed., *Jñānamuktāvalī,* J. Nobel Commemoration Volume (New Delhi, 1959), pp. 59–60, H. von Glasenapp sought to clarify the issue, distinguishing between "Unterscheidungsvermögen" for *saṃjñā* ("wobei die Bedeutung 'separates Objekt einer Wahrnehmung oder Vorstellung' mitschwingt") and "Bewußtsein" for *vijñāna.* Whilst rendering

and concepts in Buddhist thought for which no philosophically adequate translation has yet been agreed. Another kind of difficulty is presented by the Sanskrit term *pramāṇa,* which has been variously translated as right/correct knowledge/cognition, veridical awareness, valid knowledge, validating knowledge, epistemic norm, standard, and authority, all of which renderings are no doubt appropriate in some context either as denotations or, at least, as connotations of the word.[2] Until such problems associated with philosophical terminology and concepts have been first recognized to exist and then adequately investigated, lexicography and translation, as well as interpretation, will rest on insecure foundations, as will Buddhist studies in any full sense of this term.

In part, this situation might be thought to be due to what could be called a philological fallacy were one to take the word philology exclusively in its narrow sense of textual study. But since I understand the word philology in its full and comprehensive sense inclusive of content and context, I would reject the expression "philological fallacy" as a suitable tag for the problem in question. The fallacy has rather to do with the presumption that the study of the linguistic expression in texts can somehow be divorced from content.

Secondly, the issue has been complicated by the dichotomy between philosophy and religion that has been current in Western thought, and accordingly in academic structures. In the Western tradition, philosophy has indeed very often defined itself in opposition to religion, and the fact that scholars of Buddhism may regard the subject of their studies as both a religion and a philosophy has then led to the most extraordinary misunderstanding and confusion. If, for its students, Buddhism is both a philosophy and a religion in some meaningful sense of these two words, it is neither according to certain current definitions conditioned by the history of these subjects. Thus, Buddhist thought is not philosophy in the perspective of, e.g., logical positivism or linguistic philosophy as it was generally practised earlier in this

---

saṃjñā by "perceptions . . . et les notions qui en résultent," J. Filliozat rendered both senses together by "prise de conscience" in *L'Inde classique,* vol. 2 (Hanoi, 1953), p. 340 with 521; on p. 519 he explained *rūpa* as including everything which is material in the universe. In an early effort to understand Abhidharma/Abhidhamma thought, H. Guenther rendered *saññā* by "sensation" and *rūpa* by "form" and "Gestalt"; see his *Philosophy and Psychology in the Abhidharma* (Lucknow, 1957), pp. 58 and 151 (where only in his note did he provide a good explanation of *rūpa*). For *saṃjñā,* cf. also D. Seyfort Ruegg, *Le traité du tathāgatagarbha de Bu ston Rin chen grub* (Paris, 1973), pp. 76n2 and 117n1.

2. See below, section IX.

century. Nor has Buddhism normally been a religion in the sense of belief in a supreme being either as creator god or as a supernatural entity who can intervene in the natural order of things (thus giving rise to very difficult problems of theodicy). In addition, the problems of (self-)definition which the study of Buddhism has thus had to confront may have to do with the place apart in the humanities that philosophy and religious studies have so often been assigned—indeed with the place that they have sometimes been quite content to assign themselves.

Thirdly, the problem has no doubt been connected with the presumption that anything regarded as so quintessentially Greek, and hence "Occidental," as philosophy cannot possibly be found in anything "Oriental."[3] For—according to a widely held view—does not "Oriental thought" concern itself chiefly with the mystical and the irrational, or at best with what is called "wisdom" as opposed to reasoned philosophical thinking and the search for truth (defined in philosophy as the property of a proposition or state of affairs)?[4] Moreover, does not the interest evinced in mind by Indian and Buddhist philosophy place it outside the pale of true academic philosophy, so long at least as mind—that so-called "ghost in the machine"—was regarded as an epiphenomenon of the material, or of behaviour, and was not held to be a suitable subject for genuine philosophical inquiry?

A further drawback for the study of Buddhist philosophy is the fact that it has all too often been studied in isolation from Indian thought as a whole, and from Indology. It should be clear that both in its structures and its development, Buddhist thought must be investigated to a considerable extent in its relation with Brāhmaṇical and Jain thought.

Similarly, the study of Buddhist thought outside India must take account also of contextual factors such as Taoism, shamanism, Shintoism, Bon, etc.

But the undifferentiated idea of "Oriental thought," or "Asian philosophy,"

3. A discussion has turned round the question whether Sanskrit even has a word that corresponds precisely to "philosophy," and whether the concept of philosophy is an indigenous, "emic," category in Indian thought. See the valuable remarks in W. Halbfass, *India and Europe: An Essay in Understanding* (Albany, 1988); id., *Tradition and Reflection* (Albany, 1991), chap. 7.

4. Confusion has probably been created, at least for non-specialists, by the translation of *prajñā* by "wisdom" when one of the chief meanings of this term is discriminative knowledge *(pravicaya = rab tu rnam par 'byed pa)* bearing on the *dharmas*. See, e.g., Vasubandhu, *Abhidharmakośabhāṣya* i.2b and ii.24 *(prajñā dharmapravicayaḥ)*, and Prajñākaramati, *Bodhicaryāvatārapañjikā* ix.1. This confusion has then been compounded by rendering *vikalpa* by "discrimination" when this term means "(dichotomic) conceptual construction." Even for *jñāna = ye shes*, "wisdom" is a rather inadequate translation.

as some sort of monolithic entity, is of course a construct, a largely imaginary creature inhabiting the minds of some modern writers. At best, as often employed, the expression "Oriental thought" is of limited utility as shorthand.

Still, very interestingly for us as students of Buddhism, to the extent that there really is substance in the idea of an "Asian philosophy," historically it is in large part constituted precisely by Buddhism. For it is Buddhism that has linked together so many Asian civilizations from Afghanistan and Kalmukia in the west to Japan in the east, and from the northern Mongol lands to Sri Lanka in the south. At the same time, however, we have in fact long known of the enormously large and diverse ways of thought represented in Asia, which is after all a geographical rather than a cultural entity. And amongst these ways of thought we have become familiar with a very considerable number of discrete Indian and Buddhist philosophies which require to be kept distinct.[5] Several of the latter have indeed embraced within themselves some form of what has been called mysticism, and certain trends may on occasion have proved themselves to be non-rational, irrational, even anti-rational. But, after all, these are not characteristics peculiar to Asian, or Buddhist, thought alone!

II

The view that philosophy is at best of only marginal and incidental importance in Buddhism, even that the historical Buddha did not profess being a philosopher at all, claims to have support from within the Buddhist canon itself.

Holders of this view have based it in particular on the smaller *Māluṅkyāputtasutta,* where it is related how the Buddha declined to answer questions put to him by the ascetic Māluṅkyāputta relating to the permanence and endlessness of the world (*loka,* of living beings), to the link between the body *(sarīra)* and the life principle *(jīva),* and to the existence of a *tathāgata* after death. In this text, these questions set aside and left unanswered by the Buddha are described as unexplicated *(avyakata = avyākṛta)* points, and the reason for the Buddha's refusal to answer them is there said to be that they are

5. But not totally isolated from each other. Thus the concept of "Buddhisms" (in the plural), which has recently gained popularity, seems only to displace the issues, and also to avoid the question as to why so many peoples with their various world-views have in fact called themselves Buddhists.

neither relevant (*atthasaṃhita* "goal-fitted, useful, salutary") nor linked fundamentally with pure practice *(ādibrahmacariyaka),* and that they do not conduce to distaste *(nibbidā),* dispassion *(virāga),* cessation *(nirodha),* calming *(upasama),* "superknowledge" *(abhiññā),* and nirvāṇa. To illustrate this, the sūtra employs a parable that has become famous, that of the man wounded by a poisoned arrow and of the doctor called by his friends and relatives to treat his wound. According to this parable, if before allowing the removal by the doctor of the poisoned arrow embedded in his body, the wounded man were to insist on knowing just what sort of person it was who shot the arrow and precisely of what materials the arrow and the bow from which it was shot were made, he would die from his wound before all his curiosity was satisfied. But the Buddha is like a true doctor who immediately sets about removing the arrow from a wounded man's body without stopping to investigate irrelevant circumstances.[6] Here we see that the Buddha's teaching is supposed to work therapeutically—to have a salvific and gnoseological purpose—and that certain questions have been excluded from its purview because they do not serve the immediate need and are thus irrelevant.[7]

Another canonical text cited in support of the claim that the Buddha had no wish to profess himself a philosopher is the one in which he declines to reply to Vacchagotta's question as to whether an *attā (ātman)* "self" exists or not, as well as to his question concerning the unexplicated questions *(avyākatāni diṭṭhigatāni / avyākatavatthu = avyākr̥tavastu,* which have been described as "set aside," *ṭhapita,* and "excluded," *paṭikkhitta).*[8] In the case of the Buddha's silence concerning the *atman,* the tradition has sometimes

6. *Cūḷamāluṅykasutta,* Majjhimanikāya I, 426–32. In this context É. Lamotte once wrote in his *Histoire du bouddhisme indien,* I (Louvain, 1958), p. 52: "La Loi bouddhique telle que la conçoit Śākyamuni relève de la morale et de l'éthique plutôt que de la philosophie et de la métaphysique"; Lamotte's formulation was more moderate than that of some others.

7. On medicine in Buddhism and the Buddha as physician, see, e.g., *Hōbōgirin* s.v. "Byō." That the Buddhist *āryasatya*s were not, however, derived from a pre-existing medical teaching in India has been argued by A. Wezler, "On the Quadruple Division of the Yogaśāstra, the Caturvyūhatva of the Cikitsāśāstra and the 'Four Noble Truths' of the Buddha," *IT* 12 (1984), 289–337; cf. also W. Halbfass, *Tradition and Reflection,* chap. 7.

8. See the *Poṭṭhapādasutta* in Dīghanikāya I, 187 f.; the *Pāsādikasutta,* ibid., 135ff.; the *Parammaraṇasutta* in Saṃyuttanikāya II, 222 f.; the *Avyākatasaṃyutta,* ibid. IV, 374ff. (including the *Vacchagottasutta,* ibid. IV, 395 f.); the *Cūḷamāluṅkyasutta* in the Majjhimanikāya I, 426ff., and the *Vacchagottasutta,* ibid. I, 484ff.; and the *Avyākatasutta* in the Aṅguttaranikāya IV, 68ff. (on *inter alia* the *ariyasāvaka* who is *avyākaraṇadhamma* with regard to the *avyākatavatthu*s).

regarded it as pedagogically motivated;[9] elsewhere, of course, the Buddha is shown teaching that the factors of existence are without self *(anattā, anātman),* without a permanent substantial essence.[10]

In deciding whether Buddhist doctrine—either as preceptive scriptural teaching *(deśanādharma)* or as a way of life to be practised *(adhigamadharma)*—is genuinely philosophical, much will of course depend on what we think philosophy is about. Were it to be considered to be unbridled speculative thought, or about the construction of a metaphysical system, Buddhist thought would no doubt not be pure philosophy. And a doctrine like Buddhism, which has represented itself as therapeutic and soteriological, would not be counted as essentially philosophical so long as philosophy is understood to be nothing but analysis of concepts, language, and meaning (though these matters do play an important part in the history of Buddhist thought, too). But the fact remains that, in Buddhism, soteriology, gnoseology, and epistemology have been closely bound up with each other. Indeed, as a teaching concerning the Path leading to the cessation of "ill" *(dukkhanirodhagaminī paṭipadā),* Buddhism has not only had to develop a soteriological method that is theoretically intelligible and satisfying, but it has found itself obliged to identify what is this "ill" *(dukkha)* from which liberation is sought, whence it springs *(dukkhasamudaya),* and what is the nature of the cessation of ill (*dukkhanirodha,* i.e., *nirvāṇa* as the fruit of the Path). For the purpose of explicating these four Principles—the *āryasatya*s—Buddhist thinkers have brought to bear what can be described as philosophical theory and analysis alongside practice. Even their identification of a type of question *(praśna)* or matter *(vastu)* to be set aside *(ṭhapanīya = sthāpanīya = bzhag par bya ba,* as unexplicated/undecided, *avyākata = avyākṛta)* beside other questions susceptible of explication either categorically *(ekāṃsa-vyākaraṇīya),* or after making appropriate distinctions *(vibhajja/vibhajya-vyākaraṇīya)* or after further questioning *(paṭipucchā ~ paripṛcchya-vyākaraṇīya),* is itself of philosophical significance.[11] In philosophy as well as in semantics and pragmatics,

9. See, e.g., Saṃyuttanikāya IV, 400. Cf. Nāgārjuna, *Mūlamadhyamakakārikā* xviii.6, xxii.12, xxv.21, and xxvii.8 (the problem of empty [null] subject terms is also taken up in Candrakīrti's *Prasannapadā* on this passage, as it is in ix.12).

10. A recent treatment of the unexplicated points is C. Oetke, "Die 'unbeantworteten Fragen' und das Schweigen des Buddha," *WZKS* 38 (1994), 84–120, which arrived too late to be addressed here.

11. See, e.g., the *Saṅgītisuttanta,* Dīghanikāya III, 229; Aṅguttaranikāya I, 197; and *Milindapañha,* 144–45. (Cf. K. N. Jayatilleke, *Early Buddhist Theory of Knowledge,* chap.

the principle of relevance (and the maxim of relation) is also acknowledged as essentially philosophical.[12]

The canonical text in which the Buddha is shown declaring that he does not dispute with the world but that the world disputes with him, also, does not appear to justify the supposition that the Buddha was somehow anti-philosophical. The context in fact indicates that what the wise agree on as the given must provide the starting point for philosophical discussion.[13] What is rejected, then, is disputing for the sake of disputing, rather than useful discussion and analysis. The latter are in fact amply evidenced in many a Buddhist sūtra; and in so much of Buddhist tradition, scriptural authority *(āgama)* is regularly accompanied by reasoning and argument *(yukti)*. But for Buddhist thinkers reasoning *(yukti)* and disputation *(vivāda)* are not automatically equivalent.

In sum, according to Buddhist traditions, if it is true that a Buddha does not hold back, so to say in a closed teacher's fist *(ācariyamuṭṭhi = ācāryamuṣṭi)*, any relevant teaching required by his disciples, neither does he indulge in any utterance that is unwarranted and unjustified in a given philosophical and teaching situation.[14] And what he is shown as eschewing was disputatiousness and contentiousness masquerading as philosophy rather than discussion, reasoning, and analysis.

6.) For the Sanskrit, see, e.g., *Saṃgītisūtra* (ed. Stache-Rosen) iv.26; and Vasubandhu, *Abhidharmakośa(bhāṣya)* v.22, with Yaśomitra's *Vyākhyā*.

12. See for example P. Grice, *Studies in the Way of Words* (Cambridge, MA, 1989); and D. Sperber and D. Wilson, *Relevance* (Oxford, 1986).

13. See the *Pupphasutta* in Saṃyuttanikāya III, 138: *nâhaṃ bhikkhave lokena vivadāmi, loko ca mayā vivadati/ na bhikkhave dhammavādī kenaci lokasmiṃ vivadati/ yaṃ bhikkhave natthi-sammataṃ loke paṇḍitānaṃ ahaṃ pi taṃ "natthi" ti vadāmi/ yaṃ bhikkhave atthi-sammataṃ loke paṇḍitānaṃ ahaṃ pi taṃ "atthi" ti vadāmi/* . . . . For the Sanskrit parallel, and the context from the point of view of the Madhyamaka school, see Candrakīrti, *Prasannapadā* xviii.8 (370): *loko mayā sārdhaṃ vivadati nâhaṃ lokena sārdhaṃ vivadāmi/ yal loke 'sti sammataṃ tan mamâpy asti sammatam/ yal loke nâstisammataṃ mamâpi tan nâsti sammatam/; Madhyamakāvatārabhāṣya* vi.81. Cf. also the *Trisaṃvaranirdeśaparivarta-mahāyānasūtra* of the Ratnakūṭa collection.

14. See *Milindapañha*, 144–45: *natth' ānanda tathāgatassa dhammesu ācariyamuṭṭhîti. abyākato ca therena māluṅkyāputtena pucchito pañho, tañ ca pana na ajānanena na guhyakaraṇena. cattār' imāni mahārāja pañhabyākaraṇāni . . . bhagavā mahārāja therassa māluṅkyāputtassa taṃ ṭhapanīyaṃ pañhaṃ nabyākāsi. so pana pañho kiṃkāraṇā ṭhapanīyo? na tassa dīpanāya hetu vā karaṇaṃ vā atthi, tasmā so pañho ṭhapanīyo. natthi buddhānaṃ bhagavantānaṃ akāraṇam ahetukaṃ giraṃ udīraṇan ti.*

III

One of the most recent investigations known to me of the appropriateness of speaking of "Indian philosophy," and of attaching the appellation of philosophy to Buddhism, is to be found in a book by the comparative philosopher Guy Bugault bearing the challenging title *L'Inde pense-t-elle?,* which both provokes deeper thought on the matter and calls into question certain cultural shibboleths. There it is shown how—notwithstanding the very real differences between the traditions of philosophy in the West and in the Indian and Buddhist schools—there does exist a genuine sense in which we can, and indeed must, give due consideration to the philosophical dimension in the latter. Bugault's discussion turns round the questions whether what we find in India is "an other philosophy" rather than "something other than philosophy," and the extent to which a soteriology and therapeutic such as Buddhism is not wholly a philosophy but, nonetheless, a way of thinking that clearly comprises a philosophical dimension.[15]

15. See Guy Bugault, *L'Inde pense-t-elle?* (Paris, 1994), chap. 1 "La question préalable," pp. 50–51: "Après avoir essayé de montrer qu'il existe une philosophie en Inde et aussi sa spécificité, nous laissons finalement le lecteur face à la question qui nous paraît l'essentiel: en quelle mesure est-ce une philosophie, en quelle mesure est-ce autre chose que de la philosophie? [. . .] Restent les mouvements qui ne relèvent pas des brâhmanes mais des śramanes: bouddhisme et jinisme. Si on les considère dans leur totalité organique, aucun d'eux n'est une philosophie. Ce sont des thérapies, des sotériologies, mais qui comportent une dimension philosophique." G. Bugault is emeritus professor of Indian and comparative philosophy at the Sorbonne (Université Paris IV), the passage quoted being reprinted from his article "En quelle mesure et en quel sens peut-on parler de 'philosophie indienne'" in André Jacob ed., *Encyclopédie philosophique universelle I, L'Univers philosophique* (Paris, 1989), p. 1585.

An interesting recent work analysing the conditions under which Indian philosophy first attracted attention in Europe, but then came to be largely forgotten there, is also by a philosopher: R.-P. Droit, *L'oubli de l'Inde, Une amnésie philosophique* (Paris, 1989). Reference has already been made in note 3 above to the valuable studies by W. Halbfass. An older classic in this field of intellectual history is R. Schwab, *La renaissance orientale* (Paris, 1950), published (under the sign of Edward Said's problematic campaign on the theme of "Orientalism," concerning the relation of which to Buddhist studies see the present writer's remark in *JIABS* 15 [1992], 109) in English translation as *The Oriental Renaissance* (New York, 1984). Reference may be made further to G. Franci, ed., *Contributi alia storia dell'orientalismo* (Bologna, 1985). A. Tuck's *Comparative Philosophy and the Philosophy of Scholarship: On the Western Interpretation of Nāgārjuna* (New York, 1990)—notwithstanding several good observations on would-be objectivity vs. cultural relativism and on unconscious "isogesis" (defined as "a 'reading into' the text that often reveals as much about the interpreter as it does about the text being interpreted" [pp. 9–10], in contradistinction to exegesis as a conscious process)—seems to be attempting

We know of course that individual strands within Buddhist thought have been compared—if only more or less atomistically and episodically—with Socratic maieutics, Stoic and Epicurean apathia and ataraxia, or Pyrrhonic scepticism; with Berkeley's pluralistic idealism, Locke's empiricism, Hume's views on causality and psychology, or Kant's transcendentalist idealism and criticism; with Schopenhauer, Nietzsche, or Heidegger; with American transcendentalism or pragmatism; with Wittgenstein's linguistic analysis; with modern phenomenology and semiotics of various kinds; and, of course, with Derrida's deconstruction. However, although no doubt of use as intellectual exercises in a particular—and more or less limited—context, comparison of the type "Buddhism and X" or "Nāgārjuna and Y" can only take us just so far. More often than not, it has proved to be of rather restricted heuristic value, and methodologically it often turns out to be more problematic and constraining than illuminating. In the frame of synchronic description this kind of comparison tends to veil or obliterate important structures in thought, whilst from the viewpoint of historical diachrony it takes little account of genesis and context. For however much a philosophical insight or truth transcends, *in se*, any particular epoch or place, in its expression a philosophy is perforce conditioned historically and culturally.

But when saying that it is historically and culturally conditioned, I most certainly do not mean to relativize it or to espouse reductionism—quite the contrary in fact. The often facile opposition relativism vs. universalism has indeed all too often failed to take due account of the fact that what is relative in so far as it is conditioned in its linguistic or cultural expression may, nonetheless, in the final analysis have a very genuine claim to universality in terms of the human, and hence of the humanities. It seems that this holds true as much when we postulate some "Western" or "Eastern" philosophy of this or

---

to offer more than it can deliver, not least because it excludes from consideration some philosophically significant Western work on Nāgārjuna and the Madhyamaka published in this century: R. Grousset, S. Schayer, J. W. de Jong, and J. May (to mention only some) appear neither in the index nor in the bibliography even if several of them are mentioned, casually, in the text. Cf. also the review of Tuck's book by J. Bronkhorst, *Asiatische Studien* 47 (1993), 501ff.

For some observations on the relation—and the lack of it—between philosophical study on the one side and Buddhism on the other side, see also G. Chatalian, "Early Indian Buddhism and the Nature of Philosophy: A Philosophical Investigation," *JIP* 11 (1983), 167–222.

One of the most significant attempts in more recent decades to relate the study of "Early Buddhism" in the Pāli sources with philosophy was provided by K. N. Jayatilleke, *Early Buddhist Theory of Knowledge* (above, note 1). For a critique see Chatalian's article.

that period as when we consider what is now termed human rights, which by definition must transcend specific cultures in time and place.[16]

Now, it has to be recognized that our studies in Buddhist thought must indeed proceed on a comparative basis, that is, on a methodologically and phenomenologically well-founded comparativism which is, needless to say, a regular feature of scientific investigation. But a well-grounded philosophical comparison of this kind will differ very significantly from the one alluded to above by being structurally and systemically oriented, and at the same time sensitive to differences in historical genesis and context.

In the last analysis, of course, everything will depend on exactly how we actually engage in comparative philosophy. To pursue this point further would lead far afield, and I shall therefore not attempt to do so at this point.

IV

For the purposes of a philosophical study of Buddhism we are today in a probably more favourable position than formerly thanks to certain contemporary developments in the field of philosophy itself.

What is called the "linguistic turn" in philosophy and cultural studies has no doubt made investigators more aware of the complexity of linguistic issues, though one must beware of transforming this turn into a dogmatic strait-jacket or surrogate ready-made philosophy. The same applies to postmodernist relativism and to some current forms of deconstruction. At all events, Buddhist theories of interpretation and hermeneutics, and the associated problem of the canonical *vs.* the apocryphal, are in process of being addressed both more systematically and systemically, and doubtless more philosophically too. Such approaches will surely be fruitful provided they avoid the excesses of seeing so many things mainly as the expression of power relations between different trends in Buddhist thought and hermeneutics (in the wake of the "Hermeneutics and Politics" movement), or indeed between our academic disciplines. (Political forces may well have played a part in the history of Buddhist thought, but it will be a tricky task indeed to pinpoint these forces from the sūtra and śāstra sources as we now have them.)

In recent work in philosophy, some essays now collected together in the late Paul Grice's *Studies in the Way of Words* (1989) have no doubt contributed

16. Notwithstanding what some Pacific Rim politicians and entrepeneurs would have us believe about a so-called "Asian exception."

ideas and methods—not to speak of terms such as "implicature" (even if Grice's idea of the "conversational" in implicature would appear to have little relevance in Buddhist [and Indian] thought).[17]

It may also turn out that a recent book by another philosopher will not only help to make it philosophically respectable once more to address the question of the mind after the long reign of a certain Behaviorism and its reductionist cohorts, but also enable us to talk more clearly and meaningfully of consciousness and intentionality and of the mind/matter problem. I refer to *The Rediscovery of the Mind* (1992) by John Searle, who, while maintaining that the philosophy of language is in fact a branch of the philosophy of mind, has trenchantly elucidated issues in the mind/body problem while holding that monism and dualism are both false by arguing that the vocabularies and assumptions behind them are simply obsolete.

V

For my part, I am inclined to think that the approach to the understanding and analysis of our sources must initially be what has been termed "emic" rather than "etic."[18] That is, in the first instance, an effort has to be made, as far as is possible, to determine how the categories and terms of a culture relate to each other structurally and systemically, and so to place ourselves within the cultural contexts and intellectual horizons of the traditions we are studying, making use of their own intellectual and cultural categories and seeking as it were to "think along" with these traditions. This is much more than a matter of simply developing sympathy or empathy, for it is an intellectual, and scientific, undertaking. And very clearly it is not one of merely converting from one religion to another.[19] Nor is it a matter of any one-sided, or absolute,

17. Cf. D. Seyfort Ruegg "Purport, Implicature, and Presupposition: Sanskrit *abhiprāya* and Tibetan *dgoṅs pa / dgoṅs gži* as Hermeneutical Concepts," *JIP* 13 (1985), 309–25, reprinted in chapter 7 of the present volume. The concept of implicature has since been taken up by C. Oetke, "Pragmatic implicatures and text-interpretation," *StII* 16 (1992), 185–233. See also below, p. 230.

18. This terminology—inspired by the use in linguistics of terms ending in -etic as opposed to -emic—goes back to the "tagmemics" of K. L. Pike, *Language in Relation to a Unified Theory of the Structure of Human Behavior* (The Hague, 1954–60; 2nd ed., 1967).

19. This approach should therefore not become embroiled in the claim that a Buddhist is, as such, disqualified from lecturing on Buddhism in a university department of religion (where few seem, however, to be concerned about whether a Christian is disqualified from teaching courses on Christianity), nor need it enter into the opposite claim that

preference for structural and systemic—or "emic"—analysis over the generalizing and comparative—or "etic"—one which would totally reject the comparative method at every stage of work. Rather, it is one of learning how intelligently and effectively to work with, and within, a tradition of thinking by steeping oneself in it while rejecting the sterile "us" *vs.* "them" dichotomy.[20] Structural and systemic analysis is in a position to allow due weight to the historical as well as to the descriptive, that is, it may be diachronic as well as synchronic. Here the observation might be ventured that careful "emic" analysis can provide as good a foundation as any for generalizing and comparative study, one that will not superimpose from the outside extraneous modes of thinking and interpretative grids in a way that sometimes proves to be scarcely distinguishable from a more or less subtle form of neo-colonialism. It should go without saying that in proceeding along these channels it will always be necessary to steer clear of the Scylla of radical relativism—which would wish hermetically to enclose each culture in its own categories—as well as of the Charybdis of ethnocentrism, European or otherwise—which would study and judge all cultures by "our" standards—these twin extremes being travesties of the "emic" and "etic" methods respectively.

It should be emphasized again that to say this is not meant to exclude bringing together different "*épistémès*" for comparative and heuristic purposes. Quite the reverse in fact.[21]

As for the frequently made—and in some circles popular—distinction between (genuinely philosophical) evaluative study and historical (and philological) study of a philosophy or philosopher, it is evident that the first rests

---

only a Buddhist can be so qualified. These two positions are egregious examples of intellectually sterile arguments carried on with scant regard to the scientific (not to mention spiritual) issues involved.

20. The procedure may be compared with *epoché* or bracketing (*Einklammerung,* in relation to *Einschaltung*) in phenomenological method, which has occupied a prominent place in the study of religion at least since the time of G. van der Leeuw's *Einführung in die Phänomenologie der Religion* (1925) and *Phänomenologie der Religion* (1933).

21. Surprisingly, however, the (of course quite legitimate) procedures seeking to analyse and understand traditional materials with the help of contemporary theoretical and methodological concepts in anthropological, cultural, historical, literary, philosophical, and religious studies—e.g., to understand the śāstra traditions of the Indian paṇḍits through certain modern "epistemes"—is nowadays being referred to as contextualization by some Indologists. But since these procedures are by nature "etic" and comparative, it would seem that contextualization is exactly what they are not, and cannot be. For, surely, to contextualize something is to study it in its own cultural, systemic, and "emic" terms and context.

and depends on a successful pursuit of the second kind of study. The two may be theoretically distinguishable and belong to separable phases and modes of investigation, but they cannot be totally decoupled.[22]

The distinction between the "emic" and the "etic" approaches—which have to do with our modes of analysis and understanding—is no doubt parallel to the distinction drawn between the use of author-familiar as opposed to author-alien terminologies for the purposes of comparison and exposition. But these two sets of concepts do not appear to be identical because, for the expository and comparative purposes just mentioned, it may still be possible to employ author-alien terminologies even within an approach that is committed to "emic" analysis and understanding. For example, in explaining the Buddhist theory of spiritual classes or "lineages" *(gotra)* to the extent that it is based on a biological metaphor, one might evoke the idea of a (spiritual) "gene";[23] and in analysing the exegetical principle of an intended ground *(dgongs gzhi)* to which an intentional *(neyārtha)* utterance ultimately, but allusively, refers without explicitly expressing it, one might speak of a (hermeneutical) "implicature."[24] Of course, both the modern biological term "gene" and the still more recent coinage "implicature" are alien to our Indian and Tibetan sources, in which no lexeme is to be found with precisely the meaning of either of these two modern words. Yet it seems possible to evoke, *mutatis mutandis,* the ideas expressed by these new terms when seeking to explicate the theories in question. In other words, author-alien (or source-alien) terminology could very well be compatible with an "emic" approach to understanding, and it does not necessarily bring with it an exclusive commitment to the "etic" approach. (Conversely, it would in principle be possible to employ source-familiar terminology and still misconstrue and misrepresent a doctrine, thus infringing the requirement of an "emic" approach.) Furthermore, as already indicated, the use of a source-familiar terminology need not stand in the way of proceeding from "emic" to "etic" analysis.

22. For a recent investigation, from a somewhat different point of view, of the relation between philological and philosophical study, see C. Oetke, "Controverting the *ātman*-Controversy and the Query of Segregating Philological and Non-philological Issues in Studies on Eastern Philosophies and Religions," *Studien zur Indologie und Iranistik* 18 (1993), 191–212 (a reply to observations made by J. Bronkhorst in *WZKS* 32 [1989], 223–25). This article came to my attention too late to be taken into account in the present discussion.

23. Cf. D. Seyfort Ruegg, "The Meaning of the Term *gotra* and the Textual History of the *Ratnagotravibhāga*," *BSOAS* 39 (1976), 341–63.

24. Cf. D. Seyfort Ruegg, "Purport, Implicature and Presupposition," cited in n. 17 above.

In this connection, a parallel might perhaps be drawn with the questions, both musicological and musical, that today arise in recovering and performing (so-called) "early music" (mediaeval, Renaissance, and Baroque), a field in which there is also much discussion of problems of retrieval and rendition, i.e., interpretation.[25] Thus, a piece of music may have to be retrieved or reconstructed from ambiguous documents in a way satisfactory to performer and musicologist (who may or may not be the same person), and it has then to be performed in a manner pleasing to performer and listener. In the case of instrumental music, this can involve using either original instruments contemporary with the music and of the same provenance, modern copies of such instruments, or modern instruments (for instance the piano for Bach). Any of these three methods may produce results that satisfy performer and listener, though the musicologist and the "purist" performer and listener would generally prefer to use original instruments (if necessary rebuilt or reconstructed) or, if such are unavailable, modern reproductions (which may sometimes be unavoidably hypothetical).

Interpreters of classical Buddhist writings using the "emic" approach and source-familiar terminologies find themselves in a situation somewhat analogous to that of the performer of "early music" on contemporary instruments, or perhaps more accurately (because of the problems outlined above) in a position comparable with that of an instrumentalist using largely rebuilt instruments or copies. And interpreters using principally or exclusively the "etic" method and source-alien terminologies may well resemble the performer using modern instruments, and perhaps even a modern style of performance. As for the interpreter using the "emic" approach, yet perhaps having occasional recourse to source-alien terminology, he might be compared more with a musician using the first or, above all, the second kind of instrument, rather than to one playing modern instruments in modern style. (To what extent it may be possible to compare the interpreter of ancient Buddhist writings with a modern vocalist performing "early music," where the question of old and modern instruments plays no part, is another matter. Just as it would no doubt be difficult for the modern vocalist totally to remove from his mind and technique all developments in singing in the time intervening since the production of the piece he is performing, so the modern interpreter of a Buddhist text may well experience difficulty in entirely eschewing all more modern forms of thinking and all more modern problematics. In both cases, the audiences might not desire such an exercise even if it

25. The question of authenticity will be left out of consideration here because of the possible ambiguity of this concept and of the misunderstandings to which it can give rise.

were possible.) Like so many comparisons, the one offered here is of course not entirely on all fours with what is being compared, but it may at least help to illustrate the issues.

In any event, in its crudest inhibiting form as something in which the interpreter and scholar is, so to speak, imprisoned in his pre-understanding and in the limitations of his pre-judgments, the "hermeneutic circle" can, I think, be got out of if a real effort is made. And an analysis and critique in "etic" terms of philosophical thought will only become genuinely meaningful and useful once one has understood, as it were "emically," the concerns, pre-suppositions, and intentions—i.e., the problematics—of texts and their philosopher-authors, in other words the horizons and issues that have been theirs.[26] No valid principle of scientific objectivity is being thereby abandoned. And to raise this objection against "emic" methodology would be to demonstrate a rather simplistic and indeed naïve understanding of scholarly distance and objectivity—which is, as is well known, a not unproblematic thing even in the natural sciences—and a lack of awareness of certain implications of the theory of understanding in the humanities and of hermeneutics. The objection just mentioned would, then, be scientistic rather than truly scientific.

A more weighty objection against this approach is based on the hermeneutic principle that it is simply impossible for us today to project ourselves back into an age long past, that we cannot put ourselves in the skin, or in the mind, of a long-dead thinker in order to determine authorial intention—the *mens auctoris*—and that our understanding is determined by its historicality. This view has been powerfully argued by several modern writers on hermeneutics.[27] An "archaeology of the mind" is a highly challenging project indeed. But while fully acknowledging the formidable difficulties involved in any search for understanding, and while recognizing the weight of certain

26. By speaking of a crude and inhibiting form of the hermeneutic circle, reference is being made here to the negative, imprisoning effect of the circle, not to the positive nature of the hermeneutic circle as understanding in contextuality and historicality.

27. On the circle in philosophical hermeneutics, see, e.g., H.-G. Gadamer, *Wahrheit und Methode*[3] (Tübingen, 1960) and the works of Paul Ricoeur. The concept of the hermeneutic circle—found earlier with Friedrich Ast, Schleiermacher, and Dilthey—is current also in theology (Bultmann) as well as in philosophy (Heidegger). Cf. R. Palmer, *Hermeneutics* (Evanston, 1969), and J. Bleicher, *Contemporary Hermeneutics* (London, 1980). Some aspects of contemporary trends in hermeneutics have been usefully criticized by E. Betti, *Die Hermeneutik als allgemeine Methodik der Geisteswissenschaften* (Tübingen, 1962), and by E. D. Hirsch, *Validity in Interpretation* (New Haven, 1967) and *The Aims of Interpretation* (Chicago, 1976).

theoretical problems involved, I think that considerable progress can still be made in genuinely penetrating what the Buddhist tradition calls the *intention* (Sanskrit *abhiprāya,* Tibetan *dgongs pa*) of ancient authors and texts, and in understanding historically and contextually the evidence which we consider as historians of religion and philosophy. Thought forms, presuppositions, and pre-judgements as well as language may be prison-houses of sorts. But it is possible to make progress in freeing ourselves from the shackles of our mindsets, and to a significant degree also of our historically and culturally conditioned limiting horizons, if only we will—and provided, of course, we refrain from imposing currently fashionable ideas on what we are studying (a process that can on occasion come very close to neo-colonialism, as mentioned above). Surely the "us" and "them" dichotomy has been somewhat overworked in the theory of understanding.

VI

Continuities, structured patterns, and non-essentialist and lattice-like polythetic "family resemblances"—however underlying they may be—are no less interesting than discontinuities and disagreements in studying the history of thought.[28] We are, after all, trying to understand what a tradition has meant to its representatives, even in the face of synchronic intellectual and spiritual tensions and of diachronic heterogeneity present within it.

One may focus on tracing such patterns and continuities, first, within Buddhist thought and, next, between it and its Indian (Brāhmaṇical and Jain) context and, then, between this Indo-Buddhist culture and its prolongation in the "Greater India"—l'Inde extérieure—of the Himalayan area, Inner Asia, and East Asia. This kind of study has led me to think that a very large sector of Tibetan civilization, although not simply reducible to the Indian, is *typologically* (and *structurally*) *Indic* in a number of highly interesting respects, even though it has of course developed its own specific and very characteristic features and contains much that is not historically attested in India.[29]

28. See D. Seyfort Ruegg, foreword, *Buddha-nature, Mind and the Problem of Gradualism in a Comparative Perspective* (London, 1989). It is on this ground also that one can still continue to speak not of "Buddhisms" but of Buddhism. Compare below, section X.

29. The term "Indic" is used here not as an equivalent of "Indian" (as distinct from Amerindian, American Indian, "native American"), or of "Indo-Aryan," but rather to denote what is typologically and structurally Indian, without being attested (to the best of our knowledge) in our sources as having actually existed in India.

Intercultural studies of course necessarily involve the careful clarification of the modalities of relations between two worlds of thought, between peoples whose civilizations are in contact. Thus it addresses the question of how one people (the Tibetans for instance) could adopt from its southerly neighbour, and then thoroughly absorb and integrate, a religio-philosophical system like Buddhism accompanied by the not specifically religious sciences—the *vidyāsthānas* or *rig gnas*—with which this culture was closely associated in India, and with which it has continued to be linked in the Himalayan area and Inner Asia. This process of intercultural borrowing and integration raises the fascinating question not only of linguistic areas—the *Sprachbund* theory of areal in contrast to genetic relationship between languages—but also of cultural areas.[30]

VII

Let me now illustrate some of the above generalizations by a few examples relating to the philological and historical study of philosophical texts and to the philosophical and hermeneutical analysis of these texts.

Critical editions of philosophical texts

Following the publication in 1950 of the Sanskrit original of the *Ratnagotravibhāga*[31]—an important early Mahāyāna treatise counted as one of the Dharmas of Maitreya that had hitherto been known in the West mainly through E. Obermiller's work on the Tibetan sources relating to it[32]—it became apparent that this text, together with the theories of the *buddha*-nature *(tathāgatagarbha)* and of spiritual types or "genes" *(gotra)* expounded in it, could provide a valuable starting point for research which should prove to be of interest for Buddhist studies under the aspects of both philosophy and religion and historical-philological method.

Philologically speaking, the *Ratnagotravibhāga (RGV)* is of interest because the study of this work together with its extensive commentarial literature has urgently raised the question of how best to handle an old text

30. Cf. D. Seyfort Ruegg, *Ordre spirituel et ordre temporel dans la pensée bouddhique de l'Inde et du Tibet* (Paris, 1995), Part II.

31. *Ratnagotravibhāga Mahāyānottaratantraśāstra,* ed. E. H. Johnston and T. Chowdhury (Patna, 1950).

32. E. Obermiller, "The Sublime Science of the Great Vehicle to Salvation," *Acta Orientalia* 9 (1931), 82–306.

which is available in both its original Sanskrit and in (Chinese and Tibetan) translations, and which, within the Tibetan tradition, has been the subject of a vast body of exegesis from the eleventh century to modern times. That is, this text is both a literary and historical record which is some 1,500 years old and part of a living tradition. Work on it engages the question of the very nature of Indo-Tibetan (and Indo-Sinitic) philology and, more generally, what the scope and tasks of Indo-Tibetan studies are. A few decades ago these were questions that had by no means been adequately clarified, and even today uncertainty seems still to be rife concerning what Indo-Tibetan studies are about.

In Buddhist studies, critical philologically based editions are of course required of any Indian materials that may still be extant as well as of the relevant translated texts in the Chinese and Tibetan canonical collections containing sūtra and śāstra sources. In the course of this work it is necessary, *inter alia,* to draw on any proto-canonical, paracanonical, and commentarial traditions having preserved textual variants that have to be taken into account for a genuinely critical edition. By *commentarial traditions* I mean both Indian commentaries—either in their original language or as now available to us only in translation—and commentaries composed by non-Indian authors. By *proto-canonical* traditions I refer, in the frame of Indo-Tibetan studies, to textual material belonging to the time antedating the constitution of the known Bka' 'gyurs and Bstan 'gyurs, such as that found in the Tibetan Dunhuang manuscripts (going back to the ninth century) and in inscriptions and manuscripts from Ta pho (going back to ca. 1000).[33] And by *paracanonical traditions* I refer, in the same frame, to versions of a sūtra or śāstra text in editions postdating the constitution of these Bka' 'gyurs or Bstan 'gyurs, which may differ more or

33. In Dunhuang Tibetan rule lasted until 848. Aurel Stein dated the sealing of the caves to 1035. A. Fujieda, "The Tunhuang Manuscripts," *Zinbun: Memoirs of the Research Institute for Humanistic Studies* 10 (Kyōto: Zinbun Kagaku Kenkyūsho, 1969), pp. 17ff., dated (p. 22) the Tibetan materials to 782–848 (cf. *JA* 1981, pp. 65–68, where Fujieda dated the closure of the caves to shortly after 1002). But see A. Róna-Tas, "A Brief Note on the Chronology of the Tun-huang Collections," *AOH* 221 (1968), 313–16. See in general, L. I. Čuguevskii, "Touen-houang du VIIIe au Xe siècle," *Nouvelles contributions aux études de Touen-houang,* ed. M. Soymié (Geneva, 1981) 1–56; and for a recent very brief survey, see L. Petech, "The Silk Road, Turfan and Tunhuang in the First Millennium A.D.," *Turfan and Tunhuang, The Texts,* ed. A. Cadonna (Florence: Orientalia Venetiana IV, 1992), 1–13.

On the Ta pho / Tabo inscriptions and manuscripts, see E. Steinkellner, "A Report on the 'Kanjur' of Ta pho," *East and West* 44 (1994), 115–36, as well as the articles by E. De Rossi Filibek, J. L. Panglung, and H. Tauscher in the same volume.

less from the readings found in the "standard versions"—printed or manuscript—of these two canonical collections.[34] Even when already accessible, these are materials that have often been neglected when preparing editions of texts, something that is of course understandable in view of their very great abundance.

In sum, the textual transmission of fundamental works such as the *Ratnagotravibhāga* and Candrakīrti's *Madhyamakāvatāra(bhāṣya)* proves to be appreciably more complex than had been foreseen by their first editors

34. For information on the Bka' 'gyur manuscripts and printed editions, see in particular the recent work of H. Eimer, P. Harrison, P. Skilling, and J. Silk. The standard (printed) editions of the Bstan 'gyurs are those of Beijing, Snar thang, Sde dge, and Co ne, to which must now be added the so-called "Golden Tanjur" commissioned by the *mi dbang* Pho lha nas Bsod nams stobs rgyas and recently published in facsimile in China (see P. Skilling, "A Brief Guide to the Golden Tanjur," *Journal of the Siam Society* 79 [1991], 138–46).

In the case of the *Ratnagotravibhāga,* its translation in the Chinese canon (available also in the edition by Zuiryu Nakamura published in Tokyo in 1961) has been treated by J. Takasaki, *A Study on the Ratnagotravibhāga (Uttaratantra)* (Rome, 1966); some of his text-critical conclusions concerning its Indian Ur-text have however had to be reconsidered (cf. D. Seyfort Ruegg, "The Meanings of the Term *gotra* and the Textual History of the *Ratnagotravibhāga,*" *BSOAS* 39 [1976], 341–63). Even though the very useful edition of the Tibetan text with trilingual indexes published in Japan in 1967 by the Suzuki Institute was not a fully critical edition based on all existing textual materials, it had the merit of making use of the Beijing, Snar thang, and Sde dge editions of the Bstan 'gyur and referring in addition to the commentaries by Rgyal tshab Dar ma rin chen and Kong sprul Blo gros mtha' yas.

As an example of the evidence for variant readings to be extracted from Tibetan commentaries, reference may be made to the comment on the *RGV(V)* by Rgyal tshab Dar ma rin chen (1364–1432). There (fol. 42a) we find a very significant variant reading not attested in the Beijing and Snar thang Bstan 'gyur editions of this text translated by Rngog Blo ldan shes rab (1059–1109), but which is not only suggested by the sense but is actually confirmed by both Johnston's Sanskrit text of the *RGVV* (i.12, p. 12.14) and by another Bstan 'gyur edition (Sde dge). This variant is *nyon mongs pa'i sbubs las ma grol ba = avinirmuktakleśakośa* instead of *nyon mongs pa'i sbubs las grol ba = vinirmuktakleśakośa* in a sūtra passage defining the relation between the *tathāgatagarbha* and the *dharmakāya: ayam eva ca bhagavaṃs tathāgatadharmakāyo 'vinirmuktakleśakośas tathāgatagarbha ity ucyate.* Because it concerns the crucial matter of this relation, and since traces of both doctrinal views can be found in the Chinese tradition, the variant appears to be a doctrinally significant one and not to be explicable solely in terms of the textual transmission of the Tibetan Bstan 'gyur. See D. Seyfort Ruegg, introduction, *Le traité du tathāgatagarbha de Bu ston Rin chen grub,* pp. 37–45.

As for the precise contents of the concepts of the proto-canonical and paracanonical, they will be further clarified by continuing research in respect to the history of the Bka' 'gyur and Bstan 'gyur.

earlier in this century.[35] And for any truly critical edition of a sūtra or śāstra text in the Indo-Tibetan tradition, alongside the printed and manuscript Bka' 'gyur and Bstan 'gyur editions, the commentarial traditions, and any paracanonical traditions available, have to be taken into account as important *testimonia.*

The need in philosophical study for such critically constituted texts of course requires no demonstration.

Historical study of doctrinal content

With respect to the contents of the *Ratnagotravibhāga,* the historical-philological problems revealed by the examination of the *tathāgatagarbha* and related concepts have turned out to be no less challenging and interesting. These are some of them:

1. It has been necessary to trace the sources of the relevant Mahāyāna concepts in many branches of literature, Buddhist and non-Buddhist,

35. The Tibetan translation of the *Madhyamakāvatārakārikā*s and *Bhāṣya*—the only full version of these texts now accessible—was published by L. de La Vallée Poussin, *Madhyamakāvatāra* (St. Petersburg: Bibliotheca Buddhica IX, 1907–12) (evidently on the basis of the Beijing and Snar thang Bstan 'gyurs). La Vallée Poussin referred also to the translation of the *Kārikā*s alone by Nag tsho in the Bstan 'gyur and to a "paracanonical" edition which he described (p. ii) as "beaucoup plus correcte que celle du Tandjour"; but since he included no critical apparatus in his edition, it is difficult to make out what use he made of this additional material known to him. In the Beijing edition of the Bstan 'gyur are found both a translation of the *Madhyamakāvatārakārikā*s ascribed to Kr̥ṣṇapaṇḍita and Nag tsho Tshul khrims rgyal ba (b. 1011) as revised by Tilakakalaśa and Pa tshab Nyi ma grags (b. 1055) (no. 5261) and one ascribed to Tilaka and Pa tshab (no. 5262, executed in Kaśmīr), as well as a translation of the same text together with Candrakīrti's autocommentary ascribed to Tilaka and Nyi ma grags as revised by Kanakavarman and Nyi ma grags (no. 5263, also executed in Kaśmīr). And in the Sde dge edition there are found a translation of the *Kārikā*s ascribed to Tilaka and Pa tshab (rather than Nag tsho) as revised by Kanakavarman and Pa tshab (no. 3861) and a translation of the *Kārikā*s together with the autocommentary ascribed to Tilakakalaśa and Pa tshab as revised by Kanakavarman and Pa tshab (no. 3862). In Zhu chen Tshul khrims rin chen's *dkar chag* to the Sde dge Bstan 'gyur (p. 785 of the Lhasa reprint of 1985), the information on no. 3861 very strangely conflates the names of Kr̥ṣṇa and Tilaka and the names of Pa tshab and Nag tsho, as if reflecting a problem which is, however, not resolved. There exists in addition a paracanonical edition from the Lhasa Zhol par khang of Pa tshab's translation of the *Kārikā*s of the *MA.* In his comment on the *MA(Bh),* the *Dgongs pa rab gsal,* Tsong kha pa has on several occasions preferred readings from Nag tsho's translation (prose as well as verse) over the "standard" translation by Pa tshab.

including in particular any possible anticipations in the earlier scriptural sources of the Śrāvakayāna.[36] This search in turn raises the problem of continuities and discontinuities between the Mahāyāna and the Śrāvakayāna.

2. It has been necessary to trace the interrelations between the forms of these concepts found in the *Ratnagotravibhāga* together with its direct sūtra sources and those found in other Mahāyāna sūtras, in particular the Prajñāpāramitā sūtras, and in the *Abhisamayālaṃkāra*—another treatise traditionally regarded in Tibet as a Dharma of Maitreya. This in turn raises the question of a "Maitreya tradition" in early Mahāyānist thought.
3. In connection with the concept of the *tathāgatagarbha*—or the *buddha*-Element *(tathāgatadhātu)*—as empty *(śūnya)* of all heterogeneous, extrinsic, and relative factors, but as not empty *(aśūnya)* of its intrinsic, constitutive, and informing *(buddha-)dharma*s, there arises the crucial and vexed question of the historical relationship between the principle of Emptiness of self-nature *(rang stong, svabhāvaśūnyatā)* in the Madhyamaka and its sūtra sources such as the Prajñāpāramitā and the Ratnakūṭa, and the idea of Emptiness of the other *(gzhan stong: *para[bhāva]-śūnya)* in some of the *tathāgatagarbha* literature.
4. In connection with the concept of *buddha*-nature, there arises the complex question of the historical relation between the traditions of Buddhism in India and Tibet and those of East Asia. According to the former, only sentient beings *(sattva = sems can)*—the *sattvaloka*—have the capacity of becoming buddhas, whereas East Asian traditions have attributed the capacity for buddhahood also to the grasses, trees, mountains, and rivers—i.e., to the so-called *bhājanaloka.*
5. In the Sanskrit expression *tathāgatagarbha,* its Tibetan equivalent *de bzhin gshegs pa'i snying po,* and the Chinese term *ju-lai-tsang,* even the terms *garbha / snying po / tsang* have been understood somewhat differently, *garbha* being usually interpretable in the Indian and Tibetan

36. As suggested by the present writer in *JIABS* 15 (1992), 110–13, the term Hīnayāna had best be reserved as a technical one applying to cases where the *arhat* concept and the corresponding Path of the doctrinal schools *(nikāya)* is being distinguished from, and opposed to, the Path of the bodhisattva and the buddha ideal of the Mahāyāna/Bodhisattvayāna. When this is not the case, and in particular when it is the teachings of so-called Early Buddhism that are being referred to, the (non-pejorative) term Śrāvakayāna is usually a more suitable term than the potentially pejorative Hīnayāna. Needless to say, Śrāvakayāna is not coextensive with the narrower term "Sthāvira-vāda" and the even more narrow term Theravāda.

traditions as "Embryo" or "Seed," or as "Essence" *(snying po),* whereas in the Sino-Japanese tradition the value of "Womb" *(tsang)* has become established. This is not to say that the Sino-Japanese tradition's use of the word *tsang* to render *garbha* was wrong. But it has to be recognized that it has introduced a metaphor which is largely absent in the Indian and Tibetan sources, and that it is therefore quite inappropriate to import this new metaphor into the original Indian sources as is sometimes being done nowadays. This is, then, a difference that has often been overlooked in modern discussions of the doctrine of *buddha*-nature.

Philosophical And Hermeneutical Study

On the level of philosophical interpretation and hermeneutics, the *tathāgatagarbha* theory and the related problem of Emptiness of the other *(gzhan stong: *para[bhāva]-śūnya)* in relation to Emptiness of self-nature *(rang stong: svabhāvaśūnya[tā])* has given rise over recent years to a number of discussions among writers on the subject.

Thus, the doctrines of *rang stong* and *gzhan stong* have tended to be represented simply as opposed theories located on the same level of discourse,[37] but with no investigation being made of the religio-philosophical question as to the extent to which they might be complementary (as part of the Tibetan tradition has indeed thought), or whether they might perhaps be considered as what is today termed incommensurable (that is, located on different levels, or within distinct universes, of religious and philosophical discourse). What is needed in Buddhist studies is not enlistment in campaigns and polemics with schools of Buddhist thought, but careful descriptions and analyses of the various traditions establishing their sources and religio-philosophical problematics and identifying how each dealt with the philosophical and hermeneutical questions that arose in their respective schools.

In Tibet from the thirteenth century at the latest, the *rang stong* theory has been associated with dominant "majority" schools such as the "mainstream" Sa skya pas and Dga' ldan pas / Dge lugs pas, whilst the *gzhan stong* theory has been adopted by "minority" schools such as the Jo nang pas and some currents within the Rnying ma pa and Bka' brgyud pa schools.[38] Then,

37. See for example S. Hookham, *The Buddha Within* (Albany, 1991), who regards the advocates of the *rang stong* as having denigrated and distorted the *gzhan stong,* which she then sets out to defend.

38. The words "majority," "mainstream," and "minority" have been put between inverted commas because they tend to be subjective descriptions with little scientific content or

in the seventeenth century during the reign of the Fifth Dalai Lama, the Jo nang pa school in Central Tibet was suppressed and its books sealed at the time of a conflict between, on the one side, the central authorities of the Dga' ldan pho brang, who were inseparably linked with the Dge lugs pas, and, on the other side, the king of Gtsang, who was associated with the Zhwa dmar Karma pa hierarchs of the Bka' brgyud pa school. Here we have a case where considerations of state do appear to impinge on philosophical and religious ideas; and the question arises whether the Jo nang pas—whose centre was in Gtsang province and who were protected by the king of Gtsang—were in fact suppressed for political or for ideological reasons. Perhaps, however, it would be an error to opt exclusively for either of these explanations. Reasons of state may have predominated; but it is not impossible that the ideological and the political in fact reinforced each other. In any case, in a land such as Tibet, where "church" and "state" were so closely interlinked, the modern dichotomy religious *vs.* political—or sacred *vs.* profane—loses much of its relevance. And an explanation that completely subordinates one of these concepts to the other might well be too culture-bound and reductionist, and thus a travesty of the "etic" approach. The task of the historian will surely be to take account of both factors in an "emic" understanding of Tibetan Buddhist civilization—something that is admittedly not always an easy undertaking.

"Inherent Enlightenment" vs. "Critical Buddhism" as a philological, historical, and hermeneutical undertaking

In recent years it is in Japan that the most striking controversy revolving round the *tathāgatagarbha* and *buddha*-nature theory has come to the fore in discussions on "Critical Buddhism." There two respected scholars in Tokyo—Professors Hakamaya Noriaki and Matsumoto Shiro—have characterized the buddha-nature doctrine as in some way non-Buddhist.[39] According to them it represents what they have labelled by the newly coined Sanskrit term "dhātu-vāda," i.e., the *hongaku [shisō] (pen-chiao [hsing])* the-

value—the more so when proper statistics are hard to come by—and cannot in any case constitute the decisive criterion for understanding and evaluating religious, philosophical, and hermeneutical ideas.

39. See recently N. Hakamaya, *Hongaku shisō hihan* [Critique of the thought of inherent enlightenment] (Tokyo, 1989), and *Hihan bukkyō* [Critical Buddhism] (Tokyo, 1990); and S. Matsumoto, *Engi to kū: nyōraizō shisō hihan* [Causality and emptiness: A critique of *tathāgatagarbha* thought] (Tōkyō, 1989; 3rd ed., 1993), and "The Mādhyamika philosophy of Tsong-kha-pa," *Memoirs of the Research Department of the Toyo Bunko* 48 (1990) (English reworking of an article published in the *Tōyō Gakuhō* 62 [1981]).

ory of "original/inherent" enlightenment in Chinese and Japanese Buddhism. And this doctrine they hold to be incompatible with the principle of *pratītyasamutpāda* "origination in dependence." Now, origination in dependence is indeed a fundamental concept in Buddhist thought. And in their critique of the *buddha*-nature doctrine these two scholars may well be justified in reacting against a superficial or simplistic version of it current in Japan or elsewhere. But in totally rejecting this doctrine as non-Buddhist, they seem to have overshot the mark by giving scant attention to the explications of the *tathāgatagarbha* theory by Buddhist thinkers who, outside Japan, have at the same time accepted *pratītyasamutpāda* as basic.[40]

In Western reports on this recent Japanese debate, moreover, we find the Sanskrit term *tathāgatagarbha* being translated as "womb of the buddha"—a meaning which (as mentioned above) this expression simply does not have in the relevant Sanskrit texts, any more than does its Tibetan equivalent *de bzhin gshegs pa'i snying po.* And we find repeated the assertion that the Japanese technical term *hongaku* (Chinese *pen-chiao*) "original, inherent" has no Sanskrit correspondence.[41] But in point of fact, in the Sanskrit and Tibetan terms *prakṛtiviśuddhi/pariśuddhi = rang bzhin gyis rnam par dag pa / yongs su dag pa* that are well attested in the *Ratnagotravibhāga* Commentary and the related literature as expressions referring to the natural purity of ordinary beings on the level of the Ground *(gzhi)*—as opposed to the purity that is actualized on the resultant level of buddhahood or the Fruit *('bras bu) (vaimalyaviśuddhi/pariśuddhi = dri ma med pa'i rnam par dag pa / yongs su dag pa)*—the word *prakṛti* (= *rang bzhin*) is very near indeed to the Sino-Japanese term *pen-chiao/hongaku* "original, inherent."[42]

In sum, while acknowledging the contribution this debate has made to cultural and social criticism in Buddhism, it surely behoves students of Buddhist thought to refrain from carrying on a discussion of such significance for Buddhist studies as a whole on an overly narrow basis, and without paying due attention to what major Buddhist thinkers elsewhere have had to say on the philosophical and hermeneutical issues involved in the theory of the *tathāgatagarbha* and *buddha*-nature. The whole topic of the significance of the *buddha*-nature theory cannot be investigated in a vacuum, as

40. See below on the exegesis by Gung thang Dkon mchog bstan pa'i sgron me.

41. Cf. P. L. Swanson, "'Zen is not Buddhism': Recent Japanese Critiques of 'Buddha-Nature,'" *Numen* 40 (1993), 115–49.

42. See D. Seyfort Ruegg, *La théorie du tathāgatagarbha et du gotra: Études sur la sotériologie et la gnoséologie du bouddhisme* (Paris, 1969).

if it concerned only Japanese Buddhism or, at the most, the Sino-Japanese traditions of Buddhism.

In this regard, reference may be made to the thought-provoking systemic (rather than historical) exegesis of the philosophical and hermeneutical problem of the *tathāgatagarbha* in relation to *śūnyatā* offered for example by Gung thang Dkon mchog bstan pa'i sgron me (1762–1823), an outstanding Tibetan scholar who built on earlier interpretations of it current in the Indo-Tibetan tradition, and who at the same time accepted the doctrine of *pratītyasamutpāda* (on which he also wrote) without considering that it annuls the *tathāgatagarbha* theory.[43]

It does not seem, then, that the *tathāgatagarbha* doctrine can be represented as blurred and undifferentiated mysticism issuing in uncritical syncretism or in indifferentism, much less in naturalism. And it is imperative carefully to distinguish superficial syncretism of incompatible positions—not to speak of coercive inclusivism of totally disparate ideas—from the philosopher's treatment of intellectual and spiritual tensions existing

43. See D. Seyfort Ruegg, *Théorie,* 393ff. Gung thang indeed composed a treatise on *pratītyasamutpāda* (included in vol. ga of his Gsung 'bum).

On the *tathāgatagarbha* and *buddha*-nature in the Chinese Madhyamaka thought of Chi-tsang, see M.-W. Liu, *Madhyamaka Thought in China* (Leiden, 1994) 86, 160ff., 171ff.

In his interesting article entitled "What is Buddhist Logic?" in S. Goodman and R. Davidson, eds., *Tibetan Buddhism: Reason and Revelation* (Albany, 1992), 25–44, K. Lipman has rightly pointed to the historical-philological fallacy that is incurred in rejecting a given hermeneutical interpretation both because it is held to be "later" rather than "original" and because it is assumed to "favor" one Buddhist "harmonizing" exegetical tradition (objections expressed by L. Schmithausen in his critique of the present writer's *Théorie* in *WZKS* 17 [1973], 136–37). But concerning my observations of 1969 in *Théorie,* Dr. Lipman criticizes my having (supposedly) sought "the solution" where he apparently assumed I did, writing "I do not believe that the dGe-lugs-pa interpretation is the 'solution' Ruegg was seeking, and perhaps through the study of rNying-ma, Sa-skya, and bKa'-brgyud materials of the period, the dGe-lugs-pa approach will be seen in a less adequate light" (p. 25). In fact, however, the point in my book was not that, e.g., the Dge lugs pas Rgyal tshab Dar ma rin chen and Gung thang had found *the* "solution" (and *a fortiori* the last word) to any contradiction there may be between the *tathāgatagarbha* and *śūnyatā* theories—indeed I am not certain that there exists any one single "solution" to this tension which is both synchronic-systemic and diachronic—but that they had something significant to say about it in terms of philosophical hermeneutics and *Wirkungsgeschichte.* This philosophically crucial point appears to have been overlooked.

It should go without saying that, in philosophy and hermeneutics, the interest and value of what an author has to say are not simply a function of whether the author is or is not a member of a certain school (e.g., the Dge lugs pa). It is most regrettable that this basic principle is becoming overshadowed by sectarian likes and dislikes of investigators.

since early times between various strands of Buddhist thought and from his hermeneutical awareness of their possible complementarity (or, eventually, of their incommensurability). By fragmenting Buddhist studies—and in this case treating (Sino-)Japanese interpretations of buddha-nature in isolation from the history of the *tathāgatagarbha* theory as a whole—we render ourselves no longer able clearly to discern the significance in the history of Buddhist thought of an overarching set of fundamental religious-philosophical issues.

VIII

The question of the relation between the traditions of Buddhism in South, Central, and East Asia has also brought into the limelight the issue of the transcendence *vs.* the immanence of *buddha*-nature and buddhahood *(buddhatā).* In this context, it has been supposed that East Asian tradition has generally opted for immanence, with buddhahood being thought of as inborn, whereas more westerly traditions of Buddhism tended on the contrary to emphasize transcendence, with buddhahood to be reached only through a progressive and protracted spiritual and mental training. This difference has furthermore been linked with the distinction between intellectual analysis and meditative non-conceptualization, and between Gradualism—a tendency also supposed to characterize most of Indian and a large part of Tibetan Buddhism—and Simultaneism (or Subitism)—which has, by contrast, frequently been deemed a specific feature of East Asian Buddhism and of certain Tibetan traditions influenced by the latter.

Now, whether we look at these sets of contrasts only from the viewpoint of the *tathāgatagarbha* theory, or whether we additionally bring in the theme of the Great Debate of Bsam yas in late eighth-century Tibet together with the subsequent Tibetan discussions of the issues involved, the theoretical problems have turned out to be highly complex and nuanced, perhaps even somewhat intractable. At all events, it is no longer possible in this connection simply to speak of some Sino-Indian cultural frontier, and of the Great Debate of Bsam yas as a Sino-Indian controversy, as Paul Demiéville once did in his great pioneering work on the subject.[44] This is so because the traditions of Buddhism in South, Central, and East Asia are anything but monolithic, and each of them often embraces the ancient philosophical and religious polarities and tensions alluded to above.

44. See P. Demiéville, *Le concile de Lhasa* (Paris, 1952).

The Buddhist traditions themselves have of course been very alive to the philosophical and religious issues involved even if, naturally enough, they have not used our categories and vocabularies.

One old attempt at clarification was by way of developing a taxonomy of the scriptural teachings attributed to the Buddha which is based on distinguishing "Wheels" *(chos kyi 'khor lo = *dharma-cakra),* i.e., phases, of the doctrine together with a system of textual exegesis and systemic scriptural hermeneutics founded on differentiating a definitive, deep-level meaning (the *nītārtha = nges don*) from a provisional, surface-level one that requires to be further interpreted in a sense different from the *prima facie* one (the *neyārtha = drang don*). This differentiation is sometimes also expressed by saying that a given scriptural text is intentional *(ābhiprāyika = dgongs pa can)*—or that it is non-literal *(na yathāruta- = sgra ji bzhin ma yin pa)*—because (1) it has an intended ground or purport *(dgongs gzhi)* only alluded to by indirection in the Buddha's teaching, because (2) it is determined by some special motivation *(dgos pa = prayojana)* on the part of the Buddha who uttered it, and because (3) its meaning is incompatible with the true meaning *(dngos la gnod byed = mukhyārthabādha)* accepted as being the Buddha's final and definitive intention *(abhiprāya = dgongs pa)* within a given doctrinal system (or **dharma-cakra*).[45]

This hermeneutical distinction may be used in a classificatory fashion, that is, as a taxonomy. But it has sometimes also been employed in order to subordinate one body of teachings to another, as in some Chinese *p'an-chiao* classifications;[46] and this last use of the taxonomy may then include a polemical dimension.

But recourse to the distinction between *neyārtha* and *nītārtha* has not been the only possible approach to systematic hermeneutics in Buddhism. And it has been seen by some philosophically minded hermeneuticians that this division between a provisional "surface" *neyārtha*-meaning and a definitive "deep" *nītārtha*-meaning is not actually required to resolve every problem of conflicting meanings encountered by the philosopher-interpreter.

45. See recently D. Seyfort Ruegg, "Purport, Implicature and Presupposition: Sanskrit *abhiprāya* and Tibetan *dgoṅs pa / dgoṅs gži* as Hermeneutical Concepts," *JIP* 13 (1985), 309–25, and "An Indian Source for the Tibetan Hermeneutical Term *Dgongs gzhi* 'Intentional Ground,'" *JIP* 16 (1988), 1–4; reprinted as chapters 7 and 8 in the present volume, and "Allusiveness and Obliqueness in Buddhist Texts: *saṃdhā, saṃdhi, saṃdhyā* and *abhisaṃdhi,*" in C. Caillat, ed., *Dialectes dans les littératures indo-aryennes* (Paris, 1989), pp. 295–328.

46. See recently e.g., D. Lopez, ed., *Buddhist Hermeneutics* (Honolulu, 1988); and M.-W. Liu, *Madhyamaka Thought in China,* index s.v. "*p'an-chiao.*"

Thus, it has been concluded that even when we take as *nītārtha* the two doctrines of *(svabhāva)śūnyatā* and the *tathāgatagarbha,* it may still be possible to develop an interpretation—a "reading"—that allows both doctrines to be understood as congruent and compatible, without there being any need to suppose that one or the other has to be *neyārtha* and cancelled by the other. This is what Gung thang has done in his exegesis to which reference has already been made above (p. 242). Although attention was drawn to it long ago, this very important line of traditional interpretation has received virtually no attention in most recent work on the *tathāgatagarbha* and *rang stong* theories and on Buddhist hermeneutics.

IX

The matter of *pramāṇa* mentioned already at the outset (p. 219) takes us on to a further point which is of both lexical and religio-philosophical interest. This is the study of some of the things in Buddhist thought which can be subsumed—more or less "etically"—under the idea of authority current in contemporary European languages, notwithstanding the fact that Buddhism is a tradition that has regularly placed great emphasis on people's own endeavour, on their *karman* and its ripening, and on their direct understanding of reality. Thus, in the old canon we read that one has to be one's own refuge (Skt. *ātmadvīpa*), or one's own lamp (Pali *attadīpa*). And we are repeatedly told that, in the final analysis, spiritual realization must be unmediated and independent of any communication received from another *(aparapratyaya),* in other words that ultimate reality is to be directly realized within oneself *(pratyātmavedanīya, sākṣātkartavya).* Furthermore, irrespective of whether tathāgatas appear or not, it is the principle of origination in dependence *(pratītyasamutpāda)* that represents the timeless stability and fixedness of Dharma *(dharmasthititā, dharmaniyāmatā).*

Yet, at the same time, the Buddhist does take refuge in the Buddha and the Community *(saṃgha)* as well as in the Teaching *(dharma).* And the Buddha's word *(buddhavacana = sangs rgyas kyi bka')—āgama (lung)* or scripture—is regarded as trustworthy *(āpta = yid ches pa),* even as a cognitive standard or norm *(pramāṇa = tshad ma).*[47] Indeed, the Bhagavat or Buddha—the teacher *(śāstṛ = ston pa)*—is himself described as *pramāṇabhūta (tshad mar gyur pa).*[48] So, in sūtra Buddhism as well as in the Vajrayāna, the teacher—

47. See, e.g., Candrakīrti, *Prasannapadā* xv.6, p. 268.

48. See Dignāga, *Pramāṇasamuccaya* i.1.

indeed the entire line of teachers extending back to the Buddha—play a central and crucial role in Buddhist theory and practice. The spiritual master—both the proximate "root" guru *(rtsa ba'i bla ma)* who is one's immediate teacher and the more remote ones belonging to one's spiritual lineage *(brgyud pa'i bla ma)*—is accordingly no less important to a Buddhist than he is, for example, to a Hindu.

These two sets of propositions within Buddhist thought appear to belong to distinct levels of religio-philosophical discourse. Hence, although they would thus not be contradictory in the strict sense, they evidently do reflect a real tension in the idea of what we in modern parlance call authority. This is accordingly a worthwhile and fruitful subject for both lexical and religio-philosophical clarification. And the question of the function of *pramāṇa* in relation to authority proves to be of very considerable interest in attempting to demarcate what is essential to Buddhist thought intrinsically—and "emically"—from what we sometimes import into Buddhism with our own conceptual baggage when we superimpose on it either our culture-bound categories, interpretative grids, and terminologies or, alternatively, our comparatively arrived at "etic" categories.

In the Buddhist theory of knowledge, the term *pramāṇa*—though often rendered by our word "authority"—basically denotes right/correct cognition/knowledge. In the first place, it may refer to direct perception (i.e., *pratyakṣa* = *mngon sum*), a form of cognition which is defined as "congruent"—i.e., non-delusive and indefeasible/veridical *(avisaṃvādaka = mi [b]slu ba)* and hence reliable—and also as free of conceptual construction *(kalpanāpoḍha = rtog pa dang bral ba);* and its scope belongs to what is cognitively accessible immediately *(pratyakṣa = mngon gyur).* Secondly, the term *pramāṇa* may denote inferential knowledge *(anumāna = rjes dpag),* i.e., that form of right cognition whose scope belongs to what is in part cognitively inaccessible *([īṣat]parokṣa: cung zad lkog gyur)* to us because of epistemologically extrinsic obstacles such as distance, as in the case of fire the presence of which on a distant hill can be inferred from observing smoke there, in accord with the homologous example *(sapakṣadṛṣṭānta)* of smoke regularly accompanying fire in a kitchen: "no smoke without fire." Now, according to the Buddhist Pramāṇa-school of Dignāga and Dharmakīrti, *pramāṇa* has only these two basic forms of direct perceptual knowledge and inferential knowledge. Even scriptural authority *(āgama = lung)* as reliable testimony *(āpta = yid ches pa)* is not regarded as a separate and independent means of correct knowledge, but is included under that form of inferential knowledge *(anumāna)* the scope of which belongs to what is totally concealed *(atyantaparokṣa = shin tu lkog gyur)* for epistemologically intrinsic reasons connected with the transcendent nature of its cognitive object.

Still, the Buddha—though a person—does function like a *pramāṇa,* for he is stated to be *pramāṇabhūta* in Dignāga's great treatise on epistemology and logic, the *Pramāṇasamuccaya* (i.1). And a thoroughly competent teacher such as Nāgārjuna is described as a **pramāṇabhūta-puruṣa (tshad mar gyur pa'i skyes bu)* by the Madhyamaka master Candrakīrti (*MABh* vi.2). For this and related reasons such as their compassion, the Buddha and other trustworthy masters are then thought of as persons in whom one may place confidence, so that we may legitimately describe them as authorities. Thus the idea of the teacher or guru as an authority is not restricted to the Vajrayāna form of Buddhism alone.

In the Buddhist concept of *pramāṇa,* we accordingly meet once again—this time in a perhaps somewhat unexpected context—the contrast between immediacy and mediacy already encountered in the quite different contexts already mentioned above of the theory of the *tathāgatagarbha* and *buddha*-nature (on the level of Ground, *gzhi*) and of the distinction between the Gradual and the Simultaneous (on the level of the Path, *lam*). For in the case of *(pratyakṣa)pramāṇa,* the criterion is the immediacy of right knowledge free of conceptual construction *(kalpanāpoḍha).* And one prerequisite for being a truly trustworthy—and thus authoritative—teacher is the possession of this immediate knowledge of reality. That is, if the Buddha or other reliable teachers are "authorities"—i.e., *pramāṇa, prāmāṇika,* or *pramāṇabhūta*—as they indeed are for Buddhists, their being authoritative is in fact secondary and derivative inasmuch as it results from their having access to—even being, so to say, constituted by—right knowledge or *pramāṇa* relating to ultimate reality. Hence, if *pramāṇa* were to be understood as authority, this conception will inescapably involve indirectness and mediacy. For if a teacher is an authority for another cognizer, this necessarily makes the latter cognitively dependent on this outside authority (i.e., *parapratyaya*) as an external, and hence indirect, source for his own knowledge. On the contrary, being direct right/correct cognition/knowledge *(pratyakṣa) pramāṇa* is characterized precisely by its cognitive immediacy for the knower. For the Buddha, or another reliable teacher, the *pramāṇa* in question is constituted by their direct awareness *(sākṣātkāra)* of reality.

Here we are thus confronted by a curious tension—even a certain lack of perfect fit—between the above-mentioned uses of the Sanskrit word *pramāṇa* and its Tibetan equivalent *tshad ma* as (1) right/correct cognition/knowledge and (2) authority. These two well-attested values of the word—which are in fact quite distinct—come very clearly to our attention when we seek to translate *pramāṇa* into a language like English which, unlike Sanskrit and Tibetan, makes this religiously and philosophically vital distinction by employing etymologically unrelated words to express the two values.[49]

In this way, concepts which we for our part might include under the idea of authority have in Buddhism distinct philosophical (i.e., epistemological and gnoseological), religious, religio-social, and sometimes even religio-political aspects. It is therefore necessary to reflect closely on the extent to which the contemporary "standard average" idea of authority is really adequate to embrace what, basically, is cognitively direct, immediate, and (in the first place) free from conceptual construction like the *(pratyakṣa)pramāṇa*—something that is epistemologically "normal" or "standard" rather than an "authority" in the usual sense of this word.

X

It has been argued that studies in Buddhist thought may be viewed as constituting a unitary discipline even if they are also, inevitably and legitimately, multidisciplinary and, one may hope, interdisciplinary.

When considering Buddhist traditions extending from South through Central to East Asia and beyond it has, however, often been customary to think in terms of national Buddhisms (conceived of sometimes as more or less uniform and even monolithic entities). In so doing we risk falling prey to modern preconceptions. It is of course true that Buddhists themselves have not hesitated to engage very closely with and to absorb the various cultural traditions of different peoples as the Buddhadharma spread first within India and then further abroad. Yet, even if Buddhism reveals no single and universal monothetic essence throughout, its traditions show overarching continuities and what may be called lattices of polythetic "family resemblances." And it is just this that makes it possible to speak of Buddhism at all, even while recognizing that it is not a single uniform entity on the horizontal plane of its geographical diffusion in space.

As for the vertical axis of chronology, when investigating the Buddhist traditions which have presented themselves in such diverse garb over the

49. See D. Seyfort Ruegg, "*Pramāṇabhūta, *pramāṇa(bhūta)-puruṣa, pratyakṣadharman* and *sākṣātkṛtadharman* as Epithets of the *ṛṣi, ācārya* and *tathāgata* in Grammatical, Epistemological and Madhyamaka Texts," *BSOAS* 57 (1994), 303–20; and "La notion du voyant et du 'connaisseur suprême' et la question de l'autorité épistémique," *WZKS* 38 (1994), 403–19.

centuries, it has been customary for scholars to think in terms of layers of textual material where one stratum is set off from and supersedes another. Certainly, in many a case, this stratigraphical model for the history of Buddhism is appropriate. But such a quasi-geological paradigm should not be allowed to mislead. In the case of structurally contrastive oppositions—such as those between immediacy and mediacy, between inborn *buddha*-nature and progressively achieved buddhahood, between cataphaticism and apophaticism, between the non-analytically meditative and the analytically intellectual, between direct understanding by oneself and instruction communicated from outside by another—there seem rather to exist intellectual and spiritual polarities and tensions which are not best understood as conditioned only by chronology, i.e., stratigraphically. Not only have these been present in Buddhist thought from early times, but they may well be inherent to Buddhist thought throughout its history—indeed perhaps even to the Buddha's teaching as he gave it to his disciples of varying capacities and propensities.

Hence it does not seem possible simply to generalize the stratigraphical paradigm of higher criticism and to speak, in such cases, only of textual layers opposing, succeeding, and eventually superseding each other in time. If a method of textual analysis based on the stratigraphical model loses sight of its own inherent limitations, it runs the risk of postulating diachronically successive strata while overlooking the complex systemic and synchronic philosophical processes and spiritual tensions involved in the history of Buddhism. Historicist positivism does not always make good history.

XI

This last point can have a bearing as much on postulated diachronic sequences in what has been termed Earliest Buddhism, and in the doctrines of the early schools *(nikāya),* as it does on the later phases in the history of Buddhism with which the preceding remarks have been concerned.

When attempting to determine what may have constituted "original" or "earliest"—that is, "precanonical" or proto-canonical—Buddhism, let us then reflect on the circumstance that we sometimes find ourselves engaging in what may, no doubt unavoidably, be rather impressionistic inferences and atomistic reconstructions. Unless one is quite clear about the eventual role of systemically structured—and hence synchronic rather than exclusively diachronic—polarities and tensions in philosophical and religious thinking, the possibility will exist that any atomistic identification in the sources of (putative) doctrinal inconsistencies and contradictions in content—and also of formal incoherence in the textual pericopes—can, *per se,* offer no sure and reliable guide to the reconstruction of doctrinal developments that could be datable absolutely, or even relatively. (The earliest attestation of a doctrine or other piece of evidence can of course be employed as a *terminus a quo,* provided the fallacy of argument from silence is avoided.) Hence many a reconstruction, inextricably bound up as it in practice is with theoretical pre-suppositions and pre-judgments and with methodological options, may turn out to be as unfalsifiable as it is unverifiable in view of the very nature of the evidence available. And one must then carefully consider just what their scientific value and function can be. If, however, they are clearly recognized to be simply working hypotheses with a certain (albeit circumscribed) heuristic value, there may be no harm in them.[50]

Finally, an approach prepared to envisage the possible unanswerability of the question as to what "original" Buddhism was because of the very nature of our documentation should not necessarily be thought to amount to agnosticism, to relativism, or to indifferentist ahistoriscism.

By Buddhist tradition the crucial problem of the authenticity of a text or doctrine has been raised not so much in the form of the question whether doctrine *x* is "original"—i.e., that the historical Buddha Gautama Śākyamuni taught it at such and such a time—as in that of the question whether a given teaching is attested in the corpora of Sūtra and Vinaya (as in the canonical *mahāpadeśas*),[51] and whether it is both justifiable and intelligible in terms of the Buddha's soteriological purpose and his philosophical intention as expressed in his *nītārtha* statements. In Buddhist tradition, it has been considered that if these last criteria are fulfilled, a statement will be Buddha-word *(buddhavacana).*

In other words, the criterion has generally not been what the historical Buddha taught at a given time *t* in the forty-five years said to have intervened

50. At all events, recourse in such matters to arguments claiming to be based on what is rational, or plausible, will be of little avail, and often examples of methodologically naïve question-begging, unless of course it has first been possible satisfactorily to establish what, in each case, is to be considered rational and plausible. The watch-word of rationality is hardly an open-sesame, a universal pass-key which can be used anywhere. Rather, in order to avoid circularity, the relevant "rationale(s)" is (are) what has first to be discovered by investigation of the evidence in each individual case.

51. See É. Lamotte, "La critique d'authenticité dans le bouddhisme," *India antiqua* (J. Ph. Vogel Felicitation Volume; Leiden, 1947), pp. 213–22. See also R. M. Davidson, "An Introduction to the Standards of Scriptural Authenticity in Indian Buddhism," in R. Buswell, ed., *Chinese Buddhist Apocrypha* (Honolulu, 1990), pp. 291–325.

between his Awakening and his Parinirvāṇa taking place *n* years before the present.[52] For, finally, the criterion of authenticity was the idea that what is Buddhistically well-formed *(subhāṣita)* is *buddhavacana/buddhabhāṣita* "Buddha-word." Conversely, Buddha-word is *subhāṣita* in the sense of being well-formed in the philosophical meaning of this term—i.e., correctly formulated—rather than just well turned and eloquent in a literary sense. Then, in the last analysis, whatever is Buddhistically well-formed (i.e., *dharmopasaṃhita, arthopasaṃhita,* etc.) has—so to say, by definition—become Buddha-word.[53]

Needless to say, this will not have to be the point of view of the historically minded modern student of Buddhist thought. Yet, in addition to being about identifying historical origins, religious or doctrinal developments, and successive textual strata, the study of Buddhist thought is also about understanding structurally and systemically the ideas we find in the sources together with the underlying (and often unexplicit) presuppositions with which the Buddhist traditions have operated in developing these ideas. For this purpose, Buddhist hermeneutics with its theory of a "deep" definitive meaning *(nītārtha)*—as distinct from a provisional "surface" meaning

52. Attempts to answer such questions do, however, exist within Buddhist tradition, for example in the Kālacakra system and (to a lesser degree) in the taxonomy of the three Wheels of the Dharma *(*dharmacakra).*

53. See the *Uttaravipattisutta* in Aṅguttaranikāya IV, 164: *evam eva, devānam inda, yaṃ kiñci subhāsitaṃ sabbaṃ taṃ tassa bhagavato vacanaṃ arahato sammāsambuddhassa;* and the *Adhyāśayasaṃcodanasūtra* cited in Śāntideva's *Śikṣāsamuccaya* (ed. Bendall) p. 15, and in Prajñākaramati's *Bodhicaryāvatārapañjikā* ix.43ab: *yat kiṃcin maitreya subhāṣitaṃ sarvaṃ tad buddhabhāṣitam.* On the idea see É. Lamotte, *Le traité de la Grande Vertu de Sagesse,* I (Louvain, 1944), p. 80n2; D. L. Snellgrove, *BSOAS* 21 (1958), 620–21; R. Davidson, op. cit., 310; S. Collins, "On the Very Idea of the Pali Canon," *JPTS* 15 (1990), 94–95; and D. Lopez, "Authority and Orality in the Mahayāna," *Numen* 42 (1995), 27.

The parallel idea that whatever the Buddha said is well said is frequently attested. See, e.g., the *Subhāsitasutta* in *Suttanipāta* iii.3 (pp. 78–79), with the *Āmagandhasutta* in *Suttanipāta* ii.2.14 (verse 252, p. 45) and the *Kiṃsīlasutta* in ii.9.2 (verse 325, p. 56); Saṃyuttanikāya IV, 188–89. The idea is attested also in Aśoka's Bhabra inscription (ed. J. Bloch, 154): *e keci bhaṃte bhagavatā buddhena bhāsite savve se subhāsitevā.*

Although *subhāṣita = legs (par) bshad (pa)* has often been translated by "eloquent" or "eloquence," this rendering can be somewhat misleading. What is in the final analysis intended is the well-formulated, and well-formed, on the content level (though the level of expression is, presumably, not entirely excluded in the view of the tradition; cf. F. Edgerton, *BHSD* s.v.). In the passage just cited of the *Adhyāśayasaṃcodanasūtra, pratibhāna* "intelligent/insightful/inspired expression" (rather than just "elocution")—one of the four *pratisaṃvid*—is also mentioned: *caturbhiḥ kāraṇaiḥ pratibhānaṃ sarvaṃ buddhabhāṣi[tam jñātavyam].*

requiring to be further interpreted in a sense other than the *prima facie* one *(neyārtha)*—offers very considerable interest. In the philosophical study of Buddhist thought, hermeneutics too can therefore assume a place of central importance.

10. On the Tibetan Historiography and Doxography of the "Great Debate of Bsam yas"*

I

TOWARDS THE END of the eight century C.E., during the reign of Khri Srong lde b(r)tsan (r. ca. 755–94/97), there took place an event of the greatest significance for Tibetan history and culture which had an enduring influence on later religious and philosophical development in Tibet and was to shape important areas of it. This event was the famous encounter, the so-called "Great Debate of Bsam yas," between the Chinese *ho-shang* Mo-ho-yen (*hva shang* Mahāyāna) and disciples of Śāntarakṣita including the Indian Kamalaśīla and members of the great Tibetan Sba (Dba', Dba's) clan such as Ye shes dbang po and Dpal dbyangs.

Since the late 1930s this event, which is now somewhat wrapped in the mists of time, has rightly attracted the attention of European scholars such as Marcelle Lalou, Paul Demiéville, Giuseppe Tucci, and Rolf Stein. More recently it has been investigated also by scholars in America and above all in Japan. This work has been of immense importance for our understanding of this eighth-century event, although it must be said that much of the more recent research has generally tended to allow the significance of the "Great Debate" for Tibetan civilization and thought to be eclipsed by problems in the history and doctrines of Chinese Ch'an. (A noteworthy exception to this tendency is the thesis on *rdzogs chen* just published by Samten Gyaltsen Karmay: *The Great Perfection* [Leiden, 1988].)

This paper will be concerned with aspects of this encounter as either a historical event or a more or less dehistoricized *topos,* and with its significance in Tibetan historiography and doxography and for the history of Tibetan religion and philosophy.

* First published in *Tibetan Studies (Proceedings of the 5th Seminar of the International Association for Tibetan Studies, Narita 1989),* pp. 237–44. Ed. Ihara Shōren et al. Narita: Naritasan Shinshoji, 1992.

II

Several thorny questions arise as to what the exact nature of this event was. Indeed, was the encounter between Mo-ho-yen and Kamalaśīla a real event having historical authenticity? For the very existence of their reported debate as a historical occurrence has come to be questioned.[1] And one might well ask how a Chinese monk evidently unfamiliar with any Indian language could have actually discussed, much less debated, important questions of Buddhist theory and practice with an Indian paṇḍit who had only recently arrived in Tibet and could scarcely have been fluent in Tibetan let alone Chinese.[2]

Let us begin with the name given to this encounter by modern scholars. Since Paul Demiéville's path-breaking and masterly *Le concile de Lhasa* (Paris, 1952), it has frequently been called the Council of Lha sa. Now it has to be said that, as depicted in the ancient Tibetan and Chinese documents from Dunhuang as well as in the later Tibetan historical and philosophical literature, this event was no council in the proper ecclesiastical sense of the term, nor was it even a local Buddhist synod. Sometimes the relevant materials take the form of aphorisms or *logia* uttered by Mo-ho-yen (and other Hoshangs), e.g., in several Tibetan documents from Dunhuang. Alternatively, in Wang Hsi's *Tun-wu ta-ch'eng cheng-li chüeh* translated by Demiéville, we have a series of more or less polemical questions put by a "Brahman monk" to Mo-ho-yen with the latter's replies. And sometimes the materials are set out as a discussion or debate between Mo-ho-yen and (mainly) Kamalaśīla's disciples.

In the Tibetan historical literature starting with the various versions of the *Sba bzhed* and the *Chos 'byung Me tog snying po* of Nyang Nyi ma 'od zer, the event is in fact depicted as a debate *(rtsod pa, [g]shags),* with Khri Srong lde btsan in the middle acting as "witness" and presiding over the assembly. To the monarch's right were the "Simultaneists" led by Mo-ho-yen (who seemingly, according to a Tibetan tradition, wished because of his monastic seniority in Tibet to figure as the proponent). And to his left were the "Gradualists" led by Kamalaśīla but represented in the proceedings of the debate mainly by members of the Sba family—Ye shes dbang po, Dpal dbyangs, and/or Sang shi (ta)—figuring as the opponents. In other words,

1. See recently Y. Imaeda, *JA* 1975, pp. 125–46; H. V. Guenther in: W. Lai and L. Lancaster (ed.), *Early Ch'an in China and Tibet* (Berkeley, 1983), p. 351, and *JAOS* 109 (1989), p. 151.

2. See for example D. Ueyama, *Tōhō gakuhō* 35 (1964), p. 169, with P. Demiéville, *TP* 56 (1970), p. 42; Y. Imaeda, loc. cit., p. 129.

the setting is that of a classical debate with proponent *(vādin = snga rgol),* opponent *(prativādin = phyi rgol),* and witness or arbiter *(sākṣin = dpang po)* as described in the *vāda*-manuals belonging to the Indo-Tibetan tradition. Although this scenario might perhaps seem out of place at the court of the Tibetan ruler as early as the end of the eighth century, this need not be so. Let us recall that Kamalaśīla's master Śāntarakṣita had commented on Dharmakīrti's *Vādanyāya,* where procedures in debate are described. And it should be carefully noted that according to the *Vādanyāya* the procedure of debate is employed not simply out of a desire for victory at any price since it is not just *vijigīṣuvāda;* and that it concerns reflexion on what is true *(tattvacintā)* and its proclamation *(khyāpana),* serves the preservation of truth *(tattvarakṣaṇa),* and is engaged in for the purpose of assisting an other *(parānugraha)*[3] It is quite possible that all this was very well known to Śāntarakṣita's and Kamalaśīla's Tibetan disciples towards the end of the eighth century, and that a debate was arranged by the Tibetans and their Indian teacher with just such an end in view.

As for the site of the Great Debate, in the Tibetan sources it is often said to have been the Byang chub gling temple at Bsam yas, the first Tibetan monastic centre founded by Śāntarakṣita. Tucci accordingly preferred the name of "Council of Bsam yas" to Demiéville's "Council of Lha sa."[4] But more recently the appellation "Council of Tibet" has been extensively used by scholars, including Demiéville himself.[5] As has been suggested by Ueyama and Demiéville, it may well be that meetings between participants took place at more than one single place, and in more than a single session.

No cogent reason is however known to me for thinking that Bsam yas (and perhaps in particular the Byang chub gling temple which Tibetan sources have presented as the site of the encounter) was not, in the technical and legal sense, the venue and in any case the focal point for what was a debate rather than a council in the proper sense. At all events, the appellation "Council of Lha sa" is certainly a misnomer; and the name "Council of Tibet" may be more general and imprecise than need be.

Even though Kamalaśīla's three *Bhāvanākrama*s do not report in an historical fashion on any specific debate at an identifiable place with identifiable participants, they do reflect a discussion or debate in a quite dehistoricized

3. *Vādanyāya,* ed. Svāmī Dvārikādās Śāstrī (Varanasi, 1972), pp. 68–71.

4. G. Tucci, *Minor Buddhist Texts,* II (Rome, 1958), pp. 32, 285–87.

5. *T'oung Pao* 44 (1958), pp. 404–8; 56 (1970), p. 42. See also P. Demiéville in: *Essays on the history of Buddhism presented to Professor Zenryu Tsukamoto* (Kyōto, 1961), pp. 14, 24.

form. As for Wang Hsi's account in the *Cheng-li chüeh,* it refers only to a Brahman monk (*p'o lo men seng,* fol. 127a) and not specifically to Kamalaśīla as Mo-ho-yen's opponent.

The account found in the *Sba bzhed* has not only been questioned as to its historical accuracy and veracity, but it has been ascribed to the fourteenth century; and the classical Tibetan historical tradition on the subject has been described as late.[6] Despite the many problems these Sba records undoubtedly pose, such a dating would seem to be unduly late. For the account in question is found, in somewhat differing forms it is true, not only in the Supplemented *Sba bzhed* (that is, the *Zhabs btags ma* version)—which may well have something to do with Atisha's school since it concludes with his mission in Tibet, and which must, moreover, be quite late in its extant version since it refers (p. 54 in Stein's ed.) to the *Gsung rab rin po che'i [bang] mdzod,* i.e., apparently to the *Chos 'byung* of ca. 1323 by Bu ston (1290–1364), who however himself cites a *Rba bzhed*—but in the presumably earlier "Pure" *Sba bzhed* (that is, the *Gtsang ma* version), which itself includes the "Alternative Tradition" on the Great Debate used not only by Dpa' bo Gtsug lag phreng ba (1504–66) but evidently also in the works of Sa skya paṇḍi ta (1182–1251, who cites a *Dpa' bzhed* [i.e. *Dba' bzhed*] apparently in the version of the "Alternative Tradition"), Bu ston, and much of the Tibetan historical literature.

Furthermore, and most importantly, a closely related (if somewhat divergent) account of the "Great Debate" is found in the history of Nyang Nyi ma 'od zer (1124/36–1192/1204). Now, provided of course that it is authentic, this account in the *Chos 'byung Me tog snying po* goes back to a time before Sa skya paṇḍi ta. Moreover, and very significantly, it is found in the work of a master of the Rdzogs chen/Rnying ma school; and this fact militates against the supposition that the account in question of the Bsam yas Debate was simply a fabrication of the Gsar ma pas intended somehow to discredit the Rdzogs chen pas (several of whose teachings were compared by Sa skya paṇḍi ta and other Tibetan authorities with the teachings of the Hva shang Mahāyāna).

As for the main participants in the Great Debate, although according to the Tibetan sources Kamalaśīla was the leader of the Gradualists, the actual speakers on their side were mainly members of the Sba family (Ye shes dbang po, Dpal dbyangs, and/or Sba Sang shi [ta]). Hence the question as to what language Kamalaśīla and Mo-ho-yen had in common loses much of its relevance, at least from the point of view of the Tibetan sources. (It is true that in Wang Hsi's *Cheng-li chüeh* Mo-ho-yen and the unnamed "Brahman monk"

6. See Y. Imaeda, *JA* 1975, pp. 125–46.

are represented as speaking to each other; but this may have to do with the literary presentation adopted by Wang Hsi. Kamalaśīla's remarks to Mo-ho-yen could in any case have been translated into Tibetan, or even into Chinese.) It seems likely, then, that the language used in the discussions would have been mainly Tibetan, with which Mo-ho-yen was presumably familiar after his residence in Tibetan-speaking areas. Chinese may have been employed in addition between some Tibetans and Mo-ho-yen and his Chinese associates; and an Indian language might have been in use between certain Tibetans and Kamalaśīla.

By Demiéville and other scholars, the "Great Debate" has been characterized as a Sino-Indian or an Indo-Chinese controversy. This description could however lead to a misapprehension as to its nature and purpose, for the discussions were evidently set in train by the Tibetans themselves in order to clarify acute problems of theory and practice that had urgently come to their attention. The Tibetans in fact were then a major power in Central Asia; and in view of their intellectual achievements by the beginning of the ninth century (as attested, for example, in the works of Ye shes sde), it would seem to be quite unsatisfactory to regard them as nullities only a short time earlier at the time of the "Great Debate," or as nothing but an intellectual *tabula rasa* waiting to be used by others and lacking any philosophical or religious rôle of their own in organizing and carrying through the discussions. As already suggested, it may well have been organized in the way best known to Ye shes dbang po and his colleagues, namely in the above-mentioned classical Indo-Tibetan form of a debate devoted to reflecting on, proclaiming, and preserving what is true *(tattva)*.

If this is indeed so, it will also be far from the mark—and quite anachronistic—to regard the "Great Debate" as a more or less politically motivated confrontation between the Indians and Chinese as rival great powers in Central Asia. To the extent that political factors were involved, it would appear that they would have been connected rather less with any possible conflicts between Chinese and Indians than with rivalries between Tibetan clans and the regions with which the clans were linked. Such clannishness may have opposed members of the Sba clan as disciples or supporters of Śāntarakṣita and Kamalaśīla to members of the Myang/Nyang and Mnya'/Snya clans as supporters of the *ho-shang*s; the sources in fact report that Ting nge 'dzin bzang po of Myang and Bi ma / Bye ma (etc.) of Mnya' (etc.) were in opposition to Ye shes dbang po of Sba. But because of the nature of our documentation it is hard to pin this down. It has indeed to be borne in mind that a member of this Sba clan had also earlier been closely connected with *ho-shang*s, while members of the Myang as well as of the Dba' clan are stated in a Dunhuang document to have been disciples of Śāntarakṣita;[7] and in the twelfth century Nyang Nyi ma 'od zer gave an account of the Great Debate, including the defeat of Hva shang Mahāyāna, that is closely related to (if not completely identical with) what we find in the Sba records.

III

It would of course be unrealistic to pretend that the Tibetan historical and doxographical sources at our disposal have given us a full and a perfectly accurate and balanced account of exactly what took place at the "Great Debate" of Bsam yas. The relevant Dunhuang documents in Tibetan, although fairly numerous, are both fragmentary and episodic. (In this respect they differ, for example, from Wang Hsi's *Cheng-li chüeh* also recovered from Dunhuang.) And the accounts in the classical Tibetan historical literature starting with the *Sba bzhed* and the other sources more or less closely related to the Sba records, although reasonably long, are no doubt somewhat formalized and stereotyped to the extent that their authors relate what had become, in part at least, a somewhat dehistoricized *topos.*

It could nevertheless be that these Sba records go back at least in their core to a time soon after the Great Debate, and in any case to the time of the Yar klungs dynasty in the early ninth century. (The *Gtsang ma* version of the *Sba bzhed* concludes with the accession of Mu ne btsan po.) Nevertheless, if this is indeed so, this would of course apply to their contents only and not to the language of the extant versions of the *Sba bzhed* (which is scarcely the Old Tibetan of the eighth century even though it contains a number of archaisms).

The later Tibetan historical tradition would appear to have no longer had an entirely clear picture of just what had happened at the encounter between Mo-ho-yen and Kamalaśīla's disciples. There was even some uncertainty for Tshe dbang nor bu (1698/99–1755) as to whether this event took place in the reign of Khri Srong lde b(r)tsan or earlier in that of his father Mes Ag tshoms (Khri Lde gtsug b[r]tsan). After the break caused by the downfall of the Yar klungs dynasty and the end of the period of the Early Propagation of Buddhism in the middle of the ninth century, Tibetan historians evidently had as much difficulty in reconstituting their ancient history as the modern Tibetologist does. Accounts found in the Tibetan historical literature in fact seem

7. See F. W. Thomas, *Tibetan Literary Texts and Documents Concerning Chinese Turkestan,* II (London, 1951), p. 85.

to reflect the Tibetans' attempts either to rediscover their early history or to constitute tradition, or even to do both of these things at the same time. As a consequence, the "Great Debate" of Bsam yas often appears in this literature more as a semi-historical *topos* than as an historical event, and the Hva shang Mahāyāna as a more or less dehistoricized and emblematic figure standing as it were for a certain typological variety of Buddhism. In connexion with the "Great Debate," Bsam yas itself became, so to say, a "locus of memory" (lieu de mémoire).[8]

IV

Even if we must conclude that our sources on the "Great Debate" of Bsam yas are neither complete nor perfectly accurate and balanced as *histoire événementielle,* are we then to regard them merely as essentially the fabrications of anti–Rnying ma Gsar ma pas, as the interpolation of later logic-choppers *(phyis kyi rtog ge pa),*[9] as tendentious tracts, or as polemic directed against the *phyag rgya chen po* (at least in one of its forms) with its teaching described as a *dkar po chig thub,* that is, as a unique and perfectly self-sufficient Sovereign Remedy? In other words, if the Great Debate and along with it Bsam yas both became a "locus of memory," of what nature was this memory?

As reported in our historical and doxographical sources, the religious-philosophical problems that arose in eighth-century Tibet in a form evidently acute and urgent enough to make a discussion/debate and, if possible, a decision about them both timely and necessary appear to be old ones that were in no way simply the product of the particular historical juncture in question, i.e., the simultaneous presence in eighth-century Tibet of both Chinese and Indian Buddhist masters and the resulting encounter and confrontation between their doctrines.

The two traditions of Buddhism facing each other in the accounts of the Great Debate have usually been described as "Gradualism" (*rim gyis 'jug pa* etc.) and "Simultaneism" (*[g]cig c[h]ar gyis 'jug pa* etc.) or, as the latter current is often termed by Sinologues, "Suddenness" or "Subitism." This terminology is parallel to the distinction in Chinese between *chien* and *tun,* reflected in the Tibetan terms *(br)tse(n) mun/min (pa)* and *(s)ton mun/min (pa).*

Now, this Gradualism is a method of spiritual training and development

8. For this concept see P. Nora, *Les lieux de mémoire* (Paris, 1984 f.).

9. See Dpa' bo Gtsug lag phreng ba, *Chos 'byung Mkhas pa'i dga' ston,* ja, fol. 122a–b.

that is familiar from a very large number of Buddhist texts available in Sanskrit and Pāli or in translations from these languages. The term describes a course of sequential and progressive *(krameṇa)* cultivation on the Path of the factors conducive to liberation and Awakening through the mediacy of practice and means. As for its opposite, Simultaneism, it too is far from being absent in some form from the classical sources of Buddhism. The corresponding Tibetan term *cig char ba* (etc.)—derived from Tib. *cig c[h]ar = Skt. yugapad* (or *sakṛt*)—describes the immediacy and innate spontaneity of Awakening in and to the pure, original, and real nature of Mind. Such simultaneity, or spontaneous and holistic immediacy, is mentioned in a number of classical sūtras and śāstras. And typologically (if not genetically) related notions are known from both sūtras and śāstras under the names of *buddha*-nature *(sangs rgyas kyi rang bzhin), tathāgatagarbha, prakṛtisthagotra,* and natural luminosity *(prakṛtiprabhāsvaratā)* of Mind. In the literature of the Vajrayāna, related or comparable notions became especially frequent.

Simultaneism and Gradualism as two currents in Buddhism can be described in other words as immediacy in contrast to mediacy, innateness over and against reinforcement, spontaneity over and against effort, and even nature over and against nurture. To use a medical metaphor (a procedure not infrequently used in our sources in this connexion), whilst Gradualism can be described as allopathic, employing counteragents *(pratipakṣa)* as remedies against the afflictions/impurities *(kleśa)* that are the impediments *(vipakṣa)* to liberation and Awakening, holistic Simultaneism represents a sort of nature cure, consisting in face-to-face encounter with and recognition of innate and ever-present Mind. As for the Vajrayāna, using as it does the *kleśa*s to subdue the *kleśa*s, it may be described as homoeopathic. Even though it is sometimes possible to observe a tendency for these last two currents to converge—e.g., in *rdzogs chen* where, however, the simultaneist tradition of the Hva shang Mahāyāna is normally differentiated from Mahāyoga and Atiyoga—it would seem necessary in general to distinguish between the pure naturalness and spontaneous immediacy of Simultaneism and the progressively cultivated effort required in Vajrayāna traditions to achieve liberation and buddhahood in this very life and body.

Another way of looking at the matter has been in terms of the balance between tranquillity or quiet *(śamatha = zhi gnas)* and insight *(vipaśyanā = lhag mthong)*. An extreme version of simultaneist immediacy and innateness may emphasize quiet by rejecting *vipaśyanā* as analytical, ratiocinative *prajñā,* i.e., *pratyavekṣā* involving mentation *(masas[i]kāra = yid la byed pa)*. Conversely, an extreme version of gradualist cultivation of analysis may emphasize correct mentation *(yoniśomanasikāra)* and analysis *(vicāra = dpyad pa)* at the expense of quiet.[10] In general, at all events, the out-and-out "Simultaneist" *(cig char ba)* would tend to reject the need for the progressive and alternating cultivation of quiet and insight which finally leads to their total integration in a syzygy *(yuganaddha = zung du 'brel par 'jug pa)* as taught in so much of classical Buddhism. The Hva shang's simultaneist method is described in Tibetan sources on the one side as an extremely etherealized spirituality associated with a quietistic abandonment of all activity *(karman, caryā),* wholesome as well as unwholesome, as being an obstacle to realization, in the same way as white clouds and dark clouds both obscure the sun; and on the other side the Hva shang's method is associated with delectation in emptiness *(stong pa nyid la dga' ba),* which is regarded as impurity of theory *(dṛṣṭikaṣāya = lta ba'i snyigs ma).*

This is to say that two genuine components of the Buddhist Path such as quiet and insight could, if carried to excess—and when Ground and Fruit are so to say collapsed by suppressing the stages of the Path—become opposed and be regarded as antithetical extremes rather than as alternating and mutually reinforcing aspects which finally are to be integrated. The "Simultaneist" *(cig char ba)* and the "Gradualist" *(rim gyis pa)* will then appear as irreconcilable. But the co-ordination and final integration of these two currents has been amply set out both in the Śrāvakayānist and Mahāyānist canonical traditions and in śāstras. An example of the latter is to be found in the eminently "gradualist" *Abhisamayālaṃkāra,* where the progressive *anupūrvābhisamaya* (chap. vi) is followed by the single-moment *abhisamaya* of the *ekakṣaṇābhisamaya* (chap. vii), which leads on in a second and final moment to the realization of the *dharmakāya* (chap. viii).

Both these currents are moreover well attested in Chinese Buddhism itself. And there can therefore be no more question of characterizing all of Chinese Buddhism as "subitist" than there is of characterizing Indian Buddhism as exclusively gradualist. Kamalaśīla for one was evidently well aware of both currents. Not only did he comment on the *Avikalpapraveśadhāraṇī,* for example, but in the sources he cited in his *Bhāvanākrama*s they are mentioned, and their extreme or one-sided versions are rejected. But it is not clear how familiar Mo-ho-yen was with the gradualist tradition in Chinese Buddhism—a tradition which was represented for example by his (elder?) contemporary T'an-k'uang, who (like Mo-ho-yen himself) was in contact with Khri Srong lde btsan. Thus the encounter in Tibet at the end of the eighth

10. Incorrect mentation *(ayoniśomanas[i]kāra)* on the contrary is of course recognized as dichotomizing conceptualization *(vikalpa),* and as the source of *karman* and *kleśa.* See for example *Ratnagotravibhāga* i.56, and *Ratnagotravibhāga*-Commentary i.12 and 64.

century between the gradualist and simultaneist currents of Buddhism was certainly not between two homogeneous and monolithic national traditions standing in opposition to each other as Indian *vs.* Chinese Buddhism, but rather between two transmission traditions: that of Mo-ho-yen traced back to *Bodhidharma (and further to Kāśyapa) and that of Śāntarakṣita and Kamalaśīla (traced back to Nāgārjuna).

It appears that already at that time the Tibetans decided in favour of traditions the authentic transmission of which they considered they could clearly and confidently trace from reliable Indian sources, either written or living. But this did not involve the automatic anathematization of all Chinese traditions, as has been made clear by more than one Tibetan doxographer. Indeed, canonical texts translated from Chinese such as the *Suvarṇabhāsa* and the *Mahāparinirvāṇa* were received into the Bka' 'gyur; and an originally Chinese śāstra such as the great commentary on the *Saṃdhinirmocana* by Wŏnch'uk (Yüan-tse, 613–96) translated from Chinese by 'Go(s) Chos grub/Fa-ch'eng was included in the Bstan 'gyur.

Concerning the forms of *rdzogs chen* that became known in Tibet, what was especially open to criticism from Tibetan scholars such as Sa skya paṇḍi ta (Sa paṇ) and some of his successors was perhaps not any and every form of Great Perfection (though the origins of *rdzogs chen* were unclear and therefore controversial) but specifically what Sa paṇ termed in his *Sdom gsum rab dbye* the "Chinese style" Rdzogs chen *(rgya nag lugs kyi rdzogs chen)* that he linked with the Hva shang Mahāyāna. As for Mahāmudrā, it was certainly not all forms of this teaching, some of which Sa paṇ explicitly accepted, that were the object of his criticism, but what he describes as "latter-day" Neo-Mahāmudrā *(da lta'i phyag chen)* with its doctrine of the "Sovereign Remedy" *(dkar po chig thub),* which was also linked with the Hva shang. For, as already noted, in the "Alternative Tradition" of the *Sba bzhed* evidently used by Sa paṇ as well as in the *Chos 'byung Me tog snying po* of Nyang Nyi ma 'od zer, the *dkar po chig thub* is said to have been taught by the Hva shang Mahāyāna. It is perhaps not quite certain whether under this name of Neo-Mahāmudrā Sa skya paṇḍi ta was criticizing a teaching of Sgam po pa (1079–1153) or whether it was the more extremely "simultaneist" formulation of the Mahāmudrā and *dkar po chig thub* doctrine found with Zhang Tshal pa (1123–93) that he was attacking.

V

To suppose that Sa skya paṇḍi ta's use of the term *dkar po chig thub* and his juxtaposition of what he has termed Chinese-style Rdzogs chen and Neo-

Mahāmudrā with the Hva shang's teaching was mainly motivated by tendentious sectarianism and by polemics would seem to be excessive. In this matter, beside the problems of historiography mentioned above which arise in respect to the extant accounts of the "Great Debate" of Bsam yas, we are confronted by a problem in comparative religion and philosophy, and in particular by a question of typological affinity as distinct from direct genetic dependence.

As already noted, the expression *dkar po gcig thub*—which properly designates a unique and self-sufficient Sovereign Remedy—has been used metaphorically in several Tibetan sources to describe an "all-at-once" face-to-face encounter with and recognitive identification of innate and pure Mind *(sems ngo 'phrod pa, sems rtogs pa)* which restores one to one's true natural state by "curing" all afflictions and impurities. By Sgam po pa it was employed to describe an aspect of his Mahāmudrā teaching, and soon afterwards it was used by Zhang Tshal pa in a strongly "simultaneist" sense.

It is, as we know, found also in the "Alternative Tradition" of the *Sba bzhed,* in the *Chos 'byung* of Nyang Nyi ma 'od zer, and in that of Dpa' bo Gtsug lag phreng ba (following the "Alternative Tradition") in addition to the works of Sa skya paṇḍi ta and some of his followers, where the expression is used to characterize simultaneist understanding and recognitive identification of Mind in the Hva shang Mahāyāna's teaching.

Now, from a typological point of view, the doctrines in question do appear to be connected in a complex lattice of criss-crossing links. And they are furthermore connected with very much older doctrines, problems, and even controversies that are known from the Indian sources, some of them cited in Kamalaśīla's *Bhāvanākrama*s. The opposition between, e.g., the mystical and enstatic on the one side and the intellectual and analytical on the other, and that between fixation-*bhāvanā ('jog sgom)* and inspection-*bhāvanā (dpyad sgom),* which arise in some Tibetan discussions of the Great Debate, recall a tension between the mystical and the analytical currents in old canonical sources.

Doctrines that are typologically and structurally related are of course very often linked through direct historical derivation and branching. But, clearly, a pair of doctrines may, in addition, be connected with each other typologically without one having to be directly dependent historically on the other. The question then is: Are the links existing between the teachings ascribed to the Hva shang Mahāyāna and certain currents in Rdzogs chen and Phyag chen not only typological and structural but also historical in the sense of direct genetic derivation? Or are these links typological without any direct historical dependence having to be postulated?

This is not an easy question to answer. Briefly stated, Sa skya paṇḍi ta may have assumed not only typological and structural similarity but also historical dependence and continuity, and several of his successors appear to have made the same assumption. Klong chen pa (1308–63), the great Rdzogs chen master, on the other hand was evidently prepared to accept a certain typological and structural similarity between Rdzogs chen and the teaching of the Hva shang without, apparently, positing any sort of genetic dependence; this is natural for him since, as already noted, his Rdzogs chen school has differentiated between its Atiyoga tradition and the *cig char ba* tradition of the Hva shang (see also the *Bsam gtan mig sgron* of Gnubs chen Sangs rgyas ye shes). But other Rdzogs chen pas/Rnying ma pas have emphasized the differences more clearly, just as many Bka' brgyud pas have differentiated between Phyag chen and the teachings of the Hva shang.

VI

In the present state of our knowledge, the conclusion seems indicated that when the "theory of the Hva shang" was rebutted by masters of the Sa skya pa, Bka' brgyud pa, and Dga' ldan pa schools, and when some Rdzogs chen pa masters also distanced themselves from it and did not accept it unreservedly, their target was a somewhat dehistoricized position involving ethical and karmic quietism as well as an "ideoclasm" that tended towards intellectual nihilism and that form of impurity of theory *(dṛṣṭikaṣāya)* described as delectation in the empty *(stong pa nyid la dga' ba).* And the theory of the Hva shang was identified with the ethical quietism and "ideoclasm" combatted in texts cited by Kamalaśīla. In other words, the teachings of Mo-ho-yen, as known in Tibet chiefly through versions of the Sba records and related sources, have been taken as an instance of a *type* of theory and practice already rejected in classical sūtras and śāstras.

The existence of typological and structural affinities, and of "family resemblances," between the doctrines in question taught in Tibet and some much older doctrines found in the Śrāvakayānist and Mahāyānist canons—and in particular with the *tathāgatagarbha* doctrine (even though the latter doctrine is only sometimes explicitly evoked in the available sources on the teaching of the Hva shang Mahāyāna and on Simultaneism)—suggests that the acute and urgent problems that arose at the "Great Debate" of Bsam yas extend far beyond the specific frame of a particular eighth-century historical juncture when Indian and Chinese doctrines and masters met in Tibet. Clarification of the problems involved requires both religious and philosophical comparison bearing on the history of Buddhism in India since early times and the study of the ideas and modes of Tibetan historiography and doxography.

Important though each is, focussing exclusively on the problematic triad formed by the Hva shang, (Chinese-style) Rdzogs chen, and (Neo-) Mahāmudrā, on the "Great Debate" of Bsam yas as an occurrence in eighth-century Tibetan *histoire événementielle,* or on the Sino-Indian and Sino-Tibetan dimensions could have the undesirable effect of obscuring the question of typological affinity and the problem of the relationship between currents that are in fact very old in Buddhism.

To sum up: There exist certain typological affinities and "family resemblances" between the views ascribed to the Hva shang Mahāyāna and certain features in both Mahāmudrā and Rdzogs chen, especially in what has been described as "Neo-Mahāmudrā" and "Chinese-style Rdzogs chen." But links of direct genetic dependence are more difficult to establish clearly. The full significance of such similarities can only be revealed by historical and doxographical investigation combined with comparative typological and structural analysis. The Tibetologist has then to concern himself not only with trying to reconstruct what actually occurred at the so-called "Great Debate" of Bsam yas but with what the Tibetan historiographical and doxographical traditions considered to be the importance of this event and *topos,* that is, with its meaning for Tibetan civilization.[11]

11. For details see the present writer's 1987 Jordan Lectures published as *Buddha-nature, Mind and the Problem of Gradualism in a Comparative Perspective* (London: School of Oriental and African Studies, University of London, 1989).

11. Autour du *Lta ba'i khyad par* de Ye shes sde

(Version de Touen-houang, Pelliot tibétain 814)*

I

L'APPARITION sur la scène historique des Tibétains en tant que peuple possédant une langue écrite et une littérature abondante est accompagnée de problèmes qui attendent une investigation approfondie. Cet événement, qui fut aussi d'une très grande importance pour l'histoire du bouddhisme et de la Haute Asie, semble s'être produit assez abruptement, sans une longue période de préparation, dans la deuxième moitié du VIIIe siècle. L'une des questions que le tibétologue se doit donc de poser concerne les circonstances et les modalités de l'introduction et de l'assimilation au Tibet de ce qu'on pourrait appeler la civilisation indo-bouddhique.

Comme on le sait, l'historiographie tibétaine fait souvent remonter les origines du bouddhisme au Tibet à une époque beaucoup plus reculée, celle d'un roi nommé Lha Tho tho ri Gnyan btsan qui aurait vécu cinq générations avant Srong btsan sgam po (mort au milieu du VIIe siècle). Certaines sources parlent par ailleurs d'un personnage plus ancien semble-t-il, et passablement mystérieux, le maître Śrī-Siṃha de la lignée des Rnying ma pa qui aurait vécu avant Padmasambhava, peut-être même au IVe siècle selon quelques témoignages.[1] D'autre part, les Tibétains rattachent l'origine de leur écriture, qui dérive d'un modèle indien, ainsi que de leur théorie grammaticale à un nommé Thu mi/Thon mi, dont l'activité de lettré à l'époque de Srong btsan sgam po aurait rendu possible, déjà au VIIe siècle, une pénétration profonde de la pensée bouddhique au Tibet.[2]

* First published in *Journal asiatique,* Année 1981 (Numéro spécial: Actes du Colloque International, Manuscrits et Inscriptions de Haute Asie, Paris, 1979), pp. 207–29.

1. Vimalamitra et le Tibétain Vairocana sont cependant considérés comme des disciples au VIIIe siècle de Śrī-Siṃha. Le problème reste à éclaircir.

2. Voir aussi les remarques de Marcelle Lalou, «Chine et Tibet aux VIIe, VIIIe et IXe

Ces traditions plus ou moins historiques consignées dans les Chos 'byung et dans d'autres documents classiques nous donnent de l'implantation au Tibet de la civilisation indo-bouddhique sinon la «légende dorée», du moins sans doute une image quelque peu schématisée et idéalisée. Quoi qu'il en soit, il ne semble guère possible de placer avant la deuxième partie du VIIIe siècle la grande éclosion de la culture tibétaine en tant que civilisation du livre ayant des liens étroits avec l'Inde. C'est aussi à partir de cette époque que l'existence de cette civilisation est clairement attestée par de nombreux documents.

Ce sont surtout les textes tibétains trouvés dans la région de Touen-houang, notamment par Aurel Stein et Paul Pelliot, qui nous permettent d'asseoir l'étude de cette période sur la base solide de documents écrits contemporains ou relativement proches des événements relatés.[3] À côté de quelques inscriptions anciennes ils sont en effet les plus anciens documents tibétains dont nous disposions.

Les textes de Touen-houang qui concernent plus spécialement le problème de la transmission et de l'assimilation au Tibet de la civilisation indo-bouddhique sont essentiellement de deux sortes: 1° les anciennes traductions tibétaines de sūtra et śāstra (traduites soit sur des originaux indiens, soit sur des versions chinoises d'originaux indiens); 2° les ouvrages les plus anciens à caractère religieux et philosophique dûs aux premiers auteurs tibétains.[4] La majorité des textes de la première catégorie se trouvent naturellement non seulement dans les fonds de manuscrits de Touen-houang mais aussi, sous une forme plus ou moins révisée ou modifiée selon les cas, dans les éditions du Bka' 'gyur et du Bstan 'gyur que nous connaissons. Quant aux écrits anciens de la deuxième catégorie, bien qu'il s'agisse

siècles», *Journal des savants,* octobre–décembre 1965, p. 636 et suiv.

3. Voir surtout M. Lalou, *Inventaire des manuscrits tibétains de Touen-houang conservés à la Bibliothèque Nationale (Fonds Pelliot tibétain),* tomes I–III (Paris, 1939, 1950 et 1961); A. Macdonald et Y. Imaeda, *Choix de documents tibétains,* tomes I–II (Paris, 1978–79); L. de La Vallée Poussin, *Tibetan Manuscripts from Tun-huang in the India Office Library* (Oxford-London, 1962) (manuscrits de la deuxième expédition Stein). (Pour notre enquête les matériaux tibétains rapportés de la région de Khotan, Mazār Tagh, etc., par les expéditions allemandes dites de Tourfan ne semblent pas entrer directement en ligne de compte dans la mesure où ils ne renferment pas de textes littéraires; sur ces matériaux voir récemment M. Taube, *Proceedings of the Csoma de Kőrös Memorial Symposium* [Budapest, 1978], p. 487 et suiv. Sur les collections soviétiques voir V. S. Vorob'ev-Desjatovskij, *AN SSSR* 5 [1953]. et *Epigrafika vostoka* 8 [1953]).

4. Un autre document ancien témoignant de l'influence au Tibet de la civilisation indienne est la version tibétaine de l'épopée de Rāma trouvée à Touen-houang.

non pas de traductions mais de compositions tibétaines originales, plusieurs ont été incorporés au Bstan 'gyur,[5] dans la section des Ngo tshar bstan bcos.[6]

Les traductions en question sont l'œuvre notamment de (s)Ka ba Dpal brtsegs, de Cog ro Klu'i rgyal mtshan et de Sna nam Zhang Ye shes sde.[7] Elles furent exécutées par ces lo tsā ba ou traducteurs en collaboration avec des paṇḍits indiens comme Jinamitra, Śīlendrabodhi, Dānaśīla, Jñānagarbha et Prajñāvarman.

Dpal brtsegs nous est connu en outre comme l'auteur d'un des plus anciens manuels de philosophie bouddhique d'origine tibétaine: le *Lta ba'i rim pa bshad pa* conservé dans le Bstan 'gyur (six feuillets dans l'édition de Pékin, tome ngo, n° 5853) dont le titre exact selon son colophon est *Lta ba'i rim pa'i man ngag.*[8] Dpal brtsegs collabora aussi à la composition du *Ldan dkar ma,* catalogue de la bibliothèque du palais de Stong thang ldan dkar.[9]

À Cog ro Klu'i rgyal mtshan on attribue parfois le grand commentaire du *Saṃdhinirmocanasūtra* que des catalogues du Bstan 'gyur ont rattaché au nom d'Asaṅga.[10]

Ye shes sde est l'auteur d'un autre traité sur les doctrines philosophiques

5. Déjà le *Ldan dkar ma* (v. ci-dessous, note 9) contient des ouvrages d'origine tibétaine, comme le fait aussi le catalogue du Bstan 'gyur de Bu ston Rin chen grub *(Bstan 'gyur gyi dkar chag yid bzhin nor bu dbang gi rgyal po'i phreng ba,* Gsung 'bum, la, fol. 117a–118a).

6. Cf. par exemple Zhu chen Tshul khrims rin chen, *Sde dge'i bstan 'gyur gyi dkar chag,* Delhi, 1974, fol. 464a4–b2.

7. Ces trois maîtres tibétains sont mentionnés ensemble dans le *Sba bzhed* (éd. R. A. Stein, Paris, 1961), p. 73, et dans le *Mkhas pa'i dga' ston,* ja, fol. 125a, où Dpa' bo Gtsug lag phreng ba précise qu'il s'agit des trois Lo tsā ba «jeunes» (les trois Lo tsā ba «anciens» étant Vairocana, Ldan ma rtse mang et Kha che Ānanda, et les trois Lo tsā ba «intermédiaires» étant Gnyags Jñānakumāra, Khon Klu'i dbang po et Rma Rin chen mchog).

8. Cf. Bu ston, *Bstan 'gyur gyi dkar chag,* fol. 117a5. (Pékin n° 4728 est le même texte.) Dpa' bo Gtsug lag phreng ba, *Mkhas pa'i dga ston,* ja, fol. 124b, mentionne en outre le *Gsung rab rin po che'i gtam,* le *Phyi yul dran rgyud du yod par 'dod pa sel ba* et le *Mtshan nyid gsum mdor bstan,* qui pourraient aussi être de Dpal brtsegs. Avec Cog ro Klu'i rgyal mtshan Dpal brtsegs aurait aussi composé le *Brgal lan bzhi phrugs* (ibid.).

9. Voir Bu ston, *Bstan 'gyur gyi dkar chag,* fol. 117b3. Ce texte a été édité par M. Lalou, *JA* 1953 (qui écrit par erreur Stod thang au lieu de Stong thang et l'attribue a l'époque de Khri Srong lde btsan, alors que G. Tucci le place plutôt en l'an 812, a l'époque de Khri Lde srong btsan; voir Tucci, *Minor Buddhist Texts,* II, Rome, 1958, p. 46n1).

10. Voir Bu ston, *Chos 'byung,* fol. 160a–b, et *Bstan 'gyur gyi dkar chag,* fol. 117a–b; Dpa' bo Gtsug lag phreng ba, *Mkhas pa'i dga' ston,* ja, fol. 124b6. Dans le même contexte le dernier auteur mentionne aussi le *Nges pa'i don dbu ma,* le *Shes phyin mdor bsdus,* etc.

du bouddhisme remontant à la même époque environ, mais beaucoup plus long et développé que le manuel de Dpal brtsegs: le *Lta ba'i khyad par* conservé également dans le Bstan 'gyur (18 feuillets dans l'édition de Pékin, tome cho, n° 5847).[11] De cet ouvrage nous avons la chance de posséder aussi un manuscrit trouvé à Touen-houang et conservé aujourd'hui dans le fonds tibétain de la Bibliothèque Nationale à Paris (Pelliot tibétain 814).[12] Ce manuscrit, auquel manque la deuxième partie du texte (voir ci-dessous), n'indique ni le titre ni le nom de l'auteur. Pourtant, à des variantes textuelles et quelques autres divergences près, il s'agit bien d'un ouvrage identique à celui qui est incorporé au Bstan 'gyur sous le titre de *Lta ba'i khyad par.* En ce qui concerne l'attribution au *mkhan po* Ye shes sde qui est attestée dans les éditions du Bstan 'gyur, elle est confirmée par les catalogues de ce recueil par Bu ston Rin chen grub (1290–1364)[13] et par son disciple Rin chen rnam rgyal (1318–88),[14] ainsi que par l'histoire de Dpa' bo Gtsug lag phreng ba (1504–66).[15]

En tant que grand traducteur-rédacteur *(zhu chen gyi lo tsā ba)* responsable de très nombreuses versions tibétaines de sūtra et de śāstra, le *bande* Ye shes sde collabora aussi à la composition du *Sgra sbyor bam gnyis,* ouvrage qui devait servir de guide officiel à l'usage des traducteurs tibétains et qui fut

11. Comme titre sanscrit dans le Bstan 'gyur cet ouvrage porte le nom de «*Dṛṣṭiviśeṣa*», mais à lui seul le fait qu'il ait reçu un titre sanscrit dans ce recueil ne saurait prouver que l'ouvrage fut d'abord composé en sanscrit.

Le *Lta ba'i khyad par* manque dans le *Ldan dkar ma.* Un traité dont le titre est presque identique—*Lta ba'i bye brag*—mais qui est attribué à Nyi ma'i 'od figure dans le *Ldan dkar ma* n° 679 (édition de M. Lalou, *JA* 1953, p. 335); cf. aussi L. de La Vallée Poussin, *Tibetan Manuscripts from Tun-huang,* n° 607.

12. Des fragments du *Lta ba'i khyad par* se trouvent aussi dans la collection Stein de l'India Office Library à Londres. Voir L. de La Vallée Poussin, *Tibetan Manuscripts from Tun-huang,* n° 692 (= Pelliot tibétain 814, fol. 10b–11a) et n° 694 (= id., fol. 5b4 sq.).

Sur ce traité voir Y. Imaeda, *JA* 1975, p. 132sq.; et Ueyama Daishun, «Eseide no bukkyō kōyō-sho», *Bukkyō kenkyū* 32–33 (1977), p. 19–45, qui a publié les fol. 1–15a1 du Pelliot tibétain 814. La présente communication au Colloque international sur les manuscrits et inscriptions de Haute Asie du Ve au XIe siècle a été écrite sans que j'aie pu avoir accès à l'étude de M. Ueyama, qui a eu l'amabilité de me la communiquer après le colloque. Qu'il veuille bien trouver ici l'expression de ma reconnaissance.

13. *Bstan 'gyur gyi dkar chag,* fol. 117b.

14. *Bstan 'gyur ro 'chal gyi dkar chag yid bzhin nor bu rin po che'i za ma tog,* Gsung 'bum, sa, fol. 111b.

15. *Mkhas pa'i dga' ston,* ja, fol. 124b6.

écrit à l'époque de Khri Lde srong btsan (Sad na legs).[16] Ye shes sde appartint au clan illustre des Sna nam[17] qui fut lié par mariage à la maison royale—fait qu'indique le titre *(thabs)* de *zhang* avant son nom[18]—et qui fournit des ministres à l'État.[19]

À côté de l'ouvrage de Dpal brtsegs mentionné plus haut, le *Lta ba'i khyad par* de Ye shes sde est donc le traité tibétain le plus ancien du genre des Grub mtha' que nous connaissions.[20]

Comme l'autorité et l'ancienneté du *Lta ba'i khyad par* sont garanties par sa présence à la fois dans le recueil canonique du Bstan 'gyur et parmi les manuscrits de Touen-houang, ce document revêt pour nous un intérêt très

16. Voir N. Simonsson, *Indo-tibetische Studien,* I (Uppsala, 1957); D. Seyfort Ruegg, «On translating the Buddhist canon», in *Indo-Asian art and culture* (Acarya Raghu Vira commemoration volume, éd. Perala Ratnam, Śatapiṭaka Series, t. 209, New Delhi, 1973), p. 243 et suiv.

17. Voir, par exemple, le *Sba bzhed,* p. 73.7.

18. Voir, par exemple, le colophon de la traduction par Ye shes sde des *Mūlasarvāstivāda-śrāmaṇerakārikā* de Nāgārjuna (Pékin, n° 5629); Dpa' bo Gtsug lag phreng ba, *Mkhas pa'i dga 'ston,* ja, fol. 124b6; Bu ston, *Bstan 'gyur gyi dkar chag,* fol. 117b2.

19. Sur les Sna nam voir J. Bacot, F. W. Thomas et Ch. Toussaint, *Documents de Touen-houang relatifs à l'histoire du Tibet* (Paris, 1940–46), p. 82, 89 (sur une princesse du clan Sna nam comme mère de Khri Srong lde btsan; cf. P. Demiéville, *Le concile de Lhasa,* Paris, 1952, p. 9n); l'édit de Dkar chung (de 814); *Sba bzhed,* p. 40, 42; E. Haarh, *AO* 25 (1960), p. 158–63; H. Richardson, *Tibet Journal* 2 (1977), p. 10 et suiv. M. Richardson discute entre autres le clan des Sna nam en tant que *zhang* liés par mariage avec la famille royale (p. 15) et le Grand Ministre Sna nam Zhang Rgyal tsha(n) Lha snang mort en 796 (p. 18, 22), ainsi que la question de l'origine étrangère du clan (Sna nam = Samarkand) (p. 22) et ses liens avec le bouddhisme et Bsam yas (p. 21–22). Il paraît difficile de caractériser tout un clan comme favorable (ou hostile) au bouddhisme.

20. Dpa' bo Gtsug lag phreng ba mentionne en outre un *Grub mtha' dkrol ba* composé à l'époque de Khri Srong lde btsan (*Mkhas pa'i dga' ston,* ja, fol. 124b1); il doit s'agir de l'ouvrage enregistré dans le *Ldan dkar ma* (n° 727 de l'édition de M. Lalou, *JA* 1953, p. 336). Mentionnons ici en outre deux textes de Dpal dbyangs qui portent des titres semblables, mais qui sont d'un tout autre genre, le *Lta ba rin po che sgron ma* (Pékin n° 5923) et le *Lta ba yang dag sgron ma* (Pékin n° 5919). Sur le *Lta ba'i rim pa* de Nyi ma'i 'od (cf. *Ldan dkar ma* n° 679) et le *Lta ba'i sa chod* de Thogs med, voir La Vallée Poussin, *Tibetan Manuscripts from Tun-huang,* n° 607. Voir aussi M. Lalou, *Inventaire,* n° 116.

Dpa' bo Gtsug lag (*Mkhas pa'i dga' ston,* fol. 124b6) attribue trois autres ouvrages à Ye shes sde: le *Bzang spyod kyi 'grel pa bzhi'i don bsdus* (Pékin n° 5846), le *'Jig rten pha rol sgrub pa* (voir *Ldan dkar ma* n°680; le texte du même nom par Dharmottara fut traduit par Dpal brtsegs), et le *Dgongs ldem dgongs bzhi'i brjed byang* (voir *Ldan dkar ma n°* 564). Le Bstan 'gyur lui attribue en outre le *Sangs rgyas gco'i rgya cher 'grel pa* (Pékin n° 5848).

particulier, et il peut nous aider à formuler une réponse à trois questions d'une grande actualité pour la tibétologie:

- Quels sont les thèmes qui intéressèrent l'un des premiers auteurs tibétains d'ouvrages philosophiques?
- Quelles indications ce document nous fournit-il sur le degré d'assimilation de la civilisation indo-bouddhique, et notamment de sa philosophie, au Tibet vers le début du VIIIe siècle (question qui revêt un intérêt particulier compte tenu de la rapidité de l'introduction et de la propagation de cette civilisation au Tibet)?
- Cet ouvrage renferme-t-il des traits spécifiques qui le différencieraient de ses précurseurs d'origine indienne (question fondamentale pour la question de la transmission interculturelle)?

II

Avant de considérer ces questions en analysant le *Lta ba'i khyad par* de Ye shes sde, il faut donner quelques brèves indications sur les deux versions de ce traité, l'une manuscrite et l'autre imprimée dans les différentes éditions du Bstan 'gyur.[21]

Ainsi qu'on l'a déjà relevé plus haut, le manuscrit Pelliot tibétain 814 de la Bibliothèque Nationale à Paris ne porte pas de titre. Et le nom de l'auteur manque ainsi que toute la dernière partie du traité, le manuscrit se terminant (avec un *bzhi shad*) au milieu d'une phrase de la section consacrée aux huit connaissances *(vijñāna)* vers la fin de l'exposé sur l'*ālayavijñāna,* et immédiatement avant l'exposé sur le *kliṣṭamanas* (M 32b2; P 263b1). Pourtant, à des variantes et quelques autres divergences près, la partie du traité contenue dans le Pelliot tibétain 814 correspond à la première partie du texte conservé dans le Bstan 'gyur, où il porte le titre de *Lta ba'i khyad par* et est attribué au *mkhan po* Ye shes sde.[22] Des portions du texte imprimé dans le Bstan 'gyur sont en désordre.[23]

21. Dans la suite les sigles M, P et C désignent respectivement le manuscrit Pelliot tibétain 814, le Bstan 'gyur de Pékin (réimpression dans *Tibetan Tripiṭaka,* Tōkyō et Kyōto, 1955 et suiv.), et le Bstan 'gyur de Co ne (microfiches de l'Institute for Advanced Study of World Religions, New York, 1974).

22. Sur l'attribution de ce traité dans les catalogues du Bstan 'gyur à Ye shes sde voir ci-dessus.

23. C'est du moins le cas pour les éditions de Pékin et de Co ne, les seules que j'aie pu consulter. De plus, une portion de la section sur la doctrine de Bhavya (correspondant à

Comme le Pelliot tibétain 814 se termine au milieu d'une phrase et que plus de la moitié du dernier feuillet est blanc, il est possible que son scribe ait copié un original incomplet. Et il n'est pas certain que notre manuscrit représente une première ébauche, encore incomplète, du traité. Il faut pourtant remarquer que ce manuscrit contient tous les thèmes annoncés dans la table des matières figurant en tête de l'ouvrage et, en plus, une partie d'une cinquième section sur les huit *vijñāna* qui n'y figure pas. La version imprimée du Bstan 'gyur contient en outre plusieurs sections qui manquent au manuscrit, comme on l'a déjà relevé plus haut (voir aussi l'analyse du traité donnée ci-dessous).

Le Pelliot tibétain 814 est un manuscrit assez bien écrit, et presque toujours lisible. Il se caractérise par des archaïsmes orthographiques courants dans les manuscrits de Touen-houang, qui ne sont pas reproduits dans la version imprimée du Bstan 'gyur de Pékin et de Co ne. Ainsi, avant *i* et *e*, *m* s'écrit régulièrement avec le *ya btags* (exemples: *myi, myig, dmyigs, myed,* etc.). On trouve parfois la graphie *mye ngan las 'das pa* (10a4, b2), mais aussi la graphie *mya ngan las 'da' ba* (11a5). Quant au *da drag,* il n'est écrit que rarement—par exemple *gyurd pa* (1a4)[24] et *bka' scald to* (29b2)—mais on en rencontre des traces multiples—par exemple *bstan to* (27a1), *'gyur to* (29a2, à l'opposé de *'gyur ro* qu'on trouve immédiatement avant, 29a2, immédiatement après, 29a3, et passim).[25] Parfois, à la fin d'un syntagme ou d'une phrase, un *'a chung* s'écrit à la fin d'un mot après une voyelle, là où on ne le trouve pas dans l'orthographe classique (par exemple: *pa'/, ba'/, bya'/, so'//*[26]). Dans 6b5, *de'is = de yis.*

On trouve plusieurs autres graphies remarquables dans le Pelliot tibétain 814. Signalons entre autres *las (b)scogs pa = la sogs pa; phun gsum* (12a3, 28a5) = *phun sum; mngon gsum* (1a4) = *mngon sum; gsum car* (32a2) = *gsum char; the tsom* (16a2) = *the tshom; ci lta(r)* (3b1, 7b5, 24b4) = *ji lta(r); nam ka* (3b3) = *nam mkha'; tha snyan* (2b1, 7b4) = *tha snyad.*[27] On peut

---

M 7a1–b3) manque dans P et C. Il est difficile d'expliquer exactement comment le texte imprimé est tombé en désordre puisque les décalages portent aussi sur des morceaux très courts, et en tout cas plus petits que le feuillet d'un manuscrit comme le Pelliot tibétain 814.

24. Ici le manuscrit est difficile à lire.

25. Dans 13a3, l'orthographe *ched po = chen po* est à noter.

26. M 8a5, 10a1, où le *'a chung* est souscrit. M. Ueyama transcrit *rigs paḥo* (p. 34) et *rtogs poḥ* (p. 35); mais P et C portent *rigs so* et *rtogs so.*

27. Mais on trouve aussi *tha snyad* (17a4).

aussi relever la variante *rtsas bcad* (11a1) = *rtsad bcad* (P254b5).[28] Dans 10b2, *bskyab* = *bsgrub* n'est vraisemblablement qu'une faute de copie.

Parmi les transcriptions du sanscrit il faut relever 'Ba' phyva (4b5) / 'Ba' phya (5a5) = Bhavya (nom propre).

À côté du *gi gu* avec son crochet à gauche on rencontre assez souvent le *gi gu* avec son crochet à droite; mais aucune règle linguistique ne semble présider au choix de ces deux signes.[29] L'écriture n'est pas uniforme du début à la fin du manuscrit (lequel est peut-être l'œuvre de plus d'un scribe).

En ce qui concerne l'état du texte du *Lta ba'i khyad par,* on trouve des défectuosités tant dans la version de Touen-houang que dans les éditions imprimées du Bstan 'gyur. Pour établir le texte de ce traité il faudrait donc utiliser toutes les versions disponibles.

III

D'après sa table des matières liminaire (M 1a1–2; P 252a5–6), le *Lta ba'i khyad par* doit traiter succinctement *(mdo tsam zhig)* des différentes thèses philosophiques concernant l'existence d'un objet extérieur etc., ainsi que des trois Véhicules et des trois *kāya,* et ce sur la base d'enseignements recueillis par son auteur auprès de ses maîtres *(mkhan po = upādhyāya)* et puisés aux sūtra et aux śāstra. Comme on l'a déjà relevé, le manuscrit Pelliot tibétain 814 aussi bien que la version imprimée des différentes éditions du Bstan 'gyur traitent en plus d'autres thèmes. Voici l'analyse du traité.

1. *Les écoles philosophiques* (M 1a3–9b1; P 252a6 sq.)
1° *Thèse de l'existence de l'objet extérieur (phyi rol gyi don yod par smra ba = bāhyārthavāda)* (M 1a3–3a1; P 255b4 sq.). Cette théorie fait état des quatre éléments (terre, eau, feu, air) ainsi que de la matière *(gzugs = rūpa)* qui en est le résultat etc. Il y est encore question de la perception directe *(mngon sum = pratyakṣa),* autrement dit du moyen de connaissance valide *(tshad ma = pramāṇa)* qui constate l'existence objective des facteurs précédents. Puis on parle des catégories de l'analyse philosophique: les cinq agrégats *(phung po =*

28. C (220b2) porte *brtsad.*

29. Comparer, par exemple, *myed pa'ï gtan tshigs* (2a2)/ *myed pa'i dus* (3a4); *byung ba'ï/* (1a2)/ *'byung ba'i bdag* (3a2); *don dam par nï* (7a3)/ *kun rdzob tu ni* (7a2); *thabs nï/* (10a2)/ *lugs* ni/(7a1); *theg pa nï/*(9b3)/ *theg pa ni/*(10b4); *bshïg na/*(8b1)/ *bshig la/* (2a3); *'dï lta ste/*(26b1, 3)/ *'di lta ste/*(24b6); *zhï ba'i blo gros* (26b4)/ *zhi ba'i blo gros* (26a5); etc. Ces exemples sont donnés à titre indicatif seulement.

skandha), les domaines *(khams = dhātu)* et les bases *(skye mched = āyatana)* où sont incluses les facultés (cinq sensorielles et une mentale) avec leurs objets *(yul = viṣaya)* (M 1a3–1b2; P 255b4 sq.). Or, si le *rūpa* et les autres facteurs étaient aussi inexistants qu'une corne de lièvre *(ri bong gi rva = śaśaśṛṅga),* comme le soutiennent les opposants de la thèse réaliste, c'est la connaissance *(rnam par shes pa = vijñāna)* elle-même qui se manifesterait comme les objets *(de ltar snang ba);* mais s'il en était vraiment ainsi, il n'existerait pas de base objective pour une méprise à l'endroit du *rūpa (gzugs su 'khrul pa'i gzhi).* Par conséquent, on ne saurait soutenir que la connaissance se manifeste sous forme objective (M 1b3–2a1; P 255b sq.). Les arguments d'ordre épistémologique et logique cités en faveur de la thèse réaliste de l'existence d'objets ayant le même statut ontologique que la connaissance sont dirigés contre la thèse du «rien que connaissance». Et si certains sūtra ont effectivement déclaré qu'il n'existe pas d'objet et que c'est le *citta* qui se manifeste ainsi, cela signifie non pas que tout objet extérieur soit nié, mais qu'il faut avoir un contecarrant *(gnyen po = pratipakṣa)* contre la position *('jin pa = grāha)* de l'impermanent comme permanent et du composé comme corps compact *(ril po = piṇḍa)* (M 2a3–3a1; P 254b–255a).

2° *La doctrine du Vijñānamātra (rnam par shes pa tsam) ou «rien que connaissance»* (M 3a1–4b1; P 255a2 sq.). Suivant cette thèse, il n'existe pas d'objet extérieur *(phyi rol gyi don = bāhyārtha)* à la connaissance, et consistant en *rūpa,* etc.; c'est la connaissance elle-même qui se manifeste comme les objets. Ce que, dans la pratique courante du monde[30] et même dans les śāstra, on désigne comme «soi» et comme les *dharma,* n'est donc qu'une transformation du *vijñāna (rnam par shes pa gyur pa).* Les traces *(bag chags = vāsanā)* consistant en construction imaginaire *(rtog pa)* d'un «soi» et des *dharma* s'appuient sur l'*ālayavijñāna,* à partir duquel surgit la construction dichotomisante *(rnam par rtog pa = vikalpa)* qui pose l'apparition du «soi» et des *dharma;* il n'y a donc pas d'objet *(yul med do)* (M 3a3–b1; P 255a2–4). On cite à ce propos le *Daśabhūmikasūtra*[31] aussi bien que le *Ghanavyūha* et le *Laṅkāvatārasūtra* (M 3b4–4a3; P 255a). Ce *vijñāna* naît en dépendance *(rten cing 'brel par 'byung ba),* et il est permanent par continuité *(rgyun gyi rtag pa = pravāhanitya);* il existe donc au sens absolu *(don dam par yod).* Quand il s'est transformé *(gnas gyur pa'i dus na),* il est libre de l'objet saisi et du sujet saisissant *(gzung ba dang 'jin pa las dben pa),* la Gnose *(jñāna)* sans dualité *(gnyis su med pa'i ye shes)* étant ce qui est véritablement établi

30. *Jig rten na grags pa: lokaprasiddha.*

31. *Daśabhūmikasūtra,* chapitre VI: *cittamātram idaṃ yad idaṃ traidhātukam.*

(pariniṣpanna) sans erreur *(phyin ci ma log par yongs su grub pa yod do)* (M 4a3–5; P 255a–b).

3° *Le Madhyamaka, dont il existe deux divisions* (M 4b1–9b1; P 255b1 sq., avec lacune). Nāgārjuna (IIe siècle?) et son disciple Āryadeva ont tout d'abord composé les śāstra du Madhyamaka; il n'y avait pas alors de division dans l'école (M 4b1–2; P 255b1–2). Puis Ārya Asaṅga (IVe siècle) et Vasubandhu ont composé les śāstra du Vijñānamātra; ils ont établi qu'il n'existe pas d'objet *(yul)* extérieur et que c'est le *vijñāna* lui-même qui se manifeste comme objet, le *vijñāna* pur et sans dualité existant au sens absolu (M 4b2–4; P 255b2–3). Ensuite Bhavya (Bhā(va)viveka, VIe siècle), qui a reçu la tradition de Nāgārjuna, a réfuté le Vijñānamātra. Son commentaire des *Madhyamakakārikā* s'appelle le *Prajñāpradīpa;* il a aussi composé le *Madhyamakahṛdaya* (M 4b4–5a2; P 255b3–252a7). Quant à Śāntarakṣita (VIIIe siècle), il s'est appuyé sur le Yogācāra—le śāstra du Vijñānamātra—d'Ārya Asaṅga. Conformément à ce dernier il a établi le «rien que connaissance» au niveau de surface *(kun rdzob = saṃvṛti).* Mais dans son *Madhyamakālaṃkāra* il explique que, au sens absolu *(don dam pa = paramārtha),* le *vijñāna* aussi est sans nature propre *(rang bzhin med pa)* (M 5a2–5; P 252a7–b1). Ainsi le Madhyamakaśāstra s'est développé dans deux systèmes *(lugs)* quelque peu différents. Celui établi par Bhavya a reçu le nom de Mdo sde [spyod] pa'i dbu ma,[32] et celui établi par Śāntarakṣita a reçu le nom de Rnal 'byor spyod pa'i dbu ma (M 5a5–b1; P 252b1–2).

(A) Les traités de Nāgārjuna et d'Āryadeva suivent l'Ārya-prajñāpāramitā: parce que, en principe, les entités *(dngos po = bhāva)* naissent en dépendance [de causes et conditions], au niveau de surface il y a naissance simplement à la manière d'une projection illusoire *(sgyu ma = māyā);* mais au sens absolu il n'y a naissance ni de soi-même, ni d'un autre, ni de ces deux ensemble, ni sans cause.[33] Et il n'y a donc pas de nature propre. Les deux divisions du Madhyamaka se fondent sur ce principe (M 5b1–4; P 252b).

(B) L'un de ces systèmes, le Yogācāra-Madhyamaka (Rnal 'byor spyod pa'i dbu ma), est d'accord avec le Vijñānamātravāda au niveau de surface. La connaissance *(rnam par shes pa = vijñāna)* connaît l'objet *(yul = viṣaya),* et cet objet a la nature de la connaissance. En vertu donc de cette connexion [essentielle entre connaissance et objet] il peut y avoir connaissance par le *svasaṃvedana (rang gi rig pa);* au contraire, si l'on soutient que l'objet est autre [que la connaissance], parce qu'il n'y aurait alors pas de connexion avec

32. Ici (5a6) M porte *spyod,* qui manque dans P et C; plus loin cependant M lit *mdo sde dbu ma* (7a1).

33. Voir *Mūlamadhyamakakārikā* i.1.

la connaissance, cette connaissance ne serait pas possible (M 5b4–6a1; P 252b7–8). —L'auteur du *Lta ba'i khyad par* expose cette doctrine en citant de nombreux textes scripturaires tirés du *Laṅkāvatārasūtra* etc., qui doivent servir à montrer qu'elle n'est pas contraire aux sūtra (M 6a1–7a1; P 253a).

(C) Le deuxième système, le *Sautrāntika-Madhyamaka (Mdo sde [pa'i] dbu ma), suit le système de Nāgārjuna en enseignant que toute entité—qu'elle soit intérieure (psychique) ou extérieure (matérielle)—naît en dépendance. Naissant de causes et conditions au niveau de surface, une entité existe en tant que simple projection illusoire *(sgyu ma tsam du yod);* mais au sens absolu elle ne saurait naître ni de soi-même, ni de l'autre, ni de ces deux ensemble, ni sans cause (M 7a1–3).[34] Pour ces quatre raisons *(gtan chigs)* il n'y a pas de naissance [au sens substantialiste du terme]; et parler de naissance n'est donc que simple désignation conforme à la convention pragmatique (M *tha snyan brjod pa tsam,* 7b4; P *tha snyad btags pa tsam,* 253a8). Cette école réfute aussi par des raisonnements *ad absurdum* la doctrine du Vijñānamātra selon laquelle les objets *(yul)* ne sont que des manifestations du *citta (sems)* ou *vijñāna* (M7b5–8a4; P 253a–b). Elle fait en outre remarquer que des traces *(vāsanā)*—qui, selon la thèse des opposants, sont depuis toujours posées par construction imaginaire comme *rūpa* etc., et apparaissent sous forme objective en vertu de leur maturation—ne sauraient être posées de la sorte en l'absence des objets en question, et que dans ce cas ces traces n'existeraient pas (M 8b1–3; P 253b4–5). Quant au passage déjà cité du *Daśabhūmikasūtra*[35] où il est dit que le triple monde n'est que *citta,* il sert uniquement à nier l'existence d'un agent *(byed pa po = kartṛ)* et d'un jouisseur *(za ba po = bhoktṛ)* [indépendants]. Car ce qui naît, naît en dépendance; et en comprenant le *pratītyasamutpāda,* on comprend qu'il n'y existe ni *ātman,* ni *jīva,* ni *pudgala,* et que tout est Vide d'être propre *(svabhāvaśūnya),* par suite de quoi le *śūnyatāvimokṣamukha (stong pa nyid kyi rnam par thar pa'i sgo)* prend naissance (M 8b4–9a1; P 253b). Par ailleurs, selon le *Laṅkāvatārasūtra,* les enseignements portant sur le «réalisme» et sur le «mentalisme» ne servent tous les deux qu'à l'entraînement des disciples (M 9a1–2).[36]

(D) Enfin, Kamalaśīla (deuxième moitié du VIIIe siècle) est l'auteur du *Madhyamakāloka.* Selon lui, encore que les deux formes du Madhyamaka

34. Cette portion de la section sur Bhavya manque dans P et C.

35. Ci-dessus, note 31.

36. M 9a2: *dngos po don dam par yod par 'dogs pa dang/ sems tsam du bshad pas . . .* Mais P et C lisent: *dngos po don dam par yod par 'dod pa dgag pa dang/ . . .* «la négation de la doctrine de l'existence au sens absolu des entités et l'enseignement du "rien que pensée" . . . ».

qui viennent d'être mentionnées diffèrent légèrement en ce qui concerne le niveau de surface, elles sont d'accord pour dire que, au sens absolu, toutes les entités—intérieures aussi bien qu'extérieures—sont sans nature propre. Et il n'y a donc pas de contradiction entre elles (M 9a4–b1; P 254a2–3).[37]

2. *Les Véhicules* (M 9b1–15a1; P 254a3–257a6)
Les trois Véhicules *(theg pa = yāna)* sont le Śrāvakayāna, le Pratyekabuddhayāna et le Mahāyāna.

1° Le Véhicule de l'Auditeur *(nyan thos = śrāvaka)* procède au moyen des quatre vérités *(bden pa = satya)* (M 9b3–10b3; P 254a4–b4).

2° Le Véhicule du Buddha-pour-soi *(rang sangs rgyas = pratyekabuddha)* procède au moyen des douze membres *(yan lag = aṅga)* de la production en dépendance *(pratītyasamutpāda)* (M 10b4–11b5; P 254b4 sq.). Citations du *Vibhīṣaṇavyākaraṇa* et de la *Yogācāraṭīkā.*

3° Le Grand Véhicule *(theg pa chen po = mahāyāna)* (M 11b5–13a3; P 256a4–b3). Le Mahāyāna se rapporte à la compréhension de l'insubstantialité *(rang bzhin med pa)* au sens absolu de toute entité, et à la réalisation de la non-dualité *(gnyis su med pa)* de *saṃsāra* et *nirvāṇa.* Au niveau de surface on perçoit *(dmigs pa: ālamb-)* toute entité comme une simple projection illusoire, et on est alors doué à la fois de la connaissance discriminatrice *(shes rab = prajñā)* et de la compassion *(snying rje = karuṇā).* Sans rejeter le *saṃsāra* ni saisir le *nirvāṇa,* on pratique les dix perfections *(pāramitā)* pour le bien de tous les êtres animés; et on accomplit ainsi le bien parfait de soi-même et d'autrui. Le Mahāyāna consiste en les dix terres *(sa = bhūmi)* du Bodhisattva, et en la *buddha-bhūmi* comme fruit. La qualification «grand» se rapporte à la supériorité du Mahāyāna par rapport aux Véhicules du Śrāvaka et du Pratyekabuddha, supériorité qui revêt sept formes (M 12a5–13a3; P 256a6–b3).[38]

37. Il est intéressant de noter que, tout comme le *Lta ba'i rim pa bshad pa* de Dpal brtsegs, le *Lta ba'i khyad par* ne fait pas allusion à l'école de Buddhapālita et de Candrakīrti. Et les termes de Rang rgyud pa (Svātantrika) et de Thal 'gyur ba (Prāsaṅgika), qui sont devenus courants à partir du XIe siècle pour désigner les écoles de Bhāvaviveka et de Candrakīrti, sont inconnus de ces deux traités. —Cf. aussi les manuscrits 693, 695 et 607 de la collection Aurel Stein (L. de La Vallée Poussin, *Tibetan Manuscripts from Tun-huang,* p. 187, 223–24), ainsi que le Pelliot tibétain 116.

La majorité des auteurs tibétains de Grub mtha' à partir du XIe siècle font au contraire état de l'école de Candrakīrti.

38. Voir *Mahāyānasūtrālaṃkāra* xix.59–60. Cf. Asaṅga, *Mahāyānasaṃgraha,* introduction.

4° Le Véhicule Unique *(theg pa gcig = ekayāna)* (M 13a3–15a1; P 256b3–257a6). Comme des Śrāvaka ont reçu l'indication prophétique *(vyākaraṇa)* relative à leur obtention de l'état de *buddha,*[39] il y a en réalité non pas trois Véhicules absolument différents mais un seul. Certes, des Sūtra ont parlé de trois Véhicules en liaison avec cinq «lignées» (*rigs* = *gotra* ou catégories de personnes);[40] cependant, cette division quintuple concerne seulement le temps présent *('phral gyi dus).*[41] Il est vrai aussi que dans certains Sūtra il est dit que le Śrāvaka se voue exclusivement à la tranquillité,[42] qu'il ne se destine pas[43] à l'état de *buddha* même s'il y est incité par les Tathāgata, et que, ayant une fois atteint la certitude (*nges pa: niyama* etc.) dans les quatre vérités, il est immuable jusqu'à son obtention de l'état d'Arhat.[44] En outre, l'Arhat a été comparé à une semence brûlée; et il a été dit que de même qu'un morceau de verre ne deviendra jamais une pierre de *vaiḍūrya* même si on le polit, de même un Śrāvaka ne réalisera pas l'état de *buddha.* Pourtant, tout cela a été dit pour empêcher les êtres de s'installer définitivement dans le Véhicule Inférieur *(theg pa dman pa = hīnayāna).* D'ailleurs, le *Samādhirājasūtra* et beaucoup d'autres Sūtra ont déclaré que tous les êtres animés sont des *tathāgatagarbha,* et qu'ils atteindront tous l'état de *buddha*; il n'y en a pas qui ne soient pas des réceptacles qualifiés *(snod = bhājana).*[45] C'est ainsi que les deux [premiers] Véhicules sont inclus dans le Mahāyāna; il est alors évident qu'il n'y a qu'un seul Véhicule (l'*ekayāna*).

3. *Les quatre Gnoses* (ye shes = jñāna) (M 15a1–16b1; P 257a6–b7)
1° L'*ādarśajñāna* procède de la transformation *(gnas gyur pa = āśrayaparāvṛtti)* de l'*ālayavijñāna.*

2° Le *samatājñāna* procède de la transformation du *kliṣṭamanas.*

3° Le *pratyavekṣ(aṇ)ājñāna* procède de la transformation du *manovijñāna.*

39. Voir *Saddharmapuṇḍarīkasūtra,* chapitres III, V et VI. Cf. notre *Théorie du tathāgatagarbha et du gotra* (Paris, 1969), p. 178.

40. *Laṅkāvatārasūtra,* chapitre II (p. 63). Cf. *Théorie,* p. 74–75, 180–81.

41. Cf. *Théorie,* p. 195. —P et C portent *'phrin las kyi dus . . . sngar phye bar zad do.*

42. *Zhi ba phyogs gcig pa.* Cf. *śamaikāyana (zhi ba'i bgrod pa gcig pu pa)* dans *Saṃdhinirmocanasūtra* vii.24; voir *Théorie,* p. 74, 179.

43. Sur *skal pa med pa = abhavya,* qui désigne le manque de capacité spirituelle qui empêche un être de se destiner à la *samyaksambodhi* (l'état de *buddha*), voir *Théorie,* p. 94, 153n.

44. Sur *nges pa = niyama/niyāma/nyāma,* voir *Théorie,* index s.v.

45. Cf. *Théorie,* p. 209; et notre article «The *gotra, ekayāna* and *tathāgatagarbha* Theories», in L. Lancaster, ed., *Prajñāpāramitā and Related Systems* (*Festschrift E. Conze,* Berkeley, 1977), p. 291.

4° Le *kṛtyānuṣṭhānajñāna* procède de la transformation des *vijñāna* des cinq facultés *(dbang po = indriya)* sensorielles.[46]

4. *Les trois kāya* (*sku*) (M 16b1–31a1; P 257b7–263a1)

1° Le *dharmakāya* (M 16b2–18b3; P 257b7–258b3). Il a la nature de la gnose sans conceptualisation dichotomisante *(rnam par mi rtog pa'i ye shes = avikalpajñāna)*;[47] il relève de l'Ainsité *(de bzhin nyid = tathatā)* et de l'*ālayavijñāna* purifié (M 16b2–4; P 257b7–8); il correspond à l'*ādarśajñāna* (M 17a2; P 258a2). Citations du *Suvarṇaprabhāsasūtra* et de la *Buddhabhūmiṭīkā.*

2° Le *sambhogakāya* (M 18b3–19b2; P 258b3–7). Il correspond au *samatājñāna* et au *pratyavekṣaṇājñāna.*

3° Le *nirmāṇakāya* (M 19b2–21a4; P 258b7–259b1). Il procède de la transformation des *pravṛttivijñāna* (selon le *Suvarṇaprabhāsasūtra,* M 19b4; P 258b8) et correspond au *kṛtyānuṣṭhānajñāna* (selon la *Buddhabhūmiṭīkā,* M 19b5; P 259a1).

Le *nirmāṇa* revêt trois aspects: *kāya (sku), vāc (gsung),* et *citta (thugs)* (M 20a3; P 259a3)[48]

(A) Le *kāyanirmāṇa (sku'i sprul pa)* est: (1) *bdag gi lus dang 'brel pa* (par exemple le Cakravartin), (2) *gzhan gyi lus dang 'brel pa* (par exemple Māra),[49] et (3) *ma 'brel pa* (par exemple les sept joyaux [*ratna*] du Cakravartin) (M 20a5–b2; P 259a3–6).

(B) Le *vāṅnirmāṇa (gsung gi sprul pa)* est: (1) *bdag gi lus dang 'brel pa* (le *brahmasvara*), (2) *gzhan gyi lus dang 'brel pa* (Śrāvaka etc.), et (3) *ma 'brel pa* (l'*ākāśa*) (M 20b4–21a1; P 259a6–8).

(C) Le *cittanirmāṇa (thugs kyi sprul pa)* est: (1) *bdag* (compréhension de tous les *dharma*) et (2) *gzhan* (transformation d'un *citta*) (M 21a2–4; P 259a8).

Les deux *kāya* ont-ils la conceptualisation dichotomisante? (M 21a3; P259a8.) Le *dharmakāya* existe sans *vikalpa,* répond l'auteur du *Lta ba'i khyad par,* qui ajoute de nombreuses précisions sur la bouddhologie (M 21a5 sq.; P 259b2 sq.). Quant aux *nirmāṇa* des trois sortes, ils sont sans *vikalpa* et œuvrent au bien de tous les êtres animés en vertu de la grande compassion

46. Cf. *Mahāyānasūtrālaṃkāra* ix.67 et suiv.

47. La lecture *rnam par rtog pa* dans P est fautive. Sur l'*avikalpa-* ou *nirvilpa(ka)jñāna* voir aussi *Mahāyānasaṃgraha* § 8.1 et suiv.

48. Cf. *Mahāyānasūtrālaṃkāra* ix.58.

49. Cf. L. de La Vallée Poussin, *Vijñaptimātratāsiddhi: La Siddhi de Hiuan-tsang* (Paris, 1928–29), p. 765, 776 et 798.

(mahākaruṇā) (M 23b1 sq.; P 260a5 sq.). Étant sans *vikalpa,* tous les *nirmāṇa* naissent spontanément *(lhun gyis grub pa: anābhoga),* à la manière du *cintāmaṇi* et du *kalpavṛkṣa,* pour accomplir le bien de tous les êtres sans conceptualisation dichotomisante.

Les trois *kāya* sont ils permanents ou impermanents? (M 27a3; P 261b4.) Le *dharmakāya* est permanent selon les Sūtra et Śāstra, mais il n'est pas pour autant identique à l'*ātman* des *tīrthika.* En effet, ici il ne s'agit pas d'un soi, mais plutôt de la *tathatā* qu'on ne doit pas prendre pour une entité; dans ce cas il n'y a pas la substance d'une entité sous l'aspect d'une personne *(pudgala)* ou d'une chose *(dharma)* (M 27a–b; P 261b5–6). D'ailleurs, le *dharmakāya* n'est vraiment ni permanent ni impermanent, ainsi qu'il a été déclaré dans le *Laṅkāvatārasūtra* (M 27b; P 261b7).[50] Quant au *sambhogakāya,* il est sans interruption; de ce point de vue il est permanent (M 28a–b; P 262a2–3). Aussi le *dharmakāya* reçoit-il les épithètes de *nitya,* de *ātman* et de *sukha* (M 29a3–4; P 262a7). Mais en réalité la Voie du Milieu *(madhyamā pratipat)* consiste en ce que le *dharmakāya*—doué qu'il est de *samādhi* et de *prajñā,* dépassant tous les *lakṣaṇa,* sans conceptualisation dichotomisante *(vikalpa)*—n'est ni permanent ni impermanent. En fait, selon le *Laṅkāvatārasūtra,* [la dichotomie] permanent/impermanent relève du *vikalpa*[51] (M 29b–30a; P 262b). Selon le *Mahāyānasūtrālaṃkāra* et le *Mahāyānasaṃgraha,* le *dharmakāya,* qui est immuable, est permanent par nature *(ngo bo nyid = prakṛti, svabhāva);* le *sambhogakāya,* qui est sans interruption, est permanent en raison de la nondéfaillance *(mi nyams pa = asraṃsana);* et le *nirmāṇakāya* est permanent par continuité *(rgyun = prabandha)* puisqu'il apparaît toujours à nouveau. Or, comme les deux derniers *kāya* s'appuient sur le *dharmakāya,* on dit qu'ils sont permanents (M 30a3–b1; P 262b4–6):[52] L'auteur cite aussi à l'appui de son exposé le *Saṃdhinirmocanasūtra* et la *Madhyāntavibhāgaṭīkā.*

5. *Les huit Vijñāna* (M 31a1 sq.; P 263a1–265a5)

Les huit *vijñāna* sont les cinq connaissances sensorielles et la connaissance mentale *(manovijñāna)* (les six[53] *pravṛttivijñāna,* P 263a6); le *kliṣṭamanas;* et l'*ālayavijñāna.*

Par leur nature les cinq connaissances sensorielles ont pour objet *(dmigs*

50. Cf. *Laṅkāvatārasūtra,* chapitre v (p. 217.4–5), au sujet du *tathāgata.* Sur le *dharmakāya* voir aussi chapitre ii (p. 22.12).

51. *Laṅkāvatārasūtra,* chapitre V (p. 218–19).

52. Voir *Mahāyānasūtrālaṃkāra* ix.66; *Mahāyānasaṃgraha* § 10.37.

53. Dans M le mot *drug* manque.

pa: ālamb-) des objets extérieurs *(phyi rol gyi yul = bāhyaviṣaya),* mais en réalité *(de bzhin nyid = tathatā)* jamais elles n'ont pour fonction l'objectivation *(nam yang mi dmigs pa).* Elles sont entièrement liées aux impuretés;[54] mais elles sont ou *kuśala,* ou *akuśala* ou indéterminées. Le *manovijñāna* s'appuie sur le *manas* (c'est-à-dire l'un des *vijñāna* passés) et sur une chose *(dharma) saṃskṛta* ou *asaṃskṛta, sāsrava* ou *anāsrava;* il est ainsi ni avec impureté *(sāsrava)* ni sans impureté *(anāsrava).*[55] Le reste de cette section contient une discussion des *caitta (sems las byung ba),* du *kliṣṭamanas* et de l'*ālayavijñāna,* avec des citations du *Saṃdhinirmocanasūtra* et de l'*Abhidharmasūtra* du Mahāyāna.

6. *Les deux vérités* (P 265a5–b2)
Les deux *satya* sont la vérité de surface *(kun rdzob kyi bden pa = saṃvṛtisatya)* et la vérité de sens absolu *(don dam pa'i bden pa = paramārthasatya).*

7. *Les deux insubstantialités* (P 265b2–266b4)
Les deux *nairātmya* sont l'insubstantialité de la personne *(gang zag la bdag med = pudgalanairātmya)* et l'insubstantialité des choses *(chos la bdag med = dharmanairātmya).* Le terme de «personne» est une simple désignation qui ne se réfère à rien de permanent et d'indépendant par rapport aux agrégats *(skandha).* Les choses n'ont pour nature ni d'être simples *(gcig = eka)* ni d'être multiples (*du ma = aneka* etc.), ce qui veut dire qu'elles sont sans nature propre *(rang bzhin med pa).*

8. *Les trois caractères* (P 266b4–267a6)
Les trois *lakṣaṇa* sont le caractère construit par l'imagination *(kun [tu] brtags pa'i mtshan nyid = parikalpitalakṣaṇa),* le caractère dépendant *(gzhan gyi dbang gi mtshan nyid = paratantralakṣaṇa)* et le caractère parfait *(yongs su grub pa'i mtshan nyid = pariniṣpannalakṣaṇa).*

Discussion des deux inconditionnés *(asaṃskṛta)* dans le cadre du *pariniṣpannalakṣaṇa:* l'Ainsité *(tathatā)* en tant que support objectif *(dmigs pa = ālambana)* du Chemin et le *nirvāṇa*—ou l'*ālayavijñāna* purifié—en tant que but du Chemin. Le Chemin lui-même est conditionné *(saṃskṛta),* mais parachevé *(pariniṣpanna)* dans la correction *(aviparyāsa).*

54. Lire *zag pa (āsrava)* avec M, au lieu de *zad pa* (P et C).

55. Mais P et C suppriment la double négation.

9. *La production en dépendance* (P 267a6–269b1)

La production en dépendance *(rten cing 'brel bar 'byung ba = pratītyasamutpāda)* se rapporte à ce qui a une cause *(hetu)* et une condition *(pratyaya).* Elle comporte douze membres *(aṅga)* (*avidyā* «nescience» jusqu'à *maraṇa* «mort»).

Le *pratītyasamutpāda* a deux aspects, l'extérieur et l'intérieur.

Le *pratītyasamutpāda* extérieur associé au *hetu* est illustré par les cas du fruit qui naît de la fleur et de la pousse qui naît de la semence. En outre, le *pratītyasamutpāda* extérieur associé aux *pratyaya* est illustré par le cas du fruit qui résulte de l'association des six éléments *(dhātu)* extérieurs (à savoir: terre, eau, feu, air, *ākāśa* et temps).

Le *pratītyasamutpāda* intérieur revêt deux formes, l'une progressive *(lugs su 'byung pa = anuloma),* l'autre régressive (*lugs su mi 'byung ba = pratiloma* «à rebours»). La forme dite *anuloma* associée au *hetu* est décrite par les deux formules «Cela (*avidyā* etc.) étant, ceci (*saṃskārāḥ* etc.) existe» et «De la naissance de cela naît ceci». Par ailleurs la forme dite *anuloma,* associée aux *pratyaya,* est illustrée par la naissance des *skandha* à partir de l'association des six éléments *(dhātu)* intérieurs (à savoir: terre, eau, feu, air, *ākāśa* et les six *vijñāna*). Enfin, la forme dite *pratiloma* est décrite par la formule «Par l'arrêt *(nirodha)* de cela (*avidyā* etc.) ceci (*saṃskārāḥ* etc.) s'arrête».[56]

10. *Conclusion* (P 269b2–6)

Il n'est cependant pas vrai que, à cause de l'arrêt *('gags pa: nirodha)* de la nescience *(avidyā)* et des onze autres membres du *pratītyasamutpāda,* il n'y ait rien que le néant *(ci yang med pa).* Ce n'est pas davantage vrai qu'il n'y ait alors plus de *pratītyasamutpāda.* En effet, à la suite de l'arrêt de l'aspect souillure *(nyon mongs pa'i phyogs)* l'aspect pureté *(rnam par byang ba'i phyogs)* se manifeste. Si par exemple on ingère un médicament convenable, la vie ne sera pas abrégée et on sera sans maladie; on produira ainsi la longue vie et la santé. De la même façon, par l'arrêt de l'*avidyā,* la *vidyā* se manifeste. Ainsi se réalisent les fruits *('bras bu = phala)* de l'auditeur *(nyan thos = śrāvaka)* et du Buddha-pour-soi *(rang sangs rgyas = pratyekabuddha).* Étant donné la particularité qui consiste à compléter le grand équipement *(chogs = sambhāra)* en mérite *(bsod nams = puṇya)* et en gnose *(ye shes = jñāna)* issu de la *vidyā,* on s'élève d'une terre spirituelle *(sa = bhūmi)* du Bodhisattva à l'autre; et on achève l'équipement sur la terre de *buddha.* Tous les accomplissements *(bsgrub pa)* ayant été ainsi parachevés, on atteint toutes les qualités *(yon tan = guṇa)* parfaites; œuvrant spontanément *(lhun gyis grub par: anābhoga)*

56. Le *Daśabhūmikasūtra,* chapitre VI, paraît être une des sources de cette section.

pour le bien de tous les êtres vivants *('gro ba = jagat)* jusqu'à la limite du *saṃsāra,* on entre dans le *nirvāṇa* sans fixation *(mi gnas pa'i mya ngan las 'das pa = apratiṣṭhitanirvāṇa).*[57]

IV

L'analyse précédente du *Lta ba'i khyad par* permet de répondre à la question touchant les thèmes qui parurent spécialement dignes d'attention à un savant tibétain écrivant au début du VIIIe siècle.

À la question concernant le niveau d'assimilation et de compréhension de la pensée bouddhique atteint par un Tibétain de cette période, quelques décennies à peine après la pleine implantation du bouddhisme au Tibet, il est possible de répondre, en nous fondant sur le *Lta ba'i khyad par,* qu'il était déjà très avancé. Sans doute, dans ce traité, d'ailleurs relativement court, écrit pendant la première diffusion *(snga dar)* du Dharma au Tibet, ne trouve-t-on pas encore toute l'expertise exégétique, toute la pénétration philosophique et toute la finesse herméneutique qui devaient caractériser la pensée des plus grands maîtres tibétains de la deuxième diffusion *(phyi dar)* du Dharma, surtout à partir du XIIIe siècle; mais l'auteur du *Lta ba'i khyad par* n'en fait pas moins preuve d'une excellente connaissance de nombreuses doctrines fondamentales du bouddhisme. Il sait exposer des thèmes aussi difficiles que, en bouddhologie, les théories des trois *kāya* et des quatre *jñāna;* en sotériologie, le problème du Véhicule unique *(ekayāna)* vis-à-vis des trois Véhicules distincts du Śrāvaka, du Pratyekabuddha et du Bodhisattva; et, en analyse philosophique, le sens profond de la production en dépendance *(pratītyasamutpāda)* qui, tout en fondant la théorie de la Vacuité *(śūnyatā)* de tous les *dharma,* n'a rien de nihiliste.

Aussi, à l'appui de son exposé de ces doctrines et surtout de la bouddhologie, l'auteur du *Lta ba'i khyad par* peut-il citer un grand nombre de Sūtra ainsi que plusieurs des Śāstra les plus importants du Mahāyāna. Parmi les Sūtra cités ou mentionnés nous trouvons l'*Akṣayamatinirdeśa,* le *Ghanavyūha,* le *Tathāgataguhyaka*(?), le *Daśabhūmika,* le *Dharmasaṃgīti,* le *Prajñāpāramitā,* le *Buddhabhūmi,* le *Buddhāvataṃsaka,* le *Laṅkāvatāra,* le *Lokottaraparivarta,* le *Vibhīṣaṇavyākaraṇa,* le *Samādhirāja,* le *Saṃdhinirmocana* et le *Suvarṇaprabhāsa.* Du côté des Śāstra notre auteur se réfère aux *Mūla-*

57. Il s'agit ici de la voie du bodhisattva. Sur l'*apratiṣṭhitanirvāṇa,* voir L. de La Vallée Poussin, *Vijñaptimātratāsiddhi: La Siddhi de Hiuan-tsang,* p. 628, 671, 677, 683, 777, 810; E. Obermiller, *IHQ* 10 (1934), p. 230, 232, 252 sq.

madhyamakakārikā de Nāgārjuna; au *Prajñāpradīpa* et aux *Madhyamakahṛdayakārikā* de Bhā(va)viveka; au *Madhyamakālaṃkāra* de Śāntarakṣita; au *Madhyamakāloka* de Kamalaśīla; à la *Yogācāraṭīkā;* au *Mahāyānasūtrālaṃkāra* avec sa Ṭīkā; à la Ṭīkā du *Madhyāntavibhāga;* au *Mahāyānasaṃgraha* d'Asaṅga; et à la *Buddhabhūmisūtraṭīkā.* La première phrase de la section sur le Vijñānavāda (M 3a2–3; P 255a2–3) est une paraphrase de la *Triṃśikā* (1a–c) de Vasubandhu. Beaucoup de ces sources étaient particulièrement bien connues de Ye shes sde parce qu'il participa à l'établissement de leurs traductions tibétaines.

Quant à la question de savoir si le *Lta ba'i khyad par* renferme des traits susceptibles de le caractériser comme une composition originale d'un Tibétain, en l'absence de l'attribution explicite à Ye shes sde que nous trouvons dans les catalogues ainsi que dans le colophon de la version du Bstan 'gyur (mais qui manque, ainsi qu'on l'a vu, dans la version de Touen-houang), il aurait été difficile d'affirmer catégoriquement que ce traité est l'œuvre d'un Tibétain plutôt que d'un Indien. Il est vrai que le *Lta ba'i khyad par* est sensiblement moins technique, et peut-être aussi un peu moins rigoureux dans sa méthode, que nombre de Śāstra indiens de la même époque; mais en ce qui concerne son style et son mode de présentation, on peut le rapprocher de plusieurs ouvrages contemporains traduits du sanscrit et contenus dans le Bstan 'gyur (par exemple les *Bhāvanākrama* de Kamalaśīla, dont Ye shes sde fut d'ailleurs l'un des traducteurs). De plus, le *Lta ba'i khyad par* ne trahit pas son origine tibétaine par des citations d'ouvrages d'auteurs tibétains.[58]

En ce qui concerne la question de la transmission interculturelle soulevée plus haut, il semble donc qu'on puisse dire que Ye shes sde a si bien suivi le modèle śāstraïque établi par ses devanciers indiens que son *Lta ba'i khyad par* ne se distingue guère d'un traité de maint Paṇḍit indien. Tout au plus manifeste-t-il le souci, caractéristique de beaucoup d'auteurs tibétains, de composer des manuels philosophiques où sont passées en revue les thèses des différentes écoles bouddhiques de l'Inde; et à ce point de vue il est proche du genre tibétain des Grub mtha'. Pourtant, encore que les Tibétains soient effectivement devenus des spécialistes de ce genre de composition, depuis la

58. Ce fait distingue le *Lta ba'i khyad par* du commentaire du *Saṃdhinirmocanasūtra* par exemple. En effet, parce que ce dernier traité (qui serait d'Asaṅga selon certains catalogues) renvoie au *Bka' yang dag pa'i tshad ma* de Lha btsan po Byang chub rdzu 'phrul, des autorités tibétaines l'attribuent plutôt à Klu'i rgyal mtshan; voir ci-dessus, p. 269 et note 10. (Le Lha btsan po en question est identifié avec Khri Srong lde btsan; voir *Ldan dkar ma* n° 723; et Bu ston, *Chos 'byung,* fol. 160a–b, et *Bstan 'gyur gyi dkar chag,* fol. 117a.)

Tarkajvālā de Bhā(va)viveka de nombreux traités plus ou moins développés du type des Grub mtha' ont existé en Inde.

Le *Lta ba'i khyad par* se distingue de la grande majorité des Grub mtha' postérieurs dans la mesure où il consacre relativement peu de place au Madhyamaka pur et s'étend plutôt sur des doctrines associées surtout avec l'école du Yogācāra-Madhyamaka *(rnal 'byor spyod pa'i dbu ma)* et avec le Vijñānavāda. Ainsi, l'école de Bhā(va)viveka (Bhavya)—le Mdo sde pa'i dbu ma connu plus tard comme Rang rgyud pa (Svātantrika)—reçoit un traitement assez bref (M 7a1 sq.; P 253a7 sq. avec la lacune déjà signalée). Et nous avons déjà attiré l'attention sur le fait très remarquable que le *Lta ba'i khyad par* n'expose pas la doctrine de l'école du Madhyamaka pur qui remonte à Buddhapālita et à Candrakīrti, et qui fut connue par la suite comme l'école des Thal 'gyur ba (Prāsaṅgika). De plus, à la différence de maint Grub mtha' postérieur, le *Lta ba'i khyad par* ne cherche pas à classer les différents systèmes philosophiques en présence selon un ordre hiérarchique où une doctrine est censée à la fois englober et primer celle(s) qui la précède(nt); et il se borne à donner une description purement doxographique, généralement sans porter un jugement de valeur même implicite.

Il est intéressant de noter que Ye shes sde emploie dans ce traité une forme de la langue tibétaine presque identique à celle des traductions en prose du sanscrit, dont le style et le vocabulaire sont en grande mesure calqués sur la langue de leurs sources sanscrites. Il semble ainsi que la langue des Lo tsā ba ou traducteurs tibétains constituée au VIIIe siècle ait à tel point influencé le tibétain littéraire de l'époque que, dans le domaine religio-philosophique du moins, même un texte composé par un Tibétain reflète la structure du sanscrit. Cette forme du tibétain écrit *(chos skad)* a d'ailleurs été utilisée jusqu'à nos jours dans les traités des lettrés tibétains à côté d'une forme de langue plus éloignée du sanscrit, et parfois sans doute plus proche aussi de la langue parlée, qu'on trouve souvent par exemple dans des biographies, dans des textes relatifs à la pratique religieuse et à la méditation, et jusque dans de nombreux passages des Chos 'byung.

En somme, de l'étude du *Lta ba'i khyad par* il ressort que vers l'an 800 un savant tibétain fut en mesure non seulement de faire des traductions, considérées par la suite comme classiques, de plusieurs des plus importants et des plus difficiles Sūtra et Śāstra indiens, mais aussi de composer un traité qui témoigne à la fois d'une pénétration des doctrines fondamentales du bouddhisme et d'une capacité de présenter celles-ci d'une façon compendieuse et magistrale. Il s'agit là d'un exploit fort remarquable compte tenu du fait que Ye shes sde écrivait à une époque qui suivit de si près la pleine implantation au Tibet du bouddhisme par l'Ācārya-Bodhisattva Śāntarakṣita et par ses collaborateurs et disciples dans la deuxième moitié du VIIIe siècle.

La comparaison du texte du *Lta ba'i khyad par* dans la version de Touen-houang et dans celle des différentes éditions du Bstan 'gyur imprimé nous révèle enfin les vicissitudes auxquelles a été exposé ce texte du Bstan 'gyur. Les conclusions qu'on peut tirer de cette comparaison revêtent une très grande importance tant pour l'éditeur d'un tel texte que pour son interprète.

12. The Jo nang pas: A School of Buddhist Ontologists According to the *Crystal Mirror of Philosophical Doctrines (Grub mtha' shel gyi me long)**

IN THE HISTORY of Buddhist philosophy in India and Tibet, an extreme and somewhat isolated position was occupied by the Jo nang pa school, which flourished in Tibet from about the thirteenth to the seventeenth century. Amongst the earlier Indian Buddhist schools, a perhaps comparable tendency towards ontological and metaphysical development is probably to be found in the *pudgalavāda* of the Vātsīputrīyas; but the exact significance of this *pudgala* or personal element which is indeterminable *(avācya)* in relation to the aggregates *(skandha)* remains somewhat uncertain owing to the lack of original texts belonging to this school which might be expected to explain its meaning clearly and fully.[1] Somewhat later, on the other hand, one at least of Dignāga's writings, the *Traikālyaparīkṣā,* exhibits a rather remarkable ontological tendency which was, however, repudiated in his *Pramāṇasamuccaya.*[2]

* First published as "The Jo naṅ pas: A School of Buddhist Ontologists According to the *Grub mtha' śel gyi me loṅ." Journal of the American Oriental Society* 83/1 (Jan–Mar 1963), pp. 73–91.

1. Cf. *Kathāvatthu,* pp. 56ff.; etc.

2. Some resemblances are also perhaps to be found between Jo nang pa doctrines and certain works attributed to Aśvaghoṣa which are not available in either Sanskrit or Tibetan. Points in common are also noticeable between them and certain schools of Chinese and Japanese Buddhism, including Ch'an/Zen and T'ien-t'ai/Tendai. These cannot be further gone into here.

Since the present paper is intended in the first place to make more accessible the chapter of the *Grub mtha' shel gyi me long* dealing with the Jo nang pa school, prefatory matter and annotations have had to be reduced to a minimum. There is not enough space to go into detail about their theory of *śūnyatā* or the *tathāgatagarbha* and the exegesis

To judge by the accounts of their doctrines given by their critics, the Jo nang pa masters took up a specifically ontological and hence apparently un-Buddhist position by accepting in quite literal terms what appears as an eternal *(nitya, śāśvata)* and stable *(dhruva)* Element. They taught also a theory of the absolute Gnosis *(ye shes, jñāna),* undifferentiated between apprehender and apprehended *(grāhya-grāhaka: gzung 'dzin gnyis med kyi ye shes mthar thug pa),* which is constant or permanent *(nitya)* and "substantially" real (*rtag dngos; ngo bo rtag pa; rang byung du grub pa;* etc.) and which is the *parinispanna* or Absolute. Their fundamental doctrine was the Empty-of-the-other *(gzhan stong),* that is, an absolute which is established in reality and is Empty of all heterogeneous relative and phenomenal factors, as against the Empty-of-Own-being *(rang stong; svabhāvaśūnya)* of the Mādhyamika, which the Jo nang pas considered to be a merely preliminary or lower doctrine bearing on the relative *(saṃvṛti)* and not on the Absolute Meaning *(paramārtha).* Although the Jo nang pas nonetheless considered themselves to be true Mādhyamikas, the Tibetan Mādhyamikas who follow Candrakīrti—in other words the majority of Tibetan scholars—resolutely oppose and refute their theories.

Certain authorities also compare the theory of the Jo nang pas, and after them of the unorthodox Sa skya pa doctor Shākya mchog ldan (1428–1507), concerning the Empty-of-the-other with the explanation the author of the *Bṛhaṭṭīkā* gives of the *pariniṣpanna* as being Empty of the discursive and

---

of the canonical texts treating it. Nor has it been possible to furnish a full analysis of all the doctrines of the Jo nang pa school according to their own texts, since it has hitherto been necessary to rely almost exclusively on accounts of them contained in works written by their critics; it has therefore been possible to give only an outline of their best-known doctrines.

The chapter of the *Grub mtha' shel gyi me long (ThG)* translated below is one of the most comprehensive discussions available despite its comparative brevity and should thus serve as a reliable sketch of the history and doctrines of the Jo nang pas. The writer hopes to publish accounts drawn from other sources in further articles.

The best known of the original Jo nang pa sources is the *gsung 'bum* of Tāranātha (Sgrol mgon) Kun dga' snying po, who was born in 1575. (The spelling Tārānātha appears to be the invention of a few modern writers.) On Tāranātha, cf. G. Tucci, *Tibetan Painted Scrolls* (Rome, 1949, hereafter, *TPS*), pp. 128–31, 163–64. The *gsung 'bum* was printed at Phun tshogs gling, the Jo nang pa centre mentioned below (cf. op. cit., p. 163b). A collection of a Century (?) of Jo nang pa texts was apparently printed at Sde dge in a single volume under the title *Jo nang mdzad brgya;* and more or less fragmentary manuscripts of some of their works have also been preserved (v. R. O. Meisezahl, *Die alttibetischen Handschriften im Reiss-Museum* [Copenhagen, 1961]; L. Chandra, *JA* 1961, p. 513, number 103).

phenomenal represented by the "imagined" *(parikalpita)* and the "relative" *(paratantra).*[3] According to the orthodox Yogācāras on the other hand, the *paratantra* Empty of the *parikalpita* is the *pariniṣpannalakṣaṇa.*[4]

To substantiate their particular interpretation the Jo nang pa masters referred to a group of canonical texts known as the "Sūtras teaching the Essence" *(snying po)* which includes the *Tathāgatagarbhasūtra,* the *Śrīmālādevīsiṃhanādasūtra,* and the *Mahāparinirvāṇasūtra.* At the same time the Kālacakra constituted one of their principal sources. And amongst

3. The text referred to here is the **Āryaśatasāhasrikāpañcaviṃśatisāhasrikāṣṭādaśasāhasrikāprajñāpāramitā-bṛhaṭṭīkā,* which is known as the *Yum gsum gnod 'joms (che ba)* (Mdo 'grel, vol. pha) and is attributed generally to the Kaśmīrī teacher Daṃṣṭrāsena.

4. The Jo nang pas might then be described as advocates of a kind of substantialistic theory, though they are not ontologist supporters of the reality of a composite *(samskṛta)* thing. Even the Yogācāras are considered in the Tibetan histories of philosophy to be "ontologists" *(dngos por smra ba)* because they hypostasize not only the *pariniṣpanna* but also the *paratantra* as something established in reality. However, the entire question of ontology and substantialism in Buddhist philosophy requires further study before such terms can be meaningfully applied to a given school. One authority for example—Dkon mchog 'Jigs med dbang po in his *Grub mtha' rin chen phreng ba* (6b6 and 9a2)—went so far as to ascribe to the Sāṃmitīyas/Vātsīputrīyas the doctrine of the substantial existence *(rdzas yod: dravyasat)* of the *pudgala;* but this view has been questioned by followers such as Gung thang Dkon mchog bstan pa'i sgron me (*Legs bshad snying po'i mchan,* 19a).

The discussion on the *gzhan stong* refers back to the *itaretaraśūnyatā* and the sūtra text which gives as an example of one kind of Emptiness a residence for the community *(gtsug lag khang: kūṭāgāra* or *vihāra) empty* of elephants, cows, sheep, etc., but not *empty* of all monks, etc. Since the comparison made between the author of the *Yum gsum gnod 'joms* and the Jo nang pas concerns only the method of expounding Emptiness *(stong tshul),* there need be no contradiction with what is said in the *ThG* translated below concerning the Jo nang pa doctrines being a Tibetan invention.

The exact significance of this comparison for Daṃṣṭrāsena is in any case difficult to evaluate since the authorship of the *Yum gsum gnod 'joms* is disputed. Bu ston (*Lung gi snye ma,* 3a6) states that Daṃṣṭrāsena was the author of the *'Bum gyi ṭik,* i.e., the *Gnod 'joms chung ba* (Mdo 'grel, vols. na and pa) on the *Śatasāhasrikā.* But, while noting the ascription of the *Yum gsum gnod 'joms* also to Daṃṣṭrāsena, the Bu ston *Chos 'byung* (156a5–6) considers this commentary to be in fact a *Paddhati* by Vasubandhu; and this last ascription is also found in Bu ston's *Gsan yig* (17b2). (Exactly how Bu ston could attribute this work to Vasubandhu is not altogether clear. Could he possibly have had in mind the *slob dpon* Dbyig gnyen, or Vasubandhu, to whom another work of doubtful authorship preserved in the Bstan 'gyur—the *Don gsang ba*—is ascribed? But see the *Dkar chag* of the Peking edition as quoted by P. Cordier, *Catalogue du fonds tibétain,* pt. 3, p. 284.) In any case, the ascription to Vasubandhu is cogently rejected by Tsong kha pa, who ascribes it tentatively to Daṃṣṭrāsena (*Gser phreng,* 4b–5b, and *Legs bshad snying po,* 37b6). (This question has been touched on by E. Obermiller, *Bu ston's History of Buddhism,* II, p. 146n, and "Doctrine of Prajñāpāramitā," *AO* 11 [1932], p. 5n.)

śāstra works they referred especially to the stotra collection attributed to Nāgārjuna. It can thus be said that their doctrine represents an admixture of the mantra method and of the intuition achieved through practice-in-meditation *(bhāvanā)* of the Kālacakra with the sūtra and philosophical method chiefly founded on the group of sūtras just mentioned. And it was just this contestable mixture of the two methods of "metaphysics" *(mtshan nyid)* and mysticism that called forth many of the criticisms directed against their doctrines by doctors who did not reject the validity and authenticity of their intuition and understanding as such.

Thus, not only did the Jo nang pas have a tendency to hypostatize reality, but they were also thought to have, as it were, mixed their metaphors by combining together systems of expression belonging to different traditions. These traditions and their symbolical systems are all nonetheless generally held to be valid in their own domains; and only a few authorities, notably Red mda' ba (1349–1412), actually opposed the Kālacakra and the Ṣaḍaṅgayoga—perhaps much in the same way as Sa skya paṇḍi ta (1182–1251) did the later Tibetan *phyag rgya chen po* or *mahāmudrā* system—for introducing into the well-authenticated and in themselves complete methods of the great Buddhist masters extraneous and not easily verifiable notions and terms.

Another problem of fundamental and far-reaching importance was posed by the method a particular school adopted to explain the sūtras; and the application of the criteria by means of which intentional *(ābhiprāyika)* canonical texts whose provisional meaning has to be interpreted in another sense (*neyārtha* texts) can be correctly explained and distinguished from other canonical texts of definitive meaning *(nītārtha)* was thus the subject of much discussion. Various solutions were advanced by the different schools which depended on their understanding of the basic doctrines of Buddhism. The Jo nang pas, unlike many of their contemporaries, considered that the "Sūtras teaching the Essence" were of definitive and certain meaning. And in accordance with this view, they elaborated their characteristic doctrine of the *gzhan stong,* which they linked with the *ādibuddha* doctrine of the Kālacakra.

While underlining this remarkable and rather extreme position amongst Buddhist schools occupied by the Jo nang pas, it is also necessary to consider them both as one of the most renowned and as one of the most controversial of the Tibetan schools during a period of several centuries.

As the author of the *Grub mtha' shel gyi me long* informs us in the text translated below, at first, in the eleventh and twelfth centuries, the Jo nang pas appeared closely linked with the Sa skya pas, only becoming clearly distinct after their doctrines had become the object of a formal philosophical presentation, for which Dol bu pa (1292–1361) was chiefly responsible. But since both the Sa skya pa and Jo nang pa schools had their centres in Gtsang province, and since at this time the Sa skya pas were perhaps the dominant force in Tibet (though very closely rivalled by some of the Bka' brgyud pa sects), this connexion may have even earlier been above all geographical and due to the fact that the Jo nang pa masters had usually studied in the chief monastic colleges which belonged to the Sa skya pas. This is the impression conveyed at least by the passage from the *Kha skong* of the *Ngor pa chos 'byung* quoted below. At all events, theories accepted by the Jo nang pas were rejected by Sa skya paṇḍi ta in his *Sdom gsum rab dbye.*

A connexion also existed between the Jo nang pas on the one side and, on the other, Bu ston (1290–1364) and the Zha lu pa school, owing in part no doubt to their common interest in the Kālacakra; in fact, according to the *ThG,* the Jo nang pa master Phyogs las rnam rgyal (1306–86) studied under Bu ston. But from the point of view of *mtshan nyid,* or philosophical method, their doctrine of the *gzhan stong* and of the *tathāgatagarbha* was refuted both by Bu ston and his great disciple Sgra tshad pa Rin chen rnam rgyal (1318–88). It is nevertheless to be noted that in his *Mdzes rgyan* they are not attacked by name; and if Padma dkar po states in his *Chos 'byung* that Bu ston refused to discuss publicly with Dol bu pa when the latter came to see him for that purpose, this may have been because he did not wish to engage in open controversy with teachers who were regarded with great respect. A Sa skya pa authority, Ngag dbang chos grags (1572–1641), states that whereas Bu ston held that the *dharmadhātu* though real is non-existent in reality *(bden par med),* Dol bu pa proposed the thesis: The *dharmadhātu* as the subject of the proposition will exist in reality because it is real.[5]

Reference has furthermore sometimes been made to a connexion between the Jo nang pa and Bka' brgyud pa schools.[6] This does not appear to be clearly borne out by the present chapter of the *ThG,* though this text does indicate that the *gzhan stong* and the *mahāmudrā* are in certain respects comparable. Certain teachers of the Karma pa sect of the Bka' brgyud pas

5. See my Introduction to the *BNTh,* Serie Orientale Roma, p. 12, concerning the school of Mādhyamikas with which Bu ston is to be connected. Sum pa mkhan po (*PSJZ,* p. 175.2) states that he was a Prāsaṅgika; while the other authorities cited agree that he was in fact a Prāsaṅgika, they point out that some of his teachings were formulated from the point of view of the Yogācāra-Madhyamaka-Svātantrika method.

6. *TPS,* p. 128b; however, as Tucci explains, this comparison refers to the fact that Tāranātha was especially interested in the teachings of the siddhas connected in Tibet with the Bka' brgyud pa line.

however proposed an interpretation of *śūnyatā,* absolute Gnosis, and the *tathāgatagarbha* that was close to the Jo nang pa doctrine.[7]

While the question of the affiliations of the Jo nang pas with the other Tibetan schools clearly requires much further study, it thus seems correct to say that they were, to begin with, closely connected with the Sa skya pas; however, their doctrines differed from those of most of the Sa skya pa doctors. An exception was Shākya mchog ldan, whose theory of *śūnyatā* agreed with the Jo nang pa theory; for this reason his theories are often discussed together with theirs, as is done at the end of the present chapter of the *ThG.*

The above very brief sketch of some of the philosophical problems posed by the Jo nang pa school should at least be sufficient to reveal their great importance, and also to show that it is scarcely adequate to characterize them as representing chiefly "tantric magical teachings." Opinions may perhaps differ as to whether the Kālacakra, which (as seen above) was one of the pillars of their theory, was above all a magical teaching or not; but the Jo nang pa analysis of the mind *(sems),* of Gnosis *(ye shes),* and of *śūnyatā* as the *gzhan stong* clearly bears witness to a very deep concern with the soteriological, metaphysical, epistemological, and psychological problems which interested philosophers in general. That doctrines closely allied with the *gzhan stong* were also accepted by at least some Bka' brgyud pa and Rnying ma pa scholars would indicate that the Jo nang pa masters were not altogether isolated.[8]

The apparently very close relationship of the Jo nang pas with both Indian teachings and Indian teachers is also notable. It has even led one scholar to speak of "Brahmanists" in Tibet.[9] The originator and source of their

7. This is stated to be the case especially for Mi bskyod rdo rje (1507–54), who held that Maitreyanātha really had in mind the *gzhan stong* theory; his conception of the *advayajñāna* as the absolute is thus close to that of the Jo nang pas.

Karma 'Phrin las seems also to have held views on the *tathāgatagarbha* that might be compared with those of the Jo nang pas, and he refers to the views of Rang 'byung rdo rje (1284–1339) on this subject. (I owe this last reference to the kindness of Dr. H. V. Guenther. The dates are as indicated by H. E. Richardson, "The Karma pa Sect," *JRAS* [1958–59].) The link may thus have been above all with the Karma pas, as is indeed indicated by Rje btsun Chos kyi rgyal mtshan's *Klu grub dgongs rgyan. ThG* (Bka' brgyud pa chapter, fol. 46b) attributes such errors to an inability to distinguish properly between the *neyārtha* and *nītārtha* texts.

8. The Si tu Rin po che Chos kyi nyin byed is said to have at first followed the Madhyamaka theory but to have been later introduced to the Jo nang pa doctrine by a Rnying ma pa and to have then adopted the *gzhan stong* theory (see *ThG* 51b). A *gzhan stong chen mo* is said to be still accepted by Rnying ma pa bla mas.

9. E. Obermiller, "The Sublime Science," *AO* 9 (1931), pp. 106–7. Cf. also Th. Stcherbatsky, *Buddhist Logic,* I (1932), pp. 114 and 169; *TPS,* p. 92.

doctrines, Yu mo, is indeed said to have received his doctrine at Kailāsa;[10] and the chief systematizer of their doctrines, Dol bu pa (also known as Dol po pa) Shes rab rgyal mtshan (1292–1361), must have come from the Dol po region near the frontier of Nepal.[11] And such links then continued up to the time of the suppression of the school in the seventeenth century. For at that time Tāranātha was in close contact with Nepalese and Indian paṇḍits;[12] and the wall paintings he had executed in the Phun tshogs gling temple

10. See *ThG* 11b, below. On connexions with Śaivism, cf. *TPS,* p. 92.

11. The Dol po region in question used to be counted a part of Mnga' ris province, and it is mentioned together with Pu hrang, Glo bo (or Mustang, on which see G. Tucci, *Preliminary Report on Two Scientific Expeditions in Nepal*), Gu ge, and Ya tshe as part of the Stod region. See also the *Kha skong* of the Ngor pa chos 'byung, fol. 130b5. This Dol po is now part of Nepal.

The appelation Dol po pa of Shes rab rgyal mtshan points to the connexion between this Jo nang pa master and a Dol po region of Stod Mnga' ris. And the name Dol bu must be identical with Dol po—or very nearly so—for not only is Shes rab rgyal mtshan also known as Dol bu pa, but for the place name Dol po'i Ban tshang of *DNg* (tha, 11a3) the *Kha skong* (fol. 148, 'og ma, b5, translated below) has Dol bu Ban tshang (or Ban tshad?) in Mnga' ris.

The name Dol however raises a problem. It appears as a kind of surname of persons whose connexion with Mnga' ris Dol po is not determined; and, indeed, according to the *DNg* (pa 5a5), Dol is a *gdung,* or clan; but elsewhere it appears as a place name. In any case, Dol pa was the "surname" of many illustrious Tibetan masters. In the *DNg* (ca, 14a3), Dol pa Dmar zhur pa is the same person as Rog Shes rab rgya mtsho. And in many cases a precise connexion with Mnga' ris has not been established; for example, Dol pa Zang thal of the *dol gdung* was a native of 'Tshur phu (*DNg* pa, 5a5; on the 'Tshur family *[rigs]* in Dol gyi mda', see nya, 7b5; cf. ga, 34b4). However, Dol pa Dbang rgyal was from Stod (as distinct from Smad: *DNg* na, 5a4). (A La[s] stod pa Dbang rgyal is mentioned in *DNg* tha, 9b, and nya, 57b6; La stod was the province in which the early Jo nang pa master Thugs rje brtson 'grus was born, and Byang is part of it. On this see the translation of the *Kha skong* below.) Moreover, Dol pa 'Gar ston Dbang phyug grub belonged to the spiritual lineage of Yu mo, the early Jo nang pa master and teacher of the Kālacakra (*DNg* ja, 6b7, and tha, 8a; cf. also ga, 38b6, and tha, 4b4). The latter passages at least appear to establish a link between several bla mas bearing the "surname" Dol pa on the one hand and Yu mo and his lineage on the other.

It is to be noted that this area in general, and in particular the region of Kailāsa and Mānassarovar, have for countless centuries been places of pilgrimage for ascetics and yogins from India. It is then not impossible that encounters with them may have had some kind of influence on the doctrinal tendencies of the Jo nang pa teachers.

12. On the paṇḍits Gokula and Kṛṣṇa as well as Buddhagupta, Pūrṇānanda, Pūrṇavajra, etc., see *TPS,* pp. 137 and 164 (cf. p. 74–75).

are reminiscent of certain Indian schools of painting, including, curiously enough, even the modern Bengal school to a certain extent.[13]

The history of the Jo nang school may perhaps at the same time be explained, at least to a certain extent, by factors in the history of Gtsang. Under the Sa skya pas this province had for a long time assumed a preponderant position in Tibet. Separatist tendencies were later strongly asserted by the princes of Rin spungs, some of whom, though connected principally with the Karma pas and more specifically with the Zhwa dmar hierarchs, also patronized the Jo nang pas. In fact, the *ThG* links the decline of the Jo nang pas with the downfall of Karma Bstan skyong dbang po, the last of the Rin spungs princes, who was defeated in 1642 by Gu shri Khan on behalf of the Fifth Dalai Lama.[14] Given these circumstances, it may then be pertinent to consider the possibility that the Jo nang pa school was proscribed at the time of the Fifth Dalai Lama both because of the unorthodoxy of its teachings and because of some Himalayan and ultramontane connexions which might have tended to sustain local separatist movements in the southwestern areas of Tibet in which they were chiefly established. At all events it is known that the Jo nang pa centres in Gtsang were at that time converted to the Dge lugs pa order; and the only monasteries that survived were, according to the *ThG*, to be found in eastern Tibet.[15] At that time also the line of incarnations to which Tāranātha himself belonged was transferred to Mongolia, where it was recognized as the line of the Khal kha rje btsun dam pa of Da Khu re (or Hu re chen mo, Urga), which continues into the present century.[16] Tāranātha was thus the last great representative of the school.

The circumstances of this radical dispossession of the Jo nang pas in the

13. See *TPS*, pp. 189–98.

14. On the princes of Rin spungs and Karma Bstan skyong dbang po, usually referred to as *sde srid*, see *ThG* translated below and also quoted in A. Schiefner, *Tāranātha's Geschichte des Buddhismus in Indien* (St. Petersburg, 1869), pp. vi–viii (followed by G. Schulemann, *Geschichte der Dalai Lamas* [Heidelberg, 1911], pp. 135–37); Dalai Lama V, *Rdzogs ldan gzhon nu'i dga' ston*, fol. 90a ff.; *TPS*, pp. 37a, 58–64, 256n130, 651b, 697–98; H. E. Richardson, "The Karma pa Sect," *JRAS* (1958), pp. 156–57.

15. See *ThG*, 4a, below. A Jo nang pa monastery—'Dzi ka (spelling?) dgon pa—is said to exist in the district of the same name that forms part of the Rnga pa (?) region of A mdo; G. N. Roerich (*Blue Annals*, p. 777) also speaks of Jo nang pas in the Lnga ba region of southern A mdo. (It might seem that the *PSJZ* [ed. L. Chandra, pt. 3, p. 146] also refers to such a connexion with the A mdo region; but *jo nang* there is presumably an error for *jo nong*.)

16. See *KD*, za, 22a–b. Tāranātha's spiritual successor, the seventeenth in the line, was the first Khal kha rje btsun dam pa Blo bzang bstan pa'i rgyal mtshan, who lived from 1635 to

middle of the seventeenth century however present a sharp contrast with the fact that, two and a half centuries earlier, two of Tsong kha pa's teachers, Phyogs las rnam rgyal and Nya dbon Kun dga' dpal, had belonged to this school. And, although Tsong kha pa came to disagree with their teachings, and despite the fact that their tenets thus form many of the *pūrvapakṣas* refuted in the *Legs bshad snying po,* for example, the masters of this school continued to be respected. An authority like Gung thang Dkon mchog Bstan pa'i sgron me, though always rigorously opposing the unorthodox scholastic exposition of their doctrines, admits that Dol bu pa's spiritual intuition was very profound and that he was "a not inferior omniscient being because of his comprehension."[17] And as the closing lines of the present chapter devoted to them in the *ThG* clearly indicate, the author, Blo bzang chos kyi nyi ma, does not condemn them out of hand.

* * * *

As a contribution to the study of the history and doctrines of the Jo nang pas as well as of the criticisms of their interpretations made by masters of the other schools of Tibetan Buddhism a translation is offered here of the sixth chapter of the *Crystal Mirror of Philosophical Doctrines (Grub mtha' shel gyi me long).*[18] Completed in 1801 by Thu'u bkwan Blo bzang chos kyi nyi ma, this work contains a valuable if brief account of the history of the school together with notices on the lives of many of its most important teachers followed by a short outline of their doctrines and a refutation of them according to the Prāsaṅgika-Madhyamaka method of the Dge lugs pas.[19]

In this critique the author first shows that the Jo nang pa doctrines are in several respects comparable to the doctrines of the Brāhmaṇical schools and that they are consequently open to the same criticisms to which the latter were subjected by the great Buddhist teachers of India and Tibet. Thus their

---

1723. Cf. Lokesh Chandra, *Eminent Tibetan Polymaths of Mongolia* (New Delhi, 1961), pp. 15–17; C. R. Bawden, *The Jebtsundamba Khutukhtus of Urga* (Wiesbaden, 1961).

17. *Drang nges kyi dka' 'grel* (fol. 10a): *mngon par rtogs pa'i yon tan gyis mi dman pa'i kun mkhyen pa.*

18. Many references to this school are naturally to be found in the various Chos 'byungs and Grub mtha's. See in particular the Kālacakra chapter of the *DNg; KhG tsa,* 36b; and *BrCh* 127b.

19. Blo bzang chos kyi nyi ma (1737–1802) was the second re-embodiment of the Thu'u bkwan bla ma of Dgon lung in A mdo (founded in 1604) and the successor of Ngag dbang chos kyi rgya mtsho (1680–1736). Besides the A mdo edition of his *gsung 'bum,* a print of it exists in ten volumes made at the Zhol par khang. And a separate edition of the *ThG* was made at Sde dge, where it is also known as the *Bod chos 'byung.*

doctrine is first of all found to resemble that of the Word-brahman advocated by the Śabdabrahmavādins such as Bhartṛhari; and the first *kārikā* of the latter's *Vākyapadīya* is quoted according to which the *śabdabrahman* appears as the objective world *(arthabhāva)* and the source of mundane differentiated construction *(prakriyā jagatah).* It is then shown how the participation and involvement of the Absolute in the cycle of existences *(saṃsāra)* also results from the Jo nang pa theory of an eternal and immutable element of potential awakening inherent in every being in the saṃsāric condition. It is also to be noted that the tendency towards an ontological position—or at least towards an ontological formulation of a doctrine—which, as mentioned above, appears in the case of Dignāga, is also connected with the *Vākyapadīya;* for Dignāga's *Traikālyaparīkṣā* is essentially an only slightly modified version of verses taken mostly from Bhartṛhari's *Prakīrṇakakāṇḍa* (iii.3.53–85).[20]

It is next explained that the Jo nang pa doctrines are similar to those of the Sāṃkhya inasmuch as they assume what amounts to a kind of inherent liberation existing continuously from the outset in every *puruṣa,* or being. But as the author of the *ThG* shows at some length, such an interpretation has been explicitly rejected in the *Laṅkāvatārasūtra* itself in its presentation of the *tathāgatagarbha* doctrine. Similarities are also pointed out in the *ThG* between the logical consequences of the Jo nang pa theories and some Mīmāṃsaka and early Vedāntin doctrines; as regards the latter, it is also to be noted that the relative world is said to be an erroneous illusory appearance *('khrul snang [bhrānta-ābhāsa?],* but not *māyā).*[21]

20. Despite certain ressemblances with earlier Indian masters, as noted above, the author of the *ThG* (fol. 10a of the Jo nang pa chapter) and other Tibetan authorities reject the idea that the Jo nang pas continued some Indian Buddhist tradition.

The connexion between Dignāga and Bhartṛhari has surprisingly not received the attention it merits though pointed out by E. Frauwallner in 1933 (*Festschrift Winternitz* [Leipzig, 1933], p. 237). Cf. also my *Contributions à l'histoire de la philosophie linguistique indienne* (Paris, 1959), pp. 90–92, where some aspects of the question were briefly discussed.

21. It is not always easy to determine exactly to what stage of development in the history of these Brāhmaṇical doctrines the outlines contained in the Tibetan *Grub mtha*'s correspond. The description of the Sāṃkhya given in the *ThG* appears to derive from Candrakīrti's remarks in *Madhyamakāvatāra* vi.121; this form of Sāṃkhya was briefly discussed by R. Garbe, *Die Sâṃkhya-Philosophie* (Leipzig, 1917), pp. 391–92. Other sources are the *Tarkajvālā* and Jñānaśrī's commentary on the *Laṅkāvatārasūtra.* —On similarities between the Sāṃkhya and Bhartṛhari, cf. E. Frauwallner, *WZKSO* 3 (1959), pp. 107–8.

As regards the Vedānta, it maintains in its theory of error the *anirvacanīyakhyātivāda.* But the word *'khrul snang* cannot directly correspond to this term; once in the

The *ThG* moreover briefly indicates how the Jo nang pa theory is in conflict with the basic doctrine of the Buddha, for it inevitably leads both to a "nihilistic" and to an "eternalistic" position—*ucchedavāda* and *śāśvatavāda*—the two extremes which the teaching of the middle path avoids. Contradictions are also pointed out with the teaching of Nāgārjuna; and it is explained that the *Dharmadhātustava* is to be interpreted in the sense of the *Mūlamadhyamakakārikās*.

A list is then given of the chief refutations of the Jo nang pa doctrines composed by scholars of various schools. And reference is also made to some comparable points in the doctrine of the famous but unorthodox Sa skya pa scholar Shākya mchog ldan. The Jo nang pa chapter of the *ThG* does not however close on an exclusively polemical note; for, while rigorously combatting their unorthodox teachings which conflict with the Madhyamaka, Blo bzang chos kyi nyi ma also pays tribute to the part played by the Jo nang pa masters in transmitting instructions in the Kālacakra.

Translation[22]

Here begins the discourse concerning the history of what is known as the Jo nang pa doctrine,
the way opened up wide by Dol bu pa, the white banner renowned as the Omniscient One who made the entire assembly of scholars tremble greatly.

Daśabhūmikasūtra, 'khrul ba corresponds to *vivarta*. On *mithyājñāna, avidyā,* and the *anirvacanīya,* see the *Śāṃkarabhāṣya* on *Brahmasūtra* i.3.19; ii.1.22, ii.3.46; iii.2.6; etc.; cf. S. N. Dasgupta, *History of Indian Philosophy,* II, pp. 8–12 and 185. In Buddhist usage *'khrul snang* and *ma rig pa (avidyā)* are not usually synonymous.

22. The following translation of the *ThG* is based on the Zhol par khang edition compared with the Sde dge edition. In the translation of technical terms, Sanskrit equivalents, when known or at least probable, have been included in many cases because Sanskrit as the lingua franca of Buddhist studies serves to identify many terms that would otherwise be obscured in the translation. However, it should be recalled that in some cases such equivalents are given with reservations, since an absolutely regular and automatic system of equivalents does not exist; moreover, it has not always been possible to determine the Sanskrit equivalents of certain Tibetan terms because of the unavailability of a great number of relevant Sanskrit texts. As regards the English translation, in some technical passages it is regrettably only an approximation because of the lack of English (or known Sanskrit) equivalents. It is hoped that the forthcoming publication of the Tibetan text announced in India will enable the reader to achieve a more precise understanding than a translation at present allows.

The sixth chapter of the *Grub mtha' shel gyi me long* on the history of the Jo nang pa doctrine contains three sections: (1) the history of the doctrine, (2) the doctrinal method of the *gzhan stong* theory according to their system, and (3) the demonstration that this theory is bad.

1. *The History of the Doctrine*

The anchorite Thugs rje brtson 'grus[23] founded a monastery at Jo mo nang. After Dol bu pa had settled there, the doctrine spread widely; and subsequently those who maintained this tradition received the name of Jo nang pas.

Yu mo Mi bskyod rdo rje[24] was the originator of the Jo nang pa doctrine. At first a yogin, he later became a monk with the name of Dad pa rgyal po. He attended on many spiritual superiors, including Sog 'dul 'dzin, and [2a] he heard some teachings from Somanātha, the great paṇḍit from Kaśmīr.[25] From Somanātha's disciple Sgro ston Gnam la brtsegs,[26] he heard in detail the *Tantravṛtti* [the *Vimalaprabhā*] of the Kālacakra together with its *upadeśa,* as well as the *Pradīpoddyotana* [of the Guhyasamāja] together with its *upadeśa.* He then went to 'u yug and achieved intuitive-comprehension (: *adhigama*) by means of realization-in-meditation *(bhāvanā),* and the *gzhan stong* theory appeared in his mind. As a master of *abhijñā* he was very well known as an adept *(siddha),* for he many times manifested many transformations-through-artifice in the shape of a crow, a magpie, and so forth. He also composed some manuals on the Kālacakra. He died at the age of eighty-two [that is, in his eighty-second year].

The chief of his many disciples was his son Dharmeśvara.[27] Up to the age of twenty he mastered all the texts and the traditional instructions belonging to the great adept. And, attending on many scholars, he cultivated above all the Madhyamaka and logic, the Guhyasamāja, and the Kālacakra [2b]. Fully endowed as he was with transcending discriminative knowledge *(prajñā),* he is known as the manifestation of Mañjuśrī. Several of his teachings are extant.

23. Thugs rje brtson 'grus, 1243–1313 *(RM);* cf. *DNg* tha 2b, 9b; *KhG* tsa 36b; *BrCh* 127b.

24. Yu mo is mentioned in *DNg* tha 2b, 8a; ga 36a; *KhG* tsa 36b. Cf. *RM* under 1052 and 1067.

25. Somanātha was the paṇḍit responsible for the Tibetan translations of the *Vimalaprabhā, Sekoddeśaṭīkā, Sahajasiddhi,* and *Sekaprakriyā.* Cf. *DNg* tha 2b, etc.

26. Sgro ston is mentioned in *DNg* tha 2b, 7b; *KhG* tsa 36b.

27. Dharmeśvara is mentioned in the *DNg* and *KhG,* ibid.; he was born when his father Yu mo was in his fifty-sixth year (*DNg* 8a).

His great disciple was Nam mkha' 'od zer; and the latter's pupil was Dharmeśvara's son, Se mo che ba Nam mkha' rgyal mtshan.[28] Next came 'Jam gsar Shes rab 'od zer.[29] It is said that until then the scripture *(āgama)* of the Kālacakra was limited (in its diffusion),[30] but that after 'Jam gsar the teaching became generalized.

The latter's pupil was the omniscient Chos sku 'od zer.[31] His pupil was the anchorite Thugs rje brtson 'grus, who composed a treatise on the six yogas *(ṣaḍaṅgayoga)*. His pupil was Byang sems Rgyal ba ye shes.[32] Yon tan rgya mtsho, learned and reverend, was the pupil of the last two masters;[33] and his disciple was Dol bu pa Shes rab rgyal mtshan, known as the Omniscient.[34]

Dol bu pa listened extensively to the sūtra and tantra doctrines under more than thirty masters, and he studied in detail Pāramitā, logic, and Abhidharma under Skyi ston 'Jam dbyangs grags pa rgyal mtshan.[35] He then held philosophical discussions in the provinces of Dbus and Gtsang and became very well known as a scholar. From Skyi ston he heard all the mantra instructions, such as the consecration *(abhiṣeka)* itself and about seventy ancillary indications. He received the bhikṣu's ordination from the great *ācārya* of Chos lung tshogs pa, Bsod nams grags pa.[36]

Until then he had been a follower of the Sa skya pa doctrine; but at the age of

28. Se mo che ba is mentioned in *DNg* tha 2b and 8b–9a (teacher of Chos sku 'od zer).

29. 'Jam dbyangs (g)sar ma Shes rab 'od zer is mentioned in *DNg* tha 2b, 8b; cha 4b–5a; ta 2a. He was a teacher of Chos sku 'od zer, *DNg* cha 5a; tha 2b, 9a. See *RM* under 1214.

30. The Zhol par khang ed. reads *dus 'khor bka' dogs kyang;* but the Sde dge ed. reads *dog kyang,* which appears to be preferable in view of what is said later.

31. Chos sku 'od zer, 1214–92, is mentioned in *DNg* tha 9a; cha 5a; na 10a–b; *BrCh* 127b. He was famed as a master of the Kālacakra.

32. Byang sems Rgyal ba ye shes, 1257–1320, became abbot of Jo nang in 1313 (*DNg* tha 10b).

33. Yon tan rgya mtsho, 1260–1327, became abbot in 1320 *(RM);* cf. *DNg* tha 10b–11b; *KhG* tsa 36b.

34. Kun mkhyen chen po, or Jo nang kun mkhyen Dol bu pa Shes rab rgyal mtshan, 1292–1361; cf. *DNg* 11a. See also *BrCh* 127b concerning his visit to Ri phug in order to hold a discussion with Bu ston, which the latter however refused. As already mentioned above, he continued to be held in great respect—as his title *kun mkhyen pa* indicates—also by his Dge lugs pa opponents; this fact is of some significance in evaluating the doctrinal disputes which took place between the different masters and their schools.

35. Skyi ston 'Jam dbyangs, a disciple of Rong pa Shes rab seng ge: *DNg* tha 2b, 11a.

36. Bsod nams grags pa is mentioned in *DNg* tha 10b, and he appears to be identical with Bu ston's *ācārya* at the time of his *upasampadā* (v. *BNTh* 9b, and *Life of Bu ston Rin po che,* p. 78n2).

thirty-one he went to Jo mo nang and heard many consecrations and instructions—and above all the *dbang khrid* of the Kālacakra—from the learned and reverend Yon tan rgya mtsho [3a]. Henceforth he followed the doctrinal tradition of the Jo nang pas; and through his realization-in-meditation of the six yogas, the sign of perfect *prāṇāyāma* appeared.[37] He then occupied the abbatial seat of Jo nang and constructed the great *sku 'bum.*[38]

At that time he ascertained completely the theory of the *gzhan stong;* and he composed a treatise devoted to it called the *Ri chos nges don rgya mtsho.* Hence it is said that, a mountain having been heaped up, the ocean flowed forth.[39] To many scholars he preached chiefly the exposition of the *Tantravṛtti* of the Kālacakra and the *gzhan stong* theory. He showed signs of spiritual realization, such as the vision of the countenances of many divinities and the simultaneous manifestation of three bodily dispositions (: *vyūha*); and he fully accomplished the tasks of the scholar by conferring on many pupils the texts, expositions, and instructions of sūtra and tantra and by composing treatises. In general more than two thousand religious and about one thousand adepts gathered together; and it is related for example that Mchims Blo bzang grags pa perceived him in the form of Avalokiteśvara, while his disciple *(antevāsin)* Nam mkha' byang chub perceived him in the form of Mañjughoṣa.

Amongst the numberless disciples who came to him, the translator Blo gros dpal[40] and Sa bzang Mati paṇ chen[41] became his spiritual sons. Phyogs

37. *Prāṇāyāma* constitutes the third member of the *Ṣaḍaṅgayoga* of the Kālacakra (cf. also *Maitrāyaṇīyop.* vi.18). The signs mentioned are *dhūma,* etc., indicating the realization of non-duality; cf. Nāropā's *Sekoddeśaṭīkā,* pp. 29–30, 35–36; *Guhyasamājatantra* 18.

38. On this monument called the Mthong grol chen mo, see *DNg* tha 11a; *TPS,* pp. 163–64, 189–96; A. Ferrari, *mK'yen brtse's Guide to the Holy Places of Central Tibet* (Roma, 1958), fol. 22a–b.

39. This saying is found in *DNg* tha 11b.

40. Blo gros dpal, 1299–1353, revised the Tibetan translation of the "Kālacakra" together with Mati paṇ chen, according to *DNg* 11a–b. This must refer to their translation of the *Garuḍasādhana (Mkha' lding gi sgrub thabs);* in its colophon this work is called *Dus kyi 'khor lo'i rgyud.* Blo gros dpal is also known as the Jo nang lo tsā ba (*DNg* cha 10b; cf. tha 11b?), and he is referred to as Matiśrī in the copy of Rin chen chos skyong bzang po's *Rin po che'i za ma tog bkod pa* (composed in 1514) used by B. Laufer (*Studien zur Sprachwissenschaft der Tibeter,* SBayAW, Philos.-philol. Kl., 1898, pp. 529 and 575) (where it is said that he retained the orthography *kalpa* for the usual Tibetan *bskal pa*).

41. Sa bzang Mati paṇ chen Blo gros rgyal mtshan, 1294–1376, is mentioned in *DNg* tha 11a–b, pha 18a7, etc. He was the author of an important commentary on the *Abhidharmasamuccaya.* He distinguished between a *vijñāna* in the *ālaya* which is relative and one that

las rnam rgyal and many other scholars [3b] who preserved the continuity of action *('phrin las: kāritra)* also came to him.

Phyogs rgyal ba,[42] after having made his studies at Sa skya, became a great scholar. At first he did not accept the *gzhan stong* theory; but when the great Dol bu pa gave a discourse on the scriptural tradition and reasoning on the occasion of a discussion at Jo nang, he felt no disturbance and became his disciple. He heard in their entirety numerous expositions of sūtra and mantra, and above all the *dbang khrid* of the Kālacakra. He also requested many teachings from the omniscient Bu ston. He was Master of the law *(chos dpon)* at Ngam rings,[43] and he composed many treatises on Pāramitā and logic.

The great scholar Nya dbon Kun dga' dpal arrived in order to become his disciple.[44] And the omniscient master Tsong kha pa also heard the Kālacakra from Phyogs rgyal ba as well as the Pāramitā from Nya dbon.

Subsequently the current of the consecration and explanation of the Kālacakra received a very wide diffusion. But the *gzhan stong* theory was unanimously refuted by numerous scholars and adepts, and it became weak.

---

is of absolute value *(don dam pa)*, corresponding respectively to the *rnam shes* and *chos can* and to the *ye shes, bde gshegs snying po,* and *chos nyid.* (On the distinction established by the Jo nang pas between *ye shes [jñāna]* and *rnam shes [vijñāna]* in the *ālaya,* see below *ThG* 4b.) Tsong kha pa, 1357–1419, received instruction from him.

42. Phyogs las rnam rgyal, 1306–86; see *DNg* 11b–12a. Mkhas grub rje (*Rnam thar* of Tsong kha pa, 11a) states that Tsong kha pa at about the age of nineteen studied under Chos rje Phyogs las rnam rgyal; however *PSJZ* (p. 214) refers to this teacher as Bo dong Phyogs las rnam rgyal, while *RM* mentions a Bo dong Phyogs las rnam rgyal who lived from 1375 to 1450. Cf. also Dalai Lama V, *Rdzogs ldan gzhon nu'i dga' ston* 66b (*TPS,* pp. 632, 666, and n. 848).

43. The monastery of Byang Ngam ring(s), which the *RM* states may have been founded in 1225, was restored in 1354 with the permission of Dol bu pa by Byang Ta'i dben *(RM).* This is the *dpon chen* mentioned in the *Rdzogs ldan gzhon nu'i dga' ston* (fol. 66a) belonging to the family of the princes of Ngam ring who were closely linked with the teachings of the Kālacakra (*TPS,* p. 164b); cf. *DNg* tha 12a; A. Ferrari, *Guide,* n. 536. This family also helped Tāranātha in having the work on the Rtag brtan phun tshogs gling temple (below, n. 46) executed.

44. Nya dbon Kun dga' dpal, 1285–1379, is mentioned in *DNg* tha 11b, 13a; cha 7a, 9a; pha 6a. The *Rnam thar* of Tsong kha pa (11b) and the *PSJZ* (p. 214) give an account of his study of the Prajñāpāramitā with Nya dbon. Along with Brtson 'grus dpal, a teacher of G.yag phrug Sangs rgyas dpal, Nya dbon is considered the chief pupil of Dol bu pa and Bu ston (*ThG* 80a5).

However, Jo nang Kun dga' grol mchog[45] and in particular the rebirth of the *grol mchog,* Tāranātha, later revived it, spread its explanation, and composed many treatises. The latter founded Rtag brtan phun tshogs gling and established unprecedented Supports *(rten),* and he made prints of many treatises belonging to the Jo nang system.[46] Many religious assembled there.

Because the chief of Rin spungs, Prince Karma bstan skyong, became the patron, some lustre was imparted to the two systems [spiritual and temporal]. Soon afterwards the Rin spungs power declined;[47] and after Tāranātha's death, the *gong sa* Great Fifth [4a] converted the monastery to the Dge lugs pa and named it Dga' ldan phun tshogs gling.[48] The other Jo nang pa monasteries—Chos lung byang rtse and the rest—were equally changed into Dge lugs pa ones, and most of the xylographs of their scriptures were sequestred and sealed. Except that mention is made of a monastery in Mdo khams Dzam thang—which was founded by Jo nang kun mkhyen's [i.e., Dol bu pa's] pupil's pupil,[49] the *drung* and *dka' bzhi pa* Rin chen dpal—and of some monasteries which are its dependents, at the present time no foundation maintaining the Jo nang doctrine exists in Dbus or Gtsang.[50]

And, with the sole exception of the *Sgrub thabs rin chen 'byung gnas,*[51] the streams of religion of Jo nang have disappeared (literally: have become a rainbow-body).

The source of the *gzhan stong* doctrine was Yu mo Mi bskyod rdo rje. When he realized in meditation the Ṣaḍaṅgayoga of the Kālacakra, the divine Body image of Emptiness-form *(stong gzugs kyi lha'i sku rnam pa)* arose from within

45. Kun dga' grol mchog, 1495–1566 *(RM);* he was the fourteenth in the line in which Tāranātha (1575–1634/35) was the sixteenth (*KD* za 22b).

46. On Rtag brtan phun tshogs gling, see Schiefner, *Tāranātha's Geschichte des Buddhismus,* pp. vi–vii (where this passage of the *ThG* is reproduced); *TPS,* pp. 36, 62, 164, 196–98; A. Ferrari, *Guide,* fol. 21a and n. 560.

47. See note 14 above.

48. According to Sde srid Sangs rgyas rgya mtsho's *Vaiḍūrya ser po* (Delhi ed., p. 323), this refoundation took place in the year *sa khyi* (1658).

49. The Zhol par khang ed. reads *yang slob,* while the Sde dge ed. has only *slob.*

50. Cf. note 15 above.

51. This *Sgrub thabs* of Tāranātha was revised by the fourth Paṇ chen, Blo bzang dpal ldan Bstan pa'i nyi ma (1782–1853); it was also expanded by Blo bzang nor bu shes rab, a younger Mongolian contemporary of Tāranātha's successor, the first Khal kha rje btsun dam pa rin po che, in his work called *Sgrub thabs rin 'byung gi lhan thabs.*

and constituted the basis of misapprehension.[52] Relying only on the letter of sūtras of indirect meaning *(neyārtha)* as well as on some tantras, he taught that the *gzhan stong*, the truth of Absolute-Meaning *(paramārthasatya)*, permanent, stable, and eternal, pervading all that is static and mobile, is identical with the *sugatagarbha* and exists in the existential-nature of foundation *(gzhi'i gnas lugs la yod pa)*. As a result of spiritual practice employing the graded method of the Six Yogas, there arose in his conception this mass of contradiction in the direct apprehension of the *dharmatā*-Body which is the Result; and he named it the theory of the *gzhan stong*. And mixing with it the practical instruction *(khrid)* on the Kālacakra, he expounded it as a hidden doctrine *(lkog pa'i chos)*.

This explanation was transmitted from disciple to disciple down to Dol bu pa Shes rab [4b] rgyal mtshan. However, there had hitherto existed no manual devoted especially to this doctrine but only oral indications; and because the masters who upheld this doctrinal tradition were solely Yogins who had only good spiritual experiences, they had not made detailed expositions to demonstrate the scriptural tradition and arguments. Hence they were not well known.

Dol bu pa composed a treatise expounding this theory called the *Nges don rgya mtsho*, as well as many opuscules such as the *Bka' bsdu bzhi pa*.[53] After

52. The *stong gzugs* is for example realized in the Kālacakra system on the level of the fourth *abhiṣeka*. But the Jo nang pas confounded this intuition with the philosophical expression to be given to the theory of the pure *jñāna* or *citta*. The *Uttaratantra* (*RGV* i.104) indeed states that in the incarnate being there exists the *anāsrava-jñāna*, or "Gnosis devoid of impurity"; but such authentic sources may become the basis for the unfounded interpretation of the Jo nang pas, who while maintaining that the *rūpakāya* of such nature is the Self of the five *jinas* and so forth, concluded erroneously that the purified self is the negation of all relative phenomenal elements attached to a pre-existing pure *jñāna;* for according to them this negation is not the non-propositional absolute negation *(prasajyapratiṣedha)* of the Prāsaṅgikas but a really existent Gnosis Empty of all else *(gzhan stong)*. The Jo nang pas thus consider that the *stong gzugs* Body adorned with the Marks and secondary Marks is an object. And it is against this combination of two techniques that their critics took exception; see in this regard Gung thang Bstan pa'i sgron me's *Legs bshad snying po'i mchan*, fol. 12a–b: *zag med ye shes dngos su 'khrul pa yin zhing/ de nyid gzugs sku rgyal ba lnga sogs kyi bdag nyid du smra ba ni/ 'dis dag pa'i bdag zhes btags pa sngar gyi ye shes de'i steng du kun rdzob rnams bkag pa ni med dgag tsam ma yin par ye shes de nyid yin pa la mtshan dpes bkra ba'i stong gzugs kyi sku zhig 'dzin stangs su 'dod pas/ dus 'khor gyi chos skad cung zhig bsres pa yin te/*

The Tibetan critics usually stress that this theory was unknown before the Jo nang pas, and in particular before Dol bu pa, who was the first to write it down in a manual.

53. Along with the *Nges don rgya mtsho*, the *DNg* (tha 11b) mentions a *bsdus don sa bcad*, commentaries on the *Uttaratantra* and the *Abhisamayālaṃkāra*, the *Bstan pa spyi 'grel*,

having made several demonstrations of the scriptural tradition and the arguments, he established the doctrine *(siddhānta)* known as the "theory of the *gzhan stong* of Absolute Meaning."

Following him Phyogs las rnam rgyal composed the large and the small *'Khrul 'joms.* And Nya dbon Kun dga' dpal composed the *Grub mtha' 'od gsal rgyan,* etc.

Subsequently the theory and doctrine of the Jo nang pas became very well known.

2. *The Doctrinal Method of the* Gzhan stong *Theory*

In the *Nges don rgya mtsho* the following is taught. The essential nature *(yin lugs)* of all dharmas, the truth of Absolute-Meaning, is permanent, stable, and eternal. In the *ālaya* there are the Gnosis *(jñāna)* and the *vijñāna,* and it is the Gnosis; it is also the *triratna* of the *dharmatā* of Absolute-Meaning *(don dam chos nyid kyi dkon mchog gsum);* it is the divine assembly of the non-duality of "noëma" and "noësis" which exists penetrating everything static and mobile *(brtan g.yo kun la khyab par bzhugs pa'i dbyings rig dbyer med kyi lha tshogs);*[54] it is identical with the *sugatagarbha,* the Lineage existing by nature, and the hundred families *(kula)* etc. mentioned in the tantras. It has been explained in detail how it resides in the continuum of the non-duality of Ground and Result; how it exists in the three conditions *(gnas skabs)* of the *dharmakāya;*[55] [5a] and, since it is considered that it never appears *(snang ba)* in the *vijñāna* despite the fact that it always resides in the Ground, how it—the existential-nature of foundation *(gzhi'i gnas tshul)*—is the immediate apprehension of the *dharmatā*-Body of Result through the gradual practice of the Six Yogas.[56] It is stated that this is clearly expounded in the *Tathāgatagarbhasūtra,* the *Mahābherīsūtra,* the *Jñānālokālaṃkārasūtra,* the *Śrīmālādevīsiṃhanādasūtra,* the *Anūnatvāpūrṇatvanirdeśa,* the *Mahāparinirvāṇasūtra,* the *Avataṃsaka,* the *Ratnakūṭa,* and the *Suvarṇaprabhāsottamasūtra.* And this has been set

---

and the *Bka bsdu bzhi pa* as Dol bu pa's treatises expounding the *gzhan stong.* See G. N. Roerich, *Blue Annals,* p. 777.

54. The rendering "noëma" and "noësis" for the term *dbyings rig* is only an approximation. This non-dual realization of the integration of *dbyings rig* constitutes a high order of intuition relating to the level of the *dharmakāya.*

55. These are the pure condition *(shin tu rnam dag gi gnas skabs),* the impure-and-pure condition *(ma dag pa dang dag pa'i gnas skabs),* and the impure condition *(ma dag pa'i gnas skabs).*

56. Cf. note 37 above.

forth in detail in the *Uttaratantra* and its commentary, where the intention of the last cycle of the teaching is explained, as well as in the *Dbu ma la bstod pa*[57] of Ārya Nāgārjuna, etc.

The explanation given by the great masters, the realization-in-meditation of the great yogins, and the doctrines taught by the Buddha and the bodhisattvas of the ten directions of space are all without error. But all that which belongs to the relative *(saṃvṛti)*—the doctrines of the Empty-of-own-being *(rang stong)*, the Empty through destruction *(chad stong)*, and the Empty through negation *(dgag stong)*, which are the partial *(prādeśika)* Emptiness and total non-existence *(ye nas med pa)*[58]—must be rejected in all their forms by those seeking liberation.

Such is the teaching of the *Nges don rgya mtsho.*

3. *Proof that This Doctrine Is Wrong*

It is established by his reputation that the great omniscient Dol bu pa was an excellent and inconceivable being; and a basis for an intentional statement having a special motive *(dgongs gzhi dgos pa khyad par can)* may indeed exist, in accordance with an occasional declaration by Bhagavat which is intended for certain disciples *(vineya)* and according to which a *pudgalātman* exists. [5b] However, the system which accepts the doctrine literally appears quite comparable to the theses of the heterodox *(tīrthika)*.

In fact, the *tīrthika* proponents of the Word-brahman *(śabdabrahmavādin)* state that there is a transformation *(yongs su 'gyur ba)* of the *brahman* which is free from the spatial differentiations of east, west, etc., which is unproduced and indestructible, and which is the proper nature of Word; the aggregate of entities of form etc. is just this [transformation]. The Śabdabrahmavādins thus state: "The *brahman* without beginning and end is the Word-essence and the Syllable: in it is produced the world construction, and it transforms itself into the world of objectivity."[59] Since it is the essence of Word, it is

57. This may be an error for the *Chos kyi dbyings su bstod pa = Dharmadhātustava (?).*

58. Cf. below, 6b. And, as is explained later (fol. 7a), with this theory of the total non-existence of the relative—which is to be carefully distinguished from absolute negation—the Jo nang pas risk falling into the extreme of destruction *(ucchedānta).*

59. This is the first *kārikā* of Bhartṛhari's *Vākyapadīya:*

anādinidhanaṃ brahma śabdatattvaṃ yad akṣaram /
vivartate 'rthabhāvena prakriyā jagato yataḥ //

A less adequate translation of *Vākyapadīya* i.1 is found in the Tibetan version of Jñānaśrī's commentary on the *Laṅkāvatāra* (fol. 126b in the Peking ed.); this version has been noted

called *śabdatattva,* meaning that it is the true essence of Word. What is called "supreme" *(mchog)* is the Self of the *oṁ (oṁ gyi bdag nyid);* in fact, *oṁ* is known as the proper nature of all words and all things *(artha);* and it is the Veda.[60] It constitutes the means of comprehending the Veda which is present as a series of syllables and words; and it exists as the form of this [Veda]. The Śabdabrahmavādins add that this *brahman,* the supreme *ātman,* constitutes the obtaining of the supreme *dharma*-of-result, felicity *(abhyudaya)* and the summum bonum *(niḥśreyasa),* and that it is not perceived by the inner organ.[61]

Similarly, the Jo nang pas teach that the permanent, stable, and eternal taught under the name of *"sugatagarbha"*—the divinity of Absolute-Meaning *(don dam pa'i lha), mantra, tantra (rgyud), maṇḍala, mudrā,* etc., [6a] the perfection of the supreme self—which is totally pure, has the qualities of the forces *(bala)* etc. existing inherently since the beginning, and exists since the beginning pervading all the static and mobile world—is the existential nature constituting the foundation of all that is the relative *rang stong.*

Thus, just as the *tīrthika* proponents of the *śabdabrahman* maintain that all entities *(bhāva)* are transformations of the Word and that they possess its proper nature, the Jo nang pas also consider that the permanent and stable which pervades all that is static and mobile is the essential nature of all. There is therefore not the slightest difference between these two theories.

Moreover, the way in which the Jo nang pas teach how liberation is obtained does not appear to differ from the *tīrthika* Sāṃkhya philosophers. The Sāṃkhya postulates twenty-five categories and maintains that amongst them twenty-four are material *(jaḍa)* while the twenty-fifth is cognition *(shes pa)* or consciousness *(rig pa),* permanent and stable, the proper nature of the sentient being which pervades all that is static and mobile. It is unconditioned and is the self of proper nature, free from the actions of going, coming, etc. When the *puruṣa* of cognition and consciousness has a desire for the enjoyment *(bhoga)* of an object, the *pradhāna* manifests all

by H. Nakamura, *Studies in Indology and Buddhology* (S. Yamaguchi Presentation Vol., Kyoto, 1955), pp. 123f.

60. On the significance of *oṁ* and the *akṣara* in Vedāntic philosophy in general, cf. H. Oldenberg, *Die Lehre der Upanishaden* (Göttingen, 1923), pp. 134f., 227; P. Deussen, *Das System des Vedânta* (Leipzig, 1920), pp. 8–9, 143–45, 157, 213f.; recently: J. A. B. van Buitenen, *JAOS* 79 (1959), pp. 176–87.

61. The sense of this remark is not altogether clear. But "inner organ" *(nang gi byed pa)* may correspond to *antaḥkaraṇa;* on this cf., e.g., *Vākyapadīya* i.114; iii.7.41 and iii.6.23 (see H. Nakamura, *Studies,* pp. 123–24).

the aggregates of transformation; the *buddhi* which is of a material nature then becomes inclined *(zhen pa: abhiniviś-)* to this, and the *puruṣa* has the enjoyment of the object of inclination. Thus, while the solitary *puruṣa* of cognition and consciousness has never before been perceived in the condition of the cycle of existences *(saṃsāra),* by reason of the inclination together of the *puruṣa* and the objects of enjoyment, it finds itself turning about in *saṃsāra* [6b] and experiences pain *(duḥkha).*[62] Thereupon one practises meditation, and when its constant habit has been achieved, the desiring inclination that the *puruṣa* has for objects diminishes more and more. Because it is observed by the divine eye *(divyacakṣus),* the *pradhāna* no longer manifests the transformation aggregate because of shame; and the transformations are first reabsorbed in that from which they were originally produced, and the transformation is finally tranquillized in the nature of the *pradhāna.*[63] As the *pradhāna* exists in a potential state without ever being manifested,[64] all these perceptible evolutes from it having a worldly nature clarify themselves like a rainbow in space; and the self or *puruṣa* of cognition and consciousness then exists alone. When nothing else appears any more, the Sāṃkhya holds that liberation has been obtained.[65]

Similarly, the Jo nang pas also consider that the essential disposition of all *dharmas*, though existing permanently from the outset, is not seen because of conceptual inclination *(abhiniveśa).* Then, when one perceives through the practice of yoga that they have the proper nature of a mirage *(marīci),* of smoke, etc.,[66] he obtains ultimate Awakening *(sangs rgyas);* the permanent *tathatā* alone appears then, and nothing else appears. Whereas *saṃvṛti* and the *rang stong* are nothing but total non-existence *(ye med la song ba),* when nothing but the solitary Absolute-Meaning appears, Awakening is obtained.

The two preceding systems are thus quite similar; and there is not the slightest difference of superiority or inferiority between them, as any intelligent person who examines them will understand.

62. Cf. R. Garbe, *Sâṃkhya-Philosophie,* p. 367f.

63. This description of the Sāṃkhya, apparently based on the *Madhyamakāvatāra* vi.121, differs somewhat from that found in the *Sāṃkhyakārikā* and *Kaumudī* (verses 59–61) and described by Garbe, *Sâṃkhya-Philosophie,* p. 367f., and by E. Frauwallner, *Geschichte der Indischen Philosophie,* I (Salzburg, 1953), pp. 316–18, 378f. (where the doctrine described by Frauwallner is attributed—der Einfachheit halber [p. 303]—to Pañcaśikha). Cf. note 21 above.

64. This refers to the Unmanifest *(avyakta)* or *prakṛti,* a kind of natura naturans.

65. This is the *kaivalya* of the Sāṃkhya(-Yoga).

66. Cf. note 37 above.

Moreover, the Jo nang pas maintain that the whole of the octad [of *vijñānas*] consisting of the present *ālayavijñāna* etc. possesses an impure proper nature *(tshogs brgyad 'dus pa 'di dag dri ma'i rang bzhin can),* and in this they resemble the Mīmāṃsaka who accepts impurity as the proper nature of the mind [7a]. The impurity penetrates into the nature of the mind; therefore, though one may try to remedy it so as to eliminate it, this is really useless. Hence, although they have a theory of liberation, it is the cycle of existence *(saṃsāra)* that they have really established!

Moreover, the Jo nang pas, inasmuch as they maintain that the things which belong to relativity are only illusory appearances *('khrul snang),* admit that the permanent Absolute-Meaning is established if it differs from this [relativity]. Now this theory is comparable to that of the different *tīrthikas* who advocate the Vedānta and who affirm that this *('di)* is just an erroneous appearance; that the permanent and omnipresent knowledge *(shes pa)* which includes no duality between subject and object finds itself when separated from this *('di nas logs na)* in the proper nature of liberation; and that the many separately existing selves of the creatures are absorbed in the essence of the great Self when they obtain liberation. This is so because, except for a mere difference in terms, they both hold in reality that liberation is permanent and because their systems of liberation *(grol tshul)* and of [bondage in the] cycle of existences *('khor tshul)* are similar.

The theory proposed by the Jo nang pas in this respect proves to incur besides the twin fault of eternalism and nihilism. For by holding that the proper nature of the Absolute-Meaning exists as a permanent proper nature, they fall into the extreme of the eternal *(śāśvatānta);* and by accepting that the relativity which exists beforehand in the saṃsāric condition no longer exists when one is awakened, they fall into the extreme of nihilism *(ucchedānta).*

To support their doctrine of the *gzhan stong* which is truth of Absolute-Meaning *(paramārthasatya),* permanent, stable, and eternal, and which pervades all the static and mobile, the Jo nang pas also quote the *Tathāgatagarbhasūtra,* the Kālacakra, the *Dharmadhātustava,* and numerous sūtra and śāstra texts. [7b] It is however absolutely necessary to interpret texts of indirect meaning *(neyārtha)* by means of the three gates [i.e., criteria] of the intentional basis (*dgongs gzhi,* that which is intended but expressed indirectly), the motive *(dgos pa),* and incompatibility (*gnod byed,* between a literal interpretation and the real doctrine).

If it is declared (by the Teacher) that forces *(bala)* and intrepidities *(vaiśāradya)* exist in the sentient being, this refers only to the ground *(gzhi)* for their production through purification of the impurity of the sentient being, who is by nature perfectly pure *(prakṛtiviśuddha).*

If it is declared that the permanent and stable *tathāgatagarbha* exists, this is an indirect meaning pronounced with reference to the *tathatā* in order to attract the *tīrthikas*; but if it were of definitive meaning *(nītārtha),* it would not differ from the heterodox *ātmavāda.* This has been clearly declared by the Buddha himself in the *Laṅkāvatārasūtra:*[67]

> The bodhisattva Mahāmati addressed Bhagavat respectfully, saying: "Bhagavat has declared the *tathāgatagarbha.* Bhagavat has declared that the primordially pure—through purity which is luminous by proper nature since the outset and possessing the thirty-two marks *(lakṣaṇa)*—exists within the body *(lus = deha)* of sentient beings; Bhagavat has declared that, though enveloped—like a precious stone enveloped by a rag—by the rag of the *skandhas, dhātus,* and *āyatanas,* overwhelmed by concupiscence, hate, and confusion, and soiled by the impurity of unreal dichotomizing thought,[68] it is permanent, stable, and eternal. O Bhagavat, if this is so, how does the *tathāgatagarbha* doctrine differ from the *ātmavāda* of the *tīrthikas*? [8a] O Bhagavat, the *tīrthikas* also formulate a doctrine of permanence, speaking as they do of the permanent, stable, attributeless, omnipresent, and indestructible."
>
> Bhagavat replied: "O Mahāmati, my teaching of the *tathāgatagarbha* is not like the *ātmavāda* of the *tīrthikas.* O Mahāmati, for the meanings *(padārtha) śūnyatā, bhūtakoṭi, nirvāṇa, anutpāda, animitta, apraṇihita,* etc., the tathāgatas-arhats-samyaksaṃbuddhas have given the teaching of the *tathāgatagarbha.* So that the puerile may abandon their states of fear concerning non-substantiality *(nairātmyasaṃtrāsapada)*—the state of the absence of conceptualization—the domain of non-appearance *(nirābhāsagocara)* is taught by the teaching of the gate of the *tathāgatagarbha.* O Mahāmati, the bodhisattvas of the future and the present must not attach themselves in their conceptions *(abhiniviś-)* to a self. O Mahāmati, a potter, for example, makes from a single lump of clay pots of different shapes by using his hands, skill, a tool, water, a cord, and effort. Similarly, O Mahāmati, by the varied use of transcending

67. In a few points, which scarcely affect the meaning of the passage, the text of this passage of the *Laṅkāvatārasūtra* as found in the *ThG* differs slightly from that found in the Bka' 'gyur and the Sanskrit (ed. B. Nanjio, pp. 77–79).

68. The Sanskrit text has: *rāgadveṣamohābhūtaparikalpamalamalinaḥ* . . . . The Tibetan translation presupposes something like °*paribhūta*° instead of °*abhūta*°.

> discriminative knowledge and skill in means, the tathāgatas teach [8b] that reversal of all the features of conceptualization, the non-substantiality of *dharmas*, either by the teaching of the *tathāgatagarbha* or by the teaching of non-substantiality—and this by different turns of word and syllable in the manner of a potter.[69] O Mahāmati, the tathāgatas thus teach the *(tathāgata) garbha* in so far as they teach the *tathāgatagarbha* in order to attract *(ākarṣaṇa)* those who are attached to the heterodox *ātmavāda.* How can people whose minds *(āśaya)* fall into the conceptual theory bearing on an unreal self *(abhūtātmavikalpa)* attain quickly the complete Awakening in the supreme and exact *sambodhi,* possessing a mind *(āśaya)* comprised in the domain of the three *vimokṣamukhas*? O Mahāmati, it is because of this that the tathāgatas teach the *tathāgatagarbha.* O Mahāmati, with a view to casting aside the heterodox theory, you must treat the *tathāgatagarbha* as non-substantial *(anātman).*"

In this text Mahāmati is Mañjughoṣa, and in order to resolve the doubts of people of little intelligence, he respectfully asked the Teacher: If the Lord's mode of teaching the *tathāgatagarbha* is of indirect meaning, what is the intentional basis and what is the motive? If it is a teaching of definitive meaning, there will be no difference between it and the self of the *tīrthikas*. The Lord then replies: Whereas this would be true if the meaning were definitive, because the meaning is indirect, the teaching is not similar to the *ātmavāda* of the *tīrthikas*.

In this connexion the intentional basis [9a] is the Limit-of-Reality *(bhūtakoṭi).* The motive is to attract through means those whom it would be impossible to introduce to the teaching because of their fright were the essential nature to be taught straightaway, the heterodox who are from the outset attached in their conceptions to a self. They will have faith in this mode of verbal teaching conforming with their theory of the permanent self and in the

69. The *ThG* reads here *de bzhin du de bzhin gshegs pa rnams kyang chos la bdag med par rnam par rtog pa'i mtshan nyid thams cad rnam par log pa de nyid shes rab dang thabs la mkhas pa de dang ldan pa rnam pa sna tshogs kyis de bzhin gshegs pa'i snying por bstan pa'am / bdag med par bstan pas kyang run ste / rdza mkhan bzhin du tshig dang yi ge'i rnam grangs sna tshogs kyis ston te /* The Lha sa edition (Mdo ca, fol. 136b2) reads *chos bdag med pa'i rnam par rtog pa'i mtshan nyid thams cad rnam par log pa de nyid;* Bu ston seems to have read *chos la bdag med pa rnam par rtog pa'i . . .* (if the Lha sa edition of the *Mdzes rgyan,* fol. 21b6, is to be relied on). Nanjio, p. 78, reads: *tad eva dharmanairātmyaṃ sarvavikalpalakṣaṇavinivṛttam . . . .*

tathāgata, and then little by little they will comprehend the reality *(tattva)*. Thus the teaching is not faulty, and attainments will result.

If this sūtra were of definitive meaning, this would involve the enormity of an unconditioned *(asaṃskṛta)* adorned with the formal attributes of the marks *(lakṣaṇa)* and subsidiary marks *(anuvyañjana)*, of an ultimate *dharmadhātu* endowed with the two purities united with the *skandha*s and *dhātu*s having impurities *(sāsrava)*, and of a *buddha* overwhelmed by the three poisons [of concupiscence, hate, and confusion]. For, in Nāgārjuna's teaching contained in the *Dharmadhātustava* and elsewhere, the intentional basis of relativity—viz. the shining knowledge of mind, production in interdependence, that which is dependent[70]—and the intentional basis of Absolute-Meaning—reality[71]—, all that belongs to *saṃsāra* and the ground of purification *(sbyang gzhi)* from the impurities, are only discursive denominations. For otherwise there would arise a contradiction with the *Madhyamakakārikā*s.

If you object that there exists an important distinction because the *gzhan stong* of Absolute-Meaning has been expounded in the *stotra* collection whereas the *Madhyamakakārikā*s expound merely the *rang stong (svabhāva-śūnya)* and absolute negation, it will be necessary to point out that the *Madhyamakakārikā*s (xxv.4–6) reject the opinion that *nirvāṇa* is either an entity or a non-entity by stating:

> *Nirvāṇa* is not an entity [9b]: (otherwise) the characteristic of ageing-death would arise, for there is no entity without the characteristic of ageing-death. If *nirvāṇa* is an entity, it will be

70. *Sems gsal rig* is the mind in its phenomenalizing and conditioned state. Pure "luminous knowledge" is given as the distinguishing feature of Mind in its relative form, whereas the Empty is its proper-nature (*gsal zhing rig pa sems kyi mtshan nyid; gsal ba sems kyi mtshan nyid/ stong pa sems kyi ran bzin/;* etc.); and, according to some, it is the unabolished principial-manifestation of Mind (*sems kyi rang gdangs ma 'gag pa gsal tsam rig tsam sel sgong lta bu;* see Mkhas grub rje's *Lta khrid mun sel,* 13a2, 16a1 and 23b6). The definition "pure luminous-knowledge" applies to Mind as container *(rten)*, it being established by a logical proof that no upper and lower limits are to be reached for pure knowledge when it is firm *(Kun mkhyen Blo rig* 26a5: *rten sems gsal rig tsam yin la/ de brtan par rig pa tsam gyi ya mtha' dang ma mtha' thug med du sgrub pa'i rigs pas grub pa'i phyir)*.

Paṇ chen Bsod nams grags pa states (*Rgyud bla ma'i 'grel pa,* 28b) that some earlier scholars considered the *sems gsal rig* of the sentient-being to be the *tathāgatagarbha (sems can gyi sems rig cing gsal tsam de . . . bde gshegs snying por 'chad)*.

71. The Zhol par khang ed. has *de bzhin nyid (tathatā)*, and the Sde dge ed. has *de kho na nyid (tattva)*.

> conditioned; for nowhere does a non-conditioned entity exist. If *nirvāṇa* is an entity, how is it that *nirvāṇa* is independent? For nowhere does an independent entity exist.[72]

What is it then? The *Mādhyamikakārikā* (xxv.3) explains:

> That which is unrejected and unobtained, undestroyed and non-eternal, unabolished and unproduced is called *nirvāṇa.*[73]

Your thesis contradicts this statement.

If you object that this refers to the *rang stong,* your own opinion that *nirvāṇa* is the Absolute-Meaning itself, without a distinction between *rang stong* and *gzhan stong,* is untenable. Moreover, you must explain how the *Madhyamakakārikās* xxv.19–20 are to be understood:

> *Saṃsāra* is in no way different from *nirvāṇa,* and *nirvāṇa* is in no way different from *saṃsāra;* the limit of *nirvāṇa* is the limit of *saṃsāra,* and there is no distinction between them, however subtle.[74]

If all the sources which have constituted erroneous discourses concerning the system of the two truths and the theories on the indirect and definitive meanings of the three cycles were to be cited in addition, there would be a superabundance; and seeing that details about this are to be found elsewhere, we shall not expatiate on them here. It has been necessary to explain this much here because some persons who pride themselves now on being interpreters of the Dharma are embroiled in the very work of Māra inasmuch as they teach that this Jo nang pa doctrine is similar not only to the Cittamātra

72. *bhāvas tāvan na nirvāṇaṃ jarāmaraṇalakṣaṇam /*
prasajyetâsti bhāvo hi na jarāmaraṇaṃ vinā //
bhāvas ca yadi nirvāṇaṃ nirvāṇaṃ saṃskṛtaṃ bhavet /
nâsaṃskṛto hi vidyate bhāvaḥ kvacana kaścana //
bhāvaś ca yadi nirvāṇam anupādāya tat katham /
nirvāṇaṃ nânupādāya kaścid bhāvo hi vidyate //

73. *aprahīṇam asamprāptam anucchinnam aśāśvatam /*
aniruddham anutpannam etan nirvāṇam ucyate //

74. *na saṃsārasya nirvāṇāt kiṃcid asti viśeṣaṇam /*
na nirvāṇasya saṃsārāt kiṃcid asti viśeṣaṇam //
nirvāṇasya ca yā koṭiḥ koṭiḥ saṃsārasya ca /
na tayor antaraṃ kiṃ cit susūkṣmam api vidyate //

but also [10a] to the intention of the Kālacakra and its commentary and also to the essence of the *mahāmudrā* in the mantra system. The ominous talk which such an affirmation comprises is like the shameless cry of a crow;[75] and the errors in this bad theory have therefore been briefly revealed. But on the ears of those beings without desires who perceive that the good and the bad, gold and aconite, are Equal, how can such talk have the effect of even the sound of a herdsman's flute?

In Tibet, the land of snows, there exist many different philosophical doctrines, and it is necessary to identify the sources belonging to the different channels and instructions of authoritative scholars and adepts. Although some errors may exist in the manner of constructing the discursive presentation, if persons versed in the scriptural tradition and in reasoning and endowed with spiritual experience examine them with an impartial mind, the essential meaning will be in fundamental agreement, as is written in the Omniscient Paṇ chen's *Phyag chen rtsa 'grel*.[76] But because this Jo nang pa doctrine stems from a personal invention, it is not a source transmitted by the Indian scholars and adepts; and if a sentient being propounds such a bad and low theory which is incurable because the intention of many sūtras and śāstras of definitive meaning has been incorrectly explained, all the sūtras and tantras proclaim that the maturation *(vipāka)* of this is unimaginable. If the sentient being remains on the correct path, he will become the protector of numberless sentient beings. But by severing the vital artery of liberation, [10b] the cause *(rgyu)* of the *dharmakāya* of the *tathāgata* is destroyed.

Thus, because they could not tolerate this method, many excellent beings of the past who were as renowned as sun and moon composed many treatises that destroyed these pernicious views.

The omniscient Bu ston composed the refutation called *Bde gshegs snying po gsal zhing mdzes pa'i rgyan;* and his spiritual son the translator *(lo tsā ba)* composed the *Bde gshegs snying po'i mdzes rgyan gyi rgyan.*[77] The *piṭakadhara* Brtson 'grus dpal composed the *Bde gshegs snying po gsal bar byed pa'i sgron me.* Yar 'brog pa Rin chen tog composed the *Mnyam med dbang po'i rdo rje,* the *Ye shes thog tog,* the *Rdo rje'i thog chen,* and the *Rdo rje'i tho ba.*[78] The Sa

75. Just as the ominous call of a certain bird, the *than bya,* forebodes drought and calamity, so does this ominous talk indicate the presence of danger.

76. Two works of the Paṇ chen Blo bzang chos kyi rgyal mtshan.

77. Bu ston's spiritual son, the *lo tsā ba,* is Sgra tshad pa Rin chen rnam rgyal (1318–88). The writer has prepared a translation of these two works, which he hopes soon to publish, together with a study on the theory of the *tathāgatagarbha* and the *gotra.*

78. Yar 'brog pa refuted the Jo nang pa doctrines by showing that they had erroneously

skya scholar and master of the six sciences Dge 'dun dpal, the *piṭakadhara* of Bde ba can Rin chen gzhon nu,[79] and the *dka' bzhi pa* Rin chen rdo rje[80] also forcefully refuted this doctrine.

In their discourses the incomparable and great Red mda' ba[81] and our omniscient *bla ma* Tsong kha pa expounded many texts and arguments refuting this bad theory. And during the time when he was residing at Gnas rnying before going to the presence of the master, the eldest of the latter's spiritual sons, the omniscient Rgyal tshab, also composed a treatise named *Yid kyi mun sel* which defeats the theory of those who hold the extreme position of a permanent self having the name *buddha*. He then circulated in the schools of scholars a challenge called a Request for the opportunity to discuss at any place and time, saying that if a refutation of the thesis of this doctrine is not permitted, people will incline to the opinion that this is the truth and that all else is confusion *(moha);* [11a] but seeing that complete proofs exist in the scriptural tradition and in reasoning, if a discussion is permitted, once the sūtras and tantras and their instructions, the great masters of India and Tibet, and all the doctrines established by the Buddhists and non-Buddhists have been cited, they will be discussed in order to determine which are in accord.

Though there were at that time many followers of Dol bu pa's system like Phyogs rgyal and Nya dbon who were excellent debaters, nobody had the requisite skilled insight *(pratibhāna)* to refute his arguments on this matter.[82]

---

confused the mantra method of the Kālacakra with the *pāramitāyāna* and the sūtra method. His point of view is however peculiar inasmuch as he included the Prajñāpāramitāsūtras of definitive meaning in the third cycle of the teaching, while he held that the *Tathāgatagarbhasūtra,* etc., agree with the *Saṃdhinirmocanasūtra,* etc. His refutation of the Jo nang pa theory was therefore considered by the Dge lugs pas to be ineffective since he had, as it were, given up his sword to the Jo nang pas, whom he then attempted to fight with an empty scabbard.

79. A Bka' brgyud pa Rin chen gzhon nu is mentioned in *DNg* nya 140a f., but Bde ba can is a name of a school at Snye thang. (Another Bde ba can gyi mchod khang is mentioned in the *Sa skya dkar chag:* Ferrari, n. 494.)

80. A *bka' bzhi pa* Rin chen rdo rje is mentioned in *DNg* ta 11b.

81. Red mda' ba gzhon nu blo gros, 1349–1412, was a Sa skya pa master and one of Tsong kha pa's principal teachers. He was a pupil of Nya dbon Kun dga' dpal; he is known as a critic of the Kālacakra, and the three *Byang chub sems 'grels* attributed to Nāgārjuna, as well as of the *khrid* of the *ṣaḍaṅgayoga*. At first he also considered the *Uttaratantra* to be a Vijñānavādin work, but he later changed his opinion. He is especially famous for his commentaries on the Abhidharma and the *Madhyamakāvatāra.*

82. Cf. *PSJZ,* p. 271, where it is stated that, before becoming a disciple of Tsong kha pa, Rgyal tshab Dar ma rin chen (1364–1432) had studied at Sa skya, Gsang phu, Rtse thang, etc., and had defeated in discussion Rong ston and G.yag sde paṇ chen.

Later Zi lung pa Shākya mchog ldan,[83] who claimed to uphold the Sa skya teaching and who was celebrated as a great scholar, wrote in his youth the *Dbu ma rnam nges,* the *Rtsod yig tshigs bcad ma,* and so on. Moved as he was without being free in mind by the demon of passion and hate for the method of the theory established by the master Tsong kha pa—the real meaning of Nāgārjuna and his son [Āryadeva]—he thus composed many apparent refutations. And claiming he had accepted literally the texts of the *rigs tshogs*[84] and of Candrakīrti, he explained that the theory of neither being nor non-being *(yod min med min gyi lta ba)* was the doctrine of Śrī Candra.[85] But in his old age he composed the *Lugs gnyis rnam 'byed;* and, after having affirmed that Asaṅga and his brother Vasubandhu were Great Mādhyamikas[86] and that Candrakīrti

83. Shākya mchog ldan (1428–1507) was a disciple of Rong ston Shākya rgyal mtshan (1367–1449), who is stated to follow the Madhyamaka-Svātantrika doctrine.

Shākya mchog ldan is said to have at first followed the Madhyamaka, then the Vijñānavāda, and finally the Jo nang pa doctrine (*ThG* 85b3–4; cf. *PSJZ,* p. 257). His doctrines, like the Jo nang pa ones, are said to have the effect of destroying the cause of the *dharmakāya* of the *tathāgata* (see below; and above, fol. 10a); this is so because he came to reject the Prāsaṅgika theory according to which *śūnyatā* is absolute negation (which is *not* to be confused with total non-existence, *ye nas med pa*).

84. These are Nagārjuna's *Mādhyamikakārikās*, *Vigrahavyāvartanī, Ratnāvalī, Yuktiṣaṣṭikā, Śūnyatāsaptati,* and *Vaidalyasūtra.* Bu ston in his *Chos 'byung* (fol. 19b) gives a slightly different list; cf. also E. Obermiller's note 506 in his translation of *Bu ston's History of Buddhism.*

85. This general interpretation of the Madhyamaka was quite frequent amongst scholars of the Sa skya pa, Rnying ma pa, Karma pa, and 'Brug pa schools. It was also accepted by Zhang Thag sag pa, a follower of Spa tshab lo tsā ba, who introduced the Prāsaṅgika Madhyamaka into Tibet (cf. *DNg cha* 8a–b).

86. *Dbu ma pa chen po.* The term "Great Madhyamaka" *(dbu ma chen po)* is applied by certain Tibetan scholars, including the Jo nang pas and Karma Mi bskyod rdo rje (1507–54), to the theory of the Gnosis without differentiation between apprehender and apprehended *(grāhya-grāhaka: gzung 'dzin gnyis med kyi ye shes),* which is held to be the ultimate reality *(gnas lugs mthar thug pa).* This *advaya-jñāna* corresponds to the Jo nang pa definition of the *pariniṣpanna,* or absolute. According to Mi bskyod rdo rje, this doctrine of the *dbu ma chen po* was taught in the stotra collection attributed to Nāgārjuna and in Āryadeva's *Catuḥśataka.* The Great Madhyamaka is then distinct from the partial Madhyamaka *(phyogs gcig pa'i dbu ma),* which teaches absolute non-existence (*bden par med pa tsam gyi stong nyid* and the *med dgag,* or absolute negation). Mi bskyod rdo rje furthermore held that the Prajñāpāramitā sūtras and the *Abhisamayālaṃkāra* are to be interpreted in accordance with the *dbu ma chen po* of the *alīkākāra* doctrine of the Nirākāravādins Asaṅga and Vasubandhu; Asaṅga, Vasubandhu, Dignāga, and Dharmakīrti are thus considered to have maintained the *dbu ma chen po,* which is then assimilated to the *sems tsam rnam brdzun pa* doctrine. The doctrine of the *gzhan stong chen mo* also belongs to the *dbu ma chen po.*

Shākya mchog ldan apparently also accepted a comparable classification of these Indian sources inasmuch as he is stated to consider the Madhyamaka of Candrakīrti, which

and the rest were Mādhyamika proponents of the non-existence of own-being *(niḥsvabhāvatā),* he for example insisted that this *śūnyatā* is not to be practised at the time of realization in meditation because it is the *śūnyatā* of destruction *(chad stong)* and absolute negation *(prasajyapratiṣedha).*[87] [11b] He thus composed many terrible discourses.

As a result of having during his whole life studied the doctrines, at the time of his death he became aware of the bad and low theory which defeats the cause *(rgyu = hetu)* of the *dharmakāya* of the *tathāgata;* and this constitutes a sign of the great merits of Shākya mchog ldan. When he changed his field of existence *(zhing),* he accepted as retribution the fruit flowing *(niṣyandaphala)* from his act of reviling the exact vision of his youth. And in his subsequent existences he had experience of many burdens in accordance with what is expressed in a verse of the *Catuḥśataka* (xii.10): "He who is enveloped by confusion of thought procures for himself spiritual obstacles, and he will obtain neither the good nor *a fortiori* liberation."

> In the divisions of one lunation of the established doctrine *(siddhānta),* the bright fortnight brings the clear light which is the right explanation;
> and the dark fortnight comprises the thick darkness of bad theories: the Jo nang pa system includes both.[88]

---

teaches non-substantiality *(ngo bo nyid med pa, niḥsvabhāvatā),* to be a lower doctrine that does not correspond to the highest Gnosis.

Long before Mi bskyod rdo rje, Go rams pa Bsod nams sen ge (1429–89), a contemporary of Shākya mchog ldan, had rejected for the Sa skya pas the idea that the teachings of Maitreyanātha and the works of Asaṅga, Vasubandhu, Dignāga, and the other masters of this line could be considered as setting forth the *dbu ma chen po* identical essentially with the "real" opinion of Nāgārjuna and Āryadeva. Indeed, if such were the case, Go rams pa asks, what texts should we have belonging to the Cittamātra?

The background to these theories still remains to be studied on the basis of the abundant sources available both in Sanskrit and in Tibetan.

87. As already stated, according to Shākya mchog ldan, the *rang stong* or Prāsaṅgika *śūnyatā* is the Empty through destruction *(chad stong),* which is only applicable to the relative, all the appearances of which are totally non-existent.

88. According to a frequently mentioned idea, a movement in the discursus of the relative world at the same time presupposes and brings about a counter-movement; thus, on the discursive level, a truth may engender as it were a counter-truth. This mechanism is compared to the periodic alternation of the *śukla*° and *kṛṣṇa-pakṣas,* of the *vivarta*° and *saṃvartakalpas,* etc. According to the Rnying ma pas this also accounts for the existence of false *gter mas* and *gter stons* beside the authentic ones. Here the Jo nang pa doctrine is said to comprise within itself both phases of this periodic movement.

The brilliant dawn, which is the good explanation of the Kālacakra,
brings thousands of suns which are the joy of scholars;
but the darkness of the bad and incurable theory in the Jo nang pa
system obscures the path of liberation.
The refutations made by scholars constitute sometimes a shower of
hailstones, while sometimes offerings of flower-garlands of praise
are made.
After such a one as I have subjected it to a decisive examination, it is
difficult to praise or criticise [exclusively] the Jo nang pa system:
This system joining together the iron band of the theory of the
permanent, stable, and eternal and the golden band of the
consecrations of the tantras and instructions
was obtained, it is related, from Kailāsa by Yu mo in a state of
composition of mind.
The preceding discussion of this history [12a] has been made both like
a naturally shining mirror and like a needle that removes the thorns
of faults and errors.
This exposition of the history of the Jo nang pa doctrine, which is part
of the *Crystal Mirror of Good Explanations* which expounds the
sources and methods of the doctrines, is finished.
[Well-being to all!]

Appendix

History of the Jo nang pas According to the Ngor pa chos 'byung[89]

Jo nang kun spangs [Thugs rje brtson 'grus] came[90] to Dab shar in La stod Byang.[91] He was the abbot of Nyang stod Rkyang 'dur.[92] Having relinquished this function, he practised religion in mountain retreats and became

89. The following notice on the Jo nang pas, which furnishes some further valuable information not included in the *ThG,* is taken from folio 148 'og ma of the *Kha skong legs bshad nor bu'i bang mdzod* by Sangs rgyas phun tshogs (1649–1705), a supplement to the *Dam pa'i chos kyi 'byung tshul legs bshad bstan pa'i rgya mtshor 'jug pa'i gru chen* by Dkon mchog lhun grub (1479–1557). On this work see also *TPS,* p. 145.

90. The word *'byon pa* meaning "come, arrive" is apparently applied here and below to the "advent" of a master in his birthplace. On Dol bu pa's "advent" in Mnga' ris Dol bu Ban tshang, see just below.

91. This name appears as La stod byang gi dab phyar spang sgang in *DNg* tha 9a7.

92. Rkyang 'dur was founded by 'Jam dbyangs gsar ma according to *DNg* cha 4b; cf. *DNg* tha 8b4 and 9b1.

renowned as an anchorite *(kun spangs).* When Jo mo nags rgyal[93] presented a secluded place *(dgon gnas)* [to him], he founded Jo mo; and since this lord *(rje)* was a pupil of the Dharmarāja 'Phags pa and the others, Jo nang also is a branch monastery *(dgon lag)* of Sa skya. Thereafter, Byang sems Rgyal ba ye shes, Mkhas btsun Yon tan rgya mtsho, and others came.

Dol bu pa Shes rab rgyal mtshan came to Dol bu Ban tshang in Mnga' ris,[94] and he attended on Skyi ston, Mkhas btsun Yon tan rgya mtsho, and others. He occupied the abbatial seat of Jo nang, instituted the doctrinal system of the *gzhan stong,* and constructed the Sku 'bum chen mo, and [thus] the treasury of the Dharma was revealed; so he said he thought that, the mountain having been heaped up, the ocean flowed forth.

His pupil Jo nang Phyogs rgyal ba also came to Dol bu in Mnga' ris, and he occupied the abbatial seats of both Jo nang and Ngam ring. Concerning Ngam rings,[95] together with the *bdag chen* of Byang, the Tva wen chen po Nam mkha' bstan pa,[96] this master founded the residence *(bla brang),* assembly hall, etc. of Ngam ring. [149a] Thereafter there was a line of abbots at Ngam rings.

Kun mkhyen Dol bu pa's pupil Kun spang[s] Chos grags pa[97] was the son of the *dpon* Kun dga' rgyal mtshan, the elder brother of the great Yon btsun Grags pa dar, the *dpon chen* of Byang in the *g.yas ru* [of Gtsang province] belonging to the *dbon rgyud* of the Sa skya bla brang Khang sar chen mo.[98]

93. Jo mo nags rgyal is mentioned as (the residence of) one of the Bstan ma bcu gnyis who resides in Gtsang stod (*KD* ya 6b5). G. N. Roerich (*Blue Annals,* II, p. 772) explains Jo mo nags rgyal as the local deity of Jo nang.

94. It is not quite certain whether the xylograph has Ban tshad or Ban tshang, as in *DNg.* Cf. note 11 above.

95. On Ngam ring(s), a famous centre for the study of the Kālacakra, see note 43 above.

96. On Nam mkha' bstan pa (or brtan pa), see *BNTh* 28b3 (which also mentions the religious name Rin chen dpal bzang po) and 40a6; *Rdzogs ldan gzhon nu'i dga' ston,* 66a. Cf. note 43 above.

97. Chos grags dpal bzang po, the *kun spangs* or anchorite, is mentioned in *DNg* nya 57b; tha 11b, 15b, 19b, 41a; pha 18a7. (See also the *Life of Bu ston Rin po che* [*BNTh* 22b1 and 23b3]?). See *RM* under 1313.

98. On the Khang gsar (and Byang rin) see *DNg* nga 6a–b. This passage of the *Kha skong* is not quite clear concerning these persons. Compare *Rdzogs ldan gzhon nu'i dga' ston* 66a2 f., which is followed by *PSJZ,* p. 160.

According to these sources, the Byang bdag and dpon Grags pa dar was a contemporary of Se chen, i.e., Qubilai Qan. His grandson was Nam mkha' brtan pa (see above), whose son was Rin rgyan, and the latter's son was Chos grags dpal bzang, a *si tu chang gu* (1352–1417; cf. the Genealogical Table IV in *TPS*). It does not seem that this Chos grags dpal

He attended on Dpang lo, Dpal ldan seng ge,[99] Bu ston, Dol bu pa, and many other scholars and adepts. He established many religious schools *(chos grva)* including Bzang ldan, 'Ga' rong,[100] Chung kha ba, and others, and he accomplished much that was beneficial as the ornament of the teaching.

Sa bzang Ma ti ba came to Mdog dpang po [spelling?] and attended on Dol bu ba, Kun spangs pa, Dpang lo tsā ba, and others. He also was the first *upādhyāya (mkhan po thog ma)* of Bzang ldan. His learning was great, and his action was far-reaching.[101] He also founded the hermitage *(dgon gnas)* in the secluded place of Dga' ldan sa bzang.

Sa bzang 'Phags pa Gzhon nu blo gros occupied his seat there.[102] And the Vajradhara Kun dga' bzang po came together with the others and occupied this seat.[103]

---

bzang si tu chang gu is Chos grags pa, the *kun spangs,* of the same family, whose father was Kun dga' rgyal mtshan.

99. Dpal ldan seng ge is mentioned in *DNg* tha 15a–b. He was a teacher of Bu ston (*BNTh* 9a7 and 12a7; cf. *DNg* ja 11a, 15b) and a disciple of Shes rab seng ge (*DNg* tha 15b and pha 21a). Dpang lo tsā ba Blo gros brtan pa was also a great master of the Kālacakra, etc. (*DNg* tha 15b, etc.). The xylograph here reads *dpang lo dpal ldan seng ge* as if Dpal ldan seng ge were his name; but the reference is presumably to the well-known Dpang lo tsā ba, 1276–1342.

100. Tsong kha pa studied in these two seminaries (cf. *TPS,* p. 426a).

101. On Sa bzang Mati paṇ chen Blo gros rgyal mtshan, see above, and *DNg* pha 18a.

102. Sa bzang 'Phags pa Gzhon nu blo gros is mentioned in *DNg* pha 18a5 and 18b1.

103. Ngor pa Kun dga' bzang po (1382–1456) founded Ngor E vaṃ in 1429 *(RM).* On his connection with Sa bzang, see also *DNg* pha 18a5.

13. A Karma Bka' brgyud Work on the Lineages and Traditions of the Indo-Tibetan *dbu ma* (Madhyamaka)*

I

PEOPLES INCLINE to order their world and the ideas they have of their civilization and traditions in a variety of characteristic ways. In Tibet one of the most typical structures so employed is the lineage. Such lineages may be articulated into princely and royal genealogies *(gdung rabs, jo rabs, rgyal rabs)* belonging to "clans" or "races," into abbatial *(gdan [sa'i] rabs)* or magisterial *(mkhan rabs)* ones connected with monastic seats, and into genealogies of hierophanies *(sku 'phreng, sku rabs kyi 'phreng ba)* in lines *('khrungs rabs)* of rebirths *(yang srid)*. While these lineages together with the individuals who make them up might seem at first sight to be, according to the particular case, either secular or religious, they very frequently turn out to have been regarded in Tibet as possessing both a temporal and a spiritual side. Thus a sovereign or prince may be thought of as born in a lineage having heavenly, divine antecedents, and also as a king by/of the Dharma *(chos rgyal)*. On the other hand, religious heads, abbots, and spiritual masters—who occupy their positions either by heredity or through pupillary succession within a magisterial or preceptorial line (cf. *bla brgyud, mkhan brgyud, sgrub brgyud, bshad brgyud*), or again in virtue of being regarded as a link in a line of hierophanies *(sprul sku)*—are regularly invested with temporalities that are frequently considerable and sometimes indeed truly princely; very often, therefore, they are in effect abbot-princes in hierocratic lines.[1]

* First published in *Orientalia Iosephi Tucci memoriae dicata* (Giuseppe Tucci Memorial Volume, Serie Orientale Roma LVI), vol. 3, pp. 1249–80. Ed. G. Gnoli and L. Lanciotti. Rome: Istituto Italiano per il Medio ed Estremo Oriente, 1988.

1. This conception may be linked with the religio-political system known as the "conjunction of Dharma and polity" *(chos srid zung 'brel)*, or the "two-fold way" *(lugs zung, lugs*

Genealogies are given in detail in the Tibetan historiographical and hagiographical-biographical literature, and they occupy an especially prominent place in the Rgyal rabs literature starting with Sa skya Grags pa rgyal mtshan (1147–1216) and in the Deb ther literature starting with Tshal pa Kun dga' rdo rje (Dge ba'i blo gros), who composed the body of his *Deb ther dmar po (Hu lan deb ther)* in 1346; and genealogical material thus occupies much space in 'Gos lo tsā ba Gzhon nu dpal's *Deb ther sngon po* composed in 1476–78. In the "archival" works of the Yig tshang literature, too, genealogies are as is to be expected very prominent; and in a work that reflects this genealogical approach in a characteristic fashion, the *Rgya bod yig tshang mkhas pa dga' byed,* which is a collection of records compiled in the fifteenth century by the archivist *(yig mkhan)* "Śrībhūtibhadra" (Dpal 'byor bzang po?), we find listed the royal and princely lineages of India, Li yul, China, Mi nyag, Tibet, and Mongolia side by side with the lineages of the prince-hierarchs of the Sa skya, Bka' brgyud, and other schools.[2]

It was the Bka' brgyud pas in particular who developed to the highest degree the idea of combining the concepts of hierophany and hierocracy in a single line of *sprul sku* type rebirths. In the case of the Karma pa branch of the Bka' brgyud pa school, this latter development was evidently occasioned by certain political and social conditions in conjunction with the fact that the Karma pas were among the chief transmitters of the doctrine of the projection *('pho ba)* of the conscious principle into a new state of existence, one of the Six Dharmas of Nāropa (Naḍapāda). Historically as well as ethnographically, the various kinds of lineage mentioned above undoubtedly have different origins and belong to distinct systems. But in effect they appear to have merged together in a single representation in which they reinforce each other, being held together by the common theme of ancestry, biological or spiritual.

The Karma pas' propensity to view their history and traditions in terms of lineage and genealogy has evidently had a strong influence on their conception and articulation of the traditions of the Indo-Tibetan Dbu ma

gnyis), which came to be embodied in lines of temporal-cum-spiritual figures such as the Dalai Lamas in Tibet and the Jebtsundampa Qutuγtus in Mongolia. The dating of this religio-political system depends in part on the date of the *Čaγan teüke* (recently edited and translated by Klaus Sagaster); though sometimes ascribed to the thirteenth century, this work was edited (in a *recensio nova)* in the sixteenth century by Sečen Qung Taiyiǰi, an associate of Altan Qan (1507–82) who was, very significantly, a donor-patron of Bsod nams rgya mtsho (Dalai Lama III, 1543–88, who received the title of Dalai Lama from Altan Qan) and the ancestor of Yon tan rgya mtsho (Dalai Lama IV, 1589–1616/17).

2. Cf. Ariane Macdonald, *JA* 1963, pp. 58–62.

(Madhyamaka) with which this article is concerned. A noteworthy example of the combination of doxography and spiritual genealogy is found in the introduction to the commentary on Candrakīrti's *Madhyamakāvatāra* and *Bhāṣya* entitled *Dbu ma la 'jug pa'i rnam bshad, Dpal ldan dus gsum mkhyen pa'i zhal lung dvags brgyud grub pa'i shing rta,*[3] where Mi bskyod rdo rje (1507–54)—the eighth hierarch in the Zhwa nag Karma pa line—sets out the main lineages and teachings of the Madhyamaka/Dbu ma in India and Tibet. By its very title this work already clearly shows that Mi bskyod rdo rje's conception of the traditions of this school centre on the precepts of Mi la ras pa's great disciple Dvags po lha rje—otherwise known as Sgam po pa Bsod nams rin chen (1079–1153)—which were handed down to the Karma pa school of the Bka' brgyud pas by Sgam po pa's disciple Dus gsum mkhyen pa (1110–93), the first hierarch in the line of Zhwa nag Karma pas.[4]

Of particular interest to us is the fact that for each lineage and teaching, Mi bskyod rdo rje has also traced the line of transmission down to himself. This combination of genealogy and doxography thus serves to authenticate and validate a tradition for its recipient—the hierarch—and his disciples.

3. This text was published in 1975 by the Dharma Chakra Centre of Rumtek (Rum btegs, Sikkim) in 403a folios. An earlier edition in 412a folios was published in 1969, also from Rumtek. The *Dvags brgyud grub pa'i zhing rta* was begun in the author's thirty-ninth year (1545).

4. On Dus gsum mkhyen pa, the disciple of Sgam po pa and the founder of the 'Tshur phu/Mtshur phu monastery, see 'Gos lo tsā ba gzhon nu dpal, *Deb ther sngon po* (= *DNg*), na, 31b f. (G. N. Roerich, *The Blue Annals,* pp. 473–74).

Beside the *DNg* (written in 1476–78) and Dpa' bo Gtsug lag phreng ba's *Mkhas pa'i dga' ston* (completed in 1564), chapter pa, the main source for the history of the Karma pas is the *Bsgrub brgyud karma kaṃ tshang brgyud pa rin po che'i rnam par thar pa rab 'byams nor bu zla ba chu shel gyi phreng ba* by Si tu Chos kyi 'byung gnas (1699/1700–1774) and 'Be lo Tshe dbang kun khyab, contained in volumes da and na of the Dpal spungs edition of Si tu's Bka' 'bum (reprinted in two volumes, New Delhi, 1972). See also Karma Nges don bstan rgyas, *Chos rje karma pa sku 'phreng rim byon gyi rnam thar mdor bsdus dpag bsam khri shing* (brief biographies of the successive embodiments of the Black Hat Karma pa Lamas, written in the *lcags yos* year [1891] and published by Topden Tsering, Tibetan Bonpo Monastic Centre, Ochghat, H. P., 1973); H. E. Richardson, "The Karma-pa Sect," *JRAS* 1958, pp. 139–64, and 1959, pp. 1–18; N. Douglas and M. White, *Karmapa* (London, 1976); Karma Thinley, *History of the Sixteen Karmapas of Tibet* (Boulder, 1980); E. G. Smith, introduction to Lokesh Chandra (ed.), *Autobiography and Diaries of Situ Paṇchen* (New Delhi, 1968), pp. 20 f.

II

After recapitulating briefly the basic points in Madhyamaka thought (fol. 2a3–3b2), Mi bskyod rdo rje turns his attention to the origin of the lines of transmission of the Madhyamaka. In the first place, he notes that this system of thought *(lugs = naya)* had its origin with—literally it was "opened up" *('byed pa)* by—the preceptor Nāgārjuna-pāda, about whom prophetic indications *(lung bstan pa = vyākaraṇa)* given by the Buddha himself are found in the scriptures of the Mahāyāna (3b2).

Next Nagārjuna's great disciple Āryadeva is mentioned, followed by Śūra (Dpa' bo)[5] and Śāntideva. Mi bskyod rdo rje observes that since these masters have not been opposed by any proponent of the Madhyamaka, their teachings are known as the Madhyamaka of the "matrix texts" (*mātṛkā,* i.e., the basic sources of all the branches of the Madhyamaka school) *(gzhung phyi mo'i dbu ma)* (3b3).

Thereafter[6] the preceptor Buddhapālita expounded the meaning of the Madhyamaka, but he was combatted by the preceptor Bhā(va)viveka. And because this rebuttal required investigation in its turn, the preceptor Candrakīrti—regarded as a manifestation *(rnam par 'phrul pa)* of Buddhapālita himself—appeared in the world in order to explain in detail the unlimited meaning of the Madhyamaka. Later there also appeared preceptors such as the authors of the *Madhyamakālaṃkāra* (Śāntarakṣita), the *Madhyamakāloka* (Kamalaśīla), and the *Satyadvayavibhaṅga* (Jñānagarbha), all of whom differed slightly from Candrakīrti (3b4–5).

Still, with respect to their doctrine of the ultimate Madhyamaka *(mthar thug gi dbu ma'i bzhed pa),* these preceptors did not disagree in the slightest, for all of them were proponents of the Middle *(dbu ma par smra ba).*

In support of this statement Mi bskyod rdo rje quotes *inter alia* the *Prajñāpāramitāsaṃcayagāthā* (xxii.3ab) where it is stated that the Pāramitā alone is the Path of all past and future *jina*s in all the directions. And he cites, too, the words of Master 'Bri gung gling pa,[7] who declared of the *vajra-*

5. A *slob dpon* Dpa' bo is mentioned in Bhā(va)viveka's *Tarkajvālā* iii.199 (P, fol. 113b8), for example.

6. The word "thereafter" *(phyi nas)* is justified *doxographically,* from the point of view of the tradition, but of course not historically since Śāntideva, just mentioned, is *chronologically* later than Buddhapālita, Bhā(va)viveka, and Candrakīrti, who are about to be mentioned.

7. Cf. *DNg,* na, 76b (p. 577). Here and elsewhere the 1969 edition reads 'Bri khung (which is possibly the more usual spelling). This is Shes rab 'byung gnas (1187–1241).

logia of the master 'Jig rten gsum gyi mgon po 'Bri gung pa chen po (1143–1217)[8] that, in all their extensiveness, they set out just one thing, namely the real essence or nature of all the factors of existence *(chos thams cad kyi gshis sam babs kyi gnas lugs)* in conformity with the Buddha's own teaching[9] (3b5–4a2).

Here in Tibet, however, prattlers led astray by error pertaining to faulty direct perception and inference *(mngon sum dang rjes dpag ltar snang gi log shes)*[10] talk, with regard even to Mādhyamikas such as Bhā(va)viveka and Candrakīrti, about a higher and a lower degree of theory *(lta ba)* and comprehension *(rtogs pa)*, and also about a right and a wrong philosophical doctrine *(grub mtha' = siddhānta)*. But if this were correct, those described as inferior would in fact not be Mādhyamikas at all; for so long as the meaning of the Madhyamaka remains unrealized in such a way, there would be nothing but the mere names "Madhyamaka" and "Mādhyamika," as is the case with [the names] *Alīkākāra-Madhyamaka* and *[Alīkākāra-]Mādhyamika*[11] (4a2–4).

To trainee-disciples *(gdul bya = vaineya/vineya)* of higher and lower capacities attracted to the four philosophical doctrines *(siddhānta)*[12] the Buddha has accordingly taught the Dharma in accordance with the intellect of each. And for this reason the doctrines of the three lower *siddhānta*s appear to various trainee-disciples in accordance with the Buddha's having variously taught either the provisional, indirect *(neyārtha)* or the final, certain meaning *(nītārtha) (drang nges ci rigs par gsungs pa ltar)*. In the Madhyamaka, the highest of the four *siddhānta*s, on the other hand the teaching is exclusively in terms of what pertains to the ultimate certain meaning *(nges don = nītārtha)*. How then could it be appropriate for superior and inferior theories to exist in the doctrine of the Madhyamaka? For here there is found no teaching in terms of a division between *neyārtha* and *nītārtha*. To support this view Mi bskyod rdo rje refers to Mañjuśrī,[13] who has stated that whereas in the texts of the Vaibhāṣikas, Sautrāntikas, and Yogācāras there is found

8. See *DNg*, na, 85a–87a (pp. 596–601).

9. This is presumably an allusion to the *'bri khung/gung dgongs gcig*, a fundamental doctrine of 'Bri gung 'Jig rten mgon po.

10. The 1975 edition reads *log ges* instead of *log shes*.

11. On this see below.

12. The four *siddhānta*s *(grub mtha')* referred to here are the Vaibhāṣika, the Sautrāntika, the Vijñānavāda (or "Cittamātra"), and the Madhyamaka.

13. I.e., Mañjuśrīkīrti? —On Mañjuśrīkīrti, a follower of Candrakīrti, see below, fol. 8b6, and n. 69.

the quasi-true *(cung zad bden)* and the untrue *(mi bden),* the system of the Madhyamaka is entirely true (4a4–6).

Now, to the question as to which of the above-named preceptors had the greatest power of intellect for overcoming especially quickly the mental capacity of both non-Buddhist and Buddhist sectarians *(mu stegs byed = tīrthakara)* when explicating the intended purport *(dgongs pa)* of the Madhyamaka the Reverend Dīpaṃkaraśrījñāna has replied that the great preceptor Candrakīrti-pāda was without a rival[14] (4a6–b1).

Coming then to the task he has set himself, from among the independent and commentarial works composed by Candrakīrti Mi bskyod rdo rje proposes to sum up the meaning of the independent treatise called the *Madhyamakāvatāra.* And with this end in view he takes up first the topic of the persons who have transmitted this Dharma and then, secondly, the actual exposition of this Dharma which is to be explicated (4b1–3).

In this article we shall be concerned only with what Mi bskyod rdo rje has written concerning the first topic, namely the transmitters of the Madhyamaka Dharma. This section is divided into three sections[15] (4b3–32b5).

1.1. The sources of Gracious Conferment *(bka' drin)* generating certainty in respect to the three kinds of discriminative knowledge *(shes rab gsum gyi nges pa,* i.e., *śrutamayī, cintāmayī,* and *bhāvanāmayī prajñā)* pertaining to this Dharma system. This section is subdivided into three divisions.

1.1.1. The lineal transmission *(brgyud pa)* from within the Precious Preceptive Line itself *(bka' brgyud rin po che nyid).*

1.1.1.1. The lineal transmission from Lord Nāropa.[16]

Whereas it is accepted that the Bka' gdams pas were in direct relation with Candrakīrti and also with Nāgārjuna,[17] in an ancient document on the history and lives of the lineal transmission of the Four Precepts *(bka' bzhi brgyud pa'i lo rgyus rnam thar gyi yig rnying)* composed by Lord Mar pa the Translator,[18]

14. See *Satyadvayāvatāra* (P, ha, fol. 70b = gi, fol 7b), where Dīpaṃkaraśrījñāna refers in particular to Candrakīrti's *Madhyamakāvatāra.*

15. Sections 2 and 3 are actually treated together in a single short paragraph (fol. 9b1–4). In the following our translation has been condensed and abridged.

16. Nāropa (Naḍapāda) died probably in 1040. He was a teacher of Dīpaṃkaraśrījñāna.

17. This connexion was through Dīpamkaraśrījñāna (Atisha). See below.

18. On Mar pa's dates (1012–97) see G. Tucci, *Tibetan Painted Scrolls* (Rome, 1949), p. 257n163.

there is very highly praised the Life *(rnam par thar pa)* called *Excellence of the Prophetic Indication (vyākaraṇa) to Candrakīrti (Zla grags la lung bstan gyi che ba)*. According to this document, following on the nirvāṇa of the sun-like protector Nāga [i.e., Nāgārjuna], a prophetic indication was given to the effect that, after the passage of five hundred years, a paṇḍit born in a pure family and named Candrakīrti would dispel the darkness, just as the moon *(candra)* does when the sun [i.e., Nāgārjuna] has set. He is stated to have been the disciple of Āryadeva (4b4–5a1).

The following is then the line of transmission: Sambuddha-Bhagavat; Rigs gsum mgon po [Avalokiteśvara, Mañjuśrī, and Vajrapāṇi]; Nāgārjuna; Āryadeva; Candrakīrti; Mātaṅgi;[19] Tailo; Nāro; Mar pa; Mila; Dvags po;[20] Dus gsum mkhyen pa [Zhwa nag I, 1110–93];[21] 'Gro mgon Ras chen;[22] Spom brag pa;[23] Karma pa [Pakṣi, Zhwa nag II, 1204 or 1206–83]; Auḍyāyana pa;[24] Rang byung ba [Rang byung rdo rje, Zhwa nag III, 1284–1339]; G.yung ston pa;[25] Rol pa'i rdo rje [Zhwa nag IV, 1340–83]; Mkha' spyod dbang po [Zhwa dmar II, 1350–1405]; De bzhin gshegs pa [Zhwa nag V, 1384–1415]; Ratnabhadra;[26] Mthong ba don ldan [Zhwa nag VI, 1416–53]; 'Jam dpal bzang po and/or Dpal 'byor don grub;[27] Chos grags rgya mtsho [Zhwa nag VII, 1454–1506]; Snye bo[28] Go shri and Rje btsun Ras pa chen po; and Mi bskyod rdo rje [Zhwa nag VIII, 1507–54] himself (5a1–4).

19. The 1969 edition reads Mataṅgi and the 1975 edition Mātaṅgi. On Mātaṅgi as a pupil of Nāgārjuna and Āryadeva, see Tāranātha, *Rgya gar chos 'byung* (ed. A. Schiefner), pp. 70 and 164.

20. Dvags po lha rje = Sgam po pa Bsod nams rin chen (1079–1153). See, e.g., *DNg*, nya, 22a f. (pp. 451 f.).

21. See above, note 4.

22. Sans rgyas ras chen dpal grags, a disciple of Dus gsum mkhyen pa. Cf. *DNg*, nya, 34a (p. 480).

23. See *DNg*, nya, 35b (p. 483).

24. O rgyan pa Seng ge dpal (1230–1308/9).

25. G.yung ston Rdo rje dpal (1284–1365). See *DNg*, ga, 22b (p. 149); nya, 40a (p. 493).

26. Sog dbon Rin chen bzang po(?).

27. Rgyal tshab I.

28. The 1969 edition reads Snye 'og.

1.1.1.2. The lineal transmission from Lord Maitrīpāda.[29]
Having understood that the Madhyamaka of Saraha the Elder, Saraha the Younger, Nāgārjuna, and Candrakīrti is one in meaning, the sovereign *(mnga' bdag)* Jina Maitrīpāda taught it to others. And this cycle of the Madhyamaka Dharma according to his system was then known as the Dharma cycle of non-mentation *(yid la mi byed pa: amanasikāra).*

Concerning his being known as Victor *(Jina)* Maitrīpāda, he debated with Ratnākaraśānti—who adhered to the thesis of the Alīkākāra-Cittamātra—and was victorious over him.[30] Now in his *Tattvadaśaka* (verse 2) Maitrīpāda has written: "For one wishing to know *tathatā,* there is neither the *sākāra* nor the *nirākāra:* a middle not endued with a guru's instructions is only middling."[31] Therefore Sahajavajra has stated in his comment on this passage[32] that the Mādhyamika thus wishes to know *tathatā* having the mark of origination in dependence proclaimed by Ārya Nāgārjuna, Āryadeva, Candrakīrti, and the others. As was stated by the Bhagavat with this meaning in mind: What is born from conditions *(pratyaya)* is [really] unborn, there being no birth by self-nature; what is dependent on conditions is stated to be empty *(śūnya),* and he who knows Emptiness is attentive; what arises in dependence has no self-nature whatever, and whatever has no self-nature arises nowhere; no factor *(dharma)* is found which is something born, [but] the foolish hold *dharma*s that do not arise to arise. Therefore, if Maitrīpāda has stated that "A middle not endued with a guru's instructions is only middling," the remainder *(lhag ma)* after the rejection of the specific [i.e., the *sākāra* and *nirākāra* doctrines of the "Cittamātra"] is a cognitive object *(viṣaya)* that is postulated; so this teaching of the essence of the *tathatā* of *yuganaddha* endued with the excellent guru's instructions—the Madhyamaka-Bhagavatī—captivates the minds of the learned. After having rejected the specific—that is, after having rejected the Cittamātra—to assert that the postulation of a remainder,

29. See *DNg,* da, 2a (pp. 841–42), where Maitrīpa (Maitrīpāda) is said to have been born in 1007 or in 1010.

30. See also below, fol. 23a3–4. Cf. *DNg,* da, 2b (p. 842); Nag tsho Tshul khrims rgyal ba, *Rnam thar rgyas pa,* fol. 42b–43a.

31. *Tattvadaśaka* (ed. Haraprasād Śāstrī, *Advayavajrasaṃgraha* [Gaekwad's Oriental Series, vol. XL], Baroda, 1927), p. 59: *na sākāranirākāre tathatāṃ jñātum icchataḥ/ madhyamā madhyamā caiva guruvāganalaṃkṛtā//* (The Tibetan translation is in the Bstan 'gyur, Rgyud 'grel, mi, fol. 122b–123a of the Peking edition.) On Advayavajra = Maitrīpāda, see G. Tucci, *Tibetan Painted Scrolls,* p. 232.

32. Sahajavajra, *Tattvadaśakaṭīkā,* fol. 182a of the Peking edition, mi. (The text of Mi bskyod rdo rje's quotation differs slightly from the text found in the Peking edition.)

namely cognition established in reality *(shes pa bden grub),* is the Madhyamaka is then itself a middling middle, and not the very pure Madhyamaka system. It is accordingly indicated that here [in Maitrīpāda's teaching] lies the explication of the meaning of the Middle endued with the teachings of Nāgārjuna and the other superiors *(guru)* (5a4–b6).

With regard to the *Yid la mi byed pa'i dbu ma* of Maitrīpāda, there have arisen in Tibet three distinct ways of developing the intended purport *(dgongs pa skong tshul).* These are (1) practice with concentration on the Mantra Madhyamaka of the Profound and Luminous *(zab gsal sngags*[33] *kyi dbu ma rtsal du bton nas nyams su len pa),* (2) practice with concentration on the Sūtra Madhyamaka of the Profound *(zab pa mdo'i dbu ma rtsal du bton nas nyams su len pa),* and (3) practice with concentration on the Madhyamaka of the Alīkākāra-Cittamātra *(sems tsam rnam rdzun gyi dbu ma)* (5b6–6a2).

The latter (3)—which explains as the sense of the *Dohās* a cognition empty of the objective and subjective *(gzung 'dzin gyis stong pa'i shes pa)* that is self-cognitive *(rang rig),* self-luminous *(rang gsal),* and established in absolute reality *(don dam du grub pa)*—has been widely represented in India and Tibet by Phyag na (Vajrapāṇi) of India,[34] Asu of Nepal,[35] Kor Ni ru pa,[36] et al.

However, many thinkers such as the philosopher Gro lung pa[37] did not agree to interpreting this system as the Madhyamaka; and they have refuted it, saying that various systems such as that of the proponents of non-mentation etc. are not consonant with the Madhyamaka system. It also turns out that basing themselves on the mere term [non-mentation], Sa skya paṇ chen[38]

33. The 1969 edition omits the word *sngags.*

34. See *DNg,* da, 2b (pp. 842 f.); and ja, 15a (p. 384) which states that Phyag na was a direct disciple of Maitrīpāda. He was born in 1017 (*DNg,* da, 13a [p. 866]). From him comes the Stod lugs of the Mahāmudrā (*DNg,* da, 3a [p. 843] and 8b f. [pp. 855 f.]). He settled in Nepal in 1066 according to Sum pa mkhan po's *Re'u mig* (= *RM*).

35. *DNg,* da, 3a (p. 843) states that Asu spent his life in the Dbus province of Tibet. From him comes the Smad lugs of the Mahāmudrā (*DNg,* da, 10a f., [pp. 860 f.]). Cf. H. V. Guenther, *The Royal Song of Saraha* (Seattle and London, 1969), pp. 16 f.

36. (S)kor Ni ru pa (Ni ru pa ta) was born in 1062 (*DNg,* kha, 15b [p. 97]) and died in 1162 *(RM).* See also *DNg,* ga, 11a (p. 124); and da, 7b (pp. 853 f.).

37. Gro lung pa Blo gros 'byung gnas, an early Bka' gdams pa master, was the disciple of Rngog Blo ldan shes rab (1059–1109). He composed a *Bstan rim* and *Lam rim.* His Bka' gdams pa tradition was kept distinct from the Mahāmudrā teaching, a fact that differentiates it from Sgam po pa's which merged with the Bka' brgyud pa and hence with the Mahāmudrā teachings.

38. In his *Sdom gsum rab dbye* (fol. 25b–26b) Sa skya paṇḍi ta has criticized the "Neo-Mahāmudrā" *(da lta'i phyag rgya chen po)* along with the Rdzogs chen belonging to the

as well as different Bka' gdams pas have developed a hostile attitude *(sdang zhen)* to the whole non-mentation cycle, which is the Reverend Maitrīpāda's very pure Dharma;[39] and in addition it turns out that there have lived persons whose disposition was to deny *(skur 'debs pa'i skal pa can)* the Great Brāhmaṇa's [i.e., Saraha's] non-mentation doctrine—which is the meaning of the *Dohākośagīti*—as well as Maitrīpāda and Saraha the Elder and Younger (6a2–4).

The preceptive traditions *(bka' srol)* of practices 1 and 2 belong in their entirety to Lord Mar pa and Mi la [ras pa] and have been practised. The middle one (2) has in addition been concentrated on and practised by Lord Sgam po pa, and its precept has accordingly been widely propagated.

Now, in the *Samādhirājasūtra* the Sugata has himself greatly praised this Lord [Sgam po pa under the name of Candraprabha Kumāra(bhūta)] as the propagator of the Madhyamaka, which is the intended purport of the *Samādhirājasūtra.* To this Dharma-system of the Madhyamaka this tradition has therefore given the name of Mahāmudrā, the appellation Mahāmudrā being used for the Gnosis of Bliss and Emptiness *(bde stong gi ye shes),* which has its source in supreme mantra.[40] And when its Madhyamaka theory has arisen in the conscious stream, the realizing of natural awareness *(tha mal gyi shes pa mngon du mdzad)* and the realizing of *dharmakāya (chos sku mngon du byas)* are spoken of; and when it is understood that a sprout [for example] as substratum of properties *(chos can = dharmin)* as well as dichotomic construction (*vikalpa,* relating to this substratum) are not established

Chinese system *(rgya nag lugs kyi rdzogs chen)* as being nothing but a version of the teachings of the Chinese Bhikṣu, i.e., the so-called Hva shang (Ho-shang). See also the same author's remarks in his *Thub pa'i dgongs pa rab tu gsal ba,* fol. 49b–52b. In his *Gnas lugs kyi mdzod* (fol. 33b) Klong chen rab 'byams pa indeed concedes that a link exists between Rdzogs chen and the teachings of the Hva shang. For 'Gos lo Gzhon nu dpal's defence of the Mahāmudrā against Sa skya paṇḍi ta's objections, see *DNg,* nya, 141b–142a (pp. 724–25).

39. The theory of *yid la mi byed pa (amanasikāra)* was identified by many Tibetan writers with the so-called "Doctrine of the Chinese Hva shang" discussed at the time of the Council of Tibet (Bsam yas), and reputedly refuted by Kamalaśīla followed by the main lines of Tibetan Buddhism deriving from Śāntarakṣita and Kamalaśīla.

40. *Mtshan gsang sngags bla med nas 'byung ba'i bde stong gi ye shes la phyag chen du grags pa'i phyag chen de'i ming du 'dogs par mdzad pa.*

Cf. *DNg,* nga, 141b–142a (pp. 724–25), and nya, 49a–b (p. 977) on the applicability of the term *mahāmudrā,* which belongs to the mantra system, to a sūtra system such as the Madhyamaka. See also below, fol. 7a–b. It may be recalled that Maitrīpāda's (Advayavajra's) works which touch on the Madhyamaka are included in the Rgyud 'grel section of the Bstan 'gyur and not in the Madhyamaka section.

apart from *dharmatā,* this is termed the appearing of dichotomic construction as *dharmakāya.* This theory and meditative realization *(lta sgom)* is then extolled as very necessary, being the counteragent that removes the continued presence of latent tendencies towards discursive development *(spros pa'i bag nyal: prapañcānuśaya)* and of turbulence *(gnas ngan len: dauṣṭhulya)* when there has arisen the most excellent experience of the Gnosis of Bliss and Emptiness belonging to mantra. So, according to the instruction, it serves to eradicate all obscuration *(sgrib pa = āvaraṇa),* being like the medicinal substance called *dkar po chig thub* for example[41] (6a5–b3).

[Mi bskyod rdo rje here goes on to allude to the Vajrayānist dimension of this Madhyamaka, with reference being made to the preliminary character of tranquillity and insight pertaining to the third and fourth consecrations *(dbang = abhiṣeka)* and the *dpe don gyi ye shes* and to the need in addition for perfect *brda don* for the achievement of comprehension, and also to the nature of conascent Bliss *(sahajānanda)* as the theme of an exchange between Lord Phag mo gru pa and first the Master Sa skya pa and then later Lord Sgam po pa[42] (6b3–b6).]

In a logion of 'Bri gung pa chen po[43] it is declared that the Mahāmudrā in our system *(kho bo'i lugs kyi phyag rgya chen po)* surpasses the four *ānandas* *(dga' ba),* that it is superior to Luminosity *('od gsal = prabhāsvara),* and that it is untouched by the three great factors *(chen po gsum gyis ma reg pa).*[44] For

41. The *dkar po chig thub* of which Mi bskyod rdo rje speaks here and below has been identified by Sa skya paṇḍi ta with the "simultaneist" *(cig car pa)* doctrine brought to Tibet at the time of Khri Srong lde btsan by the Chinese Ho-shang(s). See his *Thub pa'i dgongs pa rab tu gsal ba,* fol. 48b, 50a. The word *dkar po chig thub* refers to a plant used by itself in the Tibetan pharmacopoeia.

42. See *DNg,* nya, 68b (pp. 558–59) for details on the meeting of Phag mo gru pa (1110–70) with, first, the *bla ma* Sa chen Kun dga' snying po (1092–1158) and, later, with Sgam po pa.

43. See above, pp. 326–27.

44. See Dbon po Shes rab 'byung gnas (1187–1241), *Dam chos dgongs pa gcig pa'i gzhung,* vi (ed. D. Tsondu Senghe, Bir, 1977, fol. 5a, in *dGongs gcig and bsTan snying Texts*). See also Dbon po Shes rab 'byung gnas *Dam chos dgongs pa gcig pa'i rtsa tshig rdo rje'i gsung brgya lnga bcu pa,* vi.8 (reprinted under the title *dGongs gcig yig cha,* Bir, 1975), fol. 9b7; and Rig 'dzin Chos kyi grags pa (seventeenth century), *Dam pa'i chos dgongs pa gcig pa'i rnam bshad lung don gsal byed nyi ma'i snang ba* (reprinted in *'Bri gung pa Texts,* vol. II, by S. W. Tashigangpa, Leh, 1972), fol. 36a ff. In these sources the expression *chen po gsum* refers to the *dbu ma chen po, phyag rgya chen po,* and *rdzogs pa chen po.* According to Kong sprul Blo gros mtha' yas, *Shes bya kun khyab,* III, fol. 204a–b, there is a correlation between the *chen po gsum* and *rim skyes* (the progressive method), *thod rgal* (the skipping method), and *cig car* (the simultaneous method).

theory and meditative realization *(lta sgom)* arise in equilibrium in the conscious stream, so that this becomes the supreme counteragent against discursive grasping *(spros 'dzin gyi gnyen po)* that posits as inferior the *saṃvṛtisatya,* the conditioned *(saṃskṛta),* the adventitious *(āgantuka),* and the *dharmin,* but as superior the *paramārthasatya,* the unconditioned, nature *(rang bzhin),* and *dharmatā.* And unless it removes such discursive development positing something superior *(mchog 'dzin gyi spros pa: parāmarśa-prapañca),* like a medicine working as poison, theory and meditative realization free from discursive development would be affected by discursive development. With this in mind the Lord [Buddha] has then affirmed that the view of a self as large as Sumeru were better than a dogmatic view of non-self[45] (6b6–7a3).

With reference to this particularity of the Dharma system of the Madhyamaka, therefore, Jñānakīrti has written in his *Tattvāvatāra* that when a person of superior faculties applying himself to the Pāramitā realizes in meditation both tranquillity *(zhi gnas = śamatha)* and insight *(lhag mthong = vipaśyanā),* and when even on the stage of the ordinary worldling he is certainly endowed with the Mahāmudrā, this is the sign of unfailing perfect understanding *(yang dag par rtogs pa phyir mi ldog pa'i rtags nyid).*[46] And in his commentary on the *Tattvadaśaka* Sahajavajra has mentioned the possession of three particularities, viz. being essentially Pāramitā, being in conformity with mantra, and being termed Mahāmudrā.[47] For conferring experiential guidance *(myong khrid)* in this Dharma system of the Mahāmudrā, the consecration *(dbang bskur ba: abhiṣeka)* of mantra is not carried out. And while the direct teaching *(dngos bstan)* of this Mahāmudrā is the Madhyamaka of non-discursive Emptiness pertaining to the sūtra system *(mdo lugs),* there is taught implicitly *(shugs las)* the ordinary and extraordinary ultimate *sugatagarbha* that constitutes the profound sense of sūtra and mantra. It is, then, in consideration of this that Lord Sgam po pa, Śrī Phag mo gru pa, 'Jig rten gsum gyi mgon po 'Bri gung pa, and other masters have declared that our Mahāmudrā treatise is the *Mahāyānottaratantra-Śāstra* composed by Bhagavat Maitreya[48] (7a3–b2).

45. See *Kāśyapaparivarta* (ed. A. von Staël-Holstein), § 64 (quoted in Candrakīrti's *Prasannapadā* xiii.8).

46. Jñānakīrti, *Tattvāvatāra,* fol. 43b5 (Peking ed., with variant readings differing from Mi bskyod rdo rje's quotation). Cf. *DNg,* nya, 142a (p. 725). On Jñānakīrti's views, see also Tenzin Gyatsho (Dalai Lama XIV) and J. Hopkins, *Tantra in Tibet* (London, 1977), p. 73, etc.

47. Cf. *DNg,* nya, 142a (p. 725).

48. Cf. *DNg,* nya, 141b (p. 724). On Maitreya, to whom the *Ratnagotravibhāga* is ascribed,

With this in mind Rgod tshang pa[49] and his disciple have declared that the initiators of this teaching of the Mahāmudrā are the Great Brahman [Saraha] and Nāgārjuna,[50] the Great Brahman having taught the Mahāmudrā under the cataphatic aspect *(sgrub phyogs nas)* and Lord Nāgārjuna under the apophatic aspect *(dgag phyogs nas).*

The great Lo tsā ba Gzhon nu dpal (1392–1481)—the tutor of the fourth bearer of the Zhwa dmar diadem[51]—has accordingly stated: "This line known as the *Dpal dvags po bka' brgyud* is a transmission of the sense *(don)* rather than of the letter *(tshig);* the sense is constituted by the lineal transmission of comprehension *(rtogs pa'i brgyud pa)* of the immaculate Mahāmudrā, the superior *(guru)* from whom comprehension of the Mahāmudrā is obtained receiving the name of *rtsa ba'i bla ma.*"[52] We approve this impartial statement. With respect to the Mahāmudrā, however, the Mahāmudrā of ultimate reality *(gnas lugs)* on the one hand and of Bliss and Emptiness *(bde stong)* on the other have been taken to constitute the separate purport of sūtra and mantra; and we have already refuted elsewhere the statement maintaining that the former is superior to the latter Mahāmudrā and is the doctrine of the Precious Bka' brgyud since this statement is altogether wrong. Thus, although according to the early (or: mantra)[53] system there exists no separate instruction on the Mahāmudrā different from the Six Dharmas *(chos drug)* [of Nāropa], those who follow this lineal transmission, being aware of this implication of the matter *(don gi dbang),* have distinguished between an instruction *(khrid)* they hold to be of the Six Dharmas and one they hold to be of the Mahāmudrā (7b2–8a1).

In addition to this Precious Bka' brgyud, the Dharma system in question has had very many propagators in Tibet. Thus, as forms of this Dharma system, there exist the three teachings—the earlier, the later, and the

---

as a *bhagavant*—in other words a *buddha*—see our *Théorie du tathāgatagarbha et du gotra,* pp. 52–53. Mi bskyod rdo rje returns to the question further on in his discussion of the interrelationship between the Madhyamaka of the sūtra-system and the Madhyamaka of the mantra-system (fol. 24a f.).

49. On Rgod tshang pa Mgon po rdo rje (1189–1258?), see *DNg,* nya, 122a f. (p. 680 f.).

50. Cf. *DNg,* da, 2a (p. 841). See also *DNg,* nya, 142a (p. 725), where Rgod tshang pa is said to have connected the Mahāmudrā of the Prajñāpāramitā also with Maitrīpāda.

51. Chos grags ye shes (1453–1524).

52. *DNg,* nya, 141b (p. 724). Cf. *DNg,* da, 2a (pp. 840–41); and na, 49a–b (pp. 976–77).

53. The 1969 ed. reads *sngar lugs,* but the 1975 ed. has *sngags lugs.*

intermediate—of what is renowned as the Good Dharma Calming Ill *(dam chos sdug bsngal zhi byed)* transmitted by the Reverend Dam pa from India,[54] and specially those Mahāmudrā traditions communicated to the bodhisattva Khro phu lo tsā ba (1173?–1225) by numerous scholars and adepts of India, such as the great adept Mitrayogī[55] and the great paṇḍit Śākyaśrī (?–1225).[56] The portion of that Mahāmudrā transmitted later, after the arrival in Tibet of the great paṇḍit Vanaratna (1385–1468),[57] to the great Lo tsā ba Byams pa gling pa, to the great Lo tsā ba Gzhon nu dpal, to Khrims khang Lo chen,[58] and to others also belongs to this Dharma system (8a1–3).

The single burden *(don po gcig)* of the Dharma has thus been given concordant expression by different persons. But masters of the Sa [skya] and Dge [lugs] as well as Bo [dong] and Dol [bu pa] have asserted that this Mahāmudrā theory and practice of the Precious Bka' brgyud only is the theory and meditative realization *(lta sgom)* of the Hva shang, whereas this has not been asserted of the system of other excellent persons.[59] How is this known? In reply it has been suggested that the working only *(phrin las tsam)* of the Precious Bka' brgyud having been transmitted, it was not available to others; and so they have not[60] made such an assertion. This is, however, not correct. Indeed, it has been stated [by the Buddha] that among the four recourses *(rton pa = pratisaraṇa) dharma* rather than an individual *(pudgala)* is to be had recourse to; but there has been a deviation from this principle because of hostility [on the part of some masters to the Mahāmudrā of the Precious Bka' brgyud] (8a3–5).

After Lord Sgam po pa the lineal transmission of this Dharma from Dus gsum mkhyen pa is accordingly the same [as above] (8a5–6).

54. Cf. *DNg*, na, especially fol. 49a (p. 976), on the link between the Zhi byed doctrine and the Mahāmudrā.

55. On Mitrayogī/Mitradzoki, a contemporary of Khro phu Lo tsā ba, see *DNg*, pha, 12a f. (pp. 1030 f.).

56. This is Śākyaśrībhadra, the great Kaśmīrī paṇḍit known in Tibet as Kha che paṇ chen. On his dates see our *Life of Bu ston Rin po che* (Rome, 1966), p. 42n1. On the date of his disciple Khro phu Lo tsā ba's birth, see p. 14n1.

57. On Vanaratna see, e.g., *DNg*, tha, 21a f. (pp. 797 f.).

58. The 1969 ed. reads: Khrus khang Lo chen.

59. Mi bskyod rdo rje turns below to the opinions of the Jo nang pa, Shākya mchog ldan, Bo dong, and Tsong kha pa on the relation between the sūtra and mantra systems.

60. There is no negative particle here in the 1969 ed.

1.1.2. The transmission from Jo bo Dīpaṃkara[śrījñāna, Atisha] (ca. 982–1054).

From the preceptor Nāga, Āryadeva, Candrakīrti, and the Elder and Younger "Vidyākokila" (Rig pa'i khu byug che chung)[61] this second transmission reached Jo bo Atisha. From him it passed on to the *kalyāṇamitra* Ston pa chen po [i.e., 'Brom ston Rgyal ba'i 'byung gnas, 1005–64], and then to the latter's disciple Spyan snga ba [Tshul khrims 'bar, 1033/38–1103] and to Bya yul pa (1075–1138).[62] From many Bka' gdams pa masters Lord Sgam po pa then heard it.

Alternatively: from Bu to ba [= Po to ba][63] it passed to the great sage Sha ra ba,[64] who then handed it down to the glorious Dus gsum mkhyen pa.[65] After the latter the lineal transmission is the same as the one already indicated (8a6–b1).

Now the question arises whether the precepts *(bka')* of the Madhyamaka having the name of Mahāmudrā transmitted from the Reverend Maitrīpāda and the precepts of the Madhyamaka transmitted from Jo bo [Atisha] are both the same Dharma system.

Our reply is that there is no difference in purport. In the latter preceptive tradition, however, fixation *(gtan la phab pa)* takes place by means of constructive analysis *(rtog dpyod);* and there is equalizing concentration *(mnyam par 'jog pa)* through discriminative knowledge *(shes rab = prajñā)* where some clear image *(gsal snang)* is achieved in the aspect of non-implicative exclusion-negation *(med par dgag pa'i cha).* But in the former preceptive tradition, fixation takes place with the discriminative knowledge of constructive analysis being entirely eliminated, like fire when its fuel is spent; and there is equalizing concentration in that which involves neither negation nor affirmation *(dgag sgrub gang gi'ang don can ma yin pa zhig).* Such is the difference between the two preceptive traditions.

So, when Lord Sgam po pa once brought to completion the theory and meditative realization of the tranquillity and insight *(zhi lhag)* of the Madhyamaka according to the Bka' gdams pa system, and when having come

61. Rig pa'i khu byug (= *Vidyākokila) is/are often mentioned as a link/links in the Madhyamaka line between Candrakīrti and Dīpaṃkaraśrījñāna. A *Vidyākokila is reported to have been a teacher of Dīpaṃkaraśrījñāna; see *DNg,* ca, 2a (p. 243); *Rnam thar rgyas pa,* fol. 4b–5a, 7a, 9a, 10a.

62. See also below, fol. 126b ff.

63. On Po to ba (1031–1105) see *DNg,* ca, 11a f. (pp. 263 f.).

64. On Sha ra ba/Shar ba pa (1070–1141) see *DNg,* ca, 15a f. (pp. 271 f.).

65. On Dus gsum mkhyen pa as a disciple of Sha ra ba, see *DNg,* nya, 32b (p. 475).

to Mi la [ras pa] he presented him with this comprehension *(rtogs pa),*[66] Mi la explained to him that, good though all this was, in the aspect of tranquillity *(zhi gnas = śamatha)* it did not go beyond the causal condition for the higher spheres *(khams gong gi rgyu)* and that in the aspect of insight *(lhag mthong = vipaśyanā)* all was in danger of falling into the four pitfalls of Emptiness *(stong nyid shor sa).*[67] Nevertheless, even though this serves as a counteragent against some part of the positing of an entity *(dngos 'dzin),* such as positing as real *(bden 'dzin),* one is fettered because of the danger of even all this quite good theory and meditative realization becoming the *jñeyāvaraṇa* since one is unable to eradicate all positing of extreme positions *(mtha' 'dzin);*[68] and, if fettered, there is then no difference between being fettered by an iron chain or a golden chain. Later Lord Sgam po pa declared that he would have risked birth as a denizen of the sphere of the Long-lived Gods had he not met the very reverend Mi la. So runs the report (8b1–6).

1.1.3. The transmission from Pa tshab lo tsā ba [Nyi ma grags] (1055–?). From Candrakīrti this third transmission passed to his direct disciple Mañjuśrīkīrti[69] and then on to Devacandra, the Brahman Ratnavajra,[70]

66. This event is placed in 1110 in Sum pa mkhan po's *Re'u mig.*

67. On the *shor ba bzhi* see Dbon po Shes rab 'byung gnas, *Dam chos dgongs pa gcig pa'i rtsa tshig rdo rje'i gsung brgya lnga bcu pa,* vi.9, fol. 9b–10a, and Rig 'dzin Chos kyi grags pa, *Dam pa'i chos dgongs pa gcig pa'i rnam bshad lung don gsal byed nyi ma'i snang ba,* fol 39b ff.; cf. Kong sprul Blo gros mtha' yas, *Shes bya kun khyab,* III, fol 204a. The sources list the four *shor ba* as *shes bya'i gshis la shor ba* (i.e., *chos thams cad stong par 'dzin pa gshis la shor ba*), *rgyas 'debs su shor ba* (i.e., *snang ba la stong nyid du blos bzo ba*), *(stong nyid lam du byas nas 'bras bu phyis dus su re ba spang gnyen dbyer med du ma shes pa'i) gnyen por shor ba,* and *(stong nyid kyi go nyams cung zad thob pa na de kas chog par bzung ste bsags sbyong gi rgyun gcod pa stong nyid) lam shor ba.* See also Sa paṇ, *Thub pa'i dgongs pa rab tu gsal ba,* fol. 50b (who speaks first of a *phyag rgya chen po gshis la shor ba* and then of a *bsgom du shor ba* instead of a *gnyen por shor ba*).

68. Cf. *DNg,* da, 2a–b (pp. 840–41).

69. A Mañjuśrīkīrti is reported to have been a teacher of Dīpaṃkaraśrījñāna; see Nag tsho's *Rnam thar rgyas pa,* fol. 9b. He is evidently the author of the commentary on the *Samādhirājasūtra* (the *Kīrtimālā*) and perhaps also the author of the *Mañjuśrīnāmasaṃgitiṭīkā.*

70. On the Kaśmīrī Brahman Ratnavajra—the father of Mahājana, the grandfather of Sañjana/Sajjana (a teacher of Rngog Blo ldan shes rab, 1059–1109), the great grandfather of Sūkṣmajana (a collaborator of Pa tshab Nyi ma grags, 1055—?), and the teacher of Rin chen bzang po (958–1055)—see J. Naudou, *Les bouddhistes kaśmīriens au Moyen Age* (Paris, 1968), pp. 139 f., 174 f.

Parahita,[71] [Ma]Hasumati,[72] Pa tshab Lo tsā ba,[73] and Lord Dus gsum mkhyen pa.[74] After him the line of transmission is the same [as the one already indicated] (8b6–9a1).

Now the question arises as to whether this Dharma system of the Madhyamaka and the Dharma system of the Madhyamaka transmitted from Jo bo [Dīpaṃkaraśrījñāna] are both the same.

Not only are they identical but the terms amount to the same. Still, in this [third transmission of the Madhyamaka], Madhyamaka theory is fixed *(gtan la phab pa)* by means of inference based on learning *(thos byung rjes dpag: śrutamaya-anumāna),* and there then predominates equalizing concentration *(mnyam par 'jog pa)* through discriminative knowledge relating to the object to be correctly cognized that has been fixed in this way *(de ltar phab pa'i gzhal bya'i don).* But in the other transmission [descending from Dīpaṃkaraśrījñāna] fixation is achieved through all kinds of reasoned knowledge deriving from learning, reflection, and meditative realization *(thos bsam sgom pa'i rig pa*[75] *mtha' dag),* and then there is equalizing concentration through discriminative knowledge without objectification *(dmigs pa)* relating to a sensory object to be correctly cognized that has been fixed in this way (9a1–3).

In consideration of the degree of superiority or inferiority relative to each other of the forms of discriminative knowledge that derive from learning, reflection, and meditative realization—and which constitute the instrument establishing *(sgrub byed) madhyamaka*—and also in consideration of whether there is an object to be rightly known *(gzhal bya)*—which constitutes the object to be established *(sgrub bya)*—some philosophers like Rma bya ba have said that there is a difference of superior and inferior degree between these two systems. Thus, between the Mādhyamika who establishes

71. Parahita(bhadra?)—a disciple of Ratnavajra and the author of a Vivṛti on Nāgārjuna's *Śūnyatāsaptati,* which he translated into Tibetan together with Gzhon nu mchog—was a teacher of Rngog Blo ldan shes rab and a collaborator of Zangs dkar lo tsā 'Phags pa shes rab. Cf. J. Naudou, *Les bouddhistes kaśmīriens,* pp. 182–83.

72. Hasumati seems to be a shortened form of Mahāsumati. He was a collaborator of Pa tshab Nyi ma grags in revising the Tibetan translation of Nāgārjuna's *Mūlamadhyamakakārikās* and in translating Candrakīrti's *Prasannapadā.*

73. (s)Pa tshab Nyi ma grags (1055–?). This is the lineage given in *DNg,* cha, 8b (p. 344).

74. According to *DNg,* nya, 32b (p. 475), Dus gsum mkhyen pa was a disciple not only of Shar ba pa, who was a supporter and auditor of Pa tshab lo tsā ba (*DNg,* ca, 15a; p. 272), but also of Pa tshab himself.

75. The 1969 edition reads *rigs pa.*

a [real] object *(don)* with respect to *madhyamaka* and the one who establishes [only] pragmatic usage *(tha snyad sgrub par byed pa)*, they have considered the Mādhyamika establishing a [real] object to be *not* the best; and the Mādhyamika establishing pragmatic usage in order to prevent erroneous constructions *(log rtog)* without, however, establishing a [real] object they have considered to be the best. Also, with regard to discriminative knowledge comprehending the object to be established—*madhyamaka* or Emptiness—they have distinguished between an inference *(rjes dpag)* as the valid means of right knowledge *(tshad ma)* and a reasoned cognition *(rigs shes)* as the valid means of right knowledge[76] (9a3–5).

Now, with respect to the way of achieving theory and meditative realization, what is the difference thus brought about between Jo bo's system and Pa tshab's system?

As to the teaching there is no difference. But there is one based on the greater or lesser capacities *(skal ba)* in energy and discriminative knowledge of persons *(gang zag)* applying themselves to the sense *(don)* of the Madhyamaka. Still, it is not altogether impossible for a follower of Pa tshab to achieve theory and meditative realization in accordance with Jo bo's Madhyamaka system. Nor is it altogether impossible for followers of Jo bo to achieve theory and meditative realization in accordance with the Madhyamaka system of Lord Sgam po pa (9a6–b1).

1.2/3. The sources of the lineal transmission of the recitation tradition *(klag lung)* and the exegetical explication *('bru sbyor 'god pa)* now current in Tibet.

Down to Pa tshab this lineal transmission is as already indicated above. After Pa tshab it is as follows: Zhang Thang sag pa,[77] 'Brom Dbang phyug grags pa,[78] Shes rab rdo rje,[79] the two brothers *(mched)* Bstan tshul[80] and Grags ldan, Bde

76. On the Rma bya bas and the question of the function in the (Prāsaṅgika-) Madhyamaka of the *sgrub byed kyi tshad ma* and the *sgrub bya*, see our article "On the Thesis and Assertion in the Madhyamaka/Dbu ma" in E. Steinkellner and H. Tauscher, eds., *Contributions on Tibetan and Buddhist Religion and Philosophy* (Proceedings of the Csoma de Kőrös Symposium of 1981, vol. 2) (Wien, 1983), pp. 205–40, esp. pp. 230–31.

77. See *DNg*, cha, 8a (p. 343).

78. Stod lungs pa Dbang phyug grags (*DNg*, ca, 14a; p. 269)?

79. Shes rab rdo rje, the disciple of Shar ra ba (*DNg*, ca, 20a; p. 284)?

80. In its lineage of the *Prasannapadā* and *Madhyamakāvatārabhāṣya* transmitted through Zhang Thang sag pa, *DNg*, cha, 8a7 has Stan tshul (Roerich's Don-tshul, p. 344, is presumably a misprint).

ba'i lha,[81] Jo btsun[,] Dbu ra ba,[82] Shes rab dpal, Dar ma shes rab, Bang ston Shes (rab) rin (chen), Bsod nams seng ge, Bang ston Bsam (gtan) bzang (po), Bang ston Gzhon (nu) bsam (gtan), Thang nag pa, Bkra (shis) seng (ge), Gzhon nu bzang po, Gsas khang pa Chos grags, Thang sag pa Gzhon rgyal,[83] Rgyal mo rong pa chen po, Byams chen rab 'byams pa, Sangs rgyas 'phel, 'Bum phrag gsum pa, and the excellent philosopher Karma phrin las pa.[84] I, the very least of the servants of the Karma tradition, was filled by the latter's Gracious Conferment *(bka' drin)* (9b1–4).

* * * *

There now arises the question as to whether there exists a Dharma system of the Madhyamaka belonging to the Mantrayāna which is different from the Madhyamaka Dharma system of the great preceptor Nāgārjuna and his spiritual son [Āryadeva] together with their followers.

With respect to the aspect of freedom from discursive development *(spros bral gyi cha)* where once the neganda *(dgag bya)*—viz. the positing of extreme positions *(mthar 'dzin)* and the positing of discursive development *(spros 'dzin)*—have been stopped *(bkag pa)* there is no establishing of anything to be established *(bsgrub bya),* there is no difference. But there does exist a differential systematization *('jog pa)* depending on whether there is or is not found some efficiency *(byed las)* of the *madhyamaka* that serves as the [yogic] instrumental path for the fixation *(gtan la 'bebs byed kyi thabs lam)* of the foregoing; and in particular it depends on whether for the beginner-exercitant *(las dang po pa = ādikarmika),* in the absence of mental effort *(yid kyi rtsol ba),* there are or are not found the theory of Emptiness endowed with all excellent modes *(rnam kun mchog ldan gyi stong nyid kyi lta ba)*[85] spontaneously free from all discursive development through the utilization of further mystical [yogic] vital points that are secret *(gsang ba'i gsang gnad gzhan bcings pa)* as well as the arising of Gnosis revealing this theory

81. *DNg,* cha, 8a–b, has Lu dbon Su ba de ba (?) (Roerich, p. 344, reads Su-kha-de-va).

82. Jo btsun and Dbu ra ba clearly figure as two persons in *DNg,* cha, 8b1 (missing in Roerich's translation), but as one person in both prints of Mi bskyod rdo rje's text used here.

83. Starting with this name *DNg* differs, reading (cha, 8b2) Thang sag pa Bsod nams rgyal mtshan, Rtse pa Kun dga' gzhon nu, Slob dpon Shākya gzhon nu, Kun spangs Gzhon nu rgyal mtshan, Dmar ston Gzhon nu rgyal mtshan, etc.

84. Karma phrin las Phyogs las rnam rgyal (1456–1539). On him see H. V. Guenther, *The Royal Song of Saraha,* Introduction.

85. On *sarvākāravaropetā śūnyatā* see our *Théorie du tathāgatagarbha et du gotra* (Paris, 1969), pp. 243, 253, 319, 351 f.

(de rtogs byed kyi ye shes 'char ba). This differential systematization depends moreover on whether there is or is not found the capacity *(las su byed pa)* in certain specific substrata *(chos can = dharmin)* of the *madhyamaka* to be the base *(gzhi)* on which discursive development is cut off. And when from the *dharmin saṃvṛtisatya* there has taken place a metaphorical transfer under the *dharmin*-name of *dharmatā-paramārthasatya,*[86] differential systematization depends further on whether there is or is not then something to be attained in the form of the fruit *('bras bu)* of transmutation as the *kāya* and *jñāna* of conjunction of the two *satyas*.[87]

This differential systematization I formerly comprehended, but without having the expository ability *(spobs pa)* to explain it because the intent *(dgongs pa)* of Lord Ras pa chen po was somewhat withheld. The withholding of this intent having however been later resolved, this is explained here in its entirety[88] (9b4–10a3).

In addition, we have the following differing doctrines concerning the varieties of Madhyamaka theory in sūtra and mantra.

The Jo nang pa [Dol bu pa Shes rab rgyal mtshan (1292–1361)] has maintained the following view.[89] The Madhyamaka of the Prāsaṅgikas' and Svātantrikas' Niḥsvabhāvavāda being Emptiness of self-nature *(rang stong: svabhāvaśūnyatā)*—which is as insubstantial *(snying po med pa: asāra)* as the trunk of the plaintain tree and not permanent—it is therefore not the Madhyamaka theory taught in the last cycle *('khor lo,* of the Dharma) and in mantra. This is because it is not Emptiness of the heterogeneous *(gzhan stong: *para[bhāva]śūnyatā),* which is the *paramārthasatya* that is unconditioned, permanent, self-existent *(rang byung),* and beyond production in dependence *(rten 'brel las 'das pa).* Nevertheless, it is not the case that the

86. See above, fol. 6b1. Like *śūnyatā*, *paramārtha* is in the Madhyamaka not a name that refers to a property-possessing thing *(chos can = dharmin).* Rather, it is nothing but a term (or metaterm) in philosophical usage for *dharmatā = śūnyatā.* See, e.g., *MMK* xviii.7, 9–11; xiii.7–8; xxiv.18. Cf. also Bhā(va)viveka, *Madhyamakahṛdayakārikā* iii.263.

87. The 1975 edition reads *chos can kun rdzob bden pa las chos nyid don dam bden pa zhes pa'i chos can zhig gi ming gis nye bar btags nas de la bden gnyis zung 'jug gi sku dang ye shes su gnas gyur gyi 'bras bu thob byar yod med kyis 'jog pa.* The 1969 edition reads at the end (fol. 10a6): ... *'bras bu'i cha 'ga' las thob par byar yod med kyis 'jog pa.* The English translation is tentative.

88. The remainder of Mi bskyod rdo rje's commentary is devoted to this explanation. Because of the complexity of the terms and the philosophical and mystical concepts to which they correspond, the translation of this paragraph given here is only indicative.

89. On the Jo nang pa doctrine and Dol bu/po pa, see the article reprinted in the present volume, chapter 12.

theory and meditative realization of these two systems [of the Prāsaṅgikas and Svātantrikas both maintaining *svabhāvaśūnyatā* in contradistinction to the *gzhan stong*] were not taught by the Teacher [i.e., the Buddha], nor is it the case that exercising *(nyams su len pa)* in accordance with them is useless; for they serve simply to remove views of conceptual attachment *(zhen lta)* that are opposed to this relative *svabhāvaśūnyatā (kun rdzob rang stong)*. However, the exercise of the theory and meditative realization in this [*rang stong*] alone does not constitute supreme Emptiness leading to the highest good *(nges legs: naiḥśreyasa)* of *mahābodhi*. This is because this Emptiness [of self-nature] is not Emptiness endowed with all excellent modes *(rnam kun mchog ldan gyi stong nyid = sarvākāravaropetā śūnyatā)* (10a3–6).

Zi lung pa [Shākya] Mchog ldan (1428–1507) has maintained the following view. When cutting off discursive development by theory relating to the Madhyamaka of both sūtra and mantra, there is no difference between the two with respect to non-implicative exclusion negation *(med par dgag pa = prasajyapratiṣedha)* where there is cut off production in terms of the four extremes *(mtha' bzhi)* of existence, non-existence [, both existence and non-existence, and neither existence nor non-existence with respect to all factors of existence] from *rūpa* to *sarvākārajñatā*. There does, however, exist the following difference when one exercises by means of meditative realization. [On the one hand,] in mantra,[90] the luminous Gnosis endowed with specific exclusively interiorized experience *(ye shes 'od gsal ba kha nang kho nar phyogs pa'i myong ba khyad can)*—the ground of the negation *(dgag gzhi)* of things such as existence and non-existence—is mantra Madhyamaka with respect to being sustained by profound mantric means *(sṅgags kyi thabs zab mo)*. And [on the other hand] the theory wherein experience derives from something even without being sustained by profound mantric means is the Madhyamaka theory that is superior to the Madhyamaka theory of the Niḥsvabhāvavāda, for it is the supreme Madhyamaka theory explained in the final Dharma *(chos phyi ma)* [i.e., the *Ratnagotravibhāga-Mahāyānottaratantra* together with the *Dharmadharmatāvibhaṅga*] of Bhaṭṭāraka Maitreya. The appellation Alīkākāra-Madhyamaka *(rnam rdzun dbu ma)* having been established for this system by both scriptural tradition and reasoning,[91] it must be so designated; and it is not right for Tibetans to extend an appellation such as "Advocate of the Alīkākāra-Cittamātra" *(sems tsam rnam rdzun pa)* to a *Cittamātrika. Indeed, Satyākāra and Alīkākāra are divisions respectively of the *Cittamātrikas and Mādhyamikas. The

90. The words *sngags su* are missing in the 1975 edition.

91. See above, fol. 5a–b.

following differences are then observed. (1) The first corresponds to the difference constituted by the [Satyākāravādin-*Cittamātrikas] accepting cognition *(rnam shes = vijñāna)* as truly established *(bden grub pa),* whereas the [Alīkākāravādin-Mādhyamikas] accept Gnosis *(ye shes = jñāna)* as truly established. (2) Whereas the two schools agree in not accepting the objectively cognized and the subjective cognition as materially different *(gzung 'dzin rdzas gzhan)* with respect to an external object *(phyi don),* there exists the difference constituted by the [Satyākāravādins'] accepting, and the [Alīkākāravādins'] not accepting, the objectively cognized and the subjective cognition as materially different with respect to internalized cognition *(nang shes pa).* (3) There is the difference constituted by the [Satyākāravādins'] accepting *abhūtaparikalpa* or the objective aspect *(gzung rnam)* as truly established, and by the [Alīkākāravādins'] accepting this as being like an illusory projection *(sgyu ma lta bu = māyopama).* And (4) there is the difference between the [Satyākāravādins'] accepting all that appears *(snang ba)* as mind *(sems = citta)* and the [Alīkākāravādins'] accepting all that appears as *dharmadhātu.* Now the *dharmadhātu* in this [theory] is not to be taken to be the doctrine of the Niḥsvabhāvavāda holding non-implicative negation *(med dgag)* comparable to empty space; rather, it is to be taken to be naturally luminous mind *(sems rang bzhin 'od gsal ba).* Since for the mind too there exist both the relative *(kun rdzob)* and the ultimate *(don dam),* it is to be taken as the latter of the two. And since there exists besides the difference between *vijñāna* appearing in the duality of objective and subjective cognitions *(gzung 'dzin gnyis snang gi rnam shes)* and non-dual *jñāna (gnyis med kyi ye shes),* it is to be taken to refer to the latter of these two (10a6–11a1).

The great Bo dong pa[92] has maintained the following view. For thorough analysis *(shin tu dpyad pa),* there is no difference at all with respect to the non-discursive theory *(lta ba spros bral)* of both sūtra and mantra; for in the case of all factors of existence belonging to both saṃsāra and nirvāṇa, no thing at all exists that is established as withstanding analysis *(dpyad bzod du grub pa).* For partial analysis *(cung zad dpyad pa),* however, the mantra Madhyamaka establishes what is to be attained—the three *kāyas (sku)* etc.—by means of what is nature *(ngo bo),* self *(bdag nyid),* and agent *(byed pa po)* possessing three special features: the *paramārthasatya* established spontaneously in nature *(rang bzhin lhun gyis grub pa'i don dam bden pa)* or the yogic relative *(kun rdzob)* of the Vajrayānists, the psychical *(dvangs ma),* and the imperishable *(mi shigs).* And thus there exist also the psychical person as

92. This may be Bo dong Phyogs las rnam rgyal (1375–1450 according to Sum pa mkhan po's *Re'u mig*).

agent *(byed pa po'i dvangs ma'i gang zag),* the insensate *(bems po),* etc.[93] But in the case of non-analysis *(ma dpyad pa),* one proceeds [simply] in accordance with what is [generally] accepted [in usage] *(ji ltar grags pa).* Although this is postulated as having the nature of the psychical person *(dvangs ma'i gang zag),* the agent in respect to *dharma*s *(chos kyi byed po),* and the self *(bdag po),* there nevertheless exists no truly real *dharma* substance *(chos kyi bdag bden);* for one must accept the non-substantiality of the factors of existence *(dharmanairātmya)* pervading (in an ontic-logical nexus, *vyāpti*) all factors of existence (11a1–4).

Tsong kha pa (1357–1419) from the east has maintained the following view. Between sūtra and mantra there is no difference of superior and inferior degree in Madhyamaka theory with respect to Emptiness, which is empty of true establishment established with respect to the sensory object itself, and unimposed by mental construction *(blo rtog pas phar bzhag min pa'i yul rang ngos nas grub pa'i bden grub kyis stong pa'i stong pa nyid).* There does, however, exist a very significant difference in degree between the Paths of sūtra and mantra inasmuch as the former does not comprise an instrument of comprehension *(rtogs byed)* of this theory through the Bliss of sensing the tangible of the *prajñā* as the instrument for ascertaining it *(de nges byed shes rab ma'i reg bya tshor bdes),* whereas the latter does comprise such an instrument of comprehension.[94] This is because the absence [of this instrument] in the sūtras makes perfect comprehension impossible *(ji lta bar rtogs mi nus pa),* so that it is impossible to overcome also the subtle obscuration to the knowable *(shes sgrib phra mo: jñeyāvaraṇa).* On the Mantra-Path on the contrary it is possible, through perfect comprehension due to this, to overcome even the subtle *jñeyāvaraṇa.* If in Awakening to supreme *bodhi* one does not augment the Sūtra-Path with the Mantra-Path, it will be impossible to attain Awakening by means of the Sūtra-Path alone. Even after his encounter with Mañjughoṣa, Tsong kha pa did not come to understand this crucial matter before he had made even greater spiritual progress through his subsequent practice of withdrawal *(dben pa = viveka)* and so forth. As a consequence there was a difference, due to his first not possessing but later possessing complete spiritual perfection *(thugs dam rtsal rdzogs),* between the [earlier] period when he composed his *Sngags lam rim* [i.e., the *Sngags rim chen mo*] and the [later] period when he composed his comment clarifying

93. See above, fol. 6b–7a.

94. For a recent discussion of this, see Tenzin Gyatso (Dalai Lama XIV) and J. Hopkins, *Tantra in Tibet* (London, 1977), pp. 20 f., 47 f., 55 f., 60 f., 69 f., 73, 110 f., 134, 205, 212; and *The Yoga of Tibet* (London, 1981), pp. 41, 233.

the *Pañcakrama (Rim lnga gsal sgron).*[95] Of these two works it is, then, only in his *Rim lnga gsal sgron* that he finally brought out the profound and specific details in the sense of mantra. This is what has been stated (11a4–b2).

In the final part of the introduction to his comment on Candrakīrti's *Madhyamakāvatāra,* Mi bskyod rdo rje critically discusses and rebuts these four opinions on the relationship between Sūtra-Madhyamaka and Mantra-Madhyamaka ascribed to Dol bu pa (fol. 11b2–13b3), Shākya mchog ldan (fol. 13b3–27b4), Bo dong pa (fol. 27b4–30b6), and Tsong kha pa (fol. 30b6–32b5). This he does with a view to establishing the Karma Bka' brgyud doctrine of the Madhyamaka in relation to the Mahāmudrā and the Vajrayāna.

III

Mi bskyod rdo rje was thus the representative—the "holder of the lineage" *(brgyud 'dzin)*—of several lines of the Madhyamaka tradition handed down in the Karma branch of the Bka' brgyud pa school and also, through Sgam po pa, in the Bka' gdams pa school.

His comment on the *Madhyamakāvatāra,* begun circa 1545 in his thirty-ninth year, can be presumed to contain Mi bskyod rdo rje's response to the searching questions and objections directed to him by Se ra byes rje btsun Chos kyi rgyal mtshan (1469–1546) in his *Kar lan Klu sgrub dgongs rgyan.* This last work by a follower of the Dge ldan pa tradition of Tsong kha pa was a close critique of Mi bskyod rdo rje's earlier comment on the *Abhisamayālaṃkāra* together with Haribhadra's *Śāstravṛtti ('Grel pa don gsal* or *"Sphuṭārthā"),* where the doctrine of Prajñāpāramitā was evidently interpreted by Mi bskyod rdo rje in terms of the non-dual Gnosis *(gzung 'dzin gnyis med kyi ye shes)* in the frame of the Emptiness-of-the-other *(gzhan stong)* theory and according to the so-called *rnam rdzun lugs kyi dbu ma chen po,* or Great Madhyamaka of the Alīkākāra system, purportedly taught in the Hymnic Corpus *(bstod tshogs)* of Nāgārjuna.[96] Like Mi bskyod rdo rje

95. The latter work is dated to Tsong kha pa's fifty-fifth year whereas the *Sngags rim chen mo* is dated to his forty-ninth year; Tsong kha pa's comment on Candrakīrti's *Pradīpoddyotana,* finally, is dated to his fifty-eighth year. The first encounter of Tsong kha pa and Bla ma Dbu ma pa Brtson 'grus seng ge with Mañjuśrī is dated much earlier, followed by a long period of meditative withdrawal. Cf. R. Kaschewsky, *Das Leben des lamaistischen Heiligen Tsong-khapa Blo-bzang-grags-pa,* I (Wiesbaden, 1971), pp. 102, 106ff., 190f., 196.

96. This work by Mi bskyod rdo rje, listed by A khu Shes rab rgya mtsho in his *Dpe rgyun*

in the introduction to his comment on the *Madhyamakāvatāra,* but in the rather different doctrinal and doxographical frame of the *rang stong* doctrine, Chos kyi rgyal mtshan has also affirmed the agreement with Candrakīrti of Maitrīpāda, Mar pa, and Mi la ras pa as well as of Tsong kha pa (*Klu sgrub dgongs rgyan,* fol. 20b3ff.); and he has examined (fol. 22a1ff.) the passage from Maitrīpāda's *Tattvadaśaka* (verse 2) concerning the inapplicability of both the Sākāra (or Satyākāra) and the Nirākāra (or Alīkākāra) doctrines to the genuine Madhyamaka endued with the instructions of the Guru—namely Nāgārjuna, Āryadeva, and Candrakīrti (fol. 22a3).[97]

The record of the lines of transmission of the Madhyamaka in India and Tibet provided by Mi bskyod rdo rje is of interest to us in several ways. In the first place, like the vast majority of Tibetan accounts of a doctrine, it places great emphasis on the preceptorial lineages responsible for its transmission. Not only are such accounts of objective historical interest in themselves—in the manner of a *rgyal rabs* or *vaṃśāvalī*—but they provide our authors with an essential means of authenticating and validating a lineage and its teachings—be it in the sūtra *(mdo lugs)* or the mantra *(sngags lugs)* system—and with an invaluable doctrinal and doxographical taxonomy that takes into account the multiple forms in which a teaching may have been handed down.

Secondly, Mi bskyod rdo rje's account brings out the links between the śāstric teaching of the Madhyamaka school and the other teachings with which it has come into intimate contact in the course of its history. In India there already existed close connexions between the Madhyamaka and the Mantrayāna/Vajrayāna; and an important line of Vajrayānist masters, beginning apparently in the seventh century with Nāgārjuna-pāda, is in fact credited with having spread the Madhyamaka and having composed treatises on it. Several such works are extant either in the original Indian languages

---

dkon po 'ga' zhig gi tho yig (published by Lokesh Chandra [New Delhi, 1963], no. 11542), is unavailable at present. Our information on it is based on the *Gsung lan* (or *Kar lan*) *Klu sgrub dgongs rgyan* by Chos kyi rgyal mtshan (Zhol par khang edition of 1944; reprinted in Delhi in 1969).

A work on the *gzhan stong* theory, the author of which is, according to its colophon, Mi bskyod dga' ba'i dbyangs, is also connected with Mi bskyod rdo rje; in addition to the third cycle of the Dharma, the *Ratnagotravibhāga,* and the *dbu ma chen po* of Asaṅga and Vasubandhu, it also quotes Candrakīrti (perhaps trying to bridge the *gzhan stong* and the *rang stong* of Candrakīrti). Its title is *Dbu ma gzhan stong smra ba'i srol legs par phye ba'i sgron me* (reprinted at Rum btegs in 1972).

97. Cf. Sahajavajra, *Tattvadaśakaṭīkā,* fol. 182a.

(Sanskrit and Apabhraṃśa) or in Tibetan translations included in the Bstan 'gyur.

This connexion was then very well established by the eleventh century when Maitrīpāda (*alias* Advayavajra) wrote works that clearly reflect the links between Madhyamaka and Mantrayāna.[98] The Karma Bka' brgyud line to which Mi bskyod rdo rje belongs regards Maitrīpāda as one of its main Indian forbears since he was the renowned master of Mahāmudrā *(phyag rgya chen po)* teachings. In Mi bskyod rdo rje's treatise the introduction to which is analysed in this article, reference has been made in particular to Maitrīpāda's *Tattvadaśaka* and to Sahajavajra's commentary on it.

Now the question whether the Mahāmudrā teachings agree with the Madhyamaka as taught for example in the *Samādhirājasūtra* as well as in the treatises by Nāgārjuna and his great Mādhyamika followers was a crucial one that has been discussed in Tibet since early times. Although Dīpaṃkaraśrījñāna (Atisha), who helped to introduce the Madhyamaka into Tibet in the middle of the eleventh century, is reported to have also on occasion taught the *Dohā*s and the *Grub snying* cycle associated with the Mahāmudrā, and although he is even stated to have received teachings from Maitrīpāda himself, his great disciple 'Brom ston is nevertheless said to have refrained from spreading it widely since he feared for the good conduct of Tibetans.[99] In Tibet, Maitrīpāda's Mahāmudrā has not infrequently been regarded as a teaching that integrates the methods of both sūtra and mantra, a view that seems to be corroborated by Sahajavajra as quoted by Mi bskyod rdo rje.[100] However, on the basis of certain Indo-Tibetan traditions, 'Gos lo tsā ba Gzhon nu dpal has chosen to distinguish the Mahāmudrā in question here from the Mantrayāna by postulating a sūtra-method Mahāmudrā.[101] But, as seen above, any attempt at radically separating the two has been criticized by Mi bskyod rdo rje (fol. 7b–8a).

A source for this linkage of one Madhyamaka tradition with Mantrayāna

98. Matrīpāda's works on the Madhyamaka are, however, to be found not in the Madhyamaka section of the Bstan 'gyur but in the Tantra section.

99. See *DNg,* da, 3a (pp. 843–44). Another early Bka' gdams pa master is reported to have declared that, even though the Mahāmudrā conveys the meaning of the *Samādhirājasūtra,* one should nevertheless neither engage in the practice of the Mahāmudrā nor deprecate it. See *DNg,* ca, 13b (pp. 268–69).

100. Fol. 6b, where Sahajavajra is quoted as saying that the Mahāmudrā is essentially Pāramitā but is at the same time in conformity with Mantra. In the same place Mi bskyod rdo rje has referred to Jñānakīrti's *Tattvāvatāra* (on which compare Tenzin Gyatso [Dalai Lama XIV], *Tantra in Tibet,* p. 73).

101. *DNg,* na, 141b–142a (pp. 724–25); and na, 48b–49b (pp. 976–77).

was considered to be the *Ratnagotravibhāga-Mahāyānottaratantraśāstra.* For a long period of time, this important text had apparently fallen into oblivion and was passed over in silence by many of the great Indian Buddhist philosophers (in particular the masters of the Madhyamaka) despite the fact that it was well enough known already at the beginning of the sixth century—that is, the time of Buddhapālita and Bhā(va)viveka—to be translated into Chinese by Ratnamati and Bodhiruci (Taishō 1611).[102] Then, according to one account, it was recovered from an old stūpa by Maitrīpāda in the eleventh century.[103] And from this time onwards the *Ratnagotravibhāga* was to occupy a most prominent place in Buddhist thought in India, and especially in Kaśmīr, where it was taught by Sajjana. It was above all Sajjana's disciples who were instrumental in introducing it in Tibet. Although the *Ratnagotravibhāga* as one of the so-called "Five Dharmas of Maitreya" *(byams chos sde lnga)* has been included by the editors of the Bstan 'gyur in the Sems tsam ("Cittamātra") section of that collection, it has very often been classified in Tibet as a work that is in harmony with and even reflects Madhyamaka thought.[104] At the same time, however, the *Ratnagotravibhāga* has figured in Tibet—and evidently in India also—as what might be described as a typologically proto-Vajrayānist work, for it expounds theories such as the *tathāgatagarbha* and *buddhadhātu*—the non-dual Ground of both saṃsāra and nirvāṇa—and the natural luminosity of mind which occupy a fundamental place in Vajrayānist thought too. As for the connexion between the *Ratnagotravibhāga* and (at least one of) the Mahāmudrā traditions, it is attested in Mi bskyod rdo rje and also, for example, in the *Deb ther sngon po* of 'Gos lo tsā ba Gzhon nu dpal.[105] And this link is as it were concretized in the dual rôle played by Maitrīpāda as both teacher of the Mahāmudrā and rediscoverer of the *Ratnagotravibhāga.* Just like the *Ratnagotravibhāga,* Maitrīpāda's Mahāmudrā, although it was held to be consonant with the Mantrayāna, is as we have just seen still stated not to have been classified by several authorities with the tantras.[106] This Mahāmudrā has indeed been equated rather with the Prajñāpāramitā.[107]

102. See D. Seyfort Ruegg, *La théorie du tathāgatagarbha et du gotra,* pp. 32 f., 443; and *Le traité du tathāgatagarbha de Bu ston Rin chen grub* (Paris, 1973), p. 18.

103. Cf. *DNg,* cha, 9b (p. 347).

104. See *Théorie du tathāgatagarbha et du gotra,* pp. 55 f.

105. *DNg,* nya, 141b (p. 724).

106. Cf. *DNg,* na, 48b–49a (p. 977).

107. See for example *DNg,* nya, 141b–142a (pp. 724–25). This has been questioned by Sa skya paṇḍi ta Kun dga' rgyal mtshan in his *Sdom gsum rab dbye,* fol. 25b ff.; cf. also the same author's *Thub pa'i dgongs pa rab tu gsal ba,* fol. 50b f.

Between Maitrīpāda and Ratnākaraśānti, a master of the Nirākāra—or Alīkākāra—Cittamātra doctrine, there existed a deep division according to Mi bskyod rdo rje, who recalls that Maitripāda is said to have defeated Ratnākaraśānti in a debate.[108] Indeed, as already noticed above, in his *Tattvadaśaka* Maitrīpāda has rejected the Nirākāravāda as well as the Sākāravāda. By Mi bskyod rdo rje this rejection is interpreted, in accordance with Sahajavajra's commentary, as a rejection of what is termed "Cittamātra" (*sems tsam,* i.e., the main Mahāyānist school opposed to the Madhyamaka). At the same time, however, Mi bskyod rdo rje has stated that one of the three lines of transmission for the Mahāmudrā concentrated on the Madhyamaka of the Alīkākāra-Cittamātra (*sems tsam rnam rdzun gyi dbu ma,* fol. 6a); but this particular tradition he connects with [Vajra]pāṇi, Asu, and (S)Kor Ni ru pa, who were among the principal transmitters of the Mahāmudrā.[109] Clearly, then, it is according to Mi bskyod rdo rje necessary to differentiate carefully between the Vijñānavāda- (or "Cittamātra"-) type Nirākāra/Alīkākāra doctrine of Ratnākaraśānti—who attempted a synthesis of the Madhyamaka and the Vijñaptimātra which, in the form of the *rnam rig gi dbu ma,* was one of the sources of the *gzhan stong* theory—and a Madhyamaka-type Alīkākāravāda considered to be consonant with the Mahāmudrā of Maitrīpāda—who represented rather a synthesis of Madhyamaka and Mantrayāna.[110] This current of thought Mi bskyod rdo rje has then explicated following the *rang stong* theory of Candrakīrti in his comment on the *Madhyamakāvatāra.* This is despite the fact that Mi bskyod rdo rje had apparently himself previously adhered to the *gzhan stong* in his commentary on the *Abhisamayālaṃkāra* together with Haribhadra's *Śāstravṛtti* on it.[111] Mi bskyod rdo rje's approach in his commentary on Candrakīrti's *Madhyamakāvatāra* may then very well

108. Ratnākaraśānti may also, in addition to Atisha, have had something to do with Maitrīpāda's expulsion from Vikramaśīlā for a breach of the Vinaya. See Nag tsho Tshul khrims rgyal ba, *Rnam thar rgyas pa,* fol. 42b–43a.

109. See for example the chapter on the Mahāmudrā in the *Deb ther sngon po* (vol. da).

110. Tāranātha in his *Bka' babs bdun ldan gyi brgyud pa'i mam thar,* fol. 7b–8b (Grünwedel, p. 23 f.) has, however, made Maitrīpāda a disciple of Ratnākaraśānti; and he casts doubt on the report of a debate between the two masters. But Tāranātha—and the Jo nang pa school as a whole—belonged to a tradition that had close links with Ratnākaraśānti and his "Vijñapti-Madhyamaka" *(rnam rig gi dbu ma).*

111. See above, note 96, where another work on the *gzhan stong* theory connected with Mi bskyod rdo rje is also mentioned.

represent his response to the criticism of his earlier work by Chos kyi rgyal mtshan in his *Klu sgrub dgongs rgyan.*[112]

Dīpaṃkaraśrījñāna (Atisha) was, for a time at least, the follower at Vikramaśīlā of Ratnākaraśānti,[113] but he appears to have later abandoned this Vijñānavādin's Alīkākāravāda doctrine; and he has indeed described Candrakīrti's interpretation of the Madhyamaka as the most satisfactory of all.[114] As for Maitrīpāda, Atisha's opposition to him on points of Vinaya discipline is mentioned in several sources; and it is reported that he was one of those responsible for expelling Maitrīpāda from Vikramaśīlā for a breach of this discipline.[115] Now, in the kingdom of Western Tibet—where he arrived in 1042 in the company of Nag tso lo tsā ba Tshul khrims rgyal ba at the invitation of *lha bla ma* Ye shes 'od, of King 'od lde, and of *lha btsun pa* Byang chub 'od—one of Atisha's first tasks was to combat certain deviant practices, such as *sbyor sgrol,* which were being spread in northwestern India and western Tibet by some self-styled mantrins who were apparently under the influence of a putative Mahāmudrā teaching that seems, however, to have been an amalgam of Śaiva, popular magical, and Buddhist elements. And a form of the Mahāmudrā is in fact explicitly mentioned in the *Bodhimārgadīpapañjikā* (P fol. 334b5 = D fol. 289a5)—a text presented in the Bstan 'gyur as Atisha's autocommentary on his *Bodhipathapradīpa*—as something to which such self-styled mantrins unjustifiably laid claim.[116] At the same time, as already

112. Mi bskyod rdo rje seems in fact to wish to turn the tables on Tsong kha pa and the Dge ldan pas by maintaining that it is their theory of *śūnyatā* that represents the (inferior) Empty-of-the-other doctrine of *itaretaraśūnyatā (gcig la gcig med pa'i stong pa nyid)* criticized in the *Laṅkāvatārasūtra* (ii, pp. 74–75) and the *prādeśika-śūnyatā (nyi tshe ba'i stong pa nyid)* criticized in the *Samādhirājasūtra* (ix, 47). And Mi bskyod rdo rje therefore remarks that this theory of theirs is not fit to serve as a basis for the Path of liberation (fol. 331a–b, 338a–b). They are indeed accused of looking for their logical negandum *(rtags kyi dgag bya)* in quite the wrong place, i.e., elsewhere than in empty *dharma*s themselves (fol. 328b–329a). On the *itaretaraśūnyatā* and the *prādeśika-śūnyatā* see also fol. 344a. Cf. *Théorie du tathāgatagarbha et du gotra,* pp. 325ff., and *Le traité du tathāgatagarbha de Bu ston Rin chen grub,* pp. 122, 126–28.

113. See, e.g., Nag tsho's *Rnam thar rgyas pa,* fol. 12a.

114. See Dīpaṃkaraśrījñāna's *Satyadvayāvatāra* (cited above, n. 14).

115. See Tāranātha, *Bka' babs bdun ldan gyi brgyud pa'i rnam thar,* fol. 8a (Grünwedel, p. 23), as well as Nag tsho's *Rnam thar rgyas pa,* fol. 12a and 43a. Atisha's journey to Tibet has even been represented as a kind of atonement for the banishment of Maitrīpāda, who was in truth a bodhisattva. See *Rnam thar rgyas pa,* fol. 43a.

116. See D. Seyfort Ruegg, "Deux problèmes d'exégèse et de pratique tantriques," in *Tantrik and Taoist Studies in Honour of R. A. Stein* (*Mélanges chinois et bouddhiques* 20 [1981]), pp. 212–26.

noted above, Atisha is stated not to have completely neglected the teaching of the Mahāmudrā in Tibet.[117] Moreover, he is reported to have received the *Ratnagotravibhāga* directly from Maitrīpāda, who had recently rediscovered it in an old stūpa.[118] And as has been mentioned above, the doctrine of the *Ratnagotravibhāga* is connected not only with the *gzhan stong* theory but also with the Mahāmudrā by Indo-Tibetan traditions.[119]

Against this background of complex, and indeed shifting, interrelationships and cross-currents, we can better understand Mi bskyod rdo rje's juxtaposition of (1) a Bka' brgyud pa tradition of the Madhyamaka descending through Sgam po pa from Nāropa and Maitrīpāda (the former of which is evidently the Six Dharma tradition, and the latter a Mahāmudrā tradition); (2) another quite distinct Madhyamaka tradition descending from Dīpaṃkaraśrījñāna through Sgam po pa, who combined the Bka' brgyud pa tradition of Mar pa and Mi la ras pa with the Bka' gdams pa tradition of Dīpaṃkaraśrījñāna and his Tibetan disciples; and (3) still another distinct Madhyamaka tradition which descended from Pa tshab lo tsā ba Nyi ma grags and represented in particular the śāstra tradition of the (Prāsaṅgika-) Madhyamaka in the sense that it was combined neither with any teaching belonging specifically to the Mantrayāna/Vajrayāna nor with any other sūtra (or śāstra) doctrine that is not specifically Madhyamaka.

Finally, Mi bskyod rdo rje's introductory remarks on the traditions of the Indian and Tibetan Madhyamaka are of special interest for the relationship between the Madhyamaka and Mantrayāna/Vajrayāna and the question whether, over and above the Dharma system of Nāgārjuna and his great Mādhyamika followers, there exists a quite distinct—and even superior—Dharma system of the Madhyamaka belonging not to the sūtra system *(mdo lugs)* and the Pāramitāyāna, but to the Mantrayāna. This problem has

---

The *Bodhipathapradīpa* is stated to have been translated into Tibetan by the author himself together with the *zhu chen gyi lo tsā ba* Dge ba'i blo gros at Tho ling in Zhang zhung; and the **Bodhimārgapradīpa-Pañjikā* is stated to have been translated by the author Dīpaṃkaraśrījñāna himself together with (Nag tsho) Tshul khrims rgyal ba. Doubts have, however, been expressed concerning the authorship of the *Pañjikā*.

117. See *DNg,* da, 3a (pp. 843–44).

118. Cf. *DNg,* da, 3a (p. 843); and cha, 9b (p. 247). Since Atisha is however also reported to have expelled Maitrīpāda from Vikramaśīlā for a breach of the Vinaya (see above, n. 115), and since Atisha's school preferred not to spread the Mahāmudrā teachings so closely associated with Maitrīpāda (see above, p. 348), the statement that Atisha could have received the *Ratnagotravibhāga* from Maitrīpāda has been questioned. Cf. Paṇ chen Bsod nams grags pa (*RGV Ṭīk blo,* fol. 2b; see our *Théorie du tathāgatagarbha et du gotra,* p. 37).

119. *DNg,* na, 141b (p. 724).

prompted much discussion and even controversy in the history of Indian and Tibetan Buddhist thought.[120] And it has a parallel in the question as to whether beside the Mahāmudrā teachings belonging to the Mantrayāna/ Vajrayāna there exists a separate Mahāmudrā teaching which belongs to the sūtra (or Pāramitā) system and is based *inter alia* on the *Ratnagotravibhāga-Mahāyānottaratantra* as a text representing a special tradition in the Madhyamaka.

It is to be noted that among the well-known and philosophically significant traditions of the Madhyamaka, no reference has been made here in Mi bskyod rdo rje's classification of the transmission lineages either to the Yogācāra-Madhyamaka descending in Tibet from Śāntarakṣita and Kamalaśīla nor to the no less important Svātantrika *(rang rgyud pa)* Madhyamaka associated for example with Rngog lo tsā ba Blo ldan shes rab (1059–1109) and the great monastic seminary of Gsang phu Ne'u thog. And there is no allusion here either to Zhan Tshes spong ba and Phya pa Chos kyi seng ge (1109–69). The only master connected with this school mentioned is Rngog lo tsā ba's disciple Gro lung pa Blo gros 'byung gnas; but this Bka' gdams pa master is mentioned in passing only and not as a link in one of the lineages.

As for the Prāsaṅgika *(thal 'gyur ba)* Madhyamaka line, there is no mention of Gtsang nag pa, a disciple of Phya pa who later joined Pa tshab and became a representative in Tibet of Candrakīrti's school; and a certain Rgya dmar ba, who evidently belonged to Pa tshab's school, is referred to only in passing. Next to Pa tshab Nyi ma grags (b. 1055) his disciple Zhang Thang sag pa is, however, mentioned in the line of transmission of the Prāsaṅgika-Madhyamaka in Tibet.

Equally remarkable is the absence of the line of Madhyamaka practice according to the *gzhan stong* theory represented by a senior contemporary of Rngog lo tsā ba, Btsan Kha bo che (b. 1021); this omission is very probably due to the fact that this tradition was not kept alive, as noted by 'Gos lo tsā ba, although a commentary on the *Ratnagotravibhāga* tentatively attributed to him apparently survived.[121] The fact that Mi bskyod rdo rje has included no lineage of the main *gzhan stong* tradition here is nevertheless highly noteworthy in view of his links with it at least in his earlier years and despite the fact that he discusses the views of the Jo nang pas and Shākya mchog ldan.[122]

120. See for example Sahajavajra, *Tattvadaśakaṭīkā,* fol. 192a5 ff.

121. See *DNg,* cha, 10a (p. 348).

122. See addendum below.

Since it cannot be said that Mi bskyod rdo rje knew nothing of these other Indo-Tibetan philosophical traditions of the Madhyamaka, their omission from the lineages of the Madhyamaka listed in the introduction to Mi bskyod rdo rje's commentary on Candrakīrti's *Madhyamakāvatāra* can perhaps be best explained by supposing that Mi bskyod rdo rje was not heir to them through the Bka' brgyud line with which the work analysed in this paper is basically concerned. In other words, the absence of a Madhyamaka tradition here may be due less to strictly philosophical and doctrinal considerations than to the factor to which attention was drawn at the beginning of this paper, namely the overriding importance for the constitution and organization of the Madhyamaka in Tibet—at least in a school like that of the Kar ma Bka' brgyud pas and possibly (if to a lesser degree) already even in India—of the preceptorial lineages which transmitted it.

Grounds for distinguishing in this manner between various currents of the Madhyamaka are provided by criteria that relate to both the forms and the contents of these traditions. Because the philosophical traditions in question are in fact often separated from each other by quite subtle doctrinal distinctions which are by no means easy to identify and isolate, in several cases it has been the demarcations formed by lines of transmission—the lineages—that have made it easiest for our authors to establish differences between them. The usefulness of such formal demarcations is especially great for a school *(chos lugs)* like Mi bskyod rdo rje's Bka' brgyud pa where—like the Sa skya pa school but in contrast to the Dge ldan pas / Dge lugs pas—several philosophical theories *(lta ba)* of the Madhyamaka have existed side by side.

Beside differences in philosophical content, accordingly, the preceptorial lineages into which the Tibetan schools have tended to articulate and classify a doctrine or textual corpus assist in defining the specific character and place of that doctrine or textual corpus for these schools. And in this way human and social factors linked with the transmission lineages, no less than strictly philosophical criteria, furnish means for differentiating between various currents of thought.[123] Alongside the interest the Tibetans have regularly evinced in lineages—biological and spiritual—this circumstance helps

123. Such a situation is not peculiar to Tibet alone, and it appears to be quite old in the history of Buddhism. The ancient "Śrāvaka" Nikāyas in fact appear not only as doctrinal schools in the strict sense, but also as Vinaya orders and as communities transmitting particular recensions of the canon, in other words as "text schools." (See our article to be published in the Proceedings of the Buddhist Studies Symposium held at the Academy of Sciences in Göttingen in July 1982.)

therefore to account for the great importance attached by Mi bskyod rdo rje as well as other Tibetan authors to the lines of transmission in Indo-Tibetan traditions such as the Madhyamaka/Dbu ma. And in the study of the Indo-Tibetan traditions, such factors with their human, social, and even psychological dimensions will have to be considered together with doctrinal and philosophical criteria on the levels of learning *(thos pa = śruta),* reflective analysis *(bsam pa = cintā),* and meditative realization *(sgom pa = bhāvanā).* Here we may have something comparable in part to what are known today as "knowledge traditions."

Addendum

Mi bskyod rdo rje's silence concerning the *gzhan stong* lineage of the Madhyamaka in the introduction to his commentary on the *Madhyamakāvatāra* (above p. 353) and his turning away in this commentary from the position he had upheld in his earlier commentary on Prajñāpāramitā and the *Abhisamayālaṃkāra* are all the more noteworthy since his predecessor, the third Karma pa Rang byung rdo rje, is often considered to have been a *gzhan stong pa,* just like Mi bskyod rdo rje early in his life. (See Rang byung rdo rje's short treatise entitled *De bzhin gshegs pa'i snying po bstan pa.*) Kong sprul Blo gros mtha' yas has included Rang byung rdo rje in his account of the *gzhan stong* traditions; see *Shes bya kun khyab,* II, fol. 276b (cf. also I fol. 173a–b).

I wish to thank Burkhard Quessel for supplying me with bibliographical references to several of the Bka' brgyud pa sources quoted in the notes above.

March 1984

14. La Pensée Tibétaine*

(accompagné d'une traduction du *Rten 'brel bstod pa legs bshad snying po* de Tsong kha pa)

LA PHILOSOPHIE TIBÉTAINE au sens propre prend pour point de départ et développe les théories des quatre écoles classiques du bouddhisme indien: les Vaibhāṣika (Bye brag tu smra ba), les Sautrāntika (Mdo sde pa), les Vijñānavādin (Sems tsam pa), et les Mādhyamika (Dbu ma pa). Il s'agit ainsi de la méthode dite de la philosophie analytique *(mtshan nyid),* mais certains éléments de la pensée «tantrique» du Vajrayāna (Rdo rje theg pa) entrent également en ligne de compte. En définitive, c'est surtout la philosophie du Milieu *(dbu ma = madhyamaka),* avec à sa base la pensée de la Perfection *(phar phyin = pāramitā)* de la sapience *(shes rab = prajñā),* que creusèrent—et que continuent aujourd'hui—les philosophes tibétains. Leur pensée philosophique se caractérise par un effort très poussé aussi bien d'analyse systématique que de synthèse. L'originalité, qui est certes présente, n'est ni revendiquée ni prisée comme un but en soi.

Au Tibet on compte usuellement cinq grandes écoles, ou plus exactement cinq «méthodes dharmiques» *(chos lugs)* principales: les Rnying ma pa («Anciens») avec les Rdzogs chen pa (Avocats de la Grande Perfection, dont les origines historiques remontent plus loin que le IXe siècle PC); les Sa skya pa (à partir surtout du XIIe siècle), dont les doctrines philosophiques sont pourtant loin d'être entièrement homogènes; les Bka' brgyud pa (à partir surtout du XIIe siècle) qui se sont groupés dans plusieurs sous-écoles distinctes ayant chacune à sa tête un disciple du poète-philosophe Mi la ras pa (Milarépa, XIe siècle); et les Bka' gdams pa (remontant à Atisha, mort ca.

* First published in *Encyclopédie philosophique universelle* I (L'Univers philosophique), pp. 1586–91. Publiée sous la direction d'André Jacob. Paris: Presses Universitaires de France, 1989.

1054), relayés par les Dga' ldan pa ou Dge lugs pa (à partir de Tsong kha pa, XIVe siècle). Les Jo nang pa, école dont les enseignements mystiques furent systématisés au XIVe siècle par Dol po pa, se firent remarquer, avec leurs congénères, par une théorie d'inspiration gnoséologique selon laquelle la réalité est Vide *(stong pa = śūnya)* de tout facteur hétérogène *(gzhan stong)* sans cependant être Vide de nature propre *(rang stong);* ils s'écartèrent ainsi du principe de la Vacuité d'être propre *(rang bzhin gyis / ngo bo nyid kyis stong pa nyid = svabhāvaśūnyatā)* préconisé par le plus grand nombre d'autorités des autres écoles (exception faite de nombreux maîtres des Bka' brgyud pa et des Rnying ma pa et par certains Sa skya pa). Il faut mentionner aussi les Bon po, école dont les maîtres combinèrent des traits bouddhiques avec des éléments d'origine non bouddhique ou para-bouddhique, et qui (à côté des Rnying ma pa) professent la «Grande Perfection» *(rdzogs chen).*

Ces écoles ou groupements élaborèrent et systématisèrent, chacun à sa manière, des doctrines fondamentales du bouddhisme. Ils développèrent ainsi des traits—tenant soit au contenu soit à la forme—qui les distinguent plus ou moins nettement les uns des autres.

Ici nous ne pourrons considérer qu'un seul faisceau de notions fondamentales du bouddhisme tibétain telles qu'elles furent exposées par le fondateur d'une de ces écoles, Tsong kha pa, qui développa des notions largement reconnues par les autres écoles tout en se démarquant de celles-ci par tel trait spécifique.

I. Production en dépendance et Voie du Milieu en philosophie tibétaine

Dans la pensée bouddhique au Tibet ainsi que dans la pratique spirituelle des Tibétains, la notion de la Voie du Milieu *(dbu ma'i lam = madhyamā pratipat)* revêt une importance primordiale. Au niveau de la philosophie proprement dite, cette notion se traduit par l'élimination des positions conceptuelles et doctrinales extrêmes *(mtha' = anta),* mais jumelles, de l'éternalisme—c'est-à-dire du substantialisme absolutiste—et de l'anéantissement—autrement dit du nihilisme. Or c'est la théorie de la production en dépendance *(rten cing 'brel par 'byung ba = pratītyasamutpāda)* qui fournit au penseur bouddhiste le moyen d'éliminer à la fois l'extrême éternaliste (car toute chose née de causes et de conditions ne saurait être prise pour une entité substantielle possédant une essence stable et perdurable) et l'extrême nihiliste (car ce qui naît en dépendance des causes et conditions, ne fût-ce qu'au niveau relatif de la réalité de surface, ne saurait être purement et simplement un néant).

Et cette double élimination se réalise par l'analyse philosophique—ou plus exactement, dans le cas du Mādhyamika tibétain, par un procédé de catalyse déconstructive ayant pour fonction de dissoudre toute vue dogmatique *(lta ba = dṛṣṭi)* qui construit dans les choses une essence ou un être propre (*rang bzhin* ou *rang gi ngo bo = svabhāva* «aseitas») positif ou même négatif. On a donc très souvent considéré le principe de la production en dépendance comme la quintessence de la pensée bouddhique, et aussi comme une des principales bases de la pratique philosophique et spirituelle des bouddhistes au Tibet aussi bien qu'en Inde.

Le texte tibétain traitant du *pratītyasamutpāda* et intitulé «Eloge de la production en dépendance» que nous présentons ici en traduction porte du reste le sous-titre de «Précis de [l'enseignement] bien-formulé»,[1] la qualité d'être bien formulé *(legs par bshad pa = subhāṣita)* définissant d'ailleurs l'enseignement du Buddha. Notre texte a pour auteur Tsong kha pa Blo bzang grags pa (1357–1419), moine et philosophe très célèbre qui fut au Tibet l'héritier qualifié et l'interprète attitré des doctrines du bouddhisme. C'est donc simultanément le thème de ce texte, son étendue conforme aux dimensions de la présente Encyclopédie, la place qu'occupa son auteur au confluent de nombreuses traditions philosophiques et spirituelles lors de la constitution définitive des écoles distinctes *(chos lugs)* du bouddhisme tibétain, et le génie de ce penseur qui ont déterminé le choix de ce «Précis» comme échantillon de la pensée philosophique tibétaine.

Ce texte se présente—de manière peut-être quelque peu inattendue au premier abord—comme un hymne d'éloge quasi dévotionnel adressé au Buddha en tant que le Maître *(ston pa = śāstṛ)* ayant approfondi et promulgué le principe de la production en dépendance. Il sera alors intéressant de considérer cette présentation en situant brièvement dans l'histoire de la pensée bouddhique le genre littéraire adopté par Tsong kha pa pour son *Précis* aussi bien que son contenu philosophique. En effet, la forme que revêt cet ouvrage n'est ni un accident ni une pure invention de Tsong kha pa ou de l'un de ses prédécesseurs tibétains.

Dans l'*Acintyastava*—hymne au Buddha attribué par la tradition indienne et tibétaine à Nāgārjuna, l'illustre père de l'école du Madhyamaka qui vécut probablement vers l'an 200 PC—nous lisons (vers 40): «La production en dépendance, tu la considères comme Vacuité [d'être propre]: telle

1. *Ston pa bla na med pa la zab mo rten cing 'brel par 'byung ba gsung ba'i sgo nas bstod pa, Legs par bshad pa'i snying po zhes bya ba.* L'ouvrage se trouve parmi les Bka' 'bum thor bu de Tsong kha pa, édition de Lha-sa, tome kha, fol. 13a4–16a3; édition du Gtsang, tome kha, fol. 15a4–18b4.

est la bonne doctrine, et le Tathāgata y est pareil.» Une version parallèle de cette stance se trouve dans le *Lokātītastava,* autre hymne attribué également à Nāgārjuna (vers 22): «La production en dépendance, tu la considères comme Vacuité [d'être propre]: qu'il n'existe pas d'entité indépendante, c'est ce que tu as enseigné par ton rugissement-de-lion *(siṃhanāda)* sans pareil». Bien qu'il ne soit pas absolument certain que ces deux stances remontent au père de l'école du Madhyamaka lui-même, elles expriment des idées qui concordent avec la doctrine des traités fondamentaux de Nāgārjuna. Ainsi, dans ses *Mūlamadhyamakakārikā* Nāgārjuna dit non seulement que la production en dépendance est Vacuité *(śūnyatā)* d'être propre mais aussi qu'elle est désignation relative *(prajñaptir upādāya)* et Voie du Milieu (xxiv.18); et plus loin il ajoute que c'est la Vue du *pratītyasamutpāda* qui constitue la Vue des quatre «principes nobles» (*āryasatya,* xxiv.40), et que le rejet du *pratītyasamutpāda* avec la *śūnyatā* représenterait la répudiation de tout usage pragmatique dans le monde (*laukika-saṃvyavahāra,* xxiv.36). Par ailleurs, selon la *Vigrahavyāvartanī* de Nāgārjuna (vers 22), Vacuité et absence d'être propre *(asvabhāvatva)* se constatent précisément au fait de l'existence en dépendance *(pratītyabhāva).*

Cette assimilation du *pratītyasamutpāda* au *dharma* et au *buddha* ainsi que le rapprochement du *pratītyasamutpāda* avec la *śūnyatā*—le fait de naître en dépendance représentant la raison qui fonde la constatation, et l'enseignement correspondant, que les *dharma* sont Vides *(śūnya)* d'être propre et non substantiels[2]—doivent être considérés de plus près quand nous cherchons à comprendre la doctrine exposée dans le *Précis* de Tsong kha pa et dans d'autres traités philosophiques tibétains.

Rappelons tout d'abord que déjà dans plusieurs textes du canon bouddhique ancien il a été déclaré que celui qui connaît le *pratītyasamutpāda* connaît le *dharma* et aussi le *buddha.*[3] Or, dans ces mêmes textes anciens nous lisons par ailleurs que la production en dépendance représente ce qu'on a parfois nommé la stabilité des choses *(dharmasthitatā* ou *dharmasthititā),* en d'autres termes leur nature (non hypostasiée, *dharmatā*) véritable et constante. Le *pratītyasamutpāda* figure donc comme un principe primordial

2. Voir l'autocommentaire de la *Vigrahavyāvartanī* de Nāgārjuna, vers 22.

3. Voir par exemple Majjhimanikāya I, p. 190–91; Saṃyuttanikāya III, p. 120; *Itivuttaka* v.3 (p. 91); et *Śālistambasūtra,* cité par Candrakīrti, *Prasannapadā* vii.16 (cf. p. 6), par Yaśomitra dans l'*Abhidharmakośavyākhyā* iii.28, et par Prajñākaramati, *Bodhicaryāvatārapañjikā* ix.14. Comparer aussi le *Suhṛllekha* attribué à Nāgārjuna, vers 112.

et régulier, une norme. En outre, il est impersonnel, car les mêmes sources précisent qu'il vaut qu'il y ait ou non naissance des tathāgata.[4]

De ces textes il ressort qu'on est en droit d'estimer que, dans l'assimilation du *pratītyasamutpāda* à la fois au *dharma* et au *buddha,* le *buddha* figure en quelque sorte comme la structuration (aspect *dharmakāya,* ainsi qu'on devait le désigner) plutôt que comme le créateur ou instituteur de cette «norme», dont la validité ne dépend aucunement de l'individu l'ayant approfondie et promulguée (aspects qu'on devait désigner par le nom de *rūpakāya*). C'est d'ailleurs dans cette perspective qu'on a pu enseigner—notamment dans les écoles des Mahiśāsaka, des Vibhajyavādin et des Mahāsāṃghika—que le *pratītyasamutpāda* est un facteur inconditionné *(asaṃskṛta).*[5]

Cependant, il ne faudrait assurément pas exciper de ces descriptions pour soutenir que le *pratītyasamutpāda* constitue une entité éternelle.[6] Les choses *(dharma)* auxquel-les se rapportent la «norme» de la production en dépendance—autrement dit les choses nées en dépendance *(pratītyasamutpanna)*—sont, de par leur définition même, construites ou conditionnées *(saṃskṛta)* par les causes et conditions présidant à leur naissance; d'ailleurs, ainsi qu'on l'a relevé plus haut, la théorie de la production en dépendance permet précisément d'écarter la position extrême de l'éternalisme. En outre, dans les textes cités ci-dessus, le *pratītyasamutpāda* a été rapproché de la *śūnyatā;* et, comme on l'a vu, il représente la raison qui permet de constater que les *dharma* («choses») sont Vides d'être propre ou d'essence (hypostasiée), la *śūnyatā* étant en quelque sorte la véritable nature (non-hypostasiée) des *dharma.*

Qu'est-ce donc que la production en dépendance?[7] Selon une définition, commune aux sources indiennes et tibétaines, la notion peut s'entendre selon la formule: «Ceci étant, cela est; en vertu de la naissance de ceci, cela naît». Cette définition concerne la théorie générale de l'origine des choses,

4. Voir par exemple Saṃyuttanikāya II, p. 25–26; *Nidānasaṃyukta* (éd. Ch. Tripathi, Berlin, 1962), p. 147–48, 164; *Śālistambasūtra,* cité par Yaśomitra, *Abidharmakośavyākhyā* iii.28.

5. Voir par exemple Vasubandhu, *Abhidharmakośabhāṣya* iii.28. Cf. A. Bareau, *Les sectes bouddhiques du Petit Véhicule* (Paris, 1955), p. 285.

6. Voir Vasubandhu, *Abhidharmakośabhāṣya,* iii.28. Cf. Tsong kha pa, *Rten 'brel bstod pa,* vers 24–25.

7. Comparer É. Lamotte, *Buddhist Studies in Honour of Walpola Rahula* (Londres, 1980), p. 118–32, et *Beiträge zur Indienforschung* (Festschrift E. Waldschmidt; Berlin, 1977), p. 279–98.

en d'autres termes la notion de la causalité «extérieure» et non personnelle dans le monde inanimé.

Il existe d'autre part une interprétation du *pratītyasamutpāda* qui porte sur l'évolution psychosomatique individuelle des êtres animés. Dans l'analyse de cette forme «intérieure» de la production en dépendance, on fait état d'une série ou chaîne de membres *(yan lag = aṅga)*—les «occasions» conditionnantes *(rgyu = nidāna)* qui sont le plus souvent au nombre de douze—dont le premier est l'ignorance *(ma rig pa = avidyā).* Ainsi, en tant que condition provoquant directement la naissance des constructions psychiques *('du byed = saṃskāra),* et indirectement la naissance des dix membres suivants dans l'évolution conditionnée des êtres animés dans le cycle des existences *(saṃsāra), l'avidyā* figure comme principe ontogénique. Or, cette *avidyā* n'est pas simple absence de connaissance, de savoir; elle est plutôt l'affliction *(nyon mongs pa = kleśa)* de la «nescience»—la connaissance fausse—à cause de laquelle on méconnaît la réalité en ne la voyant pas telle qu'elle est. C'est ce qui explique son rôle de moteur primitif du mécanisme de la production en dépendance «intérieure» en tant qu'engrenage qui pour ainsi dire plonge les êtres animés dans l'océan du *saṃsāra.* De l'*avidyā* procéderont donc finalement—après une série de chaînons intermédiaires—naissance, vieillissement et mort, autrement dit l'Agrégat de la Douleur *(duḥkhaskandha)* physique, psychique et métaphysique correspondant au premier des quatre «principes nobles» *('phags pa'i bden pa = āryasatya).* Et c'est ainsi aussi que la théorie du *pratītyasamutpāda* peut en même temps rendre compte de l'origine *(kun 'byung = samudaya)* de la Douleur, deuxième des «principes nobles». Or, parce que cet engrenage dépend en dernier ressort de l'*avidyā,* le philosophe-pratiquant est en mesure d'enrayer le mouvement ontogénique de la production en dépendance au moyen d'exercices à la fois philosophiques et spirituels servant à abolir l'*avidyā,* et qui sont constitutifs du Chemin *(lam = mārga)* conduisant à l'arrêt *('gog pa = nirodha)* de la Douleur. En d'autres termes, dans la pratique philosophique et spirituelle du bouddhisme, après avoir pénétré l'enchaînement progressif *(anuloma)*—et ontogénique—des membres de la production en dépendance, on procède à une méditation à rebours *(pratiloma)* consistant à se rendre compte du fait que, en l'absence de chaque membre immédiatement antérieur, chaque membre subséquent doit nécessairement prendre fin. Par conséquent, pour la personne ayant compris à fond, par la pratique philosophique et spirituelle, la théorie du *pratītyasamutpāda,* l'élimination de l'*avidyā* en tant que moteur de la production en dépendance «intérieure» constituera l'arrêt de toute la douleur du *saṃsāra.* Cet arrêt *('gog pa = nirodha)* de la douleur et le chemin qui y conduit sont dans l'ordre le troisième et le dernier des quatre «principes nobles» *(āryasatya).*

En ce qui concerne la relation de la production en dépendance avec la Vacuité de nature propre *(svabhāvaśūnyatā)*, à l'intérieur du domaine des choses conditionnées *(saṃskṛtadharma)* nées en dépendance *(pratītya-samutpanna)* et par conséquent Vides *(śūnya)*, la référence objective des termes de *pratītyasamutpada* et de *śūnyatā* est sans doute la même. Mais ces deux termes ne sont pas parfaitement synonymes, car le fait d'être né en dépendance est donné comme la raison permettant de constater que les choses sont Vides de nature propre. En outre, les notions que désignent ces deux termes ne sont pas coextensives parce que les *dharma* non conditionnés *(asaṃskṛta)*—l'espace vide *(ākāśa)*, par exemple, aussi bien que le *nirvāṇa*—sont Vides *(śūnya)* sans pourtant être nés en dépendance de causes et conditions.

Rappelons enfin que—conformément à une tradition de l'Inde attestée par les fresques d'Ajaṇṭā—la notion de la production en dépendance qui rend compte de l'évolution psychosomatique de l'être animé a reçu au Tibet une figuration picturale sur les murs des temples et des monastères, où les vignettes symboliques de la Roue des existences *(srid pa'i 'khor lo = bhava-cakra)* représentent les douze membres du *pratītyasamutpāda* «intérieur».[8] C'est ainsi que la doctrine de la production en dépendance a pris l'aspect d'un Dharma ou enseignement visible susceptible d'être «lu» et contemplé par tous, hommes et femmes, religieux et laïques, érudits et illettrés.

Vu leur importance capitale pour le bouddhisme tant tibétain qu'indien, les notions philosophiques en question ont fait l'objet de très nombreux exposés au Tibet. Et à la mesure de la complexité de ces notions les traités tibétains qui y ont été consacrés sont aussi étendus que touffus, car il s'agit naturellement de Sommes très détaillées et de commentaires hautement techniques. A côté de ces grands traités il existe aussi des ouvrages plus courts qui analysent, de manière non moins technique, tel aspect particulier de ces notions. Dans la place limitée à notre disposition ici il ne sera bien entendu pas possible de donner une idée adéquate de cette vaste littérature philosophique. Mais il existe aussi des sommaires, le plus souvent versifiés, revêtant tantôt la forme de chants *(mgur ma)* philosophiques et mystiques—les chants du très célèbre Mi la ras pa (Milarépa) sont sans doute les mieux connus dans

8. Comparer L. A. Waddell, *Journal of the Royal Asiatic Society of Bengal* 61 (1892), p. 133–55, et *Journal of the Royal Asiatic Society* 1894, p. 367–84; D. Schlingloff, *Études asiatiques/Asiatische Studien* 25 (1971), p. 323–34; et L. Sopa, *Journal of the International Association of Buddhist Studies* 7 (1984), p. 125–45. Voir aussi *Divyāvadāna* (éd. Cowell et Neil, Cambridge, 1886), p. 300 (histoire de Sahasodgata); et comparer p. 547 (histoire d'Udrāyaṇa, roi de Roruka).

ce genre—et tantôt d'hymnes *(bstod pa)*—dont le présent texte de Tsong kha pa est un exemple particulièrement apprécié. Imprégnés qu'ils sont des modes d'expression propres à la littérature tibétaine, ces textes sont particulièrement aptes à illustrer pour le lecteur des traits typiques de la pensée tibétaine.

Si Tsong kha pa a choisi de présenter son *Précis* de l'enseignement du Buddha sous la forme d'un hymne dédié à ce dernier en tant que promulgateur de la théorie de la production en dépendance, c'est sans doute tout d'abord parce qu'il prit pour inspiration et modèle les Hymnes attribués à Nāgārjuna cités plus haut. Aussi, selon ce qu'il nous dit en suivant Nāgārjuna, le *pratītyasamutpāda* est-il la notion clé—le noyau (vers 3 et 19)—de la pensée bouddhique; il se laisse assimiler d'une part au *dharma* et aussi au *buddha* et de l'autre à la Vacuité et, par conséquent, à la Voie du Milieu (vers 11–13, 18, 20, 26). Par ailleurs, Nāgārjuna et son successeur et commentateur Candrakīrti—le grand maître de l'école des Prāsaṅgika-Mādhyamika *(thal 'gyur ba)* qui remonte à Buddhapālita—sont explicitement cités dans le *Précis* (vers 49–51) comme les principales sources de l'interprétation de l'enseignement du Buddha proposée par Tsong kha pa, et en dernière analyse de toute sa philosophie.

L'emploi fait par Tsong kha pa dans son *Précis* de tel ornement *(rgyan = alaṃkāra)* poétique emprunté à la tradition indo-tibétaine—et notamment de la figure de sens nommée «(apparence de) contradiction» (*virodha* [*-ābhāsa*]) ou paradoxe—ne s'explique vraisemblablement pas simplement par le fait qu'il ait prêté à son texte une forme poético-hymnique, ni par la circonstance que ses modèles—et notamment les hymnes susdits de Nāgārjuna—présentaient l'aspect de poèmes. Au demeurant, si le langage figuré de la tradition poétique indo-tibétaine peut convenir, dans un traité philosophique, à communiquer la Vue *(lta ba = darśana)* théorique de la réalité *(don dam bden pa = paramārtha,* ou *de kho na nyid = tattva),* c'est que ce genre de langage a pu être censé fournir un moyen quelque peu moins inadéquat que toute autre forme de langage tenant du discursus conceptuel et linguistique *(spros pa = prapañca)* pour suspendre—et en quelque sorte pour neutraliser provisoirement—les contradictions apparentes, les antinomies et les apories que ne manque pas de susciter tout effort de prêter une expression verbale, et donc discursive, à la réalité qui est, par sa définition même, au-delà de la discursivité et qui est donc inexprimable en soi *(spros pa med pa = niṣprapañca, brjod du med pa = avācya).*[9] Du reste, sous la direction d'un spécialiste réputé de poétique et de grammaire, Nam mkha' bzang po, Tsong

9. Voir Tsong kha pa, *Rten 'brel bstod pa,* vers 13, 26 et 27, avec vers 9, 11–13 et 18.

kha pa s'était familiarisé dès sa jeunesse avec la théorie poétologique indienne dont la tradition—déjà bien connue de Sa skya paṇḍi ta dans la première moitié du XIIIe siècle—s'est définitivement implantée au Tibet au cours du siècle précédant son activité. Aussi, selon le témoignage de ses biographes, Tsong kha pa fut-il en mesure de cultiver et de gagner les faveurs de la divine Sarasvatī—patronne des lettres et des sciences—grâce à ce même Nam mkha' bzang po, qui traduisit en tibétain le *Meghadūta* du poète indien Kālidāsa aussi bien que plusieurs traités sanskrits de grammaire et de métrique.

Lorsqu'il composa en 1397, à l'âge de 41 ans, son *Précis,* Tsong kha pa venait, au dire de ses biographes, de passer par une période de très graves doutes concernant l'intelligence et l'exégèse correctes de la philosophie du Buddha et de Nāgārjuna, perplexité qui l'avait incité à se vouer à une longue et très intense réflexion philosophique et à des exercices spirituels ardus pendant lesquels il eut une vision mystico-philosophique de Buddhapālita—l'auteur déjà mentionné du premier grand commentaire des *Mūlamadhyamakakārikā* de Nāgārjuna qui nous soit parvenu en tibétain, et l'initiateur de l'école des Prāsaṅgika-Mādhyamika—et aussi de Mañjughoṣa lui-même. Ce *bodhisattva*—qu'on tient d'ailleurs pour un *buddha*—figure en effet, en tant que personnification de la sapience *(shes rab = prajñā),* comme le guide spirituel désigné, et comme l'inspirateur, du philosophe-pratiquant qui cherche à pénétrer la théorie, si profonde et absconse, de la Vacuité d'être propre enseignée dans les textes de la Prajñāpāramitā et du Madhyamaka (voir vers 49).

Certes, Tsong kha pa ne s'est pas borné à reproduire mot à mot ou à reprendre sans aperçus nouveaux ce qu'il pouvait trouver dans les sources classiques du bouddhisme indien. La contribution spécifique des penseurs tibétains a en effet consisté à tirer au clair des problèmes philosophiques et des difficultés exégétiques non explicités, ou laissés en suspens, par leurs sources indiennes, et aussi à faire ressortir des implications et des virtualités de la pensée bouddhique qui n'avaient pas été mises en relief précédemment.

Ainsi, par ses nombreux et très riches traités et commentaires, Tsong kha pa contribua de manière fort remarquable à l'approfondissement philosophique de la théorie du *pratītyasamutpāda,* et de la question de la relation de celui-ci avec la *śūnyatā.* Selon une interprétation de ces deux notions qui avait souvent été avancée par ses devanciers, le Vide *(stong pa)* doit servir à écarter l'extrême *(mtha' = anta)* de l'existence *(yod pa = bhāva)* alors que l'apparence *(snang ba)*—autrement dit ce qui se présente à la connaissance relative comme naissant des causes et conditions—doit servir à écarter l'extrême du néant *(med pa = abhāva).* Or, aux termes de l'analyse proposée par Tsong kha pa, le caractère spécifique de la théorie du Madhyamaka dans l'école de Nāgārjuna, de Buddhapālita et de Candrakīrti consiste justement à comprendre que c'est l'apparence—et partant, en dernière analyse, la production en dépendance—qui écarte l'extrême de l'existence substantielle et permanente, et que c'est le Vide qui écarte l'extrême du néant. En somme, toute interprétation nihiliste de la Vacuité ainsi que du procédé philosophique de la négation non relationnelle et absolue *(med par dgag pa = prasajyapratiṣedha)* qui permet de réaliser la *śūnyatā*—procédé qui n'implique pas l'affirmation du contraire de ce qui est nié, et qui exclut ainsi toute présupposition logique et ontologiste—est par conséquent, selon la doctrine exposée par Tsong kha pa, sans fondement et ne saurait être maintenue.

L'analyse que donna Tsong kha pa peut en conséquence être considérée, sinon comme une innovation sans précédent (notion qu'il aurait sûrement récusée), du moins comme un aperçu nouveau dans la compréhension de la Voie du Milieu et comme une pénétration en profondeur de la réalité sous les aspects de la «vérité» de surface *(kun rdzob bden pa = saṃvṛtisatya)* et de la «vérité» ultime *(don dam bden pa = paramārthasatya),* et aussi de la non-dualité de production en dépendance et de Vacuité.

II. Tsong kha pa, Éloge de la production en dépendance (Rten 'brel bstod pa), précis de [l'enseignement] bien-formulé

Hommage à Mañjughoṣa, [mon] Guru.

> Je m'incline devant celui qui voit et communique [l'enseignement de] la production en dépendance, le Victorieux (*jina,* c'est-à-dire le Buddha) qui est, au suprême degré, connaisseur en vertu de sa Vue et instructeur en vertu de sa Parole. (1)
>
> La racine de tous les maux dans la condition mondaine est l'ignorance *(avidyā),* et c'est en vertu de la Vue que ces maux prennent fin: tu as déclaré que cela constitue la production en dépendance. (2)
>
> Alors, comment une personne intelligente ne comprendra-t-elle pas que c'est la voie de la production en dépendance qui représente le noyau même de ton enseignement? (3)
>
> Ainsi donc, ô Protecteur, comme moyen pour faire ton éloge, qui trouvera quelque chose de plus merveilleux que ton enseignement de la production en dépendance? (4)
>
> Quel moyen de bonne instruction est plus admirable que ta déclaration proclamant que tout ce qui dépend d'une condition *(pratyaya)* est Vide de nature propre *(svabhāvaśūnya)*? (5)

Ce [système de la production en dépendance et de la Vacuité]—
qui, quand le sot s'y attache, resserre les liens de la prise des positions extrêmes *(anta)*—constitue, pour le sage, le moyen de détruire tout le filet de la prolifération discursive *(prapañca)*. (6)

Puisqu'on ne retrouve pas cet enseignement chez un autre [maître],
c'est toi seul qu'on désigne comme le Maître *(śāstṛ)*: [appliquée] aux sectaires *(tīrthika)* [cette dernière désignation n'est qu'] une expression fictive, comme [le nom du] lion [appliqué] à un renardeau. (7)

O Maître! O refuge! O philosophe excellent! O Protecteur.
Je rends hommage au Maître qui enseigne si bien la production en dépendance. (8)

Quand on considère comme contradictoire ou non établi ce système *(tshul = naya)* de la production en dépendance que tu as communiqué, ô Bienfaiteur, aux êtres en ta qualité de Médecin—système représentant la cause *(rgyu mtshan = hetu)* précellente pour la constatation certaine de la Vacuité *(śūnyatā)*, quintessence de l'enseignement—comment peut-on approfondir ta doctrine *(lugs = mata)*?[10] (9–10)

Selon ton [enseignement], quand on voit que Vacuité signifie production en dépendance, le Vide de nature propre et la justesse [du système pragmatique] de l'action et de l'agent ne s'excluent pas. Au contraire, si l'on maintient la vue opposée on tombe dans un abîme terrible, car l'action est impossible dans le cas du vide et le vide n'existe pas pour ce qui est actif.[11] (11–12)

C'est pourquoi la vue de la production en dépendance est bien louée dans ton enseignement: il n'y est question ni du néant total *(kun tu med pa)* ni d'être par nature propre.[12] (13)

10. Dans une inférence, la raison logique *(rtags = liṅga,* ou *gtan tshigs = hetu)* peut être contradictoire *('gal ba = viruddha)* ou non établi *(ma grub pa = asiddha),* auquel cas l'inférence n'est pas valable. Or, dans l'enseignement de la production en dépendance proclamé par le Buddha, ces fautes sont absentes.

11. Autrement dit, l'usage pragmatique *(vyavahāra)*—la «Vérité» de surface *(saṃvṛti-satya)*—au niveau de l'action et de l'expression verbale n'est pas annulé par la Vacuité—la Vérité ultime *(paramārthasatya).*

12. Ainsi, le néant (ou nihilisme) et l'être par nature propre (ou substantialisme) sont les deux extrêmes qu'évite la Voie du Milieu moyennant la théorie de la production en dépendance.

Donc, ce qui est indépendant *(nirapekṣa)* étant [inexistant] comme une fleur du ciel *(khapuṣpa)*, une chose non dépendante *(ma brten)* n'existe pas. [Or,] si [une chose] était établie par nature, elle serait [intrinsèquement] établie, ce qui exclurait sa dépendance des causes et conditions *(hetupratyaya)*. (14)

C'est pourquoi tu as déclaré qu'en dehors de ce qui est produit en dépendance il n'existe aucune chose *(dharma)*[13] et, par conséquent, qu'en dehors du Vide de nature propre il n'existe aucune chose. (15)

Parce que [par définition] une nature propre ne prend pas fin,[14] tu as déclaré que si les choses *(dharma)* avaient une nature propre le *nirvāṇa* ne serait pas possible et que toute prolifération discursive *(prapañca)* serait sans arrêt. (16)

Personne ne saurait donc invalider cette bonne déclaration—faite si souvent par toi à la façon d'un rugissement de lion *(siṃhanāda)* dans les assemblées des savants—selon laquelle [les choses sont] sans nature propre *(niḥsvabhāva)*. (17)

Les dispositions doctrinales *(rnam gzhag)* conjuguées expliquant qu'il n'existe pas de nature propre et que telle [chose] dépend de telles [causes et conditions] sont [ainsi] entièrement exactes. A plus forte raison elles ne sont pas contradictoires. (18)

Tu as si bien déclaré que, à cause de la production en dépendance, on ne recourt pas aux vues extrêmes. Et, ô Protecteur, c'est pourquoi ton enseignement est suprême. (19)

Les constatations certaines *(nges pa)* conjuguées aux termes desquelles tout est Vide de nature et tel résultat procède de telles [causes et conditions] se complètent l'une l'autre, sans s'opposer. (20)

Qu'est-ce qui est plus merveilleux, plus admirable, que cela? A condition qu'on te loue par ce moyen, tu es [vraiment] loué, mais pas autrement. (21)

Qu'y a-t-il d'étonnant à ce que celui qui te hait parce qu'il est sous l'emprise de la confusion *(moha = avidyā)* récusera le terme d'absence de nature propre *(niḥsvabhāva)*? (22)

13. Plus exactement, aucun *dharma* conditionné *(saṃskṛta)*.

14. Comparer Nāgārjuna, *Mūlamadhyamakakārikā* xviii.5.

Celui-là m'étonne qui, ayant une fois accepté la production en dépendance—trésor précieux de tes discours—ne supporte pas cette proclamation de la Vacuité *(śūnyatā)*. (23)

Si une personne, à cause du terme même de production en dépendance, prend pour nature propre *(svabhāva)* ce qui est [au contraire] le moyen suprême pour arriver à l'absence de nature propre *(niḥsvabhāvatā)*, par quel moyen devra-t-elle être conduite maintenant vers ce bon Chemin qui te réjouit—passage sans pareil franchi, à si bon droit, par les Nobles *(ārya)* supérieurs? (24–25)

D'une part nature propre—non produite *(akṛtrima)* et indépendante *(nirapekṣa)*—et d'autre part production en dépendance—dépendante *(sāpekṣa)* et produite *(kṛtrima)*:[15] comment se réuniraient-elles [toutes les deux] sans incompatibilité dans un seul substrat? (26)

C'est pourquoi tu as déclaré que ce qui naît en dépendance, tout en étant toujours dénué *(vivikta = śūnya)* de nature propre, est comme une projection illusoire *(māyopama)* du fait de se présenter en apparence *(snang ba)* comme cette [nature propre]. (27)

Aussi, s'il est déclaré que même des opposants ne découvrent pas convenablement de point faible dans l'enseignement que tu as communiqué,[16] cela se comprend fort bien par là-même [c'est-à-dire en vertu de l'exposé de la théorie de la production en dépendance]. (28)

Et cela s'explique par le fait que tu as, par cet exposé, écarté toute possibilité et pour l'imputation *(samāropa)* et pour la dénégation *(apavāda)* à l'endroit d'une entité, visible ou non visible. (29)

Par cette voie précisément de la production en dépendance—cause de la perception que ta doctrine est sans pareille—on s'assure que [tous tes] autres enseignements sont [eux aussi] des moyens de connaissance correcte. (30)

Pour celui qui te suit en pratiquant ce que tu as si bien déclaré après avoir obtenu la Vue conforme au réel, tous les dommages sont écartés puisque la racine de tous les maux [c'est-à-dire l'ignorance, *avidyā*] est [ainsi] coupée. (31)

15. Comparer Nāgārjuna, *Mūlamadhyamakakārikā*, chap. xv.

16. Comparer Nāgārjuna, *Vigrahavyāvartanī* 59, 63 et 29–30; *Mūlamadhyamakakārikā* iv.8–9 et 24.13; Āryadeva, *Catuḥśataka* xvi.25.

Si l'on se détourne de ton enseignement, on sera comme emporté toujours à nouveau par les défauts, même au cas où l'on se serait adonné longuement à des peines ascétiques. Car la vue substantialiste *(ātmadṛṣṭi)* est forte.[17] (32)

Oh! Comment une personne intelligente ayant compris la différence entre ces deux choses[18] ne se dévouera-t-elle pas de tout cœur à toi? (33)

On obtiendra une grande joie si l'on acquiert la certitude, même générale, au sujet du sens seulement d'une portion de tes enseignements. Et, à plus forte raison, cela sera vrai [si l'on acquiert la certitude] au sujet de [tous] tes nombreux enseignements. (34)

Mon esprit étant accablé par la confusion *(moha = avidyā),* bien que j'aie depuis longtemps pris refuge dans une telle masse de bonnes qualités, je n'ai pas—hélas!—pris connaissance même d'une partie de [toutes] ces bonnes qualités. (35)

J'estime qu'on est cependant fortuné si l'on a tant soit peu confiance en toi aussi longtemps que sa série vitale—laquelle tend vers la mort—ne sera pas épuisée. (36)

Côté enseignement on enseigne la production en dépendance, et côté discernement on connaît la production en dépendance: c'est toi—et non point un autre—qui les connais bien et de façon précellente, à l'instar du seigneur qui règne sur les mondes. (37)

Dans toute leur étendue les discours que tu as prononcés se rapportent à cette même production en dépendance. Comme il s'agit là du *nirvāṇa,* tout ce que tu fais est tranquille.[19] (38)

Oh! Merveille! Puisque tous ceux qui entendent ton enseignement seront apaisés, qui ne se dévouera pas en retenant ton enseignement? (39)

Chez moi se développe un engagement joyeux à l'égard de cette doctrine qui évince tout contradicteur, est exempte d'erreurs et de

17. En tant que *satkāyadṛṣṭi,* la vue substantialiste—qui saisit la notion d'un soi *(ātman)* et celle de ce qui relève d'un soi *(ātmīya)*—est un des aspects principaux de l'ignorance ou «nescience» *(avidyā = moha).*

18. Entre fautes et afflictions, y compris la vue substantialiste, d'une part, et les bonnes qualités, y compris la compréhension de la production en dépendance et la Vacuité d'autre part.

19. Le nirvāṇa a précisément pour caractère d'être tranquille ou apaisé *(śānta, śiva).*

contradictions et procure le double profit [provisoire et ultime] de toutes les créatures. (40)

C'est dans ce but que, au long d'âges incalculables, tu as maintes fois fait don tantôt de ton corps, et tantôt de ta vie, de tes chers parents et amis, et de tes biens. (41)

Infortuné est celui qui n'a pas reçu de toi ce Dharma que tu as toi-même saisi par ton esprit—tel un poisson par un hameçon—car on saisit ses bonnes qualités. (42)

Or, à cause de la force de cette douleur mon esprit n'abandonne pas—à l'instar de l'esprit d'une mère qui suit son enfant chéri. (43)

Quand, à ce sujet aussi, je considère ta Parole, et que je pense que le Maître a parlé ainsi avec sa voix sublime douée de toutes les qualités—lui qui, entouré d'un réseau lumineux, brille par la majesté des Marques et des Signes [du *buddha*]—, par suite de sa seule manifestation dans mon esprit l'image du sage est un baume, tel le rayon lunaire pour qui est affligé par la chaleur. (44–45)

La personne ignorant cette bonne doctrine si merveilleuse s'embrouille complètement, à la façon des herbes sauvages *(balbaja)*. (46)

Ayant observé ceci, et après avoir fréquenté des savants à force de nombreux efforts, j'ai toujours à nouveau recherché le sens visé *(abhiprāya)* par toi; puis, comme j'étudiais alors les divers traités de notre école et des autres écoles, mon esprit a été maintes fois tourmenté par un filet de doutes. (47–48)

Mon esprit a été revigoré quand, par la bienveillance de mon *guru,*[20] j'ai aperçu le jardin des fleurs *kunda* des enseignements de Nāgārjuna—qui devait, selon ta prédiction, expliquer exactement le système de ta Voie suprême en évitant les positions extrêmes de l'être et du néant—, jardin éclairé par les rayons brillants de la bonne exégèse du majestueux Candra[-kīrti]—disque lunaire plein de la connaissance pure—qui se meut dans le ciel de ta Parole, chasse les ténèbres spirituelles des positions extrêmes et soumet les constellations des doctrines erronées. (49–51)

20. C'est-à-dire, en premier lieu, Mañjughoṣa (voir la dédicace liminaire).

> L'action de parler est la meilleure de toutes [tes] actions,[21] et cet [enseignement de la production en dépendance] constituant justement cette [action], une personne intelligente doit te commémorer sur cette base. (52)
>
> Etant devenu renonçant en suivant ce Maître, et en tant que moine dont l'étude de la Parole du Victorieux n'est pas infime et qui me consacre à la pratique du *yoga,* je témoigne ainsi de mon respect pour le Grand Sage. (53)
>
> Une pareille rencontre avec l'enseignement du Maître suprême étant due à la bienveillance du *guru,* je dédie ce bien *(kuśala = puṇya)* comme cause pour que tous les êtres puissent être soutenus par un Bon Ami *(kalyāṇamitra)* saint. (54)
>
> Puisse l'enseignement de ce Bienfaiteur n'être jamais, jusqu'à la fin des temps, ébranlé par les vents des constructions mentales erronées, et ayant connu l'essentiel de l'enseignement puissions-nous être comblés [dans nos vœux] en obtenant confiance en le Maître. (55)
>
> Puissé-je ne jamais manquer, ne serait-ce que pour un instant, de maintenir dans toutes mes existences, et même au prix de mon corps et de ma vie, cette bonne doctrine du Sage, qui élucide le principe vrai de la production en dépendance. (56)
>
> Puissé-je passer jour et nuit à considérer les moyens qui augmenteront cet [enseignement] que le meilleur des guides [Śākyamuni] a réalisé après avoir déployé des efforts moyennant d'innombrables exercices ascétiques. (57)
>
> Puissent Brahmā, Indra, les *lokapāla,* Legs ldan Kāla[22] et les autres protecteurs m'accompagner toujours sans défaillir quand, a vec une aspiration pure, je me voue à ce système. (58)

Ce traité, intitulé *Le Précis quintessentiel de [l'enseignement] bien-formulé (subhāṣita),* hymne au Maître suprême—le Buddha, le Bienheureux

21. La mise en mouvement de la Roue du Dharma est la onzième des douze actions du Buddha selon le *Ratnagotravibhāga* (ii.56).

22. Comparer Blo bzang dpal ldan bstan pa'i nyi ma (Paṇ chen IV), *Yi dam rgya mtsho'i grub thabs rin chen 'byung gnas kyi lhan thabs, Rin 'byung don gsal,* II. Il s'agit d'une forme de Mahākāla qui protège ceux qui détiennent la Théorie du Madhyamaka (Phur bu lcog Ngag dbang byams pa).

(bhagavant) et le Grand Ami extraordinaire de tous les êtres—, qui prend la forme d'une proclamation de la profonde production en dépendance, fut composé par le moine érudit Blo bzang grags pa'i dpal à Lha zhol dben gnas lha sdings de 'o de gung rgyal—roi des monts neigeux de ce pays des neiges [le Tibet][23]—[endroit] connu aussi sous le nom de Rnam par rgyal ba'i gling. Le scribe fut Nam mkha' dpal.

23. Sur cette localité voir la biographie de Tsong kha pa par Mkhas grub rje, le *Dad pa'i 'jug ngogs*, p. 83; G. Tucci, *Tibetan Painted Scrolls* (Rome, 1949), p. 432, 632, 728–33.

15. The Indian and the Indic in Tibetan Cultural History, and Tsong kha pa's Achievement as a Scholar and Thinker: An Essay on the Concepts of "Buddhism in Tibet" and "Tibetan Buddhism"*

In memory of Jan Willem de Jong,
a great pioneer in Indo-Tibetan studies

A CHALLENGING AND very significant task before us is to attempt to clarify the ways in which Tibetans have absorbed and integrated into their civilization the various component parts of the originally Indian culture that they imported starting at the latest in the seventh/eighth century. In the study of such a transcultural relation, and of the enculturation of Indo-Buddhist civilization in Tibet, the identification and analysis of continuities and discontinuities—of homoeostasis (dynamic stability) and internal, systemic disequilibrium leading to restoration/renewal/innovation—will naturally play a major part. This should then assist us in overcoming the familiar opposition of stagnant stasis *vs.* dynamic change, a somewhat superficial and jejune dichotomy which has so frequently, and unproductively, been invoked in considering such matters.

The Tibetan absorption of Buddhism, and along with it of a major portion of Indo-Buddhist civilization, was most certainly not one of mere passive reception: even at the time when this process first came into full flower ca. 800 C.E., the Tibetan mind was clearly no blank slate, no *tabula rasa*. And the Tibetan appropriation of Indo-Buddhist civilization has been, at least in large part, a creative one in which Tibetans have indeed made a very noteworthy contribution of their own.

* This article was intended as a contribution to the memorial volume for J. W. de Jong published in Tokyo but for technical reasons could not be included in it. It was first published in the *Journal of Indian Philosophy* 32 (2004), pp. 321–43.

Such considerations clearly have a vital bearing on the relationship between Tibetan and Indian studies as two disciplines which—however distinct—are of course very closely linked. Whilst so much in Tibetan civilization cannot be adequately understood without knowledge of the Indian background, certain developments in Tibet provide us with highly interesting comparative material throwing light on similar (or, alternatively, dissimilar) developments taking place in India from comparable starting points. But what might be briefly referred to under the catchword of "Meta-India," in other words the complex of peripheral cultural extensions of India which can be said to be in especially close intellectual propinquity to India proper—and which once were major topics of historical study under the name of Greater India (or Inde extérieure) in connexion with Southeast Asia and Indonesia in particular—fell out of sharp focus until a very recent recrudescence of interest.[1]

I

Let us first very briefly review some examples of the absorption of Indo-Tibetan tradition that are drawn from various areas of Tibetan culture.[2]

Even though much work still remains to be done in tracing stylistic and technical developments and influences, as well as artistic lineages, we can readily see how Tibetan artists took over styles and techniques from the surrounding areas of South, East, and Central Asia, and even sometimes from Western Asia. Related iconographical models as well as iconological structures are fairly plain to see. Yet, at least from a certain period onwards, it is usually possible to say whether an art work we are looking at is actually a Tibetan production or one that was either imported into Tibet or perhaps produced by a foreign artist in Tibet.[3]

1. In the volume bearing the promising title *Indien und Zentralasien: Sprach- und Kulturkontakt* (Vorträge des Göttinger Symposions vom 7. bis 10. Mai 2001) edited by S. Bretfeld and J. Wilkens (Wiesbaden, 2003), we read in the foreword: "Keine Folge unserer Auswahl, sondern der Schwerpunktsetzung des Symposiums ist die Aussparung des indo-tibetischen Bereichs." Whether the question is just one of a focal point and emphasis alone, or one of a more far-reaching and fateful sea change in scientific concerns over the years, may remain undecided here.

2. For a short outline of the place of the Indo-Buddhist sciences or knowledge systems *(rig gnas = vidyāsthāna)* in Tibetan culture, see, e.g., part 2 of D. Seyfort Ruegg, *Ordre spirituel et ordre temporel dans la pensée bouddhique de l'Inde et du Tibet* (Paris, 1995).

3. Allowance has of course to be made for art work produced in Tibet by artists and

In Tibetan literary production, the translations of Indian (and eventually Chinese or other) texts found in the Bka' 'gyur and Bstan 'gyur speak for themselves in an eloquent way. But the Tibetan achievement in creating, within the time-span of only some decades during the eighth and early ninth centuries, a classical literary language—the *chos skad*—suitable for translating the most difficult works from Sanskrit (etc.) into Tibetan was a most remarkable feat both intellectually and linguistically. When we look at early indigenous Tibetan writings composed in this *chos skad,* it is, however, not always immediately obvious that they were not translations from Sanskrit. For example, in its language and style, the *Lta ba'i khyad par* by the renowned translator *(lo tsā ba)* Sna nam Ye shes sde (ca. 800) could perhaps be a Tibetan translation of an Indian original just as well as the indigenous Tibetan text that it actually is. Other works by Ye shes sde, as well as work by Ska ba Dpal brtsegs such as his *Lta ba'i rim pa,* are further examples of this situation.[4]

In this way there appears to exist a certain formal difference between the Tibetan achievement in the domain of the visual arts and in that of written texts in the *chos skad.*

In the areas of poetry and poetics, we know that learned Tibetans were inspired in their literary aesthetics by Indian *kāvya (snyan ngag/dngags)* and that their literature has indeed been informed by concepts drawn from Indian poetics *(alaṃkāraśāstra).*[5] As for narrative matter, a Tibetan version of the *Rāmāyaṇa* is already found among the Dunhuang manuscripts.

The influence of Indian grammar and linguistics in Tibet was a special

---

craftsmen of foreign origin, such as the Newars. In the first generation a Newar might be expected to continue working mainly in his ancestral Newar style(s), whilst his descendants resident in Tibet would gradually adopt specifically Tibetan styles. For a recent study relating to portraiture in particular, see H. Stoddard, "Fourteen Centuries of Tibetan Portraiture," in D. Dinwiddie, ed., *Portraits of the Masters* (Chicago and London, 2003), pp. 16–61.

4. See D. Seyfort Ruegg, "Autour du *lTa ba'i khyad par* de Ye šes sde," *JA* 1981, pp. 207–29, reprinted as chapter 11 of the present volume. Contrast for example the much less scholastic "Cycle of Birth and Death"—the *skye shi 'khor ba'i chos kyi yi ge* or *skye shi'i 'khor lo'i le'u*—studied by Y. Imaeda, *Histoire du cycle de la naissance et de la mort* (Genève-Paris, 1981); found, like Ye shes sde's text, among the Dunhuang manuscripts, this edifying composition of unknown authorship in the narrative genre is not scholastic in style, unlike the *Lta ba'i khyad par,* and it employs a somewhat less standard Buddhist vocabulary.

5. See L. van der Kuijp, "Tibetan Belles-lettres: The Influence of Daṇḍin and Kṣemendra," in J. Cabezón and R. Jackson, eds., *Tibetan Literature* (Ithaca, 1996), pp. 393–410. See also M. Kapstein, "The Indian Literary Identity in Tibet," in S. Pollock, ed., *Literary Cultures in History: Reconstructions from South Asia* (Berkeley, 2003), pp. 747–802.

case. The Indo-Aryan and Dravidian languages of India and the Tibetan language belong to genetically unrelated linguistic families; and the relevance of Sanskrit grammar for the Tibetan language is anything but evident, even if certain areal features appear to be detectable which link Tibetan with Indian languages. Nevertheless, the development of the above-mentioned *chos skad* has been marked by the frequency of syntactic and lexical calques reflecting the language of the original Indian source texts. This is readily understandable in view of the great cross-cultural enterprise that consisted in translating into Tibetan the important Indian sources of Buddhism, and of Indo-Buddhist civilization, now incorporated in the Bka' 'gyur and Bstan 'gyur. If, then, Indian languages cannot be said to have formed a linguistic substratum properly speaking for Tibetan, the existence of the influences just noted does allow us to speak of the former having possessed an, as it were, archistratal function in the history of the Tibetan language.[6] Recent work on the influence of Sanskrit grammar on Tibetan linguistic description has, moreover, sought to show how certain ideas of the Sanskrit grammarians may have had an impact on indigenous Tibetan grammar.[7]

In a different direction, mention may be made of the highly interesting case of the socio-religious and religio-political impact of Buddhism in Tibet and Inner Asia. This is evidenced for example in the close relationship existing between the spiritual and temporal orders that has been so prominent in the polities of this area, and which in a sense prolongs the old relation between the monk as donee and his lay donor *(dānapati = sbyin bdag)*. In Tibetan, the association of Dharma and temporal rule—the *chos srid zung 'brel*—is designated as the two-fold system *(lugs gnyis, tshul gnyis)* or two-fold law *(khrims gnyis)* linking a donor *(yon bdag = sbyin bdag)* with his spiritual preceptor, counsellor, and ritual officiant *(mchod gnas, yon gnas)*. Reference is made to this close association by the copulative compounds *mchod yon / yon mchod*, i.e., *mchod gnas = yon gnas* "preceptor donee" and *yon bdag (~ sbyin bdag)* "(princely) donor." Dyarchy of a ruler—the temporal power as donor—and his counsellor-preceptor and

6. See D. Seyfort Ruegg, "Notes sur la transmission et la réception des traités de grammaire et de lexicographie sanskrites dans les traditions indo-tibétaines," in N. Balbir et al., eds., *Langue, style et structure dans le monde indien* (Centenaire Louis Renou; Paris, 1996), pp. 213–32; id., "Sanskrit-Tibetan and Tibetan-Sanskrit Dictionaries and Some Problems in Indo-Tibetan Philosophical Lexicography," in B. Oguibénine, ed., *Lexicography in the Indian and Buddhist Cultural Field* (Munich, 1998), pp. 115–42 (with p. 123 for the use of "archistratal").

7. See P. Verhagen, *A History of Sanskrit Grammatical Literature in Tibet,* II (Leiden, 2001), chapter 2, together with the present writer's review in *JRAS* 13 (2003), pp. 123–27.

ritual officiant—the religious authority as donee—had more or less distant precursors in India, where it was at least foreshadowed in theory if not strictly equalled. In Tibet the complex—even oscillating and somewhat kaleidoscopic—socio-religious and religio-political link existing between a spiritual preceptor/officiant—a personage regarded as worthy of honour and of a ritual offering/fee *(yon = dakṣiṇā),* which explains his appellation of *yon gnas = mchod gnas* (Skt. *dakṣiṇīya*)—and his princely donor *(yon bdag / sbyin bdag = dānapati)* has been an important and very significant feature in polities conceived of in terms of Buddhist principles.[8] (Compare the Pāli terms *dakkhiṇeyya-puggala* and *-khetta.*) In certain favourable circumstances in Tibet and elsewhere in Inner Asia, this relationship then developed into a sort of concordat linking the spiritual and temporal orders, as in the case of the personal preceptor-donor relationship established first between the Tibetan hierarch Sa skya paṇḍi ta (1182–1251) and the Mongol prince Köden, and then between the former's nephew 'Phags pa (1235–80) and the Mongol emperor Qubilai Qaγan (r. 1260–94). In India, on the contrary, the relation between a monk-preceptor/counsellor and a ruler appears not to have been institutionalized, and lexically expressed, to the degree to which it came to be in Tibet, either with the *mchod gnas* in his personal relation to a princely donor or with the high religious officers termed *ti shri* and *gu shri* (< Chinese *dishi* and *guoshi*) in their official relation to a ruler in the imperial bureaucracy. Even in Tibet, the personal relation between preceptor and donor, well attested though it is, seems not to have become the object of a systematic theorized exposition in a treatise. Eventually Tibet was to develop a hierocratic—or more exactly a "bodhisattva-cratic"—form of government in which the hierarch regarded as a bodhisattva could combine spiritual authority with temporal power. Much if not all of this development appears to be ultimately derivable from Indo-Buddhist inspiration, but in Tibetan hands it took on a special form not exemplified in India.[9]

As an example of the Tibetan propensity to absorb imported intellectual

8. For this reason the common rendering "priest-patron relationship" is inadequate and potentially even misleading. From the point of view of political power relations (as distinct from the socio-religious and religio-political points of view), the label protector/benefactor-protégé relation would seem preferable.

9. See D. Seyfort Ruegg, *Ordre spirituel et ordre temporel dans la pensée bouddhique de l'Inde et du Tibet,* part 1; id., "The Preceptor-Donor *(mchod yon)* Relation in Thirteenth-Century Tibetan Society and Polity, Its Inner Asian Precursors and Indian Models," in H. Krasser et al., eds., *Tibetan Studies: Proceedings of the 7th Seminar of the International Association for Tibetan Studies,* II (Vienna, 1997), pp. 857–72.

property, Tibetan medicine also deserves mention because it has combined South Asian (Indian) and East Asian (Chinese) elements with West Asian elements. This being a special department in Tibetan studies that has been making noteworthy progress in recent years, it will not be gone into here.

II

It is of course very clear in the case of Buddhism that the transcultural linkage between Tibet and South Asia has been especially strong, creative, and productive. This appears to be true in various degrees for all Tibetan religious orders or schools *(chos lugs)*. Even the history of Bon shows that this religious tradition has not been without links to South Asia (as well as to western Asia, the western sub-Himalayan area, and Central Asia).[10]

The Indo-Tibetan traditions of Buddhism thus bear ample and most eloquent testimony to the many and various links between India and Tibet which have had an impact on most departments of activity—including art, architecture, etc.—and thought—from monastic discipline *(vinaya, 'dul ba)* through to logic and epistemology *(pramāṇa, tshad ma)*, philosophy, and tantra. They accordingly go far beyond the individual case to be discussed in the following lines.

III

The life's work of Tsong kha pa Blo bzang grags pa (1357–1419) as thinker and writer has been variously described as that of a reformer, an innovator (to the extent perhaps of even having been something of a maverick), and a conservative traditionalist. When reading his writings it is possible to see how such various, and at first sight contrary, descriptions can have been attached to him. Their appropriateness and justification still require careful scrutiny and evaluation. This will of course be the task for a full-scale intellectual

10. This complex matter remains the subject of investigation and discussion. On Buddhistic ("bouddhisant") features in Bon, see *Ordre spirituel et ordre temporel*, pp. 143–44. For the problem of links with western Asia (Iran, etc.), see G. Tucci, "Iran et Tibet," *Acta Iranica* 1 (1974), pp. 299–306, with the critical observations by P. Kvaerne, "Dualism in Tibetan Cosmogonic Myths and the Question of Iranian Influence," in C. Beckwith, ed., *Silver on Lapis* (Bloomington, 1987), pp. 163–74. For a recent discussion of several of these topics (with an extensive bibliography), see D. Martin, *Unearthing Bon Treasures* (Leiden, 2001).

biography—in Tibetan terms principally a *nang gi rnam thar*—of this master. Here only a few aspects of the matter can be addressed.

A major thinker in the lines of philosophy and ritual—one who embraced analytical and "exoteric" Prajñāpāramitā and Madhyamaka thought along with the "esoteric" Vajrayāna—Tsong kha pa has on occasion himself alluded to his intellectual and spiritual struggles, and to how he came to feel dissatisfied with certain views and interpretations current among his Tibetan predecessors and contemporaries. An eloquent and at the same time moving account of this intellectual and spiritual struggle is found in the *Rten 'brel bstod pa*—his well-known hymn to *pratītyasamutpāda*—where he speaks of his efforts to penetrate the connexion between origination in dependence *(rten 'byung)* and Emptiness *(stong pa nyid)*, between the surface level *(kun rdzob = saṃvṛti)* and the deep level of ultimate reality *(paramārtha)*.[11] Yet he is also known as a disciple of Red mda' ba/pa Gzhon nu blo gros (1349–1412), the renowned Sa skya master in whose Madhyamaka lineage he has been listed, as well as of a number of other Tibetan masters.[12] This picture of Tsong kha pa as a traditionalist placed in an Indo-Tibetan spiritual lineage is not in fact belied by his own writings. His biographies and hagiographies have represented him as indebted to other Tibetan masters also. Among his contemporaries was Bla ma Dbu ma pa Dpa' bo rdo rje, who is stated to have acted as intermediary (*lo tsā ba* "interpreter") for Tsong kha pa in visionary encounters with the bodhisattva Mañjughoṣa, for instance at a time when he felt overwhelmed by the difficulties he was experiencing in reaching an understanding of the Buddha's teaching and of Nagārjuna's thought, the Madhyamaka *(dbu ma)*.[13] This theme of a visionary encounter with, and of inspiration received from, a great bodhisattva is reminiscent of the role attributed to the bodhisattva Maitreya(nātha) in the traditional *Vita* of Asaṅga at a time when this Indian master too was meeting with difficulties in understanding and interpretation.[14] The *topos* of visionary encounter and

11. Cf. D. Seyfort Ruegg, "La pensée tibétaine," in: A. Jacob (ed.), *L'univers philosophique* (Encyclopédie philosophiqe universelle, t. 1, Paris, 1989), col. 1589–91, reprinted in chapter 14 of the present volume. This renowned work by Tsong kha pa has been published and translated several times in recent years.

12. See our *Three Studies in the History of Indian and Tibetan Madhyamaka Philosophy* (Studies in Indian and Tibetan Madhyamaka thought, Part 1, Vienna, 2000), pp. 60–64, 88f.

13. See *Three Studies*, pp. 89–90.

14. See P. Demiéville, "La *Yogācārabhūmi* de Saṅgharakṣa," *BEFEO* 44 (1954), pp. 376–87; and D. Seyfort Ruegg, *La théorie du tathagatagarbha et du gotra* (Paris, 1969), pp. 42ff.

teaching may perhaps be understood as implicitly alluding, in India as well as in Tibet, to a felt need for both conservative traditionalism and restorative or renovative interpretation.

IV

What then are we to make of these attested facts and widely spread traditions and allusions in so far as they relate to Tsong kha pa? Does being a traditionalist continuator, a "conservative," in fact preclude being a radical thinker, perhaps even an innovator? The word "innovator" may be problematic here, and it might be more accurate to speak of a "renewer" and "restorer," and of a "rethinker." And to be a "reformer" might imply a return to, and restoration of, old but overlaid or eclipsed tradition.[15] In other words, are these characterizations and categories, now so often taken to be mutually exclusive, truly so?

Furthermore, in a somewhat different perspective, are the things referred to as "Tibetan Buddhism" and "Buddhism in Tibet" to be regarded as entirely different, perhaps even opposed, entities?

It is useful to explore these questions in respect to Tsong kha pa's place in the history of the Indo-Tibetan Madhyamaka. And the answers to be given to such questions are of fundamental significance for the understanding of Tibetan civilization, and hence for Tibetan and Indo-Tibetan studies also. For whilst the Tibetans indubitably, and avowedly, introduced—"imported" or "borrowed"—Buddhism from India, they so thoroughly internalized and integrated it in a carefully pursued and systematic process comparable to that of *enculturation* (as distinct from acculturation) that Buddhism—the *(sangs rgyas kyi) chos*—was no longer a strange foreign import in Tibet. In this case the category of the foreign—"the other" in xenology—becomes blurred and is of doubtful pertinence.

Put otherwise, Tibetan culture embraces (at least) two co-ordinate and closely related, but withal distinct, component strands. The first consists of elements originating *historically* in India and found documented in sources that are still extant either in their original Indian language or in canonical

15. The Śākyamuni also has sometimes been described, problematically, as a reformer, but exactly what he is supposed to have reformed has not usually been made clear. That he set out to be a social reformer seems doubtful. That he was in some sense of the word a spiritual reformer, and that he in some way reformed ways of thinking, is a defensible view that requires further clarification.

Tibetan translations of Indian works. These components can of course be properly described as *Indian.* By contrast, another component strand in Tibetan culture consists of what may be called *Indic* (meta-Indian) elements. It has evidently been developed in a process of elaboration by Tibetans thinking in a style and along lines that are *typologically* Indian without being *historically* Indian in so far as this second strand is not attested in our available sources of Indian origin.[16] In this matter the Indian works included in the Tibetan Bka' 'gyur and Bstan 'gyur served both as sources of inspiration and as models, templates, or moulds. In developing their Indic elaborations, Tibetan thinkers were then able, as it were, to think along with their Indian sources.[17]

This co-existence of a component strand that is historically of Indian origin with a second strand of typologically Indic elements developed by Tibetans appears to characterize Tsong kha pa's work, just as it does the work of many of his Tibetan predecessors, contemporaries, and successors. In this way, as a searching and sometimes radical philosophical (re)thinker, Tsong kha pa may justly be described as being both a *conservative traditionalist* and a *creative restorer/renovator/innovator.* But he would surely have disavowed "originality" in its frequent modern sense of the reverse of traditionalism (see below on *rang bzo*).

Following on these observations, let us examine some cases which serve to illustrate Tsong kha pa's philosophical position and his intellectual contribution in relation to the Indian Madhyamaka sources. And let us recall from the outset that Tsong kha pa saw it as his task to penetrate, and to interpret as faithfully as possible, the final import, the "intent" *(dgongs pa),* of the thinking of Nāgārjuna—the source of the Madhyamaka school of philosophy—as well as that of Buddhapālita and, above all, Candrakīrti—the two main Indian exponents of what came to be termed the "Prāsaṅgika" *(thal 'gyur ba)* branch of the Madhyamaka, which, in Tibet, has been very widely held to be the most accurate and faithful interpretation of Madhyamaka thought.[18]

16. Compare the observations made in our *Ordre spirituel et ordre temporel,* p. 141f.

17. For the idea of "thinking along" in another context, that of modern scholarly "emic" analyses of classical Indian and Tibetan thought, see our "Some reflections on the place of philosophy in the study of Buddhism," *JIABS* 18 (1995), pp. 155–56, reprinted in chapter 9 of the present volume, pp. 229–30.

18. See Tsong kha pa's *Lam rim chen mo* (Zi ling ed.), pp. 573–74. By some authorities it has been held that it was Candrakīrti rather than his predecessor Buddhapālita who was to count as the foundational institutor *(srol 'byed)* of the Prāsaṅgika school of the

Tsong kha pa considered that in fulfilling this great task he was at the same time contributing to the clarification of the final import of the teaching of the Jina, or Buddha, himself.

For Tsong kha pa, such were indeed the stake and real issue. And he would therefore seek to eschew anything that might constitute arbitrary personal invention *(rang bzo)* having the effect of distorting the true meaning of the basic sources. By Tibetan as well as by modern scholars, Tsong kha pa has sometimes been suspected—even openly accused—of having unjustifiably, and hence unfaithfully, innovated and invented to the extent of making unrecognizable the authentic Indian Madhyamaka. No doubt, historically unfounded interpretations may occasionally be found in his writings, but hardly to the extent and in the frequency alleged by Tsong kha pa's opponents, provided of course that the cases impugned are examined philologically *and* through philosophical and hermeneutical analysis. They then frequently turn out to be well-founded systemic "readings" of the sources that are authentically grounded in careful philosophical thinking and analysis. But there may, of course, exist more than a single philosophically founded "reading" of the sources, a notorious example being the problem of the *pratijñā* "thesis" in Madhyamaka thought (on which see below). Indeed, it is on such points that Tibetan orders and schools *(chos lugs, bshad tshul)* could differ among themselves.

V

With the purpose of clarifying this situation, let us consider the following points illustrating what has been said above concerning Tsong kha pa's relation to the Madhyamaka tradition in India.

(1) Take the well-known, and often discussed, division of the Mādhyamikas, Indian as well as Tibetan, into the two branches of Rang rgyud pas—the "Svātantrikas" or Autonomists—and Thal 'gyur bas—the so-called "Prāsaṅgikas" or Apagogists. Tsong kha pa recognizes that, as it stands, this doxographical nomenclature is unattested in the Indian sources and that it

Madhyamaka. See Lcang skya Rol pa'i rdo rje, *Grub mtha',* na, p. 288. And on Bhavya's not having considered himself to belong to a branch of the Madhyamaka quite different from Buddhapālita's (and on the claim that both are classifiable as "Svātantrikas"), see ibid., pp. 287–88. (See now also W. Ames, "Bhāvaviveka's Own View of His Differences with Buddhapālita," in: G. Dreyfus and S. McClintock, eds., *The Svātantrika-Prāsaṅgika Distinction* [Boston, 2003], pp. 41–66.)

appeared in Tibet only towards the end of the eleventh century, at the time of the Tibetan Madhyamaka master Pa tshab Nyi ma grags (b. 1055). He nevertheless considers that this nomenclature, and the doctrinal division it expresses, are in conformity with Candrakīrti's own explanations.[19]

The lexeme **svātantrika*—a possible Sanskrit equivalent of Tib. *rang rgyud pa*—would not be morphologically anomalous in Sanskrit;[20] but in its specific connexion with Bhavya's (Bhā[va]viveka's or Bhāvin's) branch of the Madhyamaka, the term *rang rgyud pa* seems to go no further back than Jayānanda, the Kaśmīrī master who was active in Tibet in the late eleventh and early twelfth centuries. Still, extracted as it is from the expressions *svatantrānumāna°* (and *svatantram anumānam*) and *svatantraprayoga(vākya)*[21]—which denote respectively an "independent inference" and an "independent formal argument" (the Mādhyamika's so-called "syllogism") with which Bhavya and his Svātantrika school operated—the term "Svātantrika" would possess both philosophical justification and doxographic appropriateness as a name for this school. As for the correlative appellation Thal 'gyur ba—equivalent to Skt. *prāsaṅgika* and used in Tibet to designate the second main Indian school of the pure Madhyamaka—in extant Indian sources it does not appear to be

19. See *Lam rim chen mo,* p. 573; and *Three Studies,* pp. 95–96. Cf. K. Yotsuya, *The Critique of Svatantra Reasoning by Candrakīrti and Tsong-kha-pa* (Stuttgart, 1999).

Earlier, Tsong kha pa is said to have learnt from a visionary instruction given by the bodhisattva Mañjughoṣa in reply to his enquiry put through Bla ma Dbu ma pa (see above, p. 381) that he had not adequately understood the distinction between Rang rgyud pa and Thal 'gyur ba and that his philosophical theory *(lta ba)* was then neither. That is, he still had to reflect long and deeply before he could properly fathom Nāgārjuna's and Candrakīrti's Madhyamaka thought; and this would involve, *inter alia,* his coming correctly to appreciate the true function of an accepted position or assertion *(khas len pa = abhyupagama)*—in other words a philosophical thesis *(dam bca' = pratijñā)*—in Madhyamaka thought (see below).

Whatever the exegetical and philosophic problems attaching to the nomenclature "Svātantrika" and "Prāsaṅgika" in Tibet as well as now in contemporary studies of the Madhyamaka, and however late the origin of this nomenclature, the fact remains that it possesses a certain usefulness for taxonomic and doxographical purposes, and even a certain heuristic value. (The matter of the nomenclature "Svātantrika" and "Prāsaṅgika" has just recently been the subject of discussions and opinions, with somewhat mixed results, in G. Dreyfus and S. McClintock, eds., *The Svātantrika-Prāsaṅgika Distinction,* published in 2003 shortly after this article was written.)

20. Compare also the attested word *svātantrya.*

21. Cf. *svatantrasādhana(vādin)* in the so-called **Lakṣaṇaṭīkā*. Cf. Y. Yonezawa, *IBK* 47 (1999), pp. 1024–1022 (and the same author's introduction to the facsimile edition of Sanskrit palm-leaf manuscripts in Tibetan *dbu med* script, Tōkyō: The Institute for Comprehensive Studies of Buddhism, Taishō University, 2001).

attested at all in the meaning of Candrakīrti's branch of the Madhyamaka; and it must be judged to be a terminological innovation current in Tibet (though possibly originating in Jayānanda's native Kaśmīr). But since it is regularly derived from the technical term *prasaṅga* (Tib. *thal 'gyur*)—denoting here the apagogic procedure adopted in Buddhapālita's and Candrakīrti's school of the Madhyamaka that points up, in an opponent's theory and argument, consequences or eventualities *(prasaṅga)* undesired by the opponent himself—, it too possesses its philosophical justification and doxographic appropriateness.

Concerning the question as to whether the use of this nomenclature constitutes nothing but fanciful and hence arbitrary personal invention (that is, a *rang bzo*) on the part of Tibetan interpreters, Tsong kha pa has accordingly concluded that, even though unattested in the Indian sources as the names of the two branches of the pure Indian Madhyamaka, it is in fact not a *rang bzo* because it accurately corresponds to Candrakīrti's own philosophical procedure and explanations.[22]

According to Tsong kha pa, this terminology relates to the two ways in which the theory *(lta ba = darśana)* ascertaining the deep level of ultimate reality *(don dam pa = paramārtha)*—Emptiness *(śūnyatā)*—is generated in the conscious stream *(rgyud = saṃtāna, saṃtati)* of a Mādhyamika philosopher-practiser,[23] a process which is itself located on the level of philosophical analysis and meditative praxis that belong to the realm of pragmatic transactional usage *(tha snyad = vyavahāra),* that is, to the surface level *(saṃvṛti).* The distinction between the two terms stands then in correlation with the difference in whether, when reaching his understanding of ultimate reality, a Mādhyamika—following the method of the "Svātantrika" Bhavya—proceeds through the use of independent *(svatantra)* inferences and formal reasoning, or whether—following the "Prāsaṅgika" Candrakīrti—a Mādhyamika resorts instead to the use of the negative (or, more precisely, apagogic) procedure termed *prasaṅga* to achieve this end.

In sum, according to Tsong kha pa, the terminology and nomenclature in question, as well as much of the relevant commentarial detail, are indeed later than the foundational Indian sources. Nevertheless, for him, the philosophical procedures pointed up by the Tibetan appellations "Rang rgyud pa" and "Thal 'gyur ba" are grounded in the respective philosophical methods of

22. See *Lam rim chen mo,* p. 573.

23. See *Lam rim chen mo,* p. 573: . . . *don dam pa stong pa nyid nges pa'i lta ba rgyud la skyed tshul gyi sgo nas ming 'dogs pa* . . . .

Bhavya and Candrakīrti, the institutors *(srol 'byed)* of the two main branches of the pure Indian Madhyamaka.

(2) Another significant case where Tibetan interpreters and commentators have entered philosophical territory that had not been clearly charted by their Indian predecessors was in seeking to clarify the vexed question as to whether, in the frame of Madhyamaka thought, the true Mādhyamika—and in particular the Mādhyamika of the "Prāsaṅgika" school—is actually entitled to hold a propositional thesis *(dam bca' = pratijñā),* a philosophical doctrine *(lugs = mata),* and a doctrinal position *(phyogs = pakṣa)* of his own. The Tibetan exegetes were faced with the need to explicate Nāgārjuna's famous—and *prima facie* subversively radical—statement that he himself has no thesis whatever (*pratijñā*; *Vigrahavyāvartanī* 29). And they had to reconcile this statement by Nāgārjuna—as well as a not unrelated one by Āryadeva (*Catuḥśataka* xvi.25)—with the actual philosophical and commentarial practice of these two masters and their successor Candrakīrti, all of whom have indeed propounded philosophical propositions and statements.[24]

This issue has been a subject on which Tibetan scholars have written hundreds of pages that raise fundamental questions in philosophical language, method, and thinking. It was also a matter on which Tibetan scholars differed among themselves. The position of Tsong kha pa's school was that, although the Mādhyamika indeed has no thesis postulating the existence of any entity *(dngos po = bhāva)* whatsoever produced in terms of the "tetralemma" *(mu bzhi = catuṣkoṭi)* of ontological positions—namely origination from self (as in the Sāṃkhya's *satkāryavāda*), from another entity (as in the Nyāya's *ārambhavāda*), from a combination of both these positions, or from neither (i.e., causelessly), as stated in *Madhyamakakārikā* i.1—, which is to say that all things are Empty of self-existence *(svabhāvaśūnya)* and originate only in dependence *(pratītyasamutpanna),* as a philosopher the Mādhyamika (inclusive even of the "Prāsaṅgika") does nevertheless have a philosophical position expressible in the form of a proposition or statement. This view of the matter Tsong kha pa's school considers to be in conformity with Candrakīrti's actual philosophical procedure, for instance when the latter ascribed statements and doctrines to Nāgārjuna himself (and also to the Buddha).[25]

(3) Still another area in which Tibetan exegetes innovated—albeit in this case in the wake of some later Indian Mādhyamikas—was in effecting a drawing together or convergence between the Madhyamaka *(dbu ma)* and the logic

24. See Candrakīrti, *Prasannapadā* (ed. La Vallée Poussin), p. 16.

25. See *Three Studies,* section II.

and epistemology *(tshad ma)* of Dignāga and above all Dharmakīrti.[26] This convergence they expressed lexically by means of the copulative compound *dbu tshad* "Madhyamaka and Pramāṇa."[27]

That the balance between continuity and change has been an issue not only in Madhyamaka but also in the history of Tibetan logic and epistemology has been demonstrated in recent studies.[28]

(4) A further noteworthy Tibetan development concerns the analysis of negation. The two forms of negation recognized for Sanskrit by Mīmāṃsaka ritualists and by the grammarians were defined respectively as verbally bound sentence-negation *(prasajyapratiṣedha)* and nominally bound term-negation *(paryudāsa)*. The difference between these two kinds of negation has thus been defined in terms of syntax. And a trace of this syntactic view of the matter is found within Madhyamaka thought in the examples given in the *Tarkajvālā* (on Bhāviveka's *Madhyamakahṛdayakārikā* iii.26; D, fol. 59b) and by the exegetes who quote this influential source.

Bhavya himself held that the kind of negation found in Nāgārjuna's *Madhyamakakārikā* i.1 is *prasajyapratiṣedha* (*med [par] dgag [pa];* see *Prajñāpradīpa,* ed. Walleser, p. 10.8). And this was Candrakīrti's understanding also (*Prasannapadā*, ed. La Vallée Poussin, p. 13). Now, according to Buddhist philosophical analysis since the time of the *Tarkajvālā* ascribed to Bhavya, the difference between *paryudāsa* (*ma yin [par] dgag [pa],* i.e., relative or internal negation) and *prasajyapratiṣedha* (i.e., absolute or external negation) lies in the fact that the first is presuppositional and implicative—that is, it presupposes the existence of an entity *(bhāva = dngos po)* the relation of which to a given predicate is then negated, and it thus implies the affirmation *(vidhi, vidhāna)* for this entity of a real nature, which is different

26. Candrakīrti has criticized Dignāga, but he does not appear to know Dharmakīrti. See Candrakīrti's *Prasannapadā,* and our *Two Prolegomena to Madhyamaka Philosophy: Candrakīrti's Prasannapadā Madhyamakavṛttiḥ on Madhyamakakārikā i.1 and Tsoṅ kha pa Blo bzaṅ grags pa / rGyal tshab Dar ma rin chen's dKa 'gnad/gnas brgyad kyi zin bris* (Studies in Indian and Tibetan Madhyamaka Thought, Part 2, Vienna, 2002), p. 5 (and passim).

Concerning Jitāri/Jetāri and his congeners as precursors in India of this movement of convergence, see *Three Studies,* p. 30 with n. 56, and p. 273n65.

27. See *Three Studies,* section III, pp. 272ff., where Tsong kha pa's use of *tshad ma* has been discussed. The justification for Tsong kha pa's procedure in this respect has been the object of discussion among scholars.

28. See T. Tillemans, *Scripture, Logic, Language: Essays on Dharmakīrti and His Tibetan Successors* (Boston, 1999), especially chap. 7; G. Dreyfus, *Recognizing Reality: Dharmakīrti's Philosophy and Its Tibetan Interpretations* (Albany, 1997).

from the one being negated—and that the second type of negation is on the contrary non-presuppositional and non-implicative—that is, it does not presuppose the reified existence of the entity for which negation is stated, and being then pure negation *(pratiṣedha[mātra])* it therefore does not imply the affirmation of any real nature different from the one negated.[29] In other words, the distinction drawn between these two forms of negation is no longer defined in terms of syntax, and it rests instead on ontic, logical, and semantic analysis. According to both Bhavya and Candrakīrti, in the crucial first stanza of the *Madhyamakakārikā*s just referred to, Nāgārjuna's statement that all entities *(dngos po = bhāva)* do not originate from self does not presuppose the reified existence of an entity; nor, above all, does the negation of origination from self (the first of the four *mu = koṭi* "positions" enumerated in *Madhyamakakārikā* i.1) imply the affirmation of the contrary of this negation, namely that reified *bhāva*s originate from other *bhāva*s (the second position). In this stanza of Nāgārjuna's work, an interpretation according to the *paryudāsa* type of negation is in fact untenable within the frame of his Madhyamaka philosophy; and, irrespective of syntax, the Mādhyamika accordingly understands the negation used in this stanza as being of the *prasajya* type.

Now, Tsong kha pa has observed that, even though in the Tibetan language implicative negation *(ma yin dgag)* may correlate with negation expressed by means of the negated copula (i.e., *ma yin / min*) whereas non-implicative negation *(med dgag)* may stand in correlation with negation expressed by the negated substantive verb (i.e., *med*), this is not necessarily and automatically so. In other words, there here exists no regular and necessary isomorphism between linguistic usage and ontic, logical, and semantic analysis. Tsong kha pa has thus perceived that such analysis may in fact be independent of the linguistic form lent to a syntagma in a natural language.[30]

29. See *Tarkajvālā* (D), fol. 59b: *ma yin par dgag pa ni dngos po'i ngo bo nyid dgag pas de dang 'dra ba de las gzhan pa'i dngos po'i ngo bo nyid smra bar byed pa ste/ dper na 'di bram ze ma yin no zhes dgag pas bram ze de 'dra ba de las gzhan pa bram ze ma yin pa dka' thub dang thos pa la sogs pas dman pa'i dmangs rigs yin par bsgrubs pa lta bu'o // med par dgag pa ni dngos po'i ngo bo nyid tsam zhig 'gog par zad kyi de dang 'dra ba de ma yin pa gzhan gyi dngos po sgrub par mi byed pa ste/ dper na bram zes chang btung par mi bya'o zhes bya ba de tsam zhig 'gog par zad kyi de las gzhan pa'i btung ba btung ngo zhe'am mi btung ngo zhes mi brjod pa lta bu'o//*

30. See Tsong kha pa, *Drang nges legs bshad snying po,* fol. 108b (= Zi ling ed., p. 518): *ma yin zhes pa dang med ces pa'i tshig gis bkag pa ni de gnyis kyi khyad par min te/ bdag las ma yin zhes bkag pa med dgag tu legs ldan dang zla ba grags pa gnyis kas bshad pa'i phyir dang/ tshe dpag med ces pa ma yin dgag tu bya dgos pa'i phyir ro.* Cf. "Sanskrit-Tibetan and

Much of what has been said in the preceding is, no doubt, not exegesis in the narrowest sense but explicative elaboration—sometimes indeed innovation—offering interpretations which have not actually been explicitly set out in a thematized and theorized form in the works of Nāgārjuna, Āryadeva, Buddhapālita, and Candrakīrti. But such rethinking and restorative/renovative explication might be regarded as a form of *systemic hermeneutics,* and also as *internal philosophical reconstruction,* of Nāgārjunian and Candrakīrtian thought, as distinct from literal commentary on it. Every effort has been made by Tsong kha pa solidly to ground his internal reconstruction and hermeneutics in philosophical penetration and analysis, which were in their turn rooted in the classical texts of the Indian masters of the Madhyamaka tradition. In any case, what is often called "originality"—i.e., *rang bzo* or *rang dga' ba*—was eschewed by him.

VI

In their treatments of Candrakīrti's *Prasannapadā*—and in particular of the first stanza of Nāgārjuna's *Madhyamakakārikās*, the part known in Tibet scholastics as the *(Tshig gsal) stong thun*—the philosophical horizons of Tibetan commentators have expanded and shifted from those that were current among Indian authors. Tibetan scholars such as Tsong kha pa were for instance concerned less than Candrakīrti was with a detailed critique of the views of the Indian schools of Sāṃkhya, Nyāya, Vaiśeṣika, and Mīmāṃsā; and they tended to generalize philosophical issues which had earlier been identified by Candrakīrti with a view to criticizing or rejecting the doctrines of these schools, or eventually of Bhavya. In other words, although the Tibetan interpreters were certainly not unfamiliar with the Brāhmanical schools—as is amply demonstrated by the Tibetan doxographical (Grub mtha') literature going back to Bhavya's *Madhyamakahṛdaya,* the *Tarkajvālā* commentary on it, and Avalokitavrata's comment on Bhavya's *Prajñāpradīpa*—, they universalized doctrinal positions held historically by these earlier schools into so to say transhistorical philosophical positions and views that continue to possess an abiding significance within much later Buddhist thought.[31]

Tibetan-Sanskrit Dictionaries," (as in note 6 above), p. 126n24; and *Two Prolegomena,* p. 19n6 (esp. pp. 20–21).

31. Compare, e.g., D. Seyfort Ruegg, *Two Prolegomena,* pp. 56–57 (note). An interesting case is provided by Tsong kha pa's discussion, in his *Drang nges legs bshad snying po,* of *Prasannapadā* i.1, pp. 66–68, on *lakṣaṇa* and *lakṣya* and on Candrakīrti's famous

With regard to his commentarial method, although Tsong kha pa may on occasion supply word-for-word explanations of the text of Candrakīrti's *Madhyamakāvatāra, Prasannapadā,* etc.—providing what in Tibet is known as a *tshig 'grel* "word-commentary"—, his effort was mainly concentrated on philosophical analysis and hermeneutics—on *don 'grel* "meaning commentary"—, that is, on a philosophical reading and internal reconstruction of Nāgārjunian and Candrakīrtian thought. (The predominance of "meaning commentary" of course already characterized most of Candrakīrti's own exegetical practice.)

Tsong kha pa on occasion made use of citations of Indian sources in what—at least to strictly literalist exegesis—might seem an unexpected and philologically unnatural way. In the ninth chapter of the *Bodhi(sattva) caryāvatāra,* for example, we read: "Without having reached a (conceptually) constructed entity, its absence [i.e., negation] is not apprehended; therefore, the [positive] entity being indeed false, its absence [i.e., negation] is [itself] clearly false" (ix.140: *kalpitaṃ bhāvam aspṛṣṭvā tadabhāvo na gṛhyate / tasmād bhāvo mṛṣā yo hi tasyâbhāvaḥ sphuṭaṃ mṛṣā //*). In Śāntideva's text this statement pertains to the solidarity of binarily opposed (conceptual) things, so that the negative *abhāva* "non-entity" has no ontologically superior status to *bhāva* "entity."[32] Tsong kha pa understands verse ix.140ab as referring specifically to his theory of the need to identify *(ngo 'dzin pa)* the concept or image of what is to be negated—the negandum *(dgag bya'i spyi = dgag bya'i rnam pa),* i.e,. substantial self-existence or self-nature *(ngo bo nyid, rang bzhin)*—in order to achieve understanding of the Emptiness of self-existence, i.e., non-substantiality *(ngo bo nyid med pa = niḥsvabhāvatā, bdag med pa = nairātmya).*[33]

---

discussion of the use in ordinary language of the expressions "Rāhu's head" *(rāhoḥ śiraḥ)* and "body of the torso/pestle" *(śilāputrakasya śarīram).* In Candrakīrti's *Prasannapadā* the discussion arose in connexion with Dignāga's postulation of the two *pramāṇa*s of *pratyakṣa* (: *svalakṣaṇa*) and *anumāna* (: *sāmānyalakṣaṇa*). In the *Drang nges legs bshad snying po,* pp. 445–52, however, Candrakīrti's discussion has been linked by Tsong kha pa with his rubric of the identification *(ngo 'dzin pa)* of the negandum *(dgag bya),* followed by negation of the self-characteristic *(rang gi mtshan nyid)* and of the thing established by it *(rang gi mtshan nyid kyis grub pa),* factors attributed to Bhavya. On this theme, which was of such fundamental importance for Tsong kha pa, see below.

32. For *bhāva* and *abhāva,* cf. ix.35, where the commentator Prajñākaramati speaks of a relation of affirmation *(vidhi)* and negation *(pratiṣedha).* In his comment on ix.140 Prajñākaramati refers to the negative *abhāva* of an entity (such as a pot) as the *sambandhin* relatively to the entity to which a positive nature is imputed in conceptual construction.

33. Although there exists no full commentary by Tsong kha pa on the *Bodhi(sattva)*

Tsong kha pa's exegetical procedure was in part due to the already mentioned fact that he regarded the textual corpus of scripture and śāstra as a hermeneutically coherent set of texts located in a philosophically timeless and enduring intellectual present.[34] That is, his interpretations—however

---

caryāvatāra—the *Shes rab le'u'i zin bris* (in vol. pha of the *bka' 'bum*) being an outline manual on the ninth chapter written down by Tsong kha pa's disciple Rgyal tshab Dar ma rin chen (the author of the extensive commentary entitled *Rgyal sras 'jug ngogs*) which only alludes to its verse ix.140, while the comment on the ninth chapter subtitled *Blo gsal ba* (in vol. ma) written down by another disciple is even shorter—, "hyper-interpretation" can be found in Tsong kha pa's treatment of ix.140ab (in the numbering of the Skt. text) in the *Lam rim chen mo,* where this half-verse is explained as relating to the conceptual negandum (p. 579: . . . *bdag med pa dang rang bzhin med pa zhes pa'i don nges pa la'ang med rgyu'i bdag dang rang bzhin de legs par ngos zin dgos te/ dgag par bya ba'i spyi legs par ma shar na de bkag pa'ang phyin ci ma log par mi nges pa'i phyir te* . . .). For the *dgag bya'i spyi* related to this verse, see also Tsong kha pa, *Dgongs pa rab gsal,* fol. 71a (= p. 129: *brtags pa'i dngos po ste dgag bya'i spyi legs par ma shar na/ dgag bya de med pa legs par 'dzin mi nus par gsungs pas/ med rgyu'i bden grub dang/ gang gis stong pa'i dgag bya'i rnam pa blo yul du ji lta ba bzhin ma shar na/ bden med dang stong pa'i ngo bo legs par nges pa mi srid do//*). (Verse ix.139 of this text also contains a philological *crux,* the Tibetan translation reading *[b]sgom pa* [i.e., *bhāvanām*] against the *bhāvānām* of the Sanskrit text.) Cf. H. Tauscher, *Die zwei Wirklichkeiten in Tsoṅ kha pas Madhyamaka-Werken* (Vienna, 1995), pp. 75–81 (with P. Williams, *Altruism and Reality* [London, 1998], pp. 82ff., and T. Jinpa, *Self, Reality and Reason in Tibetan Philosophy* [London, 2002], p. 52, which do not refer to Tauscher's detailed discussion of the matter).

A further example of Tsong kha pa's "hyper-interpretation" of a classical Indian source is in his exegesis of chapter 25 of Bhavya's *Prajñāpradīpa,* on the basis of which he ascribes to Bhavya the doctrine of a *rang gi mtshan nyid (svalakṣaṇa)* and of something that is *rang gi mtshan nyid kyis grub pa* (*svalakṣaṇa-siddha;* see below).

34. This transhistorical coherence is traditionally understood in terms of certain established hermeneutical principles, the fundamental one in sūtra hermeneutics being the division of the Buddha's Word *(sangs rgyas kyi bka' = buddhavacana)* into that having a definitive sense *(nges don = nītārtha)* and that having a sense that is provisional since it requires to be further elicited *(drang don = neyārtha)* in another meaning. (This hermeneutical division is independent of, and not reducible to, the additional division between the "literal" *[yathāruta = sgra ji bzhin pa]* and the "non-literal" *[sgra ji bzhin ma yin pa].*) The *neyārtha* or provisional sense is, moreover, not set up arbitrarily, for this category is subject to the three hermeneutical criteria of (1) the really intended *(dgongs gzhi,* e.g., *ngo bo nyid med pa = niḥsvabhāvatā)*—i.e., what the Buddha had in view *(dgongs nas = saṃdhāya)* even when uttering an intentional (*dgongs pa can = ābhiprāyika,* allusive) statement—, (2) the motive *(dgos pa = prayojana)* for formulating such an intentional and hence provisional utterance, and (3) incompatibility with the intended sense *(dngos la gnod byed;* cf. Skt. *mukhyārthabādhā).* See D. Seyfort Ruegg, "Purport, implicature and presupposition: Sanskrit *abhiprāya* and Tibetan *dgoṅs pa/dgoṅs gži* as hermeneutical concepts," *JIP* 13 (1985), pp. 309–25; and id., "An Indian source for the Tibetan hermeneutical term *dgoṅs gži* 'intentional ground,'" *JIP* 16 (1988), pp. 1–4, reprinted as chapters 7 and 8 of the present volume. Tsong kha pa's major treatise on the subject was his *Drang*

unexpected and anachronistic they may perhaps be from the standpoint of literalist commentary—can be well founded and meaningful from a systemic—and transhistorical—point of view.

Sometimes, moreover, Tsong kha pa has narrowed down the meaning of a word, making, e.g., *rang bzhin / ngo bo nyid* (Skt. *svabhāva*) regularly and systematically denote "self-nature/self-existence," and bracketing out other, less technical, usages of this word even though attested in Nāgārjuna's text (e.g., *Madhyamakakārikās* xv.1–2) and, occasionally, in his own literal comments.[35] In practice, this procedure of attaching a single fixed meaning to a technical term in philosophy need not in itself be either misleading or illegitimate: quite the contrary in fact.

A contrasting feature in Tsong kha pa's exegetical method has been to extend the range of usage of the technical term *rang gi mtshan nyid* (Skt. *svalakṣaṇa*) to designate the "self-characteristic"—i.e., the ontic-logical foundational ground which is the object of a non-erroneous *(ma 'khrul ba = abhrānta)* cognition in Bhavya's philosophy. This procedure was in conformity with his understanding of Bhavya's philosophical analysis of the surface level or *saṃvṛti*.[36] He has thus ascribed to this Indian thinker the doctrine of some thing established through self-characteristic *(rang gi mtshan nyid kyis grub pa: *svalakṣaṇa-siddha)*, even though Bhavya does not in fact seem ever to have himself used this particular terminology. This is, then, a noteworthy example of Tsong kha pa's philosophical reconstruction of Bhavya's "Svātantrika" thought.[37] In Tsong kha pa's view, it was the postulation of the self-characteristic, and of a thing established through it, that

---

nges legs bshad snying po; see also the relevant section of the *Dka' gnad/gnas brgyad kyi zin bris,* together with *Two Prolegomena,* pp. 257–70 (and pp. 78–82).

35. As just seen above, this self-nature/self-existence is regarded as the negandum for principled analytical reasoning *(rigs pa'i dgag bya).*

36. Compare Tsong kha pa's description of Bhavya as a proponent, on the *saṃvṛti*-level, of a (reified) entity *(dngos por smra ba: bhāva/vastu-vādin),* one who is, however, at the same time a Mādhyamika in respect to his understanding of ultimate reality *(paramārtha).* On this, and on the matter of Tsong kha pa's acceptance of a *tha snyad pa'i tshad ma (vyāvahārika-pramāṇa),* see *Three Studies,* pp. 93–94, 237, 250, 276; and *Two Prolegomena,* pp. 6–7, 214, 236.

37. See *Three Studies,* pp. 236–38. In this study it was noted that, when considering the philosophical expression *rang gi mtshan nyid = svalakṣaṇa,* it is necessary to distinguish between three usages, those of the Ābhidhārmikas (for whom it means "specific characteristic, property"), the Buddhist logicians ("particular characteristic"), and the Svātantrikas as understood by Tsong kha pa ("self-characteristic"); see there the index s.v. *svalakṣaṇa.* (For a study just published, see M. Eckel, "The Satisfaction of No Analysis: On Tsong kha

underlay Bhavya's recourse to autonomous *(rang rgyud = svatantra)* inference. A remarkable feature of Tsong kha pa's Madhyamaka interpretation was accordingly to consider Bhavya to be in certain respects a proponent of substantialism *(dngos po[r] smra ba)* but at the same time to acknowledge this master to be a respected Mādhyamika in the final analysis.[38]

Tsong kha pa sought to remain faithful to what he understood to be the genuine import and structure, the philosophical dynamic, of the thinking of Candrakīrti even though he was prepared when analysing and expounding it to adopt a historically later (and hence strictly speaking anachronistic) terminology that had not actually been employed by that Indian master. This is because he found it to be *in conformity with* Candrakīrti's (or Bhavya's) philosophical procedure and thinking. An example is his adoption of the terms Rang rgyud pa and Thal 'gyur ba to denote respectively Bhavya's and Candrakīrti's branches of the Madhyamaka.

In sum, on the historical level, noteworthy shifts are observable between the expressed intellectual worlds of Candrakīrti, and of Bhavya, on the one side, and Tsong kha pa's own philosophical horizons on the other side. But such a historical shift does not inevitably and automatically bring with it a distortion in the overall understanding of the philosophical mainspring and import, the internal dynamics, of the Indian source's philosophical thought. Such updating indeed constitutes a kind of continuing philosophical *aggiornamento,* where Candrakīrti's discussions relating to a Brāhmaṇical school of philosophy, or again to a particular Buddhist school such as that of the Ābhidhārmikas, are linked to themes and issues which, a millennium later, continued to occupy a prominent place within the frame of Buddhist philosophical discussion, if only as universalized—and hence *ahistorical* or rather *transhistorical*—subjects of discussion and criticism.

If Tsong kha pa's writings may be said to represent a "reading" of much of the Buddhist Dharma as known in Tibet, this is because they not only provide an interpretation—a *lectio*—of a canon of fundamental scriptural

---

pa's Approach to Svātantrika Madhyamaka," in G. Dreyfus and S. McClintock, eds., *The Svātantrika-Prāsaṅgika Distinction* [Boston, 2003], pp. 173–203.)

38. Cf. Tsong kha pa's *Lam rim chen mo,* fol. 425a (= p. 705), discussed in *Three Studies,* pp. 239, 267, 280–81; and fol. 343a (= p. 573). On the Svātantrika's *rang gi mtshan nyid = *svalakṣaṇa* in general, see *Two Prolegomena,* pp. 168ff. (For two just published discussions, see T. Tillemans, "Metaphysics for Mādhyamikas," in: G. Dreyfus and S. McClintock, eds., *The Svātantrika-Prāsaṅgika Distinction,* pp. 91–124; and C. Yoshimizu, "Tsong kha pa's Reevaluation of Candrakīrti's Criticism of Autonomous Inference," ibid., pp. 257–88.)

(Bka' 'gyur) and commentarial (Bstan 'gyur) texts, as in the case of his hermeneutical treatise on the coherence of the Buddha's word *(sangs rgyas kyi bka' = buddhavacana)* and on distinguishing in it between provisional meaning *(drang ba'i don = neyārtha)* and definitive meaning *(nges pa'i don = nītārtha)*—the *Drang nges legs bshad snying po* (of 1408)—but also because they constitute a reasoned enquiry—a *quaestio*—relating to a philosophical corpus, as in the case of his two major Madhyamaka commentaries—the *Rtsa she ṭīk chen* (the *Rnam bshad rigs pa'i rgya mtsho,* 1408/9) on Nāgārjuna's *Mūlamadhyamakakārikā*s and the *Dgongs pa rab gsal* (ca. 1418) on Candrakīrti's *Madhyamakāvatāra(bhāṣya).* His great synthetic expositions of the Buddhist Path, the *Lam rim chen mo* (1402) and the *Lam rim chung ba* (1415) (not to speak of his *Sngags rim*), represent the outcome of this twofold investigation concerned with hermeneutics and internal philosophical reconstruction.

VII

In the history of Tibetan civilization, then, Tsong kha pa can be said to have embraced in his philosophical thinking the twin spheres of the *Indian*—that is, what is *historically* identifiable as having been taken over from Indian sources—and the *Indic*—that is, the meta-Indian that is *typologically* (if not historically) Indian, continuing as he did to think in line with Indian models and templates found in the canonical sources of the Bka' 'gyur and Bstan 'gyur. Yet faithfulness to what was either historically Indian or typologically Indic did not make Tsong kha pa any less Tibetan. And his insights were thus able to have a deep and fruitful impact on Tibetan thought. At the same time, his creative contribution has deeply marked the history of Buddhism, this being one of several reasons for which it is appropriate to speak of an Indo-Tibetan tradition within Buddhism, notwithstanding the fact that this tradition was very clearly not a frozen or ossified one.[39]

39. To avoid misunderstanding concerning this non-essentialist use of the expression "Indo-Tibetan," what was written in *Three Studies* may be recalled here (p. vi): "... this descriptive term is not meant to convey the idea of a single monolithic—and monothetic—entity. Rather, over a large area of South and Central Asia and a period of more than a millennium, it refers to cultural and intellectual developments marked, polythetically, by continuities—and by what may be described as 'family resemblances'—as well as by discontinuities." Whether the relationship of some Tibetan scholarship to Indian sources justifies speaking of certain Tibetan scholars as having been Indologists *avant la lettre* (see D. Seyfort Ruegg, *Literature of the Madhyamaka School of Philosophy in India* [Wiesbaden,

What has been said above may suffice to indicate that the problematics of continuity relative to change—and indeed of the very concepts of Buddhism in Tibet and Tibetan Buddhism—are more complex than might perhaps appear at first sight. The differentiations made above are more than just verbal distinctions without real difference. For, without developing clear concepts and the corresponding terminology, it is not possible to speak meaningfully about these matters. And a "rectification of names" can be essential for further progress. As for the expressions "Tibetan Buddhism" and "Buddhism in Tibet," even if there exists a certain overlap between the two, each is no doubt appropriate in the relevant context, having its application in a particular defined situation. And both expressions can be usefully employed when investigating the contribution of a thinker such as Tsong kha pa.

In the last analysis, the matters discussed in this paper are no doubt just as much issues in anthropology (in the comprehensive sense), and in the history of mental representations, as they are narrower ones of Buddhist philosophy and the transcultural history of intellectual traditions of Indo-Buddhist provenance.[40]

To sum up, in Tibet we find a complex interplay between continuity accompanied by conservative (and sometimes simply epigonal) transmission on the one side and on the other side creative rethinking/restoration/renewal/innovation accompanied by updating and new insights. In Tibetan cultural history, one or the other of these poles may stand out as predominant in an individual case. (The latter trend appears to be especially pronounced in the earlier part of the so-called Later Diffusion, the *phyi dar,* of Buddhism in Tibet, which was followed in Tsong kha pa's tradition by a re-emphasizing of classical Indian sources.) And between the two poles there are intermediate positions, as well as instances of synchronic and diachronic tension between them. Outside circumstances—social, political, and cultural—have no doubt played a part in channelling developments, these external factors

1981], p. viii) may have been called into question; but this description actually corresponds to known facts in the history of Tibetan civilization and scholarship.

40. Whether the forms of restoration/renewal/innovation considered in the present paper might be relatable to Hobsbawmian "invention of tradition" is a quite different matter requiring further clarification. An instance of the constitution/invention of tradition seems to be found in the Tibetan historiography relating to the Great Debate of Bsam yas and to the Hva shang Mahāyāna (Ho-shang Mo-ho-yen) who figures in this historiography more as an emblematic than as a strictly historical figure; see our *Buddha-nature, Mind and the Problem of Gradualism in a Comparative Perspective* (London, 1989), pp. 5, 58, etc.

being nowadays often called upon to provide the preferred mode of explanation. A cultural tradition is in fact hardly ever wholly shielded from such outside influence. But the internal dynamics of a living and vital tradition inclusive of the requirements of internal philosophical reconstruction are surely not to be neglected when we seek to account for renewal and innovation. Moreover, if there has existed a tension between these processes, it is no doubt also the case that change is not inevitably incompatible, and entirely incapable of co-existing, with a search for fidelity and continuity. Tsong kha pa's intellectual and spiritual achievements seem to exemplify these considerations.[41]

Concerning finally the question as to precisely what Tsong kha pa may have himself been hoping to achieve in his life's work of teaching and writing with regard to the above-mentioned trends and polarities, insights and glimpses are provided by his compositions, as well as by hints to be found in his *Vita*—that is, in his "internal" or intellectual biography *(nang gi rnam*

41. Indological scholarship has sometimes raised the question as to whether the writings of Tibetan commentators and interpreters of Indian authors have any truly useful contribution to make to our present understanding of these sources. And among some Indologists there has existed an inclination to play down, even to deny, this possibility. (When reading Indological reactions to publications on the Indo-Tibetan Madhyamaka [see, e.g., K. Werner's review article of H. Tauscher, *Die zwei Wirklichkeiten in Tsoṅ kha pas Madhyamaka-Werken,* in *Buddhist Studies Review* 15 (1998), 213–22] or on Pramāṇaśāstra [see, e.g., the review of T. Tillemans, *Scripture, Logic, Language: Essays on Dharmakīrti and His Tibetan Successors* by J.-M. Verpoorten, *Bulletin d'Études indiennes* 20 (2002), 322–26], it is noticeable how considerable the obstacles to scholarly communication and understanding can prove to be.) Part of the difficulty lies no doubt in the complexity and technicality of the Tibetan materials. Yet one cannot help gaining the impression that there exists a difference of opinion as to just what the endeavour of the exegete, interpreter, and philosopher-practiser might consist in when embarking—as Tibetans clearly did—on the intellectual internalization and integration of Indian Buddhist traditions, and in particular on the arduous enterprise of penetration, interpretation, (re)thinking, and internal philosophical reconstruction. Such difference of opinion may perhaps have to do, at least in part, with the pre-understanding, or pre-judgement, as to what philosophy as an intellectual exercise or practice, and also as a theoretical activity, has in fact been even within the history of Western philosophy (compare, e.g., P. Hadot, *Qu'est-ce que la philosophie antique* [Paris, 1995] on the one hand, and on the other L. Wittgenstein)—not to speak of what the scholastic enterprise in philosophy has represented. In several discussions of Indo-Tibetan traditions it has then been, first and foremost, commentarial discontinuity that has been perceived and emphasized, to the exclusion of continuity and the internal dynamics of an intellectual tradition linking India and Tibet. The possibility that the complex and very intense process of absorption, internalization, and (re)thinking could be traditional *and* yet creative, faithful in its aim *and* yet renovative and even innovative in its outcome, appears not to have received full attention.

thar), but also in his "external" biography *(phyi'i rnam thar),* where outer, "public" events in his life are narrated,[42] and no doubt even in his "secret" or intimate biography *(gsang ba'i rnam thar),* where his spiritual visions are recounted.[43] To explore all this further will be a task for comprehensive study in the future.[44]

42. It is to be recalled that Tsong kha pa refused to visit India as well as China, thus centring his external activity in Tibet while focussing his intellectual activity on the Indian (as represented by sources contained in the Bka' 'gyur and Bstan 'gyur) and on the Indic (or meta-Indian as defined above), although not of course rejecting Tibetan tradition out of hand but only if he felt it to be ungrounded in, and incompatible with, the Indian and the Indic.

43. Compare the visionary instruction from the bodhisattva Mañjughoṣa (referred to above in note 19) according to which Tsong kha pa's earlier understanding of the Madhyamaka had been inadequate.

44. Tsong kha pa's relation to the Indo-Buddhist traditions was briefly considered already many decades ago by E. Obermiller, "Tsong-kha-pa le paṇḍit," *MCB* 3 (1934/35), 316–38. On his life see also R. Kaschewsky, *Das Leben des lamaistischen Heiligen Tsongkhapa Blo-bzang-grags-pa (1357–1459)* (Wiesbaden, 1971).

In the history of Buddhist thought, a parallel (but not identical) problem—the doctrine of the *tathāgatagarbha*—which also raises highly interesting questions in systemic and transhistorical hermeneutics, and in philosophical rethinking and updating *(aggiornamento),* due to factors present within Indian Buddhism has been discussed in our "The Buddhist Notion of an 'Immanent Absolute' *(tathāgatagarbha)* as a Problem in Hermeneutics," in T. Skorupski, ed., *The Buddhist Heritage* (Tring, 1989), pp. 229–45, and in the first section of *Buddha-nature, Mind and the Problem of Gradualism in a Comparative Perspective.* There the factors determining philosophical elaboration and development were not initially ones pertaining to intercultural transmission, enculturation, and the Indic relatively to the Indian, but ones that were endogenous to Indian thought itself. Only later did the question of the Indic in Tibet arise, on which see *La théorie du tathāgatagarbha et du gotra* (cited above) and *Le traité du tathāgatagarbha de Bu ston Rin chen grub* (Paris, 1973).

English Glossary of Selected Terms

Absolute/ultimate Meaning/Sense, the correlative opposite of transactional-pragmatic, and of Surface (level). See Skt. *paramārtha,* Tib. *don dam pa.* Cf. Reality of Absolute/ultimate Meaning/Sense, Skt. *paramārthasatya,* Tib. *don dam pa'i bden pa.* (The frequently used translation of Skt. *satya* = Tib. *bden pa,* and of Pali *sacca,* by "truth" is in this case etymological and hence simply conventional. Here the word *satya* does not denote truth as the property of either a proposition, statement or sentence, or of a belief. But even the rendering Reality does not entirely resolve all the philosophical issues involved, and recourse to multiple renderings and definitions can only partly compensate for these difficulties of translation. For the use of conventional terminological equivalents in the translation of Indian and Tibetan philosophical terminology see D. Seyfort Ruegg, "La traduction de la terminologie technique de la pensée indienne et bouddhique depuis Sylvain Lévi" [2007]. In the present work, markedly conventional and technical English renderings are shown by capitalized initial letters, for example "Absolute" and "Emptiness.")

apagogic (of an argument or method). See Skt. *prasaṅga,* Tib. *thal ba(r 'gyur ba)*

Apagogist, a representative of the line of Madhyamaka thought connected with Buddhapālita and Candrakīrti. See Skt. *prāsaṅgika,* Tib. *thal 'gyur ba*

apophatic, apophaticism, a mode of thinking and expression linked with many sūtras of the Mahāyāna (such as the Prajñāpāramitā collection) and with Nāgārjuna's "Scholastic Corpus" (Tib. *rigs tshogs*).

Autonomist, a representative of the line of Madhyamaka thought going back to Bhā(va)viveka/Bhavya. See Skt. *svātantrika,* Tib. *rang rgyud pa*

autonomous (of an inference). See Skt. *svatantra,* Tib. *rang rgyud (pa)*

binegation. See tetralemma, in which a form of binegation is the (negated) fourth position. (Distinguish binegation that is *not* the fourth position of a tetralemma and which is used to describe ultimate Reality.)

cataphatic, cataphaticism. A mode of thinking and expression linked in particular with certain sūtras teaching the *tathāgatagarbha,* with the *Ratnagotravibhāga-Mahāyānottaratantraśāstra,* and with Nāgārjuna's "Hymnic Corpus" (Tib. *bstod tshogs*).

conditionship. See dependence, origination/production in —; Emptiness

deep meaning. See definitive meaning

definitive meaning (also deep meaning, the opposite of provisional or surface meaning). See Skt. *nītārtha,* Tib. *nges pa'i don*

dependence, origination/production in —. There are two sides to the very fundamental Madhyamaka concept of origination in dependence:

1. *pratītyasamutpāda,* closely linked with *śūnyatā* "Emptiness" (for which in reasoning it supplies the *hetu* or evidence) and often in effect an expression for ultimate reality; and
2. the originating/being produced in dependence (*pratītyasamutpanna*) on causes and conditions (*hetu-pratyaya*), i.e., in conditionship, thus belonging to the level of the conditioned (*saṃskṛta*) and the Surface level of the relative or conventional (*saṃvṛti*), and having the quality of being empty (*śūnyatva*).

Although closely linked with Emptiness (*śūnyatā*), origination in dependence is, nevertheless, not exactly co-extensive, and coterminous, with *śūnyatā* inasmuch as the latter term pertains to all entities (*bhāva*) and things (*dharma*) without exception—i.e., to unconditioned (*asaṃskṛta*) as well as to conditioned (*saṃskṛta*) things—, whereas to have originated in dependence (*pratītyasamutpanna*) applies to the conditioned, and the *sāṃvṛta,* only; the two terms are therefore not strictly synonyms substitutable for each other in philosophical usage. Cf. D. Seyfort Ruegg, *The literature of the Madhyamaka school of philosophy in India* (1981), pp. 44n110 and 45n113; *Two prolegomena to Madhyamaka philosophy* (*Studies in Indian and Tibetan Madhyamaka thought, Part 2,* [2002]), pp. 271ff. See Skt. *pratītyasamutpāda,* Tib. *rten cing 'brel bar 'byung ba/rten 'byung*; and Skt. *pratītyasamutpanna*

designation, relative. See relative concept/designation

Emptiness, a term expressing the ultimate nature (*dharmatā,* Tib. *chos nyid*) of all things (Skt. *dharma,* Tib. *chos*), conditioned (Skt. *saṃskṛta.* Tib. *'dus byas*) and unconditioned (Skt. *asamskṛta,* Tib. *'dus ma byas*), as being Empty of self-existence (Skt. *svabhāva,* Tib. *rang bzhin, rang gi ngo bo nyid,* i.e., aseity, hypostatized/reified existence, substantial existence). The term is an equivalent of absence of self-existence (Skt. *niḥsvabhāvatā*) and non-substantiality (Skt. *nairātmya,* literally "Selflessness"), and (in some degree) of other terms for the ultimately real. Emptiness is closely linked with origination/production in dependence (Skt. *pratītyasamutpāda*) and the fact that things are produced in dependence (Skt. *pratītyasamutpanna*) on causes and conditions (Skt. *hetu-pratyaya*), such conditionship being in fact stated to be the ground or reason for their being Empty of self-existence. It is important to note that *śūnyatā* is itself stated to be Empty of self-existence. —*Śūnyatā* is so to speak a dynamic enabling principle rather than a static and hypostatized (or reified) thing. See *VV* 70: "All things obtain for him for whom this *śūnyatā* obtains; nothing at all obtains for him for whom *śūnyatā* does not obtain" (*prabhavati ca śūnyateyaṃ yasya prabhavanti tasya sarvārthāḥ/ prabhavati na tasya kiṃcin na prabhavati śūnyatā yasya//*) (Skt. *pra-bhū-* is here rendered by Tib. *srid pa*); *MMK* xxiv.14: "All fits for him for whom *śūnyatā* fits; all does not fit for him for whom the Empty does not fit" (*sarvaṃ ca yujyate tasya śūnyatā yasya yujyate/ sarvaṃ na yujyate tasya śūnyaṃ yasya na yujyate//*) (Skt. *yujyate* is here translated by Tib. *rung ba,* and Skt. *śūnyam* by Tib. *stong pa nyid* "Emptiness"); and *MMK* xxiv.36: "In rejecting *śūnyatā* that is production in dependence you reject all worldly practices" (*sarvavyavahārāṃś ca laukikān pratibādhase/ yat pratītyasamutpādaśūnyatāṃ pratibādhase//*). N.B. The term *śūnyatā* is usually to be distinguished from the word *śūnyatva,* the state or quality of being Empty; cf. D. Seyfort Ruegg, *The literature of the Madhyamaka school,* pp. 3n8 and 45n113. (In certain textual passages, e.g., *MMK* xxiv.14d, *śūnya* appears to stand for *śūnyatā,* and Tib. renders by *stong pa nyid.*) See Skt. *śūnyatā,* Tib. *stong pa nyid*

Empty (of self-existence, Skt. *svabhāva*), a qualification of all things (Skt. *dharma*), of all entities (Skt. *bhāva,* Tib. *dngos po*), in Mahāyāna and Madhyamaka thought. See Skt. *śūnya,* Tib. *stong pa*

In the history of the Madhyamaka two aspects of the idea of the Empty are found:

1. the Empty of self-existence (Tib. *rang stong*). The advocates of this theory are known in Tibetan as *rang stong pa*s. See Skt. *svabhāvaśūnya,* Tib. *rang bzhin gyis stong pa, rang stong;*
2. the Empty of the other (*gzhan stong,* i.e., of the heterogeneous, as opposed to *rang stong*). In cataphatic thought and language, this is the true nature of ultimate reality, free from all that is heterogeneous to it—namely all adventitious (Skt. *āgantuka,* Tib. *glo bur ba*) defilements and all that is conditioned (Skt. *saṃskṛta,* Tib. *'dus byas pa*) or produced in dependence (*pratītyasamutpanna*) on causes and conditions—but still endowed with unconditioned (*asaṃskṛta*) properties that are co-essential with it. The advocates of this theory are known in Tibetan as *gzhan stong pa*s, even though they do not form a single entirely homogeneous and monolithic school opposed to the *rang stong pa*s. See Tib. *gzhan stong* and *gzhan stong pa*; also Tib. *nyi tshe ba* (Skt. *prādeśika,* i.e., "partial" Emptiness), *dgag stong* "the Empty through negation," and *chad stong* "the Empty through destruction," expressions referring in the language of *gzhan stong pa*s to the *rang stong* or *svabhāvaśūnya(tā)* of the Indo-Tibetan Madhyamaka, especially that of Candrakīrti. Compare the idea of "Emptiness endowed with all excellent modes/features" (Skt. *sarvākāravaropeta-śūnyatā,* Tib. *rnam pa thams cad kyi mchog dang ldan pa'i stong pa nyid,* etc.; see D. Seyfort Ruegg, *La théorie du tathāgatagarbha et du gotra* [1969], pp. 351ff.). And differentiate "relative emptiness" (Skt. *itaretaraśūnyatā*; Tib. *gcig gis gcig stong pa nyid*).

family resemblance. (L. Wittgenstein's *Familienähnlichkeit;* a polythetic relation, as opposed to the monothetic)

Gnosis. See Skt. *jñāna,* Tib. *ye shes*

gradualism, gradualist. See Tib. *rim gyis pa*

hypostatically established (as a reified self-existent entity). See Tib. *bden par grub pa* = *bden grub* indeterminacy, indeterminate (undescribable). See Skt. *avācya, avaktavya*. Cf. inexpressible; D. Seyfort Ruegg, *Three studies in the history of Indian and Tibetan Madhyamaka Philosophy* (*Studies in Indian and Tibetan Madhyamaka Thought, Part 1* [2000]), pp. 109ff.

inexpressibility, inexpressible (in linguistic and conceptual discursivity, ineffable). See Skt. *anabhilāpya, nirabhilāpya*; D. Seyfort Ruegg, *Théorie du tathāgatagarbha et du gotra*, part 3, chapter v with chapter viii.3 (pp. 362ff. on the positive determination of the *tathāgatagarbha* and the Absolute). Cf. indeterminacy, indeterminate

inference. Classical Madhyamaka thought was divided between Svātantrikas (Autonomists, who admitted the existence of the autonomous—*svatantra*—inference) and the Prāsaṅgikas (Apagogists, who did not).

intention (of a speaker, especially the Buddha). See Skt. *abhiprāya*, Tib. *dgongs pa*

intentional (of a meaning or teaching, especially of the Buddha). See Skt. *ābhiprāyika*, Tib. *dgongs pa can*. Cf. provisional/surface meaning

Middle, Skt. *madhyamaka*, Tib. *dbu ma*. The word *madhyamaka*—derived from Skt. *madhyama* "placed in the middle, central," itself related to *madhya* "id."—means middle, middlemost. In the sūtra for Kātyāyana cited in *MMK* xv.7 (the Pali version of which is in the Saṃyuttanikāya II 17), the Buddha is shown explaining that to say "all exists" is one extreme (*anta*) and to say "all does not exist" is a second extreme; hence he, the Tathāgata, without resorting to either binary extreme, teaches the Dharma "by the middle" (*majjhena*). This sūtra then mentions members of the chain of origination in dependence that accounts for the arising (*samudaya*) of the entire aggregate of Pain (*dukkhakkhandha*), and whose reversal leads to the cessation *(nirodha)* of this Pain. See also *Kāśyapaparivarta* § 56 ff. It is of the highest importance that the *Samādhirājasūtra* (ix.27) has pointed out that the Middle is no third position in which one might install oneself, having once eschewed the twin extremes of existence and non-existence *(madhye 'pi na sthānaṃ karoti paṇḍitaḥ)*. The word *madhyamaka* denotes, then, a philosophical Middle free from the twin extreme views of the eternal (*śāśvata*) and destruction (*uccheda*), and indeed from any hypostatized position on which one might fixate. (Compare also Śāntideva's *Bodhicaryāvatāra* ix.35: *yadā na bhāvo nâbhāvo mateḥ saṃtiṣṭhate puraḥ/ tadânyagatyabhāvena nirālambā praśāmyati//*).) Madhyamaka thought is thus neither substantialism (metaphysical essentialism) nor nihilism. Later (see *The literature of the Madhyamaka school of philosophy in India*, p. 1) the word *madhyamaka* came to designate the system or school of thought that goes back to Nāgārjuna (ca. second century C.E.) and was continued by his disciple Āryadeva and, subsequently, by Buddhapālita (ca. 500, a source for the Apagogist branch of the Madhyamaka school), by Bhāviveka (sixth century, the initiator of the Autonomist branch of the school), and by Candrakīrti (the seventh-century master of its Apagogist branch). Madhyamaka theory (and the school) may be designated also by the appellation *madhyamakadarśana*. The term *madhyamakaśāstra* denotes either a major text belonging to the Madhyamaka school or the body of this school's texts and doctrines. A Mādhyamika (Tib. *dbu ma pa*) is a person who follows this school of thought. (Wackernagel-Debrunner, *Altindische Grammatik* II, 2 [Göttingen, 1954], § 37b [p. 124], is misleading when declaring: "Auf Prākritismus beruhen buddh. [...] *madhyamika-* neben *mā-* als Name einer Schule.") Over many centuries Mādhyamikas have drawn out and explicated the philosophical implications of the Middle Way.

Middle Way, Skt. *madhyamā pratipat*, Tib. *dbu ma'i lam*. One of the oldest and most important of the central ideas in Buddhism, the Middle Way has fundamental practical and ethical as well as religious and philosophical dimensions. For Madhyamaka thought, the link between the Middle Way, Emptiness (*śūnyatā*), and origination/production in dependence (*pratītyasamutpāda*) is stated in *MMK* xxiv.18: "Origination in dependence is what we call Emptiness; it is a relative concept/designation, and just this is the Middle Way" *(yaḥ pratītyasamutpādaḥ śūnyatāṃ tāṃ pracakṣmahe/ sā prajñaptir upādāya pratipat saiva madhyamā//*; for *prajñaptir upādāya* the Tib. has *brten nas gdags pa)*. In this verse, the demonstrative pronoun *sā* in *pāda* c may refer either to *śūnyatā* in *pāda* b (as indicated in *PPMV*, p. 504.8) or to *pratītyasamutpāda* in *pāda* a (as suggested by *PPMV*, p. 504.14–15, with the gender of the pronoun being attracted to its feminine predicate *prajñaptiḥ*; cf. Apte, *Student's guide to Sanskrit composition* § 24); cf. *Literature of the Madhyamaka school of philosophy in India*, p. 17n39. In *MMK* xxiv.36 there is found the compound *pratītyasamutpādaśūnyatā*. Nāgārjuna's autocommentary on *VV* 70 refers to Emptiness, origination in dependence, and the Middle Way as equivalent (*yaḥ śūnyatāṃ pratītyasamutpādaṃ madhyamaṃ pratipadaṃ ca/ ekārthāṃ nijagāda praṇamāmi tam apratimabuddham//*). The equivalence of the first two items is stated in *Lokātītastava* 22 and *Acintyastava* 40. —In his comment on *MMK* xxiv.18, Candrakīrti specifies (p. 504.14–15) that *śūnyatā* (which is *svabhāvānutpattilakṣaṇā*), *upādāya prajñaptiḥ*, and *madhyamā pratipat* are special appellations *(viśeṣasaṃjñā = ming gi bye brag)* precisely for *pratītyasamutpāda*; cf. *PPMV* xxiv.13. And he explains (p. 504) that the concept and linguistic designation of an entity such as "cart" *(ratha: aṅgin)* is employed relatively *(upādāya)* to its parts *(aṅga)* such as its wheels: there is indeed no origination of any entity through hypostatized self-existence *(svabhāvenânutpattiḥ)*. The idea of a "cart" being conceptually (and as it were metonymically) constructed relatively to (i.e., on the base of) its component parts is regularly employed in our sources as an example in order to deconstruct the postulated concept of a *pudgala* or *ātman* (see e.g., *MA(Bh)* vi.120ff., 135, 151–61). According to *PPMV* xviii.1 (p, 344.10–11), persons who fail to understand *upādāya-prajñapti* do not comprehend that *ātman* is *nāmamātraka = ming tsam zhig* "mere name." In *PPMV* x.16 there is found the expression *upādānena prajñapyate* "[an *ātman*] is designated through [its] appropriated base," (this formula being accordingly a gloss on the expression *upādāya prajñaptiḥ*). Candrakīrti explains there that *pratītyasamutpāda* free from the twin extremes of the eternal and destruction is termed *upādāya-prajñapti*. —The four expressions *pratītyasamutpāda, śūnyatā, upādāya prajñaptiḥ*, and *madhyamā pratipat* are not synonyms in the sense that they could meaningfully be substituted one for the other in any context; but they are nonetheless said to be equivalent in the sense that they are so to say co-functional in Madhyamaka thought. (They might even be said to be co-referential provided that their "referent" is not taken to be a hypostatized self-existent entity.) They may be co-functional in the following way. (1) The expression *pratītyasamutpāda* denotes the fact that all conditioned things *(saṃskṛta)* originate in dependence on causes and conditions so that they lack any independent aseitic existence (*svabhāva*) whatsoever, and it thus refers (indirectly) to non-substantiality (*niḥsvabhāvatā* = *śūnyatā*), for which it provides a reason. (2) The expression *śūnyatā* refers (directly) to this *niḥsvabhāvatā* of all things—conditioned *(samskṛta)* and unconditioned *(asamskṛta)*—the relevant full expression being *svabhāvaśūnyatā*. (3) *Upādāya prajñaptiḥ* would also engage *niḥsvabhāvatā* to the extent that, the concept/designation being relative, it can by itself have no truly independent status—no referent having real self-existence—just as a whole (*avayavin, aṅgin* = *yan lag can*, e.g., a cart) and the component parts (*avayava, aṅga* = *yan lag*, e.g., wheels, etc.) that make up this (conceptual) whole "cart" are interrelated and hence relative to each other. And (4) the expression *madhyamā pratipat* is the Way that eschews the twin extremes of existence and non-existence—substantialism and nihilism—(see the canonical sūtra for Kātyāyana) without, however, itself constituting some fixed intermediate position in which installation might be possible (see *Samādhirājasūtra* ix.27) and on which one might mentally fixate (see *Bodhicaryāvatāra* ix.37). Being in this way as it were co-functional in Madhyamaka thought, the expressions in question are said to be equivalent in *MMK* xxiv.18 and in many parallel passages in Madhyamaka literature. In sum, the four expressions all have the function of "showing" in a meaningful way the dependent origination and hence the non-substantiality of all things, the fundamental principle of Madhyamaka thought.

negandum. See Skt. *pratiṣedhya, niṣedhya*; Tib. *dgag bya*

negation. See Skt. *pratiṣedha,* Tib. *dgag pa*. Two main types of negation are recognized in Madhyamaka:

1. non-implicative and non-presuppositional —, also known as exclusion, external or propositional negation ("it is not the case that..."), and even as one form of illocutionary negation ("I do not assert, etc., that..."). Cf. D. Seyfort Ruegg, *Three studies,* pp. 224ff. See Skt. *prasajyapratiṣedha,* Tib. *med (par) dgag (pa);*
2. implicative and presuppositional —, also known as choice, internal or predicate negation. See Skt. *paryudāsa,* Tib. *ma yin (par) dgag (pa)*. See D. Seyfort Ruegg, *Two prolegomena*, pp. 19–24 (note 6).

non-substantial(ity), (the fact of being) without self-existence (*svabhāva*) (said of all things, Skt. *dharma*). See Skt. *niḥsvabhāva, anātman, nirātman, nairātmya*; Tib. *bdag med pa (nyid)* (literally "Selfless[ness]")

origination/production in dependence. See dependence, origination in —.

provisional meaning (a surface, intentional, meaning requiring hermeneutical interpretation in a further sense; the opposite of definitive meaning). See Skt. *neyārtha*, Tib. *drang ba'i don*

Reality of Absolute/ultimate Meaning/Sense, Skt, *paramārthasatya*. See Absolute/ultimate Meaning/Sense; and compare Surface Reality, *saṃvṛtisatya*. See also Skt. *tattva*, Tib. *de kho na nyid*

refutation. See Skt. *dūṣaṇa*, Tib. *sun 'byin pa*

relative (or: conventional, transactional-pragmatic) level = Surface. See Skt. *saṃvṛti*, Tib. *kun rdzob*

relative concept/designation, Skt. *upādāya prajñaptiḥ*, Tib. *brten nas gdags pa* (cf. Pali *upādāya paññatti* and *upādāpaññatti* attested in the language of the commentaries); relatively conceptualized/designated, Skt. *upādāya prajñaptaḥ*, Tib. *brten nas btags pa* (v.l. *brtags pa*). A concept/designation that is relative to—i.e., conditioned by and deriving its employment from—its base or ground, whence it is so to say metonymical. (Cf. *The literature of the Madhyamaka school of philosophy in India*, pp. 16–17, where the rendering "conditional (pragmatic) designation" was offered.) A classical example is a self *(ātman)*, or a *pudgala*, which in Buddhist thought is only a postulated entity constructed on the base of the five Groups *(skandha = phung po)* of philosophical and psychological analysis. The term *upādāya* (Tib. *brten nas*) is similar in meaning to *pratītya* (Tib. *brten nas*, e.g., in *pratītyasamutpāda*, origination/production in dependence). At *MMK* xxiv.18, the demonstrative pronoun *sā* in *pāda* c may refer to *pratītyasamutpāda* in *pāda* a, it being in the feminine gender by attraction to its predicate *prajñaptiḥ* (cf. Apte, *Student's guide to Sanskrit composition* § 24; this is compatible with the commentaries, and with Candrakīrti's remark that *upādāya prajñaptiḥ* is a *viśeṣasaṃjñā* for *pratītyasamutpāda*); or the pronoun may refer to *śūnyatā* in *pāda* b (as indicated in *PPMV* p. 504.8). See under Middle Way; and *Literature of the Madhyamaka school of philosophy in India*, p. 17n39. —The substantive that corresponds to the absolutive form *upādāya* is *upādāna*, denoting a base, ground, or cause, as well as appropriation, attachment. Bhāviveka explains *MMK* xxiv.18c as follows (*Prajñāpradīpa*, D, tsha, 230b): *rten cing 'brel par byung ba zhes bya ba/ stong pa nyid gang yin pa de ni brten nas gdags pa ste/ 'jig rten pa dang 'jig rten las 'das pa'i tha snyad 'dod pas ñe bar len pa la brten nas gdags pa yin no*, "so-called origination in dependence, which is Emptiness, is a relative concept/designation; and since worldly and transmundane transactional-pragmatic usage *(vyavahāra)* is maintained, there exists a concept/designation *(prajñaptir)* relative to *(upādāya)* an appropriated base *(upādāna)*." Candrakīrti uses the formula *upādānena prajñapyate* in *PPMV* x.16. See also under Middle Way

relative emptiness. See Skt. *itaretaraśūnyatā*, Tib. *gcig gis gcig stong pa nyid*

self-characteristic *(*svalakṣaṇa)*. For Tsong kha pa's positing of a self-characteristic *(rang gi mtshan nyid)* in his exegesis and interpretative reading of Bhāviveka's philosophy, see D. Seyfort Ruegg, *Three studies*, section III. See Skt. *svalakṣaṇa*, Tib. *rang gi mtshan nyid = rang mtshan*

self-existence (as an entity, substantial existence, aseity). See Skt. *svabhāva*, Tib. *rang bzhin/rang gi ngo bo nyid*

Selfless(ness), i.e., non-substantial(ity). See Skt. *nirātman, anātman, nirātman, nairātmya;* Tib. *bdag med pa (nyid)*

simultaneism, simultaneist. See Tib. *c(h)ig c(h)ar (ba)* .

subitism. *See* simultaneism

substantiality, absence of —. See non-substantial; Skt. *nairātmya, niḥsvabhāva(tā)*

Surface, *saṃvṛti*, the level of the transactional-pragmatic, relative or conventional (the correlative opposite of Absolute/ultimate Meaning/Sense, *paramārtha*). Cf. Surface Reality. See Skt. *saṃvṛti*, Tib. *kun rdzob*

surface meaning (a provisional, intentional, meaning requiring hermeneutical interpretation in a further sense; the opposite of definitive/deep meaning). See Skt. *neyārtha*, Tib. *drang ba'i don*. Cf. intentional *(ābhiprāyika)*

Surface Reality, *saṃvṛtisatya*. Often rendered relative "truth" or conventional "truth," even though this is not a truth in the strict sense of the property of a proposition, etc.; but the translation of *satya* = *bden pa* by Reality is itself somewhat conventional and does not resolve all the philosophical issues involved. In Madhyamaka thought, *saṃvṛtisatya* is reality in a limited way only; see Candrakīrti, *MABh* vi.23, 28 and *PPMV* xxiv.11. Cf. D. Seyfort Ruegg, *Two prolegomena*, pp. 187n52 and 194n65. It is, then, only in a restricted, and even problematic, sense that it is possible to speak of a *two*-truth—or even of a *two*-reality—theory in Madhyamaka (as distinct from a two-level theory). In the purified cognitive sight of *ārya*s, *saṃvṛtisatya* is presented, i.e., apprehended, as *saṃvṛti[mātra]* = *kun rdzob [tsam]*, mere Surface. Cf. *Two prolegomena*, pp. 194ff. In Madhyamaka, the theory of Surface-level Reality has the effect of "saving appearances/the phenomena" (sôzein ta phainomena, *salvare phaenomena*). Cf. transactional-pragmatic. See Skt. *saṃvṛtisatya*, Tib. *kun rdzob kyi bden pa*; compare Tib. *snang stong*

tetralemma. The set of four positions in terms of which a reified entity might conceivably be postulated and defined. All of these positions and their corresponding statements have been negated by Nāgārjuna and his followers, who did not posit any such substantial entity (without the interpretation of this *prasajya*-type negation having to depend on an intuitionist or paraconsistent logic); see the entry "negation" above. Cf. D. Seyfort Ruegg, *Three studies*, pp. 109–12 (note 5), 139–47. See Skt. *catuṣkoṭi*, Tib. *mu bzhi*

thesis. In Madhyamaka thought the vexed question of the exact role and status of a thesis has been the object of much reflection and discussion; see D. Seyfort Ruegg, *Three studies*, sections II and III. See Skt. *pratijñā*, Tib. *dam bca'*

transactional-pragmatic (the "relative" or "conventional," said of discursive linguistic usage). See Skt. *vyāvahārika*, Tib. *tha snyad pa*. Cf. Surface, Surface Reality, *saṃvṛti(satya)*

"Truth" of Absolute/ultimate Meaning/Sense. See Reality of Absolute/ultimate Meaning/Sense; Absolute/ultimate Meaning/Sense; and Skt. *paramārthasatya*, Tib. *don dam pa'i bden pa*. Compare Surface Reality, *saṃvṛtisatya*, often rendered as "Surface Truth," "conventional truth" or "relative truth." (As noted above, since here there is no truth in the current philosophical usage of the word, the rendering of *satya* by "truth" is conventional.)

Publications by David Seyfort Ruegg

Books and Monographs

Contributions à l'histoire de la philosophie linguistique indienne. Publications de l'Institut de Civilisation Indienne (Sorbonne, Paris), Fascicule 7. 133 pp. Paris, E. de Boccard, 1959.

The life of Bu ston Rin po che. Serie Orientale Roma, Volume XXXIV. XVIII + 192 pp., facsimile plates. Rome, Istituto Italiano per il Medio ed Estremo Oriente, 1966.

The study of Indian and Tibetan thought: Some problems and perspectives. Inaugural Lecture, Chair of Indian Philosophy, Buddhist Studies and Tibetan, University of Leiden. 48 pp. Leiden, E. J. Brill, 1967.

La théorie du tathāgatagarbha et du gotra: Études sur la sotériologie et la gnoséologie du bouddhisme. Publications de l'École française d'Extrême-Orient, Volume LXX. 531 pp. Paris, École française d'Extrême-Orient, 1969.

Le traité du tathāgatagarbha de Bu ston Rin chen grub. Publications de l'École française d'Extrême-Orient, Volume LXXXVIII. XII + 162 pp. Paris, École française d'Extrême-Orient, 1973.

The literature of the Madhyamaka school of philosophy in India. History of Indian Literature, ed. J. Gonda, Volume VII, Fascicule 1. IX + 166 pp. Wiesbaden, Otto Harrassowitz, 1981.

Buddha-nature, Mind and the problem of Gradualism in a comparative perspective: On the transmission and reception of Buddhism in India and Tibet. (Jordan Lectures 1987.) 219 pp. London, School of Oriental and African Studies (University of London), 1989.

Ordre spirituel et ordre temporel dans la pensée bouddhique de l'Inde et du Tibet. Collège de France, Publications de l'Institut de Civilisation Indienne, Fascicule 64. 172 pp. Paris, Édition-Diffusion de Boccard, 1995.

Studies in Indian and Tibetan Madhyamaka thought, Part 1. Three studies in the history of Indian and Tibetan Madhyamaka philosophy. Wiener Studien zur Tibetologie und Buddhismuskunde, Heft 50. XIV + 322 pp. Vienna, Arbeitskreis für Tibetische und Buddhistische Studien, Universität Wien, 2000.

Studies in Indian and Tibetan Madhyamaka thought, Part 2. Two prolegomena to Madhyamaka philosophy: Candrakīrti's Prasannapadā Madhyamakavṛttiḥ on Madhyamakakārikā I.1 and Tsoṅ kha pa Blo bzaṅ grags pa/rGyal tshab Dar ma Rin chen's dKa' gnad/gnas brgyad kyi zin bris. Wiener Studien zur Tibetologie und Buddhismuskunde, Heft 54. XIV + 299 pp. Vienna, Arbeitskreis für Tibetische und Buddhistische Studien, Universität Wien, 2002.

The symbiosis of Buddhism with Brahmanism/Hinduism in South Asia and of Buddhism with "local cults" in Tibet and the Himalayan region. Österreichische Akademie der Wissenschaften, Philosophisch-Historische Klasse, Sitzungsberichte, 774. Band (Beiträge zur Kultur- und Geistesgeschichte Asiens, Nr. 58, Wien, 2008).

Articles

Védique *addhā́* et quelques expressions parallèles à *tathāgata*. *Journal asiatique*, 1955, pp. 163–70.

The term *buddhiviparināma* and the problem of illusory change. *Indo-Iranian Journal* 2 (1958), pp. 271–83.

Review article of: Gaurinath Sastri, *Philosophy of word and meaning*. *Indo-Iranian Journal* 4 (1960), pp. 173–79.

Vārṣagaṇya and the *Yogācārabhūmi*. *Indo-Iranian Journal* 6 (1962), pp. 137–40.

A propos of a recent contribution to Tibetan and Buddhist studies. *Journal of the American Oriental Society* 82 (1962), pp. 320–31.

The Jo naṅ pas, A school of Buddhist ontologists. *Journal of the American Oriental Society* 83 (1963), pp. 73–91. Reprinted (with no proofs supplied for correction) in: P. Williams (ed.), *Buddhism, Critical concepts in religious studies*, Volume 6 (London, 2005), pp. 363–91.

Sur les rapports entre le bouddhisme et le «substrat religieux» indien et tibétain. *Journal asiatique*, 1964, pp. 77–95.

On a Yoga treatise in Sanskrit from Qïzïl. *Journal of the American Oriental Society* 87 (1967), pp. 157–63.

Ārya and Bhadanta Vimuktisena on the *gotra* theory of the Prajñāpāramitā. *Beiträge zur Geistesgeschichte Indiens: Festschrift für Erich Frauwallner = Wiener Zeitschrift für die Kunde Süd- und Ostasiens* 12–13 (1968), pp. 303–17.

The dGe lugs pa theory of the *tathāgatagarbha*. In: *Pratidānam, Studies presented to F. B. J. Kuiper* (*Janua Linguarum*, Series Maior 34), pp. 500–509. The Hague, Mouton, 1968.

Le *Dharmadhātustava* de Nāgārjuna. In: *Études tibétaines dédiées à la mémoire de Marcelle Lalou*, pp. 448–71. Paris, Librairie d'Amérique et d'Orient Adrien Maisonneuve, 1971.

On the knowability and expressibility of absolute reality in Buddhism. *Indogaku Bukkyōgaku Kenkyū (Journal of Indian and Buddhist Studies)* 20/1 (1971), pp. 1–7.

Dedication to Th. Stcherbatsky. *Journal of Indian Philosophy* 1 (1971), pp. 213–16.

On Ratnakīrti. *Journal of Indian Philosophy* 1 (1971), pp. 300–309.

On translating the Buddhist Canon. In: *Studies in Indo-Asian art and culture*, Volume 5 (= Śatapiṭaka Series, Volume 209), ed. Perala Ratnam, pp. 243–61. New Delhi, International Academy of Indian Culture, 1973.

Pali *gotta/gotra* and the term *gotrabhū* in Pali and Buddhist Sanskrit. In: *Buddhist studies in honour of I. B. Horner*, ed. L. Cousins et al., pp. 199–210. Dordrecht, Reidel, 1974.

A recent work on the religions of Tibet and Mongolia (on G. Tucci and W. Heissig, *Die Religionen Tibets und der Mongolei*, Stuttgart, 1970). *T'oung Pao* 61 (1975), pp. 303–24.

La traduction du canon bouddhique selon une source tibéto-mongole. In: *Études tibétaines, Actes du XXIXe Congrès international des Orientalistes* (Paris, 1973), pp. 61–64. Paris, L'Asiathèque, 1976.

The meanings of the term *gotra* and the textual history of the *Ratnagotravibhāga*. *Bulletin of the School of Oriental and African Studies* 39 (1976), pp. 341–63.

On the supramundane and the divine in Buddhism. *The Tibet Journal* 1 (1976), pp. 25–28. Reprinted in *Buddhist and western philosophy*, ed. N. Katz, pp. 421–24. New Delhi, Sterling Publishers, 1981.

La philosophie tibétaine. In: *Dieux et démons de l'Himâlaya: Art du bouddhisme lamaïque*, pp. 28–31. Paris, Éditions des Musées Nationaux, 1977. German rendering, unseen and uncorrected by the author, in: *Tibet, Kunst des Buddhismus*, Munich, Haus der Kunst, 1977.

The uses of the Four Positions of the *catuṣkoṭi* and the problem of the description of reality in Mahāyāna Buddhism. *Journal of Indian Philosophy* 5 (1977), pp. 1–71. Reprinted (with no proofs supplied for correction) in: P. Williams (ed.), *Buddhism, Critical concepts in religious studies*, Volume 4 (London, 2005), pp. 213–77.

The *gotra, ekayāna* and *tathāgatagarbha* theories of the Prajñāpāramitā according to Dharmamitra and Abhayākaragupta. In: *The Prajñāpāramitā and related systems: Studies in honor of Edward Conze* (Berkeley Buddhist Studies Series 1), ed. L. Lancaster et al., pp. 283–312. Berkeley, 1977.

Mathematical and linguistic models in Indian thought: The case of zero and *śūnyatā*. *Wiener Zeitschrift für die Kunde Südasiens* 22 (1978), pp. 171–81.

The study of Tibetan philosophy and its Indian sources: Notes on its history and methods. In: *Proceedings of the Csoma de Kőrös Memorial Symposium held at Mátrafüred, Hungary, 24–30 September 1976* (= *Bibliotheca Orientalis Hungarica*, Volume XXIII), ed. L. Ligeti, pp. 377–91. Budapest, Akadémiai Kiadó, 1978.

Ahiṃsā and vegetarianism in the history of Buddhism. In: *Buddhist studies in honour of Walpola Rahula*, pp. 234–41. London, Gordon Frazer, 1980.

On the reception and early history of the dBu-ma (Madhyamaka) in Tibet. In: *Tibetan studies in honour of Hugh Richardson (Proceedings of the International Seminar on Tibetan Studies, Oxford 1979)*, ed. M. Aris et al., pp. 277–79. Warminster, Aris and Phillips, 1980.

A further note on Pali *gotrabhū*. *Journal of the Pali Text Society* 9 (1981), pp. 175–77.

Autour du *lTa ba'i khyad par* de Ye šes sde. *Journal asiatique*, Année 1981 (Numéro spécial: Actes du Colloque International, Manuscrits et Inscriptions de Haute Asie, Paris, 1979), pp. 207–29.

Deux problèmes d'exégèse et de pratique tantriques. In: *Tantrik and Taoist studies in honour of R. A. Stein* = *Mélanges chinois et bouddhiques* 20 (1981), pp. 212–26.

Towards a chronology of the Madhyamaka school. In: *Indological and Buddhist studies, Volume in honour of Professor J. W. de Jong*, ed. L. Hercus et al., pp. 505–30. Canberra, Faculty of Asian Studies (Australian National University), 1982.

In memoriam Arnold Kunst (1903–81). *Journal of Indian Philosophy* 11 (1983), pp. 3–5.

On the thesis and assertion in the Madhyamaka/dBu ma. In: *Contributions on Tibetan and Buddhist religion and philosophy*, ed. E. Steinkellner and H. Tauscher (*Wiener Studien zur Tibetologie und Buddhismuskunde*, Heft 11 = *Proceedings of the Csoma de Kőrös Symposium held at Velm-Vienna* 13–19 September 1981, Volume 2), pp. 205–41. Vienna, Arbeitskreis für Tibetische und Buddhistische Studien, Universität Wien, 1983.

Problems in the transmission of Vajrayāna Buddhism in the Western Himalaya about the year 1000. In: *Studies of mysticism in honor of the 1150th anniversary of Kōbō-Daishi's Nirvāṇam* = *Acta Indologica* (Naritasan) 6 (1984), pp. 369–81. Revised reprint in: A. McKay (ed.), *The history of Tibet*, Volume 2 (London, 2003), pp. 123–33.

Über die Nikāyas der Śrāvakas und den Ursprung der philosophischen Schulen des Buddhismus nach den tibetischen Quellen. In: *Zur Schulzugehörigkeit von Werken der Hīnayāna-Literatur*, ed. H. Bechert, Erster Teil (= Symposien zur Buddhismusforschung, III,1, *Abhandlungen der Akademie der Wissenschaften in Göttingen*, Philologisch-Historische Klasse, Dritte Folge, Nr. 149), pp. 111–26. Göttingen, Vandenhoeck und Ruprecht, 1985.

Purport, implicature and presupposition: Sanskrit *abhiprāya* and Tibetan *dgoṅs pa/dgoṅs gži* as hermeneutical concepts. *Journal of Indian Philosophy* 13 (1985), pp. 309–25.

Does the Mādhyamika have a thesis and philosophical position? In: *Buddhist logic and epistemology*, ed. B. K. Matilal and R. D. Evans, pp. 229–37. Dordrecht, Reidel, 1986.

An Indian source for the hermeneutical term *dgoṅs gži* "intentional ground." *Journal of Indian Philosophy* 16 (1988), pp. 1–4.

A Karma bKa' brgyud work on the lineages and traditions of the Indo-Tibetan dBu ma (Madhyamaka). In: *Orientalia Iosephi Tucci memoriae dicata* (Giuseppe Tucci Memorial Volume, Serie Orientale Roma LVI), ed. G. Gnoli and L. Lanciotti, Volume 3, pp. 1249–80. Rome, Istituto Italiano per il Medio ed Estremo Oriente, 1988.

La pensée tibétaine [accompagé d'une traduction du *rTen 'brel bstod pa Legs bšad sñiṅ po* de Tsoṅ kha pa (pp. 1589–91)]. In: *Encyclopédie philosophique universelle I (L'Univers philosophique)*, publiée sous la direction d'André Jacob, pp. 1586–91. Paris, Presses Universitaires de France, 1989.

Allusiveness and obliqueness in Buddhist texts: *saṃdhā, saṃdhi, saṃdhyā* and *abhisaṃdhi*. In: *Dialectes dans les littératures indo-aryennes*, ed. C. Caillat (Publications de l'Institut de Civilisation Indienne, Fascicule 55), pp. 295–328. Paris, E. de Boccard, 1989.

A Tibetan's Odyssey (on H. Stoddard, *Le mendiant de l'Amdo*, Paris, 1985). *Journal of the Royal Asiatic Society*, 1989, pp. 304–11.

The Buddhist notion of an "immanent absolute" *(tathāgatagarbha)* as a problem in hermeneutics. In: *The Buddhist heritage* (Buddhica Britannica, Series Continua I), ed. T. Skorupski, pp. 229–45. Tring, Institute of Buddhist Studies, 1989.

Review article on: D. Snellgrove, *Indo-Tibetan Buddhism* (London, 1987). *Journal of the Royal Asiatic Society*, 1989, pp. 171–76.

A Note on the transliteration of Tibetan. *Journal of the Royal Asiatic Society*, 1989, pp. 176–78.

On the authorship of some works ascribed to Bhāvaviveka/Bhavya. In: *Earliest Buddhism and Madhyamaka*, ed. D. Seyfort Ruegg and L. Schmithausen, pp. 59–71. Leiden, E. J. Brill, 1990.

mChod yon, yon mchod and *mchod gnas/yon gnas*: On the historiography and semantics of a Tibetan religio-social and religio-political concept. In: *Tibetan history and language* (Studies dedicated to Uray Géza on his seventieth birthday, *Wiener Studien zur Tibetologie und Buddhismuskunde*, Heft 26), ed. E. Steinkellner, pp. 441–53. Vienna, Arbeitskreis für Tibetische und Buddhistische Studien, Universität Wien, 1991. Reprinted in: A. McKay (ed.), *The history of Tibet*, Volume 2 (London, 2003), pp. 362–72.

On *Pramāṇa*-theory in Tsoṅ kha pa's Madhyamaka philosophy. In: *Studies in the Buddhist epistemological tradition*, ed. E. Steinkellner (Österreichische Akademie der Wissenschaften, Philosophisch-Historische Klasse, Denkschriften, 222. Band = Beiträge zur Kultur- und Geistesgeschichte Asiens, Nr. 8), pp. 281–310. Vienna, Verlag der Österreichischen Akademie der Wissenschaften, 1991.

The "Council of Tibet" in two early Tibetan works. In: *Proceedings of the XXXII International Congress for Asian and North African Studies* (Hamburg, 1986) (= *Zeitschrift der Deutschen Morgenländischen Gesellschaft*, Supplement IX, 1992), p. 218.

On the Tibetan historiography and doxography of the "Great Debate" of bSam yas. In: *Tibetan studies (Proceedings of the 5th Seminar of the International Association for Tibetan Studies*, Narita 1989 = *Monograph Series of Naritasan Institute for Buddhist Studies*, Occasional Papers 2), ed. Ihara Shōren et al., pp. 237–44. Narita, Naritasan Shinshoji, 1992.

Some reflections on translating Buddhist philosophical texts from Sanskrit and Tibetan. *Asiatische Studien/Études asiatiques* 46.1 (1992) (Études bouddhiques offertes à Jacques May), pp. 367–91.

Notes on some Indian and Tibetan reckonings of the Buddha's Nirvāṇa and the duration of his teaching. In: *The dating of the historical Buddha/Die Datierung des historischen Buddha*, Part 2, ed. H. Bechert (Symposien zur Buddhismus-Forschung IV,2, *Abhandlungen der Akademie der Wissenschaften in Göttingen*, Philologisch-Historische Klasse, Dritte Folge, Nr. 194), pp. 263–90. Göttingen, Vandenhoeck und Ruprecht, 1992.

Some observations on the present and future of Buddhist studies (Presidential Address to the Tenth Conference of the International Association of Buddhist Studies, UNESCO, Paris, July 1991), *Journal of the International Association of Buddhist Studies* 15 (1992), pp. 104–17.

Some observations on the present and future of Buddhist studies. In: *Buddhist studies present and future: Tenth International Conference of the International Association of Buddhist Studies*, ed. Ananda W. P. Gurugé, pp. 193–205. Permanent Delegation of Sri Lanka to Unesco, Paris, 1992.

Ahiṃsā y el vegetarianismo en la historia de Budismo. *Revista de Estudios Budistas*, No. 6 (1993–94), pp. 47–61. [Spanish translation of "*Ahiṃsā* and vegetarianism in the history of Buddhism," 1980.]

*Pramāṇabhūta. *pramāṇa(bhūta)-puruṣa, pratyakṣadharman* and *sākṣātkṛtadharman* as epithets of the *ṛṣi, ācārya* and *tathāgata* in grammatical, epistemological and Madhyamaka texts. *Bulletin of the School of Oriental and African Studies* 57 (1994), pp. 303–20.

La notion du voyant et du "Connaisseur Suprême" et la question de l'autorité épistémique. *Wiener Zeitschrift für die Kunde Südasiens und Archiv für indische Philosophie* 38 (1994), pp. 403–19.

The Tantric corpus *(rGyud 'bum)* of the Tibetan bKa' 'gyur according to a recent publication. (Review article on: H. Eimer, *Der Tantra-Katalog des Bu ston im Vergleich mit der Abteilung Tantra des tibetischen Kanjur*. Indica et Tibetica 17, Bonn, 1989.) *Buddhist Studies Review* 11 (1994), pp. 179–86.

Some reflections on the place of philosophy in the study of Buddhism. *Journal of the International Association of Buddhist Studies* 18 (1995), pp. 145–81.

Validity and authority, or Cognitive rightness and pragmatic efficacy? *Asiatische Studien/Études asiatiques* 49 (1995), pp. 817–27.

On translating Tibetan philosophical texts. In: Doboom Tulku (ed.), *Buddhist translations: Problems and perspectives* (New Delhi, 1995), pp. 75–86. [Abridged version of "Some reflections on translating Buddhist philosophical texts from Sanskrit and Tibetan," 1992.]

Notes sur la transmission et la réception des traités de grammaire et de lexicographie sanskrites dans les traditions indo-tibétaines. In: N. Balbir et G.-J. Pinault (ed.), *Langue, style et structure dans le monde indien—Centenaire Louis Renou* (Bibliothèque de l'École des Hautes Études, Sciences historiques et philologiques, tome 334, Paris, 1996), pp. 213–32.

The Preceptor-Donor (*yon mchod*) relation in thirteenth-century Tibetan society and polity, its Inner Asian precursors and Indian models. In: H. Krasser, M. T. Much and E. Steinkellner (ed.), *Tibetan studies—Proceedings of the 7th Seminar of the International Association for Tibetan Studies, Graz, 1995* (Österreichische Akademie der Wissenschaften, Philosophisch-Historische Klasse, Denkschriften, 256. Band, Vienna, 1997), Volume II, pp. 857–72.

Sanskrit-Tibetan and Tibetan-Sanskrit dictionaries and Some problems in Indo-Tibetan philosophical lexicography. In: B. Oguibénine (ed.), *Lexicography in the Indian and Buddhist cultural fields* (Studia Tibetica: Quellen und Studien zur tibetischen Lexicographie, Volume 4, Munich, 1998), pp. 115–42.

A new publication on the date and historiography of the Buddha's decease (*nirvāṇa*): a review article. (On H. Bechert [ed.], *The dating of the historical Buddha/Die Datierung des historischen Buddha*, Parts i–iii, Symposien zur Buddhismusforschung IV/1–3, Göttingen, 1991, 1992 and 1997.) *Bulletin of the School of Oriental and African Studies* 62 (1999), pp. 82–87.

Remarks on the place of narrative in the Buddhist literatures of India and Tibet. In: A. Cadonna (ed.), *India, Tibet, China: Genesis and aspects of traditional narrative* (Orientalia Venetiana VII, Florence, 1999), pp. 193–227.

In memoriam J. W. de Jong (1921–2000), *Indo-Iranian Journal* 43 (2000), pp. 313–17. Reprinted in: H. W. Bodewitz and M. Hara (ed.), *Gedenkschrift J. W. de Jong* (Studia Philologica Buddhica, Monograph Series XVII, Tokyo, 2004), pp. xiii–xvi.

The contents, antecedents and influence of Tsong-kha-pa'a *Lam rim chen mo*. In: J. Cutler et al. (ed.), *The Great Treatise on the Stages of the Path to Enlightenment by Tsong-kha-pa* (Ithaca, 2000), pp. 17–32.

On the expressions *chandaso āropema, āyataka gītassara, sarabhañña* and *ārṣa* as applied to the "Word of the Buddha" (*buddhavacana*). In: R. Tsuchida and A. Wezler (ed.),

Harānandalaharī (Felicitation volume for Professor Minoru Hara, Reinbek, 2000), pp. 283–306.

A note on the relationship between Buddhist and "Hindu" divinities in Buddhist literature and iconology: The *laukika/lokottara* contrast and the notion of an Indian "Religious Substratum," in: R. Torella (ed.), *Le parole e i marmi, Studi in onore di Raniero Gnoli nel suo 70o compleanno* (Serie Orientale Roma XCII, Rome, 2001), pp. 735–42.

The Indian and the Indic in Tibetan cultural history, and Tsoṅ kha pa's achievement as a scholar and thinker: An essay on the concepts of Buddhism in Tibet and Tibetan Buddhism. *Journal of Indian philosophy* 32 (2004), pp. 321–43.

Aspects of the study of the (earlier) Indian Mahāyāna. *Journal of the International Association of Buddhist Studies* 27 (2004), pp. 3–62.

Introductory remarks on the spiritual and temporal orders. In: C. Cüppers (ed.), *The relationship between religion and state (chos srid zung 'brel) in traditional Tibet* (Lumbini International Research Institute, Lumbini, 2004), pp. 9–13.

The Kalawān copper-plate inscription: Early evidence for Mahāyāna-type thinking? *Journal of the International Association of Buddhist Studies* 28 (2005), pp. 3–9.

The *Svātantrika-Prāsaṅgika* distinction in the history of Madhyamaka thought. *Indo-Iranian Journal* 49 (2006), pp. 319–46.

La traduction de la terminologie technique de la pensée indienne et bouddhique depuis Sylvain Lévi. In: L. Bansat-Boudon et R. Lardinois (éd.), *Sylvain Lévi: Études indiennes, histoire sociale*. Bibliothèque de l'École des Hautes Études, Sciences religieuses 130 (Histoire et prosopographie de la Section des sciences religieuses 3, Turnhout, 2007), pp. 145–71.

Editorships and Prefaces

Editor of *Monumenta Tibetana 1*: Geshé Ngawang Nyima, *Memoranda on logic (bsDus grva'i brjed tho)*. Leiden, 1970. Preface, pp. i–ii.

Editor of *Monumenta Tibetana 2*, Parts I–IV: Geshé Ngawang Nyima, *Introduction to the doctrines of the four schools of Buddhist philosophy (Naṅ pa'i grub mtha' smra ba bži'i 'dod tshul gsal bar bšad pa Blo gsar rig pa'i sgo 'byed)*. Leiden, 1970. Preface, p. i.

Preface in: Tāranātha, *Life of the Buddha and Histories of the Kālacakra and Tārātantra*, pp. i–iii. Published by Ngawang Gelek Demo. New Delhi, 1971.

Editor of the series *Tibetan and Indo-Tibetan Studies*, published by the Institute for the Culture and History of India and Tibet at the University of Hamburg. Franz Steiner Verlag, Stuttgart, 1989 ff.

Earliest Buddhism and Madhyamaka, edited by David Seyfort Ruegg and Lambert Schmithausen, *Panels of the VIIth World Sanskrit Conference* (1987). Leiden, E. J. Brill, 1990.

Tibetan Tulkus: Images of continuity. Introduction to Photographs by Martine Franck (Mme. Cartier-Bresson). London, Rossi and Rossi, 2000, pp. 1–3.

Reviews

Heinrich Lüders, *Beobachtungen über die Sprache des buddhistischen Urkanons*. Berlin, 1954. *Journal asiatique*, 1955, pp. 260–64.

Hermann Goetz, *The early wooden temples of Chamba*. Leiden, 1955. *Journal asiatique*, 1956, pp. 237–38.

P. Hacker, *Vivarta: Studien zur Geschichte der illusionistischen Kosmologie und Erkenntnistheorie der Inder*. Wiesbaden, 1953. *Journal of the American Oriental Society* 78 (1958), pp. 81–83, with Note, *ibid.*, p. 140.

K. Satchidananda Murty, *Revelation and reason in Advaita Vedānta*. New York, 1959. *Journal of the American Oriental Society* 80 (1960), pp. 374–78.

D. J. Hoens, *Śānti: A contribution to ancient Indian religious terminology I*. The Hague, 1951. *Journal of the American Oriental Society* 81 (1961), pp. 67–69.

J. Varenne, *La Mahā-Nārāyaṇa-Upaniṣad*. Paris, 1960. *Journal of the American Oriental Society* 82 (1962), pp. 88–90.

R. V. Joshi, *Le rituel de la dévotion kṛṣṇaïte*. Pondicherry, 1959. *Indo-Iranian Journal* 6 (1962), pp. 70–72.

Y. Ojihara et L. Renou, *La Kāśikā-Vṛtti (adhyāya I, pāda 1) traduite et commentée*, 1re partie. Paris, 1960. *Indo-Iranian Journal* 6 (1962), pp. 72–73.

Marie-Thérèse de Mallmann, *Les enseignements iconographiques de l'Agni-Purana*. Paris, 1963. *Indo-Iranian Journal* 8 (1965), pp. 226–27.

B. Mukherjee, *Die Überlieferung von Devadatta, dem Widersacher des Buddha in den kanonischen Schriften*. München, 1966. *T'oung-Pao* 54 (1968), pp. 164–68.

H. V. Guenther, *Tibetan Buddhism*. Leiden, 1966. *T'oung-Pao* 55 (1969), pp. 220–26.

H. Hoffmann, *Symbolik der tibetischen Religionen und des Schamanismus*. Stuttgart, 1967. *T'oung-Pao* 56 (1970), pp. 338–43.

Y. Ojihara et L. Renou, *La Kāśikā-Vṛtti (adhyāya I, pāda I) traduite et commentée*. 2e partie, Paris, 1962; 3e partie, Paris, 1967. *Indo-Iranian Journal* 13 (1971), p. 206.

Srinivasa Ayya Srinivasan, *Vācaspatimiśras Tattvakaumudī, Ein Beitrag zur Textkritik bei kontaminierter Überlieferung*. Hamburg, 1967. *Indo-Iranian Journal* 13 (1971), pp. 290–92.

S. D. Joshi, *The Sphoṭanirṇaya of Kauṇḍa Bhaṭṭa*, edited with Introduction, Translation and Critical and Exegetical Notes. Publications of the Centre of Advanced Study in Sanskrit, University of Poona, Poona, 1967. *Indo-Iranian Journal* 13 (1971), pp. 292–95.

Stuart H. Buck, *Tibetan-English Dictionary*. Washington, 1969. *Linguistics* 100 (1973), pp. 101–3.

D. L. Snellgrove, *Four Lamas of Dolpo*. Oxford, 1967. *Central Asiatic Journal* 17 (1973), pp. 81–84.

N. A. Jayawickrama, *The sheaf of garlands of the epochs of the Conqueror, being a translation of the Jinakālamālīprakaraṇam of Ratanapañña Thera of Thailand*. London, 1968. *Journal of the American Oriental Society* 92 (1972), pp. 179–81.

A. W. Macdonald, *Matériaux pour l'étude de la littérature populaire tibétaine I: Edition et traduction de deux manuscrits tibétains des "Histoires du cadavre" (Vetāla)*. Paris, 1967. *Indo-Iranian Journal* 14 (1972), pp. 137–40.

Acta Indologica II. Naritasan Shinshoji, 1971/72. *Journal of the American Oriental Society* 96 (1976), p. 151.

M. L. Matics, *Entering the Path of Enlightenment, the Bodhicaryāvatāra of the Buddhist poet Śāntideva*. New York and London, 1971. *Journal of the American Oriental Society* 97 (1977), pp. 88–89.

G. Tucci, *Minor Buddhist Texts III: Third Bhāvanākrama*. Rome, 1971. *Journal of the American Oriental Society* 97 (1977), pp. 89–90.

Y. Takeuchi, *Probleme der Versenkung im Ur-Buddhismus*. Leiden, 1972. *Journal of the American Oriental Society* 97 (1977), pp. 90–92.

Sanskrit-Wörterbuch der buddhistischen Texte aus den Turfan-Funden, Begonnen von Ernst Waldschmidt, herausgegeben von der Akademie der Wissenschaften in Göttingen unter der Leitung von Heinz Bechert, 1. Lieferung. Göttingen, 1973. *Journal of the American Oriental Society* 97 (1977), pp. 550–52.

M. Hahn, *Candragomins Lokānandanāṭaka*. Wiesbaden, 1974. *Journal of the American Oriental Society* 97 (1977), pp. 552–54.

E. Conze, *The Large Sūtra on Perfect Wisdom, with the divisions of the Abhisamayālaṃkāra*. Berkeley, 1975. *Journal of Indian Philosophy* 5 (1977), pp. 187–89.

Marie-Thérèse de Mallmann, *Introduction à l'iconographie du Tântrisme bouddhique*. Paris, 1975. *Journal of the American Oriental Society* 98 (1978), pp. 543–45.

E. Lamotte, *Le traité de la Grande Vertu de Sagesse de Nāgārjuna*. Tome IV, Louvain, 1976. *Journal of the Royal Asiatic Society* 1978, pp. 179–81.

H. Bechert, ed., *Sanskrit-Wörterbuch der buddhistischen Texte aus den Turfan-Funden*, 2. Lieferung. Göttingen, 1976. *Journal of the American Oriental Society* 99 (1979), pp. 160–61.

Saddharma-Puṇḍarīka-Sūtra (Kashgar Manuscript), edited by Prof. Dr. Lokesh Chandra with a Foreword by Prof. Dr. H. Bechert. Tokyo, 1977; and H. Toda, *Note on the Kashgar Manuscript of the Saddharmapuṇḍarīkasūtra*. Tokyo, 1977. *Journal of the American Oriental Society* 99 (1979), pp. 343–45.

L. Schmithausen, *Der Nirvāṇa-Abschnitt in der Viniścayasaṃgrahaṇī der Yogācārabhūmiḥ*. Vienna, 1969. *Orientalistische Literatur-Zeitung* 75 (1980), col. 275–76.

J. W. de Jong (ed.), *Nāgārjuna, Mūlamadhyamakakārikāḥ*. Adyar, 1977. *Indo-Iranian Journal* 22 (1980), pp. 247–49.

E. Conze, *The Prajñāpāramitā literature*. Tokyo, 1978. *Journal of the American Oriental Society* 101 (1981), p. 471.

The sDe dge Tibetan Tripiṭaka: bsTan 'gyur, dBu ma, Volumes 1–17. Tokyo, 1977–79. *Journal of Indian Philosophy* 9 (1981), pp. 101–3.

Padmanabh S. Jaini, *Amṛtacandrasūri's Laghutattvasphoṭa*. Ahmedabad, 1978. *Journal of Indian Philosophy* 10 (1982), pp. 101–3.

G. Oberhammer, *Strukturen yogischer Meditation*. Vienna, 1977. *Indo-Iranian Journal* 24 (1982), pp. 57–60.

H. Eimer, *rNam thar rgyas pa, Materialien zu einer Biographie des Atiśa (Dīpaṃkaraśrījñāna)*. Wiesbaden, 1979. *Indo-Iranian Journal* 24 (1982), pp. 74–76.

P. S. Jaini, *Sāratamā, A Pañjikā on the Aṣṭasāhasrikā Prajñāpāramitā Sūtra by Ācārya Ratnākaraśānti*. Patna, 1979. *Indo-Iranian Journal* 24 (1982), pp. 156–57.

Beiträge zur Indienforschung Ernst Waldschmidt zum 80. Geburtstag gewidmet. Ed.

H. Härtel. Berlin, 1977. *Journal of the American Oriental Society* 103 (1983), pp. 649–50.

A. Yuyama, *Vinaya-Texte*. (Systematische Übersicht über die buddhistische Sanskrit-Literatur, Erster Teil.) Wiesbaden, 1979. *Journal of the American Oriental Society* 103 (1983), pp. 650–51.

E. Waldschmidt, *Kleinere Sanskrit-Texte III/IV*. Berlin, 1979. *Journal of the American Oriental Society* 103 (1983), pp. 651–52.

H. Bechert, ed., *Die Sprache der ältesten buddhistischen Überlieferung/The language of the earliest Buddhist tradition*. Göttingen, 1980. *Journal of the American Oriental Society* 103 (1983), pp. 652–57.

Marco Pallis, *A Buddhist spectrum*. London, 1980. *Journal of the International Association of Buddhist Studies* 7 (1984), pp. 159–62.

T. Skorupski, *The Sarvadurgatipariśodhana Tantra*. Delhi, 1983. *Bulletin of the School of Oriental and African Studies* 48 (1985), pp. 166–67.

Yoshiro Imaeda, *Histoire du cycle de la naissance et de la mort: Étude d'un texte tibétain de Touen-houang*. (Centre de Recherches d'Histoire et de Philologie de la IVe Section de l'École pratique des Hautes Etudes, II, Hautes Études Orientales 15.) Genève et Paris, Droz, 1981. *Bulletin de l'École Française d'Extrême-Orient* 74 (1985), pp. 532–33.

Sanskrit-Wörterbuch der buddhistischen Texte aus den Turfan-Funden, 3. Lieferung, edited by Georg von Simson, Göttingen 1983 (?); and 4. Lieferung, edited by Michael Schmidt, Göttingen, 1984 (?). *Journal of the American Oriental Society* 106 (1986), pp. 596–97.

Yoshiro Imaeda, *Catalogue du Kanjur tibétain de l'édition de 'Jang Sa-tham*. Seconde partie (Bibliotheca Philologica Buddhica, Series maior, IIb). Tokyo, 1984. *Journal of the American Oriental Society* 106 (1986), pp. 597–98.

J. Terjék, ed., *The Collected Works of Alexander Csoma de Kőrös*. Four volumes. Budapest, 1984. *Journal of the American Oriental Society* 106 (1986), pp. 598–99.

Erich Frauwallner, *Kleine Schriften*. Edited by G. Oberhammer and E. Steinkellner. Wiesbaden, 1982. *Wiener Zeitschrift für die Kunde Südasiens* 30 (1986), pp. 189–91.

O. von Hinüber, *A new fragmentary Gilgit manuscript of the Saddharmapuṇḍarīkasūtra*. Tokyo, 1982. *Journal of the American Oriental Society* 106 (1986), p. 879.

G. M. Bongard-Levin and M. I. Vorob'eva-Desjatovskaja, *Pamjatniki indijskoi pis'mennosti iz central'noj Azij* (Bibliotheca Buddhica XXXIII). Moscow, 1985; G. M. Bongard-Levin, *New Sanskrit fragments of the Mahāyāna Mahāparinirvāṇasūtra*. Tokyo, 1986; and K. Matsuda (in collaboration with G. M. Bongard-Levin), *Sanskrit fragments of the Mahāyāna Mahāparinirvāṇasūtra*. Tokyo, 1988. *Bulletin of the School of Oriental and African Studies* 51 (1988), pp. 576–78.

H. Inagaki, *The Anantamukhanirhāra-dhāraṇī sūtra and Jñānagarbha's commentary*. Kyoto, 1987. *Bulletin of the School of Oriental and African Studies* 52 (1989), pp. 156–57.

Y. Fukuda and Y. Ishihama, *A comparative table of Sa-bcad of the Pramāṇavārttika, found in the Tibetan commentaries on the Pramāṇavārttika*. Tokyo, 1986. *Journal of Indian Philosophy* 17 (1989), pp. 207–8.

sDe dge Tibetan Tripiṭaka: bsTan 'gyur, Sems tsam (Cittamātra). Tokyo, 1979–81; and *sDe dge Tibetan Tripiṭaka: bsTan 'gyur, Tshad ma (Pramāṇa)*. Tokyo, 1981 ff. *Journal of Indian Philosophy* 17 (1989), pp. 208–9.

D. L. Snellgrove, *Indo-Tibetan Buddhism, Indian Buddhists and their Tibetan successors.* London and Boston, 1987. *Journal of the Royal Asiatic Society*, 1989, pp. 171–76.

Peter della Santina, *Madhyamaka schools in India.* Delhi, 1986. *Buddhist Studies Review* 7 (1990), pp. 142–44.

Sanskrit-Texte aus dem buddhistischen Kanon: Neuentdeckungen und Neueditionen. Edited by Fumio Enomoto, Jens-Uwe Hartmann and Hisashi Matsumura. Sanskrit-Wörterbuch der buddhistischen Texte aus den Turfan-Funden, Beiheft 2. Göttingen, 1989. *Journal of the American Oriental Society* 113 (1993), pp. 602–3.

Bhikkhu Pāsādika, ed., *Kanonische Zitate im Abhidharmakośabhāṣya des Vasubandhu.* Sanskrit-Wörterbuch der buddhistischen Texte aus den Turfan-Funden, im Auftrage der Akademie der Wissenschaften in Göttingen herausgegeben von Heinz Bechert, Beiheft 1. Göttingen, 1989. *Journal of the American Oriental Society* 114 (1994), p. 523.

Sanskrithandschriften aus den Turfanfunden. Teil 6 (nos. 1202–1599). Herausgegeben von H. Bechert, Beschrieben von K. Wille. Verzeichnis der Orientalischen Handschriften in Deutschland, Band X,6. Stuttgart, 1989. *Journal of the American Oriental Society* 114 (1994), p. 523.

Tibetische Handschriften und Blockdrucke. Teil 10: Die mTshur-phu-Ausgabe der Sammlung Rin-chen gter-mdzod chen-mo, Bände 1 bis 14. Described by Peter Schwieger. Verzeichnis der Orientalischen Handschriften in Deutschland, Bd. XI,10. Stuttgart, 1990. *Journal of the Royal Asiatic Society* 4 (1994), pp. 434–36.

Mariane Winder, *Catalogue of Tibetan manuscripts and xylographs and Catalogue of thankas, banners and other paintings in the Library of the Wellcome Institute for the History of Medicine.* London, 1989. *Journal of the Royal Asiatic Society* 4 (1994), p. 436.

Paolo Daffinà, ed., *Indo-Sino-Tibetica: Studi in onore di Luciano Petech.* Rome, 1990. *Journal of the Royal Asiatic Society* 5 (1995), pp. 146–48.

Hundert Strophen von der Lebensklugheit: Nāgārjunas Prajñāśataka, Tibetisch und Deutsch. Eingeleitet, herausgegeben und übersetzt von Michael Hahn. (Indica et Tibetica 18.) Bonn, 1990. *Buddhist Studies Review* 12 (1995), pp. 73–75.

Die Ratnāvalīṭīkā des Ajitamitra. Herausgegeben und erläutert von Yukihiro Okada. (Indica et Tibetica 19.). Bonn, 1990. *Buddhist Studies Review* 12 (1995), pp. 75–78.

Donald S. Lopez, ed., *Buddhist hermeneutics.* (Kuroda Institute Studies in East Asian Buddhism 6.) Honolulu, 1988. *Bulletin of the School of Oriental and African Studies* 58 (1995), pp. 573–77.

H. Bechert et al., ed., *Sanskrit-Wörterbuch der buddhistischen Texte aus den Turfan-Funden und der kanonischen Literatur der Sarvāstivāda-Schule.* Parts 5–8. Göttingen, 1987–94. *Journal of the American Oriental Society* 118 (1998), pp. 552–54.

Bhikkhu Pāsādika, *Nāgārjuna's Sūtrasamuccaya: A critical edition of the mDo kun las btus* pa. Fontes Tibetici Havnienses II. Akademisk Forlag i Kommission. Copenhagen, 1989. *Buddhist Studies Review* 17 (2000), pp. 222–24.

Johannes Schneider, *Der Lobpreis der Vorzüglichkeit des Buddha. Udbhaṭasiddhasvāmins Viśeṣastava mit Prajñā-karavarman's Kommentar, nach dem tibetischen Tanjur herausgegeben und übersetzt.* Indica et Tibetica 23. Bonn 1993. *Buddhist Studies Review* 17 (2000), pp. 229–32.

Tibetische Handschriften und Blockdrucke. Teile 11–12: Die mTshur-phu-Ausgabe der Sammlung Rin-chen gter-mdzod chen-mo. Nach dem Exemplar der Orientabteilung,

Staatsbibliothek zu Berlin—Preussischer Kulturbesitz, Hs Or 778, Bände 14 bis 40, 34 bis 40. Described by Peter Schwieger. (Verzeichnis der Orientalischen Handschriften in Deutschland, Band XI,11–12.) Stuttgart, 1995 and 1999. *Journal of the Royal Asiatic Society* 11 (2001), pp. 104–6.

Elena de Rossi Filibeck, *Catalogue of the Tucci Fund in the Library of IsMEO.* Volume 1. Rome, 1994. *Journal of the Royal Asiatic Society* 11 (2001), pp. 106–7.

Jens Braarvig, ed., *Buddhist manuscripts,* Volume I: Manuscripts in the Schøyen Collection I. Oslo, 2000. *Bulletin of the School of Oriental and African* Studies 65 (2002), pp. 188–91.

Pieter C. Verhagen, *A history of Sanskrit grammatical literature in Tibet.* Volume 1: Transmission of the canonical literature; Volume 2: Assimilation into indigenous scholarship. Handbuch der Orientalistik/Handbook of Oriental Studies, Section 2, Volume 8. Leiden, Brill, 1994 and 2001. *Journal of the Royal Asiatic Society* 13 (2003), pp. 123–27.

Chr. Lindtner, ed., *Madhyamakahṛdayam* [sic] *Bhavyakṛtam: Madhyamakahṛdayam of Bhavya.* Adyar (Chennai), The Adyar Library and Research Centre, 2001. *Buddhist Studies Review* 20 (2003), pp. 88–92.

J. Braarvig et al., ed., *Buddhist manuscripts,* Volume II. Manuscripts in the Schøyen Collection, Volume III. Hermes Publishing, Oslo, 2002. *Bulletin of the School of Oriental and African Studies* 70 (2007), pp. 622–24.

R. M. Davidson, *Tibetan renaissance: Tantric Buddhism in the rebirth of Tibetan culture.* New York, Columbia University Press, 2005. *Bulletin of the School of Oriental and African Studies* 70 (2007), pp. 624–27.

Indexes

Subject Index

Indian Proper Names

Chinese And Korean Proper Names

Indian Sources

Tibetan Proper Names, Place Names, and Texts

Chinese Texts

About Wisdom

WISDOM PUBLICATIONS is dedicated to making available authentic Buddhist works for the benefit of all. We publish translations of the canonical texts, commentaries and teachings of past and contemporary Buddhist masters, and original works by the world's leading Buddhist scholars. We publish our titles with the appreciation of Buddhism as a living philosophy and with the special commitment to preserve and transmit important works from all the major Buddhist traditions.

Wisdom Publications
199 Elm Street
Somerville, Massachusetts 02144 USA
Telephone: 617-776-7416
Fax: 617-776-7841
Email: info@wisdompubs.org
www.wisdompubs.org

Wisdom is a nonprofit, charitable 501(c)(3) organization affiliated with the Foundation for the Preservation of the Mahayana Tradition (FPMT).

Studies in Indian and Tibetan Buddhism
Titles Previously Published

Among Tibetan Texts
History and Literature of the Himalayan Plateau
E. Gene Smith

Approaching the Great Perfection
Simultaneous and Gradual Methods of Dzogchen Practice in the Longchen Nyingtig
Sam van Schaik

Buddhism Between Tibet and China
Edited by Matthew T. Kapstein

Buddhist Teaching in India
Johannes Bronkhorst

A Direct Path to the Buddha Within
Gö Lotsāwa's Mahāmudrā Interpretation of the Ratnagotravibhāga
Klaus-Dieter Mathes

Foundations of Dharmakīrti's Philosophy
John D. Dunne

Freedom from Extremes
Gorampa's "Distinguishing the Views" and the Polemics of Emptiness
José Ignacio Cabezón and Geshe Lobsang Dargyay

Luminous Lives
The Story of the Early Masters of the Lam 'bras Tradition in Tibet
Cyrus Stearns

Mipham's Beacon of Certainty
Illuminating the View of Dzogchen, the Great Perfection
John Whitney Pettit

Omniscience and the Rhetoric of Reason
Śāntarakṣita and Kamalaśīla on Rationality, Argumentation, and Religious Authorit
Sara L. McClintock

Reason's Traces
Identity and Interpretation in Indian and Tibetan Buddhist Thought
Matthew T. Kapstein

Resurrecting Candrakīrti
Disputes in the Tibetan Creation of Prāsaṅgika
Kevin A. Vose

Scripture, Logic, Language
Essays on Dharmakīrti and His Tibetan Successors
Tom J. F. Tillemans

The Svātantrika-Prāsaṅgika Distinction
What Difference Does a Difference Make?
Edited by Georges Dreyfus and Sara McClintock

Vajrayoginī
Her Visualizations, Rituals, and Forms
Elizabeth English